D1712850

Journey to a
Nineteenth-Century
Shtetl

Raphael Patai Series in Jewish Folklore and Anthropology

A complete listing of the books in this series can be found at the back of this volume.

General Editor:
Dan Ben-Amos
University of Pennsylvania

Advisory Editors:
Jane S. Gerber
City University of New York

Barbara Kirshenblatt-Gimblett
New York University

Aliza Shenhar
University of Haifa

Amnon Shiloah
Hebrew University

Harvey E. Goldberg
Hebrew University

Samuel G. Armistead
University of California, Davis

Guy H. Haskell

Journey to a Nineteenth-Century Shtetl

the memoirs of

Yekhezkel Kotik

Edited with an Introduction and Notes by

David Assaf

WITHDRAWN

Wayne State University Press   Detroit
Published in cooperation with
The Diaspora Research Institute, Tel Aviv University

Translated from the Yiddish by Margaret Birstein and edited by Sharon
Makover-Assaf. Footnotes to the text translated from the Hebrew edition by
Sharon Makover-Assaf and edited by Dena Ordan. Introduction translated from
the Hebrew by Dena Ordan.

Originally published in Yiddish in 1913 as *Mayne zikhroynes*. Translated and
published in Hebrew in 1998 as *Mah she-ra'iti . . . Zikhronotav shel Yekhezkel
Kotik*.

Copyright © 2002 by Wayne State University Press,
Detroit, Michigan 48201. All rights are reserved.
No part of this book may be reproduced without formal permission.
Manufactured in the United States of America.

Library of Congress Cataloging-in-Publication Data

Kotik, Yekhezkel, 1847–1921.
   [Mayne zikhroyneás. English]
   A journey to a nineteenth-century shtetl : the memoirs of Yekhezkel Kotik /
edited with an introduction and Notes by David Assaf ; translated from the
Yiddish by Margaret Birnstein.
     p. cm.—(Raphael Patai series in Jewish folklore and anthropology)
   Includes bibliographical references (p.) and index.
   ISBN 0-8143-2804-0
   1. Kotik, Yekhezkel, 1847–1921. 2. Jewis—Russia—Biography.
3. Jews—Russia—Social life and customs—19th century. I. Assaf, David.
II. Title. III. Series.
DS135.R95 K6445513 2002
947.08'092—dc21   2001008005

⊛ The paper used in this publication meets the minimum requirements of the
American National Standard for Information Sciences—Permanence of Paper for
Printed Library Materials, ANSI Z39.48–1984.

CONTENTS

PREFACE TO THE
ENGLISH EDITION

The imaginary city of Zora's uniqueness inheres in its being "a city that no one, having seen it, can forget. But not because, like other memorable cities, it leaves an unusual image in your recollections. Zora has the quality of remaining in your memory point by point, in its succession of streets, of houses along the streets, and of doors and windows in the houses, though nothing in them possesses a special beauty or rarity. . . . This city which cannot be expunged from the mind is like an armature, a honeycomb in whose cells each of us can place the things he wants to remember: names of famous men, virtues, numbers, vegetable and mineral classifications, dates of battles, constellations, parts of speech. Between each idea and each point of the itinerary an affinity or a contrast can be established, serving as an immediate aid to memory."[1]

This book invites the reader to journey to cities and towns that once existed and are no more, yet nevertheless remain alive in our memory. "I spent my youth in a small, typical shtetl," wrote Yekhezkel Kotik (1847–1921) in the introduction to his Yiddish memoirs published in 1913, "where Jews lived a poor but 'quiet,' and, if one may say, flavorful life. . . . This no longer exists today; the poetry of those former shtetls has been silenced too." Yet Kotik browses lyrically in the precincts of memory, imagination, and emotion, evoking surprisingly delicate impressions, of a quality rare in the history of the descriptions of the Eastern European shtetl.

In 1998 volume one of Kotik's memoirs appeared in an annotated Hebrew translation, titled *Mah she-ra'iti . . . Zikhronotav shel*

Yekhezkel Kotik (What I have seen . . . The memoirs of Yekhezkel Kotik; Tel Aviv University: Diaspora Research Institute). The warm reception afforded the Hebrew version of this magical but forgotten text motivated me to make this important work accessible to the English-speaking public as well.

The text of the memoirs was translated from the Yiddish by Margaret Birstein of Jerusalem. Entranced by the memoirs, she met the challenge of their translation with enthusiasm and devotion. My beloved wife, Sharon Makover-Assaf, ably edited the translation and undertook the Herculean task of translating the hundreds of notes accompanying the text. My thanks to her know no bounds. Dena Ordan translated the introduction and prepared the final draft of the book for publication with her characteristic thoroughness. Her good taste and judgment are apparent on each and every page. Thus three women brought this English edition into being, and to them I say: mine and yours is theirs (BT *Nedarim* 50a). Others assisted the "birth" of this book. It is my pleasant duty to thank my friend Dan Ben-Amos of the University of Pennsylvania, who affectionately nursed the book along from before the appearance of the Hebrew edition until its publication in English, and Arthur B. Evans, director of Wayne State University Press. To them and to the professional staff of the Press as well, my appreciation.

"The generous man is blessed, for he gives of his bread to the poor" (Proverbs 22:9). Many teachers and colleagues assisted in the preparation of the Hebrew edition of the book, sharing their knowledge, and their insights and comments have been incorporated throughout. It is my pleasant duty to acknowledge the help received from Israel Bartal, Nathan Cohen, Immanuel Etkes, Yehoshua Mondshine, Avraham Novershtern, Elchanan Reiner, Shmuel Werses, and Yair Zakovitch. Neither can I fail to express my gratitude to the late Chone Shmeruk, an eminent scholar and a true friend, who encouraged me along the way but unfortunately did not live to see this project's completion.

The aid of various institutions was also vital, in particular the archives of the YIVO Institute for Jewish Research in New York, Beth Shalom Aleichem in Tel Aviv, and the Department of Manuscripts and Archives at the Jewish National and University Library, Jerusalem, as well as the "Index to Yiddish Periodicals" project at the Hebrew University, Jerusalem.

I am deeply grateful for the support granted the English edition by my colleagues at the Diaspora Research Institute of Tel Aviv University and especially by institute director Aaron Openheimer. The Koret Foundation's generous grant was essential to the forwarding of this project.

"Torah seeks its home" (BT *Bava Metzia* 85a). Without the indispensable assistance, devotion, and wisdom of my beloved mother, Rachel Krone, the Hebrew translation would not have come to fruition. Imagine then my surprise and excitement at discovering that a peculiar twist of fate linked my mother's side of the family and Yekhezkel Kotik. My late grandfather, Yisrael Tzvi Blumberg of Warsaw, who earned his living from dealing in books and prayer shawls, had a small shop situated at 31 Nalewki Street, the very same address where Kotik's famous café was located.

I dedicate this book to the wondrous legacy of Eastern European Jewry and to the martyred souls of my grandmothers and grandfathers, uncles and aunts, who perished at the hands of murderers and in the flames of the crematoria. Although I never made their acquaintance, their images are before my eyes.

I unashamedly admit that the reading of Kotik's memoirs, following his footsteps and rendering them in translation with explanations, has given me unbridled pleasure. I can only hope that readers of this volume will share this feeling. I find the felicitous remarks of one of the world's great humorists, Jerome K. Jerome, an apt conclusion:

> The chief beauty of this book lies not so much in its literary style, or in the extent and usefulness of the information it conveys, as in its simple truthfulness. . . . Other works may excel this in depth of thought and knowledge of human nature: other books may rival it in originality and size; but, for hopeless and incurable veracity, nothing yet discovered can surpass it.[2]

David Assaf
Jerusalem 2000

NOTES TO PREFACE

1. Italo Calvino, *Invisible Cities*, trans. William Weaver (London: Pan Books, 1979), 16–17.

2. Jerome K. Jerome, *Three Men in a Boat* (Ipswich: W. S. Cowell, 1975), x.

A Note on the
Translation

otik's memoirs themselves have been translated from the Yiddish original. The introduction and notes have been translated from the Hebrew edition, with changes introduced to meet the needs of the English reader. This edition also differs from the Hebrew in that Kotik's letters to Sholem Aleichem have been omitted (Appendix 1 in the Hebrew edition).

For the reader's convenience, a glossary of Hebrew and Yiddish terms has been appended. More familiar Hebrew and Yiddish words found in *Webster's Third New International Dictionary* (1966) have not been italicized. Other foreign words are italicized throughout.

The problematic nature of the spelling of place names is well known to all those conversant with "Jewish geography." This book uses the familiar English or Jewish spellings and those found on international maps, with alternate forms (Polish, Yiddish) generally provided in the notes. By and large, the spellings found in the *Columbia Gazetteer of the World* (New York: Columbia University Press, 1998); in Gary Mokotoff and Sallyann Amdur Sack, *Where Once We Walked* (Teaneck, N. J.: Avotaynu, 1991); and in the *Encyclopaedia Judaica* were utilized. We have not striven for authenticity in reproducing personal names. These are rendered in a form that more closely reflects the Yiddish or Hebrew pronunciation; thus Yisrael and not Israel, Yaakov and not Jacob, for example, with more weight given to the Hebrew pronunciation. Similarly, in cases of words that have both Hebrew and Yiddish spellings, preference has been given to the Hebrew.

Transliteration of Yiddish follows Uriel Weinreich's system in his *Modern English-Yiddish/Yiddish-English Dictionary* (New York, 1968). For Hebrew a modified form of the general system found in the *Encyclopaedia Judaica* has been followed. No diacritical marks have been used for either *aleph* or *ayin,* or to indicate the distinction between *heh* and *het,* on the assumption that the reader who knows Hebrew will know which is appropriate.

ABBREVIATIONS

BT   Babylonian Talmud

EJD   Encyclopaedia of the Jewish Diaspora

JNUL   Jewish National and University Library, Jerusalem

LYNL   Lexicon of the New Yiddish Literature

M.   Mishnah

PT   Palestinian Talmud

RHT   Russian Historical Terms

SAA   Shalom Aleichem Archives, Tel Aviv

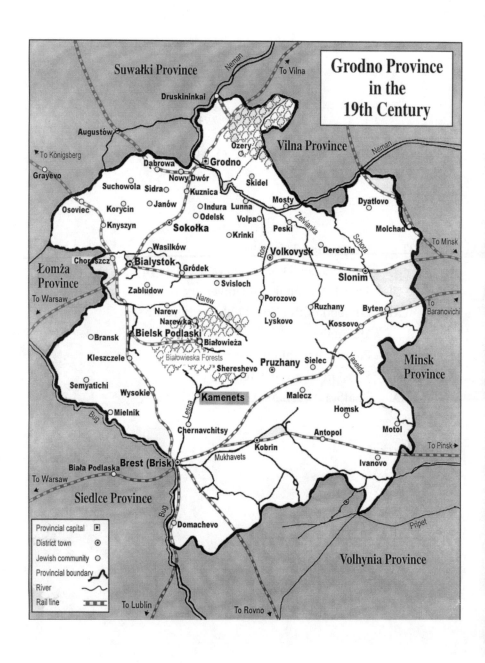

"LIFE AS IT WAS"—YEKHEZKEL KOTIK AND HIS MEMOIRS

Many things have happened in our lifetime that have not been recorded in any book only because of the foolish belief held by many people that nobody but the historians of the next generation can properly ascertain the true facts and form a correct and balanced picture. But by that time, many of the events of our age will have been forgotten. . . . The future scholar of merely ordinary human capacities, however, who will have to labor long and hard to write the chronicle of our times, will hold this generation's writers responsible. . . . And the writers who will bear the fullest share of the responsibility . . . will be those who know our people well, who are conversant with their way of life, whether high or low, and are too lazy to set it all down in detail.

Mendele Mokher Seforim ("Of Bygone Days")

"THE SONG OF THE SHTETL"

"This is not just a book—this is a treasure, a garden. A paradise full of blossoming flowers and singing birds." "I am crazed with delight!" "A simply monumental creation . . . it is a necessity that each Jewish home with an interest in the Jewish past be the proud owner of such a book." These remarks, penned by none other than Sholem Aleichem—the foremost early-twentieth-century Yiddish author— and by Yisrael Elyashev ("Ba'al-Makhshoves")—the leading literary critic of the day—represent but a sampling of the acclaim with which volume one of Yekhezkel Kotik's *Mayne zikhroynes* (My memoirs) was hailed.

First published in late 1912 in Warsaw, Kotik's *Mayne zikhroynes*—of which part one (of two) is here presented to the English reader under the title *Journey to a Nineteenth-Century Shtetl*—

can indeed be considered among the more notable and beautiful exemplars of early Yiddish memoir literature.[1] Its panoramic vista— encompassing the author's family; his childhood and youth; the community of Kamieniec Litewski (hereafter: Kamenets), where he grew up; its sites, institutions, and personalities; all those with whom he lived and those of whom he had but heard—not only provides evidence of Kotik's storytelling talent, but also makes his memoirs an authentic cultural document of prime importance, an incomparable source for the study of the history of the Jews in the nineteenth-century Pale of Settlement.

Peopled by the colorful figures of Great-grandfather, Grandfa- ther and Grandmother, Father and Mother, the author himself, his brothers- and sisters-in-law, aunts and uncles, nieces and nephews, the sixty- to seventy-member-strong Kotik clan also represents the chronological axis about which the plot of the memoirs revolves. At first glance nothing more than a four-generational Eastern Euro- pean family saga, a description of the life of a simple, albeit wealthy and influential, Jewish shtetl family, closer examination reveals that this simply serves as a pretext for Kotik to parade before the reader a gallery of varied figures and personalities, colors and sounds, fla- vors and smells preserved in his memory, described candidly and lovingly but with scant nostalgic embellishment.

Kotik vividly recreates for the reader days of joy and mourning, of hope and fear, painting his characters and plot with broad, lively strokes. A veritable pageant unfolds before our eyes. The drama of everyday life is played out before us, ranging from descriptions of panic child marriages, magic rites of exorcism and of halting an epi- demic, and the relationship between the Jews and the Russian au- thorities on the one hand and the Jews and the Polish lords on the other, to Jewish occupations. Through Kotik's mediation we make the acquaintance of a most variegated cast: the "hidden" Jews and cantonists, tax collectors and kidnappers, communal strongmen and householders, rabbis and rebbes, leaseholders and innkeepers, merchants and simple folk, hasidim and mitnaggedim, preachers and precentors, miracle workers and witches, scholars and ignora- muses, believers and freethinkers, informers and thieves, match- makers and wedding jesters, teachers and melamdim, all of whom inhabited Kotik's beloved birthplace.

Kotik's native town, Kamenets, constitutes the spatial axis of the memoirs. Viewed in the harsh glare of historical perspective,

Kamenets is perhaps nothing more than a marginal, unimportant community in White Russia. As seen through Kotik's lenses, however, it is the omphalos of the world. Like the master storyteller S. Y. Agnon's Galician Buchach, which mirrored an entire world, serving as an all-encompassing temporal and geographic microcosm, so too Kotik's Kamenets: somehow the town and its residents encapsulate the pith of Eastern European Jewish history. Not only do Kotik's memoirs relate to major historical events—the decrees of Tsar Nicholas I, the abolishment of the Kahal, the freeing of the serfs, or the Polish rebellions—they also touch upon the most basic existential questions affecting the Jews of Eastern Europe in the modern period: the undermining of the traditional world; the shift from a feudal class society to a precapitalist one; the sociocultural conflict between hasidim, mitnaggedim, and maskilim regarding the shape of the Jewish future; the collapse of traditional authority—whether religious or familial—and the growth of new sources of authority, to name but a few. Although here distilled into the context of one small shtetl, in actuality, as played out in Kamenets these transformative processes mirror those taking place in Jewish lives in hundreds of towns throughout Eastern Europe.

Perusal of Kotik's memoirs almost inadvertently evokes musings on the fate, method, and twists and turns of historical writing, broaching the question of how an "unimportant" community, whose rabbis, leaders, and internal history never received special attention in "official" historiography, can become a reflection of historical events. So, too, is history written, relying mainly on a literary-documentary tradition preserved by chance. The historian's "narrative" may be regarded as nothing more than a cleverly systematic, critical integration of the "stories" and images, documents and testimonies that have survived and come into his purview. Indeed, the stories preserved by talented writers and documentarists, either their own or others, not only shape our vision of the past, they also influence how historians determine what is "important" and what is not. In the past generation the theoretical aspects of the threefold affinity between autobiography (or memoirs), historical truth (things as "they were"), and literary invention have been subjected to intensive examination based upon exemplars from different cultural and temporal contexts.[2] The unique status of Kotik's memoirs as a historical source and the problematic aspects of their utilization are considered later in this introduction.

Let me simply note here that I prefer to define Kotik not as a historian but as a storyteller, not as a writer but as a raconteur. It is Kamenets's good fortune that its son, Yehezkhel Kotik, has recounted its history in his memoirs, that because of his talent it has achieved a position of "importance" in our repository of the Eastern European shtetl and its inhabitants.[3]

KAMENETS AND ITS ENVIRONS

The geographical twists and turns affecting Eastern Europe have determined that the formerly Polish town of Kamenets, which lies at the edge of the large, swampy, forested Polesie region,[4] is presently found within the borders of Belarus, or White Russia. Located some thirty-five kilometers north of the district capital of Brisk (Brześć Litewski; Brest), 175 kilometers south of Grodno, and 155 kilometers northwest of Pinsk, Kamenets was founded in the latter half of the thirteenth century and went into decline in the early eighteenth century.

Its situation on the eastern bank of the Lesna River, one of the larger tributaries of the Bug, placed Kamenets at the heart of a confluence of borders and cultures. Situated at the intersection of two major commercial crossroads—within the commonwealth of Poland-Lithuania, it lay conveniently near the highway that connected Kraków, the Polish capital in the south, with Vilna, the Lithuanian capital in the north—Kamenets also played a role in east-west trade between Poland-Lithuania and Muscovite Russia. Although originally part of Poland, the town's non-Jewish population was composed mainly of ethnic Belorussians and Ukrainians.[5] Furthermore, Kamenets's proximity to the popular hunting sites in the huge Białowieska Forest, and its important medieval archeological remains (a military tower known as the "Slup"), made it a popular way station and retreat for kings, nobles, and aristocrats.

Under the administration of the Polish-Lithuanian commonwealth, Kamenets was assigned to the Brisk province (*wojewodztwo*) and district (*powjat*). Indeed, until the early eighteenth century Kamenets was home to the district governor (*starosta*). Immediately following the third division of Poland in December 1795, the northeastern area of Poland, now annexed to Russia, was redefined. Under the Russian administration, Lithuania was divided into two provinces (*guberni*), Vilna and Slonim, with Kamenets

Jewish youth boating on the Lesna River
(1932). The "Slup" is in the background

assigned to the Slonim province. Eight months later, in August
1796, the Slonim province was divided into eight districts (*uyezdi*)[6]
and Kamenets was now assigned to the Brisk district. In December
1796 the two provinces were united into the "Lithuanian province,"
whose capital was at Vilna. In September 1801 this united Lithuanian province was again split into two: the Vilna and Grodno provinces. The latter, whose administrative center was located in the
city of Grodno, was essentially identical to the previous Slonim
province and its districts. This state of affairs remained virtually
unchanged until 1915,[7] when World War I reached the area. Under
Tsarist Russia, the period relevant to Kotik's memoirs, adminis-
tratively Kamenets belonged to the Brisk district of the Grodno
province.

Our first evidence of an organized Jewish community in Kamenets comes from the seventeenth century: the township is mentioned in the *Pinkas* (Minute Book) of the Jewish communities in
Lithuania as one of the communities belonging to "the border and
environs of the holy community of Brisk."[8] According to the 1847
census, the Jews of Kamenets numbered 1,451: 645 men and 806

women.[9] These data are certainly imprecise, as we must add to this figure an unknown number of "unregistered" Jews who thereby evaded conscription and taxes.[10] In 1897, out of a total population of 3,569,[11] some 2,722 Jews were registered; in other words, in the late nineteenth century, Kamenets's Jews comprised some 76 percent of the town's total population.

It is not only from a geographical-social viewpoint that Kamenets must be classed as a "border town," but from a Jewish viewpoint as well. Here the distinctive cultural-religious worlds of Lithuanian and of Polish Jews met and clashed, a conflict of which the sharp antagonism between the mitnaggedic world of Lithuanian learning and the magnetism of the hasidic rebbe and his court is but a single aspect. Kamenets was also a venue where stratified Polish society encountered the language, institutions, and conceptual world of the new Russian regime's enlightened absolutism. Varying degrees of hostility, tension, and cooperation characterized interaction between the population's various components—Polish lords, government and police officials (mainly Polish), Belorussian and Ukrainian serfs, Catholic and Russian Orthodox clergy. Often caught in the middle, for better or for worse, Kamenets's Jews were part and parcel of this social mosaic.

During the interregnum between the two world wars, the historical fate of Kamenets, then part of the independent Polish republic, differed not a whit from that of hundreds of its fellow Eastern European towns. Known as shtetls, these small towns were destined to become a symbol of culture, identity, and longing.

The signification of the polysemous term "shtetl" chosen by Kotik to describe his hometown (called in his introduction: *a kleyn kharakteristish shtetl*) has become blurred since the destruction of Eastern European Jewry. What exactly is this shtetl, most accurately translated into English as "town"?[12]

From a sociohistorical viewpoint the term shtetl refers to a physical enclave represented by hundreds of small and midsized towns in Eastern Europe whose Jewish character was in clear evidence, obvious even to the casual observer, if only from a demographic viewpoint. These towns, in some of which Jews outnumbered non-Jews, were the main form of Jewish settlement in Eastern Europe until the late nineteenth century. They are to be distinguished on the one hand from isolated villages (*dorf* or *yishuv* in Yiddish) where only a handful of Jews dwelled, and from the large densely populated city (*groyse shtot*) on the other, which became the dominant form of Jewish settlement only in the late nineteenth century.

As early as the late nineteenth century and more powerfully from the early twentieth century on, the shtetl was sometimes perceived popularly and folkloristically as an experience, a mood, a "state of mind," linked not only to a defined space but also to the soul, possessing not just physical reality but also a spiritual geography. Shtetl came to be identified, by friends and foes alike, with traditional Jewish society and with the "old way of life" created in its context as these developed in Eastern Europe. This simplistic nostalgic identification later contributed to a one-dimensional vision of Eastern European Jewry, notwithstanding its complexity and the sweeping changes that occurred in the process of its transformation from a traditional to a modern society. Nor does it fully reflect the variegated human, cultural, social, economic, and religious types it contained.

More than anything else it seems that the memory of the Holocaust and its accompanying destruction must be identified as a major factor obscuring this multidimensionality and contributing to the monolithic representation of Eastern European Jewry via the myth of "the shtetl." With the passage of time, this myth has taken firmer hold, finding popular expression in belles lettres, the plastic arts, music, television and cinema, and in the mass media. The musical "Fiddler on the Roof," a simplistic reading of Sholem Aleichem or Isaac Bashevis Singer's works, superficial examination of Mark Chagall's paintings or Roman Vishniac's photographs, or the surprising rejuvenation of *klezmer* music in recent years may be seen as signs of this popularization of the shtetl. In addition, the post-Holocaust era has seen the proliferation of personal memoir literature written by Eastern European survivors as well as hundreds of memorial books (*Yizker-bikher*) dedicated to destroyed Jewish communities, portraying their hometowns in a naive and harmonious light. All these have contributed to the shaping of a false collective memory of the shtetl: a unifying vision that avers all Jewish towns resembled each other—know one, know them all, and leads to the identification of the shtetl with an artificial sentimentalized fictional creation and to its identification with Eastern European Jewish culture as a whole, from the beginning of Jewish settlement in Poland to the Holocaust.

Kotik penned his memoirs well before these distinctions became obscured. While it is true that he limited his description to the geographically defined, "real" shtetl of Kamenets, in his introduction he also identified it with the "poetry of those former shtetls," which in 1912 was being silenced because of persecution in Russia and mass immigration to America.

I have therefore chosen to remain faithful to Kotik's original terminology (except in cases where stylistic considerations prevailed). Kotik was well aware of the distinction between city and town,[13] but he did not always use these terms precisely. Throughout his memoirs Kotik utilizes both "shtetl" (town) and "shtot" (city) to describe his hometown of Kamenets, which was, by any criterion, a midsized town.[14] Kotik refers to Kamenets as a *shtot* on scores of occasions (though never as a large town—*groyse shtot*)—and it is difficult to arrive at a systematic distinction between *shtetl* and *shtot* in Kotik's usage.

The reasons for this admixture are not solely attributable to inconsistency or imprecision on Kotik's part. Despite the obvious differences, Yiddish speakers made no clear semantic distinction between a large and a medium-sized town, referring to both as shtetl (but not as *kleyn* [small] *shtetl*). In actuality, there was not much difference between a large town, a small city (*shtot*), or a district center (*provints-shtot*). In these nineteenth-century patterns of residence it seems safe to assume that the Jewish population of both a large town and a small city numbered between two and five thousand. Population size was therefore not the distinguishing criterion; rather it was the presence in a small city of modern educational institutions (such as gymnasia) and also of government officials.[15] Another possible reason for this "imprecise" use of terminology may lie in the fact that from the inception of Jewish settlement in Poland Jews enjoyed a unique legal status similar to that of city dwellers, even when they lived in towns.

Kotik, writing his memoirs in the teeming city of Warsaw with its multitude of Jewish and non-Jewish residents, was certainly aware that most Eastern European Jews were living in cities, with all the accompanying socioeconomic problems of rapid urbanization. From his point of view, any form of Jewish life not identified with either the modern city or with rural settlements is a shtetl, which had become, even during his lifetime, not just a territorial designation but a target of yearning symbolizing the old way of life.

Perhaps small and economically insignificant, nonetheless Kamenets supported a vibrant social and cultural life. Its five hundred Jewish families, the absolute majority of the population until the Holocaust, left their indelible impression on the town. In addition to the hundreds of young scholars studying at the Knesset Beit Yitzhak Yeshiva (founded in 1897 in Slabodka, a Kovno suburb, and relocated, after many vicissitudes, in Kamenets in 1926),[16] Kamenets was home to animated national and Zionist activity, youth movements, local politicking, secular culture, and sports, among other spheres.[17]

In 1939 the Russian army conquered Kamenets, imposing the iron rule of communism. On 22 June 1941, with the outbreak of hostilities between Russia and Nazi Germany, the Germans took the town without opposition. Several days later a hundred Jews were murdered in the nearby Pruska Forest, and the remaining Jews were concentrated in a two-block, unfenced ghetto area. Time began to run out for the Jews of Kamenets. Some of its Jews were transferred to the Pruzhany ghetto and later sent to Auschwitz. The remaining Jews of Kamenets died in the Treblinka concentration camp. Only a few survived.[18] By the end of World War II, Lithuanian Jewish Kamenets, Kotik's beloved town, was no more.

YEKHEZKEL KOTIK: THE MAN AND HIS TIMES

Born in Kamenets on 25 March 1847 into a wealthy family of communal officials and leaseholders, until his marriage at age seventeen, Yekhezkel, or Khatskl, as he was known in Yiddish, lived a life of ease. Educated in the traditional manner—in the heder and by private tutors—this instruction failed to actualize his intellectual potential (something, we shall see, Kotik blamed on his father's hasidic outlook). In 1865 Kotik married Libe, an orphan from Pinsk, whom he first saw on their wedding day. His adolescent years paralleled a period of decline in the family fortunes, the result of socioeconomic turmoil in Russia: the liberation of the serfs in 1861; the suppression of the Polish rebellion in 1863; and the concomitant fatal blow to the status of the Polish aristocracy.

Whereas Kotik's grandfather and his mother's entire family belonged to the militant mitnaggedic camp that despised Hasidism and its leaders, subsequent to his marriage Kotik's father became attracted to Hasidism, becoming an ardent follower of the Slonimer

Yekhezkel Kotik, 1847–1921

and Kobriner rebbes. Although drawn to this magical world as a youth, upon attaining maturity—but prior to his marriage—Yekhezkel secretly reached a decision to abandon the hasidic world and became a mitnagged. Coming to light immediately after Kotik's marriage, this shift in allegiance created a troublesome estrangement between Kotik and his father, one that persisted throughout Kotik's life.

Following their marriage the young couple initially tried to support themselves by keeping shop, but met with abject failure. It was during this period that their first child, Avraham—later an active socialist—was born, and that we find Kotik embarking upon a series of frustrated attempts to acquire an education and a suitable livelihood. The present volume, which contains part one of the memoirs, is devoted to this period of Kotik's life: childhood, adolescence, and young manhood.

From that point onward, as catalogued in part two of Kotik's memoirs, failure, disappointment, and missed opportunities form the prevailing motifs of Kotik's life. Part two of Kotik's memoirs unfolds the tale of Kotik's plight as a young family man thwarted in his attempts at self-realization and education, and buffeted by forces beyond his control. A gentle nature, an early marriage, the need to earn a living, and family conflicts sidetracked Kotik from attaining his ambitions. Favored with economic security while growing up, for Kotik Kamenets formed the center of the world. Being forced to exchange the secure nest where his family had resided for generations for a life of wandering and sorrow in the Pale of Settlement was in his eyes tantamount to the expulsion from Eden. It should not surprise us that, given the hapless circumstances of Kotik's life, he visualized himself as a prototypical Diaspora Jew, a reincarnation of Sholem Aleichem's Menakhem-Mendl: "I am a true diaspora Jew, a wanderer, a Jew with a large sack, seeking a livelihood: a melamed, a leaseholder, a property owner, a shopkeeper, a vintner, a Menakhem-Mendl, turning hither and thither, unable to attain any goal."[19]

We can divide Kotik's life as extracted from the second volume of his memoirs and other sources into three main periods: his time as a *yishuvnik*, his time in Kiev (punctuated by brief stays in other cities), and his final station—Warsaw. Essentially, his biography can be viewed as a distillation of the processes affecting much of late-nineteenth-/early-twentieth-century Pale of Settlement Jewry.

Kotik's tale begins in 1867, when the worsening economic situation, sparked by the cancellation of leaseholds in the aftermath of the 1863 rebellion, first forced his father, Moshe, to exchange his former livelihood as a leaseholder for that of an unwilling villager. Kotik's parents took up residence in Wakhnovitz as leaseholders of a small estate, a move that cut them off from communal Jewish life and from the hasidic society so central to his father's lifestyle. Unable to envision himself as a *yishuvnik* leasing an estate or a tavern, Kotik remained in Kamenets meanwhile, and continued to dream of acquiring an education and of broadening his intellectual horizons. All his attempts to achieve this aim failed, however. Part one of the memoirs concludes with a description of how Kotik's father foiled his plans to study at the Volozhin yeshiva and to learn Russian in order to qualify for the post of "crown rabbi." In part two, Kotik describes how he tried his luck in Brisk and Bialystok, and how he began to work as a melamed in Warsaw and again met with failure.

It was not until the early 1870s that Kotik experienced some economic success, with his move to a small village in the Bialystok district by the name of Makarowsci, near the town of Krinki. There a relative of his named Sender Rosenblum lived with a Polish noble-woman who had fallen in love with him and bequeathed him all of her property. Kotik leased a dairy and a tavern from the pair and be-gan buying and selling milk, butter, cheeses, and wines, making a go of his business among the local peasants and nobility. Kotik worked hard, saved money, and spent his spare time in intellectual pursuits, reading works of Jewish philosophy and ethics and conversing with his neighbors—Jews and non-Jews alike.

The status of *yishuvnik*s underwent significant improvement in the 1870s: it was no longer shameful for a Jew to leave the town and live in the villages or forests. A series of recent socio-economic developments—first and foremost railroad construction, but also the opening of gymnasia to Jews, new commercial initia-tives, and the rapid demographic growth of the Jews in the Pale of Settlement—significantly shortened geographical distances in the Russian empire; concurrently, these developments reduced the physical and mental gap between urban and rural life. Also, the economic success many village Jews experienced totally eliminated their feelings of inferiority vis-à-vis urban dwellers.

Nevertheless, Kotik was seen as an exception among the simple, uneducated *yishuvnik*s—being both of distinguished lineage and a learned Jew. Kotik established a minyan in his home and invited his Jewish neighbors living on nearby estates to spend the Sabbath with him. Also enhancing Kotik's popularity was the fact that he sub-scribed to Hebrew newspapers such as *Ha-melitz* and *Ha-maggid*. The local Jews, hungry for the latest world and Jewish political de-velopments, transformed Kotik's tavern into a sort of social club.

Kotik took pleasure in rural life and, as noted, even enjoyed a large measure of success. Nonetheless, economic success per se did not interest him. He himself testified that he never allowed financial considerations to dictate his actions and that he always made do with the available resources. He neither knew, nor did he wish to know, how to cheat, lie, or indulge in self-aggrandizement. "What I sought was a peaceful life: easygoing, modest, without undue wealth, so that I would be able to read a book, to take care of the needs of the community, and to devote time to intellectual pursuits. Moreover, I always hated those people who devoted themselves entirely to business, their miserliness, their one-track thinking about money, their inability to find anything else of interest."[20]

The village's proximity to Krinki, and to Grodno especially, brought Kotik to the large city from time to time, where he purchased maskilic literature and made the acquaintance of maskilim and members of the new Jewish intelligentsia. At a certain stage Kotik moved his "business" to the heart of the nearby forest, where he also dealt in the sale of lumber for construction. Following the birth of their daughter, however, Kotik's wife developed tuberculosis, and involved with medicines and doctors, Kotik neglected the tavern and the dairy. Wanderlust awakened in Kotik's soul and he decided to leave Makarowsci, a decision that brought the period of naiveté and happiness in Kotik's life to an end.

Thus began Kotik's second, much more painful period as a *yishuvnik*. At that point in time, Kotik's grandfather presented him with the lease to a small estate named Kuszelewo, located between Kobrin and Pruzhany. Kotik's grandfather was misled by the Polish noble, and this "gift" became the worst disaster of Kotik's life—the remote estate lay in the heart of a thick, uninhabited, boggy forest, rampant with ravening wolves, poisonous snakes, and wild boars. Kotik and his family found themselves forced to take up residence among crude peasants and to learn agricultural pursuits. The estate's equipment and farmhouses were in a state of total rack and ruin, its fields were barren, there was no grazing land for cows, and nothing but hay could be grown there. Moreover, the damp and difficult climate destroyed their health: in the winter heavy snows brought damp and mold; in the summer, incessant forest fires also destroyed some of the dilapidated buildings. Kotik and his wife were in deep despair: far from friends and neighbors, they had no visitors and made no new friends, and they suffered terrible loneliness. The attempt to live in Kuszelewo was a stinging failure, causing them unspeakable distress.

It did not take long for Kotik, who spent dawn to dusk in the fields among the peasants, to realize that the move to a rustic milieu had been a mistake. He missed books, stimulation, intellectual life, and friendly conversations. He feared for his children's future, raised as ignoramuses among a non-Jewish population whose hostility found overt and covert expression, and bemoaned his fate. Meanwhile, his wife and children were stricken with typhus during an epidemic. The physicians summoned brought no relief, and as no one visited them, the sick family imposed a self-quarantine. For an entire month the family members hovered between life and death, hope and dejection, until the death of their infant son.

The Kotiks remained on this godforsaken estate for three years. Finally, at age thirty, burdened with responsibility for three children (two sons and a daughter), Kotik decided to change his life radically. He was ready to try his luck in the cities, based on his realization that for him it was better to be a poor townsman than a rich villager. He now joined the stream of immigrants leaving the drought- and famine-stricken northwestern provinces of the empire, following the route marked out by his hasidic brother-in-law Aharon Zailingold several years earlier. Zailingold had migrated to Kiev, where he ran an inn on the banks of the Dnieper. He now invited Kotik to join him, and, enthusiastic and naive as always, he jumped at this opportunity. Kotik sold the estate, of which he was certainly glad to rid himself, and moved his family to Kiev in 1876 or 1877.[21]

During Alexander II's liberal reign Kiev became an important Jewish center. Because of its central role in the developing economy of the awakening Russian empire, this large city was a preferred destination for Jewish emigrants from Lithuania, the Ukraine, and the provinces of New Russia. Although officially only certain types of Jews were allowed to reside in the city—rich merchants and their servants, holders of diplomas, or professional artisans—in practice many Jews without professions, like Kotik, managed to settle there, albeit living in constant fear of police raids.[22] Kotik's first venture was the purchase of a small grocery store in one of Kiev's non-Jewish neighborhoods, where he installed his family in a nearby apartment. They were the only Jews on the block and Kotik began once again to taste the sense of failure that was a constant theme of his adult life. The small non-Jewish children teased his children, the grocery business was not a success, and Kotik barely scraped by.[23] Kotik began to seek out new means of earning a living: he switched stores, engaged in sale of dried fruits, rented an apartment that allowed him to take boarders, worked as a manager in a bakery— but found no satisfaction for his growing frustration. He decided to keep wandering and to try his luck in Kharkov, where his uncle Hillel Fried, who had become a railroad magnate, resided.

Kotik remained in Kharkov for a few months, earning his living by renovating houses and working in the office of the railroad station. He lived in his wealthy uncle's house, where he was exposed to the carefree lifestyle of Jewish high society and its partial adoption of Russian culture. Kotik failed to fit in here, either; moreover, the foreman tormented him. Kotik again thought to seek his fortune elsewhere, this time in Moscow. The hopes he placed in the metropolis, however, were disappointed. Unable to find work, he decided to return to his family in Kiev.

Kotik now tried his hand at producing and selling raisin wine. To his surprise, he experienced success and his wines sold well. For the first time in years Kotik enjoyed a sense of security; from his restricted viewpoint even the political climate seemed encouraging. Yet his joy was short-lived. Under the surface the empire was in turmoil. Antisemitism was rampant in all circles; revolutionary cells and terror were endemic. On 1 March 1881 (13 March according to the Gregorian calendar), members of the revolutionary Narodnaya Volya (People's Will) murdered the beloved Tsar Alexander II. The assassination shook Russia to the core, fundamentally altering the Russian attitude toward Jews as well as their status.

An ill wind of hatred and incitement, fanned in the streets and in the press, pervaded the atmosphere. After the Jews of Yelisavetgrad and the nearby villages were attacked on 15 April came the turn of Kiev's Jews, who knew exactly what to expect. Kotik gave apt expression to the tense atmosphere preceding the oncoming catastrophe: "This must be how sheep feel when being led to slaughter."[24] Indeed, 26 April saw the initiation of a three-day pogrom against the Jews of Kiev and its suburbs, during which the shell-shocked Kotik family hid in a woodshed and an attic, fearfully watching the killing, raping, and looting in the city. Kotik's description of the mouselike emotional state of the hiding Jews, their humiliation, despair, and hopelessness, counts as one of the most impressive of its type.[25]

Volume two of Kotik's memoirs closes with the Yekhezkel Kotiks' final relocation to Warsaw in the aftermath of this traumatic experience, and with the bitter news of the death of his admired grandfather, the strongman of Kamenets, who had remained there all those years. As we shall see in the following, Kotik completed a third volume of his memoirs, which concentrated on his initial period in Warsaw, and evidently even planned to write a fourth volume. This third volume has been lost, thus we can reconstruct but a limited portion of Kotik's life in Warsaw via his other writings, newspaper articles, and later memoirs, and to some degree via the memoirs of his son Avraham.

The Kotiks arrived in Warsaw, which had become a magnet for Jewish immigration in the late nineteenth century, in August 1881.[26] Here Kotik finally achieved the stability he had sought throughout his entire adult life, immediately making his mark as a public figure, directing his energies mainly to the Lithuanian immigrant community. Having resided in Warsaw previously—Kotik had spent a number of months there as a melamed in 1867[27]— he was well aware of Polish Jewish hatred for their Lithuanian brethren. Easily distinguishable from the local Jewish population by virtue of their different dialect of Yiddish, customs, and nature, Lithuanian Jews in Warsaw suffered isolation and social ostracism. Kotik ascribed the origins of the derogatory epithets *Litvak-khazir* (Lithuanian pig) and *Litvak-tseylem-kop* (lit. "Lithuanian cross-head," meaning cunning blade, or heretic) to this period. "When a Lithuanian Jew walked down Nalewki Street," A. Litvin (pseudonym of Shmuel Hurwitz) wrote, "hundreds of Polish hasidic children ran after him derisively shouting: 'Litvak-khazir, tfoo, tfoo, tfoo!' "[28] Kotik, described by Litvin as "a living representative of the internal peregrinations of Russian Jewry,"[29] worked tirelessly within the "Lithuanian colony," becoming the adhesive that bonded its members together.

The Lithuanian Jewish immigrant society in Warsaw was made up both of "new" immigrants—those who arrived straight from the Lithuanian towns and those who were among the Jews expelled from Moscow in 1891–92—and of "old" immigrants like Kotik who came in the wake of the pogroms of the 1880s and after previous relocations. Kotik's home served as a social center for Lithuanian Jews of all types, a magnet drawing both chance guests and traveling merchants. Kotik, as we shall see, even founded a unique minyan, which prayed according to the Lithuanian custom and around which charitable and welfare societies were organized. The driving force behind this synagogue, Kotik delivered sermons, preaching to his audience a model of moral-religious behavior in the spirit of the organizational bylaws and didactic pamphlets he published.[30]

For his livelihood Kotik ran an inexpensive dairy restaurant in the heart of teeming Jewish Warsaw, at 31 Nalewki Street. A sort of café, it eventually became a meeting place and vibrant sociocultural center for young intellectuals, budding Yiddish writers, and workers' movement activists (with whom Kotik's oldest son Avraham was intensely involved). The publisher Shlomo Shrebrek penned the following description of this restaurant:

> The Yiddish writers could also be found in one café on Nalewki Street. This was not a particularly expensive eatery; one could have a satisfying lunch there for twenty kopecks. Its patrons were mainly poor merchants; agents, office clerks, and once in a while a teacher came in. The newspaper *Ha-tzfirah* was out on the table, and it seems to me that this was the only restaurant where this newspaper was available. People sat there for hours, reading the paper, meeting others, talking, sometimes doing everything at once, even those who had just met for the first time. . . . They also used to converse there about the latest literary news, the week's articles, and the manners of the writers themselves: about Frishman, Nahum Sokolow, Peretz, about "Zionism," various local matters and more general Jewish ones. All these were the topics of the day.[31]

The poet Avraham Reisen, a friend of Avraham Kotik, also noted this institution's uniqueness. Upon entering the inner courtyard, Reisen wrote, one immediately noticed Kotik's café because of its glass door. Although its bustling atmosphere was in no way distinguishable from that of any other coffeehouse, it differed in nature nevertheless. Frequented by salespeople and clerks from the commercial enterprises on nearby Gęsia Street, budding writers and Hebrew teachers, Zionists and Bundists, PPS (Polska Partia Socjalistyczna—Polish socialist party) members and the unaffiliated—a sort of political and social grab bag—this naturally sparked off debates over every trivial matter. "Tall and fat," Mrs. Kotik did not enjoy the arguments—notwithstanding their relatively mild nature—and angrily rushed to hush the contestants, fearful that the shouting would draw unwanted attention from the police. Mr. Kotik, himself a tall, well-built, and imposing figure, was much more tolerant. According to Reisen, and much to his wife's displeasure, Kotik neglected his business affairs, devoting himself instead to the publication of his pamphlets and bylaws at his own expense. He took pride in these publications, and engaged in nonstop preaching of the same principles of proper moral behavior that he published in these written works. The fact that the coffeehouse served as a reading club also made for a relatively peaceful atmosphere. Kotik supplied copies of all the leading Jewish newspapers: a special rack on the wall held copies of Hebrew, Yiddish, German, and Russian papers.[32]

The writer A. Litvin, who first encountered Kotik in the first decade of the twentieth century—that is, before Kotik published his memoirs—sheds intriguing light on his colorful personality. Litvin took particular notice of the public-spirited aspect of Kotik's personality—his involvement in initiating and forming mutual aid societies for the poor and the needy, primarily for Lithuanian Jews who felt lost and abandoned in Warsaw. Kotik could easily have used his personal connections to promote his own business affairs, becoming a successful merchant, Litvin averred. Yet Kotik had no such desire. "He lived in a different, more just and beautiful world," solely concerned with devoting his energies to how to help the poor and the weak, Litvin wrote.[33] Kotik himself echoed this goal in one of his publications: "My sole desire in life is to see them [his coreligionists] live peacefully, quietly, and happily at home and in the world."[34]

Kotik's organizational and propaganda activity revolved around the café under his management. Although he did not enjoy great profits, Litvin commented, neither did he run up large expenditures, "and there was food there at least and he would thus not die of starvation." There was also a telephone in the café—a rare commodity in early-twentieth-century Warsaw—utilized by Kotik in the service of the public matters in which he took an interest.[35] Not only did Kotik's personality combine energy with organizational ability, he was also endowed with naive idealism and strong enthusiasm for the cause of the weak. By virtue of these traits Kotik managed to persuade others to assist the associations he founded. He himself prepared their bylaws, and succeeded—with no legal training—in attending to every detail. He published these organizational charters in small brochures (see appendix A) distributed gratis to all those who frequented his café.

This propensity for organization and propaganda was already evident during Kotik's childhood. In his memoirs he recounts some of this activity—how he organized a group of youths in Kamenets to jointly purchase copies of talmudic tractates, and how this society collapsed when he fell ill; how he led protest demonstrations against the synagogue beadle; and how he even headed a group intending to colonize Palestine, to mention several examples.[36]

The first society Kotik founded in Warsaw was called Achiezer.[37]

A meeting of Warsaw physicians and philanthropists to
establish a school for midwives (Kotik, front row, center)

Formed in 1888 by a board of seven members headed by Kotik, its
main objective was to provide aid for the sick. Within a short period
of time its membership grew, reaching six hundred a year later. Yet
this society did not restrict its activities to assisting the sick. Its
members also founded a special synagogue, first in a private home,
and later at 38 Dzika Street. Kotik, the moving force behind this
synagogue, promulgated unique rules, grounded in his criticism of
the emphasis on "honors" in religious life. On this basis he eliminated special seating and militated against the prestige associated
with certain portions of the weekly Torah reading. He also preached
against the popular reluctance to being called up to the Torah when
the portions containing the execrations are read (Lev. 26:14–45;
Deut. 28:15–44, which describe the curses that will befall the Israelites if they flout the terms of the covenant) and made certain
to be called up for those portions.[38] The society continued to grow,
but, due to internal dissension, dissolved after five years. Two years
later, in 1896, after a trading clerk in a store in the Powązki quarter
starved to death, the society was revived by a group of young people who had gathered around Kotik. This time Kotik prepared special bylaws, which he even had printed.[39] The society's members

again founded a synagogue, located at 31 Gęsia Street. In 1901 the society received a governmental license and opened its offices at 27 Karmelicka Street, where it continued to function until 1914 at least. Achiezer also branched out into other areas through its subsocieties, which assisted orphans and the poor, and ran soup kitchens in Warsaw and in Otwock. This rapid growth was again accompanied by internal disagreements, instigated mainly by "Polish" activists disgruntled by Achiezer's Lithuanian flavor.[40] In the final analysis, the "Poles" split off, founding a new society named Bikkur Holim ha-Kelali (General Society for Visiting the Sick).

According to Litvin, Kotik's public activity also had its tragic aspect. Once well established, the activists involved in the societies he initiated, finding his dominant personality and obsessive attention to detail tiresome, often shook him off in short order. In addition, his avoidance of public acclaim angered those officials who engaged in public activity specifically for this purpose. This tension is well exemplified in the founding of the Moshav Zekenim (Old Age) society. This project was initiated upon Kotik's discovery that the greater Warsaw area, with its 250,000 Jews, had not a single old age home, and, as was his wont, Kotik now devoted all his energies to this idea and wrote up detailed bylaws. His efforts were crowned with success: he founded an exemplary organization whose net worth was valued at some thirty thousand rubles. Yet in the final event, Kotik was not even invited to the founding meeting. A furor ensued in the Jewish community. Goaded by a sense of shame, the officials—themselves Kotik appointees—reinstated Kotik to the board of directors.[41]

The "unknown soldier of Warsaw's humanitarian institutions" was how the publicist Zevi Prylucki, the first editor of the Yiddish daily *Der moment,* termed Kotik, whereas the writer Hirsh-David Nomberg portrayed him "as an original and creative individual," simultaneously noting that of "the 101 ideas he thought up, one hundred were impractical and only one implementable."[42] In his memoirs Prylucki described Kotik's tireless efforts to persuade others of the necessity for his plans. He even found his way to the circles of assimilated Jews in Warsaw and succeeded in drawing influential figures like the doctor Henrik Nussbaum and the banker Adolf Peretz to his projects.[43]

In the absence of precise data, we cannot assess the success of Kotik's manifold plans: neither the number of societies and welfare

Front page of Kotik's unpublished manuscript *Torat adam* (1906)

projects actually founded nor their duration, functioning, or success. A matter for separate study, such an inquiry lies outside the
purview of this book. In any event, the necrologies published upon
his death unanimously agreed "that for past decades there was no
welfare society or federation in Warsaw that was not founded at

his initiative or without his close involvement."[44] It appears that of all the societies Kotik founded or sought to found, only three functioned successfully for any length of time: Achiezer, one of the first charity societies in Warsaw, which operated as an umbrella organization on the model of general charity societies such as the Vilna Tzedakah Gedolah society, and its two offshoots, Ezrat Holim (sick fund) and Ezrat Yetomim (orphans' fund).[45]

We must also recall that a certain amount of risk inhered to Kotik's activity. In pre-World War One Russian-ruled Warsaw almost any public activity was defined as "subversive." Even welfare organizations were considered illegal, and many such activities took place underground. It is not surprising, therefore, that in each and every proposed charter he published Kotik clearly stated in the title that he hoped "to acquire a license from the exalted government."[46]

In 1909 Kotik was bitten by a new "bug." He now conceived a program to relieve the housing problem afflicting many of Warsaw's Jews, who paid high rents and lived in overcrowded and unsanitary conditions. Not content with publishing special pamphlets outlining his ideas,[47] Kotik sought to found a special Jewish neighborhood where Jews could purchase apartments at reasonable prices and implement principles of cooperative living and social justice. He even managed to persuade the editors of the new Warsaw Jewish daily, *Der moment,* but recently founded in 1910, that they could increase its circulation by backing this cause. In its quest for a readership, the management of this publication was prepared to utilize cheap publicity gimmicks, and it quickly took this campaign under its wing. In summer 1911 a suitable plot of land was found and purchased by the newspaper in the Miłosna Forest, a resort area some twenty kilometers east of Warsaw.[48] Strident daily ads promoted a special deal: readers who collected fifteen of the coupons which appeared in the paper every day would be eligible to participate in the raffling off of a Miłosna lot once every two weeks. The lots would be given free of charge, and winners had the right to build private homes on them. In his memoirs editor Zevi Prylucki affirmed that this initiative of Kotik's indeed boosted the paper's circulation. However, although the campaign lasted for several months, the grandiose plan to create a Jewish "colony" in Miłosna never came to fruition.[49]

Of another failed Kotik-initiated plan we hear from the writer Hirsh-David Nomberg: to found what Kotik called a "tabernacle" or "folkshoyz" (community center). To this end, he assembled the directors of the Jewish societies in Warsaw in an attempt to convince them to erect a large building to house their offices. He also envisioned this building as a venue for lectures, concerts, and exhibits of Jewish interest. The directors of the Jewish societies, mistakenly convinced that Kotik intended to unify all the societies into one umbrella organization, fled for their lives.[50]

Kotik's life came to a turning point in 1912 when he acceded to his son Avraham's pleas and began to write his memoirs. He wrote like one possessed, and volume one went to press but four months later. The book, which appeared in Warsaw in late 1912, was an instant success. Kotik immediately devoted himself to volume two, which appeared in Warsaw in late 1913, and then to volume three, which was never published and has evidently been lost. During 1913 and 1914 Kotik immersed himself in the writing of his memoirs, in replying to the reactions he received regarding his book, and, in particular, in the exceptional correspondence that developed between him and the writer Sholem Aleichem. We know but little of his life from 1914 on. He apparently fell ill shortly thereafter and became bedridden.

At noon on Saturday, 13 August 1921 (the Ninth of Av), Kotik died in Warsaw, following a lengthy and difficult illness, according to the Jewish press. He was seventy-four.[51] His funeral was held the next day. The procession originated from his home at 11 Muranowska Street,[52] and made its way to the Jewish cemetery in Warsaw, where M. A. Hartglas, one of the Zionist movement leaders in Poland, eulogized him.[53] The second edition of Kotik's memoirs, containing both parts one and two, which he prepared for publication during the final year of his life, was published in Berlin several months after his death.

THE RECEPTION OF THE MEMOIRS

"I Am Crazed with Delight": Yekhezkel Kotik and Sholem Aleichem

Yiddish readers greeted the publication of the first volume of the memoirs in late 1912 with surprised delight.[54] No one had imagined that Kotik, the elderly community activist, also had literary talent. "Where have you been until now?" Sholem Aleichem queried, as he had not before even heard of Kotik. The reactions of Sholem Aleichem—whom Kotik admired and whose literary verdict he accepted as binding—seem to have greatly influenced Kotik's subsequent decisions. To Sholem Aleichem's enthusiastic reception of part one we must at least partially attribute Kotik's immediately devoting himself to the writing of part two. Furthermore, it is possible that it is to his cold reception of this second part which we must attribute Kotik's decision to bury part three, including the first sixty-five pages, which had already been printed, now evidently lost.

This relationship between Kotik and Sholem Aleichem is of special interest, as the two—who had not previously met—carried on a brief but intense correspondence, of which only portions are extant.[55] The famous writer, then confined to his sickbed, revealed to Kotik the details of his illness and his mood swings, praised Kotik's writing, and encouraged him to continue writing his memoirs. For his part, Kotik saw the interest taken in him as the ultimate honor, and he shared his writing methods and his aims with his pen pal. As this relationship also had some influence on Sholem Aleichem's literary path in 1913, it warrants further investigation.

Sholem Aleichem received a copy of volume one of the memoirs shortly after its publication. It seems that in mailing the first copies of his book to Sholem Aleichem, to the critic Shmuel Niger, and

Sholem Aleichem (at right) and "Ba'al Makhshoves," Kovno 1905

to his friend the poet Avraham Reisen, Kotik experienced some confusion. The copy with a dedication to Niger was mistakenly sent to Sholem Aleichem (both were then in Switzerland), and the one for Reisen (then in the United States) ended up being sent to Niger. Sholem Aleichem, hospitalized at that time in a sanatorium near the Swiss city of Lausanne,[56] could not resist taking a look at the book, began reading, and but a few days later, on 6 January 1913, penned his first impressions to Kotik.

In his letter Sholem Aleichem informed Kotik of the mailing mix-ups and also complained of the printers' failure to bind the copies properly: he was unable to read the book without damaging the uncut pages, and finally, imbued by a passionate desire to read it, decided to cut the pages even though he knew this would make the book fall apart. In his humorous way, Sholem Aleichem suggested that Niger would be afflicted by the same evil passion and would treat the copy sent to him similarly. "I desire to read your book," he wrote to Kotik, "because my heart tells me that your memoirs belong to the type regarding which Gogol commented, that if each person seriously and honestly wrote his biography, then we would have a multitude of good books. I perused several pages and liked what I saw. . . . Today I am finishing my novel [*Der blutiker shpas*] and reciting *barukh she-petarani* [good riddance] and taking your memoirs to hand."[57]

A mere two days later we find Sholem Aleichem writing a letter to his friend Niger, then living in Berne: "It has been a long time since I have derived so much enjoyment from a book as I have from Yekhezkel Kotik's *Zikhroynes*. This is a family chronicle of unparalleled historical importance. I literally licked my fingers. I could not put the book down. I beg of you, write to me *immediately* who is this Jew? Where is he from? What does he do? Write everything you know of him. Have you looked at this book? And what do *you* say? After all, you are a critic and have more expertise than I. I am not sure of myself. It seems to me that this is capital—is it possible that I am wrong? I beg of you, write to me immediately!"[58]

It took Sholem Aleichem but two days to finish the book, according to his own testimony, reading nonstop and quickly penning a letter to Kotik (10–11 January 1913). This impressive letter, in which Sholem Aleichem doffed his hat to the memoirs' author's literary talent, was published by Kotik in the second edition of his memoirs and appears translated in full in this English edition as well.[59] In this letter Sholem Aleichem gave heartfelt expression to the great pleasure he derived from reading the book, to the outbursts of laughter interspersed by tears, to his identification with the characters, and to his admiration for Kotik's descriptive and reconstructive ability. In his words: "No! I, with my bunch of characters and all my portrayals—many of whom I knew, and many I have imagined—must admit without pretense or false modesty—I am compared to you, nothing but a poor child, a pauper!" Sholem Aleichem concluded by expressing the wish, almost an entreaty, that Kotik continue writing his memoirs:

> I am truly proud that a book like your memoirs has enriched our still young Yiddish folk-literature. Will you continue writing your memoirs? Will they be as rich and successful as the first volume? Successful—of that I am sure—rich—I don't know. I fear they might be leaner and thinner. Those Jews don't exist anymore! That is, they are here, but one doesn't notice them. . . .
>
> Please, answer me, if you can spare the time, whether you intend to go on writing more memoirs, of what period, which circles you have in mind, whether it runs as smoothly as it did up until now, and whether you will also write more about your family? There are types in your family that you must continue telling and telling about. Be well, keep your spirits up and write!

That very day, on 10 January, Sholem Aleichem penned another letter to Niger, again giving rein to his unrestrained enthusiasm for the memoirs—"I am crazed with delight!"[60]

On 13 January Sholem Aleichem again wrote to Kotik. That same day he had also received a copy of the popular Warsaw daily *Der fraynd* from 20 December 1912, in which Ba'al-Makhshoves— the pen name of the influential critic Isidor Elyashev—had written an extremely complimentary review of Kotik's book. Sholem Aleichem praised Elyashev's discerning literary taste, expressing his conviction to Kotik that sometime in the future Elyashev would make a detailed study or write a more substantive review "of your book or books. . . . After all, we know that you are writing a second part! Amen! May it be true!"

"I have yet to receive a reply from you," Sholem Aleichem complained, "and meanwhile I have the book in front of me with notes scribbled in the margins from which I hoped to prepare 'delicacies,' but 'Ba'al-Makhshoves' beat me to it."[61]

Kotik's reply, completed on 23 January 1913, reached Sholem Aleichem a few days later. Kotik, stunned by the praise showered upon his book by the famed author, first modestly replied that he felt Sholem Aleichem's estimation and recognition excessive. Personally, he had not imagined that the memoirs of a simple Jew like himself could be of value, until on one occasion after relating some episodes from his life to his son and one of his son's friends, they encouraged him to write. He began writing in winter 1911–12 and completed his work some three to four months later. "I am now hard at work on part two . . . which will present a picture of a true Diaspora Jew . . . that is of myself." In the continuation he noted that he intended to devote the third part to "Warsaw and its public workers. That must be as it represents my 'bag,' my specialty, as I founded nearly all the welfare societies operating in Warsaw. Parts of my soul disintegrated within." Kotik ended his reply with an entreaty to the admired writer: "Another letter from you is what I desire. The day I receive a letter from you is a holiday for me."[62]

Sholem Aleichem's next letter, completed on 28 January, was penned from a private hospital in Berne, to which he had been rushed ten days earlier because of the sudden onset of kidney disease.[63] "I am afraid that this letter will be a holiday whose happiness has been spoiled: I am writing this letter from the hospital in which I expected to die. . . . I have been feeling better for some days now and it seems to me that I may be able to finish my autobiography, which I began writing in 1908, [before I die]." He went on: "What will be now? I don't know. . . . I'm in terrible trouble. Yet I write and write anyhow. Most of all, I wish to write the story of my life." He recounted how in Geneva many prayed for his recovery, humorously noting his conviction that this synagogue and its prayer service in no way resembled the one in Kamenets. "Write me letters, old fellow," he concluded, "and finish your book!"[64]

Scholars have wondered what circumstances prompted Sholem Aleichem's renewed interest in writing his autobiography, the novel *Funem yarid* (From the fair) in 1913. Although begun in 1908, and despite the presence of autobiographical elements in his writing from its inception, Sholem Aleichem often declared—as he did explicitly in a letter from 1912—that he was delaying this task until his dotage, that at present he was but a youth at the threshold of his creativity. "But a year has gone by and he is writing his biography. What happened? Was this a sudden realization that he was nearing the end of his 'youth'? From whence came this feeling?" his friend and critic Niger wondered.[65] It is possible, and this surmise requires substantiation, that the fresh vitality of Kotik's memoirs, which, as noted, reached him just as he completed his long novel *Der blutiker shpas* (published in installments in *Haynt*), provided the impetus for Sholem Aleichem's renewed interest in autobiographical writing.

Comparison of *Funem yarid* and Kotik's *Mayne zikhroynes* merits study in and of itself, yet similarities and differences immediately spring to the eye. It suffices to cite a tidbit from the beginning of Sholem Aleichem's book, with its biting criticism of books of Kotik's ilk: "First, as is customary, we must introduce you to our hero's parents. So be glad I'm starting with Sholem's parents and not like other biographers with his grandparents and great-grandparents."[66]

To return to the letters: on 5 February Sholem Aleichem sent to Kotik—still from his hospital bed in Berne—a brief postcard in which he rejected Kotik's suggestion that he visit him in Switzerland in order to fulfill the mitzvah of visiting the sick (Kotik's letter was not preserved). He munificently negated the idea ("too far and too expensive"), adding, "this is a bad day for me! But do not be troubled. If I live, I shall certainly come to visit you at your coffeehouse and we'll get a little drunk."[67]

The next postcards from Berne (8–11 February) fluctuated between pessimism ("I was certain that yesterday was the end . . ."; "I had a terrible night, oh what a night!") and hope ("again, not good—but hopeful, hopeful!"). When he felt better, he directed his energies to the writing of his autobiography, "at times rolling with laughter, like a child uttering some nonsense and laughing at it."[68]

Sholem Aleichem's doctors finally concluded that an operation was not necessary and ordered him to travel to the Italian resort town of Nervi, near Genoa. From his stop in Vienna, he sent Kotik two optimistic postcards (1–2 March). The next day, 3 March, he sent another postcard, this time "from the most beautiful city in the world"—Venice.[69]

From this point on the correspondence abated somewhat. Perhaps Kotik was reluctant to bother Sholem Aleichem while he was recuperating in Nervi and awaited a sign from him. During Passover 1913 Sholem Aleichem renewed contact with an interesting announcement related to his own literary work. He had decided to incorporate his new friend into this work, explicitly using his name, and wanted Kotik's permission for this step. At that time Sholem

Aleichem had begun to publish his second series of feuilletons featuring his beloved protagonist Menakhem-Mendl in the Warsaw daily *Haynt*.[70] Although hopeful that his plans to visit Poland again and to meet with Kotik would be realized, he was aware in his heart of hearts that his health prevented this. Thus he created meetings with Kotik via his fertile imagination.

This time Sholem Aleichem transferred Menakhem-Mendl to Warsaw, where he was employed as a journalist. In his amusing letters to his wife Sheyne-Sheyndl, who remained behind in Kasrilevke, Menakhem-Mendl comments on current events and Jewish and international politics from his inimical viewpoint in the troubled pre-World War One period. And lo and behold, upon his arrival in Warsaw, Menakhem-Mendl makes the acquaintance of and becomes fast friends with one "Khaskl Kotik." Their talks, which take place in Kotik's coffeehouse, range from politics and wars to imaginary "projects" suggested by Menakhem-Mendl. Kotik, mentioned scores of times in these feuilletons, listens, argues, advises, and guides, while Menakhem-Mendl provides his wife with a weekly report:

> I take my walking stick and go to my *mleczarnia* [dairy restaurant] to drink coffee and to converse with people. My *mleczarnia* is on Nalewki, Khaskl Kotik's place. Why Khaskl Kotik's place you ask? To annoy the Polacks! . . . We sit and sit tête-à-tête, Khaskl Kotik and me, over a cup of coffee and discuss our Jewish brethren. . . .[71]
>
> I ran to my friend, to Khaskl Kotik. He is my confidant. He knows everything about me. "You seem very agitated these past few days Reb Menakhem-Mendl," says he. . . . He smiles, Khaskl Kotik that is, and turns to me in his pleasantly quiet manner: "Do not go nuts Reb Menakhem-Mendl," says he, "wait a bit," he says, "and hear of even worse things. . . ." A strange Jew this Khaskl Kotik is!

Sometimes he poked gentle fun at Kotik's literary pretensions, perhaps as a foil to his own: "How many times have I told him: 'Reb Khaskl,' I'm telling him, 'abandon all your nonsense' (like me he is involved in writing; but he does not write politics, he writes books), 'better we put our necks in the noose of war,' I tell him, 'that is what we would be better off doing!'. . . . He looks at me as if I were a madman: 'What do Jews like us, engaged in writing, have to do with war?' "

Even Sheyne-Sheyndl wondered about this new friend: "And who is this Kotik to whom you have become so swiftly attached that you are unable to live a day without seeing him? From which Kotiks is he descended? Is he married?. . . . Take care that he does not get you in trouble, or simply cheat you."

Concerning Kotik's personality, Sholem Aleichem wrote: "Khaskl Kotik likes to argue. . . ."; "This Jew has a tendency to ask questions all the time and to argue stubbornly about everything. Whatever you say to him, he must say the opposite! . . . Stubborn, willful mule"; "he becomes filled with anger—he is hotheaded, dangerous! . . . We tease each other mercilessly." Naturally, these descriptions drew upon Kotik's testimony about himself in his memoirs, such as: "Already from early childhood I was extremely inquisitive and kept pestering him with awkward questions" (chapter 8).

He also poked gentle fun at Kotik's "literary expertise" in the writing of bylaws. When Menakhem-Mendl conceived a project to publish "an entire plan with various bylaws" as a book to be distributed gratis in six million copies, "I stopped by my friend Khaskl Kotik. He has already published many such books, and he is conversant with the process, and we immediately took paper and pencil and made calculations."

When Menakhem-Mendl dreamed up a new "project"—a coffeehouse especially for Jewish writers and a professional writers' union—he informed his friend Kotik: "As soon as he heard the word 'society' he grabbed the chance and began to deluge me with advice. . . . He himself, he said, had founded innumerable such societies, more even, than the hairs on his head. For creating societies—he says—he has no equal. One society he founded is called 'Ozer Dalim' [Aid to the Poor]. If I like, says he, he will give me one, two, or three booklets of his Ozer Dalim society, so that I will learn from him and not make stupid mistakes."

Regarding Kotik's obsession with bylaws, he wrote: "This Jew, you should know, once he sticks to you, it is not so easy to get rid of him. He has stuck to me concerning this Jewish coffeehouse that I want to open with shares, that I take the bylaws he has written for me. Everything must have a legally authorized charter. What more do you need? Even for my book for the benefit of the immigrants he has also prepared a 'charter,' says he—this Jew is in love with 'charters.'"

Sholem Aleichem was uncertain as to Kotik's reaction, hoping
that he would not be angry because of the publicity he was giving
him in his hometown of Warsaw; thus he felt compelled to first
seek his permission. On 25 April 1913, Sholem Aleichem wrote to
him: "To my very dear friend, Reb Khaskl Kotik! This is the name
my Menakhem-Mendl has bestowed upon you in his second letter,
published in *Haynt,* and he will not forget you, God willing, in any
of his letters to Sheyne-Sheyndl. Every Friday, God willing, he will
mention you and I hope you are not angry with either him or with
me. I inform you of this in advance as there are those who like to
bare their teeth when their name appears in a feuilleton, and take
it amiss [as if they are being mocked] when people [in the street]
point them out. As I do not know you personally, I am writing to
you of my intent. God willing, after the [Passover] holiday, when I
arrive in your camp [Warsaw] we will have a good laugh over this
together."[72]

Kotik penned his reply immediately after the conclusion of the
holiday, on 28 April. He was delighted at the renewal of their correspondence, and as for Menakhem-Mendl—"I will let you in on a
secret. In the second part of my memoirs I present myself as a veritable Menakhem-Mendl. Thus, your Menakhem-Mendl could indeed
be my close friend." Yet the most exciting news was Sholem Aleichem's projected visit to Warsaw: "I am counting the days, and the
hours, and the minutes until your arrival," Kotik wrote. "Is it but
a paltry thing that this Menakhem-Mendl (as I see myself) should
make merry in the company of the delightful Sholem Aleichem?"
In concluding, he reported that the second part of his memoirs was
due to go to press shortly, and that he was currently engaged in
writing part three.[73]

Three weeks went by, during which more of Menakhem-Mendl's
letters appeared weekly in *Haynt.* In a letter to Sholem Aleichem
dated 21 May, Kotik treated his literary persona and its attributes,
particularly as the perennial advice-giver, humorously. "I am a little
cross with Menakhem-Mendl," he wrote. "A man too much in a
hurry to do everything without me. He asks me nothing, and pays no
attention to my advice. . . . I fear that he will make some blooper in
international diplomacy. . . . I warn you, my dear Sholem Aleichem,
that if Menakhem-Mendl does not come and consult with me, but
does everything without me, by himself instead, I will complain to
his wife. I already have her address. He will get a scolding from

her. . . . You have been silent for a long time. Why are you silent? Answer me. . . ."[74]

Sholem Aleichem sent an immediate reply (23 May), and as was his wont, countered humor with humor. His ostensibly unintelligible reply becomes clear against the background just described: "How can that be? What does it mean, he doesn't ask your advice? Whom then does he ask? To whom does he come every day? Who does he mention if not yourself? I found your brief letter incomprehensible, totally so. Why not write to me how you are? What the 'world' and the 'world-at-large' say about the 'Letters'? Write! We will soon be much closer than we are now."[75]

On 2 June Kotik replied to this missive, reacting, among other matters, to Sholem Aleichem's query regarding the response of the Warsaw man-in-the-street to Menakhem-Mendl's letters. This question was superfluous, Kotik wrote, as Sholem Aleichem was incapable of writing anything not first rate. Moreover, "the 'world' reads, grabs, swallows, and snaps up your witty, wise, and gently humorous letters."[76]

Summer 1913 saw an improvement in Sholem Aleichem's health. His wife Olga visited Warsaw in July and met with Kotik at his behest. On 4 August 1913, following a several-month-long break, Sholem Aleichem again wrote to his friend, this time from the German resort town of Wiesbaden.

> Only a letter you say? Is it not enough for you that my Menakhem-Mendl does not skip over you in any of his letters? On this Friday you will meet him, God willing, in the bylaws of the Kasrilevke *Hakhnasat Kallah* society. In short, he admires you greatly, my Menakhem-Mendl does, and even though he fights with you on many occasions, this passes quickly and he again runs to you, particularly to receive advice—but of that it is forbidden to speak! My wife brought me fond regards from you, but that is not sufficient—I myself must make your personal acquaintance. I refuse to believe that you have read nothing—your book proves the very opposite. God willing, we will meet in Warsaw after the holidays, no excuses. In the meantime, please answer me and write me letters . . .
>
> P. S. When will the second part of your *Zikhroynes* appear?[77]

In Menakhem-Mendl's reply to his wife's letter reporting the founding of a Hakhnasat Kallah society in Kasrilevke, Sholem Aleichem again poked good-natured fun at Kotik's expertise in founding societies:

I went straight to my friend Khaskl Kotik and found him hard at work—writing the bylaws for a new society. What kind of society—he prefers not to say. In the meantime, he said, it's a secret. But when it comes out this will occasion much joy in the world . . . there is nothing like this anywhere in the world. . . . For founding societies, says he, and composing bylaws, ask *me* he says, and I will present you with material! . . . Sit down please, says he, and I will dictate to you. . . . Do you think that this took forever, or that he pulled out some book or piece of paper, or what? No, orally, and without much prior thought, he just wrinkled his forehead, and just as I am writing this letter to you, it poured out of him like a hymn, fluently, smoothly, and in polished form: pearls and not words![78]

The fictional Kotik dictates the full name of the society to his friend Menakhem-Mendl: "the project of the bylaws of the Hakhnasat Kallah society of Kasrilevke, which awaits authorization from the exalted government," a typical "Kotikian" name.[79] From that point on Sholem Aleichem mocks the dozens of detailed paragraphs ("some sixty-odd") that the real Kotik used to publish in his brochures. But this droll ridicule on Menakhem-Mendl's part was accompanied by admiring respect: "Take a man like Khaskl Kotik. You may say whatever you like about him, and the elders of Kasrilevke can make as much fun of his Hakhnasat Kallah society as they like, but I tell you . . . I have learned a lot from this Jew . . . an immeasurable amount!"[80]

In his 15 August reply Kotik answered Sholem Aleichem's query regarding his knowledge of literature: "If you speak simply of belles lettres—I have read little; if you speak of works of philosophy and old Hebrew books: of these I have read quite a bit. With the works of Yiddish writers, I am largely unfamiliar. For them, I have not had any time at all, as you well know: societies, bylaws, charters, etc. were the only thing on my mind."[81] The sole author whose works he had read, Kotik confessed, was naturally none other than Sholem Aleichem. He had also resolved, as soon as he had some spare time, first to devote himself to reading Sholem Aleichem's works in their entirety and then to proceed to all the other well-known authors. As for the second volume of his memoirs, it would be published shortly, he promised.

The 1913 High Holiday season passed and Sholem Aleichem, who had not yet visited Warsaw, made do with sending a New Year's card.[82] Meanwhile, the second part of Kotik's memoirs appeared. On 30 November 1913 Kotik sent Sholem Aleichem a copy of the book.

CH. KOTIK

WARSZAWA
NALEWKI 31.

13/I 1914

A letter from Kotik to Sholem Aleichem, 13 January 1914

"You must have forgotten me already," Kotik opened his letter, "but I have not, nor shall I forget you." Anxious to hear Sholem Aleichem's opinion of the second part, he pressed him to "please take a look at the book, and grace me with a letter. I am looking forward to this like a child waiting for Hanukkah *gelt.*" An intriguing comment was appended to this letter: "My third book is already ready and will go to press shortly."[83]

Kotik awaited his pen pal's evaluation impatiently. On 2 January 1914 Sholem Aleichem sent his reply, this time from Paris. Sholem Aleichem, as we are aware, disliked the second part, but evidently sought a way to break the news gently, without hurting Kotik's feelings. He chose oblique allusion as his tactic: "Why have I not yet answered the letter sent with your second book? For two reasons: first, because I believed that I would be in Warsaw today or tomorrow . . . it all depends on the entry visa we shall receive on either the twelfth or the fifteenth of the month. And second, I wanted to look at your first book again, from which I was and remain so thrilled; perhaps because holiness pervades it, the sanctity of the ancient beloved past which has been lost forever. . . ."[84]

Sholem Aleichem, Warsaw, April 1914

Kotik failed to grasp these gentle hints, but sensed that something was amiss nonetheless. On 13 January 1914, he again begged Sholem Aleichem to send him his explicit opinion: "Your brief letter . . . disquieted me somewhat. Why did you 'suddenly' run to the first part of my book? Did you have doubts? Why no word concerning part two? . . . I anxiously await your verdict . . . like a good hasid awaiting a hint from his rebbe." By way of indicating the desired reaction, Kotik concluded with the following comment: "I. L. Peretz sent me a postcard using this very language: 'I am simply full of admiration for your second volume.' "[85]

If the truth be told, although Sholem Aleichem himself had encouraged Kotik to continue writing, in his heart of hearts he feared that Kotik would not be able to repeat his initial achievement, albeit not due to lack of talent. To recall, he had given explicit expression to these doubts when Kotik was just beginning his literary career.[86] Despite Sholem Aleichem's negative opinion of part two, somehow he encountered difficulty voicing his disappointment openly in his letters. What he only alluded to in his correspondence with Kotik, however, found overt expression in a letter to his friend Niger, to whom he penned the following "offhand" remarks: "Do you have Kotik's second volume already? What a waste. It ruined the flavor of the first for me. Such a naive Jew!"[87]

The final exchange of letters between Sholem Aleichem and Kotik that has been preserved dates to 26 February 1914. Sholem Aleichem was then in Nervi and once again evaded coming expressly to the point: "You ask for my opinion on the second volume? Can that be? After all I wrote to you long ago. What's going on with you?—robber! murderer! . . . I hope that we will soon meet in Warsaw. The 'world' is working hard at it. My agent is banging on the walls for me there—May God help him. Amen."[88]

Some two months later, Sholem Aleichem began his final tour of Russia. His first stop was in Warsaw in April 1914, where the Jewish public afforded him an admiring reception. Sholem Aleichem met with various Warsaw literary figures, and although we lack explicit proof, we can assume that the two met at this juncture.[89] Perhaps Sholem Aleichem was unable to avoid expressing his true opinion at this face-to-face meeting, and it may have been at his prompting that Kotik sent a copy of part three to Niger before submitting it to the press.[90] Was it Sholem Aleichem's and Niger's negative opinions that spurred Kotik to consign part three to oblivion? In the absence of documentary evidence this question must remain unanswered.

"The Big Spark of a True Writer" or "Silly Tales"?

Having traced Sholem Aleichem's reaction to Kotik's writing in great detail, it is time to examine how other contemporary writers received Kotik's memoirs. While many press notices and reviews were enthusiastic, particularly noting Kotik's contribution as the progenitor of a genre, others criticized the book's failings.

Regarding the opinion of I. L. Peretz, one of the central literary figures of Hebrew and Yiddish literature in general and of Warsaw in particular, we have virtually no documentation. Nonetheless, more than one hint of Peretz's enthusiasm has survived. Ba'al-Makhshoves made explicit mention of this enthusiasm in a review essay on Kotik he published in the Warsaw daily *Der fraynd:* "It has been a long time since I so enjoyed writing a review. . . . I held this book with enjoyment, taking joy in the fact that my old wish, that our grandfathers would begin to write their memoirs, has been partially fulfilled. My interest increased as I began to read the book. Although perhaps it is not fitting that a critic say so, nonetheless I must admit that this is the first time I have been so enthusiastic about a book that I paid almost no attention to the errors. Moreover, an even greater personage than I—I. L. Peretz—has shown similar interest in the book. He was then also reading Kotik's memoirs and spoke of them with enthusiasm bordering on my own."[91]

Furthermore, from the remark Kotik appended to his letter to Sholem Aleichem discussed earlier we can deduce that Peretz found the second part impressive as well. Peretz's memoirs began to appear in 1913 (first in installments in the press and later in book form) and we can perhaps conjecture a link between the appearance of and warm reception afforded Kotik's first volume and Peretz's embarking upon the writing of his own memoirs, which were, coincidentally or not, also called *Mayne zikhroynes.*[92]

The critic Ba'al-Makhshoves bestowed lavish praise on Kotik's first volume in a short review published in his "Literarishe geshprekhn" (Literary talks) in December 1912. This press review, written by a figure considered to be the foremost modern critic of Yiddish literature, evidently set the stage for the warm reception afforded to Kotik's book. The critic presented the book as the first mature and unique fruits of a truly Jewish memoir genre: "This is the first time that we find in Jewish literature such a work of memoirs. . . . In order to find something similar in Yiddish literature, we must return to the seventeenth century, when Glückel of Hameln wrote her memoirs in Yiddish. On a smaller scale we have examples of this genre in Hebrew and Russian-Jewish literature; we have Mendele's unfinished "Shloyme reb Khayims," a work combining the memoirist and the artist. . . . But such a perfect work we have yet to come across."[93]

He went on to note some of the book's distinguishing features, waxing overenthusiastic. "Grandfather Aharon-Leyzer and the great prodigy Yisrael the hasid . . . are described with strong artistic clarity, like characters in the best novels. Generally speaking we must say that the author has the big spark of a true writer, possessing the talent to tell his innermost experiences fluently and pleasantly. Sometimes I feel that the author is too literary, which is detrimental to the simplicity of the memoirs."

Ba'al-Makhshoves, who had on more than one occasion voiced his hope that the elders of that generation would write their memoirs, now indicated that Kotik's memoirs might signal the growth of a new literary genre: "When years ago I wrote my article in *Fraynd* on the importance and necessity of creating a Yiddish memoir literature . . . I myself never imagined that this natural wish of a Jewish writer would ever be realized. And now, suddenly, the Jewish reader has presented before him such a work (for the present, just the first volume, but as I have heard, it will be three volumes in toto), a simply monumental creation. Over time, it is a necessity that each Jewish home with an interest in the Jewish past be the proud owner of such a book."[94]

Of especial importance is the five-part comprehensive coverage published by the Yiddish journalist and researcher Noah Prylucki, in which he expressed his surprise that no one had as yet considered the fact that no national literature, and certainly not a Jewish national literature, could exist without the genre of memoir literature, which is the unique portrait mirroring every human community.[95] Prylucki further suggested that the best exemplars of memoir literature should be viewed as an important interpretive tool, which, like historical documents, can be utilized to enhance our comprehension of outstanding literary works.

The praise Prylucki showered on Kotik, his definition of Kotik as a "born memoirist," was accompanied by attention to the book's flaws, including its confusion and lack of order. From the outset, the reader is aware of abrupt jumps from topic to topic and the sudden dropping of a story in the middle as characteristic features of Kotik's literary style. Thus, for example, Kotik deliberately chose to open his memoirs with a description of the "Slup," a historic tower in his hometown, "since, the moment I think of my shtetl, the tower pops into my mind as some sort of sign whose meaning is incomprehensible. And now I can proceed to describe the town itself." Despite the expectations this statement arouses for in-depth explication, however, this remark remains devoid of content. The reader waits in vain for a clue as to what that symbol signifies. Instead, Kotik immediately plunges into a description of his hometown.

Also noted in Prylucki's critique are Kotik's pretensions in reporting conversations he had not witnessed and in showering a multitude of data—numbers, sums of money, and prices—on the reader, mocking Kotik's observation in chapter one that a certain Polish noble had 600 serfs. "He counted them himself," Prylucki wrote. "Not 599 or 601, but precisely 600." He also belittles Kotik's historical observations: although perhaps accurate in detail, Kotik's perspective remains limited in scope. For example, it was highly unlikely that his grandfather held the "copyright" to new solutions for the economic difficulties afflicting the Jews after the failed 1863 rebellion, as Kotik writes in chapter twenty-two.

Nonetheless, Prylucki viewed Kotik more favorably than he did the writers of the previous generation, first and foremost Mendele Mokher Seforim, whose descriptions of the Jewish shtetl from within were grounded in a polemical bias that sought to battle the negative aspects of this life and to propose correctives. Kotik's memoirs were written from an entirely different perspective. As the old shtetl had been lost in this battle, Kotik could take a conciliatory, calm, not grating or argumentative tone; that is, he could portray "life as it was," with no particular bias, without obscuring or hiding negative aspects and without aggrandizing or idealizing positive ones.

It appears, then, that the critics as a whole were in agreement that the heart of Kotik's innovation lay in the very act of memoir writing. The importance of the emergence of a new genre hitherto absent from Jewish literature outweighed the question of the quality of Kotik's writing. This was the sentiment expressed by the critic Avraham Yuditski in a long essay published in the Vilna Hebrew paper *Ha-zeman* in summer 1913. "This book is unique, of a genre not found at all in our Yiddish literature, whose lack is genuinely felt in our other literatures, the Hebrew and the Russian. This is the start of a memoir literature, which sheds light on the life of the previous generation and transports us to another world."[96] Earlier descriptions of shtetl life, "from Bogrov and Levanda to our grandfather Reb Mendele," had taken either the form of realistic or biographical stories, "made-up stories, based on facts, episodes, or events that occurred in real life. In these stories we hear the echo of the past. But the everyday life of the previous generation, as it truly unfolded, is not found in these stories."

The demand accordingly was for true-life descriptions, without condescension or polemical bias. The past as it was. Such descriptions could be provided only by "the remnants of the old generation, who still live among us, serving as living symbols of the previous period." In the stories of the elderly members of the previous generation, "we sense no artificiality, exaggeration, or hyperbole. . . . In contrast, we sense here the unadorned naked pulse of life." The writers of an earlier period had deliberately overemphasized the negative aspects of the shtetl in their descriptions: "They blackened the colors, imaginatively creating terrible and terrifying depictions in order to more forcefully denounce the despicable uglier sides of life during that period." Thus was reality hidden, both its positive and negative aspects.

Yuditski likened Kotik, bent over his desk, writing his memoirs, to the elderly denizens of the study house, who tell stories of the past between the afternoon and evening prayers. Each story evokes yet another, emerging in a disorderly and disconnected manner. Yet the very charm of these stories erases this fact. Conjoined, they reveal a comprehensive and pleasurable picture of life in the previous generation.

Aharon Einhorn, who also noted how Kotik's oeuvre came to fill a vacuum in Yiddish literature, penned a no less enthusiastic review which appeared at the same time.[97] According to Einhorn, up to that point Yiddish literature had concerned itself with great events—anti-Jewish libels and persecutions—but this focus on specific events brought in its wake disregard for the broader context and narrowed the readers' horizons. Nonetheless, Einhorn did not ignore the book's failings: perusal of the book revealed that it was not Kotik's intent to create a coherent work, but rather to present the reader with a series of independent, individual vignettes. This explained the manifold repetitions, and also Kotik's divergence from the rules of the memoiristic genre, which, unlike autobiographical writing, does not place the writer at the center of events but at their margin. In sum, however, the final result was impressive: an extraordinary gallery of characters, into whom Kotik breathed life in clear, incisive, simple, and colorful language conspicuously lacking false pathos.

In September 1913 yet another review appeared, in the important Yiddish literary journal *Di tsukunft*, published in New York. Written by M. Katz, the article opened by stating: "The Jewish shtetl is dying. This small self-enclosed world is disappearing and with it the flavor and the song of the past, which modern Jews now yearn for." To his mind, Kotik made a first attempt of its kind to portray the long-ago shtetl to his reader "as it really was," to expose the reader to an all-encompassing picture of the Jew as he truly lived and felt. "This might detract from the value of his material were it not for his unusual memory for facts, which cancels out his slight subjectivity. Kotik possesses all the attributes necessary to be a first-rate memoirist: He saw much. . . . He remembers precisely and well. . . . He remembers above all that he does not have to convince us, but simply to present the true person." However, he, too, noted Kotik's exaggerations and his uncritical recounting of the stories and traditions he had heard in his youth.[98]

Of especial importance was the reaction of the eminent historian Simon Dubnow, editor of the Russian-language journal *Evreiskaia starina* (Jewish antiquities). In the book review section Dubnow published a brief but comprehensive piece on Kotik's memoirs. He, like other reviewers, praised Kotik for pioneering the writing of Jewish memoirs and for his beautifully rich popular language. As a historian, Dubnow naturally noticed Kotik's innocent exaggerations, particularly those connected to his grandfather's all-powerful grip on the communal leadership and his status among the Polish nobles. This Dubnow ascribed to the Kotik family legacy, which overemphasized the heroic aspects of Grandfather's activity. Nonetheless, Kotik's memoirs were of far greater worth than those of "Grandmother" Pauline Wengeroff, which were aimed at an audience far removed from Judaism and lacking knowledge of its past. Dubnow predicted that Kotik's book would assume a very respectable place in Jewish memoir literature, and that historians of Jewish culture would cull valuable material from it.[99]

Favorable evaluations of Kotik's book also came from a more general audience. For example, the publisher Shlomo Shrebrek, a personal acquaintance of Kotik who also frequented Kotik's Warsaw café, wrote that the reception of the memoirs surprised not only the reading public but the author himself: "It was obvious that for a long time Yekhezkel Kotik himself was unaware of his creative ability." Shrebrek contrasted the boredom engendered by the memoirs of such famed authors as I. L. Peretz and Ahad ha-Am with the fascination provoked by the memoirs of a simple Jew like Kotik. Kotik's greatness lay in that "in all of what he wrote and published there was no exaggeration or flights of fancy so typical of the memoirist. . . . He gave voice to the simple man."[100]

Encouraged by the warm reception afforded his first volume, and particularly by the ardent support of Sholem Aleichem, I. L. Peretz, and Ba'al-Makhshoves, Kotik hastened to publish volume two of his memoirs but a year later. This second volume failed to arouse the enthusiasm of the first; we have already noted Sholem Aleichem's chilly reception. A similar literary critique appeared in a brief survey published in *Ha-tzfirah*'s "Bibliographical Notes" column. Its anonymous author observed that Kotik failed to distinguish between important and trivial matters, between private memoirs and descriptions of historical events: "The author devotes the largest portion of this second volume of the memoirs to descriptions of his various travels. . . . This volume contains living pictures of our people's life during that period, and many tried-and-true ideas, expressed offhandedly. But the author does not know how to distinguish between things of value and matters of no significance at all. And in this part the author did not maintain a proper balance; he speaks overmuch of private matters, thereby weakening the impression made by his descriptions."[101]

The contemporary reader who peruses part two of the memoirs finds this negative evaluation difficult to comprehend, for this volume is in no way inferior to its predecessor, being similarly filled with fascinating material. Nonetheless, we must note that this negative evaluation was not unanimous; there were those who did view the second part admiringly, seeing it as a natural sequel to the first—for example, I. L. Peretz, as noted earlier, and A. Litvin, who wrote: "Critics have received both volumes warmly . . . both from the literary standpoint and for their cultural-historical material. By writing these two volumes the elderly Kotik has won a place of honor among the members of the Jewish family of writers."[102]

In closing this section, it is of interest to note the attempt by

Haynt editor Shmuel Yaakov Yatzkan to cast aspersions on Kotik's "authorship" of the memoirs. To recall, at that point in time Sholem Aleichem was publishing his feuilletons on Menakhem-Mendl in Warsaw in this paper, using Kotik as a character. This angered Yatzkan, who took the trouble to apprise Sholem Aleichem of his strong objections in a letter, dated 8 June 1913:

> I have but one thing to ask of you: leave off using Yekhezkel Kotik. You obviously haven't a clue as to what kind of man he is. If you but knew what a beast and ignoramus he was, you would be inordinately ashamed to have anything to do with him. You are mistaken if you believe that he wrote that wonderful book *Mayne zikhroynes*. It's not his "fault" that this book emerged a gem. Simply by chance Kotik was lucky enough to have the artist David Kassel turn his silly tales into polished diamonds.[103] He himself cannot even write a proper sentence. You are certainly aware that he is not a competitor of mine and that I have no intent of harming him, but this is the *truth*, which is common knowledge in all of Warsaw. Leave him. The memoirs will remain a gem of our literature, but Kotik will remain Kotik.[104]

Contemporary sources do not echo this surprisingly strongly worded allegation. It received confirmation, however, some fifteen years later in an entry on David Kassel published in Zalman Reisen's *Lexicon of Yiddish Literature*.[105] Some sixty years later, in 1971, the writer Aharon Zeitlin repeated this allegation, suggesting that it was an open secret in Warsaw that Kassel had edited Kotik's memoirs, endowing them with their unique literary flavor.[106]

Is this simply an unfounded slur or was Kassel actually Kotik's editor? The answer, it seems, lies somewhere in between. Logically, as an inexperienced author, it was likely that Kotik needed an editor, and perhaps A. Gitlin, the publisher of Kotik's memoirs, who also published some of Kassel's works during those years, employed the latter's services. This was, after all, the accepted practice, and even experienced authors were not exempt from the need for editorial intervention. Moreover, Kotik himself wrote to Sholem Aleichem that it was at the urging of his son Avraham-Hirsh and another writer, a friend of his son, that he undertook to write his memoirs. Although Kotik nowhere makes mention of this writer's name, it could have been Kassel, who was one of his son's closest friends.[107]

The question at hand is the degree of Kassel's involvement as an editor—was he a ghostwriter who created a totally new text, as

Yatzkan and Zeitlin aver, or did he perhaps simply prepare the text for publication? The second possibility seems the more likely of the two. If there had been intervention by a ghostwriter, many of the clearly visible literary defects, some of which we have already noted and others of which will be mentioned in the following, would have been corrected. In addition, if Kassel's purported involvement in the actual writing was common knowledge throughout Warsaw, how is that the Yiddish critics, themselves residents of this city, well acquainted with Kotik and his book, seemed unaware of this fact? True, Kotik was a tiresome, eccentric old man, but it appears that Yatzkan, himself no saint and whose remarks are tainted by un-reliability, went overboard in repeating this bit of gossip to Sholem Aleichem.[108] Nonetheless, this allegation is undoubtedly of some interest to students of the history of Yiddish literature.

The Lost Volumes of the Memoirs

Was there really a continuation to the first two volumes of Kotik's memoirs? The existing evidence suggests that there was indeed a third volume, and perhaps even a fourth volume was planned. Concerning Kotik's intent to write three volumes we hear first from Ba'al-Makhshoves, in his article from December 1912.[109] In addition, we have the testimony of Kotik himself in his 30 November 1913 letter to Sholem Aleichem that he had completed writing the third volume, the one dealing with the Warsaw period, and that the book would soon go to the printer.[110] Yet as we have hinted before, the manuscript of volume three was never published, and efforts to trace its whereabouts have met with no success.

Additional evidence for the manuscript's existence comes from a letter dated 18 May 1914 from Kotik to the famed literary critic Shmuel Niger, then in Vilna.[111] Kotik wrote that it had suddenly occurred to him that he might send Niger a few sheets from the as yet unprinted third part of his memoirs; perhaps he would take pleasure in it.[112] Kotik requested a speedy response—whether positive or negative—and asked that, in the latter case, Niger return the manuscript. At present, a search through Niger's extensive archive has turned up no fragments of Kotik's work, and it is possible that Niger complied with this request.

It appears that Kotik decided to publish the third volume of his memoirs in 1919, when he was already seventy-two years old.

Confirmation for this somewhat unlooked for turn of events comes from the 1919 Yiddish catalogue of the Yidisher Folks-Farlag published in Kiev. According to this catalogue's advance publication information, Kotik's memoirs were to appear in three volumes, and it explicitly stated that volume three was now appearing in print for the first time.[113] Yet this plan was never put into effect. Exigencies of the time and the civil war in the Soviet Union, followed finally by financial bankruptcy, ultimately led to the cancellation of this publishing house's literary projects.[114]

In late 1920 Kotik entered into negotiations with German publishers regarding both the translation of his memoirs into German and the possible publication of a new Yiddish edition. From the two surviving contracts we learn that it was Kotik's intent not simply to have the two already published volumes translated and reprinted, but also two additional parts, which he promised to deliver within a brief time span.[115]

On 29 October 1920 Kotik signed a contract with the Berlin Welt-Verlag. The contract's first paragraph stipulated that Kotik was signing over to the publisher exclusive rights for the publication of the three volumes of his memoirs in German translation. The following comment was appended: "It should be noted that volume three has not been published before." The contract, which outlined Kotik's financial rights, stipulated that Kotik would receive half of the sum for the rights to the translation of the third volume only after this volume appeared in Yiddish, and the other half after the German translation was published.[116] In other words, in 1920 the manuscript of the third volume of Kotik's memoirs was evidently ready to go to press; in any event, Kotik had committed himself to completing it in a very short time.

A more detailed contract was signed with Klal-Verlag on 27 July 1921. The signatories were Yekhezkel Kotik and his wife Libe, on the one hand, and the directors of Klal-Verlag, on the other.[117] This agreement, which was indeed partially implemented, gives us fresh insight into the probable fate of part three of Kotik's memoirs.

According to this contract, Kotik signed over exclusive rights to the publisher to reprint the Yiddish edition of the memoirs. The first paragraph also stipulated that the author would turn the original manuscripts of the two as yet unpublished volumes over to the publisher. The paper matrices for the plates of the first two volumes, paragraph eight stated, and for the first sixty-five pages of volume three, as well as the manuscript of volumes three and four, were to be sent to the printer upon receipt of the initial payment, scheduled to take place immediately following the signing of the contract (the rights were activated from 1 August 1921 and were good for five years). It would appear, then, that in July 1921 Kotik had in his possession matrices for the first sixty-five pages of volume three and complete manuscripts of volumes three and four. The promised payment for the four volumes was 370,000 Polish marks.[118] However, Kotik died on 13 August 1921, just two weeks after signing the contract.

The fate of these initial sixty-five printed pages and the manuscript version of the last two volumes is unknown. Did the representatives of Klal-Verlag get the money to Warsaw before Kotik's death? Did Kotik send the matrices and the manuscript to Berlin? From the fact that Klal-Verlag published the first two volumes of the memoirs several months later it appears that the agreement was implemented. On the other hand, Klal-Verlag made no use of the original matrices and reset the entire book.[119] Nor do we have a hint as to the fate of the final two volumes. Perhaps the matrices and the manuscript arrived in Berlin, and for unknown reasons were not utilized.

Some open questions remain. It appears that Kotik's wife Libe and son Avraham were conducting negotiations with the Warsaw publisher A. Gitlin (who published the original edition) at the same time as the Klal-Verlag agreement was in the works. We have a copy of a contract drawn up in Warsaw on 4 July 1921 between Gitlin as one party and Libe and Avraham Kotik as the other (Kotik himself was not a party to this contract).[120] For his part Gitlin undertook to publish a thousand copies—six hundred of volume one and four hundred of volume two (indirectly attesting to the first volume's greater popularity)—of a new edition of the memoirs, for which the family would receive a sum of 85,000 Polish marks.[121] He also agreed not to distribute the books in America, and in exchange the Kotik family undertook not to allow any other publisher to print the book, effective for a year and a half from the date of publication. Subsequent to that date, the matrices were to be turned over to Avraham Kotik.

This agreement—if indeed it was an agreement and not a one-sided proposal on Gitlin's part—was never implemented. Perhaps the Kotiks found the conditions and payment offered by Klal-Verlag

more appealing. Yet why did the family engage in simultaneous negotiations with two publishers, and why did Kotik sign the Klal-
Verlag agreement and not the Gitlin one? A partial answer certainly
lies in Kotik's severe illness. Gitlin, a Warsaw resident, could ne-
gotiate with family members without troubling the now ill Kotik;
the negotiations with the Berlin publishing house were carried out
via the mails, and formal considerations affecting both the family
and the publishing house may have dictated that Kotik himself sign
the forms.

In any event, the third volume has been lost, as has the fourth—
if there ever was one (apart from the contractual obligation mentioned above there is no evidence that it was ever written). Even
the planned German translation was only partially realized. It was
not until 1936 that selected excerpts from the memoirs appeared
in German translation, published by the prestigious Judaica series
of the Schocken publishing house, which presented the German
reader with the best of Yiddish literature. The book, titled *Das Haus
meiner Grosseltern,* was translated by Leo Hirsch and contained a
total of ninety pages. Did Schocken purchase the translation rights
from Welt-Verlag, then no longer in existence? We have no answer
to this question at present, but it is noteworthy that in his afterword
the translator mentions the as yet unpublished third volume.[122]

THE MEMOIRS AS A CULTURAL
DOCUMENT AND HISTORICAL SOURCE

The Book's Structure and Main Characters

The first volume of the memoirs, presented herein, focuses on
Kotik's grandfather's rise to leadership and the growth of the Kotik
clan. A spirit of joy, optimism, and even mischief wafts from most
of its pages; in contrast, sadness, pessimism, and a strong sense
of failure permeate volume two. At its center is the mature Kotik,
portrayed against the background of the decline and breakup of
the Kotik family, a breakup that began with the death of his grandmother—the true power and brains behind the grandfather and the
glue bonding the family together—and continued with his grandfather's remarriage to a young woman. This, in turn, ultimately cul-
minated in the neglect of the family that was once his grandfather's
source of strength. Kotik's graphic account of his personal fate and

wanderings within and without the Jewish Pale of Settlement sets his family's decline against the background of economic-political events as these impacted on the Jews of the Russian Empire. Volume one of Kotik's memoirs covers the period from the late 1830s, a few years prior to the abolition of the Kahal (1844), and ends with the late 1860s. Volume two concludes in 1881 with an appalling description of the pogrom inflicted on Kiev's Jews.

Chapter one of the first volume, also the longest chapter, differs substantially from its fellows. Like other descriptions of Jewish communities in the Pale of Settlement, this introductory chapter traces the physical, institutional, human, and social topography of Kotik's birthplace.[123] It describes its main sites and institutions—the Polish gentry's estates, the churches, the synagogues and study houses, the bathhouse and the ritual bath, the poorhouse and the Talmud Torah, the river and the cemetery—and its social structure, both Jewish and non-Jewish. On the one hand, Kotik depicts the Jewish kahal and its elders, the householders, the scholarly elite and the *prushim,* the residents of the Zastavye suburb, the wealthy members of the community, and on the other, the Polish nobles and their world, the Catholic and Russian Orthodox clergy, and the peasant-serfs. Interspersed among these descriptions are human-interest episodes more typical of the continuation: the Sabbath and holiday atmosphere, studies in the heder and the melamdim, weddings and funerals, and the like.

Only in chapter two does Kotik arrive at the heart of the book, the core around which the plot of the memoirs is woven and develops—his family. The first significant personality is Kotik's great-grandfather Velvel ben Aharon, who served as communal leader (*parnas khodesh:* head elder) in the early decades of the nineteenth century. A leader from the "old" school—a wealthy, learned man, firm but generous—he enjoyed free exercise of power and the full support of the governmental authorities. His powers even extended to the right to flog or arrest offenders and lawbreakers. Kotik never knew his great-grandfather and only heard stories about him. It seems, however, that his leadership qualities, but not his Jewish erudition, were bequeathed to his son Aharon-Leyzer, Kotik's grandfather.

Aharon-Leyzer, the protagonist of the memoirs, was undoubtedly a remarkable personality: charismatic, energetic, an inventive entrepreneur, strong-willed and resourceful, albeit characterized by an unusual fusion of contrasts—meshing the cunning and cruelty of a typical Polish noble with "Jewish" gentleness and mercy. It was these qualities of a Jewish kulak that brought him, against his will, to exercise almost tyrannical rule over the town, first as *parnas khodesh* (a post inherited from his father), and after this office was abolished as the town's tax collector (*sborshchik*). He refused, however, to take money from the Jewish community, preferring to derive his income from leaseholds acquired from the Polish nobility living in the Kamenets vicinity, with whom he maintained friendly relations, enjoying their trust and serving as their confidant. Despite several attempts to resign his position as leader of the Jewish community and to devote himself solely to his business dealings, the town notables, in collusion with the district commissioner (*ispravnik*), imposed this job on him in the knowledge that without Aharon-Leyzer not only would there be no law and order in the town's affairs, its members would also indulge in harmful interminable disputes.

Thus, Aharon-Leyzer's powerful one-man rule was grounded in the enthusiastic support of the district authorities, on the one hand, and on the deferential fear of the town's Jewish residents, on the other. Although finding himself in conflict from time to time with various circles jealous of his economic success that attempted to encroach on his territory, via skillful and brutal use of his connections Aharon-Leyzer was able to push them off the playing field. He even cultivated an intelligence network of favor-currying toadies who reported on the activities of Aharon-Leyzer's opponents, whom he placed on a private blacklist. Also at his disposal were several bullies whom he engaged as enforcers. Aharon-Leyzer's control of the township extended to no less a personage than the town rabbi, whom he threatened with expulsion if he did not arrange a match between his niece, the daughter of the distinguished rabbi of Grodno, and Aharon-Leyzer's son Moshe. Notwithstanding his formidable personality, Jewish Kamenets unanimously recognized that Aharon-Leyzer served communal interests and not personal ends. Uniquely affectionate ties developed between Aharon-Leyzer and his "subjects," particularly the simple people, who viewed him as a protector and savior from internal and external wrongs.

Grandmother Beyle-Rashe was well matched to her complex husband. For Kotik, she, more than any other person, symbolized the now defunct old stable order, the archetypal Jewish mother:

intelligent, quiet, obsessively devoted to her husband and family, but also the natural behind-the-scenes ruler of the roost. Her level-headedness, sage advice, cordiality, moderation, and wisdom stood in inverse proportion to her unassuming appearance, of which Kotik made no secret: "She herself was a tiny, skinny woman whose body seemed barely to sustain her soul, but she had the drive and energy of a man" (chapter 6). It was no coincidence, Kotik noted on several occasions, that the family, previously known for its loving solidarity, began to disintegrate after her death. The dramatic description of Grandfather's pathetic, almost deranged mourning for her death does not simply symbolize the personal grief of an old man who has lost the wife of his youth, but encompasses the collective grief of the entire family, and even of the shtetl, at the conclusion of a golden age. In the absence of a central guiding hand, from that point forth the "Tsar's Regiment," as the Kotik clan was known, began its dissolution.

The source of Grandfather's power was not vested solely in his acumen and charisma; it was intricately enmeshed with the united family front and with the family's intense ties to Kamenets itself. For Grandfather, the family he headed as an authentic patriarchal figure was the backbone of his life; he insisted that all his children, even his married ones, live with him, deriving warmth, love, and pleasure from everything related to his wife and family. To the township of Kamenets, Grandfather felt a similar bond. Although well aware of the gap between his abilities and the tiny sphere in which he operated, he refused his father-in-law's offers to help him relocate to the much larger town of Brisk, a more suitable venue for a man of his ilk. Grandfather's response was that nothing, not even millions, could induce him to leave Kamenets, the place where his parents and grandparents were buried and where he had expended his youthful energies.

Next in the family gallery is Kotik's father Moshe, Aharon-Leyzer's firstborn and most beloved son, who represents the figure of the ideal hasid, used by Kotik to reconstruct the world of Lithuanian Hasidism. An ardent hasid, Kotik's father played a central role in the branch of Kobrin-Slonim Hasidism in general, and in Kamenets hasidic circles in particular. Although his chosen path totally diverged from that of his father, he did, nonetheless, inherit some of Aharon-Leyzer's qualities: he was a balanced, stable, and practical man, in contrast to the popular conception of the foolish

Libe Kotik and an unidentified young woman (probably her daughter)

and idle hasid.[124] Moshe Kotik's residence was the central gathering place for the local hasidim, constantly reverberating with celebrations and with hasidic conversation, melodies, and teachings. As the "black sheep" of the Kotik family—an active hasid from a typical mitnaggedic family in a primarily mitnaggedic town—Kotik's father lived a double life, raising his children in a perpetually tense atmosphere. Existing conflicts with other family members, over such issues as his absence from family gatherings on Rosh Hashanah because of his visits to the rebbe, were exacerbated by the shaky status of his wife Sarah within the family.

Yekhezkel Kotik's mother Sarah was indeed an atypical figure within the Kotik family context. Of distinguished rabbinic lineage, descended from a family that traced its roots to the Gaon of Vilna and Hayyim of Volozhin, her marriage to Moshe was the direct consequence of Grandfather's strong desire to find a wife from among the scholarly elite for his beloved son. The unhappy woman was out of her element in the noisy, unrefined Kotik clan. Endowed neither with housekeeping abilities nor with good looks, she was not even very intelligent. With surprising frankness Kotik wrote, "Above all, my mother, may her soul rest in peace, wasn't particularly smart herself, and one can easily imagine how much of a misfit she was in Grandfather's household" (chapter 11). Despised by Grandfather Aharon-Leyzer, she plays but a marginal role in the memoirs, receiving scant esteem. It was not oversight that led Kotik to dedicate his memoirs not to his mother but to his grandmother, "the quiet and kindly educator of our large and noisy family."

Another intriguing member of the family gallery was Kotik's uncle and Aharon-Leyzer's first son-in-law, Berl-Bendet, who managed the Polish lord Sikhowski's Czechczowa estate. Portrayed as a prototypical *yishuvnik*—a talented and engaging entrepreneur, bright and ethical, loyal to his employer even at the risk of personal danger—hardworking Berl-Bendet even took the trouble to widen his professional horizons by reading German management and agricultural journals.[125] In many respects, Berl-Bendet resembled his father-in-law; in turn, Aharon-Leyzer evinced great affection for him and regarded him as his true heir, as neither Moshe (Kotik's father) nor Yosl (Kotik's uncle) wished to follow in their father's footsteps, harboring profound distaste for his economic dependence on Polish lords and his intense personal involvement in their lives. Repulsed by the humiliation and flattery so integral to this way of life, they preferred to engage in leaseholding within the town itself.

Berl-Bendet's outstanding qualities—his devotion, talents, and courage—almost cost him his job upon first starting out. Motivated by conventional antisemitic feelings inculcated during her childhood, the Polish noble's wife could not come to terms with the "Jewish commissar's" success and sought to have him driven off the estate via a libelous ruse. Thanks to Grandfather's cunning this plot was uncovered and the proud Polish lady was forced to humiliate herself and to beg forgiveness not only from Berl-Bendet but also from her estranged husband, whose affections had been alienated by her distasteful machinations. Peace having been restored via Grandfather's active intervention, a radical volte-face took place in the Polish lady's attitude: respect and fraternization replaced contempt and estrangement. This changed relationship finds expression in the description of Berl-Bendet's daughter's wedding. Not only did the Polish lord and lady foot the bill, they also stood under the wedding canopy and participated in all the festivities: "Sikhowski and his wife never tired of all the rejoicing. Madame Sikhowski even confessed her total ignorance concerning the ways of the Jews. She had been brought up from the cradle on the saying . . . 'The Jew will snatch you up and shove you into his bag.' All her life she kept hearing Żyd! Żyd! And it scared her; she had felt threatened. Only now did she realize how amiable a people we Jews really were and how entertaining our company was" (chapter 13).[126]

This intimacy peaked during the Polish Rebellion of 1863—a literary symbol for the abortive Jewish-Polish brotherhood. By dint of his bravery and charm, Berl-Bendet not only managed to save his mistress from a cruel beating at the hands of Russian Cossacks, his wisdom also prevented his master from taking to the woods and joining the Polish rebels. Berl-Bendet's unique style of management and his fair treatment of the peasants made the Czechczowa estate the sole estate in the area to function normally while the rebellion was being quashed. It is impossible to view these episodes describing the relationship between Berl-Bendet and the Sikhowskis as anything but a symbol for the Jewish-Polish dialectic of attraction-repulsion and of amity-hostility.

Given the space Kotik devotes to his extended family, he is surprisingly reticent about his own nuclear family. Although his beloved wife Libe is portrayed briefly in the description of his wedding and of the rift with his father, Kotik pays scant attention to his siblings and to his own children. Of Kotik's three sons, only the eldest, Avraham-Hirsh, who later attained prominence in his own right, is mentioned by name.[127] One son died in infancy. We know the name of Kotik's other son, Mordechai, only from his brother

Avraham's memoirs.[128] Kotik also fails to record the name of his daughter, although he alludes to her existence in part two of his memoirs.

Kotik was keenly aware of the role heredity played in forming his personality, that he had inherited from his forefathers a variety of conflicting traits. Concerning his legacy from his grandfather, he wrote: "He was a great weeper and I must have inherited that trait from him. To this day, as soon as I hear someone crying, no matter for what trivial reason, my eyes at once fill with tears" (chapter 14). Because of his hasidic upbringing, even as an adult he did not know how to play cards (ibid.). He was also aware of his personal charisma, organizational talents, and intellectual potential, and his ability to influence his peers, all qualities inherited from his grandfather.

Yet all these issues take the back bench in Kotik's biographical musings. What lies at the core of Kotik's being—given fascinating artistic expression in the memoirs—is his perception of his life story as the inversion of his father's. As noted earlier, Kotik's father Moshe rebelled against the mitnaggedic world in which he was raised, becoming a devoted hasid. In turn, Kotik, raised in a hasidic atmosphere, rebelled against his father's world and returned to the mitnaggedic milieu, largely defined by its rejection of Hasidism—this notwithstanding his abiding love and admiration for his father. Yet the upshot of Kotik's rebellion differed substantially from that of his father. Whereas Moshe and his father—who was essentially not a spiritual personality but rather a simple, even unlearned man—managed to effect a reconciliation and to create conditions conducive to a shared life, Moshe failed to achieve this with his own son. The rift between Father Moshe—the staunch hasid who, unlike his father, was a learned spiritual individual—and Yekhezkel was never mended. His father's anger and inability to come to terms with Yekhezkel's "defection" left a permanent mark—a sense of missed opportunities and failure—on the subsequent course of Kotik's life. This tense father-son relationship also led to incessant clashes. In his memoirs Kotik recounts how he prepared himself for an intellectual-religious debate on Hasidism with his father, a debate whose irrefutable results he imagined would help his father come to terms with his spiritual conversion. As omniscient readers, we might have warned Kotik that his naive hopes were not to be realized. Kotik's father continued to place obstacles in the path of Yekhezkel's efforts at education and self-advancement, even going so far as to meddle in Kotik's marriage and to thwart his plans to attend the Volozhin yeshiva and to study Russian. A mature Kotik later manifested appreciation for his father's position: "But on second thought, I could hardly blame him. Firstly, I realized that a mitnagged could become a hasid, but the other way around—never" (chapter 25).[129]

The concluding chapter of the memoirs is of interest both in terms of the book's organization and from the standpoint of Kotik's status in the family chronicle. Longer than any of the other chapters except for chapter one, it is in some respects a disappointing conclusion. Permeated by a moralizing didactic tone, it attempts to explain the secret of Hasidism's charm and to educate the reader regarding the differences between Hasidism and Mitnaggedism. Kotik himself was aware that this "theoretical" chapter interrupted the chronological flow of the memoirs, noting: "I ought to have concluded the first part of my memoirs with Grandmother's death." Nonetheless, this chapter does contain significant autobiographical and apologetic elements. Witness the following statement: "Hasidism suited every class of people, from the poor to the rich, from the ignorant to the learned, from the old to the young. . . . But I couldn't be a hasid." Kotik, who construed his personal biography as the outcome of an unceasing battle to realize spiritual values, could not help building his writing in general, and the concluding chapter in particular, around the driving spiritual force that caused him no little suffering throughout his life—his attraction to Hasidism's socioreligious charms and his simultaneous aversion for Hasidism and its representatives.[130]

Opening the chapter with a disputatious passion more suited to the late eighteenth century, Kotik relies heavily on scriptural and midrashic references characteristic of the classic mitnaggedic anti-hasidic polemic, in which such citations ostensibly bore weight. It appears that Kotik here reproduced the principled debate he had in his youth with his father regarding Hasidism's defects, placing greater emphasis this time, however, on hasidic claims vis-à-vis Mitnaggedism. On the one hand, this chapter romanticizes and to a large degree empathizes with the positive aspects of Hasidism (identified, as we have noted, with his father); on the other, it is an almost pathetic polemical anachronism. We may attribute this duality to the retrospective treatment, in which the author's life is interpreted as a manifestation of this historic rift.

A Picture of the Past

The shtetl as portrayed in Kotik's memoirs differs from the bitter-sweet accounts of Eastern European Jewish communities found in many post-Holocaust memoirs.[131] Writing on the eve of World War I, Kotik did not view his past through the threatening storm of physical destruction. Rather, the great experiential lens shaping his perspective was the consequence of *modernity,* not *catastrophe.* The early-twentieth-century shtetl differed from the mid-nineteenth-century one: the lords were not the same lords, nor were the Jews the same Jews. Static for generations, the former reality was irrevocably altered in short order, not by the brutalities of war but rather by an inexorable organic process, of which Kotik himself—looking back with hindsight—was a part.

Some of the appeal of Kotik's memoirs inheres in his realization that the world he described was irretrievably gone. By 1912, the rapid pace of modernization and the inroads made by emigration,

An eighteenth-century wooden synagogue in Kamenets

urbanization, industrialization, and secularization made it self-evident to many that the old shtetl was disappearing. This, in turn, prompted a wave of nostalgic preservation among wide circles, including those who viewed themselves as the radical-secular avant-garde—whether nationalist, Zionist, Yiddishist, or Socialist.[132] This nostalgia for the lost shtetl—which had its inception in the late nineteenth century—found expression in a variety of spheres: historiography, the arts, ethnography, folklore, music, poetry, and literature.[133] Kotik's memoirs constitute a prime example of this trend, which does not necessarily express sorrow or wistful longing for the old world, but primarily displays acceptance of its disappearance. This acceptance was, however, coupled with some patronizing elements, similar to the condescending arrogance displayed by the Russian populists (*Narodniki*), who went "to the people" in the belief that social change could be effected only through the masses.

Several examples of the monumental changes reflected in both volumes of the memoirs, and by Kotik's biography as he interpreted it, come to mind. Of these, the disintegration of the traditional family framework, which had lost its valiant struggle to maintain its stability and solidarity at any price, is preeminent. Kotik repeatedly stressed the importance his grandfather ascribed to having all his family members under one roof; to the family holiday rituals; and to the mutual assistance and cohesion at times of celebration, sickness, or mourning. In Kotik's view, his grandmother's death represents the watershed, the breakdown of the old order she symbolized: "People also said that as a result of her constant mediations, no divorces took place in Kamenets during her lifetime. She kept a watchful eye wherever she could, did everything within her power to preserve the peace between fighting couples. Nowadays, when divorces keep cropping up like mushrooms after a rain, when relationships are deteriorating, with each side tugging and tearing at the damaged fabric until it falls apart altogether, I must admit, that Grandmother's endeavors seem rather naive" (chapter 28).

So, too, the intimacy of the Sabbath and holidays in the shtetl, their strong olfactory and visual aspect—a favorite subject of Eastern European memoirists—gave way before urban secularization and alienation. The divisive conflict between hasidim and mitnaggedim, so bitterly fought out in the eighteenth- to nineteenth-century traditional communal framework, became marginalized and anecdotalized in the even more riven twentieth-century Jewish community, no longer united by a stabilizing religious ideal or an accepted leadership. Fresh ideals sprouted alongside the classic prototype of the learned scholar, so vital to the traditional world. New conceptual systems—Enlightenment, nationalism, Zionism, and Socialism—proffered their wares, undermining previously accepted norms and revamping the hierarchy of professional prestige within Jewish society. The learned prodigy or the pious hasid no longer comprised the sole models for emulation; new figures made their presence felt on the urban and shtetl scene: maskilim, intelligentsia, and certified professionals. The premodern economy, in which Jews had traditionally functioned as leaseholders, innkeepers, and mainly as middlemen, mediating between the Polish lords and their serfs, now capitulated to the professional training, the sciences, and the factories essential to an industrialized economy. With the collapse of the stratified feudal economy the Jews inexorably found themselves in a different economic and social reality, forced to find new sources of income and to use political means to fight for their status as a national and religious minority. Thus the multigenerational Kotik family chronicle—from Great-Grandfather to Yekhezkel Kotik and his children—also represents the strong winds of change tearing at Eastern European Jewish society, forcing it to adapt to modernity.

Throughout the memoirs Kotik interjects his apprehension of the irrevocable passing of the magical past. He felt doubly constrained: by his belief in his readers' inability to even grasp the experiences of the past, and by his own inadequacy as a writer to pen an authentic description. This finds striking expression in his attempts to reconstruct the atmosphere of the holidays as celebrated in his youth. In his view, it was nearly impossible for the modern city dweller to identify with the fear of judgment so strongly experienced by shtetl Jews during the High Holiday season: "Nowadays, when the totality of the Yom Kippur experience has become diminished and the tremendous fear of this holy day no longer has a hold on us, it is difficult to describe those nights of Kol Nidre! The very walls wept, the stones in the streets sighed, and the fishes in the water trembled." Regarding the joyous atmosphere at the festive Purim meal, he wrote: "the fun we all had would be difficult to convey to people belonging to later generations" (chapter 14). What modern person could even imagine the nature of family solidarity or mutual help and concern, the intensity of the sorrow and of the joy, and above all, the quality of *time* in the shtetl, Kotik wondered. There was time aplenty in the shtetl and it moved slowly, whereas the demands of urban life set a totally different, breathlessly rapid pace. Kotik's memoirs clearly reflect his perception of the contrary rhythms of urban and rural life—not just their disparate economy and business practices and their divergent attitude toward landscape, soil, and nature, but also their effect on the texture of personal and communal relationships. Nonetheless, he also displays awareness of the obverse: the disadvantages of the alienation, competitiveness, and hostility found in the urban setting are offset by its wealth of cultural and educational opportunities, and the charm and intimacy of shtetl life are counterbalanced by its narrow provincialism.

Beyond his personal distress at his failure as a writer to recreate the experiences of the past, Kotik recognized the existence of objective changes hampering the reader's ability to understand that past. Kotik emphasized the gap between past and present on numerous occasions, of which card-playing on Hanukkah is but one example. Although they played cards in the shtetl, "it was a far cry from the scandalous and cutthroat gambling many indulge in now" (chapter 14). Nor was the modern Jewish woman cast in the mold of Beyle-Rashe, who would stay awake all night stoking the samovar so that her tired husband could have a boiling-hot cup of tea when he returned in the middle of the night. "This is how a Jewish woman lived and behaved in those days," Kotik eulogized her, "her lofty virtues barely noticeable in a woman of today. Women of such virtuous conduct used to be rare even in those days. Today there isn't even one" (chapter 6; chapter 28).

Nonetheless, Kotik was far from romanticizing the past, expressly aware that in certain respects it was inferior to the present—not only with regard to technological advances in hygiene and medicine, but also with respect to the attitude toward women, and the prevalence of superstitious beliefs in demons and ghosts, amulets and charms. Kotik also directed his barbs at the traditional educational system and its personnel on account of their low level and ineffectual teaching methods, singling out in his critique the severe beatings administered by melamdim. Kotik's account of the extreme passivity exhibited by the parents of a child who died from such a beating is a stinging condemnation of this practice.[134]

Kotik is revealed here as a direct heir to the Eastern European maskilic tradition. Many works, particularly Yiddish ones writ-

ten in the 1860s, harshly criticized aspects of shtetl life they conceived as flawed: the hasidic social and religious milieu; popular
belief in magic and witchcraft; the unsound educational methods;
the bathhouse and its brackish water; the absurd local politicking which centered on the study house, and the like.[135] However,
not surprisingly, the stock figures of the corrupt head elder and
the wealthy leaseholder—often targeted for scathing condemnation
in maskilic literature—receive a sympathetic portrayal in Kotik's
memoirs; they were, after all, his kith and kin.

Comparison of the memoirs with bylaws Kotik published sheds
further light on Kotik's dialectic view of human progress, of the
relationship between past, present, and future.

> Having read the history of civilization and having noted the extensive
> gap between humankind's former and present life, we should rejoice
> that we were born in this day and age and feel pity for our fathers, who
> lived in darkness and experienced terribly bitter lives. . . . The great
> change between human life as formerly lived and at present proceeds
> gradually. At first, people shed one mistaken idea, later—another, and
> so on and so forth until humankind reached its present level. . . . But
> do not imagine, dear readers, that people have achieved happiness,
> that nothing in their lives requires correction. . . . To our great joy this
> progress will not cease; it proceeds surefootedly on its way. In another
> hundred years the next generation will view our lives as we view former
> generations' today. They too will be amazed at our vain lives, at our
> customs and practices, as we are amazed at those of the generations
> that preceded us.[136]

Although fully cognizant of the futility—and the impossibility
and undesirability—of attempting to revive the glory of the past,
neither was Kotik willing to abandon its memory. His empathetic
documentation of this past was grounded in his perception that it
had shaped his personality and values. This warm regard notwithstanding, Kotik did not refrain from passing judgment on that past.
Put briefly, in Kotik's eyes, the shtetl never attains the status of a
"holy community." This is not simply the result of its negative qualities and undesirable citizens. Even its elite—rabbis and scholars,
communal officials and notables—is not idealized, but rather portrayed in all its human complexity, with the lights and shadows of
its existence.

Between Writer and Storyteller,
between Historian and Memoirist

Yekhezkel Kotik belonged neither to the rabbinic or intellectual elite—although their lifestyle and manners were not entirely foreign to him—nor to the class of polished professional writers. (As we saw earlier, in his letter to Sholem Aleichem he admitted to but minimal familiarity with modern Yiddish literature.) Here we have a "simple," although not uneducated man of the people, who records matters incised in his memory. Even "as a young boy I loved listening to his [Grandfather's] conversations with the grown-ups," he commented. "They liked that I stood around observing them, hanging on their every utterance, familiar with all the ins and outs of every dispute" (chapter 10). Kotik also possessed considerable acquired expertise in popular folklore: "Concerning demons and devils, evil water spirits and all sorts of sorcerers, I had already heard from Grandmother. . . . In all those things I had become a great expert, a genius. I was fluent with the smallest details of the most atrocious and horrible misdeeds" (chapter 15). These fundamental qualities of attentiveness, curiosity, and memory, found throughout Kotik's book, eminently qualify him for his chosen role as narrator and memoirist.

It is not their striking artistic level that makes Kotik's memoirs important, for alongside beautiful and moving chapters—the description of the "panic" weddings (chapter 3), the cantonists (chapter 9), and Grandmother's death (chapter 28)—we find a considerable number of disappointing ones. Rather, their strength lies in their being an authentic cultural document, which preserves, along with significant data on all aspects of life, a gallery of images, flavors, and smells. In comparison to later family chronicles, whether memoirs like Isaiah Trunk's *Poyln* or imaginary chronicles like Der Nister's *The Family Mashber,* Shmuel Yosef Agnon's *Korot bateinu,* or Isaac Bashevis Singer's *The Estate,* Kotik's literary powers fall short. Notwithstanding his story's fascinating and colorful plot, Kotik's literary expression is far from sophisticated or poetic. Nevertheless, to his credit, although he displays no interest in landscape or nature descriptions in the manner of the best writers, neither does he employ pathos or flowery language in the manner of the worst. In short, he must be defined not as writer but as a gifted popular *storyteller.* Despite his limited vocabulary and imagery, as the raconteur of his own story he is unsurpassed. "I am going to tell of *what* I have seen, but have no idea of *how* to go about it," Kotik informs us in the introduction. "The reader will forgive me the 'how' for the sake of the 'what,' and this will be my reward."

Kotik's writing is by no means without injections of humor. He often exhibits a bemused perspective on the past; for example, his account of the card game in which one of the lords bets his wife and is forced to pay off his debt by kissing an old serf's rear end (chapter 1), and his description of internal Jewish affairs—such as the informer who brought disaster upon many Jewish communities, yet who on the High Holidays prayed "with such weeping and wailing that even those not easily moved by their own prayers could not help crying and moaning with him. . . . But immediately after Yom Kippur off he marched to Grodno in order to inform on another town" (chapter 1). In Kotik's recounting, the attempt to exorcise a dybbuk from a young girl becomes a ludicrous confrontation between representatives of the traditional order and the town free-thinker. The petrified beadle, who commands the dybbuk to leave the girl via her pinky, is in strong counterpoise to the maskilic apikores, who mockingly places his face near that of the girl and calls upon the dybbuk to enter his open mouth (chapter 8).

In adopting the storyteller's role, Kotik avoided the audacity of assuming the historian's mantle, deliberately abstaining from historical writing for which he had neither training nor inclination. Nonetheless, his finely honed instincts enabled him to preserve much important data, which both substantiate and supplement other historical sources. In short, Kotik must be regarded not as a historian, but as a *memoirist.* His awareness of the importance of preserving the past—which also finds expression in his strong tendency to anecdotal oddities—manifests itself in detailed descriptions of the various melamdim, the number of their students and their tuition fees, of various foods and their preparation, and of grades and prices of cloth and jewelry. In and of themselves these detailed descriptions have their documentary value. Yet the true import of Kotik's memoirs as a historical source lies in their enhancement of our ability to check broad generalizations and historical stereotypes found in other contexts against the reality of one small Pale of Settlement shtetl. [137]

Several examples come to mind. Early in chapter one, while describing the problem of "hidden" Jews, Kotik almost unwittingly relates to a major problem facing students of Eastern European Jewish demography, in Tsarist Russia in particular: the unavailability of precise population figures before the late 1870s at least. According to Kotik, until 1874—the year Alexander II instituted conscription reforms—some two-thirds of Kamenets's Jews did not appear on the government registers. This deception benefited Jews and government officials alike—Jews because they limited thereby, insofar as possible, the number of draftees (one for every thousand residents); government officials because they received bribes and other inducements. Only in this light can we understand the statistical oddity whereby Kamenets officially had 250 Jewish households and only 450 Jewish residents (that is, an average of fewer than two persons per family!), when in actuality it had closer to 1,350 Jews (an average of 5.4 persons per family). Kotik clearly indicates that a similar state of affairs prevailed in nearby Wysokie as well, which undoubtedly substantiates our inference that this was the case for all Jewish Pale of Settlement townships.[138]

Kotik's memoirs also reveal the gap between official policy and its actual day-to-day implementation. Thus, official church policy, which barred economic dealings with Jews, in no way deterred the Polish Catholic priest from leasing some of his property to Kotik's grandfather. This clergyman, who maintained a lifestyle far grander than that of his local Russian Orthodox counterpart, even lived with his beautiful "sisters," well known in the township to be his mistresses (chapter 1).

Precapitalist rural economy, both prior to and after the freeing of the serfs in 1861, is also described in its full complexity. The Jews served as middlemen between the increasingly impoverished and disenfranchised Polish nobility and their indentured peasants, especially following the failed rebellion of 1863. The tension between the Polish Catholic majority that ruled by dint of its ownership of property and means of production and the socially and economically discriminated-against Russian Orthodox minority also placed the Jews in a difficult position. Although dependent for their livelihood on the "old" Polish lords, they were also subject to the machinery of the new Russian regime. Larger or smaller deceptions (like tax evasion or smuggling whiskey from Poland) and personal links between individual Jews and administration officials, greased by overt and covert bribery, held the consensual key regulating the relationship between the Jewish minority and the government authorities.

Like those of the Jews, the local authorities' interests lay in not rocking the boat. Jews and local officials alike viewed the annual visit by the government inspector (*revisor*) to check the accuracy of the population register or to license shops not just as a nuisance but also as harboring the seeds for disaster. The head of the Jewish community and the Polish *ispravnik* joined forces to ward off danger. In addition, we must note the agreed-upon use of bribery by all parties involved, and its employment as a shared idiom that facilitated rapid problem solving and obviated harassment. In this lawless political and social environment, the Jews bribed the government authorities to ignore unlicensed shops and unregistered Jews, whereas the Polish lords bribed the same officials to ignore their illegal mistreatment of their serfs. The amusing story of the inspector who refused to take a bribe and was run out of town by Grandfather, to the *ispravnik's* open joy, clearly illustrates this reality (chapter 4).

Generally speaking, it is doubtful whether there exists another such detailed Jewish description of the relationship between Jews and Polish lords, their mutual interdependence and involvement in each other's lives, as in Kotik's memoirs. Via the central role played by Jews in their service, the social world of the Polish gentry is unveiled. Kotik, in whose view these ties constituted a doleful episode in diaspora history, describes them with awareness of the ambivalence they created in the Jew's self-identity. Abjectly terrified in the presence of the Polish lord, who treated him with humiliation and contempt, the Jew feared the lord's wrath, hatred, cruelty, and his dogs, but was unable—and perhaps unwilling—to sever his dependence on that same lord and the estate economy. For the Jew, the lord was not simply another human being like himself, but a source of income, one that could even be inherited. Yet on his own turf, this same Jew was fully capable of displaying different characteristics, even an entirely different persona—that of an aggressively passionate individual, fully capable of entering into bitter conflict with the community and its institutions over trivial matters.[139]

Kotik's dichotomous portrayal juxtaposes the Polish gentry's cultural world to that of the Jews. Whereas the former spend their time playing cards and drinking to excess, wasting their lives on hunting, partying, and other vain pursuits (the Polish *pan* Sikhowski, who neither played cards nor drank, is presented as an unusually positive exception), the latter, clever, hardworking family men, devote their free time (Sabbaths and holidays) to intellectual pursuits, to Torah study and prayer, but also to arguments and disputes. Moreover, the lords themselves were aware of this distinction. Each "believed that the Jew was a cunning creature, sly, but essentially honest (each noble maintained that his 'little Jews' were honest, but the others were swindlers and thieves). . . . A Jew, he believed, could handle a delicate matter with greater discretion, and he would not make a move without his 'Moshko' or 'Shmulik'" (chapter 1).

The contrast between conventional Gentile and Jewish thought patterns and behavior is conveyed in small episodes—the drunken, cheating non-Jewish estate manager is opposed to the hardworking, trustworthy Jew who never drinks to excess; the almost sadistic cruelty of the Polish lord who enjoys beating his peasants, sets wild dogs on innocent Jews, and even displays cruelty to his family members is offset by Jewish moderation, as illustrated in the story of the libelous accusation against Berl-Bendet. Whereas Sikhowski's instinctive suggestion was to beat the false witnesses until they admitted the truth, Grandfather, for his part, found this punishment too harsh—his suggested (and successful) alternative was to eavesdrop on their conversation and allow them to incriminate themselves (chapter 12). Despite the intrinsically stereotypical thinking found in the memoirs, Kotik also projects his awareness of the complexities and gray tones of historical and social phenomena. "One cannot say that all nobles behaved so cruelly with Jews; there were also decent nobles whose relations with Jews were completely different," he noted.[140]

Kotik's description of the ramifications of the freeing of the serfs in 1861 and of the Polish Rebellion of 1863 and its suppression, as these affected Jewish-Polish relations and the "Jewish economy" in particular, provides a composite picture of Jewish existence in Eastern Europe in an era of change. Within the Jewish community, opinions ranged from identification with the Polish nationalist opposition to the conquering Russian regime to intense hatred for the Polish nobility due to its ingratitude and for its abusive terrorization of the Jews when the tide of victory temporarily turned in its favor.[141] Kotik was fully cognizant of the conundrum of Polish Jewish existence, its nearly total dependence on the stratified class society, exemplified by his comment that in "those days, what was ruinous for the gentry, was no less so for a large section of the Jewish population who derived their livelihood from the lords" (chapter 21),

and by his recognition of the fact that the Polish anti-Jewish attitude remained an unaltered given with which Jews simply had to
contend.

With the suppression of the rebellion came the undermining of
the estate-leaseholding-based Jewish economy, bringing the "old"
order, in which Jews had played a major role in mediating between
the lords and their peasants, to an end. Outbreaks of hatred by the
freed serfs, who were not Poles, toward their Polish former masters
were also directed, as in the past, at those whom they identified
as collaborators with the prior regime—namely, the Jews. During
the rebellion the estates were neglected, and the peasants, in the
spirit of revenge, refused to enter their former masters' employ,
even for wages. What's more, they captured Polish nobles in hiding
and turned them over to the Russians.

Kotik's wealthy family, supported for generations by leasing the
township's property from its owner, the noble Osserevski, began to
decline in the late 1850s, after the Crimean War. It was then that the
right to collect taxes on alcoholic beverages was transferred from
small-town leaseholders and concentrated in the hands of Baron
Günzburg. Yet the ultimate blow was dealt by Alexander II's reforms
and the stormy events of the 1860s, which impoverished the Kotik
family along with thousands of other Jewish families dependent on
monopolistic leasing of estates or other holdings for Polish nobles.
Concurrently, the crisis created a new stratum of nouveau riche,
composed of individuals able to turn to their advantage the opportunities presented by the changing economy, now based on competi-
tive industry and on efficient cash marketing of agricultural produce
using modern means of transportation (the railroads).[142]

Kotik testifies to the prevailing dejection among Jews during
that period: "It seemed at the time that the spring from which Jews
used to draw their livelihood for hundreds of years, had completely
dried up and the chance of finding new livelihoods was small, perhaps even nonexistent. It seemed as if everything was lost forever"
(chapter 21).[143] Notwithstanding Grandfather's inventive efforts to
rectify the family's economic distress via attempts to revive the mutual interdependence of Polish nobles (in this case, the nobles' wid-
ows) and Jewish leaseholders, he failed to resuscitate the family's
glorious past; nor did he find a place in the new economy. Consequently, Kotik's father was forced to exchange town for village and
to become an unwilling *yishuvnik*.

The world of the *yishuvnik*s is treated at length in Kotik's memoirs. His handling of this subject can be divided into two periods, with the 1863 rebellion marking the watershed. During the earlier period, represented by Kotik's uncle Berl-Bendet, "it was degrading for a respectable Jew to live in a village, that is, to be dubbed a *yishuvnik*" (chapter 12); but in the post-1863 era, represented by Kotik's own experiences as documented in volume two of the memoirs, the social status of village Jews changed for the better.

Of especial interest is the picture Kotik provides of the autonomous Jewish communal institutions, both prior to and after the official abolishing of the Kahal (the Jewish communal board) in 1844. I have already noted Kamenets's relative unimportance both in terms of the Russian administration and in the Jewish world. Yet perhaps that very lack of importance makes examination of the relationship between a mid-sized Jewish community and its surrounding villages, and between that community and the major Jewish centers in the vicinity (Brisk and Grodno) worthwhile. For instance, the memoirs indicate that the title "parnas khodesh" (see chapter 1, note 85) had become anachronistic even before the Kahal was officially abolished. Formally speaking, this official's term in office was not a month (*khodesh* is the Hebrew word for month) but three years. In essence, the head of the community could continue in office as long as this served the interests of the government authorities who approved the appointment. Both Kotik's grandfather and great-grandfather were forceful and astute communal leaders, well equipped to take a strong stand to guard their prerogatives and their status, unhesitatingly employing cruel measures when they saw fit. Not only did they enjoy broad powers—including the right to place their opponents in jail—they had the full backing of the local and the provincial authorities (the *assessor* and the *ispravnik,* respectively), who felt no compunctions about interfering in the Jewish community's internal affairs in order to ensure the appointment of an "acceptable" communal leader, that is, one acceptable to them (chaps. 2 and 10).

Also of special interest is Kotik's testimony regarding the spread of Hasidism in White Russia and Lithuania, areas traditionally regarded as bastions of Mitnaggedism. It appears that as early as the first half of the nineteenth century the hasidic movement had succeeded in gaining a foothold throughout Eastern Europe, including the northwestern regions of the Pale of Settlement.[144] Unexpectedly, we find one or more hasidim cropping up even in the most zealously mitnaggedic families. Thus, for example, despite their mitnaggedic upbringing, two of Grandfather's sons, Yekhezkel's father Moshe and his uncle Yosl, adopted Hasidism, along with their two cousins, the sons of the local rabbi, a descendant of the illustrious mitnaggedic rabbis Hayyim of Volozhin and the Vilna Gaon (chapter 4). Hasidic power and status as a significant economic and social pressure group, not just in the Kamenets area but also in the district seat of Brisk, emerges from Kotik's description of the carefully organized hasidic revenge on a mitnaggedic informer who brought about the Slonimer rebbe's arrest (chapter 15). However, Kotik's claims that his switch in allegiance to the ranks of the mitnaggedim succeeded in blocking the attraction of Kamenets's youth to Hasidism (chapter 25) must be treated with skepticism. Even if true, it is doubtful whether he alone can be credited with this development. Many factors contributed to the decline of Hasidism's attraction in the latter half of the nineteenth century—certainly not just Kotik's public debate with its representatives in Kamenets, but primarily the inroads made by Haskalah, russification, nationalism, and secularism.

As described by Kotik, Hasidism appears in all its brilliance and its shadows. Alongside a mocking description of the disputed inheritance of the office of Kobriner rebbe and the resulting rift (chapter 15), Kotik provides a sympathetic portrait of hasidic internal cohesion: its experiential world, fervent prayers, holiday celebrations and daily routines, attitude toward simple folk, and indifference to daily cares and false honors, placing particular emphasis on Hasidism's democratic and egalitarian elements. He goes so far as to attribute Hasidism's success upon its inception in the eighteenth century to social strains within the Jewish community, to the tension between rich and poor, and to the dispossession of the unlearned in institutionalized synagogue worship. By no means do these opinions constitute a profound historical analysis of the hasidic phenomenon; rather, they are a naive reflection of neoromantic notions of the hasidic past (which had already found literary expression in the works of I. L. Peretz, M. Y. Berdyczevski, Yehudah Steinberg, and others) and of socialist doctrines to which Kotik was probably exposed in his old age (mainly via his son Avraham). If in the final analysis Kotik rejected Hasidism, this rejection was primarily the result of rational appraisal: his inability to accept the cult of the rebbe, his criticism of the male milieu fostered by Hasidism that destroyed the family cell and of the inherent conservatism that placed barriers in the way of individual intellectual development, and lastly, the lack of purpose in the hasid's daily life. Nonetheless, on the emotional level Kotik remained full of admiration for Hasidism, identified first and foremost with the memory of his adored father.

Despite the foregoing comments on the importance of his memoirs as a historical source, we must be wary of accepting Kotik's "testimony" as accurate in each and every detail. Even if we assume he was blessed with a remarkably keen memory, unaffected by age, several factors detract from the memoirs' historical value. First, as Kotik devotes a significant portion of his memoirs to the period before his birth, this gives us a fifty- to eighty-year gap between the time these events occurred and their recording in 1912, when Kotik was sixty-five. Moreover, even descriptions of events that occurred in his lifetime are often based on hearsay and not on direct observation. Put briefly, Kotik is an "omniscient" narrator, with access to his heroes' innermost thoughts, who facilely quotes a conversation between two Polish nobles, or between the rebbe and one of his followers, without having actually been present.

Second, Kotik himself admits the limitations of his memory, noting regretfully that certain details have slipped his recollection. "I often think that had I been blessed with an indelible memory, and could recall all those discussions of ours, I would, perhaps, have been able to write a fascinating account of the dreams of young Jewish boys of days gone by" (chapter 19).

From the literary standpoint, Kotik's chosen genre, the memoir, which can also be viewed as involving the exercise of what has been termed "creative memory,"[145] compels the writer to intermingle three strata: (1) "objective" *testimony,* which relies on the writer's memory; (2) "subjective" *interpretation,* bestowed by the writer on the events he witnesses, which places the specific event in a broader context and provides it with a suggested significance; and (3) *narrative,* in which the writer calls upon his imagination to create fictitious links between the documentary and the interpretive bases, used to fill gaps in the testimony. Historians seeking to utilize "creative memoirs" of the Kotik type must therefore try to separate, to the best of their ability, these three intermingled layers. At the very least, they must be aware of their problematic coexistence.

There is another, ethnographic, aspect to Kotik's memoirs. We can certainly assume that Kotik recorded many episodes as he heard them from his grandfather, grandmother, or uncles. In so doing, he acted as an archivist or ethnographer who "records," documents, and preserves oral family traditions. Undoubtedly, the typical processes affecting the development of folktales from the "actual" event until their recording in writing also had a share in shaping these traditions.[146] We must also bear in mind that, as he himself constitutes an inseparable link in the chain of transmission, Kotik is not an alienated, objective "recorder." His personal emotional involvement in his family's history, along with his innocent lack of sophistication, were what forced him, consciously or unconsciously, to adopt the elastic norms of "creative memory," uprooting any attempt on his part at critical examination of his sources or of his impressions.

Kotik attempts to grab the stick at both ends. His memory does not necessarily serve as a means for uncovering the truth, but rather of recreating a "fascinating" past worthy of being bequeathed to future generations. Thus, he preserves "hard" data that might otherwise have been consigned to oblivion: tuition rates, food prices, attire and jewelry, and the like. On the other hand, as a memoirist whose real interest lies in documenting his family history, in recreating the shtetl life that was and is no more, in portraying different personalities, Kotik unhesitatingly uses his imagination to fill in the gaps, occasionally spouting absurdities that contradict data found in other sources. Alongside lack of knowledge (not to say ignorance) and internal contradictions, we find, in addition, accidental slips of the pen.[147]

Notwithstanding these qualifications, coupled with his artless naiveté, Kotik's memoirs constitute a valuable historical source and primary cultural document, not simply because they contain information verifiable from other sources but also because they preserve gems of authentic folklore and testify to unique lifestyles and customs not always documented elsewhere. All of these elements— exorcisms and superstitions, Sabbath and holiday dishes, wedding customs and ways to ward off epidemics, joy and mourning, Hasidism and Mitnaggedism, games and leisure activities, and more— form an organic part of the story.

Kotik's *Mayne zikhroynes* opened a new era in the history of Jewish memoir literature, inspiring or serving as a model for a unique branch of autobiographies, memoirs, and family sagas, whether consciously or unconsciously. Earlier I noted the possibility that Kotik's memoirs played a role in inspiring the great classicists Sholem Aleichem and I. L. Peretz to pen their autobiographies. In their wake, following the First World War, came a spate of memoir writing of the type of which Ba'al-Makhshoves had dreamed.[148] Certain motifs and anecdotes from Kotik's memoirs have even found their way into contemporary Hebrew literature.[149]

ON THIS EDITION

Excerpts from Kotik's memoirs have appeared in translation into various languages, in most cases crudely rewritten. As noted previously, the planned German translation by Welt-Verlag was only partially implemented. An anonymous translation of the chapter on panic marriages, titled "Kinderhochzeit," appeared in a 1927 issue devoted to Polish Jewry of the illustrated magazine *Menorah* (published in Vienna),[150] and in 1936 Schocken published an abridged version of volume one in Berlin. In 1945 several chapters appeared in English in an anthology of memoirs edited by Leo Schwarz, under the title "Love Found a Way."[151] Additional excerpts in English also have appeared in Jack Kugelmass's dissertation, completed in 1980.[152] With regard to Hebrew, prior to the appearance of my full Hebrew translation of volume one, only short excerpts had been translated.[153] Although Kotik's memoirs have been widely utilized for research purposes, it would not miss the mark to observe that in the absence of a full Hebrew or English translation, the work remained on the margins of the past generation's research.

This English edition was based on the 1922 Berlin edition, which was essentially identical to the first 1913 edition.[154] Because of the self-evident difficulties in rendering a work in translation, we have allowed ourselves to diverge from strict adherence to the tenses used in the original, as well as to unify or divide paragraphs or sentences as we saw fit. The note apparatus is intended to clarify, to the extent of my knowledge and the available primary and secondary literature, aspects of *realia,* customs, foods, names of places, books, and persons, as well as linguistic, geographic, historical, and folkloristic issues arising from the text. Rendering a work in translation presents its challenges, all the more so when no English equivalent is readily available.[155] I have striven for the truth, and have followed the dictum of the rabbis in that I have admitted what I do not know.

Several of Kotik's critics noted his "low," inelegant language and his long-winded style: "There is no point in seeking linguistic logic in his writing," A. Litvin commented after perusing brochures by Kotik that appeared prior to the memoirs. "Sometimes a sentence goes on for an entire page or more. Nonetheless, his Yiddish is limpid and not flowery, just as it is spoken by the people."[156] Even Noah Prylucki, notwithstanding his praise for the memoirs' piquant content, notes the stiff, unpolished writing that sets the reader's teeth on edge.[157] Avraham Yuditski perhaps best approached the truth when he described Kotik's style as "simple, popular, pleasant, and lively."[158]

This popular and "crude" style undoubtedly loses something of its vitality and charm in translation. Kotik's characters, himself included, speak and think in simple, clear, and pleasant, not high-flown language. The English translator has tried to faithfully reproduce not only the language and content of the original but also the spirit of the period, its ideas and world, even some of its language. I can only hope that this aim has been realized.

NOTES TO INTRODUCTION

1. See, for example, the assessment by Reisen, *Lexicon,* 3:425–26. Despite the affinity between the two genres—memoirs and autobiography—this work is more correctly assigned to the memoir genre, and not simply because Kotik himself used this term. "Memoirs" implies that the author does not necessarily visualize himself as the main character, that his narrative incorporates events taking place before his time, and that he does not see his work as holding the key to an understanding of his spiritual-intellectual world. Nonetheless, we can easily discern the influence of eighteenth- to nineteenth-century maskilic Jewish autobiography on Kotik. On haskalah autobiography, see Werses, "Hashalah Autobiography"; Feingold, "Autobiography as Literature"; Mintz, "Shape of Haskalah Autobiography"; Robertson, "From Ghetto to Modern Culture"; Graetz, "Autobiography"; and Moseley, "Jewish Autobiography," which contains an extensive bibliography on this genre. "Memory" and "collective memory," including the Jewish culture of memory, have received extensive scholarly attention. I cite here several seminal works of methodological importance germane to the formation of Jewish memory in various periods: Yerushalmi, *Zakhor*; Roskies, *Against the Apocalypse*; idem, "Shtetl"; Raba, *Between Remembrance and Denial*; Shmeruk, "Collective Memory"; Piekarz, "Testimony Literature"; and Zerubavel, *Recovered Roots.*

2. Given the broad scope of literature on this topic, I restrict the discussion to references to several works containing substantive surveys of the various approaches. See, for example, Marcus, *Auto/biographical Discourses*; Nalbantian,

Aesthetic Autobiography; and Barros, *Autobiography: Narrative of Transformation*. For the prevailing view that places basic trust in the truthfulness of the "ordinary" writer, see Lejeune, *On Autobiography*. For a treatment of the relationship between autobiography and truth, see Pascal, *Design and Truth in Autobiography*; Buckley, *Turning Key*; and Eakin, *Fictions in Autobiography*.

3. On the problematic nature of the descriptions of "places" in Hebrew literature, see Govrin, "Geografia sifrutit."

4. On Kamenets, see *Słownik,* 3:763–64. On its Jewish community, see Sarid, "Kamenetz"; *Zakhor nizkor; Pinkas ha-kehillot: Poland,* 5:312–15. For a survey of the history of the Jews of Polesie, see ibid., 5:209–18.

5. It was not without cause that in the 1918 treaty of Brest-Litovsk the southern part of the Grodno province—the Brest area—was assigned to the Ukrainian republic.

6. The eight districts were: Slonim, Novgorod, Lida, Grodno, Volkovyshki, Brest, Pruzhany, and Kobrin.

7. The only significant change took place in 1842, when parts of these two provinces were taken (mainly from the Vilna province) to form the Kovno province. See *Pinkas ha-kehillot: Lithuania,* 4.

8. *Pinkas medinat Lita,* 17, no. 89.

9. *Evreiskaya entsiklopediia,* 9:189, s.v. "Kamenets-Litevsk"; *EJD: Brest-Litovsk,* 425; *Pinkas ha-kehillot: Poland,* 5:312.

10. See Kotik's remarks at the beginning of chapter 1, where he states that there were 450 registered Jews, but that was only a third of their actual number. In 1847 the Grodno province had a Jewish population of 98,196. See Leshtchinsky, *Yidishe folk,* 31.

11. *Evreiskaya entsiklopediia,* 6; between pp. 792 and 793 (Grodno gubernia, table 2).

12. This topic has been treated at length by Barbara Kirshenblatt-Gimblett in her stimulating introduction to the new edition of Zborowski and Herzog's *Life Is with People*. Since its initial publication in 1952, this book has played an influential role in shaping the simplistic idealized image of the shtetl. See Kirshenblatt-Gimblett, Introduction, ix–xlviii. See also Roskies, "Shtetl," and Klier, "What Exactly Was a Shtetl?" 23–35.

13. Kotik well knew how to distinguish between Kobrin, which was a large district city (*an uyezd, a groyse shtot*), and Kamenets, which was a small town (*a kleyn shtetl*). See chapter 26, near note 2. In using the diminutive, Kotik was engaging in lyrical-nostalgic writing rather than a realistic description, as at that time the Jewish population of Kamenets numbered about 1,500.

14. I define small town as one with up to five hundred Jewish residents; a midsized town had up to two thousand Jews.

15. A similar distinction arises from Chemerinsky's memoirs, *Motele,* written in 1917. See my introduction to the new edition of this work (Jerusalem: Magnes, 2002). See also Kirshenblatt-Gimblett, Introduction, xix–xviii.

16. Zeidman, "Yeshiva Kneset Beit Itzchak."

17. On Kamenets during the interwar period, see the extensive material in *Kamenetz Memorial Book* and the Yiddish work of Falk Zolf (b. 1896; emigrated to Canada, 1927). Zolf was a native of Zastavye, a Kamenets suburb located on the other side of the Lesna River, and his description of his childhood was influenced

by Kotik's memoirs. See Zolf, *Oyf fremder erd*. On Zolf, see *LNYL*, 3:530–31 and Glatstein, "Di letste fun a dor."

18. The data for Kamenets's fate during the Holocaust comes from *Kamenetz Memorial Book* and *Pinkas ha-kehillot: Poland*, 5:313–14.

19. Kotik, *Memoirs*, 2, introduction, p. 5.

20. Ibid., chapter 20, 219. See also ibid., chapter 7.

21. His son Avraham, who reports that he was born in 1868, dates the move to when he was eight or nine (Kotik, *Lebn*, 14, 24). Kotik himself writes that he lived in Kiev for only a five-year period (*Memoirs*, 2, chapter 17). On the economic crisis in Lithuania and migration to the Ukraine, see Nadav, "Pinsk," 242–44.

22. An estimated eighteen thousand Jews resided in Kiev in the late 1870s. See chapter 22, note 21.

23. Kotik, *Memoirs*, 2, chapter 17; Kotik, *Lebn*, 14–15.

24. Kotik, *Memoirs*, 2:252.

25. Ibid., chapter 25. Cf. Kotik, *Lebn*, 19–25. On the wave of pogroms in the early 1880s and their significance for Jewish history, see Frankel, "Russian-Jewish Crisis"; and Klier and Lambroza, *Pogroms*, 39–134. On the pogroms in Kiev, see Hamm, *Kiev*, 123–27.

26. Kotik, *Lebn*, 26.

27. Kotik, *Memoirs*, 2, chapter 4.

28. Litvin, "Kotik," 2. On Litvin (1862–1943), see Reisen, *Lexicon*, 2:142–46; and *LNYL*, 5:94–97. On the hatred toward Lithuanian Jews in Warsaw during the 1880s and 1890s, cf., for example, *Ha-melitz*, 31 January 1892, 4–5; Salzmann, *Min he-avar*, 106–7; Friedman, *Zikhronot*, 263; and Freid, *Yamim ve-shanim*, 2:13–15. See also *Warsaw*, 89–90.

29. Litvin, "Kotik," 2.

30. Ibid., 3. On the synagogue founded by Kotik, see near note 37; on his didactic publications, primarily his brochure *Aseret ha-dibrot*, see appendix A, note 2.

31. Shrebrek, *Zikhronot*, 144. See also ibid., 159.

32. Reisen, *Epizodn*, 1:214–16. "Kotik's narrow sooty coffee house" was also mentioned by the Hebrew poet Jacob Fichmann, who sat over "a cup of coffee" with Sholem Asch, Reisen, and others. Fichmann noted that Kotik "was not stingy with his food and would provide credit" ("Nusah Polin," 10). The popularity of this café was also noted by Prylucki ("Mayne zikhroynes"). On the unique atmosphere in Warsaw literary circles during the first decade of the twentieth century, see Miron, *Loners*, 365–81.

33. Litvin, "Kotik," 4–5; Goldberg, "Kotik."

34. Kotik, *Aseret ha-dibrot*, 5–6.

35. Litvin, "Kotik," 9.

36. See chapters 16, 18–19 of the memoirs.

37. On the history of Achiezer and its activity, see Kestin, "Yidisher yubileum" ; R-n, "Akhiezer" ; *EJD: Warsaw*, 1:590, 592.

38. On this criticism, see Litvin, "Kotik," 3, and chapter 29 below, near notes 7–11.

39. See the list of his publications, appendix A, no. 1.

40. In 1913 Kestin ("Yidisher yubileum") reported that the three societies (Achiezer, Ezrat Yetomim, and Ezrat Holim) had a membership of eight thousand

and revenues of forty-five thousand rubles. These membership data seem much exaggerated (Kestin did not indicate what year his data referred to), particularly in light of the fact that Achiezer's annual meeting in 1914 was attended by only 49 of 729 members. See R-n, "Akhiezer." Note that Kotik does not appear as an officeholder in this article.

41. Litvin, "Kotik," 6–9. On Kotik's argumentative propensity, which often led him to resign from the societies he founded, see also Goldberg, "Kotik."

42. Prylucki, "Mayne zikhroynes"—these memoirs were written shortly before his death in the Warsaw ghetto; Nomberg, "Kotik." On Prylucki (1862–1942), see LNYL, 7:224–25; on Nomberg (1876–1927), see LNYL, 6:160–68.

43. Prylucki, "Mayne zikhroynes"; Nun, "Nussbaum." For a notice on the founding meeting of the Moshav Zekenim society, whose board members included Nussbaum, Peretz, and Kotik, see Der fraynd, 14 March 1911, no. 61: 3.

44. Ha-tzfirah 174, 15 August 1921. For a general survey of welfare societies in Warsaw during the period in question, see Shatzky, Warsaw, 3:172–91.

45. This society founded an orphanage in 1898, which in October 1912 moved to its permanent quarters at 92 Krochmalna Street, where it operated under the directorship of Dr. Janusz Korczak until the Holocaust. See EJD: Warsaw, 1:591–92 and "Yekhezkel Kotik." For this society's charter, see appendix A, nos. 3–4. Among this society's founders was Eliezer Elijah Friedman. See his Zikhronot, 259.

46. See "Yekhezkel Kotik." The YIVO Archives (New York) possess an official police permit dated 4 February 1910 granting Kotik permission to hold a meeting in his home to discuss the regulations for the Moshav Zekenim society (Zamlung shrayber, file 2721, no. 100559). On this society's charter, see appendix A, nos. 11–12.

47. Appendix A, nos. 9–10.

48. Ads began to appear in issue no. 117 (5 June 1911), and readers' queries and comments were printed in succeeding issues. See also "Kolonye fun 'Moment'"; and "Vider in Milosna." On Miłosna, see Pinkas ha-kehillot: Poland, 4:273–74.

49. Prylucki, "Mayne zikhroynes." Sholem Aleichem satirized the entry of the Warsaw newspapers into lottery wars and real estate dealings in his story "Oyfn himl a yarid," first published in Haynt, 14 July 1913, no. 151. See also Y. D. Berkowitz's mocking comments on the "'lots'—sorts of building lots in the swampy areas near Warsaw, whose winners could build summer homes, either for themselves or for income" (Berkowitz, Ha-rishonim, 261).

50. Nomberg, "Kotik."

51. This is based on simple arithmetic. The obituary published on the front page of Der moment on 14 August 1921 stated his age as seventy-six.

52. The family lived on this street from 1883. See Kotik, Lebn, 70.

53. Brief notices of Kotik's death and funeral appeared in the Warsaw Jewish press. See, for example, Ha-tzfirah, 15 August 1921, no. 174; Der moment, 14 August 1921, no. 185: 1–2, and the following day's issue, 15 August 1921, no. 186 (an unsigned report on the funeral and a necrology); Haynt, 14 August 1921, no. 185: 3, and the following day's issue, 15 August 1921, no. 186: 4 (a report on the funeral); Ha-olam 10 (1921), no. 48: 16. On 26 August 1921, Haynt published a necrology penned by Avraham Goldberg ("Kotik"). Even the Vilna children's papers, such as

Der haver (August 1921, no. 9: 428–29) and *Grininke boymelakh* (11 August 1921, no. 31: 436–37), published brief necrologies.

54. Although the book itself bears 1913 as its publication date, it is obvious that it had already been published by early December 1912. A promotional ad by the publisher, A. Gitlin, appeared in *Haynt*, on 11 December 1912 (no. 274). Ba'al-Makhshoves's review appeared in *Der fraynd* on 20 December 1912, and thus we can assume he had received the book several weeks earlier. Sholem Aleichem received his copy in early January 1913, confirming its arrival in a letter sent to Kotik on 6 January. Mail delivery from Poland to Switzerland must have taken at least a week.

55. Seventeen of Sholem Aleichem's letters to Kotik are extant. Their dates, publication, and content will be explored in detail in the following. As for Kotik, seven of his letters to Sholem Aleichem are extant. These letters are housed in the Sholem Aleichem Archives at Beth Shalom Aleichem, Tel Aviv (hereafter: SAA), LK 3/1–LK 3/7. This archive has been photographed and catalogued in the Manuscript Division, Jewish National and University Library, Jerusalem (hereafter: JNUL), 4° 1481; Kotik's letters are in file 808. These never-before-published letters, which I have translated into Hebrew, appear in Appendix 1 to the Hebrew edition of this book, 382–88. Undoubtedly, there were additional letters, as the extant ones contain references to matters not treated in the surviving ones. Moreover, in a letter from the Warsaw writer Jacob Dineson to Sholem Aleichem on 21 March 1913, the former wrote that he had seen twenty-two letters and postcards sent to Kotik by Sholem Aleichem (SAA, LD-10/101; JNUL, file 404).

56. On Sholem Aleichem's stay in Lausanne in January 1913, see Berkowitz, *Ha-rishonim,* 301ff.

57. This letter was published in its entirety in *Sholem Aleichem Book,* 244, no. 87; and again by Lis, *Briv,* no. 651.

58. Published by Niger, "Fun Sholem Aleykhems korspondents," 229, no. 15; emphases in the original. Although Niger noted that the date was not clear, in the original (SAA, MN-1/18; JNUL, file 145) the date is legible.

59. The original is no longer extant, but I found an undated copy in YIVO, Eliyahu Tcherikover Collection, file 735, no. 62300. Published again in *Oysgeveylte briv,* nos. 183–84; Lis, *Briv,* nos. 652, 654.

60. *Sholem Aleichem Book,* 245, no. 88; Lis, *Briv,* no. 653.

61. Weinreich, "Unpublished Letters," no. 15. On Ba'al-Makhshoves (1873–1924), see *LNYL,* 1:359–66. To the best of my knowledge he never did return to Kotik's book. His journalistic review will be discussed in the following. Although Sholem Aleichem admired Ba'al-Makhshoves's literary taste, others voiced harsh criticism. See, for example, the letter from Y. D. Berkowitz (28 January 1913), SAA LB-57/130; JNUL, file 340. For the citation, see Assaf, *What I Have Seen,* 36 n. 67.

62. For a Hebrew translation of the letter (SAA, LK-3/5), see Assaf, *What I Have Seen,* 383–84 (letter 1).

63. See Sholem Aleichem's Hebrew letter to his son-in-law Y. D. Berkowitz, dated 18 January 1913: "I am not in Lausanne, nor am I in Losan, but in the city of Berne, in the Lindendorf Clinic, in care of a famous expert professor, and my wife is at my side. My condition is very serious; if I had not come here I would have died, because the doctors in Lausanne are incompetent" (SAA, MB-37/19; JNUL, file 49; *Sholem Aleichem Book,* 110, no. 104).

64. Weinreich, "Unpublished Letters," no. 16; *Oysgeveylte briv,* no. 185; Lis, *Briv,* no. 657.

65. Niger, *Shalom Aleikhem,* 119. See also Berkowitz, *Ha-rishonim,* 302, 304; *Sholem Aleichem Book,* 8–12; and Roskies, "Sholem Aleichem's *From the Fair.*" Berkowitz disapproved of Sholem Aleichem's engaging in autobiographical writing in the midst of an illness and tried to dissuade him from this pursuit: "It is not good in my eyes that you are writing your autobiography at *such* a time, a time of pain, worry, and despair. I am sure this will be your book of books, the Song of Songs of your life—your youth and your maturity. Thus I believe this book of yours should not be written during such days of 'vacancy,' but joyfully, and in the creative spirit, and with a balanced mind" (SAA, LB 57/130; JNUL, file 340).

66. Sholem Aleichem, *From the Fair,* 6.

67. Weinreich, "Unpublished Letters," no. 17; *Oysgeveylte briv,* no. 188; Lis, *Briv,* no. 659.

68. Weinreich, "Unpublished Letters," nos. 18–20; *Oysgeveylte briv,* no. 189; Lis, *Briv,* no. 660. Sholem Aleichem's letters to his son-in-law Y. D. Berkowitz were more poignantly explicit. See, for example, his Hebrew letter of 1 February 1913, which he wrote "with a broken spirit, but a clear mind": "Last night I went down to my grave. But one step separated me from death. I shouted much and I wept even more at the thought that I would not see Tissy [Ernestina, his daughter and Berkowitz's wife] before I die . . . Maybe I shall recover and maybe I shall go down to the grave. . . . A man is very foolish to keep postponing from day to day the writing of his will . . ." (SAA MB-38/37; JNUL, file 49; *Sholem Aleichem Book,* 11, no. 106; English translation cited from Grafstein, *Panorama,* 344).

69. Weinreich, "Unpublished Letters," nos. 21–23; *Oysgeveylte briv,* no. 191; Lis, *Briv,* no. 661. In some of his letters (Weinreich, "Unpublished Letters," nos. 22–23, 26) Sholem Aleichem asked for Kotik's assistance in a matter concerning a widow named Zamoshtshin whose maiden name was Kotik. The request was related to some "writings" in her possession, whose nature is not clear, as Sholem Aleichem's first letter on this matter has not survived. Kotik attempted to come to his assistance (see Assaf, *What I Have Seen,* 386–87 [letter 5]) but was unsuccessful. Evidently the reference is to Berta, the widow of Paltiel Zamostsin (d. 1909), a Yiddish writer who was friendly with Sholem Aleichem in the late 1880s.

70. On this work, see Berkowitz, *Ha-rishonim,* 304–5, 312; Shmeruk, "Menakhem-Mendl-serye," 22–55 (for Kotik, see p. 26). These feuilletons, which appeared in *Haynt* over a nine-month period, were collected and published in Yiddish: *Menakhem-Mendl* (*Nyu York—Varshe—Vin—Yehupets*) and were translated into Hebrew by Arieh Aharoni, *Menahem-Mendel be-Varshah* (subsequent references to the Hebrew translation appear as Sholem Aleichem, *Menahem-Mendel be-Varshah*).

71. The citations that follow have been taken from Aharoni's translation, *Menahem-Mendel be-Varshah,* 19–20 (Yiddish ed., 46–47); 25, 27 (Yiddish, 53, 55); 34–35 (Yiddish, 65); 39 (Yiddish, 69–70); 43 (Yiddish, 75); 89–90 (Yiddish, 127–28); 107 (Yiddish, 146); 115 (Yiddish, 155–56); 123–24 (Yiddish, 166); and 141 (Yiddish, 184).

72. Weinreich, "Unpublished Letters," no. 24.

73. For the Hebrew translation of the letter (SAA, LK-3/6), see Assaf, *What I Have Seen,* 384–85 (letter 2).

74. For the Hebrew translation of the letter (SAA, LK 3/2), see ibid., 385 (letter 3). Shmeruk's conjecture ("Menakhem-Mendl-serye," 26 n. 5) that Kotik took no offense at Sholem Aleichem's use of his personality is borne out by Kotik's letters.

75. Weinreich, "Unpublished Letters," no. 25. Sholem Aleichem's curiosity as to how Menakhem-Mendl's letters were received by their Warsaw audience is related not only to the cool reception by Shmuel-Yaakov Yatzkan, editor of *Haynt,* which distressed him (see Berkowitz, *Ha-rishonim,* 305), but also to other unfavorable critiques which reached his ears and indicated dissatisfaction with the letters' literary level.

76. For the Hebrew translation of the entire letter, see Assaf, *What I Have Seen,* 386 (letter 4).

77. Weinreich, "Unpublished Letters," no. 26. (The original is housed at the YIVO Institute; a copy is found in SAA, MK-1/4).

78. Sholem Aleichem, *Menahem-Mendel be-Varshah,* 148–49 (Yiddish, 192–93).

79. Cf. Kotik's *Der proyektirter.* See appendix A, no. 10.

80. Sholem Aleichem, *Menahem-Mendel be-Varshah,* 170 (Yiddish, 218).

81. For the entire text of the letter (SAA, LK 3/4) in Hebrew translation, see Assaf, *What I Have Seen,* 386–87 (letter 5).

82. Weinreich, "Unpublished Letters," no. 27.

83. For the entire text of the letter (SAA, LK 3/3) in Hebrew translation, see Assaf, *What I Have Seen,* 387–88 (letter 6).

84. Weinreich, "Unpublished Letters," no. 28; *Oysgeveylte briv,* no. 196; Lis, *Briv,* no. 686.

85. For the entire text of the letter (SAA LK-3/7) in Hebrew translation, see Assaf, *What I Have Seen,* 388 (letter 7).

86. See his letter to Kotik cited previously (near n. 60), dated 10 January 1913.

87. *Sholem Aleichem Book,* 249, no. 97; Lis, *Briv,* no. 682. The letter is undated, and the editor (Y. D. Berkowitz) suggests a date of November 1913. However, as we have seen, the book reached Sholem Aleichem only in December of that year. Incidentally, on 13 December Berkowitz wrote to Sholem Aleichem (in Russian), inquiring whether he "had already received Kotik's part two?" (SAA, LB-57/136; JNUL, file 43).

88. Weinreich, "Unpublished Letters," no. 29.

89. In a Russian letter from Sholem Aleichem to Berkowitz, dated 20 April 1914, he mentioned his planned visit to Kotik in Warsaw (SAA MB-38/80; JNUL, file 50). On his plans to visit Russia and to stay in Warsaw, see Berkowitz, *Ha-rishonim,* 313–17.

90. Kotik sent parts of the manuscript to Niger in May 1914, requesting his opinion. See following, near nn. 111–12.

91. Ba'al-Makhshoves, "Literarishe geshprekhn" (here and in the quotes following). On Peretz's positive attitude toward Kotik's memoirs, see also Goldberg, "Kotik."

92. On Peretz's memoirs, see Roskies, "Peretses zikhroynes."

93. In such a brief review Ba'al-Makhshoves could not be precise in detail, but there were memoirs preceding the appearance of Kotik's *Zikhroynes* and not just unfinished biographical stories (like "Shloyme reb Khayims" by Mendele ["Ba-

yamim ha-hem" in its Hebrew version]) and *Aviezer* by Mordecai Aharon Günzburg. Additional examples are Solomon Maimon's autobiography (first published in 1792) and Pauline Wengeroff's memoirs (first published in 1908), in German, and the memoirs of Avraham Yaakov Paperna and Grigori Bogrov, in Russian, as well as the works of Moshe Leyb Lilienblum, Avraham Dov Gottlober, and Isaac Hirsh Weiss, in Hebrew, and of Eliakim Zunser and Rachel Feigenberg, in Yiddish. For a survey of Jewish memoir literature, see Shatzky, "Yidisher memuarn literatur"; and Meisel, "Geshikhtlekher shtof."

94. An example of Ba'al-Makhshoves' demand that the "older generation" leave off its involvement with "nonsense" like the founding of societies and turn instead to "useful pursuits," that is, writing memoirs, is found in a review he wrote of Zvi Lipschitz's *Me-dor le-dor*. See Ba'al-Makhshoves, *Skirot u-reshamim*, 1:76–81. See also his essay "Memuarn-literatur."

95. Prylucki, "Kotiks 'Zikhroynes.'" On Prylucki (1882–1941), see *LNYL*, 7:216–23.

96. A. Yud. (Avraham Yuditski), "Sirtutim sifrutiyyim," here and in the following citations. On Yuditski (c. 1885–1943), see *LNYL*, 4:252–55.

97. Einhorn, "Amol." On Einhorn (1884–1942), a journalist and publicist then at the beginning of his literary career, see *LNYL*, 1:72–73.

98. Katz, "Bibliografye," 936–37. The writer is evidently Moshe Katz (1898–1955), a well-known literary critic; see *LNYL*, 4:357–58.

99. Dubnow, *Evreiskaia starina* 6: 413–14 (in Russian).

100. Shrebrek, *Zikhronot*, 158–59.

101. *Ha-tzfirah*, 12 March 1914, no. 50. The author Jacob Dineson wrote similar remarks to Sholem Aleichem regarding volume one of the memoirs: "I am curious as to what Sholem Aleichem can write to a Jew like that, who has scattered among the many good memoirs he wrote so many personal and silly matters (Yiddish original, SAA LD-10/101; JNUL, file 404).

102. Litvin, "Kotik," 10–11.

103. David Kassel (1881–1935), a native of Minsk, was a well-known Bund activist. Following his marriage to the poetess Sarah Reisen (sister of Avraham Reisen), he moved to Warsaw in 1910, where he was employed in translation and editing. See *LNYL*, 8:84–87; Ofek, *Leksikon le-sifrut yeladim*, 568.

104. SAA LH-14/35; JNUL, file 419. The Yiddish original is difficult to decipher. For the full Yiddish citation, see Assaf, *What I Have Seen*, 54 n. 128.

105. Reisen, *Lexicon*, 3:484. Note, however, that this detail is missing both from the first edition of the *Lexicon* (Warsaw, 1914) and from the updated version (New York, 1981).

106. Zeitlin, "Fun fraytog biz fraytog."

107. See Assaf, *What I Have Seen*, 383 (letter 1). Kassel, Avraham Kotik, and the siblings Sarah and Avraham Reisen were active in socialist circles in Minsk as early as 1904.

108. Yatzkan (1874–1936) was a controversial figure, mainly because of his arrogance and his businesslike approach to intellectual matters. He promoted the *Shund* literature and crassly interfered in the work of writers and journalists (including Sholem Aleichem) who published in his journals. See Berkowitz, *Ha-rishonim*, 261–62, 281–82; Finkelstein, *Haynt*, 27–38; and Shmeruk, "Schund Literature," 337–39.

109. See above, following n. 93.

110. See Assaf, *What I Have Seen*, 387–88 (letter 6). The obituary published in *Haynt*, 14 August 1921, no. 185, also noted that the third and fourth parts of the *Zikhroynes*, which dealt with Kotik's latter years in Warsaw, would soon be published.

111. YIVO, Niger Archives: Hosafa, Algemeyns, no. 363.

112. For the original Yiddish, see Assaf, *What I Have Seen*, 56 n. 137. Niger's attitude toward Kotik and his memoirs remains unclear, as I have yet to find any documents relating to this question in Niger's archives. It is also surprising that in Niger's review of Avraham-Hirsh Kotik's *Lebn* ("Di noente fargangenheyt") he makes no mention of the fact that the book's author was Yekhezkel Kotik's son.

113. Yidisher Folks-Farlag, prospectus no. 1 (Kiev, March 1919), 9. It was the late Professor Chone Shmeruk who brought this rare catalogue to my attention.

114. Yidisher Folks-Farlag, which was founded in October 1918, apparently went bankrupt in 1920. Its editor-in-chief was Jacob Wolf Latzki-Bertoldi, and Ba'al-Makhshoves was on the editorial board and perhaps recommended that the book be published. For more details on this publishing house, see Dinur, *Milhamah u-mahapekha*, 404–9. On the exigencies of Yiddish publishing in the Soviet Union during that period, see Shmeruk, *Jewish Publications*, 70–76.

115. The contracts are housed in the YIVO Archives, Zamlung shrayber, file 2721, nos. 100560–100562. An item on the intended publication of a German translation also appeared in the necrology published in *Der moment* (see n. 53 above).

116. Kotik was to receive 2,350 marks for the first two volumes. Welt-Verlag, which was founded in 1919, specialized mainly in belles lettres. In 1921, Alexander Aharon Eliasberg, who had an unusually favorable attitude toward Yiddish literature, was appointed director. See Fuks and Fuks, "Yiddish Publishing," 422.

117. Klal-Verlag was founded in 1921 by Latzki-Bertoldi, who had been among the founders of Yidisher Folks-Farlag in Kiev (see n. 114 above). Perhaps it was he who brought the manuscript from Kiev to Berlin and contacted Kotik from there. Klal-Verlag specialized in publishing the best of Yiddish literature, both in the original and in translation, primarily for sale outside Germany. It was especially active between 1922 and 1923. See Fuks and Fuks, "Yiddish Publishing," 423; for the Yiddish titles published in 1922, see ibid., 429–30.

118. Until 1923 a temporary currency known as the Polish mark was in circulation. As inflation was tremendously high, this was not as large a sum as it seems at first glance.

119. Kotik was involved in the preparation of the second edition, and even added a brief introduction explaining why he appended the letter sent him by Sholem Aleichem to the book (this letter was slated to be included in the planned Kiev edition). Evidently the book went to press before Kotik's death.

120. This document has been preserved in the YIVO Archives in New York, in the as yet uncatalogued "New"-Old boxes sent from Vilna in 1995. The agreement bears Gitlin's signature alone; thus it appears that this was the copy given to the Kotiks, which they naturally did not sign.

121. Avraham received 50,000 Polish marks before 4 July 1921, and Gitlin undertook to pay the remainder by 15 July of that year.

122. Kotik, *Das Haus meiner Grosseltern,* 94. On this book, no. 64 of the Bücherei des Schocken Verlags series, see also Schreuder and Weber, *Der Schocken Verlag,* 274.

123. See, for example, the beginning of Yisrael Aksenfeld's novella "The Headband," 49–50; Mendele Mokher Seforim, "Of Bygone Days"; or the first chapter ("The Town N.") of Der Nister's *The Family Mashber.* Although the latter book describes a city, Berdichev, and not a town, the concentric topography of the Jewish community is the same.

124. On the other hand, in the second part of his memoirs (*Memoirs,* 2:17–18) Kotik describes an episode in which, forced to choose between pragmatic considerations and his hasidic leanings, his father incurred a seven-hundred-ruble loss to travel to the rebbe for Rosh Hashanah, the height of the agricultural season. When Kotik queried him as to this unfathomable behavior, suggesting he could have chosen a more convenient time to travel, his father replied: "You have never been a hasid, thus you cannot understand what it means to travel to the rebbe. There is no greater pleasure. The rebbe endows one with strength to go on living."

125. A parallel figure, featured in the second volume of the memoirs, is Sender Rosenblum, another family member who also managed a Polish estate with great success.

126. Kotik was intensely aware of Polish antisemitism, which he described dramatically in the context of the events of the Polish Rebellion of 1863 (chapter 21), when the Polish rebels tormented the Jews, and the lords, who hid in Jewish homes, treated them with despicable forced gratitude.

127. Avraham-Hirsh Kotik (1867–1934) was a socialist activist who engaged in publishing activity and in bringing the Russian-Jewish intelligentsia closer to the Yiddish language. From 1885 to 1887 he operated a young revolutionary circle in Warsaw with his friends Shmuel Rabinowitz (son of the historian Saul Phinehas Rabinowitz [ShePHeR]) and Yitzhak Tabenkin. He wandered throughout the Pale of Settlement (Bialystok, Minsk, Yaroslav, Vilna) and emigrated to the United States in 1925, taking up residence in New York. He published his memoirs (*Lebn*) in that same year, and attempted to realize a youthful fantasy in his father's vein: founding and directing an academic institution called the Yiddish Home-University. See his letters to Niger, 23 October 1925 (YIVO, Niger Archives, file 369). In 1926 Kotik returned to the USSR and lived in Moscow, later moving to Kharkov in 1927, where he remained until his death. On him, see Reisen, *Lexicon,* 3:418–24; Reisen, *Epizodn,* 2:46–50, 212–13; Rabinowicz, "Fifty Years Ago," 320–25; Hershberg, *Bialystok,* 1:422–23; *LNYL,* 8:42–43; "Materyaln," 169; and Mintz, *Tabenkin,* 12–13. Bluma Kotik (1908–68), one of Avraham's daughters, was also known for her literary activity, mainly translations. See *Sovetish heymland* 1983, no. 8: 165.

128. Kotik, *Lebn,* 12, 26. Kotik's wife Libe died soon after her husband. The above-mentioned book by their son Avraham, published in 1925, was dedicated to her memory.

129. Kotik gave forceful expression to his admiration for his father at the conclusion of chapter 24: "I wanted to kiss him, to cry, to ask for his mercy, to beg his forgiveness, and was ready to lay down my life for him. . . . I was well aware of how much health my rebelliousness cost my dear father whom I adore and worship to this very day."

130. In this he is an authentic heir to the eighteenth- to nineteenth-century maskilic autobiographies of development. See Robertson, "From Ghetto to Modern Culture"; Buckley, *Turning Key,* 38–53.

131. The existing studies of daily life in the nineteenth-century Jewish shtetl are based on partial observations and fragmentary sources; a full-fledged academic and systematic study is still a desideratum. The only comprehensive study written from an anthropological-folklorist perspective is now somewhat outdated and suffers from generalizations and idealization (Zborowski and Herzog, *Life Is with People*). Noteworthy among the anthologies are: Dawidowicz, *Golden Tradition;* Roskies and Roskies, *Shtetl Book;* and Kugelmass and Boyarin, *From a Ruined Garden*(excerpts from post–Holocaust memorial books).

132. The desire for preservation was restricted neither to Eastern European Jewry nor to Jews alone. A separate issue is Western European Jewry's changed attitude toward the *Ostjuden* and shtetl culture, which shifted from contempt to romanticization. See Ascheim, "East European Jew"; and Mendes-Flohr, *"Ostjuden."* We must also note that similar feelings moved Orthodox rabbis to engage in source-collecting projects. Witness, for example, the comments of the folklorist Rabbi Yehuda Leib Zlotnick: "We shall do a great disservice to our nation if we allow the memory of certain customs currently practiced to be lost, *particularly as it seems that the time for customs has ended,* for they are being pushed out of our lives one by one." Elzet (pen name of Zlotnick), "Me-minhagei yisrael," 337 (emphasis mine—D. A.). This article was written before World War One. See *Edoth* 2 (1949): 248.

133. Considerations of space permit me to mention but a few examples: Simon Dubnow's collection project, kicked off in his 1892 Hebrew article "Nahpesa venahkora" (and in Russian in *Voskhod* a year earlier) and continued in the founding of historical and ethnographical societies with branches throughout the empire; the folk song collection project of Saul Ginsburg and Pesach Marek (*Yiddish Folksongs,* 1901); Joel Engel's folk music project (from 1898); I. L. Peretz's notes made while a member of a delegation making a statistical study of the condition of the Jews in Poland (1890), echoed in his series of stories "Impressions of a Journey"; and primarily the ethnographic delegation headed by S. An-sky (1912–14). For rich material on this topic, see *Tracing An-sky.* On the link of Russian-Jewish artists like Eleazar Lisitzky and Marc Chagall to the shtetl, see Harshav, "Chagall," 9–97. It is noteworthy that we can trace a concurrent development of a similar trend with regard to Russian village life in general and among Russian scholars with regard to the chances for preservation of this life. The ethnographic documentation by Olga Semyonova Tian-Shanskaia of peasant life in late-nineteenth-century Russia is a parallel example that reflects a shared atmosphere. See Tian-Shanskaia, *Village Life.*

134. On hygiene and medicine and the attitude toward women, see chapter 1, near note 118. On superstitions, see, for example, chapter 8, near note 26; regarding exorcism of the evil eye, see chapter 15, near note 5; on customs connected to the wedding ceremony, see chapter 23, near note 8. On the cruelty of the melamdim, see chapter 1, near note 97. On teaching methods, see chapter 1, following note 104. In part two of his memoirs Kotik describes at length two types of melamdim he hired to teach his children: one, a coarse ignoramus, represented all the negative features of the typical melamed; the other, his complete opposite, was a learned prodigy who brought him happiness and satisfaction (Kotik, *Memoirs,* 2:161–73).

135. Gurshteyn, "Der yunger Mendele," 495–99.

136. Kotik, "Ezrat Holim Society" (appendix A, no. 5), 4.

137. Many historians have noted the importance of Kotik's memoirs as a historical source and as an authentic reflection of the contemporary milieu, utilizing and relying upon them in their work. Their number includes Salo Baron, Azriel Shochat, Raphael Mahler, Yehuda Slutsky, and Israel Halpern (see, for example, Levin, *Social and Economic Values*, 74). References to the works of these historians are scattered throughout my notes to the memoirs. Especially noteworthy is the collection of sources published in the USSR (1929) that makes extensive use of Kotik's memoirs as a historical source to describe Jewish life in the nineteenth-century Pale of Settlement. See Yakhinson, *Sotsyal-ekonomisher shteyger*. Kotik's memoirs were also studied in Jewish schools in pre-World War I Poland. See Greenbaum, "Undzer Kotik-ekspeditsye."

138. This was by no means a new phenomenon. Similar phenomena—primarily poll tax evasion—are attested to in earlier population censuses, like the one carried out in Poland in 1764. See Mahler, *Toldot ha-yehudim be-Polin*, 231–33.

139. See, for example, the explanation the Jew gives his wife for why he returns to the lord who abused him (chapter 1, near n. 23). When as a child Kotik commented to his grandfather that he was not willing to do business with nobles who cruelly beat their serfs, the latter replied: "'If so . . . one wouldn't be able to do business with any of the gentry. But, my dear boy, what can be done? We have no other choice'" (chapter 10). A different type of ambivalence in Jewish life is reflected in chapter 14, where Kotik fondly describes the wonderful feeling of unity that prevailed on Yom Kippur among Jews who, "fought one another viciously throughout the year over a single groshen for their livelihood!"

140. See chapter 1, prior to note 23. Indeed, most of the Polish lords described in Kotik's memoirs are cast in a positive light. On the various literary treatments of non-Jews and their image in Eastern European Yiddish literature, see Bartal, "Non-Jews"; and idem, "Gentile Society."

141. An archetypal example of this identification with the Polish nationalist opposition is that of Yisrael, the Kotsker hasid. See chapter 5, near notes 11–19.

142. One example is Kotik's relative, Hillel Fried of Kharkov, who made his fortune in railroads. On Fried and his lifestyle, see Kotik, *Memoirs*, 2, chapters 21–22.

143. See Slutsky, *Russian Jewish Press*, 1:19–21.

144. See Zalkin, "Hasidism in Nineteenth-Century Lithuania."

145. See, for example, the acute observation by the Israeli writer Meir Shalev: "The process of remembering and of reworking memory is the essence of creativity for many writers, because, among other things, remembering is not simply mechanical extraction of information from a database in the boring computer sense, but a more complicated process involving elements of change and rewriting. In *Esau* my narrator notes that every time he remembers something this elicits changes in the content of his memory, and he denotes this phenomenon 'creative memory.' Every person who has listened to himself recount childhood memories to his children is well aware of the meaning of this creative memory" (*Be-ikar al ahavah*, 201).

146. For an examination of these processes in the context of various literary genres, see, for example, Zakovitch, "From Oral to Written Tale in the Bible"; Shinan, "Aggadic Literature"; Werses, "Agnon"; Yassif, *Hebrew Folktale*, 376–80; and Shmeruk, *Yiddish*, 201ff.

147. Among such mistakes and slips of the pen, noted throughout the book, we find, for example, the description of the Kotsker rebbe taking presents (chapter 5); the exorcism of a dybbuk by mitnaggedic rabbis (chapter 8); and the description of the prodigy Yisrael Vishniak putting on twelve pairs of phylacteries (chapter 16). Among the accidental slips, we find Samuel instead of Elijah (chapter 1, note 71); incorrect dates (chapter 3, note 1); confusion regarding the titles of books (chapter 17, note 2; chapter 28, note 11); and unsubstantiated historical data (chapter 21, note 17). The questionable nature of the numerical data Kotik provides has already been noted.

148. I shall note several memoirs that emerged from the Lithuanian cultural context: Hayyim Chemerinsky (1862–1917), *Motele* (which, like Kamenets, was in the Grodno province)—see my new edition with an introduction about the man and his book in the series *Mivhar: Studies and Sources in the History and Culture of East European Jewry* (Jerusalem: Magnes Press); Eliezer Elijah Friedman (1857–1936), *Zikhronot* (a native of Kelme who was educated in the Lithuanian yeshivot); Shmaryahu Levin (1867–1935), a native of Sbislovitsh in White Russia, whose memoirs appeared in English in three volumes: *Childhood in Exile* (1929), *Youth in Revolt* (1930), and *The Arena* (1932), and in abridged form (abridged by Maurice Samuel) *Forward from Exile* (1967); Yisrael Isser Kasovich (1859–1919), *Our Years,* on his life in a remote village in the Minsk province in the latter half of the nineteenth century; and Meir Yaakov Freid (1871–1940), *Yamim ve-shanim* (a native of Kalvarija in Suwalki province), among many others. Special note must be taken of Falk Zolf's memoirs, *Oyf fremder erd.* In the introduction Zolf cites from a letter from Max Weinreich in which he defined Zolf's book as the sequel to Kotik's memoirs (p. 6).

149. This is especially evident in Yossel Birstein's Hebrew novel *A Face in the Clouds.* See, for example, 183–84 (the cantonists; Kotik, chapter 9); 189, 198 (selling half of one's portion in the world-to-come and canceling the sale; Kotik, chaps. 6–7); and 198 (the grandmother's death and the grandfather's subsequent remarriage; Kotik, chapter 28 and chapter 1 of *Memoirs,* 2).

150. The translation, which was of chapter 3, appeared in *Menorah* 6/7 (June 1927) [=*Die Juden in Polen*], 384–88.

151. Schwarz, *Memoirs of My People,* 233–42 (chapters 23–24, and part of 25).

152. Kugelmass, "Native Aliens," 125–64, 184–92. In some instances the translations found in Kugelmass's work have been utilized in the body of the memoirs. A brief excerpt from the first chapter of the memoirs appeared in *Kamenetz Memorial Book,* English section, 29–37.

153. Excerpts appeared, for example, in *Kobrin,* 51–52; *Kamenetz Memorial Book,* Hebrew section, 39–43, and small bits elsewhere.

154. Aside from the addition of Sholem Aleichem's letter to Kotik to the 1922 edition, the main differences lie in orthography. Whereas the first edition used the "old" spelling and vocalization, the second edition appeared in a more modern Yiddish orthography.

155. For a discussion of some of these difficulties with regard to hasidic homilies, see Green, "Hasidic Homilies."

156. Litvin, "Kotik," 7–8.

157. Prylucki, "Kotiks 'Zikhroynes,'" no. 37.

158. A. Yud., "Sirtutim sifrutiyyim," no. 193.

My Memoirs

Yekhezkel Kotik

Dedicated to the memory of my

beloved grandmother Beyle-Rashe,

the quiet and kindly educator of our

large and noisy family.

Instead of an Introduction

I am going to tell of *what* I have seen, but have no idea of *how* to go about it. What is old, people say, is important for what is new, and in order to build the new, one must know the old. If this is so, the reader will forgive me the "how" for the sake of the "what," and this will be my reward: I have uncovered a corner from a gray, remote, but beloved past. . . .

I spent my youth in a small, typical shtetl where Jews lived a poor but "quiet," and, if one may say, flavorful life. . . . This no longer exists today; the poetry of those former shtetls has been silenced too. The immigration to America has thinned them out, and the arduous life for Jews in Russia, which is filled with the black lead of antisemitism, has entirely ruined them. These gracious Jewish towns, which were weaker than the Jewish cities, were the first to die. . . .

Y. K.

Preface to the Second (1922) Edition

I do not think it superfluous to present here Sholem Aleichem's letter to me, which he sent after receiving the first volume of *My Memoirs.* I am not doing this, God forbid, in order to display before the reader the praises that the great Sholem Aleichem granted me, to the point that he signed his letter enthusiastically, "your grateful reader, your friend, and your pupil."

I am publishing this letter in order to underscore through it that Sholem Aleichem, that warm-hearted humorist who laughed at and mocked everything, also possessed much genuine humility. Being ill in Switzerland, and cut off from the world, he nevertheless revealed great interest and warmth in every book in Yiddish newly appearing over there, in the Old Country, and became captivated like a child by an unknown writer's depiction of characters which bring to life in his memory "his youth, his family, his heder, his holidays, and his dreams. . . ."

Y. K.

Sholem Aleichem's Letter
to Yekhezkel Kotik

My most esteemed, though regretfully, unknown colleague, Yekhez-kel Kotik!

With one stroke I dispatched two letters—one to you,[2] the other to Niger,[3] asking him for an exchange of books. But it turned out that you had already sent Niger the copy dedicated to the poet, Abraham Reisen,[4] and Reisen, happens to be, of all things, at the moment in New York, in America! Had all that taken place several years earlier when Sholem Aleichem was still nimble-footed and could have been up and about within a flash, it would have been easy as laughter for me to be on my way to America. But now, all that is rather difficult. So, what can I do, that I am captivated by reading your *Memoirs*? I have placed the entire blame on your head that I have cut Niger's book to pieces[5] and I don't have an ounce of regret.

I have taken to reading your *Memoirs* so what should I say? I can't remember the year when I had as much pleasure, as much delight—real spiritual pleasure! This is not just a book—this is a treasure, a garden. A paradise full of blossoming flowers and singing birds.

It reminded me of my youth, my family, my heder, my holi-days, my dreams, and of the types of people I knew. No! I, with my bunch of characters and all my portrayals—many of whom I knew, and many I have imagined—must admit without pretense or false modesty—I am compared to you, nothing but a poor child, a pauper! With your experiences and your family, I would have al-ready flooded the world! For heaven's sake, where have you been until now? A man possesses so many diamonds, precious stones and pearls, and nothing?! A Jew walking about "gathering *rendlekh*"[6] (as your fanatical pious ones over there call it) and no one even mentions that he has a treasure?! I began reading and could not stop. I almost went out of my mind! Who is that Kotik? I think I once heard about someone called A. Kotik,[7] a young man. But you are already a gray-bearded Jew!

What has enchanted me with your book is the holy simple truth—not artificial plainness. And the language! No! You are not

just a good, honest, and faithful guardian of an enormous and valuable treasure; you have been blessed with a God-given talent, with
the soul of an artist, yet are unaware of it. Not a few Jews were in
your Kamenets, and in Zastavye,[8] not a few of them are relatives
in your noisy, as you call it, family—why has it never occurred to
anyone to gather such recollections, as you have? Why have none of
them shown themselves to be the type of person you are, who could
produce such fervor? I imagine, do you hear, that your family—is
my family (and that is probably what every reader feels).

I know your grandfather Aharon-Leyzer, and your grandmother
Beyle-Rashe, your father Moshe the hasid, and all your uncles and
aunts, even the *ispravnik,*[9] with the *assessor,*[10] and all the lords,[11]
the good and the evil ones, the melamdim, the hasidim and the
mitnaggedim, the healers, and the rabbi, and that apikores who
was a scribe in Brisk,[12] for whom a *kerbl* was a bastard,[13] and the
two "Yisraels,"[14] and Aharon-Leybele, Khatskl and Moshke,[15] and
Berl-Bendet, the *upravliaishche*[16] of the estate—all, all of them!
All of them are alive, I know all of them and with all of them I
share in their joy and I mourn in their sadness. One needs great
restraint not to burst out laughing (and there were moments when
I held my sides with laughter), or to burst into tears. I swear to you
upon my word that I cried together with all your family, when your
grandfather blessed you all on Yom Kippur eve;[17] and when your
saintly grandmother who had passed away was laid out on the floor
and your grandfather fainted a hundred times.[18] We should have as
much joy in the redemption of Israel as I had tears in my eyes, and
not because someone died—Good God! How many people die every
day and every hour! But because your grandfather and grandmother
are also mine, mine, mine!

And because those are living and precious people, made of gold,
and because you warmed them all with your soul and placed in your
book the entire, fiery truth, I am truly proud that we possess such
a person, such a Jew as you. Thanks to you such *rendlekh* will not
be lost, which have been scattered about (and to my mind, are still
scattered about) among our people.

I am truly proud that a book like your memoirs has enriched our
still young Yiddish folk-literature.[19] Will you continue writing your
memoirs? Will they be as rich and successful as the first volume?
Successful—of that I am sure—rich—I don't know. I fear they might
be leaner and thinner. Those Jews don't exist anymore! That is, they

are here, but one doesn't notice them. They don't stand out. They have become like a drop in the ocean, especially in the big city.

11 JANUARY 1913

1,500 meters high up in the mountains of Lausanne, I ran today, quite by chance, into the writer Izbitski (Mikhailovitch).[20] I told him about the excitement that was aroused in me by a book written by a simple Jew named Y. Kotik, and how it brought me close to tears. It turns out that this Izbitski knows you very well,[21] and that you are the father of A. Kotik, and the proprietor of a coffeehouse on Nalewki Street;[22] and that everyone has known for a long time that you had written some *Memoirs*. This, naturally, begs the question: Where have they, those idiots, been all along, if they knew about it? Why did they keep silent? And where was I, the same idiot? I have also been on Nalewki, drinking coffee, as I recall, with Spektor.[23] Why didn't I know where I was? Why didn't I know whose coffee I was drinking? Why is our book market flooded with all sorts of trash, when at the same time a "treasure" like yours is hidden away in some box, drawer, or under a mattress?

I am boiling with rage at our critics every time I recall how they praise every snotnose who scribbles out some filth stolen from the Gentiles. It turns one's stomach to read the vomit belched up, like the obscenities of Artzibashev[24] and the garbage of others like him. It makes a good humorist—as they call me—angry and takes away my desire to write. I become a robber—mind you, not for long, but like a "Jewish Robber."[25] In short, I've given my tongue too much free rein.

Please, answer me, if you can spare the time, whether you intend to go on writing more memoirs, of what period, which circles you have in mind, whether it runs as smoothly as it did up until now, and whether you will also write more about your family? There are types in your family that you must continue telling and telling about. Be well, keep your spirits up and write!

Your grateful reader, your friend, and your pupil . . .

Sholem Aleichem.

The "Slup"

MY TOWN

*K*amenets, the town in which I was born, is famous for its old, historic tower, called the "Slup."[1] No one knows when it was built. It was thought to be a remnant of an ancient fortress. This tower, rising high up, was built of thick masonry with battlements for guns and cannons. In my grandfather's time cannon balls weighing ten *funt*[2] or so could still be found lying about—clear proof of their having been shot through those holes. The bricks of the tower were so solid that it was impossible to chip away even a small piece. In Kamenets they said that the walls were built with egg whites—and that's why they were so strong. . . . Whenever Tsar Alexander II[3] and his companions, the European princes, went hunting in Białowieska Forest,[4] about seven miles[5] outside of Kamenets, all the ministers and generals who accompanied him would ride into town to take a look at this historic tower.

I have purposely begun my memoirs with reference to this tower since, the moment I think of my shtetl, the tower pops into my mind as some sort of sign whose meaning is incomprehensible. And now I can proceed to describe the town itself.

About sixty years ago [c. 1850], the time at which I am starting my memoirs, Kamenets consisted of 250 old houses, black and small with shingled roofs. Yet only 450 "souls," were noted in the *skazka*[6]—the government registry. This leads to the logical question—250 houses and only 450 souls? How did this come to be? There is, however, a very simple answer. Prior to 1874, before the new conscription law was introduced,[7] almost two-thirds of the Jews were not recorded. The government had been aware of this, but, as if silently, let it go. The registration of all those unlisted souls began only in 1874, when the Tsar issued a manifesto that the "hidden,"[8] (i.e., the unregistered), would not be punished if they only entered themselves in the government registry, and commissions traveled around all the towns and villages to write down those who had not yet been recorded.

It is of considerable interest to relate how recruits were produced in those days from among the 450 registered souls of my town. At a distance of four miles from Kamenets lies the shtetl of Wysokie[9] which had in its registry about 550 souls. Wysokie and Kamenets used to supply their recruits together. Since soldiers were drafted according to a certain percentage of a town's inhabitants, say one per thousand, and since Kamenets and Wysokie had about a thousand inhabitants in all, only one recruit from both townships combined was drafted into Tsar Nicholas's army. Kamenets was required to supply somewhat less than half a recruit, and Wysokie, with a slightly larger population, something more than half a recruit. It took a bit of work for the elders of both towns to come to a compromise. Eventually, it was agreed upon that one year Kamenets was to supply a recruit, and the following year Wysokie, but once in ten years Kamenets would not have to provide its soldier. The reckoning was quite simple: Every year the registered inhabitants of the townships would be reduced by fifty, which amounted to 500 in ten years, and so there was no need to supply any recruits at all from either township. That's how recruits were produced in those days—the Jews came to an agreement among themselves.

As was common, in the middle of the town stood two rows of small stores whose front doors opened inward. The narrow alley between them scarcely had room enough for a wagon to pass through. Three or four of those stores sold cloth of a better quality for the more well-to-do Jews and the lords living on the outskirts. Three or four other stores sold aprons, large and small kerchiefs, and the like. The rest dealt in notions, tar, resin, and so on.

All the stores were run almost exclusively by women—older and younger wives, their daughters and daughters-in-law. The women usually sat outside, opposite one another or side by side, scarcely able to hide their mutual anger and envy if one of the numerous young wives pulled or dragged in potential customers by their sleeves, mainly peasants or their womenfolk. The better kind of customers—the Jews or the gentry—usually patronized particular stores and nobody dared drag them into one's own store like a herring.[10] But under their breath, the women fired curses at them and the storekeepers who made a profit from them.

Business was slack except for Sundays, because the peasants rarely came into the town during the week. So the women sat in their stores and had nothing to do. On Sundays, however, they set up a great market, and crowds of peasants came and congregated around the doors of the shops and they created such congestion, like flies around sugar-coated window panes.

The taverns did a brisk business and there were many of them in town. In addition to alcohol, the peasants could find there a bite to eat: cheese, herring, and pickled cucumbers. But sweet wine was also not lacking, which a *szlachcic*,[11] or a member of the lower Polish nobility, would permit himself. He would not be satisfied, as a peasant would, with cheese or herring after his schnapps, but would rather have some goose or fish. These taverns, like the shops, were also run by women; however, on Sundays, when profits were great, the men also came to lend a hand.

So what did the men occupy themselves with? Surely, they did not hang around idly. Kamenets was surrounded by about two hundred landlords of larger and smaller estates, and each had about two hundred serfs who slaved away for them day and night. The lords, of course, wanting to continue a life of pleasure and leisure, employed one or two local Jews each, who did their bidding. In this way, the Jews made a living, more or less.[12]

If two Jews depended on a lord, one had to be a "nice" Jew, an upper-class and respectable merchant, and the other had to be a "smaller" Jew, a person who was both less respected and had a smaller business. Both were the lord's right-hand men. The "nice" Jew served more to give advice, while the second performed various tasks by exercising his cunning and resourcefulness. But both Jews stood in great terror of their employer, even though they made a partial living from him and he protected them from the authorities. Nevertheless, one must praise God ten times a day for the fact that the Gentry-Jew relationship has passed from the world for good.[13]

When it struck his fancy, the noble would flog his Jew and then say: "If you keep quiet you'll continue to stay with me, and if not, I'll find another Jew. You won't be able to do anything against me anyway, since the *assessor* and the *ispravnik* are on my side." The Jew would keep quiet and think to himself: "So what, I got a beating. After all, he is the lord of the manor, and at least I do make some sort of a livelihood from him. If I pass away, my children will be able to get a job from him, eventually."

And that was usually the case. If the Jew happened to die, the landlord would choose either his son or son-in-law, whoever pleased him, to take his place, just as one chooses a prospective bridegroom. In that way, the son would "inherit" the landlord. Yes, the lord was a kind of inheritance.

At this juncture, it might be worth mentioning that each land-lord had his own artisan working exclusively for him.[14] There were many artisans in the town—cobblers, tailors, blacksmiths, etc.—who had a much harder time than the storekeepers making ends meet. Although they paid very little rent for their dwellings—from ten to twelve rubles a year—nevertheless a single family was not even able to pay that much, and often had to share a small house with two or three other families.[15]

In those days, the *assessor* and the *ispravnik* were the unchallenged rulers. If two Jews came to blows with one another, they, their wives, their sons and daughters, their assistants, their good friends, and their relatives would run to the *assessor* to arbitrate between them. The *assessor* would favor either the one that greased his palm with the greater amount or simply the one he liked better. If one of them, adamant and standing on ceremony, was not satisfied with the *assessor*'s ruling and took his complaint against the *assessor* to the *ispravnik* in Brisk,[16] it rarely did him much good. His life would then be worthless. The *assessor* would harass him pitilessly, going so far as to have him beaten or arrested. The *ispravnik,* of course, always sided with the *assessor.*

The *ispravnik* at that time wielded enormous power and governed the whole area. The governor,[17] on the other hand, was considered akin to the tsar in those days, and it was unthinkable to approach him on matters of Jewish interest.

A lord always had a Jewish agent who lived with him on the estate, and also a lessee, usually a Jew, too. If he owned several more estates and a number of villages as well, these, too, were run by a Jewish agent and a Jewish lessee. Such Jews, of course, stood in fear of the landlord.

In those days, if flogging male and female peasants, young and old, was a little matter, then why should beating a little Jew be an exception? One can imagine how the agent and the lessee, along with their families, were scared to death of the lord. If, God forbid, the agent and the lessee had pretty daughters, this was considered a terrible misfortune. One had to see to it that the lord should not find the daughters attractive, since, with his power, he could carry out whatever struck his fancy. Consequently, the daughters of the village Jews[18] were always dirty, unwashed, and neglected, so that their beauty would not be apparent. Only when they went into the town and had washed themselves well with soap did one know that those girls were attractive.

Anything that the lord needed was generally obtained through his Jews. He believed that the Jew was a cunning creature, sly, but essentially honest (each noble maintained that his "little Jews" were honest, but the others were swindlers and thieves). He would send his Jews on errands to his colleagues, the other nobles, and, although he had a steward who was in charge of his estate and watched over his peasants, he nevertheless preferred to send one of his Jews to do business. A Jew, he believed, could handle a delicate matter with greater discretion, and he would not make a move without his "Moshko" or "Shmulik."[19]

The Kamenets lords were not, on the whole, very wealthy. Their land was sandy and not particularly fertile. A plot of about two acres would yield at most 240 sheaves[20] containing no more than five or six pud[21] of grains. Very little wheat thrived on the soil surrounding Kamenets, yet, here and there one could find an especially fertile plot of land the size of a few square versts.[22] Then those same two acres would yield between 700 and 900 sheaves of wheat.

The nobles living within three or four versts of one another often hosted balls in their mansions, sometimes this one, sometimes that one. These were magnificent and expensive affairs, and only the best wines were served. However, such extravagant entertaining drove many of the gentry into expenses they could scarcely afford and impoverished quite a few. Needless to say, they were always hard-pressed for money.

That was why the Jews who bought grain, spirits, wool, and livestock from the nobility had to pay for everything in cash, in advance, and frequently more than the purchase was worth.

There was no lack of competitors who would run to the lord and try to outbid his steady buyer. Nevertheless, to the extent that the noble had to do the buying himself, he would purchase from "his Jews," with whom he had steady dealings, who brooked no competition.

As was the fashion, the noblemen loved dogs. Each kept several types of dogs; there were hunting dogs, and dogs that would attack a stranger without so much as a bark and nearly tear him to pieces. A third sort would bark but not bite, and there was a kind that would bark, and bite. Each lord had these categories of dogs with him on his estate, and the torments that Jews had to endure from these dogs when they visited the noble could fill an entire page in the history of the Jewish exile.

When a Jew drove to the noble, he would first stop his wagon in front of the main entrance to the estate and wait to see if he could spot a peasant. The peasant would bring the Jew to the lord's agent, who was somewhere on the estate, and from there, he would be accompanied to the lord. When the Jew was about to leave, the lord would send someone with him to the main entrance of the palace. If the Jew was worthy to go out through the main door, the lord allowed him to walk to the main gate with a servant. If he didn't have this good fortune, he had to make his own way, in deathly fear, from the palace to the lord's agent, who would then accompany him to the gate of the estate.

Not until the Jew made it to the main gate was he safe from the evil dogs. If, God forbid, the noble bore him the slightest grudge, then his life was worthless. The nobleman would have the Jew walk to the main gate completely unescorted, and he would undergo systematic mockery and torture. The lord would first send out a few dogs that only barked but didn't bite, immediately followed by another category of dogs, and after that, the dogs that were the true biters. They would attack the Jew from all sides and not let him go this way or that, and along the way they would take substantial bites. He would be scared to death and his cries would rise to heaven, while the nobleman and his entire family stood on the balcony and laughed.

Sometimes, at the noble's slightest resentment against a Jew, even a highly respected one, the same spectacle would repeat itself: the lord would send someone to escort the Jew out through the main gate, and hinting to his man, would have him abandon the Jew halfway across the courtyard. One cannot say that all nobles behaved so cruelly with Jews; there were also decent nobles whose relations with Jews were completely different.

Of course, those same Jews would come home half dead from such an experience, and many fell ill from fear. The Jew's wife, and above all, his children, on seeing their father trembling and pale, would break into heartrending wails as on Yom Kippur. A few days later, the lord would again summon the same Jew to advise him on a matter of the utmost urgency. The Jew, of course, would run to him again at full speed, since what will a Jew not do to make a living? He would console his wife, that the lord was basically not a bad person, and that one could get along with him and earn a livelihood. Only when he had his bad moments[23] was it truly unbearable. "This is all from God," he'd say. "Nothing happens without God's will. Since God wanted to punish me, he sent some capriciousness into the lord's head. Let this be the worst of my troubles, and may God protect me from now on from those evil dogs."

The nobility who lived around Kamenets attended church nearly every Sunday. On important holidays, all of the nobility would ride in, each striving to show that his carriage, with its horses and fancy leather harnesses, could outdo his neighbor's. It is difficult to describe the opulence of these carriages and horses. They would be driven in from all sides of the town, and parked along the entire length of the streets.

One nobleman would arrive in a costly carriage drawn by four expensive horses, harnessed side by side. The horses and their harnesses were embellished with gold and silver, as was the livery of the driver and footmen. Another nobleman would drive in a carriage drawn in tandem by two teams of horses, even more ornately appointed. And a third had six horses harnessed to his carriage, two on each side and two in front. If that wasn't enough, others had footmen announce their arrival in the town by blowing silver horns, and the coachmen would crack their long whips—casting fear on everyone. Even nobles who had small estates with only a few dozen serfs spared no expense when it came to a carriage and a pair of horses.

Upon leaving church, the nobles would go their separate ways. Some of them stopped at Khaytshe Trinkovski's,[24] to pick up good bottles of wine and fine tea. Long-legged hunting dogs with precious silver collars ran after the carriages.

There were two churches in Kamenets. One was a Polish church for the nobility. The Catholic peasants attended the village churches, but not, God forbid, the nobility's church. It was, in fact, forbidden for a peasant to be seen walking on the street where the church was located.

The Polish priest and his two assistants lived in a large compound not far from the church. It had a pretty garden with beautiful fruit trees and fragrant flowers. The smells rising from the priest's garden were so intoxicating that Jewish noses could hardly bear them, and they often set their heads reeling. The priest lived like a prince, with silver and gold utensils—just like a tsar. The wealthiest lords would come to the priest for breakfast after the Sunday service. He owned several carriages—both open and closed, drawn by magnificent horses. When he drove, the horses would be harnessed in tandem, two by two. The priest also owned many fields and meadows, tilled and tended for him by noblemen's serfs. He sometimes received, as a gift from a lord, a couple of peasants, who were his as long as he lived. He also had many cows and different kinds of fowl, and an artificial lake in the compound filled with fish. In addition to all that, the priest had beautiful maidservants and chambermaids, peasant girls given to him by the nobles.

When I was a boy, we used to live opposite the priest's compound, actually in his inn. It was an impressive building that the priest had built in order to augment his income. Unlike all others obliged to pay the estate owner excise duty on vodka, beer, salt, candles, tobacco, etc., the priest was exempt from this tax. Since we held the *arenda*[25] of the town, we were forced to lease the inn from the priest in order to prevent outside competition. We paid the priest three hundred rubles a year for the inn, where we also lived.

I recall that the priest had four sisters who were tall, slim, and exceptionally beautiful. They wore the most expensive clothes, and adorned and beautified themselves as did only the wives of wealthy landholders.

The priest's home was full of guests day and night, who hung around his beautiful sisters. The revelry went on nonstop. The din of the music from the various instruments, mixed with the cracking of the whips by the carriage drivers and the blowing of the trumpets by the trumpeters, made it impossible to sleep entire nights.

The poor Russian priest, who would be green with envy of the Catholic priest's wealthy, luxurious lifestyle, swore to the peasant parishioners and to the Jews that the beautiful young ladies were not the Catholic priest's sisters at all, they were not even relatives, but mistresses. Since a Catholic priest may not marry, he spread a rumor that they were his sisters. One must confess that the poor Russian priest had it right, they were indeed the Catholic priest's mistresses and not his sisters.

The Russian Orthodox church was situated on one of the hills in town (in Kamenets there were four high hills: the Slup hill, the Church hill, Adolina hill, and Palace hill, where the lord's commissioner[26] lived). The Russian Orthodox serfs prayed in this impoverished church. Of course, since there were no Polish lords who were Russian Orthodox, one can imagine how "richly" the Russian priest lived with his wife and child.

He lived in a shabby little house and went everywhere on foot. Moreover, he was a big *shlimazel*[27]: once he did buy a little horse with a wagon for thirty rubles, but the horse died on him, so again he had to travel on foot. He dressed in old faded and patched garments and carried in his hand a simple walking stick, a gift brought to him by a peasant who had cut it down from the noble's forest. It is said that when the lord found out about the gift, he sent his *assessor* to the priest to have him return the stick and reveal the name of the peasant who had given it to him. But since the *assessor* himself was a coreligionist, he could not, of course, subject the priest to such an indignity. The *assessor* did not take the stick, but the priest had to reveal the peasant's name. On account of his innocent gift, the latter received sixty lashes from the lord with a switch made of branches from the same tree.

The priest owned a small plot of land on which he would sow grain and then sell it. He was so poor that Jews would pay him in advance for the harvest even before the seeds began to sprout.

Kamenets belonged to a noble called Osserevski. He was an old bachelor, who had been an officer in the Polish army before the first uprising.[28] He owned about five thousand serfs and a large number of estates around Kamenets, as well as the town itself. In addition, he had fourteen million gulden in the bank. Some said that he had won all his possessions playing cards. It must have been true, for Osserevski was a great card player who always won. Most of the time he lived in Warsaw, where he played cards with rich nobles. Some said he was a sorcerer who won his money through magic. Once a year, Osserevski visited his beautiful estate at Pruska,[29] some eight versts distance from Kamenets.

There was a lord, whose name, I think, was Motsyevski, who once played cards with Osserevski throughout an entire night. It was a game of life or death. First, Motsyevski lost thirty thousand rubles in cash, and then he gambled away his carriages, his horses, and finally his entire estate along with six hundred serfs. He lost everything and confirmed it by signing a piece of paper with his full given name and family name. Such documents, of course, do not have any legal value, since they lack a notary's authorization. But this was enough for Osserevski, who was an intimate of the government officials in Warsaw,[30] and the general-governor[31] of Vilna province was also one of his close friends. Thus, all of the documents signed by Motsyevski were ironclad.

This, however, was not the end of that episode. After Motsyevski had, with great passion, gambled everything away, and since he had nothing more to wager, he staked his wife for twenty-five thousand rubles, and again—he lost.[32] Then he asked Osserevski, "If I shoot myself, will you come to my funeral?"

Osserevski, a typical Polish lord, responded with a subtle mixture of compassion and brutality: "I pity you, but I am willing to make a deal with you, and for a small deed I am ready to return all your losses. I want you to kiss my ——!"

Motsyevski agreed, and then Osserevski added: "You will have to do it, however, in the presence of all the lords and your wife. She will have to witness it because you have gambled her away without her knowledge."

This was more than Motsyevski had bargained for. "I'd rather put a bullet through my head," he said. "I won't let you do that," Osserevski threatened, and had him locked up in a special room, closely guarded by two of his servants.

The following day all the lords were invited to a ball. At the height of the festivities, Osserevski commanded that the impoverished nobleman and his wife be brought in. Beside the lavishly set table Osserevski told his guests about his extraordinary winnings, adding that, actually, he was in no need of them at all. His sole request of Motsyevski was to kiss him in that place which is too vulgar to mention. Should Motsyevski object to kissing his ———, he could kiss that of an old peasant.

Needless to say the rowdy noblemen liked the idea. An old peasant was brought in and the hapless lord had to kiss his ——— three times. His wife was finally taken outside, to spare her the humiliating spectacle. Osserevski then restored to him all the money he had lost, as well as the document he had signed. Motsyevski's wife refused to return home with her husband. He drove away on his own, and the following morning he shot himself. It seems that kissing Osserevski was bad enough, but kissing a serf—he could not bear to live with the shame.

Neither Osserevski nor Motsyevski's wife attended his funeral. Each hurriedly departed for Warsaw that same day. On account of the great humiliation, she never returned to Kamenets, despite the fact that her parents and most of her relatives, who were all wealthy landowners, lived there.

Osserevski owned fifteen estates surrounding Kamenets, each under the jurisdiction of a particular commissioner, who wielded absolute authority. Subservient to him were the steward and the bailiff.[33] The latter's tasks included meting out the punishment, generally floggings, imposed by the commissioner or the steward. The bailiff dared not make a mistake—in other words, he wasn't allowed to reduce the number of lashes, God forbid, but a stroke or two more was not taken into account. Complaining about it was useless, for even the slightest murmur meant another bout of flogging. The chief commissioner, who was in charge of all fifteen estates, lived in a grandiose mansion on top of the hill in the center of Kamenets.

The inhabitants of Kamenets paid an annual tax to the lord of the estate on whose land they lived. Furthermore, they were strictly forbidden to buy their beer or vodka from any source other than their lord. Apart from that, they were obliged to pay excise duty on salt, hides, etc., in short, for everything required for their daily needs. The crafty Osserevski, on strength of his contracts with the inhabitants, managed to squeeze them almost dry, and in this matter, it would seem, Kamenets was a unique town. However, Osserevski, on account of his enormous wealth, occasionally forgot about collecting the taxes. What, after all, did the measly lease taxes[34] paid him by the *Yids* amount to when he himself was stuffed to the gills with gold?

At each of the three approaches to Kamenets (the fourth was a river[35]) there was a barrier. Every Sunday or market day all those entering the township in horse-drawn carts had to pay five kopecks custom duty per horse. Along the river between Kamenets and Zas-tavye[36] was a lock and nearby were three bridges and three water mills. Those also belonged to Osserevski, and all this was leased to my grandfather, Aharon-Leyzer Kotik. It was called the *arenda*,[37] and my grandfather, his brother, and all their families drew their livelihood from it.

In his old age, Osserevski stopped coming to Kamenets. He had no one to entertain him there, so he settled permanently in Warsaw. But once in three years he came to the town and stayed for about a month. He never married and died at the age of eighty-five. When he did come to Kamenets, he brought along with him a huge wagon loaded to the top with kitchen utensils. Four horses were barely able to pull the wagon along, but during the rainy season, six of them were needed to haul it through the muddy roads.

When Osserevski turned eighty, he drew up a will dividing his substantial property among thirty of his closest friends. There were, of course, quite a number of them who could easily dispense with this addition to their already considerable wealth. Yet, not a single kopeck went to any member of Osserevski's immediate family, not even to his sisters, who were in dire need of such financial assistance.

Although Osserevski willed his money to various lords, he bequeathed all his estates, consisting of five thousand serfs as well as the town of Kamenets, to the seventeen-year-old orphan son of an impoverished noble family. In order to keep an eye on the prospective heir, Osserevski sent him for a probation period to his estate at Pruska along with a letter to the chief commissioner. In the letter the chief commissioner was instructed to initiate the young man into the running of the estates under his personal guidance, since this fellow would eventually be the master of the estates. He was to observe him closely and send back a detailed report of his conduct every month. It goes without saying that the chief commissioner should treat him as if he were Osserevski's own son, to provide him with a certain amount of pocket money, say two hundred rubles a month, but to pay close attention as to how he spent it.

The young heir arrived at Pruska soon afterward and within a short time befriended all the lords in the surrounding area. Scarcely a few months passed and he became acquainted with all the young rakes and made the rounds of the balls and parties held at the various mansions. There was, however, one snag: he could not entertain his new acquaintances at Pruska, for Osserevski had warned him that he would come into the inheritance only if he proved to be a decent, well-behaved, and modest person whose chief concern was to learn all about the running of an estate.

But once he joined the ranks of the local libertines his budget of two hundred rubles a month was a mere drop in the ocean, what with gambling at cards, entertaining friends at lavish dinners, and spending money on all sorts of trifles. Noticing how pressed he was for ready cash, his friends advised him to start going into the township in order to get to know the Jews there, from whom he could obtain all the money he needed.

That's what the young heir did. He rode into Kamenets in a splendid coach drawn by two pairs of horses in double-harness with a liveried footman at the back. He went straight to Khaytshe Trinkovski's inn, one of the better-known sites in town, and told her that he wished to take a loan at a high interest rate, and asked her to recommend to him the persons most suitable for that purpose.

She immediately informed several Jews of the matter and they wasted no time meeting the young man. He introduced himself to them as the future heir to all the estates as well as the lord of the township. Though he was not yet accredited with full authority, it was merely a matter of time, since Osserevski was already over eighty . . . and how long could a man of that age live on? . . . He had therefore come to take a loan at a high interest rate and the advancement of such a loan would certainly benefit his creditors.

It goes without saying that none of the Jews had the slightest inkling concerning the probation period accorded the young man and they readily lent this spendthrift all the money he asked for. It never dawned on them that he would squander it as fast as he could lay hands on it, spending it on frivolous merrymaking with other young lords. He kept borrowing in Kamenets time and again until they refused to lend him any more. So he went to Brisk—thank God for another town—and managed to extract an additional fifty thousand rubles from creditors there.

At first the young heir was wary of the chief commissioner, but it did not take the commissioner long to realize that he was dealing with a first-rate crook, who managed to extort such huge sums of money all over the place that it became the main subject of conversation in the entire vicinity. The commissioner informed Osserevski, and the latter had him assure all those holding promissory notes signed by the young man that they would be reimbursed in full, but whoever lent him any more could forget about getting his money back.

The commissioner sent Osserevski a list of all those in possession of promissory notes, and the former was ordered to repay each of them the amount they had lent the young man. In addition, the young rascal was to be given fifty lashes and dispatched immediately to his home in the Kalish province.[38]

Barely six months passed before a new heir—a young man of twenty-two—arrived equipped with a letter in exactly the same vein as the one sent with his predecessor. That young man was an even greater scoundrel and much more cunning to boot. He immediately realized that, unless he won the goodwill of the commissioner, he'd not achieve anything and would, most likely, end up like the former heir. He, therefore, decided to be on a good footing with the commissioner, take him into his confidence, and share with him the schemes he was hatching. In that way, he would gain a free hand in carrying out whatever plan he had in mind.

He became a frequent caller at the commissioner's mansion and impressed the commissioner's family with his ostensibly unassuming conduct. Above all, he tried to ingratiate himself with the commissioner's wife, an elderly but shrewd lady. In his chats with her, the young man did his best to convince her of her husband's harsh treatment of his predecessor. "It is forbidden to do such things," he said. "This young man, the son of one of the most noble families, has suffered great misfortune because of your husband, who wished to prove his loyalty to Osserevsvki but never considered the consequences of his actions."

"I actually told my husband," she admitted, "to ignore his dissolute lifestyle, for what business of his was it, after all, to look after the interest of this old bachelor wallowing in millions of rubles? My husband indeed confessed that, after the flogging, he regretted the entire affair."

After many more such chats with the lady, the young man succeeded in making her his staunchest ally. She had no doubts concerning his intentions and also talked her husband into trusting him. The scheme both were hatching was a very simple one: with the chief commissioner's support they could go on borrowing hundreds of thousands of rubles, for then no one would refuse to lend them the money. It would work out somehow until the old man closed his eyes for good. Besides, from every loan taken, a considerable amount would also flow into her husband's pockets. After Osserevski's death her husband was bound to benefit, for the heir to his possessions would transfer some of his holdings to him and make him a partner to the remaining property. In short, it was an exceptional piece of luck. The three of them put their heads together and drew up a plan for how to raise the funds they needed.

They decided that the young man was to travel frequently to Kamenets and contact someone there by the name of Moyshele K., a well-to-do Jew, shrewd and resourceful and able to assist in many things, especially in raising loans. The young man indeed befriended Moyshele and brought him to Pruska. On the way there, he acquainted him with his plans, and upon their arrival they discussed with the commissioner how to obtain loans. Moyshele suggested that they could borrow the money and assure the lenders that the loans would be returned after Osserevski's death, which, they assumed, was bound to happen soon since he was already over eighty, ill, weak, and likely to die any day. It goes without saying that the heir was to pay a high interest rate, which would not cause much hardship. Besides, with the backing of the chief commissioner it should not be difficult to raise the loan and keep the matter going until Osserevski's death. By then it would be possible to return the loan, take a new one, return it, and take a new one over and over again.

They liked the idea. Moyshele also advised them to employ several crafty, glib-tongued lackeys, well versed in flattery and known for their financial skill, enabling the young man to achieve his aim without having to lift a finger. They started to put his plan into practice. Moyshele himself enlisted a number of wealthy Jews who didn't know what to do with their money and were willing to loan it to them. As for the young heir, a new world opened up for him.

One day, Osserevski decided to pay a surprise visit to Pruska. Until then, the timing of his visit was usually announced three months in advance and everyone was ready for it. But this time Osserevski intended, by means of his surprise visit, to look into the conduct of the prospective heir to his enormous possessions. He had been deceived by the former heir and was now keen to find out about this one's conduct at close hand.

When Osserevski drove unexpectedly into Pruska and entered his mansion, he found the young man there in the company of the commissioner, Moyshele K., and a couple of other Jews, as well as a number of lords. His sudden appearance caused a panic among them and, judging by their faces, Osserevski at once guessed that something was going on behind his back. He took the young man into his study and subjected him to a thorough interrogation.

"What business have you got with those Jews and all the others?" he demanded of him in his most uncompromising tone of voice. In utter confusion the young man mumbled something about a business meeting of those Jews with the commissioner for which purpose he had summoned them there. Osserevski called in the servants and interrogated them one by one and made them tell him everything they knew about the young man's behavior. The young man's personal valet, who also acted as his agent and was familiar with all the financial deals he had clinched in the name of his young master, gave Osserevski a detailed account.

Osserevski summoned the commissioner and told him that he knew everything that had been going on behind his back. He knew that he and the young man had conspired to defraud him of as much money and property as they could. If he admitted his complicity in the plot, he would grant him his life; if not, he would have him flogged to death. The man fell at Osserevski's feet, sobbed bitterly, confessed his guilt, and begged for mercy. Next, Osserevski sent once more for the heir and his valet Stefan, and faced with the commissioner and the valet, he was forced to confirm the truth. Osserevski dealt mercifully with the commissioner and dismissed him, but the young man was condemned to twenty-two lashes, one for each year of his life.

Despite those setbacks, Osserevski did not give up his quest for an heir worthy of inheriting all his wealth and property after his death. Osserevski finally came up with a new heir, somewhat older than the former—he was twenty-eight. Six months after he was sent to Pruska, Osserevski died.

The heir became the lord, but then serfdom was abolished.[39] He sold off all the estates as well as the town of Kamenets to a Russian, a habitual drunkard, who borrowed money right and left and was deep in debt at his own, sudden death. All the estates were subsequently sold off, one by one, to wealthy Jews, who used Christian names for this purpose.[40]

The *assessor*, besides his salary, enjoyed a considerable income from the Jews as well. Since there were over a hundred small stores in Kamenets and only a handful, maybe four or five merchants, who were legal lessees, the *assessor* charged all the others the sum of three rubles a year. That also applied to the tavern keepers, who paid the *assessor* ten rubles a year. Everyone was satisfied with this arrangement. The *assessor*, who was usually informed of the government inspector's[41] annual visit several days in advance, would order the storekeepers to lock up their shops on that particular day. The inspector always called first at the *assessor*'s office, and the inspection of licenses would be carried out by the *assessor*, the inspector, the bailiff, and eighteen gendarmes.[42]

While walking through the alleyway of the little closed shops, the *assessor* told the inspector that these were small sheds that had been out of use for years. After that, he took him to the storekeepers holding legal licenses, and the inspector then put his official seal to the necessary documents. He was then slipped fifty rubles by someone purporting to represent the Jews of the town. This money was also an annual tax collected in advance by the *assessor*.

The *assessor* received additional income by arbitrating between parties of disputing Jews. The fee paid him might range from three to over ten rubles, depending upon the nature of the dispute. He lived in a lordly mansion surrounded by a huge garden. The mansion, outfitted with all the modern conveniences, was owned by a wealthy gentlewoman and leased to all incumbent *assessors* for fifty rubles a year. It had a number of milk cows, several horses, and an open carriage with an attendant coachman, all of which cost the *assessor* nothing. The lords around Kamenets supplied him with hay and oats for the livestock, as well as with all his household provisions. His domestics were drawn from among the members of the gendarmery under his command.

The lords knew full well what they were doing. In return for all those gifts, the *assessor* often turned a blind eye to their misdeeds and violations of the law. By keeping him supplied with all his daily needs, they easily got away with flogging a peasant or his wife to death, or inflicting all sorts of physical injuries upon their Jews. The *assessor* was a welcome visitor at their mansions, where he made even more money playing cards with his hosts. He never lost, for his hosts saw to it that he always left their homes with well-lined pockets. To pay money outright would have seemed inappropriate, so they preferred losing it to him at cards.

I remember a certain *assessor* called Sherinski, a particularly shrewd man, who knew how to squeeze money from Jews and gentry alike. He was rumored to have barrels full of gold coins amounting to thirty thousand pieces. Whoever was in need of a loan—whether Jew or nobleman—went to Sherinski, who would charge an extra ruble for every coin he lent them. In time, in return for an enormous sum, he had himself appointed *ispravnik* in Sokolka,[43] in Grodno province.

As everyone knows, the day of a Jew commences with the morning prayers in his own study house, of which there were two in Kamenets. The large one was called the "old study house" and the smaller one, the "new study house." There was, however, an additional, very small one, called "Hershl's study house," as well as a synagogue and a number of *shtiblekh* scattered around a courtyard. In front of this courtyard a large and deep ditch ran right down to the river. During heavy rains, the water in the ditch flooded the sidewalk, making it dangerous for a horse and wagon to pass by. Yet the ditch was never fenced in.

There was another study house some distance away in Adolina Street opposite a high hill. That particular one also served as a sort of club for political discussions. After prayers, some of the men devoted themselves to the study of a page of the Talmud, several others to the study of the Mishnah, whereas a few sat around a table listening to a discourse on *Eyn Ya'akov.*[44] All the rest engaged in town gossip or in recounting tales of righteous people and outstanding scholarly rabbis. The "politicians" among them were in a class of their own. They would gather around a table both before and after prayers, chat about wars and peace, about the news from the outside world, and discuss current political events. Their business affairs took these "politicians" to Brisk twice a week, from whence they brought back all the latest news.

There was another table attended by a group of gray-bearded old men. Their conversations dwelt upon the doings of emperors and empresses of days gone by, such as Catherine, Peter, and Paul,[45] and upon Napoleon's war with Russia in 1812.[46]

Around an additional table sat the very pious Jews and so-called *prushim.* [47] The latter were men who left their wives and children, while they attended study halls in other townships. They kept body and soul together by "eating days" [48] at various homes, and were held in great esteem by the community. The topics discussed around this table, in muted and somber tones, centered on the world to come, paradise and purgatory, and other stories in that vein.

Young married fellows milled about the tables. They were the married sons and sons-in-law who lived on *kest* with their more prosperous in-laws. [49] They spent a good deal of their time prattling about mothers- and fathers-in-law and the tasty meals they had just had. The Talmud lay open in front of them as if they were about to begin studying, but chatting about one thing or another was more interesting.

Every morning at ten o'clock, except Sundays, they went home for a bite and, for lack of anything better to do, returned to the study house, pretending to continue their learning. Once again, they sat in front of their open tractates, but before long dropped all pretense of studying and started talking. When a particular topic was exhausted, they turned to chatting about the sins in the town, such as the reading of "*treyfe bikhlekh,*" [50] and about people that had turned heretic.

In my time, three wealthy men lived in Kamenets—Jewish misers who behaved like beggars. One of them, M. G., had about one hundred thousand rubles but he lived in a small, thatch-roofed hovel. Instead of candles, they burned oil, they ate black bread and potatoes in their skins, and he himself walked about in a torn and tattered *kapote.* If he needed to go to the lords in order to buy supplies, he always went there on foot. He was the top dealer in wheat and vodka. His wealth, rumors had it, was acquired with the help of one Bukhevetski, the owner of the Ristitch estate near Kamenets. He handled all of the lord's business transactions, and he did the accounting in the sand with a small twig broken off one of Bukhevetski's trees. He would trace the numbers across the sand, erase them over and over again, and in the course of several years had managed to pile up a fortune.

The sudden enrichment of the second miser, Sh. S., came as a total surprise, occurring as it did during a circumcision ceremony at a friend's home. Prior to this, he milled flour at a local lord's mill and earned ten gulden a week. He then set up an oil press rotated by horses, which was worth about fifteen hundred rubles. No one could figure out from where this man had so much money. Suddenly, one night, the entire facility went up in flames. After that, he took to traveling in a carriage with A. T., the merchant. Sh. S. held the horses' reins and A. T., who had maybe one thousand rubles, suddenly turned into a successful wheat and vodka dealer. He sat inside the coach, traveled to all the lords in the area, and made business deals with them running into tens of thousands of rubles. Here, too, no one had a clue as to where A. T. got hold of so much money.

This went on for a number of years until the day when both men attended a circumcision ceremony. Several bottles of pure alcohol were brought in to prepare a punch—tea laced with alcohol—which they drank until they were good and soused. The tipsy guests started dancing around in a circle. Sh. S., who must have had a drop too much, remarked while dancing, "A. T. isn't just dancing like that for no reason. The tens of thousands of rubles he's invested in his business actually belong to me."

He and A. T. got into a fight and then agreed to take their dispute before the rabbinical court the following morning in order to divide the money. A. T. swore on the Torah scroll that the entire sum he owed amounted to no more than five thousand rubles. From then on, Sh. S. became a prosperous merchant in his own right. They now ate chickpeas instead of potatoes in his home.

The third miser, D. B., made his fortune out of the hunting expeditions of Tsar Alexander II. Such hunting expeditions were something beyond the wildest imagination, something the world had never before seen. For an entire year prior to the hunt, battalions of soldiers were dispatched to the Białowieska Forest in order to fence in an area of a square verst and to set up a kind of wild animal reserve within that compound.[51] Thousands of animals were imported for this purpose from all over the world, and the tsar and his retinue of European princes stood along the top of a rampart, aiming their guns at the animals, which had, however, plenty of room to escape the bullets.

D. B. owned a tavern near Białowieza at the very crossroads where everyone gathered for the hunt and near the soldiers' encampment. For the duration of the hunting season he charged thirty kopecks for a small glass of schnapps and a ruble for a finer sort. He charged thirty kopecks for a bread roll and a ruble for a piece of paper on which one could write a petition to the tsar. He charged whatever he saw fit and no one objected. In this way he managed to rake in a tidy two hundred thousand rubles, in addition to the sixty thousand rubles his wife earned running a business of her own.

D. B. bought an estate beside the river, some two miles outside Kamenets. He set up a water mill on it and leased it to a relative of his for sixteen hundred rubles a year. But seeing how well this relative was doing, he canceled the lease and had his own sons haul the wheat to the mill. He also made the most of the fish in the river. He hired peasants to catch them and then kept the fish in the river in large containers dotted with holes. Every Thursday fishmongers from Kamenets came to him to buy the fish for no less than twelve groshen[52] a *funt*. He made a huge profit on those fish, but begrudged himself and his family of them except for the Sabbath meals, when his wife dealt them out in tiny portions.

His stinginess extended to every aspect of his life. He would not even allow himself to taste the butter churned from the milk of his thirty cows, let alone eat it. But he was a smart Jew, even an enlightened one. Already then he used to read a Russian newspaper, the cost of which, for once, he did not begrudge himself. He also knew how to study a page of the Talmud. When he had to go to Warsaw to purchase several grinding stones from Sorkin of Praga[53] for his mill, costing three hundred rubles, he accommodated himself at a soup kitchen and shelter in Praga where he could sleep and get a midday meal for a mere fifteen kopecks. He purposely avoided visiting Warsaw itself, neither by coach nor on foot, lest he be tempted to spend some money there. So he always left Praga without taking so much as a peek at Warsaw.

First among the wealthy families exerting a great influence in the town was that of Yonye Trinkovski. He owned a lavishly furnished tavern that was frequented by the surrounding lords and gentry.[54] His wife Khaytshe was an intelligent and capable housewife, a real woman of valor, and it was she who managed the tavern. One could always find the lords at her tavern. They came in carriages drawn by pairs of expensive horses harnessed one behind the other, with liveried footmen at the helm, and accompanied by their personal servants. Some even announced their arrival by the blowing of trumpets. At Khaytshe's one could always get the most expensive wines, the choicest cigars, the tastiest meals, and she raked in the profits hand over fist. Apart from all that, Yonye, her husband, was a traveling agent for industrialists in Bialystok,[55] for whom he purchased wool in Russia. In those days, when the kopeck had the value of a present-day ruble, his income amounted to three thousand rubles a year. They lived in ostentatious luxury, and the money flowed through their fingers like water.

Whenever Yonye returned from one of his trips, he would summon the public bath attendant and give him three rubles for two cartloads of wood to stoke the furnace in the public bathhouse. He would then have him go through the streets, calling on the inhabitants to have a wash at his expense. Since that was usually in the middle of the week, everyone knew that Yonye had come home and, though he invited them to the bathhouse free of charge, they would first come to him to ask his permission to enter and, being rather vain by nature, Yonye derived great pleasure from this flattery.

In Kamenets, Yonye played the role of a Rothschild, as did his sons and daughters, their husbands and wives. The younger members of other well-to-do families felt deeply honored if one of Yonye's children so much as spoke to them, and being spoken to by Yonye or one of his children was an unheard-of compliment.

Yonye himself was never seen strolling idly about in the street. He had his own small study house in our courtyard—a small room in an attic. The cutlery at his home was of pure silver; the Sabbath candlesticks and the chandelier must have been worth thousands of rubles. But he personally didn't have on him so much as a thousand rubles in ready cash.

Another family of that class was Yonye's son-in-law, David-Yitzhak. He also ran a tavern, and played the same role as his father-in-law, only that in his tavern the "gluttony" was much greater than at Khaytshe's. At David-Yitzhak's they stuffed themselves with cutlets fried in fat, roast goose, chicken, and turkey, even in the middle of the week. David-Yitzhak's father—Yeshaya-Hayyim—was also a very wealthy man who lived in Tiktin.[56] He also owned a large tavern, and had sixty thousand rubles in cash. The silver plates in his home, people said, weighed at least ten pud. He imitated Itsele Zabludovski,[57] the well-known millionaire of Bialystok, who, among Russian Jews, was considered a Rothschild.

This Zabludovski was on familiar terms with all the governors of Grodno province,[58] who in his time were frequently replaced. If the elders of the Jewish community did not get on with a particular chief of police, they would turn to Itsele with a request to have him replaced. His reply would be: "My dear fellow-Jews, within eight days you will have a new chief of police." He would dispatch a letter to the governor of Grodno informing him of the unsuitability of the chief of police. The governor would immediately transfer him to another post and the Jews of Bialystok would receive a new chief of police.

David-Yitzhak's father—Yeshaya-Hayyim—was a great friend of Itsele's and also conducted himself accordingly. He spared no effort to help his son. When one of David-Yitzhak's sons got married, Yeshaya-Hayyim provided the bride with a dowry of one thousand rubles—a great deal of money in those days. In addition, he covered all the wedding expenses, and had new outfits tailored for the entire family. When David-Yitzhak married off one of his daughters, his father sent in advance a trunk full of silver utensils, candlesticks, and candelabras. During the wedding itself, silver lampstands, taller than the tables, were placed on the ground, and the lights from the silver candelabras and the other silverware shone brightly on every windowsill. If the wedding took place before Passover, when the streets were full of mud, large wooden planks were laid out all along the route leading from David-Yitzhak's house right down to the synagogue.

Bands of *klezmorim* flocked into Kamenets from the two district towns, Brisk and Kobrin,[59] and the merrymaking went on for days on end. Outstanding among the musicians of those days was the band of Shepsl of Kobrin. Shepsl couldn't read a single note, but when he played his instrument entire audiences dissolved into tears. The sweetness of his music was simply indescribable.

Shepsl's fame even reached the ears of Paskevich,[60] the high commissioner of Poland, who sent for him so that he might play his fiddle for him. So enchanted was Paskevich with his performance that he tried to persuade Shepsl to convert. He also asked him if he knew how to play from notes. "No, I don't," Shepsl admitted blankly. "Never mind," Paskevich slapped him on the shoulder. "I'll teach you, provided you become a Christian."

Shepsl resented the offer and said that even if he were exalted to the rank of a prince, he would never agree to become a Christian. Nevertheless, Paskevich kept him in his palace for the next three days. He invited the most distinguished noblemen, and during their meals had Shepsl play for them for two to three hours at a stretch. Shepsl would not touch any of their food, not even the wine or the brandy, so Paskevich had his meals brought in from a Jewish restaurant.

When Paskevich realized that he could not influence Shepsl to convert, he gave him one thousand rubles together with a diploma certifying that Shepsl was blessed with a divine musical gift despite the fact that he was completely unlearned. Before taking leave of Shepsl, Paskevich said that he would like to introduce him to the tsar himself, a favor that would benefit him and his family as well as his fellow Jews. But Shepsl respectfully declined the offer. With the one thousand rubles he bought himself a house and continued playing at all the weddings of the well-to-do in the Grodno province. There wasn't a wedding of a wealthy Jew at which Shepsl and the eight members of his band were not hired to play.[61]

There was also a *badkhn*[62] at those weddings by the name of Tudros, an unusually gifted fellow. He would come up with completely new rhymes incorporating all the names of the hosts' families as well as those of the in-laws. During the *badekns* ceremony, his elegiac words set the hearts of even the hardiest of men atremble. Those verses, accompanied by Shepsl's music, had everyone sobbing and weeping. During the *badekns,* the wailing reached to high heaven. Many of the women simply passed out from the emotional strain, and Shepsl and Tudros were often asked to stop their performances, since the women had no more strength to keep on weeping.

Among the bands of musicians there was no dearth of jesters. One of them was old Ruvele, whose jokes at the table had all the guests in fits of laughter. Now, the women laughed so much that in the end the jester was told to stop talking since the women had no more strength to keep on laughing.

When I was a child, I remember how, at a family wedding, Ruvele said to the guests sitting around the festive table, "I'll ask you a riddle, and those unable to come up with the correct answer have to pay me ten kopecks." A plate was placed in the middle and Reuben put the riddle to them: "How can four people divide three apples among themselves and still remain with a whole apple for each one?" Naturally, no one came up with the right answer and each put ten kopecks into the plate. After it contained eighteen rubles, Reuben picked up the plate, emptied it into one of his deep trouser pockets, and, putting the plate back on the table, said, "Dear guests! I myself haven't the foggiest notion. Here are my twenty groshen just as we'd agreed upon."[63] That, of course, drew a mighty roar of laughter, and Ruvele earned through this ruse as much as he would have earned from performing at three weddings.

After David-Yitzhak's highly competent wife—Khaytshe's daughter—died, he married for a second, and soon after for a third time. His social standing at this time started declining and he ceased to play a decisive role in the affairs of the town. His father, Yeshaya-Hayyim, continued to support him, though he never regained the commanding position he had held during the lifetime of his first wife, Yonye's daughter. She was an outstanding personality, both in business and in wisdom. But when David-Yitzhak took a second wife and soon after a third wife, the noblemen that used to frequent his tavern went over to Yonye, who had opened the first tavern in town, which existed until the Rebellion of 1863.[64] After the death of his wife Khaytshe, his daughter and daughter-in-law took over the running of the business.

The third prosperous and influential family in Kamenets was that of my grandfather Aharon-Leyzer Kotik and his brother Mordechai-Leyb. They also lived well, but the furniture in their large homes was of the simpler sort—large tables and benches—and their lifestyle was more down-to-earth. They, too, were in the liquor trade, but not of the exclusive kind. Yet, they lived a life of affluence that would not shame any wealthy family in Warsaw today.

Mordechai-Leyb Kotik, my grandfather's brother, was the scholarly type and, like others of similar inclination, had naturally never learnt in his younger days how to earn a living. After their father's death, his two sons inherited a large house in the center of the marketplace, a tavern, and three thousand rubles in cash. My grandfather gave the house with the tavern to his brother, and the money was divided among his brothers-in-law, who were great scholars, and the rest of the family. He maintained that he could easily dispense with the house and the money, since he could make a living and they could not.

Mordechai-Leyb made a good living, especially on Sundays, market days, and fairs, so that the rest of the week he passed in peace and quiet. He started a minyan in his house, which was attended throughout the week and the Sabbath by the simple folk of the town. He himself was the prayer leader, the Torah reader, and shofar blower during the High Holidays. On the Sabbath he would teach his congregants the Bible, and during the week, early in the morning before prayers, as well as late in the evening after prayers, he would study a page of the Talmud and Midrash. Throughout the day his house teemed with people bringing the latest news, chitchatting about the Rothschilds or what the tsar ate and drank. Later on, Mordechai-Leyb would join his guests in a game of draughts.

Around the big table others would go on chatting about kings and princes and the miracles wrought by our brilliant rabbis. Mordechai-Leyb, who seemed absorbed in his game of draughts, would, as if by the way, lend an ear to the tellers of those tales. He was an honest and upright Jew and, while in the midst of moving one of his gaming pieces across the board and hearing someone give free rein to his imagination, would chide him gently, "Don't lie and don't exaggerate, please, it isn't nice!"

Mordechai-Leyb was the most sought after *mohel* in Kamenets. Almost daily, from eight o'clock in the morning until midday he would make the rounds of the town and the surrounding villages, performing circumcisions. He never tasted any of the food laid out on the tables, nor took a sip of the wine offered him. What, however, he did allow himself to take away from a circumcision was some sponge cake for his wife and children. "It's a *mitzveh,*" he would say.

At family celebrations he took upon himself the role of waiter. If there was a wedding or a circumcision he would rush excitedly to and fro, perspiring all over while waiting upon his guests, occasionally assisted by young boys and girls. Before the recitation of Grace after Meals, he would raise a glass of sweet brandy in a toast and take a bite of the hard cheese he always kept with him for such occasions.

He kept a special petty cash box, from which he extended loans up to twenty-five rubles to stall keepers at the market. He personally was always short of ready cash because of his only child, a great spendthrift, who was married and indulged in a luxurious lifestyle. Mordechai-Leyb would borrow from others and lend what he could to the needy, and that's how he carried on throughout his life right into his seventies.

It is doubtful if Mordechai-Leyb, ever in his life, ate a meal at the home of a stranger, even for money. If he had to go to Brisk, some five miles from Kamenets, he would hire a two-wheeled carriage drawn by a good horse and ride there on his own. He loved to ride fast, and made it to Brisk within five hours, though he never remained there for more than ten. He always took with him a small bottle of sweet wine, some lean cheese, and several cookies, all of which he ate on the way, so as not to arrive hungry. He never traveled to any other towns, in order to avoid the possibility of having to eat meals cooked by strangers.

His wife, Haya-Gitl, was a capable and most charitable soul. She distributed alms left and right out of a leather bag she always carried with her, scooping fistfuls of coins from it without counting, giving one a handful, another a smaller amount. She provided meals at her table for six pupils studying at the Talmud Torah,[65] serving them generous portions of her best food in an unassuming manner. Apart from them, poor old Jews were welcome for a daily meal at her table, as well as itinerant preachers, cantors, and rabbis coming to Kamenets at frequent intervals.

Outstanding among their guests was a *porush* named Pant-shoshnik,[66] who had been learning at the new study house of Kamenets for the last forty years. He was known to be a kabbalist and kept at the study house a sack full of kabbalistic books from which he studied all day while chanting a special tune. His voice was so pure and penetrating that it made people prick up their ears and listen. On Sabbaths he instructed the congregants at Mordechai-Leyb's house in *Pirkei avot* and in Midrash. He told them stories about life in paradise the like of which one could find in none of the books known to ordinary Jews. About purgatory he never said a word. In paradise, everything was of the best and the food more delicious than anything ever tasted before. He related those marvels in such a sweet chant that it seemed to his listeners as if he had been there himself.

Once, when the itinerant Maggid from Kelme[67] came to Kamenets to preach for repentance, Mordechai-Leyb hosted him for an entire month. He wined and dined him so lavishly that, by the time he left Kamenets, he had put on so much weight that he looked as if he had been to a holiday resort.

Mordechai-Leyb's happy life had, however, one failing: he did not get on with his wife, Haya-Gitl. He was constantly angry with her and avenged himself by never touching the food she prepared for him. To tell the truth, his anger had become part of his character. One day he would be angry with his son, another day with one of his grandchildren. It was a trait that disturbed him, though it didn't interfere with his normal lifestyle. Apart from all that, he was probably the happiest man in the world. He was also very handsome—broadly built, with a smooth, youthful face and a long black beard—a dandy!

A fifth well-to-do family was that of Khaytshe's brother-in-law,

Simha-Leyzer, a Jew of unique qualities. He was a great scholar, extremely pious and virtuous by nature. Fortune had smiled on him, and eighty years ago he won twenty-five thousand rubles in cash in the "Saxonian lottery."[68] He divided the money in the following manner: five thousand rubles went to charity, because according to talmudic law it is forbidden to give away more than a fifth to charity;[69] three thousand rubles went for his daughter's dowry, whom he married off to a famed scholarly genius from Bialystok. But that son-in-law died soon afterward, which cost Simha-Leyzer another six thousand rubles. With the rest of the money he purchased two stores built of stone in Brisk, yielding him an income of five hundred rubles a year. He also acquired a small estate in Kamenets with fertile land around it, nicknamed by the Jews "gold dust,"[70] which provided him with a good income. His wife, Leyke, took over the management of the fields so that he could sit and study day and night. I remember him sitting in the old study house after the prayers, often until eleven o'clock. I was very fond of him.

Scholars in their own right used to come to discuss the Scriptures and to ask him for advice on certain passages that they could not interpret themselves. After that, he would walk home, a fair distance, maybe more than a verst, eat breakfast, and continue his studies. He owned books worth five thousand rubles. Although he had a considerable library even before his great winning, he added many more volumes to it afterward, all beautifully bound. He was naturally kindhearted and modest, and treated everyone as his equal. Small children adored him as though he were Samuel the Prophet.[71] He was soft-spoken, and anger was as alien to his nature as fire is to water.

Every summer at harvest time, he called on the *lomdim* of Kamenets to help him prepare the *shmurah matzah.* It is well known that this matzah is made from wheat that has not grown higher than necessary, and has been kept from any contact with water. The wheat was usually reaped, threshed, and ground by non-Jews. That, in itself, was, according to our Simha-Leyzer, a blemish on its purity. He therefore bought a number of small, sharp scythes, enlisted some twenty *lomdim, prushim,* and young newly married scholars, and together with them went out into the field and taught them how to reap the wheat.

The cut stalks were tied into sheaves and stored for drying in a special barn. When they dried up, Simha-Leyzer and his team threshed them with sticks especially shaped for this purpose. They then transported all the grain to Simha-Leyzer's home, where there was a table grinder consisting of two small grinding stones and a lever, all of which he had purchased for a few hundred rubles. Some of the men operated the grinder, others collected the flour into beautiful bowls, which they then emptied into the drawers of a large chest that had been punched through with holes. The flour was kept there until shortly after Purim, when Simha-Leyzer called together the same team of scholars and students to bake the *shmurah matzah*. He had prepared special rolling pins made of glass, and the work went on amid great merriment. Before their work they ate a sumptuous meal, during which they gave discourses on the Torah, and after they had completed their day's work they again ate and returned to their Torah study. Throughout their work a happy mood reigned over them and anyone not having witnessed the joy accompanying the reaping, threshing, and grinding of the wheat and the baking of it into matzot has never witnessed real joy in his life.

When the *shmurah matzah* was taken out of the oven, Simha-Leyzer divided among the scholars and students enough to last them throughout Passover. Since those portions were very large, they were able to sell some, thus earning a few rubles to cover their Passover expenses. That went on year after year and that was how a real Jew lived in those days: his charity, his way of performing good deeds, his splendor, all these were without measure. Simha-Leyzer did not live to a ripe old age. He was sixty when he died.

Those five families were the jewels in the crown of our town and they were also the wealthiest. But Kamenets itself was, on the whole, a poor shtetl whose overwhelming majority lived in grinding poverty, working their fingers to the bone in order to eke out a meager living. None of them ate meat in the middle of the week, and even white bread and freshly baked pastry were eaten in only a few homes. The staple diet of the poor was black bread, which they baked themselves once a week and sometimes even once in two weeks, for they held that the staler the bread, the less you eat of it.[72]

For breakfast they had *krupnik*—barley and potato soup.[73] Occasionally they threw into the big *krupnik* pot an ounce of butter, half a quart or at the most a whole quart of milk, bought for one kopeck. This was supposed to suffice for a family of six. For lunch they had borscht with bread and a piece of salted herring or a little butter. For supper it was noodles or crumbs of dough with a similar amount of milk. The poorer folks made noodles out of rye flour.

On Friday nights and the Sabbath everybody, even the poor, ate fish. The well-to-do bought large fish, and the poor, tiny fish which they ground up, mixed with onions, and shaped into patties. The fish were caught in the river next to the town and half a gulden for a *funt* was considered very expensive. If, as at times, the price was raised to twenty groshen, this would trigger a riot. The fishmongers were accused of selling most of their catch to Brisk, leaving Kamenets with a shortage of fish before the Sabbath.[74] The fishmongers were warned that if they continued this practice, and caused prices to rise, they would not just suffer bodily harm, but they could be assured of never being called up to the Torah again.[75]

A meat dish on a Sabbath might consist of veal, mutton, or beef, but it was lean. The butchers bought very thin livestock, hardly able to stand on their feet any more. One could buy a cow for six to eight rubles; ten rubles was already thought to be expensive. The well off, of course, bought beef, the poorer, veal, and the poorest of all, the melamdim and craftsmen who were not connected with the lords, made do with mutton.

There were all sorts of kugels, fatty and tasty, eaten even by the poor. In contrast to their meager fare in the middle of the week, the Sabbath meal was for them a virtual feast. Every home had freshly baked challah and *tsholnt.*

On Friday evening, just before the onset of the Sabbath, the beadle of the synagogue made the rounds of all the streets, calling out, "Bless the candles!" All the men, washed and clean, made their way to the prayer houses and afterward returned home for the festive Sabbath meal. During the meal they chanted the special Sabbath hymns. Large tallow candles[76] in their holders and in candelabra hanging from the ceiling illumined each home—there was cheerfulness on this dear and beloved Sabbath. The festive atmosphere drove away the wretchedness of their everyday lives, and throughout the Sabbath the joy and holiness were boundless. No one dared refer to business affairs or matters dealing with one's livelihood, for doing so was considered a big sin.[77]

On that day the men caught up with their sleep and their studies. After their rest, the men learned in study groups, winter and summer. At one table in the study house some learned a page of the Talmud with a teacher, at another, the Mishnah, at a third, the Midrash, and at a fourth, the *Shulhan arukh,*[78] each table with its teacher. Around the rest of the tables sat the common folk not conversant with this higher form of learning, but who knew entire passages of Psalms by heart and chanted them in beautiful tunes and with genuine fervor. They read out passage after passage, chapter after chapter of the Psalms, making for a truly touching scene. Later on, all assembled for afternoon prayers and then went home for the prescribed third Sabbath meal,[79] which for the well-to-do consisted of a piece of fish and for the rest, salted herring, and the remainder of the challah. Afterward, they returned for the evening prayer, which was always preceded by the long hymn from Psalms: "Happy are those whose way is blameless,"[80] chanted in the same sad melody which relates: here begins a new week with its worries and troubles, here the melancholy of the weekdays begins to creep back into our lives.

In the more wealthy homes it was customary on Saturday night, after the conclusion of the Sabbath, to brew tea in a large kettle and sip it while biting on a piece of loaf sugar. Such a piece was able to sweeten two to three cups of tea in a row. If they were not lazy they would brew another pot. Having finished their tea, they would turn to the accounts for the week ahead. Storekeepers together with their wives prepared the lists of goods to be purchased, tavern keepers the vodka needed for the week, and those dealing with lords planned their weekly transactions with them: what needed to be done at a particular nobleman's, how to handle him, and how best to speak with him on certain matters. All those considerations were talked over with their wives at the end of the Sabbath, and the following morning they took up, once again, their weekly pursuits.

Kamenets was renowned for its brilliant scholars, and its rabbis were counted among the greatest and most illustrious; this, despite the salary of the rabbi, which barely exceeded three or four rubles a week. As soon as a new rabbi appeared in town, the scholars of Kamenets, young as well as old, confronted him with complicated questions in order to put his intellect to the test. When the rabbi stood to deliver his first sermon he trembled with fear before the learned of Kamenets. His first sermon was a kind of test, which had to combine sharpness of intellect with sophisticated interpretations.[81] Once he lived up to the expectations of his scholarly audience, his appointment as the incumbent rabbi was assured.

In those days, young scholars would leave their wives and children and continue their Torah studies in another township, because at home they were unable to devote themselves to their studies in peace and solitude. They therefore took up abode in another town, where they could study night and day undisturbed by other considerations. How to feed themselves did not present an obstacle, since every such *porush* had his permanent "eating days" allotted to him in accordance with his proficiency in the Talmud.[82] Especially gifted scholars ate at the tables of the more well-to-do; the not-so-bright ones had to content themselves with the rather meager fare offered them in the less wealthy homes. Every householder, of more means or less, provided a scholar with one or two meals a week, and the less well-to-do provided meals for the poor pupils of the Talmud Torah. It was clear that a *porush* was better looked after than a boy from the Talmud Torah.

Apart from their studies, those *prushim* had other reasons for leaving their townships. In those days, as is well known, the community elders would supply the Russian authorities with the required quota of conscripts according to considerations of self-interest.[83] For this purpose they used to employ *khapers*,[84] who would catch and deliver to the authorities any young man or youngster the elders had put on their blacklist. The *khapers* not only ferreted them out in their own towns but also tracked them down in other towns, wherever they might be hiding. The fact that those young men were not listed in the government registry offices didn't matter one bit, since their particulars were recorded in the communal registers kept by the *parnas khodesh*.[85] Once such a poor young man, though unlisted, was caught by a *khaper*, he was given the name of one of the listed sons of a more well-to-do Jew, and it was this "son" who was conscripted in place of the real one. In this way the richer householders evaded conscription of their sons, even if they had six, and in return, they contributed money to the community's coffers—a hundred rubles was more than enough.

In those days, even men of thirty were conscripted despite the fact that they were already fathers of five or six children. A bachelor of thirty was almost unheard-of, and an unmarried youth of seventeen was thought an old bachelor, which was indeed a great shame. So the conscripts were already family men and occasionally fathers of many children.

It goes without saying, therefore, that the *prushim* were highly honored and none of them was ever handed over to the army. Despite this, they were afraid to remain in their native towns, for there was always the nagging fear of one's father or father-in-law falling out with one or another of the town's elders, leading to his conscription. When that happened, it was irrevocable and nothing could be done about it.

In Kamenets there were lots of *prushim* from other townships. My grandfathers, who used to be the *parnasei khodesh* and later on so-called *sborshchiks,*[86] never handed over any young married fellows who knew how to learn. A young man who sat in the study house and learned, no matter on what level, could rest assured that he would not be conscripted into the army.[87]

Kamenets's *prushim* were brilliant scholars. The big study house held over sixty volumes of the Talmud, even if they were somewhat torn and tattered from years of use. But the students made do with what was available. If they reached an illegible section, they would simply exchange the volume for another. In short, in the big study house there was an awe-inspiring reverence toward learning; the most talented scholars studied there, the most prosperous householders prayed there, and the older folks sat around the big tables by the large stove, rehashing tales of days gone by.

Kamenets was considered to be the most refined town in all of Grodno province. It boasted sophists and philosophers who were forever philosophizing, debating the small points in the Talmud, showing off their sharp wits. Whoever entered the study house would find Jews sitting around the tables, arguing over a page of the Talmud, *Tosaphot,* or *Maharsha.* Scholars known for their mastery of *Maharsha* were referred to as *Maharsha-keplekh.*[88] They spent days and nights endeavoring to understand completely the difficult interpretations therein.

Thanks to its energetic *gabbai,* the new study house, which was "jealous" of the old study house, succeeded in attracting *prushim* and *lomdim.* Young married fellows, the sons and sons-in-law of the more prosperous families, also learned there. The older scholars, however, and the aged did not desert the old study house. Thus Kamenets had two houses of study, full of scholars immersed in Torah learning.

Although, as already mentioned, Kamenets prided itself in being the most refined town in the province of Grodno, there was no lack of contention among its inhabitants. Matters concerning the running of the town would often split the townspeople into two opposing camps. During *hol ha-moed,* when most trade and menial labor was at a virtual standstill, people congregated in groups about the central square of the town marketplace, next to the stores, discussing some issue in order to start an argument. There were among them, of course, rabble-rousers, insolent and brash, in other words—types who were able to pull punches that landed a healthy fellow in a sickbed. When a town meeting was held, they would arrive at the old study house and disrupt the meeting with fist shaking and shouting. There was a certain bricklayer, the most notorious mischief-maker in Kamenets, who ostensibly sided with the downtrodden, but whose real aim was purely to start quarrels. He knew very well that his shouting would get him nowhere, but he kept it up, and the mob always sided with him. There were also the petty troublemakers, who never dared to open their mouths at meetings, but at the marketplace, among themselves, they did their level best to stir up a riot. There was hardly a *hol ha-moed* that didn't end up in a row. They always found something to fight about.

Kamenets was home to no small number of craftsmen, but they were very poor. The lords generally employed craftsmen from Brisk.[89]

In those days there was almost no town without its informer,[90] and in Kamenets too, of course, there was one—Itshe Shaytes. He was a tailor who patched old clothes, though he never had to make his living from it. His real work was informing. He was not content merely to inform on individuals; he informed on entire towns. He used to go to Grodno on foot and inform the authorities mainly about matters concerning the population registry. The governor would then set up a special commission of inquiry, and the town on which he had informed would be reduced to poverty. Committee members shamelessly accepted exorbitant bribes, and the payments were prohibitive. It goes without saying that Itshe Shaytes himself had to be paid off to stop him from squealing to the authorities. He simply ruined almost all the communities in Grodno province, causing much agony. For his own town of Kamenets he had, at least, a little respect. The townspeople didn't stint on flattering him, but each praised God in his heart that this informer left Kamenets in peace.[91]

On Rosh Hashanah and Yom Kippur, he would station himself on the pulpit in the synagogue and pray with such weeping and wailing that even those not easily moved by their own prayers could not help crying and moaning with him. His howling shook the congregants to the bone. He moaned like someone being beaten and tortured. I remember one afternoon service on the eve of Yom Kippur, when I was about nine years old. I burst into tears because of Itshe Shayte's wailing. I cried so much that I fainted and had to be taken home in the middle of services. But immediately after Yom Kippur, off he marched to Grodno in order to inform on another town.[92]

The suburb of Kamenets was called Zastavye. One of its outskirts lay along the banks of the river with its three water mills from which three bridges were suspended. Large logs of timber from the Białowieska Forest were floated downstream along the river. This forest supplied Europe with wood for all kinds of building purposes, including masts for ships, but the felling of very tall trees was strictly forbidden. So the timber merchants of the Białowieska Forest felled and stole those tall trees after handsomely greasing a forester's palm. That was long before Itsele Zabludovski of Bialystok had made his millions from that forest. Someone, however, denounced Zabludovski to the authorities, alleging his complicity in the stealing of those trees, as a result of which a commission of inquiry was sent from Petersburg.[93] Zabludovski bribed each of its members and thus extricated himself from a mess that could have cost him a *katorga*.[94]

The rights to cut down trees in that forest were later acquired by a German called Siegmund. He was an even greater crook. He lived in great luxury and rumors in town had it that the Kaiser of Prussia ordered his own palace to be painted in the very same colors as that of Siegmund's. He was one of the most notorious rakes in Prussia. He stole so many masts until he made a million rubles each year, and of course he managed to squander it all. When the state treasury forbade the further felling of trees in the Białowieska Forest, Siegmund purchased a large estate in Selets,[95] in Grodno province, for half a million rubles, though he himself went to live in Berlin. Living in Berlin was too expensive, so he moved back to his estate and threw balls and parties until he ran out of money. He died a pauper.

All the timber logs from the Białowieska Forest consigned to Danzig[96] used to float past Kamenets, and thanks to Siegmund and his Germans, there was an abundance of good livings to be made in the town. Whenever the logs floated past Kamenets, Siegmund would put up at David-Yitzhak's inn, enabling him to rake in a handsome profit.

Geographically speaking, Zastavye and Kamenets lay alongside each other, but in character they were worlds apart. Zastavye had neither a rabbi nor a rabbinical court, neither a ritual slaughterer nor a cemetery. Although its inhabitants traded with and bought all their provisions in Kamenets, they had, nevertheless, distinctive features all of their own. Almost everyone in Zastavye had a vegetable plot and made a living from selling its produce. Throughout the summer the married women and the maidens tended the plots, carefully watching over them. They used to eat rye bread with cucumbers and radishes there. Living frugally, they all were able to make a living.

Zastavye boasted few well-to-do and distinguished householders, the kind involved in communal affairs and whose children were well fed and good-looking. But they were a factious lot, and whenever a dispute broke out in the community it was they who fanned its flames. They had many followers, and once a quarrel erupted within the community it was likely to last for years. They were always at odds with my grandfather, who headed the council of town elders, but because they also feared him they were forced to conspire against him in secret.

The teachers of the children were, as was customary, the melamdim.[97] The foremost among them was Yaakov-Ber, and there was hardly a youngster in town that did not pass through his hands. A child of three or even younger would already begin to learn the Hebrew alphabet with him and would study with him for about two years, until he knew how to read the prayers proficiently and without mistakes. After that, the pupils passed on to teachers who taught *Humash* as well as Talmud for beginners: chosen passages from the Mishnah suitable for children, called *Lekah tov*.[98] Once they graduated from this primary stage, the pupils went on to the next one, studying with better teachers, until they reached the eminent scholars at whose tables young men and the sons of the well-to-do studied. Those melamdim were, however, also irascible and bad-tempered men.

There were two such teachers in our township. They would beat the children to within an inch of their lives, but the ultimate punishment was to make what was called "a bundle" out of the pupil.[99] In that case, the rabbi made him take off his pants, then rolled his shirt and caftan up his back and tied the ends together to make the victim resemble "a bundle." The melamed, whip in hand, would have the child recite a section of the Talmud by heart, and the moment he missed a word, down blows would rain on him, leaving his bottom black and blue. That lasted the better part of an hour. Such punishments usually took place on a Thursday, when the pupils had to go over the sections of the Talmud the melamed had taught them during the week. There was a good reason for it, because on the Sabbath the melamed would make the rounds of all his pupils' homes in order to examine them on the material they had learned.[100] A father who did not know how to learn on his own would ask one of the *lomdim* or the *prushim* to test his child, and if the child did not understand his lessons, the father would invariably blame the melamed. This, of course, was something the melamed did not like at all, and he, in turn, would take all his anger out on that particular part of the boy's anatomy that is generally not mentioned in print.

One of the angry teachers I mentioned was nicknamed David with the tangled hair, as his head was covered with a mass of knotted hair. He was hot-tempered and frightening, and often came to within an inch of killing a pupil. When particularly enraged, he would lift a child up and ferociously throw him to the ground, so that he landed like a corpse. That actually did happen once. After the funeral the parents of the deceased never dared accuse him of murdering their child. They accepted it as preordained that their son should die while learning Torah, and so did the rest of the community. No one considered the melamed a murderer.[101] Even the sons of M. S., who made it their business to ferret out sinners in the town, in order to cause strife and contention, kept silent on this matter, and David the melamed kept on teaching as if nothing had happened. Older boys and the younger sons of the well-to-do studied with him, and they all left his heder maimed for life.

The other melamed, who was a better scholar than the above, was David the blind, for he could see with only one eye. Since he was very knowledgeable, many of his pupils eventually turned into good learners, but he was also bad-tempered and used to beat his charges mercilessly. I myself learned with him, but of that in another chapter.

As already mentioned, both boys and girls were married off while very young, between the ages of thirteen and seventeen. The dowry awarded the boy was in keeping with his scholarly competence. The sum might range from between two hundred to a thousand rubles, enabling the young husband to continue his studies while the in-laws provided the young man with *kest.* A clause in the prenuptial contract[102] stipulated that the father or father-in-law was obligated to hire a melamed for the young husband, but if the young couple lived with the husband's family, he would continue learning with the same melamed he had studied with before his marriage. The melamed, for his part, would whip the young bridegroom after his marriage exactly as before.

In my time, young husbands did not return to the heder after their marriage. David the blind, my melamed, did in fact complain about this, and he longed for the good old days when he could beat up the young bridegrooms of the well-to-do. He used to tell of how he meted out punishments back then. For example, once the mother of one of his pupils came to the heder to inform her son of the birth of his son and to congratulate him. Since the front door was locked, the mother, so David told us, went to knock at the windowpane to wish her son "mazel tov." "That very moment"—David said—"I was busy with my whip in the midst of doling out some 'mazel tov's' of my own, and with every stroke I said: mazel tov on your son, you rascal, you, mazel tov on your newborn!"[103]

In the whole of Kamenets there wasn't a single professional scribe. The melamdim taught us how to write in Yiddish.[104]

The only subject taught in heder was the Talmud and its commentaries. We learned *Humash,* but only half of each weekly portion.[105] The "twenty-four"[106] were taught by only one—Motke the melamed. He taught pupils aged between nine and ten the Talmud and a little of the *Tosaphot.* One hour a day he taught the "twenty-four" and for another hour he told us of the miraculous deeds performed by illustrious rabbis. He knew how to depict purgatory in the most vivid way, but his knowledge of paradise was quite shallow. He even sketched for us a picture of Hell and its dimensions, even the side where the door to its entrance was. But he had no idea of the dimensions of paradise and on which side the door there was. Of the "twenty-four," he only taught First Prophets—Joshua, Judges, the Books of Samuel, and Kings—that was all. The other melamdim, those who taught the older pupils the Talmud with all its commentaries, didn't teach the Bible at all. They held that teaching the Bible virtually bordered on heresy.[107]

Tuition fees ranged from sixty to one hundred rubles a term.[108]

A melamed who earned a little less than four rubles a week was considered rich. Those teaching the alphabet to three-year-olds usually had between sixty to eighty pupils in their heder at one time and received one ruble a term for each child. The well-to-do paid him ten gulden a term. At the age of five the boys moved on to a different heder where the melamed taught them *Humash.* Then, he had no more than twenty to thirty pupils in his heder and received three rubles for each of them.

When a boy started to study *Humash,* his father would prepare a banquet for the melamed, attended by all the heder pupils and their families. Each father prepared the festive meal[109] according to his means. My grandfather, Aharon-Leyzer, would provide a feast for a son or grandson with largesse. He would order a calf slaughtered, and have expensive wines and assorted delicacies brought over from Trinkovski's tavern.

The pupils would study *Humash,* that is, the first chapter, or three at the most, in each weekly portion, for about a year or two, after which they moved on to a melamed who taught Talmud for beginners. This melamed had between fifteen and twenty pupils and was paid four rubles per pupil. The rich paid him five rubles a term. There were melamdim who taught *Humash* and Talmud to beginners. The pupils who excelled in their study of *Humash* would then begin *Lekah tov.*

After studying for two or three terms with the melamed teaching Talmud for beginners, the boy's father would transfer him to a more advanced teacher who taught one page of Talmud during the first term and two pages during the second term. Such a teacher had no more than twelve pupils and tuition per child was six to seven rubles per term. At the end of the third term, the boy's father would entrust his child to an even more scholarly melamed who taught Talmud with *Tosaphot.* A teacher on that level had no more than ten pupils for the fee of eight rubles per term. Each one of those teachers would begin a different section of the Talmud without asking his pupils what they had learnt before they came to him. That's why there was a complete lack of sequence in their studies, and the change in the sections of Talmud studied at each of the melamdim every year or so ruled out any orderly system of teaching.

Children who were not gifted learners often stayed on in the heder for many terms, but if they were simpleton sons of the more prosperous, they would advance to the same melamdim as the talented ones. In that case, the father of the slow learner would ask the melamed to suit his teaching to the boy's ability, rather than have him compete with the brighter pupils, as he was paying him three rubles per term more than the others. Because the more well-to-do were ashamed to have their sons, their big boys, study with a melamed who taught the smaller children, every more advanced heder had a number of simpletons and slow learners alongside better and brighter ones. But no one ever thought of shaming them. As most of the brighter children came from impoverished families, a certain balance was achieved between the children with regard to their status. The brighter ones did not show off their quick wits, and the more well-to-do did not flaunt their wealth, so they were all equal.

The pupils attended heder from nine o'clock in the morning until two o'clock in the afternoon, with only an hour's break for lunch. If they were not back by three o'clock sharp, they would catch a severe beating, slaps, and lashes. From three o'clock in the afternoon the schedule was thus: in the summer they learned until sunset, when the melamdim went to the study house for afternoon prayers. In the winter, the smaller boys stayed on until eight o'clock at night and the bigger ones until nine. In that case, the afternoon and evening prayers were recited by the melamdim and the pupils in the heder itself. That was the procedure throughout the week, except for Fridays. On Fridays in winter the pupils learned until two o'clock in the afternoon, and in summer until three or four in the afternoon. Not even on the Sabbath was the boy given a break. That was the day when he was examined in his father's presence by the melamed or some other scholar. In addition, the child was obliged to repeat by rote all he had learned during the week, and afterward he would return to the heder to study *Pirkei avot* or Midrash with the melamed. Children had no free time except for the holidays: Purim, Passover, Shavuot, Rosh Hashanah, Yom Kippur, and Sukkot. All in all, twenty-six days a year.

The Gentiles living alongside the Jews in Kamenets were not serfs, and they numbered about one quarter of the entire Jewish population. They lived on the outer fringes of the township in thatch-roofed cottages. The majority were Catholics, and only a handful were Russian Orthodox. Each had fields and a house, with a barn, livestock, and a yard full of poultry providing them with a good living.

There were among them some very wealthy families owning property worth thousands of rubles, and they sent their sons to study in Brisk. The head of one such family named Yermolovitch was so wealthy that no one knew how much property he owned. It was rumored that he was in league with devils who flooded him with all those riches. In those days, if one had no notion where someone's wealth came from, he was held to be in league with devils. Everyone feared angering someone like that, for fear that the devils would come to his defense. People also feared Yermolovitch and thus paid him the utmost respect, thanks to his devils. Everyone in Kamenets knew that he was in league with devils. People were afraid to walk past his house, just as one would be afraid to walk through a dark forest full of dangerous animals. Yermolovitch, however, managed his affairs in a deliberate and calculated manner. He sent his son, Yash, to study at the Vilna gymnasium. He was a spoiled wild brat and the Jewish and Christian children feared him. He graduated from gymnasium, won a gold medal, and, thanks to his father's influence, was eventually appointed *assessor* in a town somewhere in Grodno province.

In accordance with the then prevailing rule, an *assessor* was in charge of eighteen gendarmes headed by a bailiff.[110] At the express order of the lords, all the gendarmes had to be Roman Catholics, a ruling strictly adhered to by the *ispravnik*. The few Russian Orthodox in the township took it altogether for granted, since they were not only among the poorest inhabitants within Kamenets but belonged to a much lower social class than the Roman Catholics.

Kamenets had an excellent medical doctor, a Gentile called Lassovski, who had already made a name for himself in Vilna but had settled in Kamenets because his wife owned a small estate there near Meshtshanska Street as well as thirty thousand rubles in cash. Although Lassovski had been living in Kamenets for many years, all medications had to be brought in from Brisk. When there was an urgent need for a particular medicine, a coachman was sent specially to Brisk, a distance of five miles. Occasionally the small bottle broke on the way and the coachman had to drive back again to Brisk for another one. By the time the medicine finally arrived, the patient had either recovered on his own or died. Lassovski made his calls in a coach drawn by a pair of fine horses and charged fifteen kopecks for a visit.

There were some additional healers in town.[111] The best and most famous among them was Yoshke. He worked for Doctor

Lassovski. Avigdor, Khatskl, and David were more simple healers. They came to the public bathhouse every Friday and applied cupping glasses to anyone who asked.[112] And who did not want to be cupped by them! Dozens of Jews: the poor, the wealthy, and even the healthy. Anyone with a pain in his hand or foot, in his stomach or in his head, knew that the best and only cure for those ailments was cupping. The more, the better.[113] The blood flowed from their backs as if they had been murdered.

Wealthy householders like my grandfather or Yonye Trinkovski, did not go to the public bathhouse but had the healers come to their homes. My grandfather had himself cupped several times a year. As soon as he felt an ache anywhere in his body, he at once called for David the healer to have him apply his cupping glasses.

On Sundays, the healers, assisted by their wives, inoculated against smallpox and did some bloodletting on peasants and their wives. David and Avigdor lived on our street, on Brisk Street, and the peasants flocked to them in droves. I remember them crowding their homes, overflowing even onto the small porches. In the summer one could see inside the open windows. The healers held large bowls filled with blood beneath the patients' arms. The peasants didn't think much of cupping, which, in their view, did not draw enough blood . . . ! They set great store by having the blood flow directly from their veins. If they felt a pain, they went immediately to the healer to be bled, and the dripping blood often filled over half a *top*. The healers' wives did not know how to apply cupping glasses or administer enemas, but they did bloodletting with great expertise.

Compared to them, Yoshke was a virtual doctor. He didn't perform operations, but had an assistant who was studying to become a healer and it was he who cut the veins. When Doctor Lassovski died, Yoshke replaced him and became the general doctor of Kamenets. Now he performed all that was necessary, just as he had learned from Lassovski.

Our Talmud Torah had twenty pupils who had "eating days," with two melamdim in charge of them. Three *gabbaim* were responsible for raising funds toward the upkeep of the Talmud Torah and for collecting contributions from the village Jews living in the surrounding area. During Hanukkah, three well-to-do and respected householders would join the *gabbaim* on their rounds of those villages surrounding Kamenets in order to collect the contributions.[114] They never skipped so much as a single village, and it was those small villages that financed it, and, to be quite honest, it was run in an orderly fashion.

The Talmud Torah was housed in a nice building. The pupils studying there were well dressed, almost as well as the children from the more prosperous homes, and they were never short of food. They also had two good melamdim, one teaching Talmud to beginners, the other Talmud with *Tosaphot* to the more advanced. On a Sabbath, the *gabbaim* would bring in special scholars to examine the pupils. That kind of Talmud Torah, in existence sixty to seventy years ago, certainly puts to shame those run by the communities nowadays, even in the large cities.

Talking of the Talmud Torah invariably calls to mind the public bathhouse.[115] The one in Kamenets was situated behind the synagogue courtyard,[116] down below, alongside the river. The steam bath, to tell the truth, wasn't so awful. On one side of its entrance lay a pile of hot stones kept aglow by a stove beneath it. Whoever wanted a steam bath would pour one pail of water over the stones, then a second, and a third, until the steam rose and one got properly stewed. Inside the bathhouse itself was the ritual bath full of cold water. In the antechamber there was an iron tank whose water was kept on the boil all day long on Fridays, and everyone drew buckets full of boiling water from it. It was the bath attendant's duty to keep the tank supplied with water pumped from the well at the other end of the large antechamber.

Long, broad benches lined the walls of this chamber where everyone undressed. Its ancient walls were full of cracks and holes, and the wind blew in from all sides. People shook and shivered as they came in from the hot steam bath, and many of them caught bad chills, especially on Fridays. But it never occurred to anyone to have the cracks and holes plastered over in order to stop the freezing draft. In the winter, the steps leading to the antechamber were sheeted with thick ice and one had to walk barefoot down eight steps to the hot water tank. It's a great wonder that none of those climbing up and down those steps froze to death then and there.

The bath attendant leased the bathhouse from the Jewish town council for one hundred rubles a year. This money was used to cover part of the rabbi's salary.[117] Whoever came to the public bathhouse paid the attendant between a *draier*[118] to three kopecks for his services.

The section of the river alongside the bathhouse was shallow, rank, and green with decomposing matter. It goes without saying that nowadays, when public hygiene has become an essential part of our lives, many people would say that this brackish pool was to blame for the epidemics that raged then in Kamenets. In fact, every year, epidemics broke out among the small children, but the child mortality rate in Kamenets was much higher than in any other town. They fell ill with measles, smallpox, scarlet fever, and many other childhood diseases. Yet it occurred to no one in those days that the polluted waters of the river might cause epidemics. Diseases, people believed, were inflicted by God Himself, and the brackish pool was left to spread diseases and epidemics, year in, year out.

A little beyond the polluted swamp flowed the river along which the timber from the Białowieska Forest was floated to Danzig. Not far from the courtyard of the synagogue, opposite the big study house, the river was clean, its bottom sandy, and that's where the men used to bathe. They would undress beneath the clear sky and put their clothes and belongings on the logs the timber merchants had brought there. The stealing of personal items or watches was unheard of. After undressing, some wrapped their clothes inside their *kapotes*, while others just left them lying about on the riverbank. They would spend hours in the river and then collect their garments from wherever they had left them.

The women bathed far away from the men, but in a place where the water was almost like the water in the public bathhouse, shallow and murky. The further one went toward where the timber was floated downstream, the cleaner the water. But that was a fair distance away, and the river there was much deeper. As I see it today, the men ought to have offered their section to the women, since walking farther up the river in order to bathe in clean water would not have been as great an effort for them as it was for the women, for whom the water there would also have been too deep. They thus would have prevented the women from bathing in that awful filth. But in those days, the men were far from chivalrous or polite enough to care if the women bathed in clean water or not.

Kamenets was famous for its swimmers. The river narrowed at one point where the water was deep and calm. The children could swim along it for a verst or two, and if they got tired, they could scramble up the bank to take a rest on the meadows lining it on either side, and then swim on.

Next to the public bath was the poorhouse.[119] This house was not intended, heaven forbid, for the sick, but for impoverished itinerants or beggars passing through our shtetl who were in need of shelter. One could always find three to four poverty-stricken families there. The building's facade was awful. It looked like some kind of dilapidated ruin whose roof was about to cave in, whose shattered windowpanes were stuffed with black, grimy rags, and whose door was broken. Very often families lived there with their infants. It is hard to describe it all, but whenever I call to mind the squalid conditions and the privations suffered by the older folk and the very young living there, I cannot help shuddering. None of the respected members of the town, neither the well-to-do nor the influential members of the community, ever gave it any thought, accepting it as part of the natural order of things.

The rabbi of Kamenets was a great expert in the Talmud and on Jewish law. He was also of distinguished lineage[120]—the son-in-law of the author of *Yesod ve-shoresh ha-avodah*.[121] His father was Yekhezkel,[122] the son-in-law of the Gaon of Vilna[123] and the son of Shmuel, who was the rabbi of the Minsk region.[124] Yekhezkel and his wife, the Gaon's daughter, imposed a life of wandering and deprivation upon themselves.[125] They wandered on foot through the villages, clad in summer clothes during the winter and in furs during the summer, living on bread and water and sleeping on the ground. When his wife died due to exposure, he married the daughter of Simha, the rabbi of Grodno. This Simha demanded that the Polish prince Radziwill[126] return the one hundred thousand ducats he had loaned him, upon which Radziwill tried to have him put in jail. But Simha managed to escape in time, and later became the rabbi of Grodno.[127] Yekhezkel had four sons, all brilliant scholars serving as rabbis in various towns.[128] One of them was the rabbi of Kamenets.

This rabbi contented himself with a salary of three rubles a week,[129] so that he might study Torah day and night. He had five sons and one daughter, who, consequently, lived in the most straitened circumstances. His wife begged him to ask for at least one more ruble a week, but he refused. Only after she kept pestering him unceasingly did he agree to ask for that extra ruble. It cost him a great deal of humble pleading until the elders finally consented to call a general meeting at the old study house, where it was decided that every well-to-do householder was to contribute one kopeck before the lighting of the Sabbath candles, but the kopecks collected at sundown by the beadle every Friday barely amounted to a ruble.

This procedure, however, did not last long, and the rabbi and his family continued living in dire poverty all their lives. When he had to marry off one of his children, he would turn to his wealthy relatives elsewhere to have them cover the wedding expenses.

The people of Kamenets loved cantors and preachers.[130] The preachers, who used to travel all over the country preaching morality, never missed an opportunity to visit our shtetl. The cantors, accompanied by their choirboys,[131] also traveled from town to town to make some money, and always stopped there as well.

A preacher coming to our township on his own always went first to the rabbi to obtain his permission to speak in public,[132] such as to deliver a eulogy extolling one or several rabbis who had passed away that same year. In general the incumbent rabbi never refused such a request and even sent the *gabbai* of the big study house to announce the preacher's arrival. When the beadle announced that between the afternoon and evening prayers of that particular day a sermon was to be delivered by the preacher, the study house would be packed to capacity both in the men's as well as in the women's section.

The preacher usually commenced his eulogy with a loud wail and tears of grief that all but melted him. "The rabbi is dead. May he be the last victim, for who will now intercede with the Almighty for us poor sinners?" (He evidently forgot that twenty more rabbis would die in due course) and the congregation broke into heartrending sobs, weeping bitterly along with him.

If a preacher was capable of causing such an outburst of grief, he must be an especially gifted one. He was, therefore, invited to preach the following morning as well, once again moving everyone to tears. Every day, after his sermon, money was collected for him. But barely three days after he left the township, another preacher appeared on the scene with a new eulogy. It goes without saying that this preacher was better than his predecessor and capable of drawing more tears, which resulted in the community's sobbing and weeping all year round.

I remember a preacher eulogizing three rabbis at one and the same time. His loud and shrill voice had unusually persuasive powers. He roared that the righteous man didn't die on account of his own sins, but because of the sins of the entire nation of Israel. Since the three virtuous men died for our sins, there remained no more righteous souls on earth able to atone for our sins, and the Almighty must now therefore tear newborn babies from their mothers' arms. The preacher ended his oration with an awful scream that had everyone in fits of wailing and weeping. Now our own babies will be taken from us too! . . . The women almost fainted from crying. I had a little sister, called Faygele, aged a year and a half with a head full of beautiful hair, and whom I loved dearly. On hearing that God was about to take unto Himself all the little babes, including my own beloved sister, I broke into such a lament that I collapsed, exhausted, to the ground.

After the preacher left our township, God did in fact visit our enclave, and there was an outbreak of measles from which many children died, including my little sister Faygele. The inhabitants of Kamenets were outraged at the preacher, accusing him of having put a curse upon the town. They tried to track him down all over the district and bring him to account, but he had vanished, and the people of Kamenets went on weeping all the year round.

Several times a year, a cantor accompanied by his choirboys used to visit Kamenets for the Sabbath. They, on the other hand, brought with them a great deal of joy. Among them were such well-known cantors as Yisrael Shkuder,[133] Baruch Karliner,[134] Yoshe Pinsker, and many others. Cantors of that order would be paid twenty-five rubles for their chanting on a Sabbath.

The cantors were always invited for the Sabbath meals at my grandfather's, and their choirboys to the homes of other well-to-do families. On Saturday evenings Grandfather loved to sing Sabbath hymns. He would invite the wealthiest householders, together with the cantor and choirboys they hosted, and, while drinking tea and sharing with them the *melaveh malkah* meal, the cantor and his choirboys would keep singing till the wee hours of the morning. The next evening they did the same at the home of Trinkovski, and the night after at David-Yitzhak's. Every host would slip a silver coin into the cantor's pocket, and by the time he left Kamenets, his belly was full of food and his pockets full of silver.

It was customary for a bridegroom about to leave Kamenets in order to live on *kest* at his in-laws' in another town to take his leave of all the important householders, accompanied by the beadle of the big study house.[135]

The wedding canopy was put up next to the big study house,

and the rites were performed by the rabbi, who lived close by. Every bridegroom was obliged to deliver a sermon at the reception, which included the *badekns* ceremony. The bridegroom would prepare his sermon several months in advance. Of course, the gifted ones delivered brilliant, sharp-witted addresses, but even the simple ones could say a few words so long as it was a sermon of sorts so as to justify the *droshe geshank.*[136] This gift was intended for a real sermon.

If one is to believe what is written in the official population register, the local cemetery seemed large enough. But since many nonregistered inhabitants also died and had to be buried, a much larger cemetery was required. The place was surrounded by a wooden fence, and all the gravestones were alike, consisting of rather small, roughly hewn rock with a memorial inscription engraved thereon.

During the heavy rains before Passover, the cemetery was flooded. The gravestones toppled over, and the graves, especially of the more distinguished, were washed away. A little farther up, the rest of the graveyard lay on much higher ground and the floodwaters never reached there. But the people of Kamenets decided that that section was of inferior status, and despite the constant danger of flooding, they went on burying the more respectable dead in the lower section. They never gave the flooding much thought. All they cared about was to be buried in the lower part of the cemetery. Why? To this day, I haven't a clue.

Unlike nowadays, when we have many burial societies,[137] there used to be just one in Kamenets, which charged a lot of money for its services from the wealthy, and consequently at their banquets there was never a shortage of bread and borscht. Its members charged the more prosperous householders from three to ten rubles for a burial. I remember the case of a notorious miser whose wife died suddenly on the eve of Rosh Hashanah. The burial society demanded five hundred rubles from him in return for her instant burial. But he kept haggling with them, insisting on paying no more than ten rubles. The deceased had been lying unburied for three days when the miser came to my grandfather, then *parnas khodesh*, shouting, "You can pickle her, for all I care! I'll never shell out all that money!" But he eventually agreed to pay 150 rubles, an amount never before paid for a burial in Kamenets.

Every year during the intermediate days of Passover, the members of the burial society prepared a punch. I can still recall the hot mead,[138] which had a particularly pleasant flavor. But once in three years, on Hanukkah, they gave a big feast to which the townspeople flocked in droves.[139] They stuffed themselves with huge portions of fish and roast goose. One of the burial society *gabbaim,* a rather paunchy fellow, was an insatiable glutton to boot who knew that this was his chance to gorge himself with food to his heart's content. But what's to be done when one simply cannot eat another bite? This man would leave the hall in the middle of his meal, stick a finger deep down his throat, throw up all he had eaten, and return as if nothing had happened, in order to finish off the other half of the roast goose on his plate. Such a feast cost the burial society a great deal of money.

Our townspeople were full of superstitious beliefs. They believed in the existence of demons, devils, and evil spirits, and the melamdim would stuff the heads of their pupils with innumerable tales of devils' doings. All of them knew exactly what awaits a man as soon as he enters the world to come, and how he ascends to heaven the moment he dies. They spoke of it as if they had seen it with their own eyes: when someone dies, he is laid out on the floor, not on the bare floor, but on straw, so that each wisp pricks him like a thousand needles.[140] Then evil spirits surround him during the funeral procession. And when the body is lowered into the grave, the Angel Dumah[141] appears beside him and asks, "What's your name?"

To his misfortune, the unlucky deceased has forgotten his name.[142] The Angel Dumah rips open his belly, plucks out his guts, and flings them into his face. He then turns the corpse over, strikes it with a white-hot iron rod, subjects it to excruciating torture, and finally tears the body to pieces, and so on. Everyone believed those things as though they were irrefutable facts.

It was the custom for the deceased to be borne to the cemetery with a roster of pallbearers exchanging places along the way. In a town like ours, the news of a funeral spread fast, and since it was a sacred duty to accompany a deceased person to his grave, the entire population turned out for the funeral. The procession was headed by the chief grave digger, rattling a tin box full of large Tsar Nicholas coins,[143] which the mourners had dropped in. The coins rattled in the box while the grave digger kept wailing loudly, "Charity saves from death!"[144]

I still remember vividly the bone-piercing terror. Everyone was scared to death of the evil spirits hovering about the corpse. Everyone thought of the terrible predicament the deceased person was in and everyone knew that his own end would not be any different.

Chapter 2

My Grandfather

My great-grandfather Velvel • My grandfather Aharon-Leyzer • Yudl • Aharon-Leyzer's youth • The wedding • My grandmother Beyle-Rashe • Aharon-Leyzer undergoes a change • Great-grandfather's death • The *ispravnik* • His relationship with Grandfather • Grandfather as *parnas khodesh* • Grandmother's counsel • Grandfather as *sborshchik* • The secretary • The disagreement over the secretary • Grandfather's influence • Grandfather and the lords • The government inspector • The new *sborshchik* • The quarrel in the township • The new *ispravnik* • Grandfather once again *sborshchik*

My grandfather, Aharon-Leyzer, was a wise and competent man who wielded enormous influence in the township. He was born in 1798. His father, Velvel, the son of Aharon, had been the *parnas khodesh* in Kamenets. In those days, the Jews of each town would elect their leader once every three years, only after his candidacy had been endorsed first by the *ispravnik* and then by the governor.[1]

The *parnas khodesh* was the sole arbiter in the township concerning all internal Jewish communal affairs, as well as on matters between Jews and the government authorities. His duty was to collect all the taxes and debts owed by the community and pay them directly to the *ispravnik*. It is, therefore, easy to understand how important a role he played within the community.

With regard to his authority, I think it enough if I mention that he had the right to put a person under arrest for three days. If he wanted to prolong the detention he had to apply in writing to the *ispravnik* in Brisk, explaining why, in his opinion, it should be extended to an entire month. The *ispravnik* always confirmed his recommendation. The *parnas khodesh* could even have a Jew flogged, although he lacked official sanction for this kind of punishment. But in those days, every *ispravnik* was more powerful in his own district than the governor is in our days, and he always gave the *parnas khodesh* a free hand and supported all of the latter's decisions.

There was a case in the Vilna province where the *parnas khodesh,* a mitnagged, ordered the flogging of a hasidic rebbe who had come to visit his followers. All the pleading and wailing of the hasidim had no effect whatsoever.

Although the law required the election of a new *parnas khodesh* every three years, the *ispravnik* ignored it. Someone who found favor with the *ispravnik* was elected, and he usually maintained his position as long as he enjoyed his overlord's goodwill and confidence.[2]

Velvel, my great-grandfather, was the *parnas khodesh* throughout his lifetime. He was a wealthy Jew who lived lavishly, and his holdings were valued at three thousand rubles. He owned a liquor distillery, and since in those days there was no excise tax[3] on alcohol, he charged twelve groshen for a *top* of vodka. Later on he raised the price to eighteen groshen. It was customary to keep a number of cows next to the distillery, which were fed on the malt.[4] Each of the ten to twelve cows he kept there yielded him four pails of milk a day. So great was the quantity of milk, cheese, and butter derived from them that he was hard put to get rid of it. He also dealt in the sale of timber, and the foresters there used to bring him the honey extracted from the hives in the forest. Furthermore, he had the sole right to levy the communal taxes in the township.[5] His home virtually overflowed with milk and honey, as well as with meat, and the gluttony that went on there was rarely seen elsewhere.

Great-Grandfather was gentler by nature than Grandfather, and his attitude toward the poorer classes—the artisans and the melamdim—was one of compassion. He therefore imposed all the taxes upon the more well-to-do householders, above all, upon the most powerful ones. His hold over the community extended to all walks of life. If someone refused to attend a *din torah*, he would summon him to his home and put it to him point-blank: "I'm giving you three days to think it over." The man, not having any other choice, would go to the rabbinical court without further ado.

A case in point was that of the rich man M., who was a great scholar but a wicked person. He dealt unscrupulously with those who traded with him and never agreed to go to a *din torah*. When the people whom he had swindled complained to the then incumbent *parnas khodesh,* who was none other than my great-grandfather, he called them all together and said: "I want each and every one of you to summon him to a *din torah*, but not only on account of this year's debts, but for all unsettled matters from previous years which he has also refused to settle with you in court. Do this and you will see that it will all work out. I'll see to it that he goes to the *din torah.*"

Great-Grandfather sent for him immediately, but when this wealthy man pretended not to understand what all the fuss was about, Great-Grandfather dispatched his personal guards—three Jews named Khatskl, Moshke, and Aharon-Leyb—to him, who bound him hand and foot in his own home. No one present dared to offer any opposition, for such an act, everyone knew, would fill the entire home with more policemen. The shackled M. was hauled before the *ispravnik* with an accompanying letter requesting his detention until he approached Great-Grandfather with a written request for his release.

It is easy to imagine the commotion stirred up in the township at the sight of such a venerable Jew, a scholar, and wealthy to boot, being led, bound hand and foot, from Zastavye through the town toward Brisk Street. It set off a riot; his entire family came running along, and the tumult was great. It was, of course, a dirty deed, but it was characteristic of the times. The townspeople were quite angry about the incident, and there was a tremendous uproar. However, despite the heated reaction, no one had the courage to take charge and try to release the man by force. M. was taken to Brisk, where he was clapped in jail for the duration.

The Jews of Zastavye banded together and sent a letter of complaint to the *ispravnik* accusing the *parnas khodesh* of acting in so arbitrary a manner that it was impossible to live in peace with him. They did not, however, leave it at that. They sent a delegation of five well-respected and glib-tongued men to the *ispravnik,* but he gave them an icy reception. "It won't do you any good," he told them, "even if you turn to the governor himself. He will, naturally, ask for my opinion, and I will say that your *parnas khodesh* is a brave man. As for your insolence in coming to me behind his back with such a complaint, I will teach you a lesson." He tore up their letter in front of their eyes.

M. sat in jail for two weeks before he asked the *ispravnik* for permission to write a letter to the *parnas khodesh,* begging his forgiveness. He agreed to go to *din torah* with each of his creditors separately, even over the money he owed them from previous years. Subsequently, the *parnas khodesh* dispatched a letter to the *ispravnik* to have M. released. Straight after his release, M. went to Great-Grandfather's house, and there, in the presence of ten witnesses and with a handshake, he promised to fulfill all the conditions he had set down in his letter.

Great-Grandfather also settled accounts with the five Jews from Zastavye who had had the insolence to complain about him. He saddled each of them with a tax of seventy-five rubles—an enormous sum in those days—instead of the customary one or two rubles. No one could or would want to pay such a huge sum all at once. Within one hour, all their bedding and household utensils were brought to the council hall.[6] After much weeping and wailing, each paid twenty-five rubles, and the money went for the purchase of sets of the Talmud for the big study house.

All disputes between husband and wife, parents and children, and siblings were brought before him. In such cases he always assembled a council of wise and respected householders in order to ask their advice. In particularly difficult cases he called in the town rabbi. Great-Grandfather's verdict was equal to that of the governor.

He had especially warm feelings toward orphans, and spared no effort to ensure that they were not mistreated by their stepmothers. If such an instance came to his notice, he had the stepmother arrested, and after her release forbade her to show herself in any of the prayer houses in the township. That always had the desired effect, for then she would come to him weeping bitterly, promising to treat the orphans fairly. It was enough to restore peace within the home.

Great-Grandfather was also a scholar and never missed studying a page of the Talmud at home every day. He could quote passages from the Midrash by heart, he fasted on the eve of every new month,[7] and he observed the *hatzot* ceremony.[8]

He also protected Jews from humiliation at the hands of the lords. When someone had sustained such an injustice he immediately turned to the *parnas khodesh,* who would complain about it to the *ispravnik* and ask him, despite the hardship involved, to have this lord admonished. Since Great-Grandfather was on good terms with all of the high government officials, he was also able to exert a certain amount of influence upon the local lords. He personally had little contact with them, but if he had a special request to make on behalf of a particular Jew, he would drive to the nobleman's estate, and his request was rarely turned down.

Great-Grandfather's house was always teeming with people, especially the poor. At a time when a *top* of vodka cost eighteen groshen, and roasted or fried sausages were strung from one end to the other of his attic for them to nibble at while swilling vodka, it was certainly worth their while to hang around. They were Great-Grandfather's most loyal devotees. The well-to-do householders, on the other hand, were his sworn enemies. They hated him for his high-handed arrogance and for the exorbitant taxes he squeezed from them at his will.

The rabbi of the township was a great scholar, and Great-Grandfather helped him to earn a decent living. A frequent guest for tea at Great-Grandfather's house, the rabbi used these visits to seek his counsel. In those days, Kamenets enjoyed a large measure of law and order and its Jewish inhabitants lived more or less in peace with one another. Great-Grandfather Velvel was probably the best and most honest *parnas khodesh* the township had ever had.

Velvel had two sons and two daughters. The eldest son, Aharon-Leyzer, who is in fact the central figure of my memoirs, was my grandfather—a very bright youngster who showed no inclination toward studying. He easily got away with it because his father usually looked the other way and the melamdim feared him as they would the Kaiser. They all figured that if the boy refused to study, it was, after all, none of their concern.

That's why Grandfather Aharon-Leyzer wasn't a scholar in spite of the fact that he had a good head on his shoulders. He was not even familiar with the Talmud, ample proof of his father's leniency toward him and of the boy's own willfulness. However, he liked to read the Bible, although learning it was, in those days, considered akin to heresy. Occasionally, he would skim through a chapter of the Mishnah and *Eyn Ya'akov*.

At the age of eleven he was married to the daughter of Yudl of Semyatich,[9] in Grodno province. This Yudl was a very learned man and could recite several hundred pages of the Talmud from the tractates of *Nezikin.* He was, as well, somewhat of a philosopher and also read a great deal about astronomy as it was understood in those days. He was a merchant by trade and traveled to Leipzig twice a year in his own coach, drawn by three horses and driven by a special coachman. He used to lug along with him a large container full of silver coins, and a smaller one full of gold coins, not to mention several tractates of the Talmud and books of philosophy, which he looked through on his long journey. He had a weakness for musical instruments, especially the clarinet, which he particularly enjoyed playing.

Some time afterward he ceased trading in Leipzig and became a supplier for the army.[10] That often used to take him to Petersburg, from whence he returned full of stories, especially about the tsar and his family. I was already twelve years old when he died. I remember that when we were searching through the drawers of his desk we came across letters from suppliers of military goods from all over the Vilna region. In several those suppliers granted him power of attorney to represent them in their claims for debts owed them by the state treasury and requested that he travel to Petersburg to state said claims. There were also letters from communities of various townships inviting him to take up residence among them, where he would be held in great esteem by the inhabitants. But by then he was already an old man.

The young couple, my grandfather and grandmother, who were eleven and twelve years of age, respectively, lived on *kest* at my great-grandfather's home in Kamenets. Grandfather, a mischievous youngster, used to race through buildings under construction and bounce wildly up and down on the scaffolding. But Grandmother, who was fond of him, yet scared of his pranks, never let him out of her sight. He would hide from her or run off somewhere beyond her reach. Once, she told us, after searching for him for a long time, she eventually caught him sitting high up on the scaffolding, rocking back and forth. Seeing her standing below him gave him such a fright that he gave a long leap and landed, badly injured, on the ground at her feet. When his "wife" burst into tears, he promised her solemnly never to do that again.

If Grandfather at the age of twelve or thirteen was nothing but a wild and spoiled child, Grandmother, on the other hand, was unusually level-headed for her age. Slowly and patiently she began weaning him of his wild antics, and after their wedding, when they had already become the parents of several children, she told him that it was time he exercised the self-control befitting a father. Since lots of people used to come to his father's house on matters concerning communal affairs, she advised him to join them and listen to what they had to say, and eventually take part in their discussions. He took her advice, and thanks to her gentle and persuasive efforts, he became a *mentsh* and started taking an active interest in his father's private and communal affairs, and his efforts were rewarded.

His father was naturally happy upon noticing the great change in the conduct of his son, Aharon-Leyzer. He was now able to share his concerns regarding communal affairs with him, which had often demanded a great deal of his time. He also had preoccupations of his own and he gradually handed all the town's affairs over to his son, something that earned the young family man the respect and admiration of his fellow townspeople. Once his father even bragged in the presence of a large assembly about now having "someone to whom I can hand over the town" (as if the town and its people were his private property). That was how Grandfather Aharon-Leyzer began to take part in the town's matters and eventually became someone who worked for the public benefit. That was the basis of his future career.

Grandmother Beyle-Rashe[11] was what people used to call— wise, kind-hearted, and gentle. The young wife kept a close watch on her husband's conduct but she pretended to understand nothing. She never corrected him in public, even when she knew he was about to make a fool of himself like a little boy. In the privacy of their room at home she pointed out to him the blunders he'd committed during the day. But, before taking the matter up with him, she always begged him not to take amiss that a simple woman like herself dared to instruct him, an intelligent man, on what to do and how to behave.

"After all, you're only human," she gave him gently to understand, "and still very young. Everyone makes mistakes and often acts foolishly. I'll therefore keep a loving eye on your deeds and will only point out to you things that you do well and where you are at fault." And so she convinced him, henceforth, of her quiet and sure ways. Her gentle and wise words often had such a moving effect upon her husband that they made him burst into tears. Then Grandmother would say, "Sh-sh . . . don't cry, my beloved. You'll still do lots of good deeds in your life. But it is the duty of a good and loyal wife to talk to you about your mistakes."

From that time, Grandfather never embarked upon an important business deal, throughout their married life, without first consulting his wife. In any matter brought before him he would state that he must think it over and that he would give his final answer only the next day. And, after consulting his wife in the evening, he would act upon the decision they had reached together. The fact that he consulted his wife on all public and private affairs was common knowledge in the township and applauded by all as a praiseworthy deed. A husband, they held, should try to live in harmony with his wife and share his concerns with her.

As Aharon-Leyzer grew older and had a growing family to support, he started thinking of setting up a business of his own. It was difficult to make a living from shtetl business; in fact, most of the householders in the town could barely make ends meet themselves. Besides, he was beginning to tire of communal affairs and had no inclination to draw his livelihood from them any longer. His father's timber trading was on a rather small scale and held no attraction for him, and he hated the distillery and the cows more than anything else.

Observing the lavish lifestyle of the lords living around Kamenets, it occurred to him that he could do business with them. They knew him as the son of the *parnas khodesh* and always treated him respectfully. If so many other Jews prospered working for them, there was no reason why he should not succeed as well. In the township it was assumed that this new business venture of his had originated in Beyle-Rashe's head.

In short, the young man asked his father to give him three hundred rubles, and he began making the rounds of the estates, visiting first those of the gentry who knew him personally and lived in the vicinity of Kamenets. They always received him cordially and, before long, even took a liking to him, which enabled him within a short time to enter into business ventures with them. His earnings were small at first, for he was cautious and did not want to arouse the least suspicion in their minds that he was, God forbid, out to cheat them. Another person in his stead, people said, would already have made a fortune, but Grandfather had the following answer for them: "Anyone else in my place would not even have been allowed to cross their thresholds. I prefer to let them get used to me gradually. I'll have plenty of opportunities to make money and can afford to bide my time since I'm not that hard up at the moment." Gradually, more and more of the lords took a liking to him and appreciated the composed and tactful manner in which he handled their business affairs.

Grandfather Aharon-Leyzer had a brother six years his junior who was generally considered somewhat unlucky. Communal affairs didn't interest him at all. He and his family lived on *kest* at his father's home, and from time to time he lent a hand to whatever needed to be done. Great-Grandfather didn't like him much, for Aharon-Leyzer was his whole world. He also had a particularly soft spot for his wife, whom he always referred to as the "righteous one." Great-Grandfather also had two daughters, whom he married off to great scholars. Those two scholars, however, cost him a fortune. In those days, he could still afford to provide each of his daughters with a dowry of one thousand rubles and allow his sons-in-law—young men of genius—to live on *kest* in his own home, enabling them to spend their days and nights studying Torah. However, Aharon-Leyzer no longer cared to stay in his father's home and share his meals and lodgings with his sisters and brothers-in-law. He set up house on his own and devoted most of his time to doing business among the gentry in the area.

Grandfather was by nature a generous person. His only wish was that from his pockets money would pour out for the benefit of all and sundry. He was by now the father of a number of children, and the township was keen on getting him more involved in communal affairs. His pleasant appearance and resolute character were of great advantage in a position of that kind.

Great-Grandfather Velvel died at the age of sixty. Upon hearing of the severity of Great-Grandfather's condition, the *ispravnik* was greatly upset. He came to visit him and did not leave the township. Before his death, Velvel called for the *ispravnik* and asked him to appoint a wise and honest *parnas khodesh* who could take over the handling of communal affairs in his stead. He set before him a list of several decent householders, but the *ispravnik,* who already had his eye on Grandfather, said, "To my mind, your son Aharon-Leyzer seems the most suitable candidate despite the fact that he is still rather young." Velvel burst into tears. "Leave my beloved son alone," he said. "The task is too burdensome for him. No matter how

fair you try to be, it is never appreciated, and you make enemies of
the people around you instead."

The *ispravnik* said farewell and departed. Several days later the
parnas khodesh passed away and the *assessor* sent word of the sad
news to the *ispravnik*. The *assessor*, the *ispravnik,* and the district
prosecutor accompanied the funeral procession to the very gates of
the graveyard.

The next day the *ispravnik* summoned Grandfather Aharon-
Leyzer—then twenty-eight years old—to his office and offered him
the post previously held by his father. But Grandfather turned the
offer down then and there, claiming to be far too young for such
a responsible position. "Besides, I have a business of my own," he
told him. "I sleep well, and enjoy my food. But this additional task
is more than I can cope with."

The *ispravnik* was adamant. "Listen to me," he reasoned with
Grandfather, "the only other candidate is M., your most outspoken
enemy. If he becomes *parnas khodesh,* he is bound to cause you and
your family no end of trouble. Since I was very fond of your father,"
he went on, "and also know you to be a brave and efficient young
man, I can't accept your refusal. Once M. becomes the *parnas
khodesh,*" he warned him in a friendly manner, "he will spare no
effort to make your life in the township intolerable." The *ispravnik*
well knew how to talk with a Jew.

That was something Grandfather hadn't reckoned with. M. was
indeed the sworn enemy of his late father, as well of his entire family.
He was the man Velvel had clapped in jail for refusing to go to a *din
torah*. It weakened his resolve and he asked the *ispravnik* to give
him a day to think things over.

He discussed the matter with his Beyle-Rashe, but neither could
decide, and their thoughts wavered between what courses to pursue.
Accepting the position was bad enough, but turning it down was
much worse. They spent hours mulling it over, weighing the pros
and cons, eventually reaching the conclusion that the only alternative was to accede to the *ispravnik*'s demand. It goes without saying
that, had M. not been the sole candidate, Grandfather would certainly have refused the position. Now that he was to be the *parnas
khodesh,* they decided that Grandfather would conduct the affairs
of the community in a calm, cautious, and reasonable manner.

When Aharon-Leyzer informed the *ispravnik* of his decision,
the latter kissed the top of his head with the typical candor of those

days and wished him good luck in his new position. He called for a general assembly in the town in order to elect Aharon-Leyzer as the new *parnas khodesh* in place of his late father. The assembly readily "elected" him. Actually, they did it without reservations. They liked Aharon-Leyzer for his intelligence and competence.

Soon afterward, the *ispravnik* took him to Brisk in his private coach. He kept him there for several days to familiarize him with the details of handling the administration of a township and was absolutely delighted with the novel ideas put forward by the young man.

Aharon-Leyzer returned to Kamenets and took charge of communal affairs as his father had done before him. But he was more prudent and more efficient, and the elders, who had hitherto wasted entire evenings on endless discussions, now felt redundant. Aharon-Leyzer handled the town's affairs with such efficiency that he gradually dispensed with the committee of elders altogether and called them together only on matters of particular urgency that could not be put off. "Maybe you have a better alternative?" he would ask them. "My advice is such and such . . ."

But his chief counselor was his wife, Beyle-Rashe, with whom he spent evenings on end discussing current communal affairs. It was wonderful to see this powerful and authoritative man take no step unless he first talked it over with his wife. He considered her counsel indispensable and never failed to act upon it.

Two-and-a-half years later, the post of *parnas khodesh* was abolished and this marked the end of the absolute rule of those who held that post. The *parnas khodesh* ceased to be responsible for the administration of the entire township and was given the new title of *sborshchik* instead.[12] He was now in charge of tax collection on behalf of the state treasury, and even in this capacity he was not solely responsible, but the entire town. Aharon-Leyzer didn't want to take over this job, but once again, the *ispravnik* pressed it on him, with the assurance that his control over the town's affairs would not be affected. As far as the inhabitants themselves were concerned, this post was a complete mystery. No one knew how to relate to it or what the task of *sborshchik* entailed. But, once again, they unanimously "elected" Aharon-Leyzer to the post.

Even after becoming *sborshchik*, Aharon-Leyzer didn't change his ways. I don't know if in the whole of Lithuania there was another *sborshchik* possessing the power he did. But there were a number of householders who started looking askance at this situation. In their opinion Aharon-Leyzer assumed rights and privileges in blatant violation of the law, and so Grandfather won himself enemies.

But Aharon-Leyzer ignored them. He had the backing of the *ispravnik* and that was enough for him. Although he was beginning to tire of this occupation, he couldn't find anyone else suitable to take over. Besides, it contradicted the wishes of the *ispravnik,* who was well aware that only Aharon-Leyzer was capable of exacting the government taxes from his fellow Jews. Therefore, Aharon-Leyzer's retention as *sborshchik* was of paramount importance to him.

Seeing no other alternative, Aharon-Leyzer decided to employ an efficient secretary to whom he could delegate the management of the community. This would enable him to pursue his private business among the gentry. After all, he needed to be able to make some kind of a living on the side, and his expenses were great. He traveled to the *ispravnik* in Brisk to inform him of his intention and to enlist his help in finding such an efficient and suitable person, maybe even someone from Brisk. The *ispravnik* actually found the right person for him—one by the name of Y. F.—who was a scrivener[13] and also appeared in court for plaintiffs; in short, a sort of unqualified lawyer. Grandfather liked the man and took him back with him to Kamenets. The former secretary, who was a rather simple man and wrote a faulty Russian, was fired. But Grandfather bought him a house for two hundred rubles and a tavern to go with it and said, "There's no need for you to procure a license to sell liquor, and you'll have a far better income than you've ever had."

The new secretary entered Kamenets like an aristocrat, clad in a short coat and with a ring on his finger. He remained bareheaded even in the council hall. The entire township was outraged but it was Grandfather who bore the brunt of their wrath. So great was their anger that they found justification for the murder of Aharon-Leyzer even on Yom Kippur.[14] The only obstacle was the *ispravnik.*

Grandfather, as usual, ignored these threats and transferred the management of communal affairs to Y. F. The latter was an intelligent young man, a good learner, and even knew how to open a Talmud. But once he began to acquire secular knowledge and became a "lawyer," he turned into an agnostic.

The secretary administered the township, and Grandfather took up his dealings with the lords once again. Three days a week he made the rounds of the estates, and on the remaining days he helped the secretary in the running of the community. He told the secretary to tax his enemies ten times the amount they had been paying formerly. It was a way of avenging himself but it soon triggered a rebellion among them. It fanned the flames of dissension throughout the township. "Can it be true?" they shouted angrily, "Aharon-Leyzer took a Gentile for his secretary!"

Beyle-Rashe was greatly upset over all this. She couldn't bear listening to the slander accompanied by clamorous curses aimed at her husband and tearfully implored him to resign from his post as *sborshchik*. "The town isn't your private property," she wept, "Nor are the Jews living in it. You don't have to be their provider. Let them fend for themselves as they see fit. I can't stand to see you in this position. Oh, what a disaster!"

That was when Aharon-Leyzer went to see the *ispravnik* and reported on this new state of affairs, giving him to understand in no uncertain terms that he was determined to give up the post. The townspeople were not willing to accept the new secretary he hired, they were no longer satisfied with his performance, and his wife was constantly weeping and wailing. It was more than he was willing to endure.

The *ispravnik* sympathized with him greatly. "But," he said, "Beware that I don't appoint you *sborshchik* again, in spite of it all, since there is simply no one who can fill your post."

The *ispravnik* actually took the trouble to travel to Kamenets, where he summoned all the elders to a meeting. He ordered them to elect another *sborshchik* in place of Aharon-Leyzer by the next day. The secretary would, however, stay on, he told them. That was a clever trick on his part. "What do you mean?" they shouted in indignation. "It's the secretary we want to get rid of! We're willing to pay him two hundred rubles to have him quit the job!" The *ispravnik* called for the secretary and put it to him point-blank: "Stay on, or take the two hundred rubles and leave." The secretary's response was no less startling. "Even if they never paid me a groshen, I wouldn't stay and work for such beastly morons a minute longer." This man was a real heretic.

The township was overjoyed: a new *sborshchik* and a new secretary. Things began to calm down.

Grandfather was now free to travel among the lords and carry on his business with them. His reputation among them was so great that they even handed him some extra commissions and recommended him to other lords in the district. In time they put so much trust in him that he became a sort of "rabbi" for them all. He gave them counsel, taught them cunning schemes of enrichment (after all even lords cheat sometimes), and it would not be an exaggeration to say that thanks to Grandfather not a few of the gentry, impoverished by gambling at cards, recovered much of their lost property. Distilleries for vodka and beer, oil presses, sawmills, and mechanized water mills started appearing on the grounds of lords' estates, all of which were the result of Grandfather's ingenious business acumen.

Nevertheless, Grandfather had one incomprehensible fault: he cared little about himself, his chief aim being to keep the lords rolling in money. His reasoning was just as strange and hard to comprehend. "If the lords are prosperous it will also benefit the Jews," he used to say. "Where, after all, will all their money end up? With the Jews, of course!" Therefore, whenever two lords were at loggerheads with one another, it was Aharon-Leyzer they called in to adjudicate in their courts, and whenever a lord and his wife had a row, they called for Aharon-Leyzer to restore the peace between them.

Grandfather now, truth be told, made lots of money, but he was also a great spender. Above all, both he and Beyle-Rashe were happy that he had finally gotten rid of his preoccupation with communal matters. It was no longer his concern as to who was willing to go to a *din torah* and who wasn't, who of the wealthy paid their taxes and who didn't. And that's how their life went on for the next three years.

He'd make the rounds of the estates daily in his own coach, drawn by two horses and driven by his personal Jewish coachman. He was home most evenings now, spending his time drinking tea and conversing with the many visitors who came to his house to chat, or to ask his advice, or merely for the light refreshments offered them. Gradually, others who had shunned him earlier once again sought his company, and those who had suffered injustices at the hands of one lord or another could not get on without Aharon-Leyzer's intervention.

There was, however, one particular difficulty no one in the township except Grandfather knew how to handle. And that concerned the annual visit of the government inspector, who would come to check the list of the 450 residents of Kamenets recorded in the government population registry. Grandfather was truly proficient in "talking" to the inspector. In that respect he had no equal in the entire township. Such a "talk" invariably ended with slipping the inspector the sum of two hundred rubles, which rapidly sank into the deep pocket of his greatcoat. On inspection day many houses were locked up, their tenants fled, and scarcely a living soul was seen in the streets. The place resembled a ghost town—a cemetery. The inspector, accompanied by the entire town gendarmery, counted all those left behind, but never came up with more than four hundred souls. Fifty were missing. They, he was told, were out of town on business. So, like every prior year, the inspector left Kamenets after signing the protocol that everything was in perfect order.[15]

This annual "talking" it over with the government inspector remained Grandfather's task even after another *sborshchik* had taken his place. There were times when, at odds with the township, he threatened to give it up, but in the end he always yielded to their pleadings to carry on. After all, he couldn't leave his township in the lurch.

The new *sborshchik* and the new secretary took all the accounting ledgers, the legal documents, and the seal, and set to work. The *sborshchik* convened all the deputies[16]—that is, the committee of elders—elected to handle communal affairs. The first thing they did was to conduct a thorough examination of the township's taxpayers. It turned out that the only ones paying taxes were the rich, whereas the common folk were completely exempted. It was, therefore, promptly decided to impose taxes also on the middle and lower classes and reduce the amounts formerly levied only from the wealthy.

Tax collectors were dispatched to the artisans and the poorer classes and they did not overlook a single soul. Once again this sparked a riot. Hardly a day passed without someone bursting into the council hall, screaming and shouting. Women ran in weeping and cursing. "How can this be? How can we pay taxes," they shrieked, "when we don't even have bread to eat! Aren't there enough wealthy ones in the township that can easily afford to pay you?" They were boiling with rage, but to no avail. On the contrary. Before long all their domestic possessions—pots, pans, candlesticks, and all kitchen and household utensils—were confiscated. The shrieks of protest reached such proportions that the *assessor* had to be called into the office to arrest the poor. (The *assessor* had two stables at his disposal—one was small and meant for horses, the other was used as a kind of temporary lockup for light offenders.)

That restored law and order. The poor moaned and groaned and gnashed their teeth, but paid up, whereas the more prosperous were obviously pleased with the new *sborshchik*'s actions.

That idyllic relationship between the *sborshchik* and the wealthy householders did not last long, however. The town elders wanted him to dance to their tune. After all, they were the privileged class, so why not use him to further their own interests? But the *sborshchik,* despite his vulnerable position, refused to be ruled by them, and every meeting with the elders ended in a contentious uproar. The *assessor* informed the *ispravnik* that matters were out of hand and that the townspeople were fighting with each other all the time.

The elders eventually divided into two camps: one opposing the taxation of the poor, the other supporting it. Each side had its adherents, and gradually the entire community was engulfed in a whirlpool of recriminations and hostilities—a virtual war. The conflict became ever more fierce, obliging the *ispravnik* to come to Kamenets in person. He arrested three of the elders and five of the mob and sent them to Brisk, where he clapped them in jail for a whole month. Only then did the fighting subside; if not among themselves, at least, for appearance's sake, to the outside world.

The *ispravnik* from Brisk was transferred to the district of Slonim,[17] and the one from Slonim replaced the one from Brisk. Before stepping into their new posts, they naturally exchanged information concerning the character of the Jewish communities as well as that of the lords. The one from Brisk painted a gloomy picture of the Jews of Kamenets, but was full of praise for Aharon-Leyzer, the only Jew who, to his mind, was prudent and businesslike. No sooner did the new *ispravnik* come to Kamenets than he summoned the *sborshchik* and the elders to a meeting. He lectured them about the negative report he had received from his predecessor concerning the scandalous behavior of the townspeople. He then summoned Aharon-Leyzer to appear before him and offered him the post of *sborshchik*. But when Grandfather proved adamant in his refusal, he asked him to look him up the next time he happened to be in Brisk.

At that time, the election of a new *sborshchik* and deputies took place,[18] and one A. B. was elected to the post. He was more resolute than his predecessor and at first seemed to adopt a more conciliatory approach toward the more respected townsmen. But scarcely six months had elapsed before they all began to quarrel—a virtual repeat performance. For, when it was the turn of Kamenets to supply a recruit,[19] and the choice fell upon a tailor, the father of three small children, the flames of contention flared up again.

Military service in those days lasted twenty-five years, and it was an absolute calamity for the young family. There was a huge outcry, all the windows of the council hall were smashed, and the *sborshchik* and the town elders suffered murderous blows. Things reached such a peak that the *assessor* dispatched a special runner to the *ispravnik,* urging him to come to Kamenets without delay. He came, docketed thirty of the most respected members of the town, and then placed them under arrest. He threatened to put them on trial in Brisk for insubordination unless they accepted Aharon-Leyzer as their new *sborshchik*. Failing that, he would hand over the management of the township to the *assessor* and his assistants.

They asked to be given twenty-four hours to think it over, to convene a general assembly and see what the mood of the township was. In view of the commotion that ensued there, many people came to the conclusion that ever since Aharon-Leyzer had left the post, the township had been like a rudderless ship that had lost its bearings. There was no order in the town. The prayer houses and— not to mention in one breath—the public bath were run down and neglected. People were constantly at one another's throats. Aharon-Leyzer, on the other hand, was a respected householder, and treated everyone as his equal. Under his leadership there would be no more taking of opposing sides. Above all, he was on a good footing with the *ispravnik,* which was a great advantage in and of itself. They therefore accepted the *ispravnik*'s suggestion and wanted Aharon-Leyzer to take on the post. "You go and offer it to him yourselves," he told them, "for he refuses to take it on."

The elders and the more respected householders, headed by the rabbi of Kamenets, went to Aharon-Leyzer and pleaded with him to take the reins of the township back into his hands. Once again he refused. Only after the *ispravnik* threatened to hand over the running of the township to the *assessor* and also to conscript a member of his family into the army did Grandfather give in to his demand. All that night, he and Beyle-Rashe weighed the pros and cons of the situation, and both reached the conclusion that he had no other choice but to step into the post once again. "To my mind," Beyle-Rashe lamented tearfully, "it's a punishment sent us from above."

Aharon-Leyzer called for a new vote, which resulted in his unanimous election. The first thing he did was to recall the former secretary from Brisk, who practiced there privately as a "lawyer" although his wife and children still lived in Kamenets. Grandfather ruled the township in the same imperious manner as before, and communal affairs soon began to function properly once again.

As he had done before as *parnas khodesh,* but long forgotten by the township, he called the elders together only for form's sake. They simply sat there in silence, scared to open their mouths and oppose him. They feared his keen intellect and his power. Besides, it was common knowledge that he did not receive any payment from the community till, that he had a large income of his own, and that money played no role in his deliberations. In short, he was reliable, and once he promised something, he stuck by it.

Grandfather had a number of faithful adherents who kept him informed as to what the people in the township thought of him. But if there was someone who expressed so much as the slightest opposition, he was immediately put on his "blacklist," that is, he was made to pay ten times the amount of taxes, as before. But all those who were loyal and belonged to his circle of good friends were practically exempted from paying taxes, and their sons were never conscripted into the army.

He did not neglect his business dealings with the lords, since all the communal affairs were now handled competently by his secretary. In that way, many years passed without any communal strife.

As mentioned above, Aharon-Leyzer lived a life of abundance. He profited from the tariff on meat and therefore meat did not cost him anything. When he married off a daughter, he sent messengers to all the prayer houses in the surrounding towns, calling on the poor to come to Kamenets and partake in the great wedding feast. Such a feast would last three days. He ordered calves slaughtered, and the poor were able to stuff themselves with mountains of meat.

On two of Kamenets's hills—the Slup hill and the Adolina hill—the meat was cooked in huge cauldrons, as if for an entire army, and the poor flocked there in droves, turning the town into an encampment of paupers.[20] The music was provided by the musicians from Kobrin,[21] and none of the town's householders dared to absent themselves during the seven days of celebration.[22]

CHAPTER 3

THE "PANIC"

The "Panic" • Isaacle the Butcher

One of Aharon-Leyzer's daughters was married off during the days of the "panic." Suddenly, a rumor spread throughout the surrounding townships concerning a new decree, forbidding marriages below the age of twenty. It was that decree of 1842[1] which caused the infamous "panic" all over Lithuania and Volhin. Whoever had an eight-year-old son or daughter wasted no time in marrying him or her off. In order to keep the police in the dark, the marriages took place in utter secrecy and without lavish ceremony.

The parents of the "young couple" set up the wedding canopy at one of the homes, in the presence of the required quorum of ten, blessed the union with a glass of wine and a piece of cake, and that was that. Following the marriage, the father of the boy bought him a prayer shawl, and the next morning he prayed wrapped in the prayer shawl, though without tefillin.[2] Likewise, the father of the girl took her to have her head shaved and bought her a caplike headdress with a ribbon in front.[3] The "little wife" and "little husband" were completely unaware of the fact that they were henceforth a married couple.

The in-laws would arrange frequent meetings between the children—that is, the "husband" and the "wife"—in order that they get to know one another. The "young couple" used to play together and fight as children do, and if they were neighbors, carried on playing hide-and-seek and other children's games as before. It often happened that the "little husband," in the heat of a childish tussle, tore off his "little wife's" cap and made fun of her shaven skull, calling her "scabby." She would run home crying, but there they would put her headdress and ribbon back on, explaining to her that it was forbidden to go about bareheaded and warning her that if she ever came home again bareheaded, she would get a whipping. On turning twelve, it was revealed to the young couple that they were husband and wife, and they were blessed with the hope that they would produce a new and worthy generation. The wife was taught the laws for women, the couple was secluded,[4] and they were taught all that naturally transpired from that.

During the year of the "panic," all the small children in Kamenets were married off. Householders would meet of an evening and make up among themselves to become in-laws that very night. Around ten o'clock at night they would awaken their children. "Get up! It's time to go to your wedding," they said to their weary children.

Isaac, the butcher, I remember well, told us how he got married.

"I was then only eight years old and lay asleep fully dressed on my bed. All of a sudden, my mother awakened me: 'Isaacle! Isaacle!' she called out. 'Get up and go to your wedding!'

I had no idea what she was talking about. What wedding? Whose *huppah*? I didn't want to get up. Mother called in Father to wake me and he screamed at me as only a father can: 'Get up, Isaac! You're going under the wedding canopy!' I said, 'I don't want to go anywhere. I want to sleep.' He said, 'Are you going to get up yourself or shall I make you?' I said, 'No, I won't!' My father pinched me furiously and shouted, 'Get up!' I started to cry. So Father went for the whip and gave me a thrashing. By this time I was, of course, wide awake, and I got up, my tired eyes full of tears.

I asked, 'Where are we going?' Father answered: 'To your wedding.'

'Where's the wedding?' I asked.

Father answered: 'At the in-laws. That's where they'll put up the wedding canopy.'

I still couldn't make out what Father meant by 'in-laws,' and 'the wedding canopy.' And once again I said, 'I don't want to go.' But when Father reached for the whip a second time, I was silent.

Mother washed me, buttoned up my pants, helped me into a jacket, and told me to put on my hat. But the hat was gone. I'd lost it somewhere playing games and running about before turning in.

That set off a frantic hunt for the hat, and Father said, 'If you didn't have to go to the wedding now, I'd give you a good whipping because of that missing hat!'

Meanwhile people were sent by the in-laws to find out what was taking us so long. Everyone was now looking for the hat, and when it failed to turn up, it caused a commotion. What's to be done? It was already midnight. Mother and Father had a bad feeling that the other party might renege and call off the wedding. They were at a loss for what to do.

They started thinking which of the neighbors they could wake up in order to borrow a boy's hat until the next morning. They thought and thought but couldn't think of anyone willing to do them that favor. It was getting late, and there was still no hat.

The situation was very bad. No hat, no wedding. Mother and Father could not bear the distress any longer, but there was nothing to do. Having no other alternative, Father went to the in-laws and asked them to put the wedding off until the following night, giving the excuse that his wife had suddenly taken sick. Father stayed away for a long time, and Mother was getting restless. But, God be praised, he came back to tell us that the wedding would take place the following night at ten o'clock.

The next day they bought me a new hat. To the heder I went in Father's yarmulke. I told my fellow pupils that my father was going to take me to my wedding the night before but that it was put off because I didn't have a hat. Today, he'd buy me a new hat and then I could go to the wedding. Beynish, the blacksmith's son, told me that he had been to his own wedding the day before; that he'd stood under the *huppah* with Dvorah, Baruch the carpenter's daughter. Everyone kept circling around him, chanting something, and then they gave him a ring, and then he put it on Dvorah's finger, and then his father recited a blessing with him, and then everyone danced and ate cake, and cookies, and salted herring, which was very tasty.

When I returned home from the heder, Mother placed the new hat trimmed with tassels on my head. I asked her, 'When are we going to the wedding?' She answered: 'Just don't fall asleep tonight the way you did yesterday. It was impossible to wake you up.' I answered her, 'Tonight I won't fall asleep before the wedding.'

But by nine o'clock I was again fast asleep and they could hardly wake me. Then I went to the wedding with Mother and Father. As soon as I entered the house, I caught sight of Zisl, the girl I'd had a fight with the Saturday before at her uncle's house. She was a nasty girl and we weren't talking to one another.

They put up the *huppah* and had me stand under it. A few minutes later Zisl was led in and placed beside me. I ran out from under the *huppah,* shouting, 'I don't want to stand next to Zisl. I'm angry with her!'

Mother said, 'But Isaacle, she's your bride.' I retorted, 'I don't want her for a bride! Give me another one,' and I refused to stand beside her under the *huppah.*

Father, in his usual manner, spoke to me in his angry tones, but I wouldn't listen. He said, 'If you don't go and stand under the *huppah* this very minute, I'll send someone home to fetch the whip. Or else, I'll get a switch and teach you a lesson you won't forget in a hurry!' And Zisl said, 'Excellent. That's exactly what he deserves! He pulled me by my hair last Saturday and I'm not going to stand next to him under the *huppah!'*

Now the same thing started all over again with the bride. First her mother pleaded, then her father threatened to give her a thrashing.

To make a long story short, that went on for several hours since the bride and the groom would not stand side by side under the *huppah.* The invited guests got impatient and wanted to go home. A broom was brought in and its twigs were being plucked—intended for Zisl and me. We both burst out crying and stood, bawling at the top of our voices, under the *huppah.*

I was told to take hold of Zisl's forefinger and place the ring on it. But I didn't want to touch her finger. Father slapped me across the face, and only when he threatened to beat me with the broom did I take hold of Zisl's finger. Full of rage at being forced to take hold of her finger, I pinched it so hard that she started to squeal. Then, in order to get us to make up, Zisl's father handed her two gulden, and my father handed me two gulden. After that I took hold of her finger, slipped on the ring, repeated the blessing after Grandfather, and said mazel tov. Then everyone started dancing. Afterward, they seated me and Zisl at the head of the table and we all had cake with jam.

Suddenly Zisl began crying. 'What's the matter?' her mother asked. 'I've got to p . . . ,'[5] Zisl said. She was led outside. Then I said, 'I've also got to . . . ,' and was led outside. Later on, seated next to each other once again, we fell asleep. My sister Haya took me home, and Zisl, too, was put to bed straight afterward.

If there was something about all this that made me feel good for a while, it was my not having to go to the heder from Tuesday to Sunday. The following day, my new in-laws and Zisl came to us for the midday meal. Zisl's shaven head was covered with a cap reaching down to her eyes. Mother cooked a chicken for dinner. We never had meat in the middle of the week except for special celebrations. Then the host would order a bullock or a calf from the butcher, haggle over the price, and finally pay. There was only one butcher in the town, who slaughtered a small bullock to last him throughout the week. But that was meat ordered by the lords, high government officials, and the wealthy. Whatever meat was left over, he usually sold to the lords' servants.

After dinner, Zisl stayed on at our place. I didn't like her in that cap of hers. When we started playing games, the first thing I did was to tear it off. And here, what did I see but a white, shaven skull, and I started to shout, 'Feh! You look scabby. Scabby!'

Zisl got insulted and started to cry. Enraged, Father gave me a whipping in front of her (Father beat me at every possible opportunity), and with every lash he repeated my offenses in my ear: 'The boy will never dare to pull off Zisl's cap again or call her scabby. . . .' Screaming and crying while the blows rained down hard and fast, I promised, 'Father, I'll never do it again! I'll never do it again!'

And Zisl, looking on, started laughing through her tears. She was taken home soon afterward, and we went on being cross with one another. She because I'd insulted her and I because of the thrashing I got on her account.

The following day, my mother and father paid the in-laws a return visit, but I refused to join them. The in-laws were quite satisfied with one another, but Zisl and I did not meet. On the Sabbath, my father-in-law hosted a special minyan at his home and Father took me along for the prayers. I was called up to the Torah to read the sixth portion,[6] as is accorded the bridegroom after his wedding. I stood on a footstool placed next to the table where the Torah was read, and Father said the blessing along with me. I wore the small prayer shawl Father had asked David the wagoner to bring me from Brisk. After the prayers, cake and vodka were brought in. We all sat around the table but Zisl wouldn't sit next to me.

Several months went by and we continued to be angry with one another. It was Passover and Mother invited Zisl over. Everybody wanted us to make up already. My mother and mother-in-law gave us walnuts[7] so that we would play together. Since I was an only child, I asked the four questions.[8] Zisl liked that, and for the first two festival days[9] we played the customary nut game together. On the last days of Passover I was invited to visit the in-laws. Mother brought me over there. I played with Zisl all day, and in the evening Mother came and took me home to bed. The next day we did the same thing. On the very last day of Passover, I lost all my nuts to Zisl. She was a smart one and played almost better than I did. I was furious and pulled off her cap once again and, in spite of myself, called out 'Scabby! . . .'

With this deed I sealed my own fate. Zisl ran crying to her mother, who angrily slapped my face, and Zisl's father promised to have my melamed in the heder give me a proper thrashing. I ran home, and Zisl's father came as well in order to complain to my father about me. 'How can your son be so wicked?' he demanded of him. 'He ought to be given a whipping he'll never forget!'

My teacher in the heder was told to give me a proper whipping for pulling off Zisl's cap and for calling her scabby, and he fulfilled his duty with great eagerness. From then on I never touched Zisl's cap nor called her names ever again. But we weren't on speaking terms that whole year until the following Passover.

My mother-in-law brought Zisl to our place once again and both mothers were dead set on making peace between 'the couple.' We made up and didn't fight again. Zisl's hair had meanwhile grown back, and she often took off the cap herself in order to keep her nuts in it while we played. Until then, we used to keep them in my yarmulke.

When we turned twelve,[10] my father and Zisl's mother revealed to us separately the secret that we were husband and wife, and we were brought together. Zisl's mother taught her how to behave toward a husband, and my father taught me how to behave. And, God be praised, we've remained husband and wife to this day. Although she gives me the rough edge of her tongue every now and then, I've gotten used to it and keep my own mouth shut. And now, God be praised, we're about to marry off our daughter. May it be in a lucky hour."

That story, of which I have given you a true and detailed account, was characteristic of those days. That's how most of the married couples carried on. The little boy remained at his parents' home and the little girl at hers. They were often brought together to play games or, if they were neighbors, they squabbled and fought each other as before, and if the "husband" tore off his "wife's" cap, his father usually gave him a thorough whipping.

The whipping of children was a common form of punishment, and it was meted out for the most trivial of reasons. Young boys were beaten, and even young newlyweds, as well as mothers of children often no older than fourteen or fifteen.

Strange as it might sound, truth be told, most of those young couples, after growing up, became accustomed to one another. Husband and wife showed respect and affection toward each other. Only a small number among them went on fighting and eventually divorced.

The above-mentioned "panic" lasted only one year.[11] When the rumor spread to Kamenets, the elders of the town came to Grandfather for counsel on how to act. In those days such a rumor was taken most seriously, and Grandfather Aharon-Leyzer traveled to Brisk to ask the *ispravnik* what he knew concerning the issue. He was told that something to this effect had indeed arrived from the minister. A paper had arrived for the governor from Petersburg in which he was requested to inform the government at what age the Jews married off their sons and daughters. It had become known to them that the overwhelming majority of Jewish recruits were already fathers of several children. Consequently, the *ispravnik* assumed that the ministry would issue a decree forbidding marriages between boys or girls below the age of twenty. No sooner did Aharon-Leyzer return from Brisk than the "panic" seized everyone.

Although this panic had already taken hold of Brisk some time before that, nobody in Kamenets knew anything about it. They took Aharon-Leyzer's words for granted, and, since he himself didn't want to be an exception, he married his own daughter off at the age of eleven.[12]

CHAPTER 4

MY FATHER AND HIS
ATTRACTION TO HASIDISM

My father Moshe • His attraction to Hasidism • The match • Leyzer,
the rabbi of Grodno • My mother • My father, the ardent hasid • His
flight to the rebbe • His quarrel with Grandfather • The leaseholding
• The government inspector • The hasidim of Kamenets

Moshe, Aharon-Leyzer's son, was a particularly bright
boy, and when he turned twelve, Grandfather began
to invite matchmakers. He told them to find for his
son the daughter of a rabbi, not just any rabbi, but a great and
renowned one.

The matchmaker, Berl-Mikhl, told him that the rabbi of Kamenets[1] had a brother by the name of Leyzer who was a *dayan* in
Grodno.[2] Leyzer was the son-in-law of Rabbi Hillel,[3] and Hillel himself was the son-in-law of Rabbi Hayyim of Volozhin,[4] and this was
a most distinguished lineage. Leyzer had a daughter who was available for a match, but the matchmaker doubted if there was any point
in talking to him about a match with the son of a *sborshchik*. "If you
could enlist the aid of our rabbi," the matchmaker explained, "and
if he favors it, a match is likely to result."

Aharon-Leyzer liked the idea and sent the matchmaker to the
rabbi. But the rabbi promptly drove him out of his house. "What a
nerve!" the rabbi said angrily, "to suggest a match with the *sborshchik* of Kamenets to my scholarly brother!"

Aharon-Leyzer was not to be deterred. On the contrary. He went
to the rabbi himself and said in these very words: "You know, Rabbi,

that I have a very bright son of twelve. . . . You must have heard of him. . . ."

The rabbi replied in an amiable tone: "Of course, I've heard that your son has a good head on his shoulders."

"And I've heard," continued Aharon-Leyzer, "that your brother, Leyzer, the rabbi of Grodno, has a daughter much sought after by matchmakers. I want our families to become in-laws. Money is no problem; I will pay whatever it takes. I'd like you to arrange the match yourself. I'm certain that if you advise your brother so, he will surely listen to you."

"The matchmaker Berl-Mikhl told me," Grandfather went on, "that you drove him away in anger for suggesting a match between your brilliant brother and a *sborshchik*. So, let me tell you briefly, my dear rabbi, you have two alternatives: either you arrange the match, or find yourself another town. You have until after the Sabbath, and if you refuse to help make this match, you must leave Kamenets that very day."

In this instance all of Grandfather's despotism and wildness was revealed.

The rabbi was left stunned, white as chalk. He was well aware that once Aharon-Leyzer had made up his mind, it was irrevocable. With him, it was no sooner said than done, and who dared contradict him? He therefore asked for two weeks before giving him an answer, and Aharon-Leyzer agreed.

The rabbi called together several of the more important householders, told them of his talk with Aharon-Leyzer, and asked their advice. They were aghast at Grandfather's cruel conduct, because it was a murderous deed to force such a learned man to arrange a marriage with a *sborshchik*. Consider as well that he was related on all sides to the greatest scholars: the great scholar Rabbi Leyb-Itshe was his wife's brother;[5] Rabbi Hillel—her father; Rabbi Hayyim of Volozhin—her grandfather; Rabbi Itshele of Volozhin—her uncle.[6] The great scholar Rabbi Yekhezkel, who was the son-in-law of the Gaon of Vilna, was Leyzer's father; Shmuel, the rabbi of the Minsk region—his grandfather; Simha, the former rabbi of Grodno—another grandfather.[7] In addition, three of his brothers were themselves great scholars and served as rabbis of large towns. The idea of Leyzer's daughter marrying the son of a *sborshchik* was simply unthinkable. But it was a lost cause. Aharon-Leyzer had spoken, and there was nothing anyone could do. They had no advice to offer.

There was nothing left to do but to write a letter to his brother Leyzer, and whatever his brother replied he would do. He sent the letter, and received a completely unexpected reply. Its gist was as follows: "I see, my dear brother, that it has been ordained by the Almighty, and it is probably His will. Therefore, we ought to be satisfied with His judgment. Is the prospective bridegroom at least a good boy? If he can be expected to turn into a real Torah scholar, there is no reason not to go through with the match."

The rabbi took the letter and showed it to Aharon-Leyzer, who was overjoyed upon reading it. "Now, my dear Rabbi, I'll add a ruble a week to your salary," he said, rubbing his hands together. "I intend to travel to Grodno to take a look at the girl, to make sure she's not, God forbid, a cripple or ungainly. I love Moshe very much, so I want him to have a pretty wife, not just a girl from a good family."

To Grodno he went, together with the rabbi. He liked the girl, and the marriage contract was drawn up, with the dowry set at the sum of one thousand rubles. The young couple would live on *kest* in Kamenets for three years, and Aharon-Leyzer undertook to hire a private teacher for his son. After that, the couple would be sent to Grodno so that the young man could study with his father-in-law. He also undertook to cover all the expenses for the couple's board and lodging in Grodno.

At the time when the marriage contract was drawn up, Moshe was thirteen years old and the bride, Sarah, eighteen or nineteen. No wonder her father immediately agreed to the proposed match.

Rabbis from all the branches of the family came to the wedding, and the entire town indulged in revelry lasting eight full days. Vodka was brought in by the barrel, and the crowd drank and drank without limit. The in-laws and the rabbis left the festivity well satisfied. They had never seen such a lavish wedding celebration, attended by an entire township. But it never occurred to them that most of those attending the wedding feast did so out of fear rather than out of love.

Aharon-Leyzer looked for an outstanding scholar to teach his son Moshe. He wanted Moshe to become a rabbi himself. After all, it's no small matter to belong to such a circle of famous rabbis and scholars. He brought down from Brisk a great scholar by the name of Arele and had three more youngsters from wealthy families join the study circle. Arele received one hundred rubles a term to teach those boys, themselves also bridegrooms. In those days, twenty-five rubles per pupil was a small fortune.

But Aharon-Leyzer, it turned out, was badly deceived.

It never entered his mind that Arele might be a zealous hasid who was likely to turn his charges into hasidim rather than rabbis. In fact, Arele sowed the seeds of Hasidism in his pupils' hearts and turned them into devoted hasidim, the type that make a pilgrimage straight after their wedding to their rebbe, Moshe of Kobrin,[8] Arele's mentor.

Aharon-Leyzer was, needless to say, an ardent mitnagged, and the rabbi of Kamenets an even bigger one. So much so, that when a woman complained to him that her son had become a hasid, he ordered her to rend her clothes and sit shivah[9] for him. The rabbi's brother, Leyzerke, was, of course, a devoted mitnagged. After all, they were both descendants of Hayyim of Volozhin!

As could be expected of Moshe, he sneaked out of the house soon after his wedding and drove to his rebbe in Kobrin. Moshe, who knew his father well, did so in spite of the big row he was certain would await him on his return. He also knew what a calamity he brought upon the heads of all his father-in-law's family of mitnaggedim. It was an exceptionally severe blow to his pious father-in-law, who had fervently hoped he would become a rabbi, something that was now definitely out of the question for a hasid. Moshe, however, threw all those considerations to the wind and stuck to his resolve. He did not take after his father at all and was the very opposite of him in character. He was a thoughtful child, quiet and extremely pious. Although he knew that by embracing Hasidism he was bound to cause his family a great deal of distress, he did not take this into account. He followed an irresistible inner urge.

Needless to say, this was a sudden and heavy blow indeed for Aharon-Leyzer. His son had ruined all of his best-laid plans. How much effort had gone into having his son marry into a family of outstanding minds and to having him become a rabbi himself. What more did one need? Suddenly it all collapsed about him! It would never have dawned on him that such a terrible misfortune could happen to his own son.

Arele, the melamed, knew full well that once Moshe's trip to the rebbe became common knowledge, Aharon-Leyzer would rake him over the coals. He therefore wasted no time and took himself off as fast as he could. Aharon-Leyzer, unaware of Arele's flight, sent two gendarmes to bring him to his house. But as soon as he learned of Arele's escape, he asked the *assessor* to provide him with six gendarmes who would execute whatever orders he gave them. Such an act was not within the *assessor*'s jurisdiction, but taking into account Grandfather's good standing with the *ispravnik,* he fulfilled his request. Aharon-Leyzer dispatched those gendarmes to the house Arele had acquired upon his arrival in Kamenets, with an order to have them pull down the roof. But Mordechai-Leyb, Grandfather's brother, was strenuously opposed to such an arbitrary act. "Don't do it," he reasoned with him. "It's not the way Jews treat one another." Undoubtedly, had Mordechai arrived on the scene but one hour later, they would have razed Arele's house to the ground.

Immediately afterward, Aharon-Leyzer sent one of the most respected householders as a messenger to Kobrin, to warn the rebbe that if he wanted to live peacefully in Kobrin and continue as a hasidic rebbe to his followers, he was to send his son Moshe to his father-in-law without delay and swear never to lure the young boy to himself again. But the rebbe was powerless. Fourteen-year-old Moshe became an ardent hasid and told his rebbe with pious devotion, "Rebbe, my soul is irrevocably tied to your soul. I won't leave you unless I die."

The messenger had no alternative but inform Moshe in his father's name that unless he returned home at once and swore to abandon Hasidism for good, he would never again be allowed to cross the threshold of his father's house.

Staying at the court of his rebbe for a few weeks turned Moshe into an even more zealous hasid. Knowing full well that he was unable to return home, he wrote to his father's in-law, Zelig Andarkes,[10] asking if he would agree to take him in and protect him from his father's wrath. Zelig consented and promised to take the responsibility upon his own shoulders. He could come back to Kamenets and stay at his home. So Moshe remained for several months with his rebbe in Kobrin and spent several months at Zelig's home.

Moshe's father-in-law, Rabbi Leyzer of Grodno, was completely unaware of this turn of events. Nobody wanted to cause him distress.

Meanwhile, Sarah, Moshe's wife, gave birth to a son, and when the news reached Leyzer, he came to Kamenets for the circumcision ceremony and stayed at his brother the rabbi's house. Only then did he learn about the affair, which cost him his health. To be double-crossed like that! The in-law—a *sborshchik,* and what was even worse—the son-in-law a hasid. It was as clear as daylight that once the father was a hasid, his children and their offspring would also be hasidim, and generations of hasidim were bound to follow in their footsteps. He therefore decided to have his daughter divorce her husband—that is, if she agreed. When he came to Aharon-Leyzer's to see his daughter, he was given a royal welcome. He tried to talk to her and to judge the situation from her reactions but all his efforts were to no avail. He came to the conclusion that she was passionately in love with her husband and weeping her eyes out over the fact that he had to live the life of an outcast because her father-in-law wouldn't let him into the house, not even to attend their son's circumcision.

Leyzer realized that it was a lost cause. He took it for a punishment inflicted by God, and if that was His will, so be it. Therefore he, the sworn mitnagged, undertook to effect a reconciliation between Aharon-Leyzer and his son Moshe. Only after unceasing efforts did he succeed in persuading Aharon-Leyzer to be reconciled with his son. The rabbi, Leyzer, and Moshe went together to see Aharon-Leyzer. Moshe fell weeping into his father's arms and, as often before, begged him to be his beloved father once again. The only thing though he told his father could not be altered was his remaining a hasid. It was something he was unable to give up, not even if he were threatened with death. His father's heart softened, he gave in to his son's pleadings, and peace was restored between them.[11]

Aharon-Leyzer held the circumcision ceremony in grand style. When the baby had to be given a name, Leyzer wanted him named after his father, Yekhezkel, the son-in-law of the Gaon of Vilna. But Aharon-Leyzer insisted upon his own father's name, Velvel, the former *parnas khodesh*. They eventually agreed upon a combination of both names: Yekhezkel-Ze'ev.[12] The newborn they were wrangling about was myself, and my father was only fourteen-and-a-half years my senior.[13]

Grandfather became once again extremely fond of his son, and my father was able to practice his Hasidism without restraint. He went daily to immerse himself in the bathhouse, even on winter days when the freezing wind blew in through the large cracks and holes in the walls and one had to descend the eight ice-coated steps leading to the cold well. He also traveled to Kobrin to ask his rebbe to make a special trip to Kamenets to persuade his father to have Arele return and become their teacher again.

His rebbe, Moyshele, did just that. He traveled to Kamenets straight to Aharon-Leyzer's house, together with his son. The rebbe of Kobrin was very active among the other hasidic rebbes. He received a friendly welcome, and Aharon-Leyzer even acceded to his request. A letter was sent to Arele allowing him to return and he did not have to be asked twice. He started teaching the sons of the more well-to-do once again, and slowly but cautiously increased their number to twelve, "turning" all of them into hasidim.[14] Among them was also Yekhezkel, the son of the rabbi of Kamenets, a young prodigy of brilliant intellect.[15]

Before long, those "freshly baked" hasidim rented a separate *shtibl* in which to conduct their own prayers. Father was able to get special permission from his father for the hasidim to pray separately. My father had already given up studying the Talmud and had started studying the *Zohar* and Midrash and practicing the hasidic custom of ritual bathing and singing joyful songs.[16] Thus he spent all his days and nights—and there was no more talk of his becoming a rabbi.

Grandfather wanted to take him along on his trips to the lords' estates, to get them acquainted with him, but his son had no inclination to follow in his father's footsteps. He did not want to have anything to do with the menfolk there, and even less so with their wives. Having no other choice, Grandfather started thinking of setting his son up in a small business of his own.

Meanwhile, Grandfather made preparations to marry off his second son, Yosl. This time he chose as his in-law an aristocrat from Bialystok. His name was Shimon "Daitsch" because he already conducted himself like an aristocrat.[17] He had several pretty daughters, and the prettiest among them was the eldest—Yokheved. Since his first daughter-in-law, the rabbi's daughter, was not particularly pretty, nor did he have a great liking for her, Grandfather now sought to ally himself with a family of a different sort, one that wore diamond rings on their fingers and strings of genuine pearls around their necks.

Yosl was also a hasid, and there was an urgent need to provide livelihoods for both sons. That was when the following scheme took shape in Grandfather's mind. The inhabitants of Kamenets and the surrounding district could not buy vodka or beer from anyone except from Osserevski, the wealthy landowner. As already mentioned, they had to pay him excise duty as well on salt, tobacco, candles, and the like. Furthermore, he was paid five kopecks for every horse that entered the town for the Sunday fair. The same applied to the use of the three water mills. All this income belonged to Osserevski, who employed a special overseer to collect the taxes.

But this overseer managed the business in such a way that Os-serevski was left with almost no income. The overseer preferred to let the money flow straight into his own pockets, and, as was common practice in those days, cheated and swindled the lord.

Once, when Osserevski visited his estate, Pruska, Grandfather went to see him there. He proposed that Osserevski hand over to him the leases for all of the above. For these leases, Grandfather was willing to pay Osserevski 1,200 rubles per annum, since all he had gotten out of it until now, he told him, wasn't worth a fig. Osserevski liked the idea and they signed a three-year contract.[18]

Grandfather's acquisition of the lease to collect the taxes was something altogether new in the township and people stood in awe of his daring. For who would have the resolve to antagonize an entire township? And what would happen if anyone smuggled in vodka and didn't want to pay up? And who was so iron-willed as to undertake such a difficult enterprise, to keep a watchful eye upon the entire population, make them pay up punctually, and prevent the hitherto accepted custom of cheating and stealing?

No sooner did Grandfather take over the lease than he told the beadle to announce in the old study house that a general meeting was called for Tuesday evening. As usual, the whole town showed up. When Aharon-Leyzer calls a meeting, no one dares to stay away. If you do not come you will end up having to pay more taxes. He sent for the community scribe, to announce from the pulpit that hence-forth it was prohibited to buy vodka except from Aharon-Leyzer, and the cost of each *top* would amount to twenty-seven groshen for tavern keepers and eighteen groshen for individual customers. He ordered that with regard to beer and other goods, they would continue to pay what they had been paying up till now to the lord's former overseer. From now on, he was the sole leaseholder. In addi-tion, he would donate three hundred rubles to the town's treasury for charity. At first the news caused an uproar among those gath-ered, but since no one dared to speak up or raise objections, the uproar died down and the gathering dispersed.

After that, Aharon-Leyzer summoned all the bartenders and their employers and ordered a total reorganization in the sale of vodka. Up until then, the tavern keepers had sold their vodka cheaply to the peasants; this often caused them to go bankrupt, since they charged only four groshen per glass. From now on, Grandfather told them, as the lease was in his hands, the vodka could be bought only from him at twenty-seven groshen a *top,* and they were warned not to buy it from any other source. If they followed his instructions they would soon make up for their former losses.

He again cautioned them, "In the past, when the foreman, Patshoshe, caught you stealing, you got a whipping. With me, you won't get flogged, God forbid, but whoever is caught smuggling vodka can forget about keeping a tavern. From now on, the price of a glass of vodka will be three kopecks. Here, I've brought you special glasses from Brisk. They look like large glasses but hold less. You will sell drinks only from these glasses and under no circumstances from any others. You will all have the same glasses, and you will all make a living. The main thing is that there is no need to compete against each other; everyone will be assured of a decent livelihood."

The tavern keepers gathered at Grandfather's once again and fixed their number for the next three years, which was not to be exceeded. Each of them had to obtain a license entitling him to sell vodka freely. Accordingly, Grandfather undertook to lend money to any tavern keeper who did not have sufficient funds in order to purchase a license. Grandfather was an expert in organizing his business deals. After everything was arranged, he handed the lease over to my father in partnership with his own brother Mordechai-Leyb, and the lord agreed to supply them with all the vodka they required.

This is how the excise duty used to be levied:[19] an excise official[20] working in the brewery supervised the amount of liquor sold to the tavern keepers. If the buyers brought along a barrel, the supervisor measured the number of pails it was likely to hold, stamped it with the customs seal, and issued a certificate for that amount. Then he would record the number of pails sold. Once a month, the duty on it was forwarded by the distillery owner to the excise office in Brisk. There was another inspector at work in the town whose task it was to ensure that the vodka sold by the tavern keepers came solely from the barrels stamped with the customs seal. If he came upon a barrel that had not been stamped, there was no doubt that its contents had been smuggled in.

Grandfather opened up a tavern in Kamenets, and huge barrels of vodka were brought in—fifty pails to a barrel, in other words, about two hundred *tep*. Since this was really a huge order, the lord was loath to take upon himself the handling of the excise accounts, so Grandfather took up the task. Once a month, he would send to Brisk the tax money, which he kept in the grain storehouse in sacks filled to bursting with copper and silver coins. Several horses were needed to transport the money. On Fridays, the entire township came to buy vodka and wine for the Sabbath. On that day Grandfather's whole family was enlisted to cope with the huge sales. Tubfuls of vodka were placed there, from which it was measured and poured out into bottles.

Now that Grandfather was in charge of handling and accounting for the excise duty, the government supervisor worked alongside him, stamping the barrels with his seal. When the tavern keepers arrived, each with his own barrel, the supervisor put his seal upon them, keeping a wary eye on anyone trying to outsmart him. Then Grandfather stamped each barrel with his personal seal to ensure that none of the bartenders sold vodka obtained elsewhere. Thus, each barrel had two seals on it as well as a long stick measuring the amount of pails it contained. Once or twice a week or at unexpected times, Father and the supervisor made an inspection of the taverns in the township. They would remove the seals and check the amount of vodka left in the barrel with the measuring stick.

This is how they conducted themselves: sometimes, when they wanted to make a surprise inspection, they sent Khatskl, his burly servant, together with a few gendarmes. But there was never any need for the police. Grandfather, with the help of the *ispravnik*, could count on as many gendarmes as he needed from the *assessor*. His request was never turned down. However, the tavern keepers were very careful; besides which, they were often with us in the room which served as the accounting office, and they did their best to pass themselves off as good friends of ours, thus reducing the inspections to a minimum.

The tavern keepers sat with us in the accounting office, and vodka, of course, was ever available. Someone was usually sent to fetch portions of roast goose, and everyone was happy and content. It is worthwhile mentioning that all the tavern keepers in close contact with Grandfather did very well indeed, several of them becoming quite prosperous.

As for the excise duty on salt, candles, tobacco, and the like, Grandfather took no interest in it, and so was able to handle his vodka trading in an orderly fashion.

Once, Grandfather was visiting the *ispravnik* in Brisk, who told him about a rumor that had reached him that the governor intended to send an inspector equipped with special powers to examine the population registries within the entire province. Hints dropped by informers indicated that more than two-thirds of the Jewish population was not registered at all.[21] The *ispravnik* feared that within the district under his particular jurisdiction the government inspector would discover a great number of unregistered souls, and that was likely to cost him his post. Grandfather wanted to know if he knew the said inspector personally, and the *ispravnik* answered that he knew him well. He was an arrogant man and not very smart, and he took every trifle as a personal insult, but he was fair and honest. "Well," Grandfather said, "if that's the case, you have nothing to worry about. Tell him to start his inspection of the Brisk district in Kamenets. Things will work out all right."

The day arrived when the inspector started his tour of the province, and it was no secret that he found lots of phony registrations in many townships, and the dread of exile to Siberia kept haunting all their elders. . . . It goes without saying that great fear fell over the province. Everyone saw in the government inspector a harbinger of disaster.

Although the *ispravnik* placed a great deal of trust in Grandfather, he nevertheless dreaded the inspector's visit. It was no small matter for a man of his standing to have it made public that his population registries were phony. Acting on Grandfather's counsel, the *ispravnik* dispatched a letter to the *assessor* of Kamenets, telling him to arrange lodgings for the inspector at Yonye Trinkovski's inn, instead of, as was the custom, in his own home. The *assessor* was to keep his distance from him and not to station a police guard outside his lodgings. In short, he was not to betray by the least hint that he knew what the present visit was about. All this was in compliance with the advice given him by Grandfather.

The inspector finally arrived, and the *assessor* who welcomed him brought him to Trinkovski's inn, where lavishly furnished rooms equipped with silver plate, usually reserved for the lords, awaited him.

Grandfather knew of the inspector's arrival two days in advance. He assembled all of the distinguished householders and advised all those not lawfully registered to leave town immediately together with their wives and children. The inspector must not find even one person who was not legally registered. It was the accepted rule to pay an inspector two hundred rubles. This time Grandfather intended to pay him three hundred rubles instead, in hopes that everything would work out just as before. Following his advice, the elders started sending all those whose names were missing from the register out of the town.

At ten o'clock in the morning the government inspector drove into Kamenets in his own coach, drawn by three horses. By twelve o'clock Grandfather sent a Jewish servant to the inspector's room to inform him of the *sborshchik*'s wish to speak with him. The inspector ordered him to be led in. Some time before that, Grandfather had instructed Trinkovski, the innkeeper, to make sure that everybody vacated the adjacent rooms so long as he was in conference with the inspector. He entered and closed the door behind him.

Grandfather started the conversation in his characteristically unique and audacious manner. "My dear lord," he said, "the registration of the Jews is, indeed, not exact, and even the tsar is aware of this, ample proof that nothing can be done about it. That's how things have been carried on since time immemorial. Every inspector who comes annually to inspect the list receives two hundred rubles, puts his signature to it certifying that everything is in the best of order, and leaves without much ado. Only because you are more obstinate, I will give you three hundred rubles, and you will leave us alone, for I am a Jew to be reckoned with and you'll achieve nothing at all. But if you insist, you will do us a great injustice by causing many people to be jailed."

The government inspector was boiling with rage. "I'll have each one of you crooks exiled to Siberia!" he screamed, "and you'll be the first!"

Undaunted, Grandfather gave him two ringing slaps across his face, and stated in a calm but mocking aside: "You should be aware that behind that door my own 'tough guys' are ready and waiting to carry you out of here feet first. And that'll be the end of you. . . . But if you wish to get out of here in one piece, I demand one thing of you: swear that you will leave immediately and forever give up your swindling post." In order to scare him even more, Grandfather shouted, "Kivke! Khatskl! Moshke! Berke! Quick!"[22]

Still stunned by the slaps, the inspector stood there with head hanging and knees buckling. Scared out of his wits, he swore to Grandfather that he was getting out of town then and there. After partially regaining his composure, he left the room together with Grandfather and ordered his horses harnessed. Half an hour later, the inspector was already far beyond the borders of Kamenets.

A few days later Grandfather received a grateful and complimentary letter from the *ispravnik,* who asked him to call at his office in Brisk as soon as possible. Upon Grandfather's arrival in Brisk, the *ispravnik* told him that the government inspector had been to see him and had reported on his impressions of the tour. He never mentioned the slaps. It was his opinion, however, that the population registration all over the province was fraudulent, and in order to update it a different registration method ought to be adopted. The annual inspection, to his mind, was pointless. One of the Jews there, the *sborshchik* from Kamenets, had even told him explicitly that the registries had always been phony. . . .

At this juncture, Grandfather told him about the slaps and the threats. The *ispravnik* was so delighted that he kissed Grandfather's head again and again amid gales of roaring laughter.

"You are the shrewdest man in the world," he kept praising Grandfather. "There's no one that can measure up to you. But tell me, all the same, how could you risk your life by pulling off such a dangerous feat?"

Grandfather then told him that he had based himself upon the *ispravnik*'s own remarks concerning the man; that he wasn't particularly smart but very vain. Such a character, he held, was easily intimidated by physical force. The easiest part was the slaps in the face, since he would never own up to such an insult. The *ispravnik* was enchanted.

Several months later, another inspector arrived in Kamenets. Grandfather slipped him the usual two hundred rubles, and he left without stirring up any fuss.

Grandfather consolidated the business of his leaseholding on vodka. He leased out at nine hundred rubles a year the other incomes, from the mills and sundry other enterprises. In this way the entire leaseholding on the sale of vodka cost him no more than three hundred rubles. Grandfather and his brother were both owners of separate taverns, for which neither had a license. . . . They plied their trade without interference. In return for this freedom and his willingness to assist him whenever necessary, Grandfather paid the *assessor* five rubles a month.

The purchase of large amounts of vodka usually entailed a great deal of excise payment, which often proved a great burden. So Grandfather used to buy massive quantities of vodka in Poland, where no excise duty was levied, and transfer it to the barrels in the dead of night. They would cunningly borrow the seal from the inspector by telling him that they didn't want to see him work too hard. They would then prepare numerous wax impressions of the seal, and stick the faked seals on the bungs of the barrels. In this way each barrel always had a seal on it confirming the payment of the excise tax. Sometimes the overseer would leave the seal in the office after work. Why bother dragging it home every day? After all, he was paid fifteen rubles a month by Grandfather, in addition to his normal salary.[23]

So, the alcohol was brought in from Poland and sold together with the vodka on which there was an excise duty. The Polish vodka had a wonderful aroma, which was also its shortcoming, as it was a sure giveaway of its source. In order to avoid discovery, a rumor was spread around the township that especially aromatic drops were added to the vodka. This immediately increased sales. Every two weeks another inspector arrived to examine the excise books, but they all accepted bribes easily and readily confirmed that everything was in the best of order.

Grandfather took all his children into the leaseholding business and they made a good living from it. The general manager was my father, Moshe, who was also in charge of the bookkeeping. Grandfather kept an eye on the business only from afar and ceased to be involved in the day-to-day affairs.

During that period, Grandfather devoted most of his time to looking after communal matters. He even abandoned his business dealings with the gentry, though quite a number of them were unwilling to sever their connection with him.

Grandfather now spent evenings at home. The room was always thronging with people come to take counsel with him, one on a personal issue, a second concerning community matters, and a third to vent his anger on someone, a fourth simply to ask advice. Consequently, the house always resounded with a deafening din of voices.

My father played an altogether different role in the community. He was gentle, soft-spoken, and renowned for his honesty. He was sparing of speech, seldom said more than a word here, a word there, but once he expressed an opinion, it was worth listening to. Whenever a dispute had to be ironed out between two parties, they engaged him as arbitrator. With his moderation and endless patience, he always succeeded in pinpointing the offending party and achieving the kind of compromise that left each side—the accuser and the accused—satisfied. So popular an arbitrator had Father become that people came to him from Brisk and from as far as Bialystok, some thirteen miles away from Kamenets.

The sweet smile that always hovered on his lips was the reason why people took to him so easily. When he said something, they pricked up their ears and took his words seriously. He conducted his lifestyle at home according to hasidic tradition. He prayed in the hasidic *shtibl,* and on Friday evenings he had scores of his fellow hasidim sitting around his table, sharing the Sabbath meal with him. They ate and sang and danced until the small hours of the morning, returned for the midday meal on the Sabbath, feasted on all sorts of kugels and drank vodka, then sang and danced once again until late in the afternoon, after which they went back to the *shtibl* for the afternoon prayers. There, they partook of the "third meal," consisting of a large challah, salted herring, and several bottles of vodka that Father brought in for them from his home. After this, the singing and dancing went on again until the evening prayers. An hour after the Sabbath ended, all the hasidim went to Father's house once more, cooked a *krupnik* soup with pieces of meat thrown in; enough wine flowed to bathe in. They sang and danced once again throughout the night. At dawn, on their way home, the tipsy hasidim kicked up such a racket that it roused the entire neighborhood.

I remember how, as a young boy, I used to run after them. I liked the way they woke the people up from their sleep. They knew well with which lord each householder conducted business. This is how, for example, they awakened Leyzer Prusker, a wealthy and respectable Jew: "Leyzer," they would shout, pounding on the shutters of his house, "Dimanski is looking for you!" Of course Leyzer got up immediately. Terrified, he opened the door, where he was confronted with the mocking laughter of the hasidim, who told him to do something which it is rude to spell out.

That's how they used to rouse the wealthy householders, though none of them were offended by it. It was, after all, nothing but an amusing diversion on their part, and the awakened householders had a good laugh at it themselves.

Innumerable candles burnt at Father's home on Friday nights, and the merriment, the riotous revelry that went on throughout the night and the Sabbath following it, is practically indescribable. I doubt if there was, in any other place in the world, the kind of joyfulness like that in our home on a Sabbath.

Six to eight well-known hasidim used to pass through Kamenets every year, and all of them, naturally, were accommodated at our house. Each one would remain for about a week, and a holiday atmosphere pervaded our home the entire time. One guest would leave and not even a few weeks would pass before another turned up and the revelry started all over again.

Once a year, the rebbe himself came to Kamenets. His arrival was preceded by three weeks of preparations, for in his wake hasidim from Brisk and all the surrounding shtetls would flock in. When the rebbe arrived, people stood in awe of him, as if he were the tsar himself. Hundreds of them ran to meet the carriage that brought their rebbe, and they led him into the township with great ceremony. I already mentioned that every hasid trembled before the rebbe and felt the awe-inspiring presence of royalty before him. The rebbe drove straight to Father's house, an honor that cost Father a few hundred rubles. Young bullocks, geese, and turkeys were slaughtered to feed some three hundred men at the special feast. They ate their fill, sang songs, and tried to grab the leftovers.[24]

Throughout the couple of days the rebbe lodged with us, none of his followers gave the least thought to their business affairs. My father, usually so reticent, threw all restraint to the wind and let himself go in his eagerness to serve his rebbe. I am at a loss to describe the enthusiasm and the riotous rejoicing that took hold of the hasidim. In his followers' fancy, the rebbe was surrounded by angels and cherubs. They trembled with emotion at the merest contact with him and worshiped him as though he were God Himself. When the rebbe left, all his fellow hasidim dispersed as well, leaving Father utterly exhausted. Small wonder! He had worked hard, day and night, for a full week.

The number of hasidic adherents began to increase steadily in Kamenets, and slowly but surely their numbers rose to as many as thirty. Most of them were Slonimer hasidim, but three were Kotskers, four Karliners, and several others Neshkhizers.[25]

They always had one reason or another to make each day a festival. One had to commemorate a famous rebbe's *yahrzeit*,[26]

another, the memory of still another rebbe, and then came the
yahrzeit of Moses himself.[27] Then there was Hanukkah, the new
moon, the Tenth of Tevet, the Fifteenth of Shvat, Purim, Shushan
Purim, Passover, Lag ba-Omer, and Shavuot! On the Ninth of Av
pails of water were spilled beneath the socks of the praying congregants.[28] They would fling burrs[29] at one another that got entangled
in their beards and were very hard to remove, which caused uproarious laughter. Afterward they would go to the graveyard, where
those burrs grew on low bushes and again got stuck in their beards
and hair. In short, the Ninth of Av was a day of laughter and amusement.[30] The Fifteenth of Av[31]—more feasting, and for the first *selihot,*[32] a special feast was prepared—*krupnik.*

All those who traveled to the rebbe for Rosh Hashanah drank
wine for days on end, from the conclusion of their prayers until
midnight. On the eve of Yom Kippur they sang, on Sukkot, *Simhat
bet ha-shoevah*[33] and throughout the intermediate week of Sukkot,
the guzzling and singing went on uninterruptedly. And all that took
place at Father's home.

Father smoked a pipe, which didn't leave his lips for days at a
time. A constant smile played on his face, during days of rejoicing
as well as during days of mourning. No one had ever seen him cry.
Of course he had his moments of sadness, but it never showed on
his face. He was a good and true hasid, out of true awareness of his
inner self. For the privilege of spending one hour in the company
of his rebbe, he would have given the world. He was never known
to lose his temper. He'd walk about, his pipe in his mouth, and
smile good-naturedly. There was nothing guileful about him. Toward
women, young wives, and maidens he was courteous, paying them
compliments or engaging in playful banter with them.

He was free of financial worries, that is, he shrank away from
them in the deep conviction that this world was but a narrow passage and that the troubles besetting a man, as well as his good fortune, were nothing but vanity of vanities. He never forgot this, even
while running his business, and never considered himself a genuine
businessman.

CHAPTER 5

YISRAEL, THE POLISH PATRIOT HASID

Yisrael • His songs and musical compositions • His role among the hasidim • Yisrael as a mathematician • The bet • His patriotism for Poland • The marches he composed in honor of the Polish victory • The betrothal agreement with the hasid • Winning the lottery • The death of Yisrael

One of the most interesting figures among the hasidim of Kamenets was Yisrael. He lived at Grandfather's home with his wife and daughter. Yisrael had a brilliant mind, and already in his youth he was considered a genius. Many years before, he had received a dowry of two thousand rubles and *kest* at his father-in-law's, a very wealthy Jew. The latter had hoped that his son-in-law would in time become a rabbi in a large town and, by marrying his only daughter, would bring him a great deal of satisfaction.

But Yisrael preferred to become a Kotsker hasid.[1] He abandoned all his studies, drove to the rebbe, and stayed at his court almost the entire year. Thanks to his great scholarly ability, his brilliant mind, his good nature, and his extraordinary talents, he became the leader of the hasidim at the rebbe's court.

One of his great gifts was revealed in singing and musical composition. He composed his own songs, and if the rebbe asked for one in honor of the Sabbath, he composed three in a row, each complete, separate, and unique. He did not know how to read notes, yet each of the songs he composed was perfection in itself and never failed to captivate his listeners.

So long as his father-in-law, Eliezer, was alive he spent more time at his rebbe's court than at home. After Eliezer's death, his two sons inherited fifteen thousand rubles, and Sarah-Beyle six thousand rubles. Although in those days in Lithuania no money was willed to daughters, her father did not neglect her.[2]

As soon as Sarah-Beyle got hold of the money, she traveled to the rebbe with the request to make her husband come home so they could set up a business of their own. They "invested" the money in a store selling cloth. Yisrael, however, spent all his time in the hasidic *shtibl* and the Sabbaths at my father's home; the running of the store was something he couldn't have cared less about. Before long, their money ran out, their financial situation went from bad to worse, and they were reduced to living on handouts from their families, which was little indeed. Now he traveled to the rebbe only twice a year, on Rosh Hashanah and Shavuot, and was forced to practice his Hasidism at home.

His wife, Sarah-Beyle, was an extremely pious woman. She used to fast every Monday and Thursday during those weeks of the year when the following portions of the Torah, *Shemot, Va'era, Bo, Beshalah, Yitro, Mishpatim, Teruma, Tetzaveh,* were read.[3] Apart from that, she attended the afternoon and evening prayers in the communal study house, insisted on counting the forty-nine days of the *omer,*[4] and recited the *selihot* prayers. She never missed a single one, let alone the afternoon and evening prayers. She always wept on reading the Psalms, the *Taytsh-khumash,* or the *Tze'enah u-re'enah.*[5]

Yisrael, on the other hand, always prayed in the hasidic *shtibl,* rushing through the prayers in less than ten minutes. Everyone was waiting for him there, for after he finished they all drank a *lehayyim* and Yisrael began entertaining his fellow hasidim. He sang his enthralling songs and the hasidim joyfully "licked their fingers." He was also a good speaker, both on worldly and religious matters, and his fellow hasidim used to stand around him listening to his beautiful hasidic lore.

Among the scholars in the township he enjoyed a special status. If they came up against a particularly difficult interpretation in the *Maharsha*[6] or a tricky point in the Talmud, or in rabbinical literature, they would turn to Yisrael. With his ingenious mind, he solved those problems, as was the practice, with sophisticated *pilpul.*[7] He knew how to turn things around and around until one was hard put to follow those lofty ideas. In each adroit interpretation one saw his extraordinary genius and knowledge.

The scholars delighted greatly in his interpretations, though in the end they were none the wiser. The questions remained unresolved or even more intricate than before. All his justifications, all the twists and turns of his brilliant mind, failed to give their queries a precise definition, and they went away with a bad feeling—*he* knew and *they* didn't, and there were no answers at hand.

Yisrael stemmed from the town of Siedlce,[8] that is, he was a Polish Jew. He knew Polish perfectly and always read the Warsaw newspapers. Only a short while after settling in Lithuania he also had such a good mastery of the Russian language that he could read a Russian newspaper effortlessly. He was a great expert on politics and was familiar with the ins and outs of the diplomatic game. Apart from that, he knew the size and strength of the various armies and their military composition: the artillery, the home guard, the infantry, as well as the names of all the distinguished generals of those armies, and so on.

He had a map of the country and knew geography. If asked the location of a particular town, he at once pinpointed it on the map. Above all, he was a gifted mathematician. Large calculations, difficult mathematical equations, or measurements he solved in his head within seconds. Working with a pen was, for him, a waste of time.

Yisrael loved to sit in Grandfather's home, especially when it was full of people. Grandfather held him in great esteem and loved to chat with him about politics. Both men were extremely intelligent, and they shared many interests. Yisrael would listen to people's conversations with a characteristic smile. Aharon-Leyzer was well aware of its meaning: how paltry those people are, how trivial their words and deeds.

I remember one occasion when Grandfather's house was packed with men, among them Kamenets's elders and scholars. The talk focused exclusively upon accounting. Yisrael got up and announced that he would solve the most difficult accounting problems within one minute, no matter how irregular and complex. I also remember clearly the question that was put to him: If Rothschild gives a loan of 1,365,000 rubles at a yearly interest of 2.5 percent, what monthly percentage does he earn?

It took Yisrael no more than a split second to come up with the answer. Everyone else took pens in hand and wrinkled their brows, sweated and reckoned, sweated and reckoned, and found his answer to be correct.

They set him a second question: If someone has one thousand pud of saffron at 425 rubles a pud, and he sells half an ounce at 37.5, 38.5, and 39.5, what is the sum total of his profit? Yisrael literally came up with the solution within a couple of seconds.[9]

He visited Father almost every evening. They sat and chatted about hasidic lore till late into the night, and he often stayed at our home from Friday night until Sunday morning. He used to sing only the songs he had composed himself and which those who gathered there knew well by then. As was customary among artists, he did not think much of hasidic songs composed by others. When they sang his songs, he would accompany the singing by waving his hand, listening intently, and if he caught a false note, would stamp his foot angrily. The songs he composed were complicated, with rising and falling scales in rapid succession, but they penetrated your very bone marrow.

When Father asked him to compose a song in honor of the Sabbath eve or a festival, he would eagerly respond. It often happened that while all the hasidim were sitting together in a group, Father would ask him to compose a melody on the spur of the moment so that the hasidim could sing it that very evening. Then he would pace back and forth in the room, raising and lowering and twirling a finger, and within half an hour compose a song that would enthrall all those present. He was certainly a unique Jew and a one-of-a-kind fellow.

In the year 1863, during the Polish uprising, Yisrael was one of its most ardent supporters. He was a true Polish patriot and most optimistic concerning Poland's chances in the uprising.[10] He was convinced Poland would once more become a great kingdom, even greater than it had been before its partition. He put a great deal of trust in Napoleon III,[11] and hoped that once the Poles succeeded in weakening the Russians, he would come with his army, help the Poles to retrieve their homeland, and make the Russians lose a considerable part of their territory.

The Poles, in Yisrael's opinion, had money worth billions. They had already paid Napoleon three hundred million francs, and they would achieve their aim. He knew the exact deployment of the Russian and Polish armies and how many soldiers each side com-

Of all of Yisrael's compositions, which still live in my memory, I present here the notes to two military marches that he dedicated to Poland. The reader will find the reasons why those marches were composed among the pages of this book. I would like to thank Mr. Pesah Kaplan,[12] who took the trouble to record the musical notes for those marches, which I sang to him from memory.[13]

manded. The Russian soldiers, he held, were illiterate, and their officers had no notion of military tactics. Napoleon had already sent a contingent of officers to the Polish rebels, and with their help they could overcome all obstacles.

He was thoroughly convinced of the Polish army's military superiority, and on reading in the newspapers of Polish victories

in scattered battles, no one was more elated than he: as though it meant the conquest of Jerusalem itself. But when he read of Polish defeats here and there, his spirits flagged though he didn't despair. He had no doubt whatsoever that just as two and two equals four, Poland would be victorious in this war.

He even composed three marches in anticipation of the Polish victory. The first—in honor of the day the tsar signs an agreement of withdrawal from all Polish territories and the victorious Polish army marches into Warsaw; the second—an accompaniment for the French contingent leaving Warsaw on its way back to France; the third—to commemorate the coronation of the Polish king and the drawing up of a new constitution. . . . He assured everyone that an independent Poland would have a liberal constitution, based on the fact that Poland had been the first country in the world to have introduced a constitution at all.[14]

Ten versts from Kamenets, in the Czemeryn Forest,[15] small skirmishes took place between the Russians and the Poles, and I still remember the salvoes of gunfire, which were heard clearly in the township. The leader of the Polish rebels in Lithuania was Oginski,[16] a great military tactician, something that caused rather a panic in the Russian camp. The Russians had two regiments encamped in the Czemeryn Forest, equipped with artillery, which they turned against Oginski's army. Oginski, on the other hand, had, I think, no more than three thousand men, without even a single cannon. Oginski was defeated and fled on his horse with three Cossacks in hot pursuit. In the midst of his flight, Oginski suddenly turned his horse around and shot all three Cossacks. From there, he fled to Pinsk. The Russians took prisoner all the important Polish noblemen who had cooperated with Oginski, killed their Polish soldiers, and took the officers with them to Kamenets. I remember that they brought them to town on a beautiful Sabbath day. About seventy men sat on the ground in the marketplace, their hands tied, and Russian soldiers stood guard over them.

When the two Russian regiments with their artillery entered Kamenets, the town began to hum with activity. Yisrael, witnessing the Polish defeat, wept like a child. I clearly recall how, that Saturday night, when many people gathered at Grandfather's house, Yisrael traced on the table, with a piece of chalk, the deployment of the Polish and Russian armies in those places where the uprising was still going on.

"This is only the beginning," he said. "The defeat in Czemeryn is nothing. Muravyov[17] will hang the noblemen, but that, too, is nothing. In comparison with the wealth and might of Poland," he said, rubbing out with one hand the Russian army he had earlier traced on the table, "the Russians are less than nothing."

Meanwhile, Russian soldiers arrived at the door. They wanted brandy, and this was, after all, a tavern. The door was bolted and someone had to open it, but everyone was seized with fear and no one dared. This was nothing to be trifled with—those were soldiers! Yisrael stationed himself at the door, preventing anyone from removing the bolt. The soldiers didn't wait and immediately broke the door down. The first person they set eyes upon was, of course, Yisrael. They landed him two blows in the face that made the blood ooze from between his teeth.

After the soldiers had left, someone said to Yisrael, "Didn't you, this very minute, give us an account underrating the Russians, declaring them to be nothing and not worth reckoning with . . ."

"Those are soldiers?" Yisrael answered bitterly, "Those are bandits!"

After a while, when the Poles suffered one defeat after another, it became clear that there was no more room for hope. Yisrael took it very much to heart. He started drinking, drowning his melancholy in the bitter drop. When this heavy drinking began to affect his health, he decided to travel to his rebbe, from whom he returned in high spirits. The rebbe had advised him to drink vodka mixed with some olive oil—the alcohol to cure the soul and bring joy back to it; the olive oil to cure the body, it would heal the heart and strengthen it.[18] From then on, whenever Yisrael came to Father's house, he brought with him a small bottle of olive oil, and when the time came for the hasidim to drink a *lehayyim,* he always added a few drops of it to the drink. For this reason, Yisrael used to drink a great deal and also composed new tunes.

Once, during a visit to the Kotsker rebbe, Yisrael was having a chat with a close friend from one of the surrounding shtetls. Between one sip and another, Yisrael told him, as was common among Jews, that he had a three-year-old daughter, an only child, for God hadn't blessed him with a kaddish.[19] He fervently wished this daughter, on coming of age, to marry a righteous Jew. His friend replied that he had a three-year-old son with a bright head on his shoulders and suggested that they arrange a match between the children then and there, since they would certainly be able to turn his son into a true hasid.

Yisrael was taken with the idea, and both fathers confirmed the engagement with a handshake. The betrothal contract would be drawn up as soon as both children turned twelve, and when David, the future groom, was bar mitzvah, they would perform the wedding ceremony.[20] This understanding was sealed with several glasses of the choicest wine, after which both men went to the rebbe to obtain his blessing. Yisrael and his friend, Baruch, had been among the first Kotsker hasidim, and they always sat at the head of the table, near their rebbe. The rebbe himself poured three glasses of wine to drink to the success of the match, hoping that the boy, David, would turn into a pious Jew and that this match would produce a generation of true hasidim and righteous men.

On returning to Kamenets, Yisrael congratulated his wife on the match he had arranged with the rebbe's blessing. Sarah-Beyle, a sober, no-nonsense woman, turned livid with rage and showered him, as never before, with a barrage of curses. "May you have only a black dream on your head! You crazy idiot! Fancy taking two three-year-olds that haven't even measled and pocked as yet and arranging a match between them!"

Yisrael also lost his temper and for the first time in his life shouted at her. "The nerve of you! When I tell you that the rebbe himself blessed the match, you should have faith. You fresh mouth!"

They had a big row. Yisrael left the house and went to Father to tell him the whole story. Father did not, of course, justify Sarah-Beyle's behavior and her lack of faith in the rebbe, but tried, though unsuccessfully, to restore the peace between them. Yisrael threatened to leave home and stay at the rebbe's court until the children grew up. Only when they got married would he go back to his wife.

Father, who was strangely fond of Yisrael, realized that once he went to live at the rebbe's home, he was not likely to return. At the rebbe's he would be content; he would sit at the zaddik's table, eat, drink, compose melodies, and dance—he would lack for nothing at all.

Father then suggested that he move into our place. He'd give him a room, and they would keep each other company as before. Yisrael readily accepted the offer, for he, too, loved my father dearly. Vodka flowed like water at our home, and it was always full of hasidim. And so he moved in with us.

It had been Father's intention to bring about an eventual reconciliation between him and his wife. Sarah-Beyle was, after all, a rare woman, intelligent and pious. Prior to this incident they had lived happily together, despite the fact that her childhood wish of becoming a rabbi's wife had not materialized.

But there is a God in Heaven and He came to their assistance. A new year came, and in the month of Tevet the prospective father-in-law, Baruch, won fifty thousand rubles in the Polish lottery. He immediately sent a wire to Kamenets. Sarah-Beyle, forgetting her quarrel with her husband, ran in all haste to Father's house to happily inform her husband of the great news. She begged his forgiveness and said, "Now I certainly believe in your rebbe." Only then did peace reign once more in their household.

The prospective father-in-law sent the bride small necklaces of gold, rings, and pearls, and enough silk cloth for several dresses. And Zisl, the little three-year-old girl, walked about adorned like a princess. Yisrael looked up his in-laws living in Mezeritz,[21] and from there they traveled together to the Kotsker rebbe. In his presence they once again confirmed the match with a solemn handshake, and Baruch presented the zaddik with a gift of twelve thousand rubles.[22] Yisrael returned home, happy and content, and Sarah-Beyle was, of course, delighted as well.

When Zisl turned twelve, Yisrael and Sarah-Beyle took the bride along with them to Mezeritz to sign the betrothal contract. But by that time Baruch was no longer so rich. The dowry he could afford was now no more than a thousand rubles. When both children turned thirteen, the wedding was held in Mezeritz, and Zisl remained on *kest*[23] at the home of her in-laws. Yisrael and Sarah-Beyle returned home to Kamenets. Now he was completely free to spend all his days and nights with his fellow hasidim at Father's house, sipping his vodka laced with olive oil, and composing melodies.[24]

After Sarah-Beyle's death, Yisrael tired of the company of his fellow hasidim, gave up drinking and composing, and started writing a book of casuistic commentaries to the talmudic tractate *Pesahim*. He took the manuscript to great rabbis for their approbation,[25] but he did not succeed in obtaining even a single one. The reason was that the ninety-page book contained no more than six commentaries, and none of the rabbis had the patience to plow through even one of Yisrael's highly profound, deep, and intricate expositions.

Rabbi Isaac of Slonim,[26] who had a great sense of humor, told him that his book was aimed at the minds of angels rather than those of human beings. Yisrael was deeply insulted by this remark. From too much mental exertion he became ill in Warsaw and died there. The Kotsker rebbe and many followers were at his side during his final hours,[27] and a throng of hasidim from Warsaw attended his funeral.

CHAPTER 6

THE HANDSHAKE

Our family • Grandmother • Her love for her husband • Her treatment of others • Yudl • Community affairs • Lipe • The handshake

randfather loved to quote a particular proverb—"May the earth spew forth the bones of one who gives up his own child."[1] In fact, there was an extremely close relationship between Grandfather and his brother. This brother, his only child, and his family lived in the same house together with Grandfather's own children and grandchildren like one extended family. If a member of this family happened to take ill, all the others stood by his bed, not leaving the sick person on his own for even a moment.

Our family was known for its singular brotherhood, ruled by the gentle and tactful hand of my beloved grandmother, Beyle-Rashe. It was she who kept a constant watch over a sick family member. If a daughter-in-law was about to give birth, this mother-in-law was at her side; a daughter—this mother. If a child or a grandchild took ill—it was this grandmother. She was the one to consult a doctor or a healer. If the sick person needed anything, it was she who arranged it all.

In her house, food was always available for the children and grandchildren; and whoever entered the house was immediately given something to eat. She, herself, never ate, but was simply waiting for someone—for this or that grandchild, or a daughter-in-law—to drop in so she could feed them. Feeding others seemed to satisfy her. Only rarely was she seen eating anything herself. If she was cooking a savory dish, she contented herself with the tiniest of tastes before dividing the rest among her guests. Although she had two maids to help her, she did all the baking, roasting, and frying herself. She was a wonderful cook. Day after day, she sent pots full of food to the community poorhouse. Nor did she forget to help the individual poor and destitute, to whom she provided food in secret, lifting their spirits. She herself was a tiny, skinny woman whose body seemed barely to sustain her soul, but she had the drive and energy of a man.

Her husband, Aharon-Leyzer, was as dear to her—as the women's saying goes—"as the Sabbath." Grandfather loved to be pampered and to eat well. So Grandmother used to cook a special dish for him every day. Her greatest misfortune was for him to discover, God forbid, a fly in the food. He'd then refuse outright to go on with the meal, and Grandmother would hurry to her sister-in-law's in hope of finding some tasty dish for Grandfather. Failing that, she'd return and beg him to wait no more than "a minute" till she prepared another choice dish for him. But he, as if to annoy her, would be unwilling to wait, something that caused Grandmother a great deal of distress.

Grandfather loved a glass of good tea, so she always made sure that his tea was especially strong and aromatic. If he made the rounds of the estates, he had to tell her at what time he'd be back— preferably the approximate hour—so she could prepare the samovar for him. If, for example, he returned at midnight on a Monday, she would take the samovar upstairs to their bedroom. Since the maid would be asleep by then, Grandmother used to sit beside the samovar, feeding it with pieces of coal every now and then to keep the water seething and ensure that, as soon as Aharon-Leyzer came home, he'd have a glass of boiling-hot tea to drink. That's the way a Jewish wife used to behave in those days.

That was how she watched over the samovar all night long, so that it would boil properly. Occasionally, Grandfather stayed over for several nights at the home of one of the gentry. Then, she would doze off fully dressed, awaken with a start and add another piece of coal, and then doze off again. During the day the maid was ordered to keep the samovar constantly on the boil.

Aharon-Leyzer was a very stubborn man. If he said "yes," there were no two ways about it, and if he said "no," no amount of pleading would change his mind. If he were in the company of other people at a time Grandmother needed him on some urgent matter, she would approach him meekly and with great humility, apologizing for intruding while he was preoccupied. On such occasions, he would wave her away impatiently with his hand. She would, of course, do as he wished, never taking offense.

It often happened, however, that people coming for advice to Aharon-Leyzer asked for his wife to be present during their consultations, for she was known all over the town for the astute advice she gave whenever asked. He would then call her in and say, "Those people want your advice on a certain matter." They would put the problem to her and she would give her opinion, though not before a speaking a little preamble of her own: "I'm actually no more than a foolish woman, but it seems to me that this is what you ought to do. . . ." In most cases they took her advice.

She never sat down beside her husband but stood respectfully in front of him, despite the fact that he owed her his social standing, and she directed much of his dealings with the lords. She took care not to have him commit a folly in his dealings by pretending to be the fool herself, not he. In short, Grandfather relied on her advice in most of his business affairs, while she acted as if she had no hand in them at all.

Her father, Yudl, became a widower in his old age, and none of his children lived with him. His three sons were Torah scholars but not well-off, and each lived in a different township. Grandmother Beyle-Rashe was his only daughter, and she asked him to come and live at her place for a while. He was a highly intelligent Jew and extremely popular with his fellow townsmen, so much so that Aharon-Leyzer would not have him live anywhere else but at his home for the rest of his life. The old man sold off his house in Semyatich with all his belongings and went to live with his son-in-law in Kamenets, who treasured him like the apple of his eye.

Great-Grandfather Yudl closely followed his son-in-law's pursuits and came to the conclusion—which was not particularly difficult to arrive at—that his preoccupation with communal affairs was making him crazed. Day and night, he noticed, his home hummed with people pestering him with various matters concerning the community. It was a pity, the old man thought, that Aharon-Leyzer was wasting his business acumen on trivial things, more numerous even than in a much larger township. He therefore thought it advisable for his son-in-law to give up his preoccupation with communal matters and devote himself exclusively to his dealings with the gentry, which, at least, were of a profitable nature. If not, then it would be better for him to travel to Brisk, where he would, before long, be known for his competence and good sense. To be a leader *there,* in a large city, would be much more preferable to *here,* in little Kamenets. There, at the very least, he would busy himself with the issues of a city full of respectable and intelligent men, of Torah scholars and enlightened people.

The old man, Yudl, kept nagging his daughter, Beyle-Rashe, to explain this to her husband. But Grandfather's response was that under no circumstances would he leave Kamenets. Here, his father and father's forefathers lay buried, as would he when his time came. Here was where he'd devoted his entire life and dispensed most of his energy. Even if given millions, he would never leave Kamenets. Though as far as communal affairs were concerned, he agreed, he ought to give them up. They were getting more and more difficult for him to handle. He invested so much effort into them and it still wasn't enough.

He decided once again to resign from his communal duties and was only waiting for an opportune moment. As soon as word got around that Aharon-Leyzer intended to resign his position, all the important householders gathered at his home and begged him to continue. If he found it difficult, let him divide up the work between them and they would be happy to assist him. They talked and talked and would not take "no" for an answer until he agreed to continue for a while longer, if only to see whether this eased his burden. After some time, Grandfather himself changed the rules of management. He called a general assembly to be attended by all the town elders and began to apportion out various tasks, which they accepted willingly.

Aharon-Leyzer was able to free himself of a great deal of thought-diverting entanglements, thanks to his father-in law, Yudl, who himself didn't have much else to do. Yudl began handling the many people that still came to Grandfather's home, giving advice, listening to their complaints, and so on.

Grandmother, who, until then, out of respect for her husband, had never intervened when he was talking unless called in by him for consultation, now felt freer to do so with her father having taken over much of her husband's functions at home. She now expressed her opinions without the former constraints, and between them she and her father succeeded in relieving Aharon-Leyzer completely of his communal duties.

Once again, Grandfather was able to devote most of his time to his business with the lords, and Grandmother could no longer undress at the end of the day. Instead she would doze off fully dressed, getting out of bed again and again to add more coal to the samovar, so that Grandfather would have his hot cup of tea the moment he returned home.

Grandfather had a brother-in-law, an eminent Torah scholar by the name of Lipe. This Lipe was a pauper, and he once sent a letter to his brother-in-law, to Grandfather, requesting his help to find him some sort of livelihood. Grandfather invited him to come to his house and proposed a deal that would benefit him greatly; he would not lack a thing, and even Grandfather would gain something from it. Lipe gave him a puzzled look, unable to get to the bottom of Grandfather's intentions. What did he mean, "providing him with a livelihood from which he, Aharon-Leyzer, also gained something for himself?"

This is what Grandfather told him: "Let's make the following 'deal.' I will see to all the needs of your wife and children, and you will sit and study Torah. But you have to give me a signed statement, whereby you agree to hand over to me half of the rewards you are entitled to in the world to come on account of your studying the Torah here on earth.[2] I, God be praised, have been nothing but a simple man, a man of this world throughout my life, but have gained no reward from it. I'll at least be assured of a small part in the world to come. I fear that once I enter the next world, my fate will be a miserable one. No *ispravnik* or *assessor* will be there to support me."

Lipe was speechless. Words failed him. He was unable to fathom why Aharon-Leyzer, who enjoyed this world to the full, should also want to secure a place in the next world. He told him that he had to talk it over with his wife, Furiye, Aharon-Leyzer's sister.

Several months went by, but neither Lipe nor his wife was ready to hand over half of Lipe's share in the world to come to Aharon-Leyzer. They suffered a great deal of privation. Their small children were in need of shoes and clothing, tuition fees, and other such daily necessities. Aharon-Leyzer supported them, but with only just enough food to keep body and soul together. They lived in dire poverty but refused to enter into any partnership concerning the world to come. Aharon-Leyzer was ready to reduce his share of the partnership. He now asked for only half of the time Lipe devoted to his studies, and made no demands whatsoever on the other religious obligations Lipe performed.

Aharon-Leyzer, of course, resented this kind of behavior toward him. First of all, he was passionate about getting his share of the next world, and second, he was not used to having his wishes denied. He therefore decided to do a little something about it: he cut off their food support altogether. As a result, Lipe, his wife, and children were left without even a crust of bread or a potato in the house, and the family was reduced to virtual starvation.

Their condition became unbearable. They suffered torments, struggled along, and finally lost heart. That was when Furiye submitted to the proposed deal. "Go and give up to that evil man half of your share of the next world," she said to her husband. "I can't bear to see the children starve any longer." So, greatly dejected, he went to Aharon-Leyzer and told him that he agreed to the proposed deal.

He agreed to the terms . . . but Aharon-Leyzer, who was by then quite offended, disdainfully answered, "I am no longer interested in the deal. Before, you refused to hand over half your share of paradise?! Now it's too late. Get out of here and start worrying yourself about how you are going to support your wife."

It was obvious that Aharon-Leyzer's heart was set on getting his share of the next world. He understood full well that it was his sister who had opposed the deal, and he wanted his sister and only his sister to come to him and plead with him to change his mind. He also wanted her to endorse this agreement by putting her own signature to the same statement he'd make her husband sign.

Lipe failed to understand Aharon-Leyzer's intentions. You can imagine with what a heavy heart he returned home. The house was full of weeping and wailing, of children begging for a morsel of bread to eat, and there was nothing to give them. As though they were being led to the slaughter, Lipe and his wife dragged themselves to Aharon-Leyzer. They wept before him and pleaded that he agree to the partnership.

"So be it," Aharon-Leyzer replied calmly. "Let's go to the rabbi and sign a contract for life. I'll see to all your needs no less than I would for my own children, and you, Lipe, will give me half your share of the world to come from your Torah study." But Lipe agreed to only three years, not a whole lifetime. They finally compromised upon a five-year period.

They went to the rabbi and drew up a contract according to the agreement they had reached. Lipe and Furiye signed, the rabbi and the *dayan* signed as witnesses. The parties to the agreement vowed on a solemn handshake, according to which Aharon-Leyzer was to provide the family generously with all its needs and Lipe would, in return, give up half his share of the world to come that he earned through his studies. Lipe promised to devote his time exclusively to studying the Torah day and night and do nothing else, and the agreement became binding.

Aharon-Leyzer returned home filled with indescribable joy. This was no trivial matter—Aharon-Leyzer's happiness. Such luck! Had he been offered all the riches of the universe he would not have exchanged it for his half-share in the world to come.

Lipe and Furiye, on the other hand, returned home with mixed feelings. Nevertheless, there was the gleam of a twenty-five-ruble coin in Lipe's hand, which did account for something, after all.

From now on, Aharon-Leyzer kept their home lavishly provided, virtually flowing with milk and honey. When Lipe and his brood ate their fill at home for the first time in their lives, the deal he'd made took on an altogether different complexion, one that he began to like.

CHAPTER 7

THE SCANDAL WITH
THE *ASSESSOR*

The excise tax • Baron Günzburg • The "only child" • The scandal with the *assessor* • The *ispravnik* sides with Grandfather • Lipe reneges on the agreement

In those days the levying of the excise tax passed from the government to Baron Yozel Günzburg.[1] He leased it for a specific sum of money paid annually to the government.[2] The clerks Günzburg employed in the excise offices were all Jews, from the highest down to the humblest position in some backwater village.[3]

By that time, Grandfather had stopped smuggling vodka in from Poland. He was delighted at the fact that the government had placed such a contract in Jewish hands. As it happened, at that time, his business was doing so well that he decided not to smuggle in any more vodka lest such an act bankrupt the Baron! . . . It would also harm the Jews in general and give the Jew-baiters an excuse to slander all Jews, accusing them of thievery.

Besides, the Baron's attitude toward his fellow Jews was most commendable. By appointing them as clerks, he provided a living for thousands of them.[4] It simply warmed the cockles of one's heart to see Jews working as officials in the government treasury offices.

From that time on, Grandfather purchased all his vodka from local distilleries, as a result of which the family's income was greatly reduced. The profits made on the Polish alcohol had amounted to thousands of rubles! And since Grandfather's children as well as those of his brother derived their livelihoods exclusively from the leaseholdings, their incomes dwindled considerably, forcing Grandfather to cut down on his expenses.

Grandfather, in order to conserve his resources, found that the five rubles he paid the *assessor* every month had now become superfluous. First of all, the lord's steward put at his disposal as many peasants as were needed, and he very rarely required the *assessor's* help. Furthermore, Grandfather had nothing to fear from the *assessor*, for the *ispravnik* was on his side and rendered the *assessor* powerless.

This, naturally, greatly infuriated the *assessor*. I remember one day, I was then but a small child, the bailiff and three of his gendarmes entered our tavern and demanded a bottle of vodka. It was a Saturday evening, when Grandfather's house was usually packed with people and Grandmother was serving them tea. It was a task she took upon herself despite the fact that she had enough servants to do it for her. She never tired of handing each his glass of tea, even a second, and a third. . . .

Grandfather's nephew, the "only child,"[5] idolized his uncle, meaning my grandfather, and was ready to follow him through fire and water. Grandfather, too, was very fond of him, and consequently he was the most dominant member within the family. If anyone needed a favor from Grandfather, he would turn to this "only child"—Arye-Leyb—to act as a go-between.

He was a tall, strapping fellow and even knew how to study Torah (though his heart wasn't in it). But he was a kind-hearted man. When Arye-Leyb said he would get something from his uncle, one could be certain that he would. Furthermore, he had a sharp and witty tongue, and when Grandfather needed to inform either the *ispravnik* or the *assessor* of something, he would send glib-tongued Arye-Leyb to them. All those qualities added to his popularity, and he was liked and respected by all who knew him.

When the bailiff ordered that bottle of vodka and Arye-Leyb asked his uncle if he should give it to him, Grandfather consented. He was given the bottle, which disappeared quickly into his deep pocket, and he hastily left the tavern with his peasants in tow. Arye-Leyb did not catch what was going on and asked Grandfather: "Shall I run after them to retrieve the bottle of vodka?"

"Yes, do so this very minute," Grandfather ordered him, "and if necessary, use force."

We had a couple of "tough guys" working for us then, one was Khatskl and the other Kivke. The latter, especially, was famous for his strength. Arye-Leyb took both along in his pursuit of the bailiff and his men.

Fifteen minutes passed and Arye-Leyb returned, happy and content, with the bottle of vodka in his hand as well as the bailiff's cap. He told us that they had caught up with the gang on the very porch of the *assessor*'s house. A minute later and they would have been inside and saved their skins. But they came in for murderous blows instead, and here was the cap to confirm it.

"Did I do the right thing, Uncle?" Arye-Leyb asked.

"You did," Grandfather replied.

Early Sunday morning, Grandfather set out, as usual, on his rounds of the estates. Around midday the *assessor* arrived with eighteen gendarmes and entered my uncle's house in order to make out an official report to the effect that he was running an unlicensed tavern. Arye-Leyb gave him a proper dressing down and warned him that if he wrote out that report he would break his bones then and there, and raised a threatening fist. . . .

What would an *assessor* accompanied by eighteen gendarmes usually do in such a case? Catch the fellow, arrest him, and send him in chains to Brisk. But he did no such thing. He evidently recalled whom he was up against, the *ispravnik* and Aharon-Leyzer! He went away and penned a letter to the *ispravnik,* describing in detail what had been going on.

In reply, the *ispravnik* wrote him a letter reprimanding him for his lack of common sense in getting into a row with such a wise Jew as Aharon-Leyzer. He advised him to apologize to Grandfather and make his peace with him. But if the *assessor* turned down this advice, on his visits to Kamenets, he, the *ispravnik,* would put up only at Aharon-Leyzer's, not at the *assessor*'s home, as was the custom of all *ispravniks*. That would, of course, greatly offend the *assessor.*

The *ispravnik* also sent a letter to Grandfather in which he asked him to reserve a couple of rooms for him on his arrival in Kamenets. Grandfather promptly prepared them for him at his brother Mordechai-Leyb's home, with a separate entrance. After Grandfather notified him that everything was ready, the *ispravnik* arrived in Kamenets with four horses and a ringing bell, and made straight for Uncle's house. He also put up in those rooms for a day or two whenever the need arose.

Humiliated and humbled, the *assessor* was obliged to call on the *ispravnik* there, and often Grandfather was there in his company. All this was done with the aim of demonstrating his close relationship with Grandfather to the *assessor.*

A year and a half passed before the *assessor* gave in and apologized to Grandfather in the *ispravnik*'s presence. Only then did the latter put up once again at the *assessor*'s home, as he used to years before.

Meanwhile, Grandfather delegated a great deal of the communal affairs to the town elders, instead of carrying the entire burden on his own shoulders. He asked the *ispravnik* to hand the seal and the books over to the new *sborshchik,* and he himself would intervene only when necessary. He would do all in his power to see that everything functioned properly, as it had up till then. Now Grandfather simply acted in the capacity of advisor to the new *sborshchik* and the town elders. Only when some especially sticky problem cropped up did they come to Grandfather for help. Things settled down and peace and quiet reigned in the township.

Whenever the *ispravnik* was due to arrive, the *sborshchik* first went to Grandfather for consultation before calling on him. Only if there was a particularly important matter to discuss did Grandfather join him on his visit, to bring things to a positive conclusion.

While Grandfather carried on his dealings with the lords, his half-share of the world to come via Lipe's scholarly efforts grew apace. It spurred Grandfather to work harder and contributed greatly to his peace of mind. The knowledge of his half-share in the next world kept him alive. But Grandfather's contentment was to be short-lived. At the end of the fourth year, his brother-in-law Lipe sent him a letter canceling the handshake and the five-year partnership. He had been newly appointed *dayan* in the town, following the death of the former incumbent, and now had a steady income without strings attached, so he no longer saw the need to give up half his share in the next world.

The letter was a severe blow for Grandfather. Throughout the following six months until Yom Kippur this wise man was sunk in a deep depression and melancholy. On Yom Kippur he cried bitterly during prayers, and only after that did he calm down. But he cut off his relationship with his sister for the rest of his life, and blamed her for all his troubles.

CHAPTER 8

MY MELAMDIM

My first melamed • The questions I raised • My second melamed • My Uncle Yisrael • Yisrael the prodigy • How the prodigy Yisrael flogged us in the meadow • With Motke the melamed • Hell • Winter evenings • Tales about magic • My piety • The dybbuk • Lipe Zukerman

*W*hen I was two and a half years old my mother handed me over to Yaakov-Ber, the infants' melamed.[1] She didn't have the patience to wait until the summer when I'd turn three, but enrolled me in the heder straight after Sukkot. Already as a toddler I was most keen on learning and kept hanging around Yaakov-Ber even when it was time for me to go home. I would sit on top of the stove in the heder where it was pleasant and warm. He had about a hundred pupils, and when the boys from the more well-to-do homes got fed up with learning, they climbed on top of the big stove and played games. I felt so good up there that I didn't want to get off. But when all the boys were taken down, I couldn't stay up there on my own. I was taken home by the melamed's assistant.[2]

But Yaakov-Ber was not satisfied with me. Already from early childhood I was extremely inquisitive and kept pestering him with awkward questions, which the poor man was at a loss how to answer. For example: When he started teaching me the *alef-beys* he made me repeat endlessly, *komets alef*—"o"; *komets beys*—"bo"; and *komets veys*—"vo." I asked what need there was to repeat *komets veys*—"vo" and *komets vav*—"voo."[3]

"When you grow up," the melamed replied unwillingly, "you'll understand."

There are children who keep asking their mothers and fathers, "Why does one need this, why that?" I was like one of those children, nagging my teacher with questions, such as, "Who made the table?"

"The carpenter," was the reply.

"And who made the carpenter?"

"God."

"And who made God?"

"God!" he shouted in exasperation, "God has always been! And nobody made Him!"

"Did God make Himself?" I asked, looking the melamed straight in the eye.

"You're still a foolish child," he said, all but murdering me with his eyes.[4]

When the melamed told Father about my constantly pestering him with such questions, Father told him to rebuke me as soon as I started asking. "Tell him," he suggested, "that a small boy doesn't need to ask any questions. A small boy should just learn and keep quiet."

Nevertheless, my questions, the questions of his young son, troubled Father. He feared that such a child might, God forbid, turn into a heretic. Perhaps it would be better for the child to learn a little less. Maybe it was preferable to turn him over even earlier than usual to hasidic teachers, who would teach him to be a God-fearing hasid.

After learning with Yaakov-Ber for three terms, I was already able to pray as fluently as an older pupil, and then Father brought me to the hasidic melamed, Shaye-Bezalel, who taught Bible and Talmud to beginners.

When I started learning the Bible with this melamed, Father gave a feast in honor of the event for all his fellow hasidim. The whole day they sang, drank vodka, and ate like kings. Grandfather, however, did not join the merrymaking, for he never sat down with hasidim.

I was a bright pupil, and my melamed started teaching me *Rashi*.[5] So easily did I master everything I was taught, by the time I turned six I was ready to begin the Talmud. But my teacher thought it was too early for that.

"It is enough that you begin studying Gemara at age seven," said the melamed.

So I used to hang around the table where the boys were studying the Talmud and listen intently to their lessons instead of joining in the games of the younger children still learning the Bible. I listened closely to what was being said, so that, come Thursday,[6] I told the melamed I was ready to repeat by heart all the Talmud he had taught throughout the week. I began to recite from *Lekah tov:* "If Reuven stole from Shimon, does this mean he also stole money from Shimon?" I remember that it flowed smoothly, like water. The melamed was truly astonished, and coming to see Father in the evening, told him what a gifted son he had, who, without learning, simply by listening, was able to repeat the entire lesson by rote, word for word.

But Father was far from pleased. He was a fanatical hasid who set no store by learning as such. All he wanted me to know was the Bible and a little bit of the Midrash. There was no need to know more than that so long as I became a pious Jew—in other words, a hasid.

Shaye-Bezalel started teaching me the Talmud and I, who had a nimble mind, was an outstanding pupil. I was so quick on the uptake that every Thursday I easily rattled off all of the *Lekah tov* I had learned during that week. After some time I felt that Shaye-Bezalel with his little bit of *Lekah tov* was no longer good enough for me. I wanted to study with a more advanced melamed who taught a column, or even an entire page of the Talmud.

But Father was in no such hurry. He kept me with Shaye-Bezalel for nine terms, and I had to grind out the same lessons together with the younger pupils again and again. Father believed that I would eventually know how to learn on my own, and in any case one need not study too much. The main point was that I become a true hasid. I pleaded with him to let me learn Talmud, that I had had enough of *Lekah tov,* that I wanted to study together with the older boys. But Father was deaf to all my entreaties, for precisely that reason.

Father had a younger brother called Yisrael who was my age. Grandfather put him in my father's charge, and he sent both of us to the same heder, had us wear each other's clothes and sleep in the same room. Yisrael was even smarter than I but did not like to learn. He could not have cared less that our melamed was Shaye-Bezalel. Actually, he preferred it, since he did not have to exert himself at all. In spite of his unusual intelligence, he did not even know the bit of *Lekah tov* for the Thursday examinations; all his efforts were expended on playing pranks on others.

In our family there was another boy also called Yisrael, two years older than I, but who had the mind of a real genius.[7] His father was Yoyzl Vishniak, a renowned scholar and the nephew of my great-grandfather Yudl. He held a post in Lublin, whereas his wife, Bashe-Fayge, lived with her children at her father Zelig's home.

Their son, eight-year-old Yisrael, exhausted the best of melamdim. On each and every small talmudic phrase he asked endless questions, for which none of them could provide answers. It goes without saying the whole family was very proud of him. He spent most of his time at our house, eating, drinking, and playing games with us. Because of him, everyone ignored Yisrael and me, giving all their attention to him, and only to him.

But I and my pal Yisrael, who was, as you may remember, my uncle as well, disliked him intensely. Were it not for his presence in our house, we might have been considered the brightest kids in the township, and the family would have been even prouder of us. Yet, in spite of our dislike of this Yisrael, we also had a great deal of respect for him. We even felt strangely honored if he deigned to talk with us. But he had a wicked streak in his character, and the boys of the township preferred to steer clear of him. If he beat us up, we didn't show any resistance; we were resigned to the beatings, just like pupils in the heder submitted to their melamed's raps.

I remember one Friday, after we were released from heder, when he decided to examine several of the more well-to-do boys of the town in their knowledge of the Talmud. I recall him choosing for that purpose the tractate *Bava Metziah,* and setting out with twelve boys across the meadow leading toward Simha-Leyzer's house.

It was a beautiful summer's day. Yisrael put the Talmud down beside him and cut with his pocketknife several tender but long birch twigs. He allotted each boy a different passage, and whoever did not know how to interpret it to his satisfaction had to lie down on the ground and submit to as many strokes as Yisrael deemed necessary.

No one cried. Everyone was restrained. We received his punishment gratefully, and to tell the truth, we were all absolutely convinced that we deserved the thrashing he gave us. We were all ignorant goyim, did not know our Talmud, whereas he, Yisrael, was the true scholar. Even when we could no longer bear the pain and started crying out, Yisrael would not let up, but hit even harder, shouting,

"That's what you deserve, a goy like you! That's what you deserve!"

He left our bodies black and blue and covered with dried blood. He told me to repeat the chapter *Ha-mafkid*,[8] but at that time I had not yet started learning Gemara and was still chewing over sections from *Lekah tov*, so I knew nothing of what he asked. He gave me eighteen lashes—for the number *hai*,[9] he said—but they were so brutal and painful that I still remember them to this day.

Some time later we all returned home, practically beaten to a pulp, with tearful eyes, shamed and humiliated, but without a word of complaint—after all, we had deserved it! The boys began to be more scared of the floggings Yisrael gave them than of those of the melamed. The melamed, at least, did it with some degree of mercy, and his switch didn't have such tender, fresh, and long twigs as the ones Yisrael cut down in the meadow.

But God took pity on us, and a short while later Yoyzl took his son back home to Lublin because there was no teacher in Kamenets capable of keeping up with him. Our joy in getting rid of that Yisrael was boundless.

When I turned eight, Father sent me to study with Motke the melamed, whose heder I ought to have attended two years earlier. He was an excellent teacher, and did not flog his pupils a great deal, and they did well in their studies. He studied the Talmud with his students and worked wonders. Above all, he used to spend one hour a day telling us tales about great scholars, and all about the world to come, and how the wicked are tormented for hundreds of years after their deaths. And he held forth at length about the trail traversed by the dead; how the angels of destruction pounce upon a wicked soul on its way to Hell; the levels of Hell; how the wicked are burnt, and so on, and so on.[10]

He told us that every righteous soul has to suffer the torments of *hibut ha-kever*,[11] which I described earlier.[12] After this each one is told to proceed to Hell, where they, including the most virtuous among them, are forced to remain for twelve months.[13] On their way to Hell they are intercepted by angels of destruction, who smite them with iron rods and then hurl them into a mountain of fire. From there they are thrown into a mountain of ice and then back and forth again.[14] Especially wicked souls are hurled from one angel of destruction to the next, a distance of twelve hundred years; in other words, it takes twelve hundred years before such a soul finally drops onto the above-mentioned mountain of fire. And, as if that were not enough, on his way there he will encounter sixty thousand additional angels of destruction, each of whom will flog him with a red-hot iron rod. Only then is he ordered to enter Hell, where he must purify himself for the next twelve months. No one stays there for more than a year. By the time one reaches Hell, things are not that bad any more, but until one gets there, one has to endure hundreds of years of fire, water, and ice, torture, and suffering. . . .

Our melamed, trying to be absolutely realistic, even took up pen and ink and traced for us the full extent of this inferno on a sheet of paper. According to his estimation it is twelve hundred years long and four hundred years wide.

Another obstacle on reaching Hell is that no one has a notion as to where its exit is. Did one but know it, one could go straight there and evade the constantly raining blows of the angels of destruction. Instead, everyone gropes about in a vain search for the door, catching blows right and left.

The melamed demonstrated to us with a finger how a person standing right by the door then begins to move backward all the time. Now he'll have to retrace his steps for 400 years along one side, and 1,200 years along the other, then another 400 years lengthwise, as well as 1,199 years and 11 months, because the door is so tiny and so well-concealed that the poor man keeps turning round and round among the rod-wielding angels of destruction for 3,199 years. The righteous soul, on the other hand, finds the door sooner or later and need not spin around for so many years.

Apart from all that, the melamed loved telling us about the miraculous deeds of the Gaon of Vilna, who was familiar with the seven wisdoms.[15] He would gaze at the stars, and if he wanted to ascertain the size of a particular star and what was taking place on it, he would simply bring all the stars down upon his table and study them assiduously.[16]

Once, our melamed told us, the Gaon of Vilna attended the wedding of a very wealthy man, who asked him to do something that would amuse the bride and groom. "I'll sit down next to the musicians," said the Gaon. He sat down beside them and listened intently to their music. After several moments, he asked for a hole to be pierced into the clarinet of one of the players, and pointed to the exact spot on the instrument. The clarinet would sound much better, and the guests would derive more pleasure from it. After an additional hole was pierced into the clarinet, and the musician started playing on it, the music sounded so sweet to the ears of the listeners that many of them fell into a swoon, and the hole had to be stopped up again.[17] These were the stories Motke the melamed used to tell us every day,[18] and we sat there completely entranced. . . .

In the winter we would return home from the heder between eight and nine o'clock in the evening. I would snatch a quick supper and hasten straight to Grandmother Beyle-Rashe's rooms, where the entire family usually gathered. Frequently, the women would sit there with Leybke the beadle,[19] who lived in Grandmother's kitchen together with his wife, the cook, and listen to the tales he told about demons and the devil's sons, about sorcerers, marine creatures,[20] and the like.

He once told us about a carter who had to travel to a particular destination with a cartload of Jews. On their way they caught sight of a big, well-fed goose. It goes without saying that the carter caught the goose and took it home with him. At night, while everyone was asleep, the goose started running amok, scattering articles all over the place. When the carter lit a candle, he saw to his astonishment that the body of the fowl was half human, half goose. More dead than alive, he rushed to the rabbi, who immediately summoned a minyan to chant psalms at the top of their voices. When they finished the entire Book of Psalms, the goose spread its wings and flew away.[21]

"Demons," he said, "love to ride on horses, not on those belonging to the lords, but on horses belonging to Jews. When a Jewish carter enters the stable of a morning, he occasionally notices his horses dripping with sweat, puffing and panting from exhaustion as if they had just returned from a long ride. He might also find, every now and then, on entering the stable in the morning that his horse has dropped dead, the wheels of his cart are smashed to pieces, and the reins are ripped into shreds."[22]

He had no end of stories dealing with witchcraft. Once, so he told us, there was a Jewish woman in Kamenets whose husband, a tailor, had gone off to Odessa. At first he used to send her money and letters, but then ceased sending her money or letters. She looked up a sorcerer living in Shereshov,[23] a town near Kamenets, who said that for the payment of ten rubles he would restore her husband to her at the end of a long poker. And that's what really happened. The following evening her husband knocked on the window, weeping and pleading with her to take him in. He was exhausted from the long trip and on the verge of collapse. She quickly opened the door and he rode in on the end of a poker. He fell over and fainted then and there. His wife started screaming, and kicked up such a racket that all the neighbors gathered around her and at once set to chanting the Psalms. The tailor came out of his swoon and told the gathering how, suddenly, in the middle of the night, a large iron hand had gripped his arm, dragged him from his bed in Odessa, seated him on the poker, and commanded, "Go home to your wife this very night and ask her to forgive you." He burst into tears. How could he cover such a distance in a single night? Such a distance took at least six weeks to traverse! But the order was imperative. "You are commanded to do it!" So, he set out on his way, that is, he flew across mountains and valleys, above roofs and rivers, and here he was with scarcely a breath left in his body. [24]

I remember one story that seemed even more bizarre. Once, a man died, and after enduring torments for hundreds of years for all his earthly sins, he was brought before the Heavenly Tribunal, which was to decide if he deserved to enter Paradise. The head of the court was on the point of ruling in his favor, when the Devil appeared and told him that this man was still guilty of one great sin—of having eaten two pud of tallow. [25]

"What do you mean?" the man cried out. "I? Two pud of tallow? When? What are you talking about! It's a false accusation!"

But the Devil proved to the court that, while smoking his pipe, this man always lit it from a candle. A tiny amount of tallow always mingled with the smoke he inhaled, so that, in the course of his life, two pud of tallow had accumulated in his body. He was immediately hurled back into the hands of the angels of destruction, and once again they tormented him, in order to atone for the tallow he'd absorbed while smoking his pipe.

Such were the terrifying tales I heard at my wise Grandmother's place, told by Leybke. You can imagine in what an atmosphere of fear I spent the days of my childhood. We were terror-stricken of demons, of evil spirits, and of the next world, where even the most righteous of men suffered *hibut ha-kever* and had to endure twelve months of torment in Hell, a place four hundred years in dimension and where you are roasted and burned, where the men are suspended by their tongues and the women by their hair and breasts, and all are fried over a fiery oven.[26]

I remember that once my *tzitzit* happened to be defective, and the following morning, due to my shenanigans the evening before, I'd forgotten to put on another pair. At night, before falling asleep, I noticed that I was still wearing the defective garment. It was close to the Days of Awe, and on Yom Kippur—how pious I was then!— I sobbed bitterly over this great sin, over the defective tzitzit. At the end of Yom Kippur I returned home from the hasidic *shtibl* for the meal breaking the fast. I was then no more than eight years old and therefore completely overwhelmed by my sinfulness about the defective garment. After the meal, I went to Grandfather. It was a bright night. The houses, standing in a row close to each other, were drenched in moonlight. When I reached Grandfather's place and was about to mount the steps onto the porch, I suddenly caught sight of the neighbor, Hershl Meirtches, standing next to the small porch of his own house. I was happy to see him standing so close by, but as I was about to step onto the porch, I saw Hershl ascend, higher and higher, rising above the roof, and he was as white as snow. Terrified, I took him for a demon, not Hershl. With the last of my strength I ran across the porch until I collapsed and passed out. In Grandfather's house they had heard the thump of my fall and found me lying unconscious outside. It caused a commotion and people came running and tried to revive me. I was put to bed, and promptly fell asleep.

They brought in the famous doctor, and with him came Yosl the healer,[27] who, together with my grandmother, stayed at my bedside throughout the night. Next morning, feeling much better, I told Grandmother the incident with the demon, who had just prior revealed himself as Hershl Meirtches. I also confessed that I knew why the demon appeared in front of me: because I had worn those defective *tzitzit*.

At that time, every one was talking about the dybbuk[28] of Novogrodek[29] who had invaded the body of a young girl. She was taken to the greatest rabbis and to the most righteous and God-fearing of men to have them exorcise the dybbuk. All of Lithuania was in turmoil over the harrowing tales told about him. Here, the dybbuk recited the Psalms, there, he learnt Mishnah, and elsewhere Gemara and Midrash. Such were the tales bandied about all over the place.

The young girl was taken from town to town until, finally, they also reached the rabbi of Kamenets. He sent them to the graveyard, and all the townspeople—men, women, and children—flocked there to witness the exorcism.

The rabbi ordered Beynush the beadle to recite the appropriate passages and command the dybbuk to leave the young girl's body in accordance with the verdict pronounced by the rabbi and in the name of all other rabbis. I also wanted to come along to the cemetery and see the exorcism of the dybbuk with my own eyes. But Father forbade it because dybbuks are surrounded by evil spirits. Beynush, the beadle, came to the graveyard and recited all the passages and the commands,[30] but the dybbuk shrieked, "I don't want to come out! I feel fine just where I am!"

From Kamenets they took the young girl to the rabbi of Brisk, Yaakov-Meir,[31] a brilliant and most righteous man.[32] He, too, sent the dybbuk to the cemetery, and, as was the case in all other places, all the Jews of Brisk, young and old, flocked there. They were all keen to catch a glimpse of this extraordinary dybbuk that so obstinately refused to quit the body of this young girl.

Rabbi Yaakov-Meir sent Leyb, the beadle of the rabbinical court, to the dybbuk and he commanded him to quit the body immediately in accordance with the sentence issued by the town's rabbi. The rabbi had instructed the beadle to tell the dybbuk to exit through her pinky.[33] That's what we had been taught by the kabbalah, it being the easiest place for the dybbuk to get out. And indeed Leyb told all this to the dybbuk. When the dybbuk began to weep that he didn't want to come out, Leyb explained to him that if he refused to obey, all the rabbis would excommunicate him and he would be condemned to the middle of the sling[34] for all eternity, without any hope of reprieve. At that, the dybbuk said in a tearful voice, "I'm coming out, but let the rabbi tell me where to enter next."

Completely bewildered, Leyb remained rooted to the spot, not knowing what to tell him. He was about to return to the rabbi to ask him whom the dybbuk was to enter next. Standing beside him was Lipe Zukerman, a wealthy Jew, both a scholar and something of a heretic who was acquainted with the governor. He was also renowned for remembering several hundred pages of the Talmud by heart. This Zukerman, who loved to joke around, had come to the graveyard to poke fun at the people there. He heard the dybbuk weeping and begging to be told where to go next and saw that Leyb was about to run to the rabbi for advice. Suddenly Zukerman said, "Stop! Stop! I'll tell him where to enter next. I've got a good place for him."

He stepped up to the girl, opened his mouth wide, and said, "Hop into my mouth." His gaping mouth was right over the girl's face.

Leyb was deeply shocked, scared the dybbuk might actually leap into the heretic's mouth. But the dybbuk failed to respond. It was obvious that he "didn't want" to enter him. But the people crowding all around were alarmed and amazed that a Jew dared to challenge the dybbuk and offer his wide-open mouth for him to enter! Had it been anyone other than Zukerman, they'd have killed and buried him then and there. But they were all scared of Zukerman. Only the rabbi was sorry that the dybbuk had refused to enter the heretic's mouth. Let him know what it meant to hold such a matter up to ridicule! The rabbi, however, felt rather humiliated. He had wanted to take the dybbuk to the Lachovicher rebbe.[35] How the case of the dybbuk was resolved, I don't remember anymore.

CHAPTER 9

THE KIDNAPPERS

The kidnappers • Aharon-Leybele, Khatskl, and Moshke • Yosele •
Military service in those days

Precisely at the time I turned eight, the infamous decree was issued,[1] whereby all eight-year-old boys[2] were to be conscripted into the army with the aim of converting them to Christianity. The recruitment of such little boys lasted for no more than a year, when it became clear that it had been a mistake. Only 1 percent of all the boys converted, and even that just barely.[3] Despite the terrible sufferings those soldiers endured, perhaps only one in a hundred eventually converted. The mothers of those boys went to inordinate lengths of self-sacrifice to prepare their sons for such an eventuality. They cautioned the cantonists[4] not to convert for any price, and they provided each child with small phylacteries. Their mothers' grief-stricken faces became so deeply implanted in the hearts of those little soldiers that they stubbornly refused to abandon their Jewish faith.

In Kamenets there were at that time three kidnappers.[5] One of them, Aharon-Leybele, was as vicious as a murderer, and devoid of the least spark of pity in his heart. The other two were Khatskl and Moshke. Their task was to kidnap eight-year-old boys and supply them as recruits to the army.

Among the children of the wealthier families in Motke the melamed's heder was Yosele, the orphaned son of a prosperous wagoner. He was an amiable and gifted boy, and his mother, a well-to-do widow, was ready to pay the high fee so long as her son had the opportunity to study with a good melamed and to mix with the sons of the township's elite.

One day, two of those kidnappers entered our heder in the middle of the day, stopped on the threshold, and attentively scanned all the pupils learning there. I and my uncle Yisrael understood immediately that they had come to kidnap Yosele in order to conscript him into the army.[6] Grabbing the melamed's wife's candlesticks to hurl at their heads, and kicking up such a racket, we warned them that if they dared show their faces in our heder again, we'd flatten their heads then and there. Though threatened by mere children, they nevertheless turned around and beat a hasty retreat.

One midday while all of us were on our way home for lunch, Aharon-Leybele tried to kidnap Yosele. Realizing it within a split second, Yosele at once leaped onto my shoulders. Aharon-Leybele gave up but I still managed to fling a stone after him, which struck him so hard in the shoulder that he suffered from it quite some time afterward. I then took Yosele by the hand, led him to my home, and asked Mother to let him stay at our house, that he eat, drink, and sleep with me, until the danger had passed. All of us were very fond of Yosele on account of his intelligence and gentle nature. Apart from that, he was a particularly good-looking boy, with rosy cheeks and a peachy complexion.

But the elders of the township had authorized the kidnappers to catch Yosele and none other. They did not have permission to catch anyone in his place, so they lay in ambush for him wherever possible. One of them lay in wait close to our house for days and nights on end, in case Yosele inadvertently left the house of Moshe and Aharon-Leyzer on his own.

Yosele hid away at our place for fully three weeks. But as ill luck would have it, the boy was so homesick for his mother that one day he sneaked out of the house into the street unnoticed by us and ran off in the direction of his mother's home. That was when Moshke pounced upon him, and nothing could be done about it. His mother grieved bitterly over her loss. You can easily imagine her anguish; a young child marching alongside of rough soldiers, all goyim; until the age of twenty he'd be forced to become a swineherd somewhere, and after that he'd be conscripted for another twenty-five years![7]

For two weeks Yosele was locked up inside a small chamber next to the big study house, behind a barred window and an iron door. This was the place where they held all the kidnapped boys until dispatching them to the *ispravnik* in Brisk. In this chamber Yosele never ceased crying, while his mother, standing outside the window, all but went out of her mind with grief.

Later, the *assessor* brought up a wagon, guarded by three of his gendarmes, to cart little Yosele away. The small boy resisted violently, but beaten almost unconscious and bound hand and foot, he was cast onto the wagon. His mother kept passing out time and again and never stopped bewailing her child, lest, God forbid, he be forcefully converted. Even if they burned and roasted him, even if they beat him and tore his body apart, he must remain strong and bear up to the physical torture—until his holy soul rises up to Heaven.

The heartrending cries of mother and son could be heard all over the township and spread a devastating air throughout the community. Soft-hearted men could not withhold their tears and joined the weeping and wailing women. All the pupils of our heder (those of others were not allowed to come out) were on the spot to witness little Yosele being dragged out of the small chamber and hurled onto the big wagon drawn by a team of horses. His mother hastened after him to Brisk in another wagon and was in a constant swoon all the way there until some Gentiles managed to bring her to.

Little Yosele had no more strength to keep on crying and lay more dead than alive inside the wagon. Needless to say, he hadn't tasted any food for several days in a row.

When they reached Brisk, the bailiff told the *ispravnik* what he and his three men had had to put up with on the way on account of the boy's mother—her endless wailing and constant fainting fits. The *ispravnik* therefore ordered her to be sent back to Kamenets without fail. She returned home, lay in bed for two days, and died.

The *ispravnik* was issued strict orders not to reveal to anyone where those cantonists were being sent. They were sent far away, deep into the Russian hinterland.[8]

A cantonist who had been converted told me how they had baptized six such boys out of a group of thirty in Saratov.[9] It happened thus: when the commander of the battalion realized that the floggings didn't help, he had an idea how to break down the boys' resistance to baptism. He crowded the thirty cantonists into a bathhouse and had them step up the steam to such a degree that it became unbearable. Six of the boys broke down and agreed to be baptized, whereas the rest lost consciousness. When they were taken out

some time afterward, they found that three of them had died of suf-
focation. My cantonist was full of wrath against God. To his mind,
there must be no God if He could allow such torments and suffering
to take place. And if there is a God in Heaven, He is nothing but a
God of Evil. . . .

As mentioned earlier, it was only during 1855 that boys of eight
were conscripted into the army. After a short time it became evident to all that, on the one hand, such procedures were altogether
ineffective, and, on the other, it was too difficult a task to convert
a Jewish boy, even though he was only eight years old. And so the
decree was revoked.

Yosele vanished as though he had drowned in the ocean's depths.
But a year later, during Hanukkah, a battalion of soldiers bivouacked
near Kamenets for several months. As was usually the case, every
two or three months a new battalion arrived, remained for a few
months, and then left, and in its place, another came.

We were stunned to learn that Yosele the orphan was to be found
among these soldiers. Arye-Leyb[10] at once asked the commanding
officer to bring Yosele to us. He came to Grandfather's house escorted by several soldiers. Yosele entered barefoot, clad in a large,
coarse peasant shirt that reached down to his ankles but without
any pants, and over it all a long military greatcoat. His face was
swollen and pale, like that of a corpse.

On seeing him we all broke into tears, and I wept more than the
others. After all, he had been one of my closest friends, and I dearly
loved him.

I went up to him and said, "Yosele! Yosele!"

But all my attempts to arouse him were futile—he didn't respond. He had become like a log. No matter how much I talked and
pleaded and called out his name, "Yosele! Yosele! Yosele!"—there
was no response. They brought him a glass of tea and a sweet roll,
but he refused to eat or drink. It was a lost cause.

You can imagine what lamentations broke out in the township.
Not many people were able to see him with their own eyes because
his officer had allowed only a mere handful to come and talk to him.
I was heartbroken and crushed and bewailed his fate for weeks and
months afterward.

When the officer was asked how this little cantonist came to be
among the soldiers encamped here, he explained that when all the
other cantonists were about to be sent off deep inside Russia, Yosele

was taken ill, the reason being that he had refused all food and kept weeping for days and nights on end. He lay in a hospital within one of the fortresses for quite some time. As he took no nourishment, and on account of his incessant crying, he had turned into an idiot.

However, it stands to reason that what had brought him to this state had, above all, been his mortal fear of the kidnappers. Is this something to be trifled with? Should an eight-year-old child know he must be constantly on his guard lest he be captured like a mouse caught by a cat? What could be more terrifying? He was never able to understand why they kept trying to catch him. All he could think of was: Here, they're going to *catch me! catch me! catch me!*

Once he had turned into a simpleton, he was finally able to eat normally and stand on his feet. He was released from the hospital and handed over to the soldiers. They took him with them, but not long afterward the commanding officer sent him back to the fortress. What need was there to drag this idiot along with them from place to place? The soldiers were even likely to kill this Jewboy one of these days!

In the following year, 1856, this decree was rescinded.[11] But then a new calamity struck the Jews: a new directive was issued whereby each town was allowed to cull its quota of Jewish soldiers from among the inhabitants of another town.[12] That set off an unprecedented bout of kidnapping among the Jews. The name of the game was kidnapping, only that it turned into an uncompromisingly bloody one. The kidnappers would come from out of the way towns and catch soldiers. They would arrive in the dead of night and pluck well-to-do youngsters, themselves already fathers of several children, from their beds.

Those were the most savage scenes ever witnessed among Jews. The kidnappers would arrive in the town quietly, unnoticed by anyone. They then appeared before the police with permits issued by their town's *sborshchik* and *assessor* confirming them to be kidnappers. The police supplied them with as many gendarmes and soldiers as were necessary, and in the middle of the night they would pound on the door. If the door wasn't opened immediately, they would break the locks with tools brought along especially for that purpose. They entered quickly, dragged the young man outside with unheard-of brutality, and left.

When they heard the police knocking at the door, the family was seized by mortal terror. Occasionally, they even resisted the kidnappers with axes, knives, iron bars, and hammers prepared in advance, and as soon as the kidnappers entered the house, all the members of the family attacked them with murderous blows.[13]

But the kidnappers, for their part, came equipped with sticks and iron rods, and gave as good as they got. The house turned into a virtual battlefield and blood flowed like water. Both sides fought until their strength gave out, and victory went to the one that held out longest. Naturally, that was usually the kidnappers. Once they put their sights on someone, and "marked" him, the matter was irreversible. All this caused untold damage, for even the kidnappers risked their lives; they either succeeded and snatched the victim or they were maimed for life.

The mothers of these recruits often died of grief, and their fathers and wives were crippled as a result of the bloody feuds. The cries and lamentations of these families rose to high heaven. In addition, these people were tried in the civil court for resisting the police, for murder, for assault with iron rods, and so on. They were forced to sit in jail and to be tried in court. They lost their wealth; even quite prosperous families were completely destroyed and impoverished. Nevertheless, it is easy to understand why members of a family frequently ran the risk of losing their lives and property in order to save a son of theirs from the jaws of the military. In those days the cruel maltreatment a recruit had to endure while serving twenty-five years in the tsar's army was common knowledge.

I remember once a half-battalion of recruits was stationed in Kamenets, and only then did I understand what it meant to serve in Tsar Nicholas's army. The soldiers underwent grueling drills in the market square. If a soldier didn't hold his rifle in the proper way, or stood a fraction out of line, his sergeant would twist his ear, pull his nose, or kick him mercilessly. We were sure that the soldier's ear or nose would remain in the sergeant's hand. At times he would strike a soldier with the iron barrel of his rifle until he doubled up, writhing with pain. They would flog a soldier savagely in public view for the most trivial reasons. Fresh birch twigs were brought in from the forest every day. Each lash from such a switch literally tore strips of flesh from the victim's body.

I remember a particular officer lodging at Moshke's inn who was an especially brutal sadist and murderer. The inn was a nice building and had a stable big enough to shelter a large number of carriages. Moshke hired the entire inn out to the officers, who also used the large stable for flogging the soldiers. I remember those birch twigs well. Every day one could hear the shrieking sound of those whips cracking in the air. Sometimes it was a single soldier; at others, three in one go. When, after the floggings, we boys stole into the stable, we would find the ground there drenched with blood.

Once, this officer flogged three soldiers to death. He had ordered five hundred lashes for each, but after eighty or ninety lashes they had given up the ghost. The officer stood beside them, shouting, "Go on! Hit harder!" If the officer had ordered five hundred lashes, five hundred lashes it had to be. Two men did the flogging, and a third counted the strokes.

The army bread was black, coarse, without salt, and tasteless. One could hardly swallow it. The officers, on the other hand, went short of nothing. They simply stole what they could from the soldiers, who never tasted any meat unless it was from the bones of a carcass. The officers sold anything they could lay their hands on or would give the suppliers of provisions receipts for flour and meat for only a third of the amount brought in. The soldiers were constantly on the verge of starvation, which accounted for the widespread thieving against which no amount of flogging did any good. They were famished, mere skin and bones, both from lack of food and the floggings. It is no wonder, therefore, that on witnessing the miserable life and the long years of service a soldier of Nicholas's army had to endure, an entire family was ready to stake its life in order to snatch a son of theirs from the clutches of such cruel beasts.

This kind of kidnapping by foreign kidnappers did not, however, last for long. After two years, it had proven to be so ineffective that the authorities also revoked this decree. Once again, each town provided its quota of recruits only from among its own "souls" and not from other towns. But since many people did not live in their native towns, special kidnappers were sent to a particular town to catch only their "own" inhabitants. There was, of course, a certain amount of deception involved here. Towns handed in the names of people who were not registered anywhere. All the "nonregistered" were then caught and delivered to the army. In addition, every town added many fictitious names to the population register. That, too, was a cunning but very simple ruse. In those years every Jew usually had two or three names. For example: A certain person was called Yaakov-Yosl-Leyb Mintz. Thus one Jew was issued a passport under the name of Yaakov Mintz, the second under the name Yosl Mintz, and the third under the name Leyb Mintz. And for another, they simply invented a name. That's how affairs were managed among the Jews in Russia until 1874.[14]

If someone hadn't left the township and was to be handed over to the army, he, too, had to be kidnapped. Such a person did not enlist voluntarily, but once he was caught it was a lost cause. It is therefore easy to understand the uncompromising battles the families of potential recruits waged against the kidnappers. Words cannot describe what kind of hearts made of stone those kidnappers must have had. They were a lot more loathsome and hated than the hangman of our day.[15] Every attempt at kidnapping involved atrocious beatings and severe physical injuries. The wailing and weeping of the fathers, mothers, sisters and brothers, and other family members left those callous kidnappers cold and indifferent.

The kidnapper Aharon-Leybele was a beast in human form. His very face proclaimed him a murderer. Everyone hated him, and his name was used to frighten and threaten unruly children. He served as everyone's example of revolting contemptibility. The foulest of curses was, "You are just like Aharon-Leybele!" and it was an unforgivable insult.

I have already told you above how, in my youth, I once "fought" with kidnappers.[16] I did so out of an inner feeling of repugnance at witnessing their foul methods. Here is another story: one day while standing with a group of boys next to the preacher's house I saw David the carpenter pass by us with an unusually strange gait. It at once occurred to me that Aharon-Leybele must be at his heels in order to kidnap him for the army. And that's what it was. Aharon-Leybele had almost caught up with him when, instinctively, I ran toward him, put out a leg, and tripped him up. He fell and his nose was bleeding like a pig's. All the other boys took flight, and I stood there shouting, "Aharon-Leybele, may you croak a violent death!"

He got up, wiped his bleeding nose with a filthy cloth, but didn't dare to curse me. He only complained about me to my father, who slapped my face and said, "Even though he is Aharon-Leybele, you shouldn't have tripped him."

Grandfather gradually distanced himself from all communal affairs. Only if they required something urgent from the *ispravnik* did the elders come to Grandfather asking him to write a letter concerning the matter, for they knew that the former never refused any of

Grandfather's requests. But, during the difficult days of the recruitment, the families of a potential recruit would plead with Grandmother Beyle-Rashe to use her influence on her husband and have him do something to free the soldier. They did not turn to the *sborshchik* or to the elders, but only to Grandmother. They knew that Aharon-Leyzer was not involved with the recruitment and did not even know who the candidates for recruitment were. Nevertheless, they were sure that if he recommended the freeing of a particular recruit, he would be released at once and someone else would be taken in his stead. This had happened in the past, and therefore they always came with tearful eyes to Grandmother, who simply lacked the strength to live on.

CHAPTER 10

THE GREAT DISPUTE

Zastavye • The great dispute • The oath • The swindle • Grandfather's battle • The peace • The lords and the peasants • The flogging of the peasants

The young generation of Zastavye were great troublemakers. They lived too much of the good life. They were wealthy, and behaved arrogantly and insolently because they lacked for nothing. Sparking quarrels and disputes in the town became their favorite sport.[1] They refused to accept the fact that Aharon-Leyzer and his children made such a good living from their many leaseholdings in the town. Why should they agree to let Aharon-Leyzer have things so easy, when it was clear to all that he paid almost nothing for those leaseholdings? So, when the time neared for the lord Osserevski to arrive, they organized a large delegation which was to offer him three thousand rubles instead of the twelve hundred Aharon-Leyzer was paying annually. It had to be a strong delegation to challenge Aharon-Leyzer, for they knew full well whom they were up against. The most aggressive and defiant elements banded together and agreed to cooperate. They became infected by some kind of mania that forced them to stop at nothing to divest Aharon-Leyzer of the leaseholds—if necessary, even by force. No matter at what material cost to themselves, even to the point of bloodshed, so long as they wrenched the leaseholds out of Aharon-Leyzer's grip.

As soon as Grandfather got word of this campaign against him, he at once went to the *ispravnik* to have himself appointed *sborshchik*. The *ispravnik* came to Kamenets right away, took away the books and seal from *sborshchik* B.,[2] and handed them over to Grandfather. Grandfather set to work immediately. First off, he sent gendarmes to confiscate from the homes of the Zastavye "opposition" all the pots, pans, candlesticks, clocks, and whatever other moveables they owned, even the bedding, though he had no legal right to do that. But who dared to challenge Grandfather? And to whom, if anyone, did he ever listen? After all, he had the *ispravnik* on his side!

In addition, Grandfather dug up old debts the township owed and demanded that the entire amount be paid then and there. Once again, he exacted large tax payments from the townspeople, which many of them were unable to meet. It sparked a riot in the township, but to no avail. They realized that it was beyond their power to pick a quarrel with Aharon-Leyzer. Besides, those same people had not behaved decently toward him: they were the ones who wanted to deprive him of the leaseholds, for no good reason at all.

They sent the rabbi to Aharon-Leyzer to plead with him to give up the post of *sborshchik* for the sake of peace, and they were ready to swear any oath in the world never again to lend a hand in depriving him of his leaseholdings. Grandfather refused to even consider a reconciliation. But Father, my uncle Mordechai-Leyb, even Great-Grandfather Yudl, and Grandmother Beyle-Rashe all prevailed upon him to restore the peace in the township.

It was decided that all those that had conspired to take the leaseholdings away from Grandfather—some seventy in all, according to Grandfather's calculation—were to appear in the big study house wrapped in their prayer shawls and *kittels*,[3] Torah scrolls in hand, and swear solemnly—amid the blowing of the ram's horn and the lighting of candles[4]—never again to conspire against Grandfather. It was one of the most awesome of oaths ever sworn.

I remember the entire township flocking to the old study house. A sea of people surrounded the study house and flowed over into the street. Grandfather arrived only after all the members of the "opposition" were present and had sworn the oath as he had demanded. In that same oath they took upon themselves the promise—and not only upon themselves but for everyone else—to never again approach Osserevski in order to persuade him to hand over the leaseholdings.

The following morning, Grandfather sent a letter to the *ispravnik,* informing him that he wished to resign from his post as *sborshchik.* The *ispravnik,* who had known all along what had been going on, accepted his resignation.[5]

Nevertheless, the Zastavye gang tried to swindle Grandfather. When the time came to renew the contract and Osserevski came to town, the people of Zastavye brought in two Jews from Bialystok, who approached him, offering eighteen hundred rubles on the spot for the leaseholdings. When Grandfather called on him, Osserevski asked: "Are you ready to pay me eighteen hundred rubles?"

"Yes," Grandfather answered.

The two Jews, who were present, immediately raised the amount: "Two thousand and four hundred rubles!"

But Osserevski told them: "As far as I'm concerned, a few hundred rubles more or less doesn't make any difference to me. The lease will remain with the present holder. He's been holding my lease for so long now, let him continue to hold it as long as I live. . . ."

The leaseholdings, therefore, remained with Grandfather not just for three years, as was common practice, but in perpetuity, in other words, for as long as Osserevski was alive. But the extra six hundred rubles he had to add on account of those Jews from Bialystok infuriated him. It was a clear violation of the oath. He was boiling with rage and started probing the contract with the lord Osserevski for all the outstanding payments owed by the town. And indeed, he found in the contract a clause that had not yet been implemented, according to which payment was due him for the skinning of cattle hides.[6] That gave him a free hand to act. He informed all the butchers that before slaughtering any cattle they had to obtain from him a receipt for payment of ninety kopecks for a full-grown cow, and thirty kopecks for a calf. The butchers were well aware that once Aharon-Leyzer gave an order, it had to be complied with. They immediately raised the price of meat, which triggered an unprecedented panic in Kamenets.

The Zastavye "opposition" incited the entire township. It wasn't the increased price of meat that concerned them, but the stirring up of discontent among the inhabitants. If they had been unable to best Grandfather in the matter of the leaseholdings, when they had not conducted themselves decently, maybe now they could do something. After all, weren't they taking up the cudgel in favor of the entire township against the injustice caused them by Aharon-Leyzer? The dispute turned into an all-out state of war. People stopped buying vodka from us. A gang of fifty men went out of town, brought back a barrel of vodka, placed it in the center of the marketplace, and sold vodka to all and sundry.

Several hundred men surrounded the barrel, ready to fight Aharon-Leyzer's policemen to the death. Grandfather recruited thirty peasants from the manager of the estate, and the *assessor* added ten gendarmes, and together with his own two "tough guys"—Khatskl and Kivke—they all marched to the marketplace to confiscate the barrel of vodka. That, needless to say, sparked a fierce and ugly brawl, injurious to both sides.

Grandfather hired a secretary, someone by the name of Twersky,[7] whose task it was to write out daily reports and forward them to the *ispravnik*. Every day a new barrel was smashed and the vodka spilt on the ground. But barely two hours later, another barrel was hauled in, guarded by a hundred men. Not a day passed without a bloody battle around it.

Grandfather had all the reports sent to the *ispravnik,* in accordance with the latter's demand. The opposing faction, on the other hand, sent slanderous reports to the governor. They accused Aharon-Leyzer of having robbed the township for many years by taxing them for merchandise not mentioned in the leaseholding contract between him and the lord, and so on, and so on. The governor took the matter up with the *ispravnik,* who, of course, decided in the leaseholder's favor, that is, in Aharon-Leyzer's favor—whereas the informers were nothing short of rebels. That in its turn set off a spate of letters to the governor accusing both Aharon-Leyzer and the *ispravnik* of dividing the spoils up between them.

This feud went on daily for six months; for days on end fights broke out and blows were exchanged, though no one dared raise a finger against any of us. Our entire family walked about the streets, to and from the study house, completely unmolested, and no one dared to utter even one bad word to us, for they greatly feared antagonizing Aharon-Leyzer.

Nevertheless, the governor saw fit to send a commission of inquiry, in order to determine who was guilty and who was innocent. The committee was made up of six men, headed by the *ispravnik.* As usual, several weeks before the arrival of the commission, the *ispravnik* informed Grandfather to be well prepared, and to reserve lodgings for two members of this commission: himself and someone else. The other four would be put up at the *assessor*'s home.

In this feud, Grandfather took advantage of every means at his disposal. First of all he rallied around himself all the commoners,[8] who had always been his loyal supporters and were willing to walk through fire and water for him. He made sure to provide them with as much vodka as they could drink and feed them roast goose, and they stuffed themselves to their hearts' content. . . . It was explained to them what they were supposed to say, and each received a small bottle of vodka to drink on the way.

Our "only child" spent an entire day teaching them what to say and how to speak to the commission. Although they didn't know a word of Russian, they learned all the words and sentences they were instructed to pronounce by heart.[9] The "only child" organized a team of teachers to teach these simple folks how to speak, and he presided over them all. Grandfather prepared a list of all the witnesses on his behalf and sent it to the *ispravnik*. His opponents also sent a list of their own witnesses but kept it until the arrival of the commission in order to submit it to them on the spot.

The commission arrived in Brisk and notified the *ispravnik* of its presence. The latter hosted the honored guests in his own home for several days. In accordance with the then prevailing custom, he wined and dined them royally, and only then gave them his own version of the affair.

The commission finally arrived in Kamenets. The *ispravnik* and one other member lodged at Uncle Mordechai-Leyb's house, and the remaining four at the *assessor*'s home. On the first day the *assessor* treated all the members of the commission to an official dinner at his home, and the following day the same ceremony was repeated by the *ispravnik* at Mordechai-Leyb's. The expenses for both were, of course, covered by Grandfather, who didn't scrimp on the lavish dishes or save on the choicest bottles of cognacs and wines.

On the third day the commission started its investigation, whose hearing was attended by the entire community. The town's chief clerk called out the names of all the witnesses according to the list Grandfather had prepared in advance. Those witnesses—as mentioned before, who were there on Grandfather's behalf—packed all the rooms and corridors of the *assessor*'s home. They were called before the commission one by one and treated with utmost politeness. After all, they were Grandfather's witnesses.

The town's witnesses, on the other hand, assembled out in the street, in front of the *assessor*'s house. They stood there, on their feet, for three days running, in the rain and the wind, for it was autumn. In the *assessor*'s courtyard the "favorable" witnesses were treated to vodka and tasty snacks, while those waiting outside remained hungry and finally became completely worn out from the long wait. That had a bad effect on their testimony. And, if one factors in the rough and insulting treatment awarded them, the curses and screams they endured, it is easy to appreciate their difficult state.

An air of gloom settled over the community, for which they blamed the *ispravnik*. The townspeople's testimony was not even heard in its entirety, further fanning their hatred for the *ispravnik*. Once, while the *ispravnik* and his functionary were on their way from the *assessor*'s home to their own lodgings and already stood on the front porch, they were pelted with stones and mud clots. They hastened to the upper balcony and disappeared inside. But all the walls were splashed with mud blotches.

As expected, the *assessor*, accompanied by gendarmes and soldiers, appeared on the scene shortly afterward. The *ispravnik* stood on the balcony and ordered the arrest of all those standing in the market near his lodgings and their instant dispatch to Brisk. The first to be caught was Shlomo the melamed, a great *shlimazel* and a pauper to boot. When he was tied up he pretended to fall into a faint. Those standing by started a racket, shouting that Shlomo the melamed was dead, killed by the gendarmes. The *ispravnik* ordered him to be taken to Khatskl the healer, who lived nearby. When even he failed to revive the melamed, the *ispravnik* ordered that he be taken back to the marketplace, where Khatskl would give him an enema on the spot. At hearing that, the melamed leaped up, fully awake . . .

The *ispravnik* was about to leave Kamenets. Now, however, this was no longer a matter of a simple investigation but a matter of rebellion . . . and that was altogether a different story.

All the respectable householders of Kamenets hastened to Grandfather, pleading with him to stop the impending trial. They asked to be pardoned and forgiven and promised to reimburse him for all the expenses he had incurred. But Grandfather refused to be reconciled with them. Failing that, they turned to my father, my uncle, Great-Grandfather Yudl, and, above all, to Grandmother Beyle-Rashe. They invested enormous efforts and kept nagging the family unceasingly until, finally, peace was restored. Even people who had no part in the feud took an interest in this effort at reconciliation, and the most important influence in bringing it about was my dearly beloved Grandmother.

After peace was restored, Aharon-Leyzer submitted a detailed account of all the expenses incurred, and they paid up, as promised, to the last kopeck. Both sides signed a document of mutual forgiveness underwritten by sixty men. In this document they solemnly undertook never again to oppose Aharon-Leyzer in anything, and pledged to come to his assistance whenever required. That's how the feud ended, and because of the peace the payment on hides was canceled.

Grandfather prevailed on the *ispravnik* to forget all about the incident and cancel the trial. The documents were still in Brisk, because the commission had not managed as yet to complete its investigation, and Grandfather succeeded in obtaining his request.

From then on peace reigned in Kamenets. Grandfather could now devote all his time to his own business. Only when his intervention was required did the elders turn to him, though he had completely distanced himself from all communal affairs.

We were once again the unchallenged leaseholders until the Polish Rebellion in 1863. After the rebellion was put down, all the leases on behalf of the Polish gentry were revoked.

As mentioned above, Grandfather was particularly fond of me because already as a young boy I loved listening to his conversations with the grown-ups. I was especially interested in what Grandfather had to say to them, and they liked that I stood around observing them, hanging on their every utterance, familiar with all the ins and outs of every dispute.

When Grandfather traveled to one of the adjacent estates, he liked to take me along, and kept chatting with me of things a young child like myself could easily understand. I remember us arriving at Rimenitch, the estate of a lord whose name I've forgotten. By the time we reached his mansion it was one o'clock. We saw the commissioner standing beside the porch.

When Grandfather asked, "Where's the lord?" he replied with a smile, "He's whipping a peasant before having his dinner." It occasionally happened that when a lord had no appetite, he simply gave one of his peasants a thorough flogging and afterward was able to eat with great relish.

We were ushered into a room where we waited for a full hour.

The lord entered, still enraged, his face flushed, and his eyes burning with anger. But on seeing Grandfather, he calmed down and held out his hand in welcome: "How are you, my dear Pan Kotik? And who's the boy?"

"My grandson," Grandfather replied.

The man patted my cheek and said, "You're still so young and have already got such a fine-looking grandson." He and Grandfather entered another room to discuss some business, after which we returned home.

I didn't quite understand what the commissioner told Grandfather about the flogging, so on the way home I asked: "Why did the lord storm into the room with his face so flushed with anger? What was wrong with him?"

Grandfather explained to me at length the history of the lord-peasant relationship, and it was then that I first learnt about the miserable existence of the serfs, of their merciless floggings and their brutal treatment at the hands of the lords.

"Flogging a person just for the pleasure of it!" I said to Grandfather. "They must have hearts of stone! Don't they have any fear of God? I wouldn't conduct business with a lord like that!"

"If so," Grandfather replied, "one wouldn't be able to do business with any of the gentry. But, my dear boy, what can be done? We have no other choice."

Once I accompanied Grandfather to the estate of Pruska, whose lord was called Vilevinski.[10] As soon as we arrived, he and Grandfather went straight to the vodka distillery and I joined them. Next to the distillery a peasant was chopping wood, and the moment he caught sight of his lord, he flung the ax away and remained rooted to the spot. His face was drained of blood, like that of a corpse, and his body was trembling as if he'd seen a wolf. It was an awful spectacle, one I will never forget. Only then did I realize what it meant to be a lord and what it meant to be a serf.

I remember another appalling incident, which left an even deeper impression on my mind, so much so that an icy-cold shiver still runs down my spine whenever I recall it. That same year, the commissioner of that particular lord—a tall and very fat Gentile (he must have weighed at least twelve pud) called Patshoshe—decided to repair the dam alongside the three bridges between Kamenets and Zastavye. The dam had been damaged before Passover, during the great floods, and Patshoshe ordered five hundred wagons filled with soil and branches to fill in the gaps. I remember it was on a Sabbath around ten o'clock in the morning when I came there to watch them bring up the wagonloads of the necessary materials. Patshoshe stood there and supervised the repairs. One of the peasants happened to come an hour late. Patshoshe immediately ordered him to lie down on the ground, took the peasant's own whip, one of excellent quality which he used to steer his horse, and set to flogging him mercilessly then and there. After the fiftieth stroke, the peasant was dead. But Patshoshe, completely unmoved, coldly ordered the peasant's son and wife to cart the corpse away in his very own wagon, and no one dared to cry or moan.

One day, I drove with Grandfather to the estate of a lord several versts from Kamenets. This estate, called Starschev,[11] was a fairly small one, surrounded by a few fields and a meadow, but its soil was of superior quality, a virtual "gold mine" about one hundred dessiatines in all, with wonderful orchards and a small pond full of fish in its clear water. The mansion, too, was small but beautiful.

On our way home I told Grandfather how much I liked the look of the place, especially the fact that it was not far from our township. Grandfather then told me about the childless lord who had lived there nine years before. Shortly before his death, the lord summoned the local priest and Grandfather to have them witness the drawing up of his will. This lord owned several other estates apart from this little one, which he intended to present to Grandfather. But Grandfather turned it down. Instead, the man made him a gift of three thousand rubles. "Now," Grandfather said, "I'd gladly have leased this property for one thousand rubles a year. . . ."

When I asked him why he had turned down such a valuable gift, Grandfather replied that in those days it had been a degrading thing for a Jew to live on a lord's estate and not in the town. Twenty years later, after the liberation of the serfs and after the Polish Rebellion,[12] Grandfather did, however, obtain the lease of this property for fifteen hundred rubles a year.[13]

CHAPTER 11

MY MOTHER'S UNHAPPINESS

My mother • Rabbi Leyzer • My mother's unhappiness • The Rabbi
of Kamenets • Grandmother's advice

My mother's presence in Grandfather's house was like
a thorn in his flesh. She simply did not fit into the
household. She had grown up with a completely different type of father, Rabbi Leyzer of Grodno, who, already from
the age of eight would not look at the face of a woman. And when
he succeeded his father-in-law, Rabbi Hillel Fried, the son-in-law of
Rabbi Hayyim of Volozhin, as *dayan* in Grodno,[1] he always had the
beadle walk ahead of him and drive all the women off the sidewalk.[2]

Grandfather Leyzer used to go to the public bathhouse every
Friday, and made a point of undressing beside the poor. And, noticing a poor man's shoddy boots, he would at once exchange them
for his own and, seeing a frazzled shirt or tattered pants, he'd give
away his own garments to the poor man and put on his shabby ones
instead. Coming home, Grandmother could scarcely recognize him.
All his clothes were tattered and torn, with the exception of his
kapote and *shtrayml*, which, he maintained, one mustn't give away.

Grandmother would fly into a rage, for it was an expense she
couldn't afford. In those days, the township paid the rabbi only a
measly salary, barely enough to keep body and soul together. Even
if she sewed him a new set of garments every Friday, it would go
down the drain like all the others. He, on the other hand, would
console her, saying that the poor man was in greater need of good
boots than he because that poor soul had to make his living walking
about and wearing them out. As for the torn pants and ragged shirt,

he was likely to catch his death of a cold, and one could hardly expect him to find work wearing such tattered clothes.

Not wishing to upset him further, Grandmother would go into her own room and cry to herself. The matter soon became the talk of the township. Fortunately, a prosperous townsman, claiming to be their relative, came to their assistance. And if Grandfather happened to give away his clothes, this same man would send Grandmother a new suit on Friday before sunset.

Leyzer owned a great number of books, valued at thousands of rubles. He had inherited them from his father Yekhezkel and from his father-in-law Hillel, and they filled up all the rooms of the house. Most of the time he'd lock himself up inside his room and study. The chamber had a tiny door, which he would open only if his wife, the rebbetzin, knocked on it. If a woman had to ask the rabbi a question, the rebbetzin would hear it first. She would pass the question on to her husband through the tiny door, and he would inform her of his decision, to be handed on to the woman. If the question concerned the kashrut of a fowl, the rebbetzin would hand "the problem" itself to him through the door. He would examine the fowl and let her know his decision. On account of this procedure, the rebbetzin became quite proficient herself in handling questions of that kind, and it was usually she who decided whether or not to disqualify a fowl. Her husband listened to her evaluation and queried her, and finally granted her the license to handle the easier kinds of questions. She also knew well how to study a page of Talmud, for which people greatly respected her and even considered her a true scholar.[3]

Grandfather Leyzer used to pray with his congregation only the *shema* and the *shmoneh-esreh*[4] prayers. But even that was too much of a burden for the other congregants. It would take him a long time to get through the prayers, often as long as an hour. The rest of the prayers he would say "to himself," and that lasted fully two hours. Even the Grace after Meals would take him an hour when, at every word, he would roll his eyes up toward God, directing his supplications to Him with his heart and soul. He was a great expert in the responsa literature, and rabbis from all over the Vilna region used to come to consult with him. Besides, his library contained rare copies of responsa that were unavailable elsewhere.

His house was constantly filled with the hubbub of rabbis and *lomdim.* The scholars of Grodno also liked to discuss passages from the Torah with the rebbetzin, as it wasn't always easy to get to Leyzer himself. She had a keen, scholarly mind and only when she came up against a really tricky question would she consult her husband, when no one was around.

My mother had been much sought after by matchmakers as soon as she turned twelve, only that Grandfather Leyzer, although he had a good eye for human nature, could never make up his mind. He was evidently looking for a son-in-law who was both a great scholar and of distinguished lineage. And if he had already set his sights on such a one, it was Grandmother who didn't like him. She didn't want her daughter to marry some sort of *shlimazel*. She held that a rabbi who was unlucky would be of no good to his wife and children.

He greatly respected her opinion. She was an assertive and intelligent woman. It was only thanks to her that he could be as good and pious a Jew as he had hoped. She suffered greatly from his devotion and good nature. If poor people entered their house during mealtime, Leyzer would invite them to share the food with him and offer them the choicest tidbits on the table. He would say that poor men without even a crust of bread to chew on were for him a heartbreaking sight. . . . He, therefore, often invited as many as twelve paupers to his table. Then, the rest of the family, who were themselves famished, would have to give up their places in order to make room for the guests. And if there wasn't enough food to go around, he would send someone to buy bread and rolls to ensure that none of his guests left the house on an empty stomach. His wife would wring her hands, weep, and complain that she was unable to put up with these expenses, despite the assistance given her by her own, not well-off family and by wealthier members of the community. But even that was never enough for Leyzer, and the welfare of "his" poor was closer to his heart than that of his wife and children, who, more often than not, went hungry on that account.

By the time the match between his daughter and my father was arranged, she was already an "old maid" of eighteen, or, as some held, of nineteen. . . . Her mother kept bewailing the fact, as was customary in those days, that there was an aging spinster in a family full of scholarly geniuses. No wonder, therefore, that they readily consented to the proposed match, all the more since both the rabbi and the rebbetzin liked the looks of the prospective bridegroom. There was only one drawback: the father-in-law was a Jew of no consequence, an aggressive householder and *parnas khodesh* of his community—it was a heavy blow and a blemish on the entire family.

But there were two weighty considerations in favor of accepting the match. The girl was, indeed, already an "old maid," and Leyzer's brother was in danger of losing his rabbinical post.[5] With no other options available, Leyzer, therefore, gave the young bridegroom an oral examination of what he had learnt so far and concluded that he was a gifted lad who would eventually become a great scholar.

Father was an intelligent youth, and his father, Grandfather Aharon-Leyzer, instructed him on how to behave in the presence of his prospective father-in-law in Grodno. Father pretended to be full of naiveté, scarcely able to put two and two together and knowing nothing whatsoever beyond learning Torah and serving God.

Before his trip to Grodno for the betrothal ceremony, Father was no more than a boy of twelve. He went through the entire book of *Yesod ve-shoresh ha-avodah*,[6] and though by nature a healthy and robust boy, he arrived in front of Leyzer pious-faced with a wrinkled forehead. In short, Leyzer and his wife took a liking to him. The prospective mother-in-law, seeing how bright he was as well as good-looking, was convinced that he would also become a famous rabbi in time.

My mother, growing up in such a pious home full of righteous men and Torah scholars, landed in a household where one never heard even a quotation from the Scriptures. Of all those coming to her father-in-law's house there was nary a rabbi nor a scholar, nor a pious one among them. Just plain and simple Jews, Jews, Jews. And a Jew who wasn't a rabbi was worthless in her eyes. She saw herself surrounded by Jews who had nothing else to do but hang around all day long, neither praying nor learning, Jews who had no respect for, nor even a drop of *Yiddishkeit*. Simple men who cared only about their Sabbath meals, the kind who engaged in constant tittle-tattle or in disparaging gossip about their fellow townspeople. Above all, my mother, may her soul rest in peace, wasn't particularly smart herself, and one can easily imagine how much of a misfit she was in Grandfather's household.

However, she loved her husband no less than she loved her parents, because he was kindhearted, virtuous, and soft-spoken. Grandfather Aharon-Leyzer was not very fond of his daughter-in-law, to say the least, and he kept her at arm's length. Nor was Grandmother Beyle-Rashe satisfied with her. My mother was far from being an efficient housewife, didn't know to cook or to bake, as was the norm for wives in those days, when even the wives of the wealthy used to do all their cooking and baking themselves. She had no notion of sewing or doing any needlework, which even small girls knew well. In short, my mother was good for nothing.

On the other hand, she was extremely pious. She never learnt Talmud, but knew by heart practically all of *Hovot ha-levavot*[7] and *Menorat ha-ma'or*.[8] So engrossed was she in the book *Hovot ha-levavot*, that nothing beyond it concerned her, not even the fact that her husband had meanwhile become a fervent hasid. Father, who turned to Hasidism straight after his wedding, soon realized that his wife had no intention of making an issue over it. He appreciated her attitude and was grateful to her.

In time, Mother adjusted to the household and got used to its callers. She always kept with her a small volume of *Hovot ha-levavot* in order to deter the guests from speaking ill of a fellow townsman or indulging in idle gossip, making a laughingstock of others, or using abusive language. No sooner did someone begin speaking slander-ously, than she would at once lecture him on the virtues of good morals and read out to him a passage from *Hovot ha-levavot,* which considered this vice the greatest of sins. She simply drove them mad. At first they couldn't bear to have such a pious woman in their midst. But gradually they got used to her moralizing and refrained from using their normally rough language in her presence.

Her uncle, the rabbi of Kamenets, often came to visit her. He simply came to her without much ado, which was something un-usual for him, since he never called on anyone in Kamenets. He did it at the behest of his brother, who wanted him to befriend his daughter and keep an eye on her. Her father understood that she had landed in a home where the atmosphere was alien to the up-bringing she had received. And indeed, the rabbi was able, through his frequent visits there, to soften Aharon-Leyzer's heart and reduce the dislike he felt for his daughter-in-law.

After three years had passed, Grandfather despaired of having his children marry into families of great rabbinical pedigree. He hardly viewed the match between his son and the daughter of a rabbi as a success story. He soon realized that it would be unjust toward his other sons to have them marry incompetent wives only because of their distinguished lineage. For his son Yosl he had al-ready arranged a match of the highest aristocratic level. From now on, what mattered most to him were practical considerations, such as beauty, fame, and capability. And all those qualities he found before long in the daughter of a respectable merchant living in another town; in addition she was a great beauty.[9]

The wedding celebration proceeded without a hitch. The bride entered Kamenets in a four-horse-drawn coach, like a noblewoman. The entire township turned out to get a glimpse of the beautiful bride, and everyone was taken with her charm and elegance and admired the costly jewels she was wearing. Aharon-Leyzer's happiness was indescribable. Furthermore, she was a very bright girl, well brought up, and knew how to endear herself to everyone. In short, she was perfection itself. Grandfather was curiously fond of her and never let her out of his sight, and he valued her more than any of his other children.

With Yokheved's arrival, Mother's status in the house went from bad to worse. Not especially liked even before that, the family nevertheless had taken pride in her distinguished lineage. Now, with the arrival of her new and beautiful sister-in-law, the rabbi, her uncle, no longer came to see her, and Grandfather scarcely bothered to hide his dislike of her. The difference between the daughter of the rabbi and the daughter of Shimon Daitsch was too blatant to be ignored. Grandfather was literally bewitched by the latter's charm.

Mother's situation was becoming unbearable. She was eaten up with envy. Everybody loved her young sister-in-law and made a big fuss over her. What irked Mother above all was that her father-in-law never stopped cooing over Yokheved and wouldn't even glance in her direction. She was constantly on the verge of tears and no longer came into the room where her father-in-law sat in the company of his fellow townsmen. The townsmen, for their part, were not sorry at having gotten rid of one that kept interfering with their lives and preventing them from speaking as they liked.

The new daughter-in-law introduced a new order into the household in accordance with her aristocratic upbringing. She cooked and baked all sorts of new never-before-tasted dishes and kept herself busy every moment of the day. Here she was embroidering something, there she fixed the undergarments of all the members of the family, or sewed dresses for the women and pants for the men. The household was transformed, cleaner, and everyone wore clothes that were certainly more elegant.

Mother often ran to her uncle, the rabbi, to pour out her heart to him and complain about her bitter lot. He tried to console her as best he could, pointing out how much more worthy her own husband was than Yokheved's husband. True, though Yosl was kind-hearted and honest and even knew how to study, Moshe, my father, was much brighter, more capable than he, and of much higher moral integrity.

When Mother was in tears in her own room, Father would console her with words similar to those of the rabbi. But it didn't relieve her misery—nothing helped. Father, therefore, came to the conclusion that he had to leave Grandfather's house; that setting up house for himself would put an end to the animosity and envy—she'd be able to go on reading her *Hovot ha-levavot, Menorat ha-ma'or,* and *Sefer hasidim* [10] to her heart's content, and peace would reign within his family once again.

But Father, apprehensive about raising the matter with Grandfather, first sought Grandmother's advice. He knew how much influence his mother exerted over his father, and that he usually followed her advice on even more important matters.

His mother advised him to write a loving letter to his father, describing Sarah's unhappiness, which kept her in tears for days on end, and explaining that that was why he wanted to live in a house of his own. In addition, he should add that he was terrified of his wife's tears, who was left an orphan since her father's death. There was no other way to calm his wife than to set up house for themselves. "If you write a letter in that vein," his mother was sure, "it will touch his heart. He is, after all, a kindhearted man, and such words as 'tears' 'aged parents now deceased,' and 'righteous Jews' are sure to make a strong impression on him. He'll probably tell me about the letter and ask what to make of it. And I'll certainly know what to advise him."

My father followed her counsel, and Grandfather received the letter. At first he was angry with his son for daring to challenge the ironclad rule of his life, which was to have all his sons live under the same roof with him. He had always said he would not give up this custom for all the wealth in the world. But the tears of the distinguished rabbi's orphaned daughter did touch his heart. Besides, he was afraid lest the dead spirits of such pious people as her deceased parents invoke a curse against him. He was in a quandary and decided to talk things over with his wife, Beyle-Rashe.

The wise Beyle-Rashe told him that she herself was greatly worried over Sarah's constant weeping; that one ought not to take lightly the influence such righteous people are likely to have should, God forbid, their daughter's tears reach them up above. "I'm trembling with fear of them," Grandmother said, "and apart from that, I'm sorry for our Moshe. Why should her tears ruin his life?" Grandmother agreed with him that the match had been a mistake and that she was a good-for-nothing, unable even to tie the tail to a cat.[11] But all that could not be changed, it was a lost cause, and now all that remained to be done was to let them live their own lives in peace and quiet. Grandmother knew well how to appeal to Grandfather's conscience and make him see things her way.

Father prevailed in the end. He rented an apartment from Sholem Yores: three rooms with a kitchen for twenty rubles a year. A new world now opened up for my mother. Only now could she live her life according to her own wishes and tastes; in other words, she could devote herself wholeheartedly to her books without having her sister-in-law and her father-in-law and his fellow townspeople constantly under her nose. Occasionally she would visit her uncle and spend hours on end talking with the rebbetzin.

Unlike other women, Mother never worried about making a living. She was totally unconcerned about everything. She never knew what was cooking for the midday meal or when it would be ready—she couldn't have cared less. It was pointless to talk about the sewing or mending of a shirt. Even the Sabbath or holidays came and went without her taking any interest in them or lending a hand, as if not she but someone else was the head of the household.

In that way, Father and Mother lived peacefully alongside each other for thirty years without any change. For nine months she was pregnant, for two years she suckled the newly born, and a new baby every three years. She only took care of the child at her breast and read *Hovot ha-levavot*.

Father never talked to her about the business and never asked her what there was for dinner that day. He knew she hadn't the faintest idea. But when he came home, she would tell him stories from *Menorat ha-ma'or* and how one ought to serve God according to *Hovot ha-levavot* and from other holy books. Father would listen patiently and keep silent.

CHAPTER 12

THE LORDS

The Lords • Berl-Bendet • The Estate of Czechczowa • Sikhowski • Berl-Bendet's loyalty • The false accusation • The feud between the lord and his wife • Bogoslawski • The end of the frame-up

*G*randfather wanted to acquaint his sons with the estate owners in the area, but failed in his efforts. My father refused to have anything to do with them. He found their dissolute ways distasteful and had no wish to earn his livelihood via direct dealings with them. He preferred the leaseholding business. His brother Yosl was not so inclined either. He did not wish to flatter or fawn on them like a puppy, and also preferred the leaseholdings, which provided him with an ample income.

Grandfather, however, insisted on handing his business over to a member of his family, and his choice fell upon the elder of his two sons-in-law—Berl-Bendet[1]—who, during the days of the "panic," had been married to one of his daughters at the age of eleven.[2]

He was a man to Grandfather's liking. Already in those early days, Berl-Bendet had the makings of a social climber. He was a great dandy, all spit and polish, and above all, he had the gift of the gab. Grandfather started taking Berl-Bendet along with him on his visits to the landowners, who took a liking to him almost immediately.

One day they drove to Czechczowa, the estate of a lord called Sikhowski.[3] He took to Berl-Bendet the moment he set eyes on him and offered him the post of commissioner of his entire estate then and there. The post had hitherto been held by a Christian who was a drunkard and had tricked his master out of a great deal of income. Sikhowski was a levelheaded man and thought it best to put a Jew in charge of his estates. A Jew never drinks to excess, and Berl-Bendet seemed to him the most suitable person for the job.

Although Grandfather spoke highly of Berl-Bendet's competence, he held that he was still too young for such a responsible position. Sikhowski did not share this opinion. True, he was young, but also the very person he required for a post of this kind.

"If you like," Sikhowski said, "you can remain here with your son-in-law for a short while to teach him the ins and outs of management, though to my mind, that is hardly necessary. Let him stay on right away. I'll send a special coach for his wife and children and a cart for all his household belongings. He will live in the former commissioner's house, will be provided with three cows, three maids, and a manservant. In addition, he will have at his disposal the coach-and-four formerly used by his predecessor."

In those days it was degrading for a respectable Jew to live in a village, that is, to be dubbed a *yishuvnik*.[4] But being offered such a tempting post for his son-in-law and by none other than Sikhowski himself, renowned for his decency and, in particular, for his friendly attitude toward Jews, greatly flattered Grandfather. Nevertheless, he told him that he had to talk it over with Berl-Bendet's father—Zelig Andarkes—as well as with their wives, and that he would send him his reply via special messenger by the following week.

No sooner did Grandfather reach home than he took counsel with his wife, Beyle-Rashe. She, too, favored the proposition, and had no doubt as to Berl-Bendet's suitability and capability of managing the estates to Sikhowski's complete satisfaction.

Apart from that, such a position would ensure her daughter's future, allowing her to live like a gentlewoman. Above all, she held that it was no disgrace to be a *yishuvnik* and there was no need to feel ashamed on that account. It was a far more respectable manner of earning one's living than that of a leaseholder and battling every Monday and Thursday with the townspeople, dealing with the tavern keepers, or with brawling drunks and all sorts of nasty types. That was Grandmother's advice, and it was, therefore, decided to accept the post.

Grandfather dispatched a letter to Sikhowski informing him of his son-in-law's acceptance, whereupon Sikhowski urged the young man to be ready with his wife and children and his belongings within three days for the coach he would send to fetch them.

On Wednesday, the coach, drawn by four horses, arrived for the family, along with three wagons, each drawn by two horses, for all the luggage and household belongings. Grandfather went along as well.

As soon as they arrived, Sikhowski ordered the steward to help them settle into their new dwelling while he took Grandfather aside to give him a detailed account of the duties expected of his son-in-law. "First of all," he told him, "Berl-Bendet must keep the steward and the peasants at arm's length, adopt a haughty posture toward them, and act as though he were the landlord himself. He must make them forget that he is a Jew and handle the management of the estate with great self-confidence." Grandfather, who was deeply concerned over the well-being of every member of his family, promised Sikhowski to remain beside his son-in-law for a week and undertook to initiate him during that time into all the tasks required in the management of such an enormous enterprise.

Sikhowski was by nature a kindhearted man. He was extremely wealthy and liked a peaceful existence. All he asked was that he need not do or think about anything. His overriding passion was hunting, for the purpose of which he owned all sorts of rifles and a huge pack of big, tall hunting dogs, famous throughout the district. He had a special, large hall where each of those rifles and assorted hunting equipment adorned the walls, in addition to precious tapestries depicting various hunting scenes. He had two horse stables full of specially trained hunters along with costly trappings worth thousands of rubles. His wife, on the other hand, was a hardhearted woman who closely managed the household and hated Jews. But she hadn't the slightest influence over her husband.

Their mansion was of royal dimensions. The ballroom itself could accommodate hundreds of people, and its walls gleamed with gold. They kept entertaining guests from the surrounding estates, and the nights were spent in eating and drinking, though very little vodka was consumed because Sikhowski hated excessive drinking and card playing. If his guests did play, he made sure they didn't lose too much. He and his wife were fine pianists and often played and danced together.

Sikhowski and his wife lived a comparatively tranquil sort of life, devoid of excesses, which certainly accounted for their robust health. They had an only son. Every afternoon, husband and wife went out horseback riding both for their enjoyment and to keep fit. Apart from the estate he lived on, Sikhowski owned two others, many fields, forests, barns full of wheat, and countless serfs.

Grandfather spent a week with Berl-Bendet, long enough to acquaint him with the management of the estate, the handling of the peasants working on it, and the duties demanded of a commissioner. They set to work immediately, issuing the steward new instructions and introducing new rules and improvements on this as well as the two other estates. Grandfather and his son-in-law did not rest for a moment. It did not take Grandfather long to realize how competent and industrious Berl-Bendet was and that the job suited him to the ground. He spared no effort to urge him on, though that was hardly necessary. Sikhowski, on his part, came to see them every day and was delighted with the way things were being handled and with the new order introduced into every sector of the estate, so badly neglected by the former commissioner.

Before the week was over, the idea of setting up a brewery on the estate took shape in Grandfather's mind. The farmyard was cluttered with empty buildings merely requiring certain interior changes, all of which would greatly augment Sikhowski's income. His land yielded him plenty of potatoes,[5] and if an additional supply for the brewery became necessary, more could be grown, for the soil was of superb quality. There was no lack of serfs, for whom there was not enough work. Moreover, perhaps Berl-Bendet could benefit as well. His salary was five hundred rubles a year, apart from all household expenses. He might increase it thereby to one thousand rubles a year or be granted a percentage of every pail of vodka. It had all the makings of turning into a most profitable enterprise, and Berl-Bendet was just the man for the job. Moreover, even the lord himself would have no objection to the additional income of a few thousand rubles a year.

Grandfather suggested the idea to Sikhowski, who was keen to act upon it at once. They set to work, and within a matter of a few months a fully operational brewery was ready. The first requirement, however, was the purchase of seventy oxen to devour the stacks of malt.[6] For that purpose, Berl-Bendet harnessed the lord's coach-plus-four and drove to the market in Kamenets. Sikhowski was pleased with the purchase, for Berl-Bendet had bought the oxen cheaply, with an expert's eye, and, above all, had dealt with him honestly. After grazing the cattle in the meadow for another ten weeks,

Berl-Bendet sold them for ninety rubles each, though he had paid only forty rubles a head for them earlier.

Before the winter set in they managed to buy and sell oxen twice over and make a handsome profit on those transactions. The vodka business was working out well, and before winter set in Sikhowski raked in a clear profit of twenty thousand rubles, a great deal of money even for a wealthy lord like himself. It goes without saying that Sikhowski was delighted with Berl-Bendet's performance and entrusted him with the wheat sales for all his estates. All the grain dealers that had formerly dealt only with Sikhowski were now sent to the young Jewish commissioner, who had become the sole authority responsible for the sales and purchases on the estates. Sikhowski, sucking at his long pipe, walked about the grounds in a peaceful frame of mind, devoid of the slightest worry. He could now devote himself exclusively to his hunting and to playing host to his many guests.

The only one who looked askance at all this sudden prosperity was Sikhowski's wife. What peeved her above all was that a Jew lorded it over the estate as if he were the very master himself. Besides, Berke—that's what everyone called him—was a handsome man, tall, and well dressed. He wore clothes of a much better quality than her husband, who couldn't care less about his appearance and usually walked about in sloppy suits, never bothering to order a tailor to take his measurements, and this, too, vexed the lady of the manor. But Berl-Bendet had hardly anything to do with her. All his dealings were with Sikhowski and no one else.

However, she did not let matters rest there, but was constantly searching for an opportunity to blame him for something. She kept sounding the steward out about the young commissioner's conduct, and asked to have any dishonesty or attempts at stealing brought to her attention.

The steward was quick to realize that his mistress was dead set on getting rid of Berl-Bendet and began making up, for her benefit, all sorts of stories: that he was carrying on as though he were the landlord himself, was puffed up with such arrogance that even the peasants themselves were hard put to distinguish between their real lord and his imitator.

"Keep your eyes open and try to catch him at thieving," his mistress hinted, "and then Berke will also get a proper flogging in the bargain."

The steward understood that the mistress expected him to simply fabricate some wrongdoing on Berl-Bendet's part. He found three crafty peasants who were put to carting the vodka to Grandfather in Kamenets, and instructed them to say that each wagon loaded with barrels for Aharon-Leyzer also contained several meant for Zelig Andarkes, Berl-Bendet's father, who also kept a tavern. The steward was well aware of the fact that Sikhowski would not believe the peasants' story about smuggling vodka to Aharon-Leyzer himself, for Aharon-Leyzer was well known among the landowners in the district for his honesty. But the tale about Zelig Andarkes, he reckoned, Sikhowski was more likely to believe and would result in the complete discrediting of Berl-Bendet. He gave the peasants three rubles each to testify that they were the ones who delivered the barrels of vodka to Zelig Andarkes.

After carrying out his scheme, the steward went to his mistress and told her a story that went something like this: the peasants are carting stolen vodka to Berl's father. The lady, who could scarcely conceal her delight, ordered the peasants to appear before her. They confirmed that in the wagons of vodka meant for Aharon-Leyzer were barrels for Zelig as well. "Are you ready to swear to this?" she asked them. "Yes, we are," they replied.

During that time, Sikhowski was away hunting, and on his return his wife told him with unconcealed eagerness that his commissioner was nothing but a petty thief. Sikhowski had the peasants appear in front of him, and they repeated the story about the smuggled vodka. He did not believe it, yet confronted Berl-Bendet with the following words: "Even though I don't believe a word of that story, nevertheless you must prove to me that the peasants are lying."

Berl-Bendet was greatly alarmed. This was probably the first time that he had ever lost his confidence, and it seemed that he was at a total loss how to react. It was such a far-fetched, foolish, and ugly fabrication. But how could he prove that the peasants were telling an outright lie? When he told his wife about it, she broke into tears, and an air of despair settled over the entire household.

Berl-Bendet's wife promptly traveled to Kamenets to fetch her father and have him put matters back on track. The first thing Grandfather did was to give Sikhowski a piece of his mind and reproach him for believing such false charges, maintaining that had Berl-Bendet any intention of stealing, he would have stolen

things of much greater value than several barrels of vodka. But on
the contrary, he was so meticulously honest that he even turned
down every kind of commission offered him by dealers come to
do business. More than once had he sent costly gifts back to their
donors and refused to have any further dealings with them.

"You yourself know," Grandfather went on, "how dearly he loves
you and puts your welfare above that of his father and mother, wife
and children. There is no doubt that it is a trumped-up charge by
someone plotting to undermine him."

"But three peasants have sworn to it," Sikhowski said, adding,
"though I myself cannot believe it. But, I have an idea. Let's flog the
peasants . . . and then we will know. We will beat them so hard until
they confess the truth."

"That's too severe a punishment," Grandfather said. "But I have
a simpler suggestion. Put the three men to work together in one of
your barns and place an honest but smart person behind the wall
to eavesdrop on their conversation. Peasants, if they are in together
on a dishonest deal, often like to chat about it amongst themselves.
It stands to reason that those three will talk about the false oath and
the truth will come out."

Sikhowski liked the idea and said that he would stand behind
the wall himself. "For, after all, my personal honor is at stake," he
said. "All the landowners in the neighboring estates keep poking fun
at me for employing a Jewish commissioner and warning me that I'll
still pay for it dearly in the end."

Immediately, the three peasants were put to work in a barn close
to the mansion, and Sikhowski stationed himself behind its wall to
eavesdrop on their conversation. He stood there for a long time,
probably several hours, for at first they chitchatted about trivial
matters, but at a certain moment one of them expressed his regret
at having let the steward talk him into swearing a false oath. After
all, the commissioner was a decent man, so why did he deserve such
a raw deal? One word led to another until all three thought it best
to confess to swearing that false oath. At that juncture Sikhowski
entered the barn. The peasants, of course, stood there with their
mouths agape, as still as corpses.

"Well, now, perhaps you'll tell me yourselves who is behind that
plot, for I've heard everything you said."

They fell to their knees, wept, and told him the truth from
beginning to end. Sikhowski at once sent for the steward, and as

soon as he arrived he asked, "Did you invent that story yourself or did someone put you up to it? I want to hear the truth and only the truth, because if you lie to me, I'll beat you until I break every bone in your body."

The terror-stricken steward at once admitted that it was—with all due respect—the landlord's own wife who had goaded him into the plot and that he was not the guilty party. Not wasting any time, Sikhowski went to his wife and confronted her with the steward's allegations. She did not deny them and admitted that she had prodded the steward into cooperating with her in order to get rid of Berke, whom she disliked heartily.

The end of the affair was as follows: the peasants were given sixty lashes of the whip, as was the steward, who was, in addition, deprived of his stewardship and reduced once again to serfdom, from which status he had only recently been released. And, to make amends for the great distress caused Berl-Bendet, Sikhowski planted a kiss on his head, promising him that he'd never again listen to idle rumors.

As mentioned above, Sikhowski was a most decent person and was deeply shocked at his wife's conduct. He stopped talking to her and would not even live under the same roof with her. He ordered Berl-Bendet to have one of his houses renovated, and meanwhile went to live on one of his other estates.

Berl-Bendet promptly set to work, and himself supervised the interior decoration of the new house. He traveled to Brisk to order from a furniture dealer the most expensive furniture sold in Warsaw itself. So elegantly and tastefully did Berl-Bendet fit out the new house that it aroused the admiration of the neighboring gentry, who had never credited a Jew with possessing such exquisite taste. Sikhowski now visited Berl-Bendet every day, driving up in his splendid coach, and Berl-Bendet's wife always had a tasty meal ready for him. He was greatly appreciative and had nothing but praise for her. She was a tiny creature and as skinny as she had been when she had married Berl-Bendet at the age of eleven. But she was a smart woman and very industrious. She was physically the very opposite of her tall, broad-boned, and handsome husband and looked a mere child beside him.

Sikhowski now went on visits to his aristocratic friends instead of entertaining them in his own home. They were familiar with every detail of the scandal. The mistress's condition was much less congenial—her husband had left her, and all the gentry gossiped about it.

Sikhowski's father-in-law was Bogoslawski, a wealthy landowner in the vicinity of Kamenets. He was a respectable character, though not as kindhearted as his son-in-law. But he was shrewd, and all the landowners in the area considered him a well-balanced and experienced man. He had a son, a great charlatan and one of the most dissolute playboys among the wealthy gentry. He was an enormous spendthrift to boot, squandering since his early youth a great deal of his father's money. His prudent father thereupon deprived him of all authority over the estate and warned all those who did business with him—the stewards and the Jews—not to trust his son in anything, because his father had no intention of paying out even a penny for any deal his son might have concluded with them.

This son, Sikhowski's wife's brother, had heard of what had been going on at the estate and came to Czechczowa to see his sister. She never stopped crying while pouring out her heart to him, whereupon he offered to kill the commissioner. "After all, killing a *Żyd*," he said, "is no great crime."

But she talked him out of committing such a folly, fearing that he might have to pay dearly for it. Above all, such measures would never succeed in bringing her husband back to her. Her profligate brother agreed with her on that score and both decided to travel to their father.

Their father was fond of Sikhowski and knew that he was extremely pleased with the performance of his Jewish commissioner. When he had heard all about the fabrications his daughter had tried to concoct, he greatly resented such indecent behavior on her part. But he pretended not to know anything about it and had, therefore, abstained from visiting his daughter. He was sure that, eventually, she'd be forced to ask him to intervene.

When they came to him he was alarmed at seeing the great change in her. But he ignored it and asked why she had come without Sikhowski. At that she hung her head and remained silent while her brother started giving their father a very one-sided account of the affair, making certain to put his sister's part in a positive light. At that, the old man cut him short. "Let her tell her own version," he said and told his son to leave the room.

When they were alone, he gave her a proper dressing down, reminding her of what a precious husband she had, and that he himself was very fond of him, as dear to him as any of his own children, and now he was deeply distressed at her unseemly conduct. What did she have against this Jewish commissioner, and why did she want to cause him so much harm? Was he any worse than a drunken Pole, and so on, and so on?

The daughter listened to her father, and his words pierced her heart. He spoke to her at great length, and she now recognized her misdeeds. She understood that she had brought this calamity upon herself and it was she who had ruined her marriage to such a good man as her husband. Again she broke into tears, at which her father gave her the following advice. "It isn't too late to patch matters up again. Do you know how? Do it through the commissioner himself. You ask him and he will surely agree to put an end to the whole affair."

That, however, was just too much. To ask such a favor of the little Jew she despised—she would never agree to do that! But the old man calmed her down. "You don't have to talk to the commissioner personally," he said. "Talk to his father-in-law. He is a very astute man and will certainly succeed in setting things straight again." After all, the father-in-law is not the son-in-law, but something different altogether. She was beginning to favor the idea but couldn't make out why old Aharon-Leyzer should agree to bring about a reconciliation, knowing that she had acted so cruelly toward his son-in-law.

"Don't worry," her father said. "He will be keen to do it. I told you that he is a very wise Jew and he is bound to agree to the plan because the present state of affairs is just as unpleasant for the commissioner himself. He won't last long in his post when his landlord is at odds with his wife on his account. And I have one more piece of advice for you: don't you ever concoct any more intrigues against the commissioner. Let this be the first and last time. Remember that! There's no one around here that can boast of a better commissioner, of one that handles the affairs of the estate with more devotion than he does." Finally, he told his daughter to return home the following day and leave the matter to him and Aharon-Leyzer.

Bogoslawski sent a letter to Grandfather, asking him to come and see him, not on business but on a personal affair. In his reply Grandfather wrote that this week was out of the question since he had prior engagements, but promised to call on him straight after the Sabbath. Grandfather was well aware that Bogoslawski wanted him to intercede and effect a reconciliation between Sikhowski and his wife. He had learned from his daughter that Sikhowski's wife was deeply distressed over the fact that her husband had left her and that he spent most of his time in the company of Berl-Bendet. Grandfather put off his visit on purpose, to have the wife fret over her wrongdoing a week longer.

When Grandfather finally arrived, Bogoslawski welcomed him warmly, and ordered tea and the best cigars, as though he were one of the distinguished gentry. Their conversation finally turned to the affair of his daughter, whom, Bogoslawski told him, he had given a piece of his mind; he had had a long talk with her and confronted her with the severity of her actions; she had wept a great deal and was now full of regret for her foolish conduct, and it was now high time to restore peace between the couple. Bogoslawski held that there was no one better suited to bring this about than Grandfather himself, whom he trusted unreservedly, and that there was no point in prolonging this scandal.

At this juncture, Grandfather launched into a lengthy speech of his own expressing regret over the entire affair but doubting if such a reconciliation would guarantee the prevention of similar acts in the future. "Let's not delude ourselves," Grandfather said, "the younger loose-living sons of the gentry and, if you will forgive me, also their wives, cannot accept the fact that there is a Jewish commissioner who has been given, by the lord himself, sole authority over the estate. None of them is ready to believe that there are Jews as honest as my son-in-law, for instance. As far as your own daughter is concerned, I fear that deep within her heart she still hates Jews and is likely to hatch some new intrigue against the commissioner."

"Notwithstanding all that," Grandfather continued his address, "domestic peace ought to be restored, and I'm ready to carry out your request. A Jew is always in favor of peace. Leave it to me," Grandfather added, "but for your part, see to it that from now on your daughter behaves better to the commissioner and judges him by his achievements. Take a look yourself around the estate and compare its former mismanagement with its present condition. Now things are in order, a real pleasure. Apart from it all, the commissioner has increased the income from the estate to a level the landlord himself had never thought possible."

"I've told her all that myself," the old lord replied, "and have no doubt that she'll change her attitude toward him."

Grandfather traveled at once to his son-in-law at Czechczowa. No sooner did he arrive than a servant asked Pan Aharon-Leyzer to go straight to the lord. Sikhowski received him most politely. He told him how furious he was with his wife for almost ruining the lives of Berke and his family. But he was willing to let bygones be bygones and would never again lend an ear to such foolish diatribe against his commissioner that might have caused the deaths of innocent people.

Grandfather was not slow to realize that in spite of his great anger at his wife, Sikhowski was ready to make up with her again; that he only needed someone to act as go-between. Grandfather talked long and frankly and steered the conversation toward the necessity for a reunion. First of all, he said, his conduct was unseemly for a gentleman like himself, and second, he was sure that his good example would rub off on his wife.

"Who the most suitable person to solve this problem might be, is hard to tell," Grandfather remarked, "but I'm willing to undertake this mission without loss of face on your part or an affront to your honor."

Sikhowski agreed, and in order to conclude this unpleasant interview, he said, "Now, let's change the subject and talk about the new brewery."

"That's something I'm not ready for, as yet," Grandfather told him. "But there's plenty of time."

Grandfather's interview with Sikhowski lasted for quite a while longer, and after taking his leave of him he went to see his son-in-law. He wanted him to talk with Sikhowski about a reconciliation. This matter must be put to rest, and if his son-in-law would also push for it, the whole affair could be finished off in no time.

After Grandfather left him, Berl-Bendet went to see Sikhowski and talked with him about a truce. Berl-Bendet assured him that he would treat her with the same respect as the lord, and that he was willing to forget all that had passed between them. Sikhowski was delighted to hear this and said that he agreed to whatever Berl-Bendet suggested.

So, Berke went to look up Sikhowski's wife. She was just then in the company of her brother, the scoundrel, who had been staying with her throughout the time of her troubles. As soon as he set eyes on the Jewish commissioner, he got up and hastened into the next room. Madame Sikhowski received Berke politely and they talked for a long time. At the end of their interview Berke told her that he no longer bore her the slightest grudge, and all he wanted was to restore peace between her and her husband. The whole affair, he told her, had already cost him enough health. She, thereupon, asked his forgiveness. "I know," she said, "that you are an honest man, so let's put all that behind us."

After his talk with Madame Sikhowski, Berl-Bendet sent his wife to her father, Aharon-Leyzer, to give him a detailed account of the conversation he had had with both husband and wife. Aharon-Leyzer had, by then, already worked out a plan for how to bring about this reconciliation. He promptly traveled to the estate owner Vilevinski, who, together with his wife, were close friends of the Sikhowskis. He knew that during their estrangement Sikhowski had called on the Vilevinskis several times. Vilevinski, too, was one of the more decent landlords, and it would seem that that may have accounted for his friendship with Sikhowski, with whom he drank and played cards, but in moderation.

Sikhowski had never breathed a word to him about the dispute between him and his wife but he had heard about it from others. Now, however, Grandfather gave him a precise account of the entire affair, adding that in his opinion the couple was ready to make up and that they were waiting only for the right opportunity. "I therefore suggest," Grandfather said, "that you invite your friend to your home one evening, whereas your wife will invite Madame Sikhowski. But your wife must make sure that the lady arrives here first, and only then may you send for the husband, who must be kept in the dark about his wife's presence in the house at the same time. As soon as he arrives, start talking to him about a possible reunion. Only then will I come to your assistance, and you can tell him that it was I who told you all about it."

Vilevinski was all in favor of Grandfather's plan. Madame Sikhowski was the first to arrive, and Sikhowski himself a short while after her. Vilevinski took his friend into another room and carefully broached the subject with him. Meanwhile, Grandfather also arrived but did not enter the room. Vilevinski got up and said, "My wife doesn't feel too well. Let's go into her room and see how she's doing."

When they entered, Sikhowski was taken completely by surprise at seeing his wife sitting beside Madame Vilevinski. It was an embarrassing situation. Sikhowski, who was about to leave the room, was held back and invited to sit down instead. The servants brought in refreshments—tea and cookies—and while they were drinking and talking Vilevinski remarked, "I've also invited Kotik, let's call him in here, it's always pleasant to be in his company." Grandfather was led in and sat down at the table. After a while, Vilevinski and his wife withdrew under one pretext or another, and Grandfather, not beating about the bush, went straight to the point.

He naturally spoke warmly in defense of Madame Sikhowski, claiming that she was not the only one to blame for what had happened, and so on, and so on. He finished his little speech by calling on Sikhowski to reach out for his wife's hand and to put an end to the affair once and for all. He gave a little cough, at which the Vilevinskis reentered the room. Vilevinski took hold of Madame Sikhowski's hand, his wife that of Lord Sikhowski, and they forcefully drew the couple together. They shook hands and kissed. The joy and jubilation was great indeed.

Before long the horses were harnessed to the carriage and all of them drove straight to the Sikhowski mansion, where they celebrated the reunion in great style. And so the feud ended.

Good times began for Berl-Bendet's and Madame Sikhowski's relationship. Now he often called on her to report about conditions on the estate and the holdings in general. She behaved toward him in an entirely different manner and even allowed herself to chat with him about the outside world and what was written in the newspapers. She spent many hours in his company.

Berl-Bendet applied himself to work with renewed zeal. He was a very industrious person, who got up at six o'clock in the morning in the winter and at four in the summer and immediately started on his supervisory rounds, not wishing to rely upon the steward to do it for him. In summer he rode about on his horse all day long, visiting every corner and issuing instructions. In winter he spent most of his time in the brewery. Everything there was shiny and clean, and the excise officials visiting it were full of admiration. Cleanliness was the watchword everywhere—in the farmyard, in its various sectors, in the cellars, barns, and storerooms.

This tidiness and efficiency became so famous among the estate owners in the district with breweries of their own that they came to take a look for themselves and maybe learn how to apply them to their own works. They constantly complained to Sikhowski about their inability to introduce such a regime of order on their own property.

That same meticulous cleanliness was also the rule within the farmyard. There was no lack of workers, and they were always at work sweeping the ground and spreading clean sand over it, and Sikhowski, needless to say, took great pride in the tidiness and orderly management of his estate. As a result, many landlords would have liked to employ a Jewish commissioner. But they thought it was not right or proper and they went on losing money as a result. Their estates were managed in the old, timeworn manner. There was no one who thought of introducing new ideas, or improving production methods. Berl-Bendet, however, ordered economic and management journals from Germany and put into practice many of the ideas suggested therein.[7]

CHAPTER 13

BERL-BENDET'S LIFE
ON THE ESTATE

The life of Berl-Bendet • His daughter's wedding • The Polish rebellion • How the mistress was about to be flogged • Berl-Bendet saves the mistress • Shmuel

*M*y uncle Berl-Bendet had four daughters and a son. He and his wife were only twelve-and-a-half years older than their eldest daughter, Brakha. Their five children were born within five years and they had no more after that. They lived lavishly at Czechczowa, and after the incident the Sikhowskis treated them like members of their own family. Sikhowski entrusted Berl-Bendet with the keys to his entire holdings. In Berl-Bendet's office there was a large oak chest serving as a safe, in which he kept the jewelry only seldom worn by Madame Sikhowski, as well as all her husband's cash.

Berl-Bendet also saw to the clothes his landlord wore. Sikhowski never had a notion as to what kind of garments he needed for which occasion, and Berl-Bendet would travel to Brisk to order the cloth for his suits and, sometimes, also for the dresses of the lady. Berl-Bendet, or Berke for short, dressed his lord and lady in clothes finer and more costly than those of any of the neighboring gentry.

Whenever he went to Brisk, he brought back for Madame Sikhowski jewelry worth hundreds of rubles. He once brought her a bracelet valued at fifteen hundred rubles and a string of coral beads worth two thousand rubles, and all that finery was in the chest in Berl-Bendet's office. In return for his devoted service, the lord ordered expensive clothes for Berke and his entire family whenever the tailor came to the estate.

When Berke's eldest daughter, Brakha, turned fifteen, Sikhowski thought that it was time to find her a husband. "I will," he said, "provide her with a dowry of 1,000 rubles (which in those days was considered a very respectable sum), pay for her entire wardrobe, and for the wedding expenses."

Berl-Bendet therefore had matchmakers look for a suitable bridegroom. This was shortly accomplished, and the betrothal contract was drawn up soon afterward at the estate. Sikhowski suggested that the 1,000 rubles he had promised for her dowry be deposited with a trustee in Brisk, and also had a gold watch attached to a golden chain bought for the bridegroom at the cost of 150 rubles.

Two carriages and three wagons were sent from the estate to bring all the guests to the betrothal ceremony. Sikhowski and his wife sat together at a small table and participated in the festivities with all the guests. The following day, all the guests were invited to a dinner at Sikhowski's. The food, prepared beforehand at Berl-Bendet's home, was taken across to the mansion.

The wedding itself was set for the first day of the month of Nissan, when all the work at the brewery came to a complete standstill, since alcohol could not be produced during the summer. The entire family—myself included—arrived for the wedding in coaches and wagons sent by Berl-Bendet. I remember sixteen teams of horses, harnessed to all different types of coaches, carriages, and wagons. Scores of merchants came to the wedding, and Berl-Bendet saw to it that all of them had adequate lodgings for the night. They were followed by the musicians from Kobrin, headed by Shepsl and Tudros the wedding jester.[1]

Our family arrived three days before the wedding, just after the brewery stopped working. Its large basins were now filled with hot water, in which I, my uncle's son Shmuel, and my father's youngest brother Yisrael, took a dip. Not far from us there was a basin of cold water, and one of the peasant boys kept splashing it at us. Yisrael and I took it good-humoredly and laughed it off, but Shmuel, Berke's only son, didn't think it was funny. He threatened to tell his father, who'd have him flogged for his impudence.

The young fellow didn't take the threat seriously and continued splashing us with the cold water. But it turned out to have been no empty threat. Returning home, Shmuel told his father tearfully that Andrey had splashed cold water on us while we were in the hot basin. Because of him we could have caught a serious cold.

His father didn't bother to make any inquiries but promptly sent for the man administering the floggings and ordered him to give Andrey fifteen lashes of the whip. The order was carried out without fail. Andrey then came to the little boy Shmulik, fell to his knees, and pleaded for his forgiveness. It was an ugly spectacle. But what impressed us above all was the authority wielded by Shmuel's father.

The wedding was held in great style: the feast consisted of the choicest food, with an enormous variety of meat dishes. Sikhowski ordered all his silver dishes and cutlery to be laid out so as to enhance the splendor of the celebration.

Both Sikhowski and his wife stood beside the canopy, and the wedding feast lasted from six in the evening until six in the morning. On the next day, Sikhowski invited all the guests to a dinner at his mansion to the accompaniment of musicians. He was altogether in raptures over Shepsl's music, maintaining that he'd never heard the likes of it during his entire life. The revelry at the mansion went on throughout the following night. Sikhowski danced with Berke and with the merchant Yisrael-Shmuel from Brisk, a shrewd Jew as well as a great joker, and the jokes he cracked had Sikhowski as well as his wife and the guests in stitches.

On the third day after the wedding, all the merchants and friends of the family left for home. We, the relatives, a few dozen of us, stayed on for the prescribed seven days of feasting, as did Shepsl and his band.

Sikhowski and his wife never tired of all the rejoicing. Madame Sikhowski even confessed her total ignorance concerning the ways of the Jews. She had been brought up from the cradle on the saying, "Żyd weźmie do torby," that is to say, "the Jew will snatch you up and shove you into his bag."[2] All her life she kept hearing Żyd! Żyd! And it scared her; she had felt threatened. Only now did she realize how amiable a people we Jews really were and how entertaining our company was.

The seven days of feasting came to an end and everyone returned home. Sikhowski presented Shepsl with 100 rubles and a diamond ring worth 150 rubles, in return for which he made him promise to come whenever sent for. Subsequently, Shepsl and two other players would perform four times a year at the balls given by the Sikhowskis for the surrounding gentry and would be paid one hundred rubles each time. They took their meals at Berl-Bendet's.

Shepsl's fame spread rapidly among the many landowners, who also invited him to play for them. But Shepsl declined most of those invitations under the pretext that he couldn't leave a Jewish wedding without musicians. He was willing to play only for the good-hearted Pan Sikhowski.

Shepsl never drank any vodka, taking only a sip or so of sweet wine—like a woman—and then no more than a single cupful. He had a pleasant and quiet air about him. He rarely spoke and then only a few words at most. He was never heard to laugh out loud. When Ruvele the jester would crack jokes right and left, and everyone would be rolling in the aisles with laughter, only then could one detect the tiniest hint of a smile on his lips, like on my father's.

That's how my uncle Berl-Bendet lived on the estate of Czech-czowa. But that is far from the whole story. Berl-Bendet's greatest service to his landlord was when he saved his life during the famous Polish Rebellion,[3] when many of the landed gentry were hanged or shot. During the rebellion Berl-Bendet persuaded Sikhowski against walking through the forest, lest he pay for it with his life.

The infamous Muravyov[4] appointed two military rulers in each district in the Vilna region. He supplied them with many Cossacks whose task it was to make the rounds of all the estates in the district to find out which of the landowners had remained at home and which had joined the rebels in the forests. Those military rulers were empowered by Muravyov to beat the lords, their wives, and even their children, and by force of those beatings to extract information as to the whereabouts of their menfolk. And those Cossacks meted out the lashings, sparing neither the noblemen, nor their wives, nor their children above the age of ten.

When the military ruler of Shereshov reached the Czechczowa estate, and with him fifty Cossacks, he did not find Sikhowski at home. He had left the house only a short while before. The officer angrily asked the wife where her husband "the rebel" was. Terrified, her face pale with fear, she replied that he had only just left and would soon return. Unwilling to wait, the officer screamed to his Cossacks, "Lashes! And don't stop until she tells me where exactly her husband can be found."

The Cossacks stood ready to beat her: oh, what a spectacle that would be! And were about to begin counting the strokes when Berl-Bendet burst in and told the commander that his landlord had left him that very moment and would be back almost immediately. "I guarantee it," Berl said confidently, "Keep me, and if he doesn't return within fifteen minutes you may flog me instead, or even shoot me."

Berl-Bendet sent servants to bring Sikhowski back without delay. He knew that he always liked taking a stroll on his own around the avenues behind the courtyard.

The commander looked at Berl-Bendet—a tall man, full-bodied, handsome, and well dressed. He liked what he saw. Besides, Berl spoke a good Russian, something quite rare among the Polish gentry. He asked, "Who are you?"

"I'm the commissioner of the estate," Berl replied.

When he asked if he was a Pole and learned that he was a Jew, the commander liked that as well. He told his Cossacks to release the lady for the time being, and continued his chat with the Jewish commissioner.

Meanwhile, Sikhowski entered. "You owe your Jewish commissioner a great favor," the commander said. "If not for his intervention, your wife would have come in for a proper whipping." He warned Sikhowski not to dare leave the compound after he and his men had gone, for he was likely to come back on a surprise inspection, and should he not find him at home, he wasn't going to wait for even ten minutes and his wife and children would be brutally beaten—"I won't spare you a second time, rebels like you!" After eating and drinking their fill and feeding their horses, they took along with them a ten-*tep* barrel of vodka and headed for the neighboring estate.

Madame Sikhowski took ill from the shock and the humiliation and her condition was critical. Berl-Bendet, who was greatly concerned over the state of her health, sent a coach to Brisk every day to fetch various doctors to administer to her. Within a few months the mistress resumed her strength.

Only then did Sikhowski tell her, in the presence of the commissioner, "Now can you see how lucky you were when your intrigues against him failed? You wanted to have Berke flogged and have him driven off the estate. Now it is he himself who has saved our lives. Imagine what those Cossacks could have done to you with their iron rods, if it hadn't been for Berke."

Sikhowski stayed indoors and did not leave the mansion as long as the rebellion lasted, and Berke managed the estates by means of hired peasant labor. They liked him and were willing, but only for him, to work in the fields, in return, of course, for generous wages.

In the fields of the surrounding estates nothing was sown, and in places where grain crops did grow, all the seeds virtually poured out of the stalks' ears, for it was impossible to find reapers, even for good wages. The peasants stayed away on purpose, in order to aggravate the lords, and if they did turn up it was only to bind them and flog them in revenge for what they had had to endure throughout the years.

Berl-Bendet, on the other hand, had more work than usual during the days of the rebellion. Apart from the peasants, whom he had to keep calm, he also had to contend with the landlords of other estates, lest they drag Sikhowski along with them to the forest. In return for his exemption from actual participation, Sikhowski awarded them—at Berl-Bendet's advice—financial aid, each time about ten thousand rubles. Thus, he was kept safe, more or less, from both dangers.

In light of all this it is not hard to guess why Berl-Bendet gained such gratitude from the Sikhowskis. After the suppression of the rebellion, when Sikhowski was once again able to drive about in an open coach-plus-two, Berke did likewise. In that way, he lived for some thirty-odd years on Sikhowski's estate. Sikhowski helped him to marry off his five children and also contributed toward their dowries, though he could give each of them only five hundred rubles, since he had lost a great deal of money during the rebellion.

Berke died at the age of fifty or so. None of his children were competent enough to step into his post. His son Shmuel was a decent person, but he lacked his father's intelligence and drive. Sikhowski put him in charge of his second estate, which was much smaller than the one at Czechczowa. Though he managed, by this means, to support his growing family, it was a far cry from his father's achievements.

When both Sikhowski and Shmuel died (Shmuel died very young), Madame Sikhowski and her son presented Dvorah, Berl's widow, with the sum of five hundred rubles, and she returned to Kamenets. She also inherited her father-in-law's large house, in which she lived for the rest of her life.

CHAPTER 14

HOW WE CELEBRATED
THE HOLIDAYS

Rosh Hashanah and Yom Kippur • Feelings of awe • Floggings • The
blessing of the children • Fear in the prayer houses • With the hasidim • Sukkot • Simhat Torah • Holidays in general • How we celebrated the holidays

*L*ike all the *yishuvniks,* Berl-Bendet and his entire family
spent all the High Holidays in Kamenets.[1] They put up at
Grandfather's, and three rooms were set aside especially in
their honor. He would haul along a cart full of kitchen utensils as well
as plates and cutlery, and that's how the family always spent Rosh
Hashanah and Yom Kippur together. Grandfather's family consisted
of five daughters, three of whom were married and had children of
their own, and three sons, two of whom were married and also had
children of their own. It was a fun-filled time.

Berl-Bendet preferred taking his meals separately, with his own
family, but, on the New Year, upon returning from the prayers, he
was obliged to take part in the kiddush in Grandfather's quarters.
The tables were laid out with all kinds of tarts, piroshki,[2] egg-cakes
filled with almond crumbs, and sugar-topped fritters, a specialty
of Grandmother's, famous all over the township for their delicious
flavor. The house was teeming with people—all members of our
family.

Early on the day before Rosh Hashanah, around three o'clock
in the morning, all the children and grandchildren, even the seven-
and eight-year-olds, as well as Grandfather's brother's family, would

gather at Grandfather's home, where tea, cakes, fruit preserves, and sweet wine were served. Everyone ate and drank, and afterward went to the study houses situated in the synagogue courtyard in order to recite *selihot*. At the head of the procession walked the menfolk and their sons, followed by the wives, daughters, daughters-in-law, and the small grandchildren. I remember once counting the members of my family on that occasion: Not one, not two, not three.[3] I counted more than forty.

The procession to *selihot* was such a merry one, it must have looked almost like soldiers marching in time. They already referred to us in the shtetl as the "Tsar's Regiment" on the march again, because in the study houses no one dared to start *selihot* before the "Regiment's" arrival. Only on reaching the courtyard of the synagogue did the family split up, some heading for this, others for that study house.

Grandfather used to say the *selihot* prayers on the eve of Rosh Hashanah and the eve of Yom Kippur at the large, old study house. He had a place reserved for him along the *mizrah* side, next to the rabbi, a second one at the corner of the *mizrah,* and a third one on the southern side, next to the first window. On Rosh Hashanah and Yom Kippur Grandfather prayed at the synagogue where he had three reserved seats in the *mizrah:* one for himself, one for his brother Mordechai-Leyb, and one for his brother's "only child." Berl-Bendet attended the new study house, where Grandfather also had two reserved seats: one in the *mizrah* and one in the south, also a respectable location. Only my father was absent, as he always traveled to his rebbe for the New Year.[4]

On the night preceding Yom Kippur, no one went to bed. The entire family gathered at Grandfather's for the *kapparot* ceremony. Grandmother had already bought several dozen cocks and hens for that purpose. The more respectable householders used to send their own *kapparot* to Grandfather's house, because the ritual slaughterer, who spent the entire night making the rounds of the houses, always started off at Grandfather's. For this purpose, Grandfather prepared a large shed, to which—with Grandfather's approval, of course—many householders brought their own fowls for slaughter.

That evening the table was set with sweet wine, cakes, and fruit preserves. Those present were able to start with the *kapparot* ceremony. Some did it for themselves, others together with their small children. At the end of the *kapparot* ceremony, everyone, including the ritual slaughterer, drank a *lehayyim* and ate a little something, after which he set to work. The ceremony lasted several hours. At four o'clock in the morning everyone went to say *selihot,* except for the young boys and girls, who went home to sleep.

Grandfather started taking me along for the *selihot* prayers after I turned seven, but not his son Yisrael, who was my age. He was not at all interested in this ceremony, but to me it was most precious and important, so I kept nagging Grandfather to take me along with him. When Grandfather recited the *selihot* prayers together with me on the eve of Rosh Hashanah, he wept bitterly, and I, too, having no alternative, wept with him. Rivers of tears flowed down my cheeks, and Grandfather was pleased to see that his grandson was weeping. Maybe, thanks to the child's tears, God would protect us all.

During the *selihot* prayers Grandfather wept so hard that his knees started trembling. Perceiving this, I pressed my own knees hard against his in order to arouse a similar trembling in mine. That had such an awesome effect that I broke into heartrending sobs that rose higher and higher, to the highest level. Grandfather, it seemed, was pleased, and always took me along with him, even if I hadn't asked. He was a great weeper, and I must have inherited that trait from him. To this day, as soon as I hear someone crying, no matter for what trivial reason, my eyes at once fill with tears.

On Yom Kippur eve, at midday, Grandfather went with the entire family for the afternoon prayers. On that occasion he gave fifty rubles to charity, his brother thirty, and the rest of the family fifteen or twenty rubles each. The women contributed separately. In that way my family gave away a great deal of money to charity.

The floor of the synagogue was strewn on that day with hay, and a small heap of it lay piled up beside the door. Each of the important householders prostrated himself on it in turn, and the head beadle, wearing a *kittel* and wielding a big whip, stood beside him, meting out forty strokes, which he counted in Hebrew: *ahat, shtayim,* until forty.[5] Each man stretched out full length, wearing only his outer garments, and the beadle administered the strokes, first on the bottom, then on the top—on the back. While they were being whipped, the prostrate also beat their breasts.[6]

The poor took no "pleasure" in those strokes, because in return for their penance they would have had to pay the beadle a generous fee. When many householders arrived at once they waited patiently in line. The wealthier householders received their lashings first. When Grandfather himself arrived, he promptly lay down and the beadle started counting. It always filled me with rage, seeing Grandfather lying prostrate and the beadle beating him. . . .

About half past one in the afternoon, we all returned home for a hasty meal of chicken and noodles and a hurried Grace after Meals. After that, Grandfather began to bless the children on one side of the room, and Grandmother those on the other.[7] Grandfather started calling out each one by name and in the order of seniority: first his grown-up sons and sons-in-law, after that his daughters and daughters-in-law, after that the daughters of his daughters and the daughters-in-law of his daughters-in-law. For this blessing ceremony even two-week-old infants were brought in. The males were first, ranging from the eldest son to the tiniest infant, whose mother still carried him around in her arms on a small cushion. He would place his hands over its head and pronounce the benediction. After that, he blessed the women, again in the order of their seniority.

During the blessing, Grandfather burst into heartrending wails that could have melted a stone. It goes without saying that everyone cried along with him, old and young together. The air was filled with a mixture of varied and strange weeping voices—deep, thin, and screeching sounds. A casual observer might well have thought that he was witnessing the destruction of the town.

No sooner did Grandfather conclude his part of the blessing than everyone stepped over to Grandmother's side. Her eyes were also overflowing with tears, but no sound was heard. She merely placed a bony hand on each one's head, letting the tears wash her cheeks silently, silently, silently.

The blessing ceremony took over two hours. Grandfather always arrived late at the synagogue, which, by then, was already packed with the congregants waiting for him to commence with the Kol Nidre prayer.

Oh, those Days of Atonement of long ago. Good Lord, what went on then!

The congregants in the synagogue during the Kol Nidre prayer seemed to be gripped by a sense of excitement and fear. They were on their feet, ready as though expecting that very moment to set out on their journey to the world to come. All wore white *kittels*,[8] and gold and silver embroidered girdles, and wrapped themselves in prayer shawls and yarmulkes with similar trimmings. Grandfather's own girdle and yarmulke cost tens of rubles, and there were others wearing even more beautiful ones. Even the poor wore white yarmulkes trimmed with colored silk thread.

So many candles glimmered in the candelabras suspended from the ceiling by ropes. Candles were also placed on the tables, inside small sand boxes. Everyone wished to light a candle in memory of his late parents, which were kept burning from the onset of Kol Nidre until the following evening after the concluding *Neilah* prayer. The light glittered back and forth from the gold, silver, and silken trimmings on the yarmulkes, the white *kittels* and prayer shawls, and cast an aura of holiness over the faces of the congregation. No thoughts of impiety, of worldly or daily affairs crossed their minds.

The crowd was weeping and wailing and pleading before God to forgive them their sins, bestow upon them a good year, a year of health. Each one poured out his heart amid a river of tears to his Creator. The heartrending wails from the women's section penetrated down to that of the men, who joined their womenfolk and broke into a chorus of wailing themselves, just like the women.

Nowadays, when the totality of the Yom Kippur experience has become diminished and the tremendous fear of this holy day no longer has a hold on us, it is difficult to describe those nights of Kol Nidre! The very walls wept, the stones in the streets sighed, and the fishes in the water trembled. How fervently those people prayed— those very same Jews who fought one another viciously throughout the year over a single groshen for their livelihood! No hatred and no envy, no greed and no cunning, no cursing or evil gossip, no food and no drink. All hearts and eyes were turned heavenward, and there was only spirituality—mere bodiless souls. From the cantor's lectern, stirring melodies flowed down to them, penetrating to the core of their hearts.

At age twelve, my father took me to the Kol Nidre prayers in the *shtibl* of his fellow hasidim. Kol Nidre there was conducted in an altogether different manner, and I liked it much better than that of the mitnaggedim. One never heard any weeping, sobbing, or lamenting in the hasidic *shtibl.* The prayers were chanted with great fervor. Those possessing agreeable voices raised them joyfully, while those without prayed silently and in a dignified manner, and all joined in the same heartfelt chanting. There was no cantor, nor cantorial singing. The prayer leader chanted the words in a pleasant melody and everybody repeated them after him.

At the end of the Kol Nidre service many of the hasidim, both old and young, stayed on and even slept in the *shtibl* on the hay strewn all over the floor. That was something unusual and aroused my curiosity. I loved spending the night lying on the hay together with them. The hasidim lay about and continued chanting heartfelt melodies throughout the night; a sweet feeling accompanied our sleep. Their mellifluous murmuring rang within my ears, inducing in me a light but pleasant slumber, rousing me off and on, while all around me singing, singing, softly, softly.

On Yom Kippur morning the prayers commenced around ten o'clock, amidst noise and clamor, like soldiers on parade, and the praying was conducted with a great deal of good taste and simplicity. They started with a kind of common outcry that came straight from the heart, and all the hasidim stood up and remained on their feet until around twelve o'clock. This was followed by the auctioning off of the *aliyot,*[9] just as was customary among the mitnaggedim. But even this auction was done in a more tasteful manner.

Once again, the hasidim, the choirboys, and the elderly lay down on the hay and started chanting, not just one melody but several; one kind by those in this corner, another kind by those in that corner, each according to the tunes sung by their own rebbes— the Karliner hasidim, their melody, the Slonimer, theirs, and one single hasid, a follower of the Lubavitcher rebbe,[10] chanted his tunes all by himself. And all those fervently chanted tunes melted into a single melody and spread through all one's limbs.

Soon it was time to begin the *musaf* prayers. Many of the hasidim had no patience for *piyyutim.* They preferred chanting their soulful songs to intoning the conventional prayers, and went on humming their own tunes silently, under their breath.

I liked the Yom Kippur service among the hasidim so much that I also went to their *shtibl* on Rosh Hashanah, though without my father. (He always traveled to his rebbe then.)

At the close of Yom Kippur, after the evening prayer, all the children and grandchildren gathered at Grandfather's home. Once again we had cakes, wine, and fruit preserves, after which we ate the chickens used earlier for the *kapparot* ceremony. Then Grandfather's brother arrived with his entire brood and the merriment lasted until late into the night.

Only my father, as I stated earlier, was absent on the New Year; he was with his rebbe. First he traveled to the Kobriner rebbe, and after his death, to the Slonimer rebbe. On the eve of Yom Kippur he came to Grandfather's just for the blessing ceremony—and that was all. Yom Kippur he spent with his fellow hasidim in their *shtibl,* and on account of that, the joy in Father's house on the outgoing of Yom Kippur was even greater. Already by eight o'clock all the hasidim had begun to gather at our place and kept drinking, singing, and dancing all night long.

I, therefore, had two different ways to celebrate: at Grandfather's, and at my father's home. I was drawn to wherever it seemed merrier, but tried to put in an appearance at each place in turn.

The following morning, a coach arrived from the estate of Czechczowa for Berl-Bendet and his wife, a wagon for the children and servants, and a cart for all the household belongings. The entire family turned out to see them off, and once again we had lots of fun.

As a rule, on every holiday the entire family was required to come to Grandfather's home. The adults would have the two major meals in their own quarters, but the children had to take those festive meals together with Grandfather. The large room was packed with big and small children, eating and drinking and kicking up such a racket that Grandfather had to give up his customary afternoon nap. He sat with them at the table for hours on end, delighting in their company. He loved it, and the noisier and more frolicsome the better. The laughing voices and the constant banter of old and young were deafening, and he sat there simply self-satisfied. He kept changing places, passing from one group to another, following their amusement with a joyful face.

Grandmother used to buy bags full of nuts for the holidays and kept dealing them out to the children, first to play with and then to loudly crack open; others poured wine into tumblers. It was, in a word, *noisy.*

At Father's place the rejoicing was in true hasidic fashion. Throughout the Sukkot holiday, the very house was carried aloft on the wings of songs and dances lasting entire days and nights. After the hasidim finished praying in the *shtibl* and snatched a hurried meal at their homes, they at once made for Father's place, and then the singing and dancing began.

Simhat Torah was the opportunity to perpetuate a time-honored custom. Two Kotsker hasidim, Yankl and Shepsl the scribe, accompanied by scores of young boys, went from house to house, removing from the ovens whatever they could lay their hands on—the roast geese, the tzimmes,[11] the pastries—and bringing them to our house, where the feasting surpassed all limits.

I must admit that I myself was among the boys assisting the two hasidim in their pogrom against the ovens of neighboring houses. I remember us storming into a house and clearing the oven of all it contained. The housewives resisted, but who listened to them? We simply grabbed as much as we could carry, and hurried on. And all that "stolen" food was brought straight to our house.

Several weeks before Hanukkah people started playing cards,[12] but it was a far cry from the scandalous and cutthroat gambling many indulge in now. Back then, the entire family gathered at Grandfather's and each of the players named a child for whom he was playing. Everyone sponsored a different child and handed over all his winnings to him or to her. Only rarely did anyone lose more than ten gulden. The normal losses amounted to between thirty and seventy-five kopecks.

That's how the family spent the evenings together during the days before Hanukkah, a few hours every day, and on the holiday itself they sometimes played on until midnight. The games took place every evening through the night of *nitl,*[13] on which it was considered a holy duty to play cards; also, it was the custom not to study Torah on that particular night. But the card games ceased altogether straight after *nitl.*

I remember how much I wanted a member of the family to play for me. But Father would not allow it and always preferred to make a deal with me. He would ask me: "How much money would you get out of it, Khatskl—thirty kopecks . . . half a ruble . . . and sometimes nothing at all. Take half a ruble and forget about the card game." But he never gave me the money outright, preferring to buy me something the next morning—a penknife, a wallet, or something suitable for an eight-year-old boy.

The girls used to play a game called *Okeh*[14] all day long.

Father took special care to prevent me from playing cards and paid me for it handsomely, in other words, by buying gifts instead. He got me so used to it that to this day I don't know one card from another and have no inclination for that kind of amusement.

At age seven or eight I made a name for myself as a great "reckoner," meaning I could calculate in my head, as quick as lightning, such multiplication as six times six, fourteen times seventeen, eighteen times twenty-nine, and so on; I would come up with the correct answer on the spot.

I remember once on Hanukkah, instead of playing cards, they tried to quiz me in "mathematics." The whole family gathered in Grandfather's room and, standing around me, put problems to me, all of which I solved immediately. It earned me a great deal of respect, lots of cheek-pinching, and a silver coin from each one present.

I was asked how many seconds there were in a year, and I supplied the answer in less than half an hour. But when my great-grandfather, Yudl, asked me how much two-and-a-half times two-and-a-half was I was at a loss, having no notion how to begin calculating that kind of sum and being ashamed to admit it. Father saw my bewilderment and explained that even greater "mathematicians" than myself would have found it difficult. Only after he taught me how to calculate fractions did I calm down.

On Purim, Grandfather had some kind of a "monopoly" over several dozen of the more well-to-do householders in Kamenets, whom he invited for the holiday feast. Naturally, none of Grandfather's own family—his sisters, their husbands, and sisters-in-law—were absent from the occasion. The tables were laden with bottles of wine and vodka and an assortment of roasted and baked dishes, and the fun we all had would be difficult to convey to people belonging to later generations. Among the guests was also the cantor of the town together with his choirboys. Actors performed the *Purim-shpil*,[15] and staged acts taken from their "artistic" repertoire. Musicians strummed their instruments, and the audience listened, ate, drank, and celebrated till the small hours of the morning.

At the beginning of the month of Nissan, Grandmother started with the preparations for the entire family toward the approaching Passover holiday. She had already strained off the *schmaltz*[16] during the winter. She began fattening the geese, and throughout the winter she would fry *schmaltz* for all the members of the family. Straight after Purim she started brewing the mead and wine for the entire "Tsar's Regiment." Her mead, like everything else to which she put her hand, was famous throughout the township.

Eight days before Passover, Grandmother baked matzah for everybody. She reserved an entire day—from dawn to dusk—at the matzah bakery and took with her some thirty maidservants to help with the labor. None of the menfolk—neither her sons nor her sons-in-law—took any part in the Passover preparations. Grandmother sent everyone everything he needed.

Before baking the matzos, the floors of the dining hall and two other big rooms were given a thorough scrubbing and were then covered with a layer of hay, which remained there until Passover eve. The *chametz* meals were taken in the other rooms, and we children loved to roll about on the hay in the large hall. Three days before Passover, all the boys were released from their studies, and what fun we all had playing pranks on one another on the hay-covered floor! It was the greatest amusement of the entire year.

Throughout Passover, all the families with their children, from the youngest to the eldest, stayed over at Grandfather's home. We ate latkes,[17] drank mead, and cracked nuts.

Our whole family was bound to one another, connected and united—unlike today. We were like one person with a single soul. If someone took ill, everybody rushed to his bedside, and often stayed there for nights and days on end. Three to four family members sat beside him and the rest bedded down on the floors in the other rooms. If the sick person needed a particular article, several of his relatives were ready to fetch it for him.

If his condition worsened, everyone was in tears; and when he died—child or adult—the wailing often reached to high heaven. During the shivah the house hummed with constant coming and going of family members. Many spent the night sleeping on the hay dispersed all over the floors, all aimed at keeping up the spirits of the bereaved family. And, in contrast, during a happy event—a circumcision, a celebration for the birth of a daughter, a betrothal ceremony, not to mention a wedding, or the expected arrival of a prospective bride or groom—the rejoicing was so great so that it is difficult to describe today. Everyone was together and almost out of his or her mind with joy.

In Grandfather's house there was a large hall on one of the upper floors, which served as a kind of reception room for the more important visitors, like one of the gentry, prospective in-laws, or the more respectable members of the community. In this room, which was always well furnished and kept meticulously clean, the younger members of the family learned to dance.

If a wedding was in the offing within the family, the dancing lessons started three months in advance. I remember myself as quite a nimble dancer in my younger days, and there were many occasions for celebrating: a circumcision here, the birth of a baby girl there—we all felt that each other's celebrations were like our own. Grandfather, of course, enjoyed seeing the children turn the house upside down. It was his greatest pleasure.

If, on a Shabbat or other holiday afternoon, he wanted to take a nap, he didn't go upstairs to his own bedroom, isolated from the noise in the house, but lay down in a chamber near the large room where all the children, big and small, kicked up a terrific racket, leaving the door slightly ajar so he could hear their uproarious laughter and endless chatter.

For Grandfather's great devotion to his family, one must "blame" Grandmother, as one must for many other things. This wise, competent, and good-hearted woman did everything in her power to ensure that our large family remain united, that we remain loyal to one another and, above all, that we see in Grandfather the merciful and forgiving patriarch. But I must admit that after Grandmother's death, the family loyalty and warmth began to spoil, and many things which had characterized the "Tsar's Regiment" changed.

If Grandfather married off a daughter or a son, he asked my father, Moshe, and Arye-Leyb, his brother's "only child" to compile a list of all the garments needed for the bride or the bridegroom, and for all the members of the family. Then all the children and grandchildren, from the tiny tots to the older ones, once again assembled at Grandfather's, and each was asked what kind of garment he or she would like.

The high-pitched outcries of the smaller ones, "Grandpa, I want this!" mingling with the deeper voices of the older children, "Grandpa, I want that!" not to be outdone by the clamor of the women and young girls for a garment of their own, would fill the room with earsplitting noise. Yet, among the shrill chorus of voices, the only word clearly audible was "Grandfather! Grandfather! Grandfather!"

It was impossible to introduce some semblance of order, and therefore it was decided to compile a list of the names of all the males down to the age of two, and another one of all the females, from the eldest to the youngest—and according to the list, like in an army roll call, every name was called out separately and each was asked: "What garment would you like?" Not unexpectedly, every one wanted more than was his due. Then the bargaining began. "So many? *No!* The rest you'll get some other time."

"Now!"

Tempers ran high. Some of the more sensible children quickly sought the help of the "only child," who had great influence over his uncle Aharon-Leyzer and was usually able to achieve his aims, even if these ran counter to his uncle's own wishes. And of course in this matter as well he could aid us.

My father and Arye-Leyb traveled to Brisk in order to purchase the required cloth. The expense for it often amounted to six hundred or even seven hundred rubles, apart from what was bought in Kamenets itself. The material for the garments was somewhat cheaper in those days than today; in other words, the highest quality woolen cloth cost thirty to forty kopecks an ell;[18] the best velvet cloth, three rubles an ell, and pure silk cloth, between one and one-and-a-half rubles.

Uncle Mordechai-Leyb insisted on dividing the expenses equally between him and Aharon-Leyzer, and that was the rule observed for many years. If Grandfather married off a son or daughter, the expenses for the meals during the seven days of rejoicing were borne on an equal basis: one day the festivities were paid for by Grandfather, the next by Uncle, and so on.

CHAPTER 15

THE REBBE IS DEAD!

My father's hasidic conduct • My melamdim • The rebbe is dead! • The denunciation • Twersky • Leyb • The fine

In my father's eyes all joyful family events and worldly pleasures paled in comparison to the delights of Hasidism. There was no greater enjoyment for him than to sit around the table with his fellow hasidim and sing soulful hasidic songs—then he really got excited. He was unreservedly devoted to his rebbe, Moshe of Kobrin, and after the rebbe's death, to Avraham of Slonim,[1] both of whom, in his opinion, were blessed with the Divine Presence and were constantly surrounded by holy angels. For Father, the main thing was Hasidism; thus, he had no interest in my really knowing how to learn. He was perfectly satisfied with the religious education I was receiving, and therefore never considered that at the end of each term I should be turned over to a better melamed.

I had, as mentioned above, a good head, and after learning a term with one melamed, ought to have advanced to the next stage with a more knowledgeable teacher. But Father kept me with each melamed for two years, and I therefore stayed at the same level, unable to advance in my studies in accordance with my natural abilities. Indeed, this was almost a "favor" to me, since I was always the best pupil and did not have to exert myself.

I stayed with Mote the melamed for two years and could already learn an entire page of the Talmud with *Tosaphot* on my own. He taught us very little because he himself knew next to nothing. I was keen on starting to learn *Tosaphot,* and when I mentioned this to my father, he said, "What do you need to know that for? You are already learning the Talmud. To be a pious Jew is all you need, that's the main thing."

Instead of this, I learned from Mote the melamed all about Hell, down to its architectural details. I also knew everything about the "middle of the sling" and about the angels of destruction, and about all the terrible and awful torments the wicked endured in the world to come. About Paradise and its fine accommodations Motke the melamed knew hardly anything at all. But I knew a great deal about that place from the "Patshoshnik,"[2] the *porush* who spent every Sabbath at Uncle Mordechai-Leyb's house and loved to describe it: chairs made of diamonds, precious gilt palaces, and delicacies, delicacies, delicacies, that no mouth could describe! The *schmaltz* alone, dripping from the goose of Rabbah bar Bar Hanah,[3] the fine oil and the specially aged wine, the bunches of grapes, each individual orb yielding whatever kind of wine one's heart desired!

Concerning demons and devils, evil water spirits, and all sorts of sorcerers, I had already heard from Grandmother and Leybke, the beadle of the synagogue. In all those things I had become a great expert, a genius. I was fluent with the smallest details of the most atrocious and horrible misdeeds and had a thorough knowledge of everything connected with the "evil eye."[4]

There were two people in our township who knew incantations against the evil eye. One of them was David the carter, who delivered flour from the mills to the shops. He used to neutralize the evil eye by means of small bones from a human skeleton. To this day it remains a mystery to me how he came by those small bones. If anyone's face swelled, in other words, if his cheeks swelled up due to an infected tooth, as it is called, or if he suffered from a sore throat, he would go to David the carter. He would take hold of those small bones and circle the swelling with them, all the while whispering incantations to himself. And the patient was convinced that, if not at once, then the next day or the following week or so, the swelling would disappear. There was no doubt in the minds of the town's inhabitants that the swelling was caused by the evil eye.

The other person who knew how to neutralize the evil eye was Golda, the preacher's wife. The preacher was steeped in Torah learning, an expert in Talmud, and of his wife it was said that she too knew how to learn Gemara. She would cancel out the evil eye by means of two eggs, one in each hand, with which she would circle the swelling or the sore throat; she too whispered incantations to herself.[5]

This "medicine" was cheap—ten groshen; six for the poor. I remember my own face swelling up several times, obviously from toothaches. I was then taken to David the carter, who was considered more effective. I remember that he scratched me with those small bones. They were rough and sharp and I nearly fainted from the pain. He would run quickly, round and round, the small bones placed over the face of the patient. I pleaded to be taken to the preacher's wife: she did the same thing—but with eggs—and the procedure was so simple and easy, a virtual "pleasure." But no one listened to me. "Foolish child," they said, "though he might hurt you a little, you'll get rid of the swelling much faster. With the method used by the preacher's wife it takes much longer to heal."

Sometimes I was "lucky." David the carter would be away from home carting flour from the mills or to Brisk, and I'd be taken to the preacher's wife instead. I was truly "overjoyed" at that. It's no fun having someone run your swollen face over with the jagged tips of little bones.

When I turned nine, my father took me and his youngest brother Yisrael out of Motke the melamed's hands and transferred us to the care of Beynush-Leyb. This melamed, though a learned man, was, however, a proper sleepyhead. He'd doze off where he sat at the table with his pupils and start snoring right in front of them. We were six boys studying Gemara and commentaries with him. He taught pretty well, but in the middle of the lesson he would doze off. He had one other failing: instead of teaching us Rashi, who interprets every line in the Gemara and clearly explains the abbreviated and difficult words, he taught the abbreviations out of context, unrelated to the point in question. We would go through a page of the Gemara, then through a page of Rashi. The result would be total confusion in our minds concerning the points in the Gemara clarified by Rashi in his commentary. The talmudic sages argued amongst themselves, and Rashi explained the reasons for their disputes; however, our melamed didn't teach them in tandem.

The melamed's dropping off in the middle of a lesson did have certain advantages. Of course we had to remain in our places while he was asleep—for if on awakening he did not find a pupil with the open Gemara in front of him, this boy would surely get a slap across the face and sometimes even lashes. Still, at such times we'd feel less pressured and more at ease.

Every year an emissary from the Volozhin Yeshiva[6] would be sent to Kamenets. This yeshiva was famous for its large number of gifted students, and is to this day still very popular among Jews. I remember that when the emissaries from Volozhin heard what a gifted son my mother Sarah had, they begged her to let me go to Volozhin, where I'd be treated like a prince. But Father didn't even want to hear or think about Volozhin. Due to Rabbi Hayyim's influence, all the students of the yeshiva were fervent mitnaggedim,[7] and from Father's point of view a mitnagged was akin to a heretic, even if he was a great rabbi.

Father took care to have me beside him whenever he was among his fellow hasidim and was pleased to see me adopt their ways. I always listened to their hasidic teachings, and the question of whether I knew or did not know how to learn was of no consequence to him whatsoever. He tried to find a hasidic melamed for me but, fortunately, there were none in Kamenets except for Shaye-Bezalel, the beginners' melamed.

I remember, while in heder, having once overheard someone say that Moyshele of Kobrin, Father's rebbe, had died. I was sure that Father's rebbe was someone like my own rebbe in the heder.[8] I promptly ran to Father to inform him of the "good news," bursting into his office with the joyful announcement: "Father, your rebbe died! . . ."

But the effect was in complete contrast to what I had expected. Father blanched and almost fainted away. Not losing any time, he traveled to Kobrin, where all the members of the Kobriner *Kolel*— some six thousand of them—had gathered.[9] They appointed six men, my father among them, whose task it was to name a new rebbe. He remained in Kobrin for five weeks, during which time they chose Avraham of Slonim, a former melamed and good scholar but—may I be forgiven for saying so—something of a fool.[10] From among eight candidates it was he who was chosen as the new rebbe.

But the Kobriner and Brisker hasidim—nicknamed "the light ones," accused by others to be merely passing themselves off as true hasidim—wanted a rebbe closer to home. Having to travel as far as Slonim was too much of an effort for them. They claimed to have heard the rebbe mention, just before his death, his grandson Noah

as being worthy to succeed him.[11] That was, of course, an outright
lie. Nevertheless, in spite of this, the youth, barely eighteen years
of age and of a doubtful reputation, was crowned as rebbe by about
one hundred hasidim.

Father returned from the "coronation" ceremony, and on Friday
evening during the Sabbath meal we usually had before the arrival
of his fellow hasidim, he talked with Mother about hasidic affairs,
making sure that I too should hear what he had to say.

"What do you say to that, Sarah?" he turned to Mother. "Noah,
the late rebbe's grandson, who is barely eighteen years old and a
far less gifted learner than our own Khatskl, has been made rebbe
by those impudent upstarts. They fabricated such lies, that *he,* may
his memory be blessed, named him as his successor. If you only
knew what an absolute nonentity that fellow is! There's no doubt
in my mind that had *he,* may his memory be blessed, named the
bath attendant—forgive the comparison—to be the new rebbe, we'd
surely have carried out his will. But he did no such thing!"

My father had, of course, no inkling whatsoever that with those
very words he was sowing the seeds in my mind from which, at a
later stage, would grow my objections to Hasidism and its zaddikim.
But at that time of my life, at the age of eight or nine, I was a
fervent hasid. Whenever the more well known hasidim, returning
from their visit to the rebbe, stopped over at our place, I would not
leave their presence for a moment after having been released for
that purpose from attending heder. For Father would send a note to
my melamed requesting him to release me for the duration of his
important guests' stay at our home.

About six months after his inauguration, the rebbe Avraham
himself made the rounds of his hasidic adherents in order to raise
funds for Eretz-Israel.[12] He spent one Sabbath at our home, and I
didn't stray from his side. I stood next to him, looked into his eyes,
and listened.

Once, during breakfast, I was standing beside him and observing
him.

"Khatskl," he questioned me suddenly, " tell me—do you know
how to study?"

"Yes," I replied innocently.

"And are you a pious Jew?"

"Yes." . . . and to all his questions I replied with a clear and
simple "Yes."

Several hasidim went at once to my father, who was in the next room, supervising the food to be served, and told him that I had answered the rebbe's questions rudely—as though he were a common Jew, with "yes," "yes," "yes." What kind of a boy doesn't know that he must stand in fear and awe of the rebbe?

After breakfast, I went to Father, who sat in the next room, and he gave me a proper dressing down in the guise of a moral lecture.

"Khatskl," he said, "You stood in front of the rebbe and looked him straight in the eye as though he were an ordinary man. . . . Do you know that when the rebbe looks at me my hair stands on end and my fingernails turn over! It's no trifling thing! The rebbe! And all you can say in answer to the rebbe's questions is 'yes,' 'yes'?! Shocking! And to top it all, you said that you were a pious Jew! Do you even have a notion what, according to the rebbe, a pious Jew is? A boy your age ought to have more sense than you have shown."

His words affected me so deeply that I felt like a true sinner, as though I'd committed the worst crime. So overcome was I with shame that tears started welling up in my eyes. "I'll go in to the rebbe and ask his forgiveness," I said to Father, sobbing bitterly.

"There's no need to do that," Father said. "The rebbe knows without having been told that you're crying and regret what you've done, and he has already forgiven you. But remember, a rebbe is not to be trifled with, and when you grow up, you'll understand for yourself what a rebbe stands for."

Now the hasidim went to the rebbe and told him that my father had severely reprimanded me and that I was in tears over it, deeply regretting my sinful behavior. He had me brought in and said, "Don't worry, my child. I can see for myself that you will grow into a pious Jew."

From that time on, I became a devoted hasid. I had always been good at arguing, and often entered into debates with the young mitnaggedim, trying to prove to them that their emphasis on learning was as worthless as their prayers, and that a hasid's single groan was more edifying than all the piety and fasting of a mitnagged.

I remember one occasion when Avraham-Yitzhak, an adherent of the Slonimer rebbe, spent the Sabbath at our place and the house was teeming with hasidim. In the morning, at the table, he related many hasidic teachings, and I listened attentively.

" . . . And the Rizhiner said," he told his listeners, "had I wished to be a great Torah scholar, I could have easily done so, but I didn't want to tear myself away from God for even an hour."[13] " . . . And the Lachovicher said that if Rabbi Shimon bar Yohai had not written the *Zohar,* I would have written it myself . . ."[14] and so on and so forth. Those tales made a tremendous impression on me at the time, but since I was born, as it were, with an unhasidic nature, those very tales became the basis for my subsequent antihasidic convictions. . . .

But what does it matter, for in my youth, I was an ardent hasid. I knew all the hasidic melodies—some two hundred of them—and I jumped and danced with the hasidim. I drew great pleasure from them, and my father likewise from me. He was convinced that I'd remain a devoted hasid all my life.

The following year the Slonimer rebbe spent the Sabbath at Father's; over three hundred hasidim came in his wake, and a magnificent celebration was prepared for all. The rebbe arrived on Thursday and stayed until the following Tuesday. But what went on during those days is hard to describe. The hasidim brought along their own wine, and vodka, of course, was never lacking at Father's. It was a great celebration.[15]

On Tuesday all the out-of-town hasidim left for their homes, whereas the rebbe, together with the Kamenets hasidim, drove to the village of Kruhel—about two miles from town—in order to visit a wealthy *yishuvnik* called Leybl. He was a devoted hasid and very charitable. Leybl, of course, threw a sumptuous feast in honor of the rebbe and his fellow hasidim. They were all sitting around the table, eating, drinking, and singing, when suddenly an armed police officer accompanied by ten gendarmes and headed by the *assessor* of Kamenets entered the hall. They surrounded the tavern, and the officer asked, "Where is the rebbe?"

It was, after all, easy to identify the rebbe among the terror-stricken gathering, and the officer ordered him to be guarded at once. They started rummaging among his belongings, inside the chests in which lay twenty-five hundred rubles, the amount collected for Eretz-Israel, along with the account books and the letters from people living in Eretz-Israel. They stamped and sealed the chests and ordered the arrest of the rebbe, who was to be sent to Brisk. Father asked the *assessor* not to take the rebbe to Brisk but to keep him under guard here. After having fifty rubles slipped into his hand, the *assessor* talked it over with the officer and acceded to Father's request.

Grandfather, the sole person able to intervene, was away from home at that particular time, and therefore Father's brother Yosl went to Brisk to look up the *ispravnik* and persuade him to "dissolve" the affair and release the rebbe. After slipping him two hundred rubles, he came away with a paper ordering the rebbe's instant release. When asked who had been responsible for the rebbe's arrest, the *ispravnik* said that the informer had been a Jew. The *ispravnik* had received a document signed by a Jew to the effect that there was a rebbe in Kamenets raising funds for Palestine. That was a breach of the law, punishable by imprisonment and confiscation of all the money. "If not for your father's sake," he told Yosl, "I'd not have released the rebbe under any circumstances."

Yosl returned with the authorization, and the rebbe was released. From then on, the rebbe no longer undertook to raise funds for Eretz-Israel in person but sent emissaries to do the job in his stead.[16]

The entire affair infuriated the hasidim and in particular my father, first of all, on account of the terror to which the rebbe was exposed, and second, because it destroyed the chances that the rebbe would make annual visits to Kamenets, which had become a kind of tradition. The rebbe's visit was of great significance for the Kamenets hasidim, and no trifling matter. The hasidim therefore decided to investigate the situation, to track down the informer, and to get even with him. The informer was revealed, but turned out to have been of a rather distinctive kind.

In Kamenets there lived a man by the name of Twersky, who worked there as the secretary of the communal council. Grandfather had brought him down from Brisk—if the reader recalls—at the time of his dispute with the inhabitants over the vodka tax. Grandfather needed someone to give him a daily account of the men who smuggled in vodka illegally and refused to pay the required tax on it, and so on. After the feuding parties had reached an agreement, Twersky remained in Kamenets and earned his living by penning petitions for the Jews in the township. He frequently performed this service for the gentry as well, when they fought each other over the gaming table, or over a young girl.

Twersky himself had a brilliant mind, had been a scholar in the past, and was well versed in the Talmud and the Midrash as well. But he had afterward "gone astray" and become a nonbeliever, as was the case with many enlightened Jews in those days. He turned to secular studies, but on account of his more advanced age, was obliged to suspend them in the middle. In the absence of any other alternative, he took to earning his living as a writer of petitions, and made it his profession. He was so good at it that even residents of Vilna employed him in judicial matters of great importance. He made quite a reputation for himself all over the district. If someone was involved in a particularly intricate judicial affair, he would have Twersky come to him to compose the petition and put all his official documents in order.

He never made a fortune from his profession. First of all, he was too honest, had a gentle nature, did not bargain with his clients but accepted whatever they paid him. Second, he was a great spender and squandered his money without giving the least thought to the future. Spending all he had today was his motto, and if he had any money to spare, he'd divide it among the needy. He was known for his charitable nature, and the heavy-hearted in the township knew of his good nature and clung to him.

He was capable of giving away his last kopeck, not even leaving himself enough for a meal. But when he had some money to spare, he loved to dine on a quarter of a roast goose and giblets and wash them down with a glass of beer. And on running out of cash, he'd content himself with a buttered roll and a cup of tea. When he didn't have enough money for butter, he ate the bread dry; and when there wasn't enough for tea, he drank water. Only a moment before he might have given someone in urgent need three, five, or even ten rubles, not giving it another thought. Like all enlightened people of those days, he had a strong urge to promote secular culture and enlightenment among his fellow Jews, in order to weaken their "fanaticism" and open up the outside world for them.

As he was thoroughly conversant with Talmud and Midrash, had read all the haskalah literature in Hebrew, as well as Russian literature, in addition to being a persuasive talker, he naturally had a collection of listeners standing around him licking their lips with relish over the wonderful and exciting tales he told. He never finished a story on the same day and often kept his listeners in suspense for three days in a row. The endings of his stories were always unexpected: slowly and quietly he would lead his tale to heresy. . . . He simply poked fun at religious beliefs, cast aspersions on all the talmudic sages, and on the rabbis of his day even more so. His older listeners would either disperse or block their ears. The younger and more inquisitive ones, on the other hand, would often stay on, hanging on his lips to the very end.

Yet, despite his firm struggle against religion, there were two personalities he greatly respected. They were Hillel the Elder[17] and the Gaon of Vilna. For others he had nothing but contempt.

The extent of his skill and brilliant mind can be judged by the fact that the head of the Brisk Jewish community—Yudl Hakadir[18]—brought him from Vilna to Brisk on account of a complicated and scandalous affair in which the town was involved. It was an ugly story concerning forged passports, "so-called respectable Jews," and denunciations. Only Twersky, with his judicial know-how, actually succeeded in clearing up the mess, which had held the entire township in the grip of terror. For this alone he was worth thousands of rubles to them, but he was paid no more than three hundred rubles for his services, and those he promptly divided among his friends, keeping only twenty-five rubles for himself, which he squandered within one week. The following week he was once again going hungry until the next time he earned some money.

He usually told his stories in the home of Uncle Mordechai-Leyb, a house which was "as spacious as a field," and packed to capacity. He'd start telling a story at three in the afternoon and finish it at seven or eight in the evening. People would go out for a short while and be back soon after—so long as he didn't broach the subject of heresy.

The most interesting story, I remember, dealt with the French Revolution.

I remember him once talking about our Holy Patriarchs, from Abraham down . . . and everyone took to their heels. My father was the only one to stay on. Father never took his heretical words seriously, not even when he started to abuse his own rebbe, Avremele. He rather liked this heretic, because he was an intelligent and honest man with a heart of gold and a charitable nature. Twersky, for his part, was fond of my father on account of his warmheartedness and fine manners, and for his tolerance toward one less religious than himself.

Nevertheless, it occurred to Father that the denunciation of the rebbe might have originated with Twersky, and although it was hard for him to believe that Twersky himself was the informer, he suspected Twersky of knowing who was, in fact, responsible. He recalled an occasion when several hundred adherents had gathered

around their rebbe and he had overheard Twersky refer to them as
several hundred blockheads who had gathered to pay homage to the
fool. It left Father with a bitter taste in his mouth.

After a great deal of doubt and indecision, Father had Twersky
come to him, and asked him point-blank who the informer was, and
if it was he, let him confess immediately.

"You're right. It was I who did it," Twersky said, completely
unruffled.

Father was stunned.

"How could you do such a despicable thing?" Father said in a
trembling voice. "After all, you're an honest man who knows well
the words: What is hateful to you, do not to your neighbor."[19]

Twersky answered him without batting an eyelid. "Avremele
deserves a proper thrashing. Let him stop deceiving thousands of
people and wrangling their last groshen out of them. To be quite
honest, I would not have informed on him for my own sake, though
it would have been a 'holy duty' to do so. But I did so on behalf
of a certain person whose life the rebbe had completely ruined.
He was not just an ordinary man but one respected by everyone
in the community. I once heard him declare in David-Yitzhak's
tavern that he'd give twenty-five rubles to anyone willing to give
the rebbe twenty-five lashes of the whip. And that's how the whole
thing started."

Father quickly understood that this was the work of Leyb Meirs.
He immediately convened a special meeting of all his fellow hasidim,
which was also attended by their leader, Arele, then head of the
rabbinical court in Kamenets.[20] It was decided to turn Leyb over
into the hands of the rebbe, may he live long, and all held it a holy
duty to make his life as miserable as possible. How the rebbe had
managed to ruin him will be dealt with presently.

That same Leyb lived in Zastavye. His father, Meir, was a respected Jew and an outstanding personality whose wealth was valued at twenty thousand rubles. His son Leyb was a scholar, well
versed in the Hebrew language, wealthy himself, and an ardent mitnagged. He had a most gifted son called Hershl who, straight after
his marriage, went to the Slonimer rebbe's court, stayed there for
two months, and returned an ardent hasid.

He arrived back home one midnight and knocked on the door.
Recognizing his voice, his father refused to let him in, but his young
wife opened the door to him in defiance of her father-in-law's wishes.

When Hershl lay down in his own bed he felt that the eiderdown was warm and asked who had been sleeping in his bed. Told by his wife that she herself had slept in it, he at once grabbed the eiderdown, ran out of the house, and rolled it in the snow in order to rid it of all traces of his wife's body.

At that his wife burst into tears, and his father, hearing her voice, entered their room and asked why she was crying. She told him what his "beloved son," the hasid, had done. This time his father gave him a thorough thrashing, and the young man once again ran off to his rebbe in Slonim. But his wife, who loved him, regretted her outburst of tears, which had led to the row between him and his father. Who knew when he would return, if at all? She therefore traveled to Slonim and begged the rebbe to order her husband to return home. The rebbe acceded to her request. Hershl returned home and even patched up his differences with his father.

But Hershl remained a most zealous hasid. In winter, he went daily to the freezing cold ritual bath and kept praying devoutly, screaming at the top of his voice. He contracted a throat infection as well as a severe heart condition on account of his immersions in the freezing bath and his screaming during prayers. Night and day he went on celebrating his Hasidism with great exultation. He kept away from his wife, and hovering between heaven and earth, he finally went out of his mind from exaltation. The treatment of his mental and physical condition cost his father a fortune until, not long afterward, Hershl died. That same Leyb had a son-in-law, the son of a mitnagged, but he, too, became a hasid, left his young wife, and spent more time at his rebbe's court than at home.

Seeing his whole family going to pieces, Leyb wanted to revenge himself on the rebbe, who, to his mind, was responsible for all his misfortunes. Naturally, he had no respect whatsoever for the rebbe, and, blind with rage, conceived the unfortunate and despicable idea of denouncing him to the authorities.

Those same hasidim who had decided at the meeting that it was permissible to mete out the most grievous of punishments in the end made do with a rather "trivial" penalty. Leyb was a prosperous flour merchant who had control over and took commission from all the big flour mills in the district. He supplied the flour on credit to most of the stores in Kamenets, Brisk, and other places. It was a common practice of his to provide the goods without demanding immediate payment. After the storekeepers paid up, they received the next supply of flour, again on credit. That was the very opportunity to be taken advantage of and cause Leyb a great deal of trouble. They notified all the storekeepers not to pay up. Leyb would be forced into bankruptcy, and his demise would be bitter. The storekeepers themselves would not be harmed; they'd receive the flour, since the mill owners would procure them a new supplier in Leyb's stead. A man was dispatched in the name of all the hasidim of Kamenets to the hasidic community of Brisk, consisting of about two hundred adherents, informing them of their decision.

Their scheme succeeded beyond all expectation. When Leyb—ignorant of the plot against him—came to Brisk soon afterward to collect the money and take new orders, he was unable to get anything. No one paid him even a groshen and on top of that he was greeted with shouts of: "Informer! Get out of the store! For a Jew to inform against a rebbe!" And if he didn't get out of the store fast enough he was driven out by the younger sons of the hasidim, who chased him through the streets, throwing stones and mud balls after him. Thus they forced him to leave Brisk in a hurry, saddled with a debt of over six thousand rubles. He had enough money of his own and refused to declare himself bankrupt. He paid all the mill owners what he owed them. But since he could no longer supply the flour on account of the "ban,"[21] he also forfeited all the commissions. He lost all his money and dared not visit Brisk for fear of losing his life as well.

After some time, he sent a letter to my father, written in Hebrew and most cleverly phrased. It made a great impression. In it he expressed his desire for a reconciliation as well as his reliance upon my father's and Arele's judgment. He was ready to comply with whatever conditions they saw fit to impose.

Father called in the elders among the hasidim, headed by Arele, for a consultation. It was decided by them that Leyb take his three sons—aged between ten and fifteen—along with him to the rebbe's court at Slonim, walk into the presence of the rebbe in his socks, and beg his forgiveness. In addition, he was to pay four hundred rubles—for the bribes and expenses—and a fine of five hundred rubles to be donated toward the Eretz-Israel fund, all of which amounted to nine hundred rubles. They also wanted him to give them his word of honor that he would take his sons to the Slonimer rebbe's court every year until they married. After that, they would already visit the rebbe on their own. . . . He was also to donate a new Torah scroll to the Kamenets *shtibl* and was obliged to come from Zastavye every Sabbath to pray there. In other words: he was to become a hasid! Nothing short of a conversion. . . .

He agreed to pay the fines, though he could scarcely afford it by then. He'd willingly sell all his wife's, daughters', and daughters-in-law's jewelry, but traveling to the rebbe's court every year was something to which he would not, under any circumstances, agree. He came to my father with the tears streaming down his face.

"Moshe," he said. "You're a reasonable and kindhearted person who can understand the mental anguish of his fellow man. Tell me yourself in all honesty whether, as a result of all my troubles and misfortunes, I could ever be made a hasid by force. Is it at all possible, all at once and by force, to turn into something else, especially since I don't believe and will never believe in Hasidism? It goes against my nature altogether. You yourself know that all I did was talk to Twersky, and talk is far from committing the deed. Isn't it enough to have deprived me of my livelihood and turned me into a pauper? And now you want me to deny my faith as a mitnagged, which is as dear to me as Hasidism is to you? Money, I'm ready to pay to the last groshen, and I'm ready to visit the rebbe and ask his forgiveness. That ought to be enough. What more do you want of me? Moshe, you have a compassionate heart. You've got to understand my situation and do something to help me."

By now Father felt deeply sorry for him and promised to talk the matter over with his fellow hasidim. After a great deal of further deliberation, it was finally decided, thanks to my father's insistence, to alleviate the punishment. But on one point, they would not budge: He was to travel to the rebbe at least once—on Rosh Hashanah.

CHAPTER 16

THE FATE OF A PRODIGY

My studies • Booksellers of bygone days • My first association •
Yisrael Vishniak • Yisrael's public examination • Yisrael's career •
The fate of a prodigy

On summer evenings, when I was twelve, I loved to go to the
study house after our release from heder. There, between the
afternoon and evening prayers, I would mix with all the lads
learning in the study house and get to know the new *prushim* and all
the newly wed young men. We would chat about all kinds of issues—
those having to do with Jewish communal affairs and also just about
life in general. I would open up to a page of Gemara and talk the
whole time—sitting one evening at this table and the next evening
at another table. I enjoyed myself immensely.

There, I would also enter into heated discussions about the
advantages of Hasidism. I have always been drawn to the company
of those older than myself, and felt on an equal footing with them.
It didn't matter to me that I was the youngest among them; I simply
loved listening to the wisdom of my elders. Maybe that was what
gave me the courage to take part in their disputes about Hasidism,
and since I was a persuasive debater, I held my own in proving a
point more than once.

There were many volumes of the Talmud in the study house, but
they were all ripped and in bad condition. I remember it was a big
problem: the students and *prushim* kept complaining about their
inability to study the Gemara, since every volume was in tatters
and falling apart.

Once, booksellers used to travel from place to place with a sorry old nag, much as in Mendele Mokher Seforim's *The Mare.*[1] The wagon was packed with an assortment of religious volumes as well as many storybooks. The booksellers would come to the courtyard of the study house and spend the night at some cheap inn. Early the next morning, around the time of morning prayers, this bookseller would be present and accounted for, along with his horse and cart, in the synagogue courtyard. Occasionally, a bookseller would rent a table for several rubles, place it at the entrance to the big study house, and put his books on display there, while his partner, if he had one, made the rounds of the adjacent villages with the rest of the books.

Those booksellers often brought along advertisements for all sorts of editions of the Talmud, annotated by various commentators, and printed on high-quality paper. Once, a bookseller put about a flyer from the printer of Slavuta,[2] announcing the printing of a new and complete edition of the Talmud, including all the commentaries, printed in clear type and on first-quality paper—a "deluxe" edition. The price of such a set was seventy-two rubles, payable over a year in monthly installments of six rubles.

It then occurred to me to band together a company of youths, each of whom would donate four kopecks a week, in order that we might buy the new Slavuta Talmud for the big study house. The bookseller showed us a sample copy of this particular edition. It was a beauty!

The association was founded; Yosele, the son of a wealthy man, was appointed treasurer and I was the *gabbai.* Over every ten boys we appointed a "gendarme," whose task it was to collect the money every week and hand it over to Yosele. One of us did the bookkeeping and made sure that everyone paid up on time. The money was then handed over to Moshe-Aharon, the preacher's son, and he was responsible for delivering it to Slavuta. Right after the individual tractates arrived we sent them to the bookbinder to have them beautifully bound.[3] In that way we eventually acquired six volumes.

This was the first association I set up in the course of my life,[4] and, in all modesty, I must admit that without me the association failed to function for long. At one stage, after I took ill, it simply fell apart. Yosele and Avraham, the bookkeeper, were unable to handle its management without me, and those six volumes in the study house were just a reminder of our activity—we didn't order any more.

Yisrael Vishniak, the young prodigy who used to spank us with birch twigs for not knowing the texts as well as he did, became, after four years in Lublin, a very famous scholar. He studied under Rabbi Hershele of Lublin,[5] who wrote in his book of responsa: "My brilliant pupil Rabbi Yisrael. . . ."[6] This "Rabbi Yisrael" was then only twelve years old,[7] and it so happened that he intended to visit his grandfather, Zelig Andarkes, in Kamenets.

On the way the wagon drivers stopped in all the large cities they passed. Yisrael took the opportunity to call on the various rabbis there, and discussed Torah teachings with them. He put questions to them that they were at a loss for how to answer. While in Brisk, he called on Rabbi Hershele of Lemberg,[8] a brilliant scholar himself. For fully three hours Yisrael engaged him in discussions of talmudic issues, and the rabbi was amazed at the keenness of his mind. By the time Yisrael eventually reached Kamenets, the entire township was astir because of this young prodigy.

By that time, Yisrael considered it beneath his dignity to mix with the ordinary youngsters of Kamenets. He selected some of the brighter students, myself among them. We all looked up to him with enormous respect, and in our eyes the fact that he was willing to play with us was considered a great privilege. More than once, in the midst of a game, students would come to him to discuss talmudic matters. He would barrage them with numerous questions on the Talmud to which they did not have the answers.

He visited as well, as was his custom, with the rabbi of Kamenets, and put a question to him. The rabbi did not answer immediately, and Yisrael, who was quite short, climbed onto the rabbi's knees, seized his long, white beard with both hands, and, shaking it up and down, said, "What sort of a rabbi are you when you can't even think up a simple answer to the question of a twelve-year-old boy . . . ?"

Yisrael's impudent behavior toward the old rabbi—a well-known expert in talmudic studies—soon became the talk of the town and angered all the scholars of Kamenets. They called a meeting headed by Moshe Katz, Yosele, the brother of the rabbi of Karlin[9] and himself an outstanding scholar, as well as Leyb Meirs,[10] and decided to confront Yisrael with one of the most difficult problems in the Gemara. Should he fail to provide the answer within the shortest possible time, he would be subjected to a severe spanking.

The examination was to be held in the big study house, and Yisrael was ordered to show up the following day at two o'clock sharp. As he was full of arrogance, one might even say that he looked forward to the event. He had not the slightest doubt as to his ability to cope with the most intricate of questions. Yet, deep down, he was a little apprehensive—maybe this time he would bungle it and in the end receive a real thrashing. When he came to the conclusion that this was indeed the situation, he quickly ran to me and asked me to help him—I shouldn't let them spank him. Naturally, I did not refuse. By one o'clock I was already at the old study house, accompanied by eight of the toughest boys of our gang. . . .

I remember the occasion as though it were taking place now. The study house was packed to capacity with all the students of Kamenets, the *prushim,* and all the young husbands on *kest* learning at the study house. The crowd was enormous, and the small boy Yisrael stood apart in a separate group with us. Moshe Katz and Yosele arrived and called on him to face his examiners. They took a volume of the Talmud in their hands and opened it up—I remember clearly—to tractate *Pesahim* 66b[11] and told him to examine that page with its *Tosaphot,* and as soon as he finished reading it, they would set him the question.

Little Yisrael climbed up onto the table, passed his fingers rapidly from the top to the bottom of the page and then along the *Tosaphot.* All this took less than five minutes, following which he came up with the correct answer to the question they had set him. The scholars were so surprised and totally amazed at the sharp wits of this young boy that, instead of spanking him, they covered him with kisses.

"How could you possibly read the entire page of the Gemara, including the *Tosaphot,* with such speed?" they asked him in great wonder. "You show me the most difficult responsa," he replied, "I'll pass my fingers over the page and repeat by heart what's written on it."

They now put the *Pnei Yehoshua* in front of him.[12] He passed his fingers rapidly from top to bottom of the page, and once again repeated word for word what was written on it.

In the wake of this event, everyone in the township treated Yisrael with enormous respect, which soon filled him with an overbearing conceit. He started looking down contemptuously at the people around him, unable to grasp anything of a more profound nature. He spent a few weeks in Kamenets, during which time he was the talk of the town. Everyone spoke only about that young boy Yisrael, who was already a genius!

He returned to his father's home in Lublin and began to study kabbalah. Since the Talmud and rabbinic literature held no more attraction for him, he now devoted himself to kabbalah. And that was his undoing. Had he continued studying the Talmud, its commentaries, and responsa, like other prodigies, he might have become a second Vilna Gaon—outstanding among his generation. But, unfortunately, he started delving into the kabbalah much too early. A year later, he sent me a kabbalistic tract he had written and published by age thirteen.[13] I read it but couldn't understand a word. As far as I was concerned, the kabbalah was an alien element, and this booklet was a typical example of a kabbalistic book.

In Semyatich, within the province of Grodno, there lived at that time a very wealthy man called David "Breiter." His name, "Breiter," referred to his generous, openhanded nature. He lived like a prince. What, however, he desired above all else was to marry his daughter to a great Torah scholar. He had heard about Yisrael, the young prodigy, and sent a matchmaker to his father, Yoyzl Vishniak— a great scholar in his own right—suggesting a match between his son Yisrael and his own daughter. He would provide her with a dowry of five thousand rubles as well as ten years *kest* for the young couple.

Yoyzl made the necessary inquiries about the family, bargained, and finally the match was agreed upon. David Breiter set the day for the betrothal ceremony and invited the greatest rabbis and the most brilliant scholars from all over Lithuania to attend the celebration entirely at his own expense. It was an opportunity to exhibit his liberality and, above all, to show off to the learned gathering the kind of son-in-law he had chosen.

The betrothal ceremony was attended by tens of great rabbis, and Yisrael, the prospective bridegroom, engaged them all in such intricate casuistic debates that they virtually stood in awe of his brilliant mind, and were delighted at the privilege of witnessing the ingenuity of a fourteen-year-old youngster. The betrothal ceremony was held in royal style, and David Breiter's joy was boundless.

Since the bride was herself no more than fourteen, her father thought it best to put the wedding off for two years. He had merely wanted to "snatch up" the great genius and, having achieved this, could now afford to wait until his daughter turned sixteen.

Meanwhile, the Polish Rebellion broke out. The Poles entered Semyatich and conquered the town. But not long afterward, the

Russian army arrived, and David Breiter lost his life in an exchange of fire. Almost all his wealth went down the drain, and all his business dealings with the lords went to rack and ruin during the rebellion. All that was left amounted to thirty thousand rubles. He had, moreover, many sons and daughters, and the money had to be divided among them. They still married off their sister, providing her with the promised five thousand rubles, but without the *kest*.

After his marriage Yisrael went to live in Bielsk,[14] a district capital within Grodno province, not far from his uncle Leyzer Vishniak,[15] a wealthy man and outstanding scholar. Yisrael never gave a thought about entering some sort of business, let alone investing his money in interest-bearing loans. He rented a large apartment and slowly, slowly used up the money. It never occurred to him that one of these days it would run out.

Meanwhile he began to assume the role of a rebbe. Young students gathered around him to hear his teachings and his subtle, hairsplitting interpretations. In the township he was considered something akin to a holy man. Even his uncle Leyzer started calling him rebbe. From day to day his reputation as a genius, a saintly man, and a kabbalist increased. He discovered a new path into the kabbalah and wanted to set up a special yeshiva for its study. Day and night, his home swarmed with students, and young married students were ready to "stand on their heads" in order to listen to expositions of his Torah and kabbalistic teachings.

Throughout that time, he was living off of his rubles. His wife had begun to worry about their money running out and what would happen when it was completely gone. But he had become a saint and it was next to impossible to exchange even a word with him. He refused to discuss matters of daily life, and his wife often cried to herself in her room.

So immersed was he in his study of the kabbalah that he started putting on twelve pairs of tefillin simultaneously in order to do justice to all opinions regarding this ritual.[16] He made himself twelve small pairs of those tefillin and wore them all on his head even while walking in the street, and his young students would surround him on all sides to prevent people from ridiculing this behavior. In the township, as mentioned earlier, he was considered a saintly man, and people began to flock to him like to a rebbe, in order to receive a blessing, but he drove them away without so much as listening to their requests.

The money had run out by now,[17] and his relationship with his wife went from bad to worse. They had nothing more to live on, and she could not even talk to him about the situation. He did not want to hear about such matters, and the moment she dared to broach the subject and became more defiant, he called her an "insolent creature"! He sent for the rabbi to write out a writ of divorce. His wife sobbed bitterly, and when he handed it to her she fainted away. She returned to her brothers in Semyatich, and I have no idea what became of her afterward.

Yisrael eventually went to pieces. He had no alternative: the rabbinate—no; a hasidic zaddik—no; a merchant—no; business— no. And so what was left? He fell into a deep depression. After a great deal of hard thinking, he decided to prepare himself for the university entrance examinations. Since studying presented no difficulties for him, he hoped to become a professor in time. In one year he would complete all the gymnasium courses. For this purpose he bought himself a Russian dictionary and, in less than a month, he knew all its words by heart.

His uncle Leyzer, realizing that Yisrael was entering a dangerous path, sent a wire to his father, who came and took him back home to Lublin. In a state of complete exhaustion and total confusion he was taken to the zaddik Leybele Eger,[18] and was turned into a hasid. Leybele made him happy, and Yisrael became a hasid. Now he devoted himself completely to Hasidism. He married a second time. His wife owned a store, and he began living the simple life of all the Jews around him. And so—a boy prodigy turned into an ordinary Jew.

CHAPTER 17

THE GARMENTS OF THOSE DAYS

Other melamdim • Ephraim the melamed • Our love for Ephraim • The garments of those days • His "new" tales • The expulsion of the rabbis

From Beynush-Leyb the melamed, with whom I barely advanced but tread the same ground over and over, I passed on to David the blind, who was sightless in one eye. He was no less of a "murderer" than David with the tangled hair.[1] I studied with him for three terms and advanced rapidly. He himself was a scholar and taught very thoroughly, and it was thanks to him I acquired the reputation of an outstanding student.

From him I advanced to the class run by my uncle Ephraim, a great scholar who wrote Hebrew in a most distinguished style. He, however, had no luck in business. Unable to flatter the landed gentry, he did not get on well with them and therefore remained a very poor man. Grandfather Aharon-Leyzer kept supporting him, but how long can one get by living on relatives' handouts? He had, moreover, five grown-up daughters and, like any man of his kind without any means, had no other choice but to become a melamed. That said, he was the most excellent among them. There were just four of us in the group, and we were considered the best pupils in the township. In just two terms I learned tractate *Hulin* with its *Tosaphot, Maharsha,* and all the other commentaries, as well as *Magen Avraham* and *Shitah mekubetzet.*[2]

Of all the heders I had attended throughout the years, I never enjoyed learning more than in the one run by my uncle Ephraim. First of all, he taught us the Gemara in an intelligible manner; and when we failed to follow the hairsplitting arguments and different methods of approach, he explained them to us patiently, in clear and simple words, using parables and comparisons. And, above all, he never lost his temper. It was a real pleasure to learn under him. If, at times, we tired from learning the Talmud and the commentaries, he would allow us a rest period. Then he would start telling us of things going on in the outside world.

He was a well-read man, knew a great deal about the natural sciences, and occasionally even read a book in Russian. But his wife, a most foolish woman (may I be forgiven for saying so), constantly put obstacles in his way. He wasn't really scared of her, only of her foolishness. If she noticed something that displeased her about her husband Ephraim, she spread the tale among the entire family and gossiped about it among the womenfolk. And since it was, at that time, considered an offense to read a book in Russian, he preferred to abstain from doing so. But in comparison with his contemporaries, he knew a great deal of what was happening in the world around us. While we rested from our Talmud studies he explained to us the latest scientific developments and told us of events that occurred in earlier times, but only true and correct accounts of these events.

His income from teaching the four of us was ninety rubles a term: he was paid twenty rubles for each of the other two pupils, and fifty rubles for both Yisrael and myself. That was, of course, nowhere near enough to make ends meet, and he remained poor and destitute. He often complained to us about the high cost of food nowadays and recalled with great longing his boyhood days, when the price of an ox was only six rubles, of a cow—three rubles, a goose—eighteen groshen, a chicken—six to eight groshen, five eggs—one groshen, a *funt* of butter—six groshen, and a *top* of milk—two groshen. . . . In those days every Jew who had a few kopecks to spare would build himself a small distillery for brewing vodka, with a few cows to eat the malt, and thus he had plenty of milk, too, enough even to bathe in.

The garments of those days were made of such durable cloth that they were handed down from father to son. There was a certain kind of cloth called *regn-kamnet*,[3] strong as steel and tough and stiff like tin. If you wore a *kapote* or topcoat of such cloth, every crease would start rattling so noisily that your approach could be heard almost a mile away.

This material came in an assortment of colors and varying prices, the cheapest was sixty kopecks an ell, but always of the same toughness, and impossible to rip. Maybe after fifty years of wear the garment became a bit shabby, the colors might have faded, and it would then be handed down to one of the sons. It was considered a great honor to wear such a faded *kapote* and was seen as a piece of memorabilia from someone now deceased. When, several decades later, it looked really faded, it nevertheless came in handy as a workman's overall or for protection against wind and rain. But there was never a rent in the cloth.[4] I still remember those *kapotes* worn by the elderly. I myself wore one at the age of eight, after it had been altered to fit me. It used to belong to Grandfather, who had inherited it from his own father.

There was also a wool cloth called "lasting." Nowadays, it is called "half-lasting" but it has nothing in common with the former. Garments of lasting were worn by the well-to-do. The cloth used exclusively in making men's garments consisted of four different kinds of *regn-kamnet,* two kinds of lasting, three kinds of velvet, four kinds of satin, and several kinds of silk.

The women wore garments made of a calico cloth costing seven or eight kopecks an ell, or of wool at thirty kopecks an ell at the utmost. But woolen cloth was worn only by the more well-to-do among them.

The furs worn were of the finest quality and consisted of muskrat, gray squirrel, *shoorkes,*[5] and beaver. The women wore furs of foxes, sable, and marten. The jewelry of the day was pearls. Even the poorest women wore strings of pearls around their necks costing some thirty rubles. On their fingers they wore rings, and around their necks hung golden brooches the size of a ruble.[6]

My uncle the melamed used to tell us stories about the eminent rabbis among our people but he neither exaggerated nor attributed supernatural deeds to them; only events that actually happened—clear and logical facts. He knew how much money great rabbis and sages earned years ago: up to eighty groshen a week, the same sum earned by the rabbi of Minsk[7] and the Gaon of Vilna.[8] And if, at times, the rabbi's salary was raised, it was by ten groshen a week.

He also told us how those rabbis were at the mercy of the town's elders. More than once it happened that they chased the rabbi—who was a great scholar—out of town over a most trifling dispute. The *parnas khodesh* would simply call a meeting of some of the leading householders of the township and recommend that they punish the rabbi. If they decided to expel him, the order was promptly carried out.

In Minsk, for example, they drove the *Sha'agat Aryeh*[9] out of their town. After the Gaon of Vilna he was perhaps the greatest man of genius of his generation, and was expelled in a most shameful manner. The expulsion took place one summer on a Friday at twelve noon. He was put on a cart drawn by two oxen and led out of the town.[10] My uncle told us about a woman who went to meet the rabbi at the outskirts of the town in order to hand him three challahs for the oncoming Sabbath.[11] He asked her if her husband knew about the challahs she had brought him.

"No," said she.

"Then I can't accept them," said he.

He was taken to a Jewish tavern but did not want the owner, a *yishuvnik,* to know that he was the rabbi of Minsk. This energetic woman, however, ran ahead of him to inform all the villagers that the man arriving in their midst within a short time was none other than the rabbi, the great man of genius, whom the *parnas khodesh*—may his name be erased—had driven out of their town.[12]

From Brisk they expelled the *BaH,* the brilliant scholar who was the author of an important book of commentaries on the Talmud.[13] He served as rabbi there, and this was what happened: one Saturday night the *parnas khodesh* met with the distinguished householders of the town in the communal hall. The candle suddenly went out at midnight and it was impossible to find a light in the entire town. Everyone was asleep by then. The *parnas khodesh* instructed the beadles to go to the house of the rabbi for a lighted candle to be placed inside a lantern, and to bring it to the communal hall. They came to the rabbi's house but were astonished to see it enveloped in darkness. He, too, had gone to bed. Upon their return they reported this to the gathering, and then the *parnas khodesh* and the householders at once decided that if the rabbi was already fast asleep at midnight, he ought to be driven out of the town. And, indeed, they drove him out of Brisk.[14]

CHAPTER 18

MY FIRST REVOLT

My "melamed" Yitzhak-Asher • Our "studies" • My first revolt • My growing reputation in the township • The end of the affair

$\mathcal{I}$n Kamenets there lived a miserable, poverty-stricken, and excessively pious hasid. He didn't work to support himself and his wife didn't give him a moment's peace. She kept nagging him to become—like other *shlimazels*—a melamed.[1] When he poured out his heart about this to my father, a brilliant idea sprang into Father's head—wouldn't Yitzhak-Asher make a wonderful melamed for his Khatskl! It was doubtful whether Khatskl would indeed learn anything with him, but on the other hand, Khatskl would surely learn to be a great hasid. Although I was a hasid at heart, I was, however, drawn to what my father called "this world."

I spent much of my free time at Grandfather's and I often dined with them on the Sabbath and holidays. I was used to praying with Grandfather at Uncle Mordechai-Leyb's home, and we would already be finished by ten o'clock in the morning. Mealtime didn't last long at Grandfather's, and when Father returned from the *shtibl* at twelve o'clock, I went home for another meal. I was always where things were best for me, and on account of that Father called me "a man of this world." He regretted having sent me to study under Uncle Ephraim, who was a mitnagged and "philosopher" to boot, and most likely a heretic at heart. Father also noticed that I was beginning to know too much about matters of the world; he was afraid that my uncle would turn me, heaven forbid, into a heretic as well.

Father would have taken me out of Uncle Ephraim's hands much sooner had he not been afraid of his father, Aharon-Leyzer. He therefore cast about for an excuse to remove me from this heder that would not arouse Grandfather's objections.

When he accidentally stumbled upon Yitzhak-Asher, Father took no notice of any obstacles. He was convinced beyond a doubt that with this particular melamed I would learn first and foremost how to be a true hasid. He and a fellow hasid, Shmuel-Sholem, hired Yitzhak-Asher as melamed for their two sons—myself and Mordechai—and paid him a fee of fifty rubles a term. We would learn in Hershl's study house in the synagogue courtyard. No one studied there during the day, neither *prushim* nor yeshiva students. It was a quiet place where one could learn hasidic lore without outside interference. But his youngest brother, my friend Yisrael, Father did not take out of Uncle Ephraim's hands.

The morning after the festival of Sukkot, at nine o'clock, I arrived at Hershele's *shtibl* in order to commence learning with my new melamed: at this hour everyone goes off to heder. Our melamed hadn't arrived yet, and my friend and I waited. He arrived straight from the ritual bathhouse at eleven o'clock and at once began praying. He stomped with his feet on the floor and pummeled the wall with his fists; that's how he used to pray. This went on for an entire hour—he nearly broke through the floor and the walls, and shouted himself hoarse. Only after that, at half past twelve, did he start learning tractate *Kiddushin* with us. He never had any breakfast, since he had only just eaten his supper at daybreak.

We started learning this Gemara, though we already knew it well from our previous studies. We finished reading an entire page, and he stared straight ahead into space—was he listening or was he perhaps turning something over in his own mind? It was hard to tell. When we turned to the *Tosaphot,* he could no longer remain detached but had to look at the small letters himself. We had also learned those *Tosaphot* before, and though he was looking at the words he kept mumbling to himself, and it was obvious to us that he hadn't the slightest notion what they meant. He just sat there, holding his small head between his hands, wrinkling his narrow forehead, and mumbling the *Tosaphot* to himself over and over again. But we had the feeling that he really had no idea what he was reading, and then he would think again, and again talk to himself, and then think again for another half an hour. Eventually, when we were fed up with sitting idly in front of him, we said, "Rebbe, we'll explain the *Tosaphot* to you. They're actually quite easy to understand." "For you," he shouted at us, "everything's easy! Only for me everything's hard," and once again he took to musing to himself.

Meanwhile we slipped out of the heder and went to the large study house. We chatted for a while with the students there, and when we looked at the clock we realized that an entire hour had gone by. We weren't at all afraid of this *shlimazel* rebbe, but to prevent him from telling Father about our leaving in the middle of a lesson to go to the study house, we hurriedly returned to the *shtibl*.

On entering the *shtibl* we saw him still sitting there, holding his little head between his two hands, muttering deeply to himself. We went home for lunch, and when we returned we found him in exactly the same position he had been in when we left. Now we interrupted his brooding. "Why does the rebbe keep thinking such a long time?" we asked. "We know those *Tosaphot* well. We learned them quite a while ago. . . ."

It was obvious to us that he still didn't understand them, but, ashamed to admit it, he just kept silent. We went on reading several more passages, and again he was silent. Meanwhile, it was time for the afternoon prayers, and he began his very strange preparations. . . .

Again we went to the study house, where we played with our friends and the other boys. Yitzhak-Asher arranged with my father to teach us only until the onset of the afternoon prayers, unlike all the other heders, where the boys studied until nine o'clock in the evening during the winter. We romped about in the study house, prepared some of the Gemara and *Tosaphot* we were to learn the next day, and asked the *prushim* to explain to us what we couldn't understand.

The following morning when we began our studies, the melamed got stuck once again on the *Tosaphot* and, like the day before, retreated into himself. We sneaked out for three hours this time, and were back exactly half an hour before the beginning of the afternoon prayers. . . . Once again, we explained the *Tosaphot* to him and he kept silent. And that was how we spent the entire winter.

Meanwhile, I became a permanent resident at the big study house, and got to know all the other students, the *prushim*, and the young husbands studying there. As I had not much else to do, I started to argue with them about all sorts of issues, and in so doing fomented a minor "rebellion." It started in the following way:

As already mentioned above,[2] all the volumes of the Talmud in the study house were torn and tattered. Shabtai-Hirsh, an old man who had served as the *gabbai* there for over thirty years, used to keep the good, complete volumes under lock and key in a small chamber with an iron door and iron bars across the window. It was the same chamber where, several years earlier, they used to lock up the young boys kidnapped for service in the tsar's army.[3] Later on, a kind of prison was built, not in the synagogue courtyard, where everyone could hear the howls and screams, but near the *assessor*'s home. In that chamber Shabtai-Hirsh kept the best-preserved volumes and other books, leaving only the torn ones in the study house. When I begged him to take out the volumes of the Slavuta Talmud we had purchased and bring them to the study house, he simply refused.

I then pulled a little prank: I incited all the *prushim,* yeshiva students, those living on *kest,* the young sons-in-law of the local householders, to forcefully demand that Shabtai-Hirsh hand over to them all the new volumes of the Talmud and other books. Why did he have to leave us only the books that were completely torn? It was impossible to study from them; everything was ripped! "Over there in the chamber he keeps the new books only for the mice to nibble at!" I shouted.

"We, the *lomdim,* have no other choice," I fired up the crowd, "but to find ourselves another study house. The new study house is out of the question—Shabtai-Hirsh's son is *gabbai* there. How about if we move to the study house on Adolina?[4] The *gabbai* there, Moshe-Reuven, will be overjoyed if we sit and learn in his study house. And should there be a lack of Talmud volumes, he won't rest or be silent. He himself will comb the town and look after our every need."

I had all the time in the world for this propaganda, since my rebbe Yitzhak-Asher was still wrinkling up his forehead over those *Tosaphot,* and those wrinkles would not be smoothed out until I returned to explain the literal meaning of those *Tosaphot* to him. What a rebbe he was!

I went to Moshe-Reuven and told him about the entire affair: this and that happened and, because we are given only the torn volumes, we want to move to your study house. True, it is somewhat further away, but on the other hand, we'd have proper books to study from, and if something were missing you would provide us with whatever we needed.

Moshe-Reuven was overjoyed at this turn of events but doubted if the townspeople would agree to have the big study house remain empty of learners. The beadle would give in eventually and make up. But meanwhile it would cause him a great deal of pleasure if his study house were to be filled with Jews wishing to learn. And even if they studied there for no more than a couple of days, that would satisfy him, it would bring him great joy.

The following day around noon I had everyone leave the big study house. Not a soul remained behind. I brought everyone over to the study house on Adolina. There were over fifty students, the rich and the poor, the old and the young! Moshe-Reuven's delight was beyond description. We immediately handed him a list of the Gemara volumes we required, as well as the books of commentaries, the books of responsa, and so on.

Moshe-Reuven took with him three fellows from Adolina and by the end of the day had brought us all the books we had asked for. They carried the books until ten o'clock at night and on the following morning the walls of the study house resounded with the heartwarming singsong voices of the learners, which reverberated throughout Adolina. I convinced everyone to refrain from chattering, but to keep learning at the top of his voice. The entire neighborhood of Adolina, the women and the children, hung out the windows, looking in wonder at the chanting learners. For lack of space we also took over the women's section of the study house, except during the mornings, when twelve particularly pious women came in to pray. And Moshe-Reuven was jubilant.

When the *gabbai* Shabtai-Hirsh came to the big study house for the afternoon prayers, he was stunned. The place was dark and empty, and when other householders arrived, they were utterly bewildered. They had no idea of the rebellion. They thought that some calamity must have happened. Frightened out of their wits, they asked Shabtai-Hirsh, "What's going on here?" And he told them that the son of Moshe, son of Aharon-Leyzer, had instigated a revolt, taken out all the learners and transferred them to Moshe-Reuven's study house on Adolina.

"But why? There must have been some reason for it. Things don't happen without some provocation."

"That little troublemaker simply took it into his head," Shabtai-Hirsh said, boiling with rage, "to make me hand over the new Zhitomir Talmud volumes.[5] Once I do that, they will all be in tatters in less than three weeks! Hand over such a treasure!"

An uproar ensued. None of the householders believed him. It was too trivial an excuse for a revolt! I knew that once the householders turned up for the afternoon prayers, it would cause a commotion; that between the afternoon and the evening prayers they would fall out with Shabtai-Hirsh altogether. So I purposely came to the study house for the evening prayers. No sooner did they set eyes on me, than everyone shouted for silence. "Quiet! Quiet! Khatskl is here. Let him tell us his version of the affair!"

I plucked up courage and led the more prosperous among them to the book-filled shelves lining all the walls, and to the tables heaped with dilapidated volumes. I took down all the books and said, "Take a look at them and find me just one Gemara one can study from. They're all torn. Is it right for Shabtai-Hirsh to keep twelve good volumes of Talmud, all those books of commentaries and responsa, under lock and key while all the books here are completely in shreds? Who is he saving all those new books for? Every year several wealthy Jews pass on and bequeath their sets of Talmud to the big study house.[6] And he hides them all in his little chamber in the *shtibl,* locked behind the iron door!"

On hearing my arguments, they admitted that I was right and that Shabtai-Hirsh should open up that chamber and hand out whatever books the students needed for their studies. But the elderly Shabtai-Hirsh, a seventy-odd-year-old man, who behaved as if he were the emperor himself when it came to the study house, refused to give in. He resented a fourteen-year-old boy gaining the upper hand. Never before had anyone ever dared to oppose him or challenge his opinion. The householders coming in for morning, afternoon, and evening prayers did not conceal their anger, and the entire township turned out to look at the empty study house. They all said that Khatskl was right. That made Shabtai-Hirsh even more obstinate. He fell out with everyone; although no one took his side, he stuck to his resolve.

The following Sabbath, the congregants called for a delay in the Torah reading,[7] and the rabbi said that were Khatskl a stranger he would have immediately said that justice was on his side, but since Khatskl was his brother's grandson, he had to commit himself to silence. At that, the congregants decided unanimously to convene a general meeting that same evening and deprive Shabtai-Hirsh of his post. But Shabtai-Hirsh mounted the pulpit and, striking his hands hard on the table, as he always did before the reading of the Torah commenced, said, "Fellow townsmen! I'm willing to hand the keys of the chamber over to the rabbi and he may do with the books as he sees fit. Now, let's begin the reading!"

And that's what he did. He sent the keys to the rabbi that very day, and my uncle asked me to come to his house. "I'm proud of you, my child," the rabbi said, "seeing you standing firm and holding your own for a righteous cause. Shabtai-Hirsh is certainly wrong, and I've heard complaints for quite some time that there is not even one complete volume of the Gemara to be found . . . but Shabtai-Hirsh has now handed the keys over to me, and tomorrow I'll send Beynush the beadle over there, and by about eleven or twelve o'clock in the afternoon you and all the students can come back to the study house. Nevertheless, my child, it is better not to provoke controversy. It is better, my child, to avoid it."

On Saturday night I went to Moshe-Reuven and told him what my uncle had said to me, that I must return all the students to the study house.

"If the rabbi ordered it," he said, "so be it."

On Sunday morning we were all back at the big study house. We chose ten young men from among us who were to go to the chamber to choose the books. When we entered and saw all the books lying there, our eyes lit up. There were not just twelve sets of Talmud there but seventeen, as well as the most valuable responsa books!

We discovered there, to our great delight, a veritable treasure trove. Among the volumes we came across a particularly rare find—a set of the Talmud from the Kopust printing press, over three hundred years old.[8] We also found there the source telling the complete tale of Jesus the Christian from beginning to end.[9] Now our study house was adorned with new volumes of the Gemara: twelve complete sets of the Talmud, and many other priceless books, responsa, commentaries, and valuable Bibles. Our joy was indescribable. We took whatever we needed and locked the door, and my uncle sent the keys back to Shabtai-Hirsh. Thanks to that undertaking, I acquired quite a reputation all over the township.

On the one hand, that hasidic melamed of my father's caused me harm in that I didn't learn anything, but on the other hand, I derived great benefits as well. I would have learned much better with Ephraim, but I would have had to sit in the heder all day long. With the hasid I was free all day, and thus I was given the opportunity to take up things more in keeping with my nature. This fact was to be of utmost importance for me.

I started taking a particular interest in philosophy, and I took from the chamber all the books dealing with the subject, such as *Moreh nevukhim,* the *Kuzari,*[10] all the books of the great Jewish philosophers, *Behinot olam,* with its excellent commentaries,[11] *Hovot ha-levavot* along with books of homilies,[12] and took to reading them with great vigor.

I left the rebbe to himself, holding his head in both hands all that time, meditating on the *Tosaphot.* Within ten minutes I would conclude my studies and couldn't care less whether I understood a passage or not. Later on, I asked one of the yeshiva students to explain it to me. I felt that it was a shame to waste time on the Gemara and the *Tosaphot.* I immersed myself in philosophy and gathered around me a whole group of youngsters: *bahurim, lomdim,* and *prushim.*[13]

Throughout the day we read philosophical books, philosophizing, debating, and arguing all the while. Thanks to this new activity of mine, I gained two good friends—Yosl, the son of the town's wealthiest man, and Shmuel Meirims.[14] They were brilliant learners, very pious, and kindhearted. We spent entire days poring over the philosophy books, and in the evenings we opened a Gemara and talked. Not a soul was to know that we were passing the time in the study of those books.

At a certain stage, Yosl suggested: Why should we study philosophy here and always be in fear of those old cows? (That's what we dubbed the old householders: "old cows.") It would be best to go to his place, to Yosl's. His father's library was much richer than the one in the little chamber, nothing less than "bird's milk."[15] We could study there undisturbed as long as we liked, and in a pinch we could also go to their barn and carry on our debates and philosophizing there. In this way we founded a kind of study circle. We read and debated a great deal. There were just the three of us in the circle, three youths so engrossed in their reading and debating that they completely forgot to eat.

CHAPTER 19

THE IZBICA HASID

The Izbica hasid • *Mei ha-shiloah* • My awkward problem • The
answer of the hasidim • My acquaintance with the preacher's son •
Ha-maggid • The woodcutter • Our meetings • The beginning of
my public activities

ather employed a man named Y. V. to assist him with
the bookkeeping and such other tasks as he was asked to
perform. This Y. V. was an Izbica hasid.[1] He was given a
room within the compound of the priest's tavern where my own
family lived and where we kept a storeroom for our vodka. Thus, he
lived right next door to us. He was an intelligent and energetic man
but rather dissolute and impudent.

He never missed a chance at taunting Mother over her brilliant
forefathers, the mitnaggedim. He would, for example, refer to her
late grandfather, Rabbi Hayyim of Volozhin, as "Reb Hayyim, may
his memory stink . . . ,"[2] or prick the nose of the Gaon of Vilna in
the picture hanging at our house.[3] Mother often burst into tears of
rage at his insolence, whereas Father, as was his wont, would only
smile good-humoredly and say, "You little fool! What do you care!
The more upset he sees you are, the more spiteful he'll become."
One must not forget, by the way, that Father was on his side. He
was, after all, a fellow hasid!

Father was very pleased with him. He could order him to do any
manner of things and the orders would be carried out to his complete satisfaction. He never learned. His prayers lasted ten minutes.
He drank quite a lot of schnapps and he played cards. But all this
never interfered with business.

One Sabbath afternoon I entered his room. He was asleep on the sofa, and beside him lay the book *Mei ha-shiloah*[4] by the rebbe of Izbica. I picked it up and leafed through it. My eyes lighted on the weekly portion of *Pinhas*. It was written there that, in the affair of Cozbi daughter of Zur,[5] Zimri son of Salu acted in accordance with the law because he recognized her as his soulmate from the first six days of creation. Further down I read that Pinhas had stabbed Zimri without knowing the exact details of the affair, and that Moses condoned his deed because he was Pinhas's uncle.[6] That was more than I could bear. I took the book and brought it to my uncle, the rabbi, and asked him to explain the literal meaning of those passages to me.

The rabbi read the book and pulled at his hair. Was it possible that the author, himself a rabbi, could write such things about our Moses? What would a simple Jew make of it? "You see, my child," he said, his voice quivering with agitation, "how far those hasidim have gone astray. I want you to show this passage to your father this coming Sabbath when he's sitting around the table with his fellow hasidim. Even more so, ask him to explain it to you."

At noon the following Sabbath all the hasidim gathered at our house. There was a guest among them, one Shlomo-Itsl, a smart and rich hasid. They all sat around the large table, drinking wine and exchanging hasidic tales. I left the table, brought in the book *Mei ha-shiloah*—my hands were shaking—handed it to my father and, pointing to the particular passage, said, "Father, could you explain this to me? I don't understand it."

Father read the passage and looked quite bewildered. He was extremely honest. He wasn't able to cheat anyone, least of all his own children. His fellow hasidim were eager to know what was going on, and Shlomo-Itsl, a shrewd man, at once perceived from the look on Father's face that he was at a total loss for what to tell his son. Father handed him the book. He flipped through the pages and began to bang his hands on the table.

"It's true! It's true!" he shouted.

He handed the book to other hasidim, and they, too, began to shout: "It's true."

When I asked what was "true," I was told that when I grew up, I would understand it myself. But they were completely wrong about that. I had no intention of waiting that long. Those banging hands and shouts of "It's true!" about something that seemed absolutely repugnant, absurd, and barbarous to me, alienated me from all that Hasidism stood for. From that moment, every hasidic teaching pierced my heart, from top to bottom, and I was unable to calm down. I started thinking to myself about all their hasidic sayings—everything came out all strange and jumbled. It made me turn in exactly the opposite direction, drawing me ever backward.

I started frequenting the house of the preacher, where all the sworn mitnaggedim used to assemble. His son, Moshe-Aharon, was a prodigy, and a devoted mitnagged who never tired of agitating in favor of Mitnaggedism. While I was still a fervent hasid, I always kept my distance from the house of the preacher and his sons, despite the fact that they were the greatest scholars in the township. I couldn't bear to hear how they belittled the hasidim, the zaddikim, and the Ba'al Shem Tov. But now I revealed to them the secret that I was no longer a hasid and that they were right in their opposition.

I befriended Moshe-Aharon, who had recently returned from Minsk, where he had become—at the age of twenty—the head of a yeshiva. He had fallen ill, and the rabbi of Minsk, Gershon-Tanhum,[7] whom the Baron Rothschild admired, took Moshe-Aharon to Frankfurt and introduced him to the Baron.[8] He at once sat down for several hours and learned with him. The Baron took an immediate liking to Moshe-Aharon and arranged for him to recuperate at the medicinal baths at his expense. After that he sent him back to Kamenets with a plentiful supply of special drinking water. The doctors forbade Moshe-Aharon to study because his mind was too sharp and this was likely to prove harmful. They ordered him to drink plenty of water and take frequent walks, and he was now looking for a companion. He chose me although I was some six to seven years his junior. I must have appealed to him. He saw how I was trying to understand and find the right path, and he, therefore, talked with me a great deal.

Throughout the summer, I remained with Yitzhak-Asher, who went on wrinkling his forehead over the *Tosaphot* and kept behaving in his "pious" way. My father was completely unconcerned. I had all the time I needed to do as I saw fit, and certainly take those two-hour strolls with Moshe-Aharon. He pointed out to me all the places in the Talmud that ran counter to hasidic teaching. I also spent a lot of time reading philosophy with Yosl, the wealthy householder's son. I would return for an hour to Yitzhak-Asher—my melamed of the narrow forehead—go over a page of the Gemara and its *Tosaphot* with him, and—"So long! Have a good day!"

Just at that time, Simha-Leyzer, Yosl's father, became a subscriber to *Ha-maggid*[9] and we read it religiously. It enabled us to get acquainted with what was going on in the Jewish world at large and learn about the numerous efforts to acquire land for Jewish colonizers in Palestine.[10] Someone figured out that one could acquire an entire colony for the sum of six hundred rubles. That was exciting news for me, and Yosl and I started enlisting some sixty householders in Kamenets who were ready to sell their houses and emigrate to Eretz-Israel. There were among them also several who were able to raise the sum of three thousand rubles. I remember that Yosl and I wove together a society promoting Palestine. It consisted of simple workers, young people, and even a scholar who made his living from woodcutting.[11]

This woodcutter was a particularly interesting character. First of all, he took a keen interest in the philosophy we were reading; and second, we were greatly flattered that this man, so much older than ourselves, sought our friendship. I recall that on numerous occasions we would come up with the correct answer to a question the woodcutter had raised, which had puzzled us not a little. We then ran joyfully to him and usually found him standing on a wood block, pulling the saw back and forth across a log, and, greatly pleased with ourselves, we would tell him that today we'd found the answer to this or that problem in a certain book, dealing with it at great length. We would explain it to him in a clear and lucid manner. He would then climb down from the stump and listen to us attentively. At times we even brought the book along, since he liked to see the things written black on white. We would stand beside the block and he would be holding the saw in his hand.

That same woodcutter (whose name I've unfortunately forgotten) was enthusiastic about the idea of Jewish settlement in Eretz-Israel. He was a great agitator and a spellbinding public speaker, and thanks to him we managed to create quite an impression in the township. Almost everyone was ready to sell his property and set out for Eretz-Israel. This encouraged us to send a wire to the editorial board of *Ha-maggid* in Lyck,[12] inquiring whether the work in Palestine was by then already under way. We also sent them a list of all the people willing to give money in return for the necessary guarantees.

We worked on this for several months. The meetings took place at Yosl's home, which was always packed with old and young. We spoke heatedly and passionately, and when the woodcutter himself delivered his address, everyone burst into tears and said as if with one voice: "We will all go, young and old.[13] Finally, we have been granted the opportunity to purchase Eretz-Israel in our lifetime."

However, we received no reply from *Ha-maggid.* The newspaper suddenly ceased to arrive and all our efforts started going down the drain. I went to my uncle Ephraim and asked him to draft a letter to *Ha-maggid* in which he was to report precisely how much money was available and how many people were ready to move, and so on. But there was no response from the editorial board this time, either. I now began to have serious doubts concerning the entire affair. As a last resort we decided to send someone to the editorial office at our own expense. There was no one more suitable to carry out the mission than the woodcutter. After estimating all the expenses involved—including his travels and the upkeep of his family during his absence, each of the sixty members of the circle was to contribute up to ten gulden. We had already collected a ruble and ninety when, to our great dismay, *Ha-maggid* suddenly announced to its readers that the entire affair was postponed for the time being. Our woodcutter had to return to his chopping block, and in his free time he would come to see Yosl and me to philosophize and discuss what was going on in the world at large.

I remember how, together with a group of youngsters, we used to take outings in the meadows during the summer, spending our time probing deep issues. I often think that had I been blessed with an indelible memory, and could I recall all those discussions of ours, I would, perhaps, have been able to write a fascinating account of the dreams of young Jewish boys of days gone by.

My father seemed most content with his Yitzhak-Asher. He hadn't the slightest inkling as to how I was getting on with my studies, how I spent my time, what I was doing, or what I was thinking. He knew nothing of my almost turning into a member of the preacher's family, the very place where the most devoted and uncompromising opponents of Hasidism used to gather. He was pleased with my activities in the cause of Eretz-Israel, but that was all he knew about my doings. If, at times, he asked Yitzhak-Asher, "Well, what do you have to say about my Khatskl?" the rebbe would reply, "He's a good boy and has a fine head on his shoulders." That was all he wanted to hear, for throughout the week he was preoccupied with his leaseholding business and with his fellow hasidim.

CHAPTER 20

MARRIAGE NEGOTIATIONS

Marriage negotiations • Yekhezkel, the rabbi's son • I am tested • The lineage • My anonymous bride • The letter • The blows • My uncle • At my uncle's side • Preparations for the debate

F ather began to think about a match for me. The matchmaker had already brought him all sorts of proposals from wealthy men who were ready to pay a dowry of one or two thousand rubles, including five to ten years of *kest*. Father, however, had set his heart upon getting a hasidic in-law, but when such matches were suggested, it was Grandfather who objected to them. Meanwhile a lot of time passed and no suitable match was found, that is, none that satisfied both my father and my grandfather. I was growing into an "old bachelor" of fifteen. It was quite unpleasant. All my friends were already young married householders.[1]

Mother kept nagging Father about being so fussy even when a large dowry was being offered and long years of *kest*. "You want Khatskl to have a hasidic father-in-law," she argued, "but you know very well that my father-in-law refuses to have a hasid as an in-law, and he will prevail. Khatskl is getting older and it's just a disgrace for him to be going about like this."

She went on reasoning, and Father, as was his way, listened and was silent. He neither promised nor refused, he just smiled to himself, and then the other half calmed down a bit. But Mother could bear it no longer and went to pour out her heart to her uncle, the rabbi, as she always did when she was troubled.

"You should see to it," he advised her, "that Khatskl marries a wealthy mitnagged who will give him many years of *kest*. After all,

Khatskl excels in his studies, and if he has many years of *kest,* he will be able to learn and your hopes of his becoming a rabbi may be fulfilled."

The rabbi had a son named Yekhezkel (we were both named after the same grandfather), a great prodigy who could easily have filled the post of rabbi, even of a large city. But he was a hasid, and because of that he was just a *dayan* in Kobrin.[2] This Yekhezkel traveled a great deal in order to raise funds for Eretz-Israel, as the Slonimer rebbe had ceased to travel ever since the denunciation.[3] Whenever Yekhezkel came to Kamenets, Father's house resounded with riotous jubilation. The hasidim especially rejoiced: wasn't he after all the rabbi's son! I did not leave the table for even a minute, and listened attentively to everything that was being said. However, while now seated at the table with the hasidim, I had an entirely different agenda. I now purposely listened closely to what they were saying, so that later on, I'd be able to criticize them.

Yekhezkel was fond of me. He took me for a soft-spoken young boy and once, pinching my cheek, said, "Khatskl, if you become a true hasid, I'll give you a fine bride." I blushed and kept silent. At heart I had long been envious of my fellow students, who were, by then, already husbands and young householders. Only I, on account of the squabble between my father and grandfather, was still a bachelor.

After dinner, Yekhezkel called Father aside and told him that he had a good match for me—a relative of his, his wife's sister. She had been raised in the house of her brother-in-law, Aharon Zailingold,[4] a true hasid, a wealthy scholar, and a favorite of the zaddik Aharon of Karlin.[5]

"It looks to me like a match from the six days of creation,"[6] he added.

Father, strange as it seems, was enthusiastic about the match. Since the bride was an orphan, without a father or mother . . . , Grandfather Aharon-Leyzer could hardly object to it. That the brothers-in-law were hasidim was not so important, the main thing was the father-in-law was not a hasid. There was distinguished lineage as well, as Father knew that Hadas, the rabbi's daughter-in-law, stemmed from an honorable line. Father replied that he was not opposed to the match, his way of hinting that he liked the idea, and Yekhezkel asked for a Gemara in order to test my proficiency.[7] Though he'd heard, he said, that I was a good student, he nevertheless wanted to find out for himself since he and his wife—the bride's sister—were determined on getting nothing less than a true scholar for the girl.

Yekhezkel took out the tractate *Kiddushin,*[8] and luckily for me, opened it up exactly to the page dealing with an issue I had already learnt with David the Blind, and once again with Yitzhak-Asher, and even on my own. I was quite an expert on the *Tosaphot* and the *Maharsha,* and when he asked me to repeat the Mishnah with the *Tosaphot,* I reeled them off smoothly. He asked me to explain the difficult problem posed by the *Maharsha,* and I answered accordingly. He shut the Gemara and pinched my cheek once again, saying, "I've got a beautiful bride for you." I blushed as before. He took my father into the other room to discuss the details, such as the dowry, and so on. Then Father sent Yekhezkel to Grandfather.

When Yekhezkel came to Grandfather to talk about the proposed match, Grandfather said, "My Khatskl is a good boy. His mother stems from a distinguished line; she is one of the grandchildren of Rabbi Hayyim of Volozhin, and I don't intend to put such a lineage to shame. Although I trust the rabbi and if he put the match together with your help—and you of course are such a great scholar—it is certainly good enough for me, but nevertheless, I need to know more about your wife's ancestors."

Yekhezkel then gave him a detailed account of his wife's illustrious forebears:

His father-in-law was called Hirsh-Yoel Reitzes.[9] His father, Mordechai of Ostróg,[10] played an important role in Volhin, like the pious Rothschild in Frankfurt.[11] He had been driving about in a coach-and-four for years. The coach and the horses' trappings were made almost entirely of silver. He virtually washed his coins in silver basins.[12] He had been a devoted hasid, and financed all the zaddikim of Volhin. He always played host to the zaddikim; one rebbe would leave and another would take his place. He lived grandly, and the zaddikim often stayed with him for months. The house was always humming with the voices of hasidim and zaddikim—in short, it was a hasidic earthly paradise.[13]

He dealt in the sale of timber; but once he suffered a great disaster. He had sent rafts of timber worth six hundred thousand rubles to Danzig, but they began breaking up in the water, one by one, sending the logs floating in all directions. That year there was a great flood in Kraków—the Vistula River broke its banks and it was impossible to ship even a single raft to Danzig. Apart from that, that same year the timber trade with Danzig slumped badly, and he had a large surplus stock of timber there from former years. In short, that year Mordechai incurred a tremendous loss, amounting to between seven hundred thousand and eight hundred thousand rubles.[14] Notwithstanding the loss, he still remained wealthy enough to continue contributing to charity and keeping open house, though not as lavishly as before. He ceased his financial support of the zaddikim, and they didn't come to visit him much, either.

His son, Hirsh-Yoel, had married the daughter of the rabbi of Dubno.[15] This son, who went on living at his father's house, was an outstanding scholar and a kindhearted man, but not inclined toward Hasidism. At his father's death, he came into a certain amount of money, but since his father's losses in the timber trade had resulted in his greatly diminished fortune, he didn't want to engage in it himself. He preferred to make a living from contracting. He began working as a subcontractor for Baron Günzburg's famous excise duty.[16] He was given the concessions in two districts—Bialystok and Bielsk—and took up residence in Bialystok. He had two daughters[17] and a son. The eldest daughter, Hadas, became Yekhezkel's wife, and her father provided a generous dowry and many years of kest for him.

Hirsh-Yoel enjoyed a most respected status in Bialystok and, like his father, contributed to charitable causes and kept open house. But, unlike his father, who hosted only hasidim, he hosted only mitnaggedim. He had ten guests for dinner on a Sabbath, among them the most respectable men in the town, who were even paid to attend such a meal. At least three honored guests joined him daily for the midday meal.

He was also a famous mohel and practiced this craft throughout the town. A poor man who had his son circumcised received a sum of money from him, enough to provide a month's worth of food for the newly delivered mother. He kept a book in which the names of five thousand infants he had circumcised were inscribed.[18] So highly respected was he in Bialystok that he was always asked to officiate at the weddings of the most important people in the town. This was considered one of the greatest honors, and a privilege granted to only the most outstanding and worthy Jews of those days.

The contract for collecting the excise duties did not last long, because Baron Günzburg no longer wished to divide the excise duty into small portions and hand them out to subcontractors. The Baron intended to be the sole tax collector within the Jewish Pale.[19] So Hirsh-Yoel traveled to Brisk, where he became one of the provisioners for the fort there.[20] He also opened a large tavern in the town for all the officers living in the compound and made a good living from it. Once again he was able to pursue his charitable activities, his hospitality, and circumcisions among the poor, for which he paid handsomely.

In 1855, during the War of Sebastopol,[21] all the regiments stationed within the fortress left to go to war. The officers urged him to join them on their way to Sebastopol. One of the generals even offered to secure him a special army contract for supplying the front lines, from which he could certainly make a fortune. But he turned the offer down, not wishing to make money in a place where people were getting killed and wounded, despite the fact that most of the officers that went to war owed him a lot of money. One of the officers left him with a promissory note amounting to three thousand rubles—all of which greatly diminished his wealth.

He had a son of seventeen, a real "jewel," a much sought-after bachelor, and a rare prodigy. He surpassed both his grandfather, Mordechai, and his own father in kindliness. A month before his wedding the young man fell ill, and soon afterward died. The entire town was in mourning over his death; the stores in Brisk closed during his funeral. His father took it so much to heart that he fell into a deep depression and died two weeks after him. His mother also suffered for a few months, and then she, too, died.

At the time of these tragic deaths, their daughter—my future bride—was only six years old. Her elder sister, a young girl herself, took her to stay at her home in Pinsk. She was the daughter-in-law of a very wealthy man. Her husband, Aharon Zailingold, was a great scholar and philanthropist, and most respected in the court of the zaddik Aharon of Karlin as well as in the community. In the wake of those terrible misfortunes and tragic deaths within the family, all its wealth and holdings went to rack and ruin. Eventually, they were able to collect some of the lost money and some promissory notes for the orphaned girl.

That was what Yekhezkel told Grandfather, who, after hearing about the tragic chain of events, consented to go through with the match. The following day the final arrangements were made. I was then fifteen years old. Yekhezkel wrote a letter to Pinsk to his sister-in-law Peshe to come to Kamenets in order to put her signature to the betrothal contract.

Not a soul within the family had seen the bride, least of all I myself, and this grieved me greatly. I thought that I already loved her, but I had not even set eyes on her. . . . I never heard when she was spoken of, whether she was pretty or ugly, intelligent or foolish, and I was forbidden to ask any questions.

Grandfather bought two diamond rings in Brisk and gave them to Peshe, who was to present them as a gift to my intended bride. The following month I received a gift from my future brother-in-law, Aharon Zailingold—a silver spice box[22] and a set of beautifully bound Mishnayot with *Tiferet yisrael*.[23] From my intended bride I received a tefillin bag embroidered with silk thread.[24] My father told me to send a letter of thanks to the in-law, that is to my bride's brother-in-law.

I knew Hebrew back then as well as I knew Turkish.[25] I went to my uncle Ephraim and he wrote a flowery letter in my name. I can still recall the opening sentence, for I liked its florid rhetorical style. This is how it began: "A voice told me to call out, and I answered, what shall I call the one I do not know and can only evoke in my mind his exalted and honored image, running the risk of belittling by a hair's breadth his honor and thus committing a sin, and then I consider it in my heart that surely in accord with his great honor is his great humility, and surely he will not blame me if idleness I do speak."[26]

The rest I've forgotten. But I remember spending three whole days copying and recopying those few lines, tearing up the page time and again until, God be praised, I managed to copy word for word a faultless and perfectly phrased letter in the old-fashioned style of our holy language to my future in-law.

At exactly that time a teacher arrived in the town, who instructed the young children in writing Yiddish and Russian. He came daily to Grandfather's house in order to teach his daughters how to write.[27] Father objected to my attending those lessons, but I would sneak into the room exactly when the teacher was there and learn with my father's sisters, without my father's knowledge.

Once that teacher said to me, "Why don't you write a letter to your intended bride?" I liked the idea. I gave him half a ruble and he wrote for me in Yiddish[28] the following words:

I send heartfelt greetings to you, my beloved bride-to-be. I thank you for the precious gifts you sent me.
From me, your loving bridegroom,
Yekhezkel

And to ensure that the letter was penned in a flourishing script, I once again spent days copying those few words. Here, there was an inky blotch, there, the word did not flow uniformly, and everything had to be rewritten from scratch. It took me five days to turn out a satisfactory page, after which I showed it to Father to have him add his salutations. He took one look at the letter and, without prior warning, landed me two resounding slaps in the face.

"A '*Daitsch!*'[29] Is that what you've become!" he shouted and shredded the letter into tiny bits. "You tell me this minute who wrote this for you!"

I, unwittingly, told him.

"So it's he who's going to turn you into a '*Daitsch*,' is he?"

He at once saw to it that no one within the family continued learning with that teacher. The rumor that he was turning all the children into heretics spread like wildfire throughout Kamenets, and he was promptly driven out of the township.

The rabbi of Kamenets had a son in Pinsk[30] who came to visit his father and brought with him a sixteen-year-old girl. When my mother came to her uncle's home she asked the girl whether she knew her son Khatskl's intended bride from Pinsk. She knew her well, the girl replied, and told her that she was ugly, had a pockmarked face, spoke with a nasal twang, and was a great *shlimazel* to boot. Mother was greatly upset and broke into tears, but it was too late to do anything. At that time, nullifying a betrothal contract was worse than dissolving a marriage.[31]

When Mother told Father what the young girl had said about the bride, he replied, "What do you care if she's ugly? What they need is luck, and that will make her beautiful." Hearing her mention the word *shlimazel,* he smiled, and said, "And between me and you, what are you, exactly?" Then he broke out in laughter.

Word soon spread throughout the family, and eventually reached me as well. My ordeal was impossible to describe. I had always envied those who had beautiful wives and felt sorry for the young householder whose wife was ugly. To my mind, life with an ugly wife wasn't worth living.

My whole family now started taking an interest in my bride—trying to find out if she was really that ugly, and after much inquiry they concluded that the bride was actually very pretty . . . in fact she was very skillful and an expert needleworker. All that, however, became common knowledge only a year after the betrothal contract was signed. But throughout that year I was miserable; I couldn't ask anyone about her, let alone mention her name.

My betrothal period lasted two and a half years. As pointed out earlier, she was an orphan, and her adoptive parents were under the impression that the Kotik family, one of the most respectable in Kamenets, was clad in the finest and most expensive garments. They were apprehensive about putting together a suitable wardrobe . . . not to mention depositing the dowry.[32] The entire affair was very complicated.

On our side, as well, there were obstacles. Serfdom was abolished around that time,[33] the lords were greatly impoverished, and the Polish Rebellion loomed on the horizon. Our leaseholdings were canceled and we lost our most lucrative income. So, the wedding had to be postponed.

Earlier, I had been greatly upset over having an ugly bride, and after having been assured that she was actually very pretty, I was upset about the postponed wedding. I started longing for a person I didn't know, and must admit, to my great shame, I was most eager to get married! I lost the desire to keep on learning, least of all, to study philosophy.

I was still learning with Yitzhak-Asher, the "wrinkled forehead," as I and my fellow pupil had dubbed him. At that time, my uncle, the rabbi, started having trouble with his eyes. He traveled to Warsaw in order to have them checked and the doctor told him that his eyes were weakened due to excessive reading. He must now cover one of his eyes altogether, and if he refrained from reading, the other eye might still serve him indefinitely.

His relatives in Warsaw[34] bought him a tall chair for his studies, and he returned home with the chair. Now the rabbi needed someone with whom to study the Gemara, halakhic literature, and responsa. He was not ready to sit around idly all day long. But to find someone willing to do this without payment was quite difficult, and he had no money. It then occurred to him that I could be the one to learn with him. He would not have to pay me anything for it, and thus it was a perfect solution. And I indeed read for him, clearly enunciating the words, while he sat in his tall leather chair, his head propped on his hands, nodding as if to say "Yes, yes." He urged me on with these gestures, and I read out loud to him quickly the Gemara, *Tosaphot, Sha'agat Aryeh, Pnei Yehoshua,* in short, everything. I read and he nodded his head. I had no time to inquire into the more intricate problems arising here and there. He knew most of it by heart, thus I was no more than a good reader for him. I ran through the Gemara but understood nothing at all. And so my fate was sealed to waste away my youth and my excellent intellect on such a useless task, something I have not ceased to regret to this day.

Fortunately, people came to the rabbi in connection with all sorts of arbitration matters or to ask his advice about their business affairs. He therefore decided that we should learn together for only six hours a day. The rest of the time I spent at Moshe-Aharon's house, preparing myself for the great debate against Hasidism.

Ever since my betrothal, I had attended the prayers at the hasidic *shtibl,* sung and chanted all their melodies together with them. I did it to please my father, who took me for a most devoted hasid. It goes without saying that until the wedding I still needed his assistance. Father thought that once I was married and had begun to visit the rebbe's court regularly, he would finally be assured that his son was truly following the hasidic path.

I had made up my mind not to enter into any controversial arguments with him. First, it was not appropriate, and second, I felt rather sorry for him. I put everything off until after the wedding, when I'd take the matter up with him. I took my father for an honest and learned man and was sure that he'd understand me, that our clash over it wouldn't last too long. Nevertheless, I was scared of the eventual debate, at which several learned hasidim, like Arele and my uncle's son, meant to participate. Consequently, I prepared myself assiduously over the course of two years toward that day. I went through the Talmud and other important books, all of which categorically opposed Hasidism.

CHAPTER 21

LIBERATING THE SERFS

The proclamation of the serfs' liberation • The flogging of the peasants • The impact of the proclamation on the lords • Hard times for the Jews • My grandfather and the lords • The Polish rebellion • "Russia has been conquered!" • The Polish rebels • Their attitude toward the Jews • Oginski • The suppression of the rebellion • The revenge of the peasants

In 1861 the famous proclamation liberating the serfs was issued.[1] It happened to fall on a Saturday, and on that very day the *ispravnik* arrived in Kamenets. On Sunday at twelve noon, when the market was teeming with peasants, the *ispravnik* and the *assessor* came there together with the *klyutsch-voyt*,[2] who beat a copper gong with a hammer, and when all the peasants had rallied around them, the *ispravnik* read the proclamation out to them.[3]

After hearing the proclamation, the peasants went home and refused to work, although, according to the proclamation, they were supposed to do so until the end of the summer. They didn't want to wait until then, and, since the lord was also forbidden to flog them, they instigated a revolt.

The lords informed the *ispravnik,* and he came to Kamenets at the head of a battalion of soldiers. He dispatched them, along with policemen, in order to round up the peasants from the surrounding villages. Afterward he sent for a wagonload of birch twigs, used for flogging, to be collected from the forest. The *ispravnik* asked the peasants if they were willing to work throughout the summer. They were not. And then the beatings began, in the middle of the marketplace, three peasants at once. Their howls could be heard a mile away, and the flogging went on until the men gave in and agreed to go back to work.

The estate owners were greatly upset at this turn of events. It was no laughing matter to be deprived overnight of one's slaves, who had given of their sweat and blood, had performed the drudgeries of a horse or donkey, and had lived in total subjection to their lord's least whims.

In those days, what was ruinous for the gentry was no less so for a large section of the Jewish population, who derived their livelihood from the lords. And now all this affected them as well. The estate owners were, after all, still left with "some" of their holdings even after such "destruction." But for those Jews it proved to be outright disastrous. They were now confronted with the fateful questions: What are we to do? Where do we turn? Where do we go from here? Not only the poor faced such questions but also the prosperous classes, who had lived a life of luxury, devoid of any financial worries. The question was put before the wealthy in the harshest manner.

Poverty became widespread, and many Jewish families neared starvation. Those families that had some capital in reserve lived off it, and those that didn't became totally impoverished. It seemed at the time that the spring from which Jews had drawn their livelihood for hundreds of years had completely dried up, and the chance of finding new livelihoods was small, perhaps even nonexistent. It seemed as if everything was lost forever.[4]

The estate owners themselves were no less affected by the new circumstances, and some of them were not ashamed to shed bitter tears.

The only ones that did not feel the pinch were the tavern keepers, who, even before that, had made a good living from the peasants coming on Sundays—market day—to sell their produce and get drunk. Actually, their income increased considerably, for the peasants could now allow themselves to drink more vodka. They no longer feared the lord's flogging if they were still drunk on Monday. But not every Jew owned a tavern; yet there were others able to derive benefits from the peasants.

During the first winter after their liberation, when the peasants were free to do as they pleased, they took to learning various crafts, such as barrel making, pottery, and the like, whereas their womenfolk started spinning and weaving towels, tablecloths, and material for skirts, to supplement their income. And when they came to the market of a Sunday, they slowly began to buy luxury goods, such as colored silk ribbons, glass beads, and kerchiefs. The men frequently allowed themselves to wear boots instead of the tattered sandals of former days. Little by little, thirty new stores sprang up in Kamenets. Those who had a house opened up a tavern there and were able to make a living of sorts. Naturally, all those Jews who had dealt exclusively with the landed gentry remained altogether without any means of making a living.

A year later, in 1862, a government commission toured the entire region in order to parcel out the land among the peasantry and specify for each the famous mortgage, repayable to the government treasury within forty years.[5] Now conditions worsened for those few Jewish families who, as mentioned above, had lived a life of luxury and had called the tune in the township. They stopped living the high life, and the merchants who had catered luxury items exclusively to the gentry were left with all their stock on their hands. Go and throw it into the dustbin. . . .

Grandfather made the rounds of the estates, "to pay his condolences" to the landowners. They had been, poor souls, literally hurled from heaven to earth, and those who felt the brunt of it above all were their womenfolk. It was no trivial matter to be suddenly deprived of their ability to lord it over others! And they cried bitterly. To tell the truth, what the lords found altogether unbearable were those very peasants who had hitherto crawled to them on all fours. The lord had been allowed to flog an entire family, mother and father, sons and their wives, daughters and their husbands, all of them, all at once, under one roof, and even after the beating, the peasants would kiss their feet and beg forgiveness. But now those same peasants walked about free and easy, defiant, and the lord was forbidden to even raise a finger to them. Not even one lash! And if the peasant wasn't in the mood, he need not even tip his cap to a lord. The lord now was required to ask the peasant to agree to work his fields for wages, and whatever the peasant demanded, he would have to pay.

In the face of all that, Grandfather kept consoling them, not denying the "misfortune," but it was only the beginning, he told them, and they had no other alternative but to get used to the new situation. "You still own considerable property and enough land," he calmed them down, "and although you'll have to pay the peasants for their work, it only seems difficult at first. Believe me, they will remain the same slaves as before, only that now it will be the 'kopeck' that's going to rule their lives, and in order to earn it, they'll still crawl to you on all fours."

"To my mind," Grandfather continued to "console," "the gentry itself will derive considerable benefit from the liberation of the serfs. You'll start to live a more stable existence, to manage the estate on your own, and you will be everywhere keeping an eye on the workers, making sure they don't cheat you. You'll have to give up gambling as well as throwing wasteful and meaningless balls. From now on your lives will be much improved."

Aharon-Leyzer's words took the edge off their fears, for they realized that there was a great deal of truth in them. Those who couldn't overcome their dismay over the changed circumstances on their own sent especially for Grandfather to allay their fears. So Grandfather made the rounds of all the estates for almost a year, trying to alleviate their worries and make them feel easier. But he couldn't pluck up enough courage to talk about his own business affairs with them. He earned nothing at all throughout that entire period. He even left some of his own money with some of the more impoverished lords, preferring to wait until the stormy period had passed.

Our own family, too, started feeling the pinch. We were left with only the income from the leaseholding, and that business had to support a family of about sixty souls.

At the beginning of 1863, rebellions broke out all over Poland and Lithuania. For the Jews this was an outright disaster. The lords and the *szlachta* escaped to the woods, formed armed bands, and began "occupying" those small townships in which no Russian soldier had as yet set foot. As soon as they entered a township, they pulled down the emblem of the Russian eagle from the government administration building[6] and replaced it with the symbol of Poland[7] amid shouts of "Russia has been conquered!" As for the Jews, the revolutionary gentry singled them out for "special treatment."

The Jews in the township were panic-stricken. They were scared to walk about in the street, and if a Jew did venture outside and ran into a Polish soldier—that is, a nobleman, not even an officer, just someone who had once been a lord—he had to quickly take off his cap and bow with great humility. And if it was an officer—even more so. Then he had to fall down on all fours and prostrate himself. If something in the Jew's prostration did not meet with the nobleman's approval, he was at once hauled by his beard before the colonel[8] to be tried and sentenced. Meanwhile they teased him about his tzitzit, and about his beard and sidelocks, tore at his clothes, threw him to the ground, and humiliated him. The Jew had to put up with these torments until the colonel ordered them to stop torturing the *Żyd,* and after all that he still was forced to swear allegiance to the Polish government.

The rebel army did not remain in a township for long. Two to three days later Russian soldiers—Cossacks—arrived with their artillery, and the rebel-lords took to the woods. Many hid with Jews—in their attics, cellars, chicken coops,[9] inside stoves. But in constant fear of being given away by the Jews, they took a Jewish hostage with them to the chicken coops, to the attic, or whatever hole in which they happened to be hiding. And this is not only a legend: the nobleman hiding away with his Jewish hostage in those holes made him take off his hat and lie there bareheaded; after all, he was lying in the presence of a lord! He was even forbidden to cover his head with a yarmulke.[10]

The Russian army started hunting down the Polish gentry. They hanged them or maimed them, but to eliminate them completely proved too difficult. No sooner did the Russians leave a township than a new band of rebel-lords popped up, and throughout that year bloody battles were waged between the Russians and the Poles.

The peasants themselves were full of terror lest the Poles defeat the Russians. They feared that such an eventuality would reduce them to serfdom once again. They also were afraid to leave their villages, because they might be caught and forced to join the rebellion.

But the lords did not take the peasants. They were too unreliable. Only a few lone peasants who had happened to be passing along a road or in the woods were abducted, and they were given menial tasks but were never given any weapons.

As far as the Jews were concerned, their own lot was incomparably worse. If a Jew was caught while peddling his wares in the courtyards, or while out and about, looking for work, he was tried by the most deathly frightening experiences. First he was told that he would be hung, after which the *Żyd* was subjected to humiliating mockery. When they tired of ridiculing him, they usually looped a rope slowly around his neck and told him to make his last confession,[11] while they rolled on the ground, holding their sides with laughter.

The Jew would recite his confession to the sound of their bestial laughter. All that dragged on interminably with the bloodcurdling brutality of the Inquisition. After several hours, when the Jew had finished his confession and rivers of tears had flowed from his eyes, and he was too exhausted to shed any more, they would untie the rope from around his neck and say, "Żyd, you know that we're a kindhearted people. Did you really think for one moment that we were going to hang you? That's what the Russians would've done,[12] but not we, the Poles. Swear that you'll remain loyal to us. And should you run into a Russian on your way home, don't you dare tell him that we are here. Now go . . . !"

The Jew who had been captured would return home, his face white as chalk, more dead than alive, and his appearance would frighten the wits out of his wife and children. There were several who died soon after the "fun" those "kindhearted" Poles had had with them.

This is how the military campaign was waged. If the Poles outnumbered the Russians—by three or four to one—then the battles were bloody and lasted until the Russians, being a regular army, overcame the Poles or took the survivors prisoner. If, however, the number of the Poles was not much greater, then the combat was brief. The Poles either surrendered or took to their heels. Many times the Russians would raid an entire forest, encircle it, and afterward take all the Poles prisoner.

Not far from Kamenets, near the Chernavchitsy Forest,[13] the Poles caught a Jew, and, as was their custom, they tied a noose around his neck. At that very hour a battalion[14] of Russian soldiers accompanied by a squadron[15] of Cossacks arrived on the scene. The Poles numbered no more than a few hundred men, among whom were some of the most distinguished aristocrats. The Russians surrounded them and as they approached they saw the Poles getting ready to hang the Jew. After the Jew was released, the Russian colonel asked the Polish colonel, "Why were you going to hang that Jew?" "Just for fun," the Polish colonel replied. Now, naturally, the Russian colonel started "having his fun" with his Polish counterpart. . . .

General Muravyov became the dictator of the entire region of Lithuania.[16] All the captive gentry were flogged, hanged, or shot, or cast into jails or mildewed cellars, into which swarms of mice and rats were released. The prisoners were tortured to such a degree that none of them managed to survive more than three months.

In the Czemeryn Forest, ten versts from Kamenets, there was a large encampment of Poles. In this encampment also lived the leader of the Polish Rebellion—a man by the name of Oginski—whom I mentioned earlier. He lived there with his entire staff of officers, among them the greatest members of the Lithuanian aristocracy. Oginski himself had been a candidate for the Polish throne.[17]

A rumor had sprung up from somewhere after Rosh Hashanah that, on Kol Nidre night, the Poles intended to overrun Kamenets and slaughter all those in the synagogues and study houses, just as in the days of the 1648 Chmielnicki massacres.[18] People were panic-stricken. But Grandfather Aharon-Leyzer managed to calm them down to a certain extent, maintaining that "nobody has heard as yet of the Poles slaughtering an entire Jewish community. True, at times, they terrorized individual Jews, but under no circumstances are they cold-blooded murderers. Don't you believe it," he went on, adding, "True, they're a proud people, but. . . ."

After that, two Russian army regiments arrived in Kamenets, headed by a well-known colonel sent expressly from Petersburg to catch Oginski. The latter was relentless in his fight against the Russians, and even the Jews who lived in close proximity to where the battles took place used to tell legends about him. The Russian colonel intended to catch Oginski alive, for that was what Petersburg expected. Then the battle in the Czemeryn Forest broke out. We could hear the echo of the gunfire in Kamenets. The battle lasted for a long time and ended in victory for the Russians. But Oginski gave them the slip. The Russians found his saber, and I saw it myself. It was of an unusual kind, not particularly large, semicircular like a sickle and studded with large pearls. The Russian colonel took it for himself.

The colonel, with his two regiments and four squadrons of Cossacks, set out in pursuit of Oginski right up to Pinsk,[19] where a renewed battle broke out. The Poles were beaten, and Oginski escaped once again. He found shelter with a peasant in a village, paying him one thousand rubles for it. The peasant hid him inside the stove, and immediately sent a messenger to the Russian military command in Pinsk informing them of Oginski's whereabouts. Oginski was apprehended the following morning, but before he was led out in chains he managed to tear into shreds the sum of two hundred thousand rubles he kept on himself. He was taken to Petersburg. After Oginski's capture, the Poles lost heart. They were no longer able to raise an army in one place, only small bands in the woods, which turned tail at the approach of Muravyov's army.

My cousin, Lipe's[20] son, had a married son who lived in Semyatich. Rumor had it that 1,500 Poles had entered the township and, as was the rule, exchanged the Russian eagle for the Polish one and "conquered" Russia. Within a short time, Russian troops, along with Cossacks, had surrounded Semyatich and had indiscriminately gunned down Jews and Poles alike. This rumor sprouted wings, and when it reached my uncle's home, everyone went into in mourning. My uncle, risking his life, drove to Semyatich and reached it two days after the battle. The sight he encountered on entering the township resembled the rumors. The town was in complete chaos, and not a living soul was to be seen. Polish corpses lay about all over the ground, some of them still in their death throes. He walked on and saw a Jew wandering around aimlessly, and, scared out of his wits, asked him: "Where are all the inhabitants of Semyatich?"

"They're all in the graveyard," was the answer, and the Jew led him there, where he found his son with his wife and children. And these were the events that had taken place:

The Russian army had encircled the township, and the Poles, seeing them, did not confront them at once. The colonel ordered all the township's inhabitants to leave their homes and go to the graveyard. The Jews went to their graveyard and the Russian Orthodox to theirs. During the ensuing battle the Poles were killed to the last man. The colonel was forbidden to take prisoners since all the jails were overcrowded. It was preferable to kill them on the spot.

The inhabitants in the graveyards waited for the colonel's order to return to their homes, which he issued only on the third day. My uncle was told that nobody was harmed in the graveyard. The only Jew who lost his life was David Breiter, of whom I have already written above.[21]

The Poles fought with great courage and heroism. When the Jews returned from the graveyard they saw dead and wounded Poles strewn all over the ground. One Pole—according to my uncle—lay dying, his belly ripped wide open, whispering with his last gasp, "I'll never surrender!"

Muravyov dispatched two officers to every province to act as military governors. Each officer, accompanied by a *sotnia*[22] of Cossacks and a wagonload of firearms, made the rounds of all the estates to check which of the owners had remained at home and which hadn't. If the landowner could not be located, his wife and daughters came in for a flogging by the Cossacks, to make them reveal his whereabouts.[23] The officers kept on hand supplies of medals issued directly by Muravyov to be presented to those lords who revealed the locations of Polish rebel bands.

At the beginning, as mentioned before, the peasants lived in dread of the Poles and avoided leaving their villages out of fear of being forced to work for them at the front line. But gradually the number of Polish rebels waned, and those who survived were scared to return to their homes. They were already a marked lot by the military governor and therefore preferred to stay in the woods. It was then that the peasants started taking revenge on the lords. They would raid a lord's home in the dark of night, drag him out of his bed, tie him with ropes, kick him mercilessly, then haul him in front of the military governor and tell him that they had found him hiding in the forest. There is no need to go into detail about the fate of that lord.

Thus the peasants avenged themselves. Many lords fell victim to their former serfs, who made short shrift of them. They were hanged, shot, tortured, maimed, or exiled to Siberia and the four corners of Hell. Many of the estates were confiscated, and Russian officers acquired enormous properties for a hundred rubles. An estate later leased for three thousand rubles a year cost the Russian a minimal sum, and sometimes not even that. The destruction of the Poles was one of the most horrifying events of the last several centuries.

CHAPTER 22

THE JEWS AFTER THE
POLISH REBELLION

My uncle as a "miracle worker" • Berl-Bendet and Sikhowski • The rumor about the miracle • My uncle's reputation spreads • Grandfather's plan • The situation of the Jews after the rebellion

*D*uring the rebellion, the situation of the Jews, as mentioned previously, utterly deteriorated. They lost their means of livelihood. The stores were empty, for neither the gentry nor the peasants came into town—the latter, out of fear of the Polish rebel bands. The impoverishment of the Jews was indescribable. They were scared to venture out of town, and all sources of income had completely dried up. Craftsmen went to live in Odessa[1] and the Volhin province.[2] They sold their houses for a loaf of bread and pawned whatever valuables they still possessed; all that just to keep body and soul together.

Their only hope was that this uneven conflict wouldn't last too long; that the more powerful Russians would break the Polish resistance, thus holding out the chance of starting life anew; that God, who never deserted His people, would not forsake them now, either. This is what the Jews in the study houses believed. But, meanwhile, they were nervous, dejected, and confused, groping about in the dark. They talked of nothing but the rebellion and eagerly followed the political events.

In those days I was still reading to my uncle, the rabbi. I remember how, one day, my uncle Berl-Bendet stormed into my uncle's home, shaking with agitation. The previous night, he told us, a band of gentry had burst into his lord Sikhowski's house, had eaten and drunk their fill, and then had made him hand over three thousand rubles in cash. He, Berl-Bendet, intending to clear his landlord's name, had informed the military governor in Shereshov of the matter and, according to Muravyov's decree, Sikhowski deserved a medal. But instead of receiving the medal, the governor had dispatched three Cossacks to arrest him, and Berl-Bendet feared that his lord might come to harm. He therefore had come straight to the rabbi to have him pray for Sikhowski's release. Should the rabbi's prayers be answered, he would deposit eighteen rubles in the charity box of Rabbi Meir Ba'al ha-Nes.[3]

But the rabbi, a wise man, evidently realizing that no harm would come to the gentleman, merely asked, "How many miles is it from the estate of Czechczowa to Shereshov, and how far is Czechczowa from Kamenets?"

"It's two miles from the estate to Shereshov, and three miles away from Kamenets."

"Well, by the time you get home," the rabbi said, "you'll probably find your lord there, safe and sound and wearing a medal."

Several hours later, Berl-Bendet's son-in-law Yisrael-Aharon came to the rabbi with the joyful news that his father-in-law had found his landlord at home, wearing the medal, and therefore he was donating eighteen rubles to the charity box. The story spread quickly and the rabbi's prophecy was considered nothing short of a miracle.

Within the town and its outlying neighborhoods the "miracle" was publicized along with many lies and exaggerations, and the rabbi quickly turned into a real "miracle worker." From that time on, he was given no rest. If a woman was about to give birth, her relatives came to the rabbi, tearfully begging him to pray for her, and returned several hours later to inform him joyfully of the successful birth of a boy or a girl. If someone was dangerously ill, one immediately turned to the rabbi, who would bring out the charity box, into which everyone dropped whatever he could afford. If the sick person recovered, the rabbi's reputation grew apace—he was simply a resurrector of the dead and a miracle worker.[4]

Meanwhile, my readings to him were suspended, and I, too, became something of a miracle worker alongside my uncle. When I could no longer bear the meaningless twaddle and claptrap and the interminable gabbling of the women, I would tell them, in the words of a miracle worker: "The rabbi grants you his blessing, go home and put your trust in God's mercy. . . ."

The difficult situation after the rebellion was instrumental in spreading the rabbi's reputation as a miracle worker, resulting in the arrival of tens of carriages from Brisk at his house. People came in droves from all over, and he could no longer devote any time to his learning with me. He therefore set aside four hours a day—from twelve o'clock to four—for that purpose. During those hours, I bolted the door and read to him. Meanwhile the entire synagogue courtyard became black with people. Everyone was waiting for the miracle worker, and with every passing day, the multitude grew. It was cramped and crowded, and people from as far afield as Bialystok started to come. The rabbi could no longer handle the crowd by himself and had to enlist the aid of his son Simha, from Pinsk, who arrived soon afterward with his entire family. Now they started with the little notes and petitions,[5] which the rabbi's son would write,[6] and more people were needed in order to escort the petitioners in and out. Beynush the beadle was not able to do the job alone, and therefore he was joined by his son, to help him keep the people from rushing through the door all at once. And these supernatural phenomena grew by leaps and bounds.

In those days the Neshkhizer rebbe[7] also became known as a miracle worker and was considered the greatest miracle worker among all the rebbes of his day. Before long, however, his reputation was completely overshadowed by that of the rabbi of Kamenets. I no longer learned with him, and in fact I didn't learn at all, but devoted all my time to preparing myself for the big debate with my father and the other hasidim about Hasidism and Mitnaggedism.

After the rebellion, the government abolished the lords' monopoly on the production and sale of alcohol, including all those leases in Kamenets. This deprived us of our last means of a livelihood, but within the Jewish Pale of Settlement there was a feeling of relief—as if the winds of freedom were blowing, both in the economic and in the spiritual sense. A new epoch was in the offing for the Jews. Instead of being at the mercy of the lords, who had been, until then, their sole source of income, it was now the rich Jews who became the lords, and the big traders in timber and wheat. In fact, Jews took to commerce in a big way.[8]

After the suppression of the rebellion, almost 90 percent of the estates remained in the hands of the landowners' wives. The lords themselves died tragic deaths. Their wives, left on their own, did not know how, nor were they able to even begin to administer the estates with the hired labor, the very peasants who had once been their serfs. Those same ladies, accustomed to a life of luxury, of giving balls and engaging in coquetry, could hardly be expected to turn into practical landowners overnight. They hadn't the slightest notion how to handle their estates.

Grandfather was the first to work out a plan that would extricate those ladies from their difficulties and benefit the Jews at the same time. In other words, Jews would take out leases on the estates of those landladies who were unable to manage them. For the latter, it would be a salvation; they'd be assured of a steady yearly income without having to worry about their ruined estates. It would take a burden off their shoulders.

Grandfather at once drove to all the landladies of the estates he had dealt with formerly and presented his plan to them. He explained that in difficult times like the present, it would be advisable on their part to lease out their property to the Jews, and they, the landowners, would have a steady income. He considered the small number of landlords who, after the rebellion, remained in their homes, dejected and depressed. Broken in body and spirit, they were totally incapable of handling the husbandry of their estates, nor did they know how to relate to their former serfs, who were now their hired labor. It was, therefore, worth their while, Grandfather argued, to lease their property out to the Jews. It goes without saying that such advice was, at that time, the only reasonable advice, dictated by life itself.

Grandfather wasted no time and leased several estates, one for each of his children. For himself he reserved the estate of Pruska belonging to Vilevinski, (there were two estates by that name: one belonged to Osserevski and one to Vilevinski),[9] four versts away from Kamenets, which already had a brewery within its compound. During the first couple of years, Grandfather's family lived in the township, while he himself stayed on the estate throughout the week to supervise the workers, returning home only for the Sabbath.

In that way, the more well-to-do Jews took out leases on the estates, and within a short time Jews occupied at least 65 percent of the estates within Grodno province. No doubt, the landladies and the few landlords were highly pleased with these new Jewish settlers.

At first the leases on the estates were fairly cheap, but not long afterward, when the price of wheat started soaring, it also caused the leases on the estates to rise considerably, so that within ten years the Jewish leaseholders were not making such great profits from farming. Landladies and landlords also started selling off their forests, something not ignored by many Jews who had become big timber traders. They bought all types of logs; some for sale on the spot, some for use in building houses. They supplied building materials to the larger towns, and within a short time they also sent large transports of timber as far away as Danzig. This was a brisk and bustling business.

However, the same phenomenon that had earlier affected the leases on the estates repeated itself with the sale of the tracts of forest. Whereas earlier good forest tracts could be bought up very cheaply at two hundred to three hundred rubles a dessiatine, within a few years the prices rose exorbitantly, encouraged by the Jewish timber merchants themselves. Scores of buyers used to come to the forests, and the keen competition contributed to the eventual ruin of the trade. Now, a dessiatine of forest no longer fetched two hundred to three hundred rubles, but a tidy twelve hundred! . . .

At that time, the government treasury also started selling off its own forest tracts as well as those confiscated from the landed gentry. Those government officials did not treat the Jews as badly as they do now, but traded with them just as they did with the non-Jews.

After quelling the rebellion, Muravyov issued a decree forbidding Poles to acquire land in Lithuania. He did not forget about the Jews, and forbade them this right as well.[10] This prohibition put obstacles in the way of those Jews who drew their living exclusively from that trade. However, during those turbulent times, Jews managed to install beer breweries and vodka distilleries in many places, and to construct large water- and windmills, sawmills, olive compressor plants, and the like. They also kept large herds of sheep and cattle so as to fertilize the soil. Now, the soil yielded 600 sheaves of wheat per two acres instead of the mere 240[11] when the estates were run by the gentry. Jews owned large dairies, and raised horses of first-rate pedigree to ensure offspring of the best quality. They also introduced mechanical plows to cultivate the soil and all sorts of innovations meant to simplify and speed up labor.[12]

The estates were entirely transformed. Their soil became more fertile, and the most insignificant thing was turned into a money-maker. The wheat harvests represented but a small part of the gains, compared with the variety of produce grown by Jews applying all their energy, know-how, and hard work. They were engrossed in this business day and night, constantly on the lookout for ways to wrest an ever-greater yield from Mother Nature.

Landlords returning after some time from the Siberian jails, broken in body and spirit, couldn't believe their own eyes. Their estates looked so different—spotlessly clean, with many more sheds, and stables, and new agricultural machinery. They literally crossed themselves at the sight of this Paradise created by the Jews. Their wives had nothing but praise for the Jews' energy. Everybody worked, they said—the husband spent days and nights on the job, putting to work his sons and daughters, their husbands and wives. Everything was devoted to work, and nothing went to waste. This was nothing like when the lords were in charge, ignorant of what was going on, relying only on their drunken stewards. The landlady said that she now received 3,500 rubles a year from their holdings whereas she used to make only 1,200.

There were landlords who, envying the Jews' achievements, fired them and took over the running of the estates themselves, trying to copy and apply their methods of management. But within barely two to three years the estates reverted to their former ruinous condition. It wasn't the same thing; it wasn't successful. The whole business became neglected and eventually went to rack and ruin and they were obliged once more to lease their estates to Jews.

This period, however, was not only characterized by commercial growth but also by a drive among Jews to gain a secular education. The government opened up all its educational institutions to them.[13] A large number of Jews became doctors, jurists, and engineers. The government even permitted them to hold government posts, and in many cities Jews became judicial investigators,[14] and physicians,[15] and even assumed the rank of colonel, general, and the like.

This was, undoubtedly, one of the best periods experienced by the Jews in their Russian Diaspora. They began to spread out into the larger towns of Russia, and wherever they settled, they engaged in commerce in a big way.[16] Within a short time, a large Jewish community comprising some fifty thousand Jews sprang up in Moscow, and they played an important role in that city's industrial development.[17]

In the days of Nicholas I, a Jew was afraid to be seen in the streets of Kiev.[18] Even the sailors on the barges sailing by on the Dnieper from Pinsk to Nikolayev[19] slept aboard ship when they passed Kiev. They did not dare put up at an inn in town. And if one happened to sleep in an inn, he couldn't even risk looking out of the window. When a Jew came to Kiev to buy merchandise on a Sunday—from a Russian, of course, since there were no Jewish stores in the town—he had to pay the exact amount asked for by the storekeeper then and there. And if he started bargaining, he was asking for trouble. He would immediately be rewarded by a punch in the mouth, and the innocent victim dared not utter a word in protest, since he was, after all, on forbidden territory! . . . Not much different from the situation nowadays.[20] But later, during the reign of Alexander II, Kiev had a Jewish community of about fifty thousand,[21] among whom there were millionaires, magnates of the sugar trade.[22] The dried fruit industry also prospered there.

After the suppression of the rebellion, when all the leases in the townships were abolished, we rented estates and started cultivating the land ourselves. It barely sufficed to keep body and soul together, and we never got accustomed to it. Grandfather's business acumen was of no use here. There were no more lords! Grandfather never bothered putting away any cash reserves, expecting the gentry and leaseholdings to last forever. We did not live on the estates, for it was considered rather shameful to settle in a village. We therefore hired laborers to till the farmlands and we traveled to the estates every day.

CHAPTER 23

"KEEP IN STEP!"

The eve of my wedding • I see the bride • The sermon • The first
step on the foot • "Keep in step! Keep in step!" • The splitting up of
the hasidim and mitnaggedim at my wedding

In 1865 Father thought that it was high time for me to get married, since I was by then already an old bachelor of seventeen and it was disgraceful to be seen in public in such a state. He therefore set the wedding date for the month of Elul. The wedding would be held at our home, because the bride was an orphan, without father or mother.[1]

When it came time to order the wedding garments, Father insisted that I wear *pantofl*, stockings,[2] and a satin *kapote*. In addition, he refused to hire the musicians from Kobrin because Tudros, the master of ceremonies, was a mitnagged. He preferred the musicians from Brisk, whose leader was a well-known hasid.[3] He also wanted to bring a hasidic wedding jester.

For months prior to the wedding I tried desperately to convince Father. I boiled with rage and cried: "I don't want to stand under the *huppah* in *pantofl* and white stockings, and I want only Shepsl and his band to play at my wedding." It was only with great difficulty, and finally after enlisting the assistance of Arye-Leyb, "the only child," that I was able to convince Father to let me wear high boots. Shepsl and his band of musicians arrived on Thursday, the day before the wedding.

My bride, along with the in-laws, also arrived that day. They put up at my uncle Mordechai-Leyb's, where the wedding was to be celebrated. In those days, it was customary for all the women and young girls to gather at the bride's home at noontime on the wedding day and perform a special kind of dance to the music played by the musicians. Later, toward dusk, all the men would gather and proceed with the band to the bridegroom's home. The groom would deliver a sermon and the assembled guests would be treated to sponge cakes, fruit preserves, and wine. After that, the groom would be led through the streets to the music of the band right up to the house of the bride for the traditional rite of *badekns*, and from there to the study house, where the wedding canopy would be set up. From there, all the guests, along with the musicians, would repair to the bride's home for the wedding feast, dancing, and festivities, until the crack of dawn.[4]

If the wedding took place on a Friday afternoon,[5] the couple was escorted from the *huppah* to their home, with band in tow, and the guests left for the Sabbath eve services. After the prayers they would reassemble for the seven days of feasting, but of course, not everyone would come. The next day, Sabbath morning, all the bridegroom's close friends, relatives, and in-laws would come to lead him to the study house, where he would be called up to read from the weekly Torah portion. The dancing and the feast would take place after the outgoing Sabbath.

My father, a devoted hasid, saw no reason why I should be introduced to my bride before the wedding.[6] Upon her arrival in town, the entire family, young and old, rushed to see her, with the exception of myself. In fact, everyone, the whole town, hurried to see the bride, and they all happily told me what a beauty she was . . . ; not a pockmark was visible on her face. But there were some who were not totally convinced that this was so and decided to go again to inspect the bride. They returned and joyfully confirmed that she was without blemish, but I, on the other hand, was full of anger at not being allowed to get so much as a glimpse of her.

Once again, I asked Arye-Leyb, "the only child," to do a favor for a poor soul in dire straits and come with me to my uncle's house in order to see my bride. Early the next morning, before the women gathered there, I managed to see her. She was, indeed, beautiful. Although I felt embarrassed, I nevertheless plucked up enough courage to wish her mazel tov and ask her how she was feeling. . . . I wanted to sit down and keep looking at her beautiful face a little longer, but Arye-Leyb pulled me away by the hand, saying, "Come, it is forbidden to visit with the bride now. . . ." Sad at heart, I left to return to my "quarters" at Grandfather's home.

My uncle the rabbi was present at the reception. I delivered my sermon—all of Kamenets was wildly enthusiastic about it—and the mood was truly jubilant.

While we stood under the wedding canopy I felt the bride step on my foot. It never occurred to me that she had done it on purpose.[7] Immediately after the ceremony the bride's relatives snatched her from my side and brought her to the house so that she might be the first to set foot across the threshold. They considered this act an efficacious means of ensuring that she would rule over me. Popular belief gave great credence to those sorts of things then. The bridegroom or the bride—the first to set foot over the threshold upon returning from the wedding ceremony—will rule the other.[8] But Arye-Leyb and my family, not wishing to be outsmarted, started racing at full speed in order that I reach the house before the bride and her party. The latter, on the other hand, were determined not to lose their "dominion," and then the mad dash began, may God preserve us. I was wearing a *kittel*[9] above my satin *kapote*, and a coat on top of both. But Yehuda-Leyb, the tailor, had made the coat a shade too tight, so that during the race it came apart at the seams and my *kittel* was visible underneath. I was terribly embarrassed.

The bride and her party had, meanwhile, reached the porch of the house while I was still a short distance from the six steps leading up to it. It was then that Arye-Leyb insisted that the bride come down from the porch and that we cross the threshold together, as equals. The bride and her party had no other choice but to comply, and to join us at the foot of the stairs, from where both sides watched closely and made sure that we both stepped into the house at one and the same time. We walked up the stairs to the porch amid cries of: "Keep in step! Keep in step! . . ."

But the bride was quick to place the heel of her foot over the threshold of the room, thus she would preside over me! . . . but Arye-Leyb saw what happened and of course would not allow this. He ordered the two of us to go back down and enter together, as equals. And again amid the cries from both sides: "Keep in step! Keep in step!"

It reminded me of a military drill exercise. At heart I laughed at the whole procedure and deliberately let my bride step across the threshold before me. Why not? Let her enjoy herself! And, indeed, she was again the first to set foot into the room. That, however, incensed Arye-Leyb greatly, who now insisted that the bride and bridegroom were not to enter the room at all but were to be led to the groom's quarters, meaning Grandfather's house. And should she attempt to enter ahead of me—this would simply not be permitted, he wouldn't hesitate to make us repeat the act time and again, even if it took all night long. So, we were led a bit further to Grandfather's house, accompanied by the musicians. There the porch was just as high, but her relatives were by then quite exhausted and no longer so keen on competing with Arye-Leyb. Though they did not exert themselves as much, here, too, they shouted, "Keep in step! Keep in step!" They all kept a watchful eye on our feet, and luckily, this time everything went off smoothly and we stepped across the threshold together.

The "golden soup"[10] for the bride and bridegroom was brought from my uncle's to Grandfather's house, since after the wedding ceremony it was the custom to place the newlyweds together in a separate room.[11] We ate the famous soup at Grandfather's.

The band of musicians split up: several of them, together with Shepsl, performed at Grandfather's, and the rest at my uncle's. Meanwhile, the Sabbath had descended and the women lit and blessed the candles. The majority of the guests departed for the evening prayers, whereas we, the family members, prayed at home.

Grandfather and Father were still at odds regarding inviting the hasidim to my wedding. Grandfather objected, and Father was finally forced to agree. Therefore the hasidim came on Friday evening and Saturday morning and night. They sang and told hasidic tales and teachings, while I listened closely to what they were saying. They, who hadn't the slightest inkling that I was already an ardent mitnagged, seemed so strange to me in their hasidic ways.

The musicians played throughout most of the week, and for the next seven days, feasts were given, as was the custom, for the entire township.

CHAPTER 24

THE DEBATE

Rosh Hashanah at the rebbe's court • Father's anger at my refusal
to travel to the rebbe • My troubles on account of Hasidism • My
struggle against Hasidism • The debate • The impact of the debate
upon my family

Father spent Rosh Hashanah at the rebbe's court in Slonim.
Immediately after my wedding, Father started treating me
as an adult. He no longer told me what to do, and assumed
that I knew for myself what my obligations were. He always spoke
to me with his eyes; in other words, I looked into his eyes and knew
what I must do or say. He thought it unnecessary to tell me outright
that I must travel to the rebbe, since after the wedding all the sons
of the hasidim customarily traveled to him. Now, as he himself was
going, he was certain I would join him and say, "Father, I'm coming
with you." But I did not say a word to him and it was as if a dagger
had pierced his heart. He traveled to the rebbe alone.

Father was filled with shame there, for he could not hide from
the rebbe the fact that his son, married three weeks earlier, on the
tenth of Elul, had not come with him. After all, the rebbe knew
me well, had even predicted that I'd be a faithful hasid, and now
my father had come without me! It was a bitter pill for Father to
swallow.

When he returned from Slonim after Rosh Hashanah, he was furious and let me know it by means of abrupt sentences and sarcastic
asides filtered through his teeth. "A great share of Paradise I'll have
because of you. . . ."

That was when I decided to put an end to my pretense once and for all. I'd have it out with him by means of a debate, in hopes that this would iron out our differences and put an end to our mutual antagonism. To debate the matter with him was something different, and I had no doubt that I would triumph. Moreover, I wanted him to know that I was a mitnagged and would never be a hasid—he would eventually get used to it.

But it was far from easy, and altogether different from what I had imagined, especially with one so gentle and angelic as my father, who had always guided me by a look. How could I go against Father, and such a one as this, and prove to him that his way was mistaken? It was a dilemma as hard to face as death. I was constantly looking for an opportune moment that would give me the courage to tackle this difficult task.

As bad luck would have it, my young, beautiful wife herself leaned toward Hasidism. She had grown up in the home of her brother-in-law, a devoted Karliner hasid.[1] She was fond of telling about the fish she'd once cooked for the zaddik Aharon of Karlin when he was a guest at her brother-in-law's home (the people of Pinsk were famous for the way they prepared fish). The rebbe tasted the fish (he was, bless his soul, no small eater),[2] and said he had not tasted fish that good for a long time. "Who cooked it?" the rebbe asked.

When told that she was a fifteen-year-old orphan, and that not only her fish, but everything she cooked had a heavenly taste, he blessed her that her future husband would be a great hasid. It's therefore not difficult to imagine her disappointment at realizing that I was no hasid and would not travel to the rebbe's court.

My wife played an important role in our household. Everyone admired her for her beauty, her competence, and her intelligence, and my father expected great things of her and sincerely hoped that she would eventually succeed in returning me to Hasidism.

On the Sabbath and the holidays my wife and I usually dined at Grandfather's. Had I remained a hasid, I would not have been able to afford him that pleasure. Now I grasped at this opportunity. At Grandfather's, as in the homes of all mitnaggedim, we ate rather early in the day. Looking through the window afterward, I would catch a glimpse of Father passing by Grandfather's house on his way home from his prayers in the *shtibl*. I would return home with Libe, my young wife, and Father would talk with her about Hasidism, but send stinging remarks in my direction, which pained me.

But my good father, bent on having my wife sway me toward Hasidism, went too far. He did everything to humiliate me in front of her, while praising her to the skies, not realizing that he was creating a rift between me and my wife. This hurt me very much. It seemed as if he had made up his mind to ruin my life if I did not remain a hasid.

On Simhat Torah, Libe and I dined at Grandfather's. It was one o'clock when we made our way back home from Grandfather's, and Father was already leading a whole bunch of fellow hasidim to our place. On that day, Yankl Essigmakher[3] and Shepsl the scribe would make the rounds of other homes, taking whatever was cooking there from the ovens and bringing it to our house for all the hasidim.[4] Oh what a beloved day!

I saw Father with the hasidim and I heard Yankl's voice. They were all rather tipsy by then and advancing upon us. Libe and I crossed over to the other side of the street, and Yankl, intending to insult me, yelled out for the entire street to hear, "And that is why a man leaves his father and his mother,"[5] and then screamed at the top of his voice, "*Hund Tate, Hund Mame, and cleaves to his wife, mit der frau,*"[6] repeating those words over and over again until we reached home.

At home, when I asked Father why he let Yankl insult me like that, Yankl interrupted and said, "What? When? All I did was interpret a passage from the Bible for him, like in the version of the heretic Desser." He was referring to the German translation of the Bible by Moses Mendelssohn, dubbed Moshe of Dessau.[7]

"*Und Tate, und Mame,*" he cried.

"But you called me *Hund!*" I shouted at him.

"Not true," he remarked jokingly, "I said *und, und*. . . . "

"Well," I thought to myself, "Today is the day for me to put an end to the entire affair. I'll get drunk and start the debate. A drunk has more courage."

On the outgoing night of Simhat Torah, the preacher usually gave a festive dinner for all the town's householders at the community's expense.[8] Everyone gathered there earlier for afternoon prayers followed by a great banquet of roast duck, fruit, wine, and vodka. The bottles of wine had already been sent over by the householders themselves on the eve of the holiday, and everybody had a great time at the preacher's house, eating, drinking, singing, and dancing until well after midnight. This was an age-old custom, performed yearly. The preacher's son, Moshe-Aharon, and son-in-law held a separate feast on Simhat Torah for the young *lomdim* in the town. There, too, the revelry continued all day, with fine vodka, wines, and roast geese. I had made up with Moshe-Aharon beforehand that this time I would not go with my father and the hasidim. Rather, I would openly celebrate with him and with all our young fellow scholars.

Meanwhile the feasting had started at Father's house. Everyone, myself included, sat down around the table, though I sat there as if on pins and needles. Not long afterward, I sneaked out to join the festivities at Moshe-Aharon's, which were by then in full swing. I must admit that that day was one of the happiest in my life, and there were not too many like it afterward. There were twelve of us, the most outstanding learners in the town. We danced, kissed, and sang. We felt a kind of spiritual kinship drawing us together and we would have kissed each other endlessly. . . . We celebrated until eleven o'clock at night and, rather tipsy by then, went to the householders and drew them into a circle dance with us.

I remember catching hold of one Shmerl, a Jewish householder, the father of a friend of whom I was especially fond. I hugged him and pressed him to me with great love. I was a pretty sturdy fellow and I almost choked him to death. He was unable to escape my embrace and it took several people to pry him out. After that, I dropped to the floor dead-drunk—it was quite a disgraceful thing. I was dragged into another room to sleep it off. At one o'clock in the morning Moshe-Aharon woke me up in order for me to go home.

By the time I got there, the hasidim were busy eating the fish, and were in the midst of their revelry. Yankl, the Kotsker hasid, always drunk as Lot, was the first to set eyes on me. "Khatskl!" he called out. "You've returned from Moshe-Aharon's. May the devil seize his father!" On a sudden impulse, I retorted, "And may the devil seize your rebbe's father!"

This was a particularly vulgar Jewish insult. . . .

Had the infuriated hasidim not been scared of my grandfather, they would have beaten me then and there to within an inch of my life, and my father would probably have been quite pleased. But they were afraid of Grandfather, so they simply gnashed their teeth. No one uttered a sound. A deadly silence ensued. I went into my bedroom, where I found my young wife dissolved in tears. She accused me of having spoiled the hasidim's festivities, which were to have gone on all night long. Fear spread through to my very bones, woe to the ears who heard the son of Moshe, son of Aharon-Leyzer, thus curse the rebbe through his father!

I left the house with my wife through a side street that led to the Polish church. She did not stop crying for a moment, and my heart was breaking inside me. I could no longer bear her bitter tears. "I love you, Khatskl," she said tearfully, "but I wish I were dead. I can't go on living with you. Not that I want to divorce you, God forbid, but after hearing you curse Yankl's rebbe, the Kotsker rebbe, through his father, I am afraid to live under the same roof with you. . . ." And she burst into tears once again. I kept silent, but her sobs and whimpers made me shudder all over.

On returning home, I heard the voices of the hasidim, who were about to leave the house. They kept talking about "the misfortune," and did not sing on their way home, as they would otherwise have done. The words from my mouth had shocked them. I had, indeed, ruined their celebration.

I was about to enter our bedroom when Father called out, "Sit down here, Khatskl," and ordered my wife to go to bed. "What's the matter with you, Khatskl? What's gotten into you?" he asked, in a quiet but trembling voice.

I took one look at his face and was deeply shocked. A deathly pale face. Bloodshot eyes. I'd never seen him in such a state. I saw no trace of anger in his face—the feeling of anger was foreign to him—only sorrow. I had already seen him after the death of a child, a sister,[9] but a look as awful as this I had never seen before. I wanted to kiss him, to cry, to ask for his mercy, to beg his forgiveness, and was ready to lay down my life for him. I'd rather have suffered being stabbed in the heart than see that look on Father's face. I was well aware of how much health my rebelliousness cost my dear father, whom I adore and worship to this very day. He was, poor soul, not to blame for the distress I was causing him. I must admit that whenever I am about to do someone the least harm—something that happens to everyone—Father's image rises in my mind's eye and I immediately regret my earlier intentions. But, unfortunately, Father's image does not appear every time.

I'd have given my very life, my body, my blood to appease him, but what about my soul? How could I believe in something I didn't believe in?[10] Yet, how could I ruin the lives of the two people—my father and my beautiful young wife—whom I loved so dearly?

"Why do you keep quiet?" Father finally demanded. "Talk! And get it off your chest! That's all you and I can do. It's all my fault. I should have told you more about the aims of Hasidism. I took it for granted that an intelligent boy like you knew all about it and there was no need to talk about it too much. Now I see how wrong I was. I never talked to you about Hasidism. Had I done so right from the start, you might never have come to this."

It was way past midnight. The shutters were closed and a single candle was burning. Then I started to talk. . . .

I talked and talked, and when I saw his lips moving to say something, I took the words out of his mouth, knowing in advance what he was going to say. I talked passionately while he sat there motionless, listening attentively without interrupting the flow of my words. This was his greatest virtue. When I finally stopped talking, it was already daylight. I looked at the clock. It was seven o'clock in the morning!

He saw himself suddenly confronted by an entirely new person. How had it come about? He thought that by handing me over to Yitzhak-Asher, he had done his duty by me, and had been totally unaware of the change I had undergone during that time. He saw me as someone who was involved in everything. But he made one tiny error: he thought I would be a hasid who was involved in everything; instead I had turned into a mitnagged who was involved in everything. He collapsed onto the bed as if in a faint and groaned deeply.

My heart was aching as I left Father's bedroom, and I burst into tears. It took me a while to compose myself, and, before entering my bedroom, I wiped away the tears so my wife would not notice that I'd been crying. But on entering, I was shocked to see my young and beautiful wife thoroughly distraught, and realized that she hadn't slept a wink that night. The pillows were drenched with her tears. When I came in, she burst once again into such loud weeping that my parents came rushing in, utterly alarmed. Father, taking one look at her, grasped immediately what was going on and quickly left the room again.

There was no way for me to comfort her. Good God! I had done my share,[11] the debate with Father—to which I had dedicated the last year and a half, and had done nothing but that: I neither learned, nor progressed in my study of philosophy—that, too, was over. And what now? I thought that Father, after he calmed down, would reconcile himself to the situation and we would be able to go on living side by side. I would begin to study, as I had promised Father. I secretly decided that now I would devote myself to my studies as never before. Years of *kest,* after all, I have; for my wife, I need not worry. Father loves her desperately, she will be well taken care of, and I might sit and learn and prepare myself for the rabbinate. Finding a rabbinical post would not present any difficulties. The grandsons of Hayyim of Volozhin were at that time rather influential in the Jewish world. I had no doubt that the head of the Volozhin Yeshiva would eventually find a suitable position for me in some town, and my beautiful young wife would be a rabbi's wife! [12]

My mind was made up, though my wife's tears nearly drove me mad. But I was sure that her crying would stop, eventually. I plucked up the courage and went to pray in the study house. This was a most difficult night, indelibly etched in my memory.

CHAPTER 25

"CHILDREN, GATHER
THE COINS!"

The debate with the hasidim • I intend to study in Volozhin • Father's objections • Setting my wife against me • My wife falls ill • We fall out with one another • Peace is restored • My total absorption in my studies • "Children, gather the coins!" • "The palace" • "Khatskl's generation"

𝓜y wife begged me to go on praying in the *shtibl,* if not for my sake then for hers. On Friday night, in the midst of the prayers, my cousin Simha asked me to come to his place to debate the hasidim. I agreed. About thirty hasidim were there, headed by Arele. They had already prepared themselves for it several days in advance. It was of utmost importance for them to bring me back into the hasidic fold. I had, according to them, "a finger in every pie," was enterprising, liked to dabble in all sorts of communal affairs, and was able, therefore, to influence many of the recently married young men to become hasidim. They feared that once I remained a convinced mitnagged, it would be the end of converting the youth of Kamenets to Hasidism, and this was a matter of life and death for them.

I won the debate "hands down." I had an answer to each and every question they raised, but they had no answers for the questions I put to them. "The rebbe will find the answers to all your questions," Simha retorted angrily.

"Why should I accept Hasidism, keep on asking questions, and look for someone to answer them," I said, "when my heart is not in it? I prefer sticking to the old ways without having to ask any questions."

"And what are the questions you're so keen on asking us?" said Simha.

"The need to travel to the rebbe, for example."

"I'll give you fifty rubles for your travel expenses," Simha promised. "Go and visit the zaddik Aharon of Karlin, and he'll explain it all to you."

He shook my hand and promised to give me the fifty rubles as soon as I decided to travel to the rebbe. That's how the debate ended. I came out the victor and earned everyone's respect.

I would pray at the *shtibl* on Saturdays, and throughout the week at the new study house together with all the outstanding young students. For a long period of time, I conducted discussions after the service regarding Hasidism, and I had a large following of young people eager to hear how I had won the debate. I explained to them the basic principles of Hasidism and my criticisms. I was also asked to talk at the old study house, where I repeated the same things. I must confess that as a result, in the course of the following decades, not a single person joined the ranks of the hasidim, and Kamenets has remained a town of zealous mitnaggedim to this day.

As mentioned earlier, I was quite mistaken about the consequences of my debate with Father. I thought Father would eventually come to terms with my decision to join the mitnaggedic camp, but things did not turn out that way at all. He became vindictive, something that had never been part of his nature. He kept throwing biting remarks in my direction and did all he could to turn my wife against me. That was absolutely unfair. He had no compunctions about ruining my marriage to the woman I so loved.

Matters went from bad to worse, and when I realized that Father was bent on causing a rift between us, I decided to go and study in Volozhin. It had, after all, long been my intention to prepare myself for the rabbinate! In Volozhin I would lack for nothing, and it would finally put an end to the squabbles with my father. To be quite honest, I didn't like the idea of leaving my beautiful eighteen-year-old wife scarcely a few months after our marriage—but all was lost! To carry on as though nothing had happened was impossible.

I wanted to procure a passport. I was a bit cocky and did not want to travel about without a passport, though it was not required at the time. The first passport may not be issued without the parent's knowledge; however, I figured that, being by then quite well-known despite my young age, Yaakov, the *sborshchik,* would issue me the passport even without my father's knowledge.[1] Indeed, he promised to do so, but secretly told my father about it, which quickly brought home to me the folly of my actions—the result of my overweening pride. I should have known he would ask Father.

Father immediately interrogated me: "Khatskl, what do you need with a passport?"

"To travel to Volozhin . . ." I replied with downcast eyes.

All of a sudden, his patience snapped and, right in front of my wife, he landed me two ringing slaps across the face.

"Less than two months after your marriage," he screamed, "you already want to desert your wife and live like a *porush* in another town!"

I suspected that he wasn't so much concerned over the fate of my wife at that moment as he was with stirring up trouble between us. "Is that what you intend to do?" he ranted on and on, "abandon your orphan-wife! Whoever heard of such a thing! What outrageous cruelty! Besides, how dare you plan all this without consulting your father! That you would do such a thing without your father's consent is one thing, but what about your wife? . . . You claim to be a pious Jew. Don't you know what's written in the Torah? That you should stay beside your wife for at least one year, even in times of war![2] And now you want to leave her so as to be free to study! Why can't you do that at home? Nobody's going to stop you. But there must be another reason. Maybe you've stopped loving your wife," he said with a diplomatic smile that made my blood boil. To think that I stopped loving my lovely young wife, for whom I would gladly have given my life! Why did he have to pour salt on my wounds?

He went on abusing me in front of her, determined on setting her against me. He kept talking for a long time, raking me over the coals, depicting me as the worst possible person in the world. After all, anyone willing to abandon his wife right after the wedding couldn't be human. How can one define such a person?

My wife, as usual, broke into tears, but Father, although unhappy at seeing her so distressed, went on stoking the fire. She cried so much she nearly fainted. Finally, when she complained of a pain in her head and her face was burning up, he became alarmed, stopped talking, and sent for Yoshke the healer. But the "doctor" was not at home and the house was in an uproar. The entire family quickly gathered. They put her to bed, and I felt the blood draining from my face. Only now did it become crystal clear to me how much he hated me for having turned into a mitnagged, and how cruel he could be to those who opposed him.

Once, on catching Yitzhak-Ber with a spare key to our safe, from which he had been pilfering money, and who knows how long that had been going on, Father remained unperturbed, never uttering an unkind word to him. He merely asked him as if by the way, "Tell me, Yitzhak-Ber, how long have you had that key, and did you at least steal from me with compassion?" Later on, after having returned the amount he had pilfered, Yitzhak-Ber said that he was now without any means of a livelihood and didn't even have the money for his fare home to Brisk. Father handed him a hundred-ruble note, wished him good luck, and so on . . . in such a kindly manner that one might have taken him for a zaddik rather than a common thief.

But in Father's attitude toward me I saw clearly, for the first time, a cold-blooded vengefulness. I was, after all, no street urchin. I had quite a reputation in the town, and people showed me a great deal of respect. So why did he treat me with such cruelty? He truly wanted to destroy me!

But on second thought, I could hardly blame him. First, I realized that a mitnagged could become a hasid, but the other way around—never. A mitnagged is no more than a pious Jew. A hasid, on the other hand, believes that God, Heaven, and Paradise exist only for his sake; and the more ardently he loves Hasidism, the more intensely he hates Mitnaggedism. He would no longer concern himself with this child—who in my case was no longer a child—if he attached himself to those hateful mitnaggedim. Because I was the eldest son and had four younger siblings, Father feared I would also turn them into mitnaggedim. He was right. All my brothers became mitnaggedim.

As bad luck would have it, my wife sided with my father, and he took advantage of it. He fought me through her. If she hadn't been so beautiful, Father would have bitten his lips and given up. But knowing how much I loved her gave him added incentive to continue his struggle against me. My wish to study in another town scared Father, for it dashed all hopes of returning me to Hasidism with the help of my beloved wife. Once I was no longer around, all his efforts were bound to prove futile. However, once a father and son are at loggerheads, the former usually loses the battle. He succeeded only in making my blood boil with rage and in ruining my life, and instead of giving in I became even more obstinate.

My clever father failed to comprehend that just as he would not abandon his Hasidism for all the gold in the world, I, too, refused to give up my own convictions under any circumstances. It was not in my nature to pretend, to deceive, to lie—as others did: dressing up in long hasidic coats, traveling to the rebbe, wearing a *shtrayml*—all in order to please their wives, their parents, or their in-laws. At heart they thought the opposite: smoking cigarettes on the Sabbath and committing all sorts of religious transgressions on the sly. I could not do it.

The day I wanted to get a passport was one of the bitterest of my life. My wife took ill and my father spared no effort to restore her to health. She lay in bed, crying nonstop, and she simply refused to speak to me. Her illness disconcerted me altogether. It goes without saying I would have done anything for her, but Father would not let me get near her. The entire family kept fussing around her, helping and consoling her—all except me!

Afterward, when she had recovered, her attitude toward me changed, maybe out of pity for me. My father had already tormented me enough, and clearly she was saddened by my need to get away and travel; after all, we had only just married and I could not even enjoy my life.

We patched up our differences . . . I explained to her why my father had no right to persecute me in this way. He could never force me to become a hasid when my convictions lay elsewhere. In any case, he had no basis for his accusations against me, and he should never have treated me in this awful manner.

"He has been trying to hurt me through you. He thinks I will back down, or lose my nerve," I reasoned in her ear. "No, my beloved wife, I am willing to do everything except pretend to believe in something I truly do not believe. As for my intention to study in Volozhin and leave you at home," I went on, "you know yourself how much I love you; my soul is bound together with yours, my spirit with your spirit, and this is the very reason why I want to study in Volozhin. I want you to be happy, contented, to make certain that, God forbid, you never want for anything. We haven't much money nor the promise of new business. The little property we do have isn't enough to make a living on. I can't just start up a little enterprise and make a livelihood from it like the Jews here in Kamenets do. There's just one hope for me—to become a rabbi. That's what our own uncle, the rabbi, would tell you if you asked him. I must "thank" my father for not sending me to Volozhin three years ago. I could already be a rabbi by now. But it's not too late. I'm eighteen years old and we still have three years of *kest* with my parents. And it would not be a terrible misfortune if we were to live apart for a while. Everyone here loves you, and you won't lack for a thing in Father's house. Within five years at the utmost and God willing, I'll be a rabbi and you will be a respectable rabbi's wife."[3]

In short, my darling wife, who was practical by nature and, above all, bent on eventually gaining an independent livelihood, agreed with me. She had never doubted my devotion and loyalty toward her, she said. Finally, seeing that we lived in peace with one another again, my father stopped tormenting me.

I had made up my mind to study Talmud and all the rabbinic literature with a view to becoming a rabbi in the end. I began studying at the new study house and applied myself in earnest to my studies. Immediately after the evening prayers, that is, from early afternoon until eight in the evening, I went on learning. I then lay down beside the stove with an old prayer shawl beneath my head and asked a young student to wake me up before they all went home around ten or eleven o'clock. After everybody had left and I remained on my own, I went on learning, standing at the pulpit until the crack of dawn, and when I raised my head from the Gemara, I heard the prayer leader intone the early morning prayers and realized that a new day had dawned. That's how I studied throughout the winter.

I slept at the study house no more than three hours a day and spent the rest of the time studying.[4] Only on Friday nights did I go home to spend the Sabbath with my family, according to the law for Torah scholars.[5] To tell the truth, I was pretty scared to stay alone in such a large study house throughout the week, because I still believed in demons and other harmful creatures.[6] In those days, a crazy woman by the name of Rashele used to roam the streets of Kamenets for nights on end. As soon as she saw a young man opening his door in the middle of the night to go outside, she would sneak through the open door, straight into his bed. It would, of course, create uproar, until, not without much ado, she was dragged out again. This was her mania, and I lived in constant fear lest this Rashele also catch me spending the nights at the study house. As for keeping away the demons, I used to light all the candles in their holders suspended from the ceiling. I remember that there were eight large candelabra, each containing eight, ten, or twelve sockets for the candles lit during the Sabbath and the holidays. I lit about two *funt* of candles every night, and no one dared to stop me. On the contrary, all those householders who prayed in the study house, as well as all the other Jews, seemed pleased at seeing someone there so devoted to his studies. It's certainly no trivial matter—all night long with the Talmud.

In addition to all that, I became ever more pious, so much so that I abstained from eating meat throughout the week, making do with nothing but black bread without butter and some stew. I started reading all the books of Jewish ethics; I especially enjoyed the one called *Yesod ve-shoresh ha-avodah*,[7] and followed all its precepts to the letter of what to do while praying: to weep during the reading of certain sections and to show joy during the reading of others.[8]

I also behaved in the manner the sage Rabbi Judah suggested: "One must not hold his hands below his belt,"[9] in other words, below his *gartl.* I remember looking compassionately at the men I passed on my way home and back again. What do they know? From what books do they learn? I thought to myself. And then, looking at the sky full of twinkling stars, I was seized by a kind of awe of God, recalling how the *porush,* the Patshoshnik,[10] used to repeat time and again the phrase, "Children, gather the coins. . . ." If someone were busy picking up coins in the street, he wouldn't take the time to chat with others along the way, but would be intent on picking up the coins. "Children, gather the coins. . . ."

With the commandments a man performs down on earth he builds himself a "palace" in the next world. Not for even a second must he stop learning, for he may, God forbid, die suddenly and not have managed to complete the building of the "palace," leaving it with a missing porch, cornice, or window. That's why he has to keep building nonstop to the last drop of sweat, until he finally gives up his soul.

I did as I was bidden. I built my "palace," and didn't allow myself to exchange even a single word with anyone. I "gathered the coins," and conducted myself according to the dicta of the author of *Yesod ve-shoresh ha-avodah,* and still I didn't feel I was fulfilling my duties. I kept thinking all the time how to become even more pious.

My piety and learning left no impression whatsoever on my father. "If only I had died, if only Khatskl had died," he kept saying, "before being awarded this 'honor.' All his learning and piety are worthless in my eyes if he doesn't believe in the rebbe."

In the township, on the other hand, householders started urging their sons and sons-in-law to copy my example. They actually envied Moshe, the son of Aharon-Leyzer, for having a son who was both a diligent learner and extremely pious. It had the desired effect on many of the young people, and gradually, by Hanukkah, more and more young scholars used to pack the study house at night. They transferred from the large study house to the new study house, and now I was no longer alone. Candles no longer burned from the hanging candelabra, but from the brass candlesticks placed along the tables close to the volumes of Talmud we were studying.

We used to study to such heartfelt melodies that even today, on recalling them, a sweetness spreads over my limbs. Throughout that winter all the young fellows and sons-in-law of the town's householders studied with me. For a long time afterward, when talking about it, people would refer to us as "Khatskl's generation."

To tell the truth, there had never been anything like it in Kamenets. Now I was utterly and truly devoted to God. I remember that on Purim I got drunk, as the law commands us,[11] and kept shouting that I had a passport straight to Heaven, because I had finished learning the three tractates: *Bava Kama, Bava Metziah,* and *Bava Batra.*[12] But when sober, I prayed to God to grant me the means that would enable me to sit and learn throughout my life.

CHAPTER 26

THE IMPACT OF
THE BIBLE ON ME

The store • My trip to Kobrin • The home of Yoshe • His sons-
in-law • Leyzer, the maskil, and Zalman-Sender, the prodigy • Two
kinds of households • My closer acquaintance with the Bible • My
impressions from the Bible • The impact of the Bible upon me •
My return home • My noble intentions • The store goes bankrupt
• Haskalah books • Father once again

My family held that, on account of my studies, I would not be able to support my wife and children, and since my wife was such a competent person, it was decided that she become a storekeeper. We'd invest our dowry in a store and I could even help her a little during my free time.

To my misfortune, it happened that someone wanted to sell his haberdashery and notions store. This person wanted to leave Kamenets, and we would have a livelihood. We jumped at this opportunity before anyone else could get the chance, and brought the owner to settle the deal with my father. We were to take over the store during *hol ha-moed* Passover. Father gave him a deposit of fifty rubles and undertook to pay him the full amount the moment the store passed into our hands.

Meanwhile, I was obliged to interrupt my studies and ordered to travel to Kobrin, where my uncle's son-in-law, Yoshe Minkes,[1] lived, in whose keeping the dowry had been entrusted. I was rather unwilling to stop my studies and prayers, but had no other choice.

My wife, despairing of becoming a rabbi's wife, grasped at the chance of turning into a storekeeper. So, I traveled to Kobrin.

Yoshe's house was famous all over the Grodno province as one where learning and grandeur existed side by side.[2] His wife, Esther-Gitl, the daughter of the rabbi of Kamenets, was a clever and competent woman. They owned an inn combined with a tavern, something like the one run by Khaytshe Trinkovski in Kamenets. The only difference was that Kobrin was a large district town whereas Kamenets was only a shtetl. Gentry from all over the district used to put up at her elegantly furnished inn or stop by for drinks at her well-run tavern. The inn's furniture was beautiful, and it also had a ballroom with a piano for the use of the lords. At one time, before the Polish rebellion, the whole concern had been a virtual gold mine.

They were also very charitable, and the poor from all over the district came in droves for the bread, up to ten pud, baked for them especially and handed out to all and sundry. It goes without saying that their hospitality was a household word everywhere. They kept open house all the time, and nobody ever left it empty-handed. Their generosity was unequalled throughout Lithuania.

Esther-Gitl had given birth to no less than twenty-two children, thirteen of whom died in infancy. Among the nine that survived were three sons[3] and six daughters. The daughters were all married off to outstanding scholars.

One of those sons-in-law was Leyzer,[4] a one-time prodigy who gave up learning straight after his marriage. He was "caught"[5] as they used to say. They thought he was a heretic, a maskil. He collected about him many of the young lomdim of Kobrin, and his home became a center of Enlightenment. There they ridiculed all the zaddikim, hasidim, and other religious fanatics, a popular maskilic pastime in those days. Apart from being a great scholar and an enlightened person, this Leyzer also spoke a perfect Russian. His library was full of secular literature in both Hebrew and Russian, and he was a fiery orator to boot. In time he succeeded in gathering an ever-growing number of young adherents around himself.

Yoshe had another son-in-law—a relative of mine—the grandson of Hayyim of Volozhin.[6] Yoshe simply traveled to Volozhin and picked out the best from among the lomdim. Being a great scholar in his own right, Yoshe examined all his prospective sons-in-law in person. However, he gave up testing this youngster right at the beginning, realizing that he was much more knowledgeable than himself. Today, this boy is a substantial Jew—Zalman-Sender, the rabbi of Krinki[7]—and is reputed to be an outstanding personality, considered by many a true miracle worker.[8]

Yoshe wasted no time and took this prodigy home with him. He fitted him out in the most expensive clothes, set aside a dowry of three thousand rubles, and provided him with five years of *kest*. His wedding took place at exactly the same time as mine. This Zalman-Sender carried on a correspondence regarding Torah teachings with the greatest rabbis in Russia.[9] He lived in a home of his own which attracted young scholars.[10] It was in striking contrast to the one headed by his brother-in-law, Leyzer.[11]

And so, in this manner two of Yoshe's children ran two households; however, these two homes were as incompatible as fire and water. The maskilim poked fun at the fanatically pious, while the latter held Leyzer and his freethinkers in utter contempt, in turn. Yet, Leyzer was one of the most popular figures in town and on a familiar footing with the *ispravnik*, the local arbitrator,[12] as well as with all the high-placed government officials there. The landed gentry, too, held him in great esteem.

Yoshe's home and those of his two sons-in-law became the spiritual centers of the town. Each hustled and bustled with activity. In Yoshe's house happiness reigned uninterrupted. His daughters were thought to be great aristocrats, and though Yoshe himself was not so affluent, his daughters, nevertheless, continued making a splash in the expensive clothes they insisted on wearing.

I arrived in Kobrin after Purim, but it turned out that Yoshe, to whom my dowry had been entrusted, was unable to pay me the money just then. Though, since I was a sort of relative of theirs, a good learner and a naive young man, no one mentioned the dowry to be paid out. Instead, they made a show of welcoming me with open arms, wining and dining me generously. In their home life was one big round of merrymaking, and I must admit, in spite of all that, I was rather pleased that they were unable to pay the money I'd come for. "Have a good time here," they said, "It's always fun to stay with us."

And I took their advice. I forgot all about the Gemara and the precepts of *Yesod ve-shoresh ha-avodah*, stopped "gathering the coins" in order to keep building my "palace" in the next world, which Heaven forbid shouldn't be missing a cornice. . . .

Since I was by nature easily carried away and inclined to "keep a finger in every pie," I entered heartily into the hurly-burly of life in those three homes. At Esther-Gitl's I threw myself into the hilarious merrymaking of that family; at Zalman-Sender's, I learned together with all the other young students, who were all mitnaggedim, and also spent some time at the home of the older son-in-law, Leyzer, and his enlightened circle. I enjoyed myself there. They were all warmhearted Jews and, though not observant, they greatly appreciated the Bible, stressed all the humane values of mankind, the relations between man and his fellow man, believed in the brotherhood of men, and in making the best of the world in which we live.

As mentioned before, I personally had never studied the Bible. In those days, Bible learning was considered heresy, especially among the hasidim,[13] and particularly by my father, who was immersed in Hasidism head over heels. Only at Mote the melamed's did I learn Joshua, Judges, and Samuel. That was all. Scared of my father's reaction, I did not dare to look into the Bible at the study house. I had no notion of the significance of the prophets, of the poetry of their language, and only now for the first time did I become aware of its depth and beauty, which left me spellbound.

Isaiah the prophet speaks in the name of God: "Who has asked that of you? Trample my courts no more. . . . Your new moons and your fixed seasons fill Me with loathing. . . . Though you pray at length, I will not listen. Your hands are stained with crime—Wash yourselves clean. . . . Learn to do good, devote yourselves to justice" (Isa. 1:12–17),[14] and so on, and so on.

And more: "Is such the fast I desire . . . ,"—Do you call that a fast? "Is it bowing the head like a bulrush, and lying in sackcloth and ashes? Do you call that a fast, a day when the Lord is favorable?"— To wear a sack and put ashes on your head? Is this the kind of fast God wishes? "No this is the fast I desire: To unlock the fetters of wickedness, and untie the cords of the yoke, to let the oppressed go free, to break off every yoke. It is to share your bread with the hungry, and to take the wretched poor into your home; when you see the naked, to clothe him; and not to ignore your own kin" (Isa. 58:5–7)—No, the Lord says, I choose this fast: to remove the rope from around the necks of the suffering, to set all the oppressed free, to share your bread with the hungry. Let the poor and needy come to your home. If you see a naked person—clothe him. Then your light shall break forth like the dawn and when you call to Me, I shall answer, "Here I am" . . . (paraphrase of Isa. 58:8–9).

That's what Leyzer's maskilim taught the young hasidim who accidentally fell into their nets. I listened to it all and thought to myself: Why do Zalman-Sender's followers poke fun at the maskilim, calling them heretics, may their names be obliterated? Actually, the very opposite is true. They talk wisely and intelligently. And I was completely ignorant of the fact that the prophet could speak in the name of God, that He absolves His Jews from constantly having to pray to Him, from strictly observing the Sabbath, weeping with hands stretched out to heaven, or fasting to atone for imaginary sins.[15] The only thing that God does command the Jews is to help one another, to break the yoke imposed by the rich upon the poor— this truly moved me. The pietism of *Yesod ve-shoresh ha-avodah* seemed to me at that moment so superficial. Flat and hollow. . . .

I started falling under the influence of Leyzer's maskilim, unable to grasp how, throughout all those years, I had been led astray, doing nothing but learning, praying, weeping, fasting, and tormenting myself. I'd been convinced that that was what God demanded of me. Only now did it dawn on me that what God demanded of his creatures was for each to assist his fellow man, to be charitable, and alleviate his suffering. Up until then, I never bothered with, or even took notice of the poverty-stricken class in Kamenets. This poverty did not seem to trouble anyone; each individual worried about his own business and was perfectly willing to swallow up his neighbor. If someone managed to make a good living, he wasn't left alone, but if someone starved to death, no one could care less. In short, I was confused and made up my mind that as soon as I returned home, I would immediately take up the cause of the downtrodden and help the needy. Never mind, I had the will and energy for it and was sure that all the young men around me would follow my example.

They finally returned the money to me, and I left Kobrin a changed man. I had never seen such interesting study circles as I saw there, combining learning and grandeur, true piety and secular knowledge, and to my mind it all fit together. My stay in Kobrin had been an invaluable experience, one worth all the gold in the world.

Upon my return to Kamenets with the dowry in hand, I decided first of all to set aside a tenth of it for charity.[16] Father wanted me to donate half of that amount to the Slonimer rebbe but I wouldn't hear of it. Nevertheless, he managed to squeeze ten rubles out of me for just that purpose. The rest of the money I divided in the following manner: first of all, I found some respectable people who were in financial straits, and I discreetly gave some of the money to them. Only then did I pay the storekeeper, and my worthy wife finally became the owner of a store.

A new epoch began in my life. I went to pray every day, then studied Talmud for one hour, and again for another hour between the afternoon and evening prayers, and the rest of the time I spent sitting alongside my wife in the store. There were hardly any customers except for a peasant or two dropping in now and then. It was immediately after the rebellion and there wasn't a trace of a lord anywhere. If one happened to show up in Kamenets in a battered carriage drawn by a team of drab and dirty-looking horses, he would pass through the town like a shadow. All we had to offer were luxury items, and we might as well have cast the entire lot out into the street.

I stopped "gathering the coins" to build that "palace," and even my intention, on returning from Kobrin, to live according to Isaiah's principles came to naught. I got involved in running a store crammed with old and useless stuff, remnants of cloth for which no one had any need. For all those rags we paid—so inexperienced were we—hundreds of rubles. God only knew when, if ever, we would actually manage to sell something. First off, we had to acquire new and entirely different merchandise, simpler, for a peasant clientele, and my merchandise—send it off to a museum. It was a depressing situation, all the more so since my father and grandfather were themselves rather hard up for money.

My wife started picking on me for being such a *shlimazel* in business affairs, on account of which she had to run a miserable store in Kamenets, not for the well-to-do but for coarse peasant women with whom she had no interest in dealing. One had to act tough with them, and return "tit for tat." It was altogether beneath her dignity.

In short, things could hardly have been worse. I still enjoyed *kest* at my father's, but he, too, found it hard by now to make ends meet. We would gladly have set up house on our own, but could just have about said kaddish[17] on the little money we had invested in the store.

When I saw things going from bad to worse, I abandoned my plans to become a rabbi or to help the needy. I decided to become a *Rabiner.*[18] With that aim in mind, the first thing I did was to make a thorough study of the Bible, but without my father's knowledge. I studied the Bible ten times over and this was my method: I started out by learning chapters one through ten, then I went over them again. I moved on to chapters ten through twenty and again studied from the beginning, and so on until I knew all twenty-four books by heart. Only then did I take up the study of Haskalah literature. My friend Yosl, the son of one of Kamenets's wealthiest families, had a large library of those books, and we began to read in earnest.[19] We began to order maskilic books from the library in Bialystok, for a borrower's fee.

In Bialystok there lived at that time one of the most famous maskilim, by the name of Eliezer Halberstam,[20] the son-in-law of Itsele Zabludovski.[21] He was an enthusiastic supporter of the Haskalah movement, and because of him Bialystok became famous as an Enlightenment center. Fanatically pious young men abandoned their studies and, with Halberstam's encouragement, turned to the study of secular literature instead. This period was also notorious for its numerous divorces. It was the father-in-law who drove his son-in-law out of the house, without taking his daughter's opinion into account. The father informed the daughter that her husband had become a heretic and she must divorce him.[22]

At that time we had all the secular books we wanted sent us by post and paid the required fee for reading them. When we finished, we sent them back and received a new consignment. We received a handwritten list of all the new Haskalah books available. I was most keen on beginning to learn Russian, but there was not a single teacher of the language in Kamenets. Even had there been one, Father would never have permitted me to learn.

I had, however, become proficient by now in writing Hebrew and even acquired a distinctive style of my own. My father did not approve of this new preoccupation of mine, but soon realized that it was a lost cause. He also abandoned all hopes of my wife being able to return me to Hasidism. To make matters worse for him, my wife's own devotion to Hasidism had started to cool. Her chief concern now was to make an independent living, and she was convinced that the lives of the wives of hasidim were utterly miserable. Their husbands spent days and nights on end in the *shtibl*, dancing, singing, eating, and drinking, while their wives and children all but starved to death. She saw my father's fellow hasidim doing the same at our place every Saturday night, leaving their wives and children to fend for themselves, hungry, cold, and alone in their homes. She saw me casting about for a means of making a living to support her and our growing family, knowing full well that, had I remained a hasid, her lot would have been like that of all the other wives. She even blamed my father for placing obstacles in my efforts to find a way to support her.

In those years, the Enlightenment movement gained a great deal of ground among the Jews, and many of them sent their sons to the government-run gymnasia. Consequently, many of their graduates entered the free professions, becoming physicians, lawyers, and engineers. I kept reproaching my father for always preventing me from bettering my lot. I was neither a rabbi nor a doctor. But amidst my own troubles, a new misfortune, an even greater one, befell us, dwarfing all my worries about how to support my family. I am referring to the outbreak of the cholera epidemic in 1866, which claimed three million lives within a matter of several months.[23]

CHAPTER 27

THE CHOLERA EPIDEMIC

The cholera epidemic • Old-time remedies for the prevention of cholera • The death of the rabbi • The rumor of his revival • I look for someone willing to buy the store • Wakhnovitz • My wish to become a *Rabiner* • Slaps in the face

he cholera epidemic arrived in Kamenets from Brisk,[1] as though it were a living creature, and spread with frightening speed. In Brisk two thousand people died between the months of Elul and Kislev,[2] and the situation was not much better in Kamenets. Among its first victims was the rabbi's granddaughter, Simha's daughter, who was quite a young woman. Her death was followed by at least two to three more daily, until, eventually, the number reached as many as eight a day. Every morning when we woke up we heard about several more people who had passed away during the night.

It is, of course, no wonder that so many died during this epidemic. In those days, the need for sanitation and disinfectants was totally unknown. The dead were washed and purified at home, not at the cemetery.[3] For this purpose, a great deal of warm water was required, which was then sloshed out into the street. It's an even greater wonder that everyone didn't die. No matter how you look at it, many died. During that time, my father's fourteen-year-old sister and two-year-old daughter died of cholera.[4]

Due to the cholera epidemic, Jews resorted to all sorts of remedies; in other words: a crippled, mute virgin was married to a blind man.[5] The wedding ceremony was held in the graveyard in the hope that they would produce a generation of righteous offspring.

Another way of remedying this scourge was, I remember, the bearing of Torah scrolls through the town on a Friday, in a kind of procession, amid the chanting of the *Ketoret* prayer.[6] But those remedies did nothing to alleviate the situation.

No one had heard yet of the newer remedies used in Poland just fifteen years ago, during the cholera epidemic in Lublin.[7] Everybody wore *lulav* rings on their fingers;[8] they hitched four young girls to a plowshare and had them plow a plot of land lying in the path of the advancing epidemic.[9] In addition, a Gentile was stationed at the gate to the graveyard for three rubles a day and ordered to call out the moment a corpse was brought for burial, "There's no more room here!"[10] But being a proper yokel, he said exactly the opposite. As soon as a body was brought in for burial, he called out, "There's plenty of room here"—you can bring all the Jews here.[11]

But as mentioned above, no one in Kamenets had as yet heard about plowing one side of the town with four girls hitched to a plowshare, nor of the rings worn in Lublin. Even the *assessor* and the *ispravnik* themselves knew as much about what to do as we know about what's happening on the moon.

However, I can't refrain from relating something verging on a miracle. In Zastavye not a single inhabitant died! It was as if it had been cordoned off to prevent the Angel of Death from entering. It was a curious and incomprehensible phenomenon. On the other side of the same township, in Wysokie, the epidemic was raging as furiously as in Kamenets. And the inhabitants of Zastavye, who spent all day long in Kamenets, returning home only at night, remained entirely healthy. . . .

On the first day of Sukkot, my uncle, the rabbi, died of cholera within an hour.[12] The entire town turned up to lament his death, and rivers of tears flowed from everyone's eyes. His house was full of mourners and I remember that one of his fingers moved suddenly. People began shouting to one another that the zaddik had come alive again. All the windows were open, and the rumor that the zaddik had risen from the dead sprouted wings and made its way throughout the town. But his funeral took place just a few hours later.

When I returned home, Grandmother Beyle-Rashe asked me in her pleasing voice, "Khatskl, you were beside your uncle. Is it true what people relate, that he actually sat up in bed and said, 'Don't cry my children, with me the earth will close'?" I told her what had really happened. But that didn't matter a bit and the townspeople all confirmed the truth of the rumor. But that night the epidemic claimed another fifteen lives. The cholera epidemic kept raging uncontrolled, and because of that the rumor about the rabbi soon died down.

The cholera epidemic lasted perhaps until Hanukkah. Everyone stood on the threshold of death. One moment you were here, the next in the world beyond. During all those months, no one bothered his head about making a living. Those who had the wherewithal contributed more money to charity, and others sold their last shirt for a crust of bread.

The town set aside a chamber where cauldrons of hot water were kept on the boil. There was also a company of "scrubbers"[13] who spent days and nights scrubbing the sick and keeping them warm. But all of the members of that company succumbed to the epidemic to the last man, together with their leader, Yosl, who was a great hero. By the time the epidemic subsided, Kamenets was left almost empty of inhabitants.

Despite all the above-mentioned troubles, one had to make a living somehow. Father was forced to leave his fellow hasidim and his *shtibl* for the estate of Wakhnovitz, one of the estates Grandfather had leased from the Count of Turna,[14] about three miles away from Kamenets.[15]

I remained in Kamenets with our store. But it became obvious to us before long that we could continue to sit like this in the store until all the rest of our money went down the drain. We didn't carry goods suitable for peasants and were unable to drag them into the store by the sleeve as many other storekeepers did. We simply waited for them to come in of their own accord, but it was useless.

Although we weren't great spenders, employed only one maid, and had all our food sent us by my father from the estate, nevertheless, the little money we still had simply ran through our fingers. I personally had no notion how to cut down on expenses. It was a "family defect" and it was clear that, before long, we would scarcely be able to keep the wolf from the door.

God never throws bags full of money from the sky, and bread does not grow on trees. Before the bread reaches your mouth, you have to toil hard for it: fertilize the soil, plow and sow, mow and reap, then dry the wheat, thresh and winnow it, then grind the seeds into flour so it can be kneaded into dough and finally baked into bread.[16] It seems that man must work hard in order to obtain a piece of bread.

So, my wife and I sat in our store, looking at each other. We were not interested in pulling the peasants and their wives in by their sleeves—we obviously were not going to earn a thing this way, and we were still going to have to pay the rent on the store and on the house. Still, we were reluctant to give it up. The only "reform" we introduced was employing a young girl to drag the peasant women into the store. But even that did not improve matters.

At that time, my wife gave birth to our first child,[17] and the circumcision ceremony was held in great style, with plenty of food, drinks, and alms for the poor, which brought us to the brink of bankruptcy. The store was entirely neglected. We relied on that young girl, who had, it seemed, if the reader will excuse me, "long fingers," and that was the last straw for me. My wife had an infant to care for and could no longer work in the store, and I, too, decided that I was not cut out for this kind of business. I could not get accustomed to dealing with the peasant folk and was repulsed by having to bargain with them over the smallest item. I had made a decision to sell the store and join Father on the estate. My intention was to prepare myself to become a "crown rabbi,"[18] but I kept it a secret from both my father and my wife for the time being.

I was on the lookout for a potential buyer but was unable to find one. After much agonizing, I sold all the stock to a relative of mine for a third of its value, which she was supposed to pay off in installments. Only then did I move to my father's house in Wakhnovitz.

My father, the fervent hasid, was extremely unhappy living on the estate. He tried to strike up a merry atmosphere on Friday nights and throughout the Sabbath day. He sang and the children danced. But it was a sad merrymaking indeed, uninspired and artificial, and the habitual smile on his lips had disappeared altogether. It was obvious that he was flickering and going out like a candle in this dull village life, deprived of his fellow hasidim.

I had made up my mind to prepare myself for the examinations toward my appointment as a "crown rabbi." I traveled to Brisk and made the acquaintance of a writer, a known maskil, who supported all young men drawn to the Enlightenment.[19] He took a liking to me at once, but insisted that I learn Russian.[20] He told me what books I needed and even presented me with several of them.[21] I bought a Russian dictionary and returned home with the intention of preparing myself for the examination. I was well aware of my father's violent objection to my learning Russian, not to mention my wish to become a *Rabiner*. But I never imagined that his opposition would be as fierce as all that. When he caught me studying Russian, he landed me two ringing slaps across the face, shouting, "We have gotten along, thank God, all this time without knowing Russian! And now you want to learn the language! Under no circumstances will I allow you to do that!"

CHAPTER 28

GRANDMOTHER'S DEATH

Grandmother's sudden death • Its impact on the family and the township • Her funeral • Grandfather's lamentations • Sitting shivah • Grandmother's enormous reputation • Her charitable deeds • Our family falls apart after her death

Even before settling in Wakhnovitz, we suffered a great catastrophe. Late one night, someone pounded on the shutters of our house. "Moshe! Moshe! Get up! Mother is dying!"

We immediately broke into a loud lament and, greatly alarmed, hastily pulled on our clothes, our hands trembling uncontrollably as if we were paralyzed. Father, Mother, I, my wife, and all my brothers and sisters pulled on whatever came to hand, weeping all the while. Only Father did not weep, he was pale and his eyes glistened with moisture. We all rushed to our beloved Grandmother. Huffing and puffing from running, stumbling constantly on the steps of the porch, we picked ourselves up again and ran straight into her house. But by the time we entered, Grandmother was gone. She had suffered an internal hemorrhage. All her lifeblood had spurted from her throat, causing her death within fifteen minutes. The house was crowded with all her children, her older and younger grandchildren, Grandfather's brothers and sisters and their entire families. Everyone was there. The wailing and weeping had the whole town on its feet. Women we did not recognize came rushing to the house and joined in the general lamenting, as if all the town's inhabitants had been massacred by an enemy.

Grandfather's frequent fainting fits, causing an even greater turmoil, had everybody rushing to his side in order to revive him.

Yoshke the doctor and his two assistants[1] were prevented from leaving the house but had to keep a watchful eye on Grandfather lest he faint away again.

Grandmother was laid out on the floor of the room, and Grandfather threw himself beside her. He lay lengthwise, next to Grandmother, resting his head on hers, soaking her with an ocean of his tears. Grandfather had always been a great weeper,[2] but now a large wellspring seemed to have burst open, with his tears gushing forth in an unending stream. His moans broke everyone's heart. His weeping and wailing grew louder and louder, until finally the whole town was awake, keening over the death of this wise and charitable woman who had not made a single enemy during her lifetime.

Early the next morning people started crowding into the house, onto the porch, and around all the windows outside. Their laments virtually rent the heavens. Father immediately sent a messenger on horseback to Czechczowa to inform his sister Dvorah and her husband Berl-Bendet of Grandmother's death. They arrived within less than three hours with all their children and grandchildren, and their weeping added a heightened pitch to the general wailing.

There was indeed a reason for those expressions of grief, since it was this tiny, skinny woman who had kept the entire family intact like a single body. She had been the life and soul of the family, instilling in all of us a sense of togetherness and love for one another, and had seen to it that our large family remained modest and charitable at heart. She had taught us to control our tempers, to accept everything with love, and never to succumb to despair. And now my dearly beloved grandmother lay lifeless on the floor, covered with a black cloth, never to rise again.

The first light of dawn broke through the sky, but for us it was dark as night. It is humanly impossible to convey the painful spectacle of Grandmother lying on the ground with Grandfather's head resting on hers, washing it with his tears, all the while sobbing and whimpering like a child and everybody weeping together with him.

Every now and then he suddenly stopped weeping and became very quiet. Everyone rushed up to see what had happened. He had swooned again, and amid the huge outcry, the healers rushed over with bottles of cold water. He came to, sank to the floor, his head on hers, and again the weeping renewed like an overflowing spring, then the moaning, until he again fell silent.

Afterward the women from the burial society arrived to perform the purification of the body. Everyone was asked to leave the room,[3] but Grandfather refused to be separated from Grandmother. His head seemed to be glued to hers, and he violently resisted all attempts to remove him. He lay there for a long time, his face deathly pale, and it seemed as if he were about to pass away alongside her. But, finally, Arye-Leyb, "the only child," and Berl-Bendet, two sturdy men, came up and dragged him away from the dead body. He fell into a swoon once again, and the shrieks that followed sounded like the cries of people trapped in a burning house. This shrill outcry brought the people outside rushing into the house. Grandfather was carried out in spite of his violent resistance and put to bed in another room. But even there, he threw himself on the floor—he wanted only to lie there. He screamed: "I want to be buried together with my Beyle-Rashe."

After the corpse had been duly purified, another, shocking spectacle of leave-taking took place. Everybody fell to his knees beside the deceased asking, as was customary, forgiveness for any wrong done her and begging her to be his or her mediator in the next world as she had been in this world.[4] Grandfather lay down once more beside her on the floor, soaked through with the cleansing water, resting his head on hers as before. It was an awesome experience for all of us.

The entire town turned out for Grandmother's funeral. All the stores and taverns were closed[5] and not a single woman remained indoors, not even those living in Zastavye. Grandmother's body was borne at the head of the procession, and immediately behind it, in a semiswoon, Grandfather was led along, supported in turn by his sons, brothers, and sons-in-law, with the healers, bottles in hand, right behind them.

I witnessed only two large funerals in Kamenets in my life. The first was that of my uncle, the rabbi of Kamenets, which took place during Sukkot, and was, of course, attended by the entire township.[6] The second was that of my grandmother, which was incomparably larger. For, unlike the rabbi's funeral, all the women in and around the township had come to attend it, for the prevailing custom at the time was that women who were not among the mourners did not attend the funerals of deceased males.[7]

As the body was about to be laid to rest, a shocking scene took place. Grandfather seemed to have taken leave of his senses. He lunged forward and would not let them lower his Beyle-Rashe into the ground. Only with great difficulty was he dragged away, and when she already lay in the open grave, he lunged forward once again, screaming at the top of his voice: "Let me be buried together with my Beyle-Rashe!" He fell into a faint, which finally enabled him to be removed from the graveside.

After the funeral, Grandfather had to be carried home the entire way and was put to bed. But as before, he threw himself on the floor and would not allow himself to be put back in bed. He lay there in a state of semiconsciousness until he fell asleep. The healers thought it best to let him sleep it off. All nonfamily members had left, and his sons and daughters, their husbands and wives remained beside him. Now the weeping became softer until there was total silence. Everyone lay on the floor,[8] and the tears kept flowing. Grandfather awakened now and again from his fitful sleep, shouting that he wanted to be buried together with his Beyle-Rashe. He became feverish and started to hallucinate, screaming, "You scoundrels! Why did you bury Beyle-Rashe without me!"

Throughout this dark day, no family member dared taste any food, not even so much as a cup of tea, not even the six-year-old children. The second night was no easier. More than seventy members of the family lay on the floor, keening without a break, soaking the wooden floor beneath them with their tears. Grandfather slept through most of this night, and when he woke up early in the morning, he looked somewhat more relaxed.

"But Beyle-Rashe," he whimpered, "take me along with you. You were such a loyal wife, devoted to me with all your heart and soul. Give me proof of your loyalty one last time and beg the Lord to take me to where you are now!" And, once again, he fell to sobbing and whimpering and trembling all over, so that all those present, the young and the old, were themselves affected by it, and their cries merged into a single wail like that heard during the blessing ceremony on Yom Kippur Eve.[9]

Grandfather had not prayed during those two days. His sons, comprising more than a minyan on their own, held prayers in the morning, in the afternoon, and in the evening. Everyone cried during the services also. Father led the prayers from the reader's desk. He, who was so strong and did not cry openly, chanted the prayers in a quiet and touching tone more powerful than tears. At first the prayers were held upstairs in Grandmother's bedroom, but on the third day, the services were transferred to the large hall below because Grandfather could not bear to have us pray in their bedroom. He now led the prayers from the reader's lectern himself, but tears kept choking his words like a small child, and he kept fainting and had to be led away.

Members of the family began casting about for a medicine that would curb his constant weeping. It was enough to drive one crazy. Town householders started dropping in to pay condolence visits. The large samovar was kept constantly on the boil, and the maids offered hot tea and rolls. But few took advantage of it, and Grandfather wouldn't accept even so much as a cup of tea. "I want to die," he insisted time and again. "I want to lie in the ground beside my Beyle-Rashe."

On the third night, Grandfather actually fell asleep, but it was fitful, like that of an ailing man, and Yoshke the doctor was constantly at his side. Those of the family unable to fall asleep sat down in a circle on the floor, and everyone started telling in turn what he recalled about Beyle-Rashe, her charitable deeds, her irreproachable virtues, her generosity, her unshakable devotion to both next-of-kin and strangers, and above all, her miraculous ability to restore the peace among all those turning to her for help.

When she married off a daughter, a son, or a grandchild, she always invited the young couple, each one separately, for an intimate chat after the seven days of feasting. The session with the young wife took especially long, during which she explained to her why she must always consider her husband as the head of the family. For it was he who had to provide a living for them and look to the education of their sons, and that a wife's honor lay solely in the respect she held for her husband. "Apart from the fact that you love your husband," she went on, "you have to show him this love unreservedly. It is natural to want to cause pleasure to the one you love, but he has to see and feel how dearly you love him as if he were the apple of your eye. But even if, God forbid, he does not treat you well, or even betrays your trust in him, simply ignore it and don't bear him a grudge. For, sooner or later, even the worst of husbands will make it up again with you. You must set aside your views in favor of your husband's, as it is written in *Pirkei avot,* that you should set aside your will in the face of your friend's in order that he may set aside his will for yours—and especially the husband! [10] In order to ensure his devotion to you, you have to be the first to show your own devotion to him, by accepting his word as though it were the Lord's very own. . . . If he claims that it is now dark as night although it is broad daylight, agree with him. . . . Sooner or later, he will admit his mistake and will love you all the more for not having put him in the wrong. Always talk to him gently and never show off your own wisdom. If you act in this manner he will always say you are wise—and indeed you are. And if he does exactly the opposite of what you advised him, with undesirable results, don't rub it in, for that's likely to make him angry. But on the contrary, console and encourage him so that, eventually, he'll regret not having listened to you. Your duty is to glorify your husband, to crown him king, support and stand by him. That will give him the incentive to carry on his affairs. But if, God forbid, he fails to provide you with a decent livelihood, don't ever hold it against him, but keep your worries to yourself. Encourage and support him so that he won't lose his self-confidence. If you utter, God forbid, even the slightest criticism, he may lose his spirit and your life together will be difficult and hard."

That's how she lectured every young woman—a daughter, daughter-in-law, or a granddaughter. She also asked them to confide in her concerning the conduct of their husbands toward them, and wherever needed, she would spare no effort to soothe tempers and smooth out disagreements between the couples.

With the young husband she adopted an altogether different tone, urging him to hold his wife as dear as the apple of his eye. He ought to keep in mind his wife's suffering during her pregnancies and the pangs of childbirth, which are beyond a man's ability to imagine. "The child is circumcised," she said, "and you become a father without agony or pain. But how much does your wife pay for this? And later, when she is suckling the infant and spending many sleepless nights beside it? Only she is burdened with discomforts while you can walk about free of worries, look to your affairs, chat with people, spend time praying and learning in the study house. Your wife, on the other hand, is constantly bound to the house beside the newborn infant, who sucks the lifeblood out of her, the marrow from her bones, and if, God forbid, the child is ill, how much health does this cost her? She can neither eat, nor drink, nor sleep. Even though you share some of that burden with her, this does not compare with what she goes through. You can always escape into your own affairs. And if, God willing, your wife gives birth to many more children, just think of how it wears her down. Although you are very much in love with each other now, that love is an essential factor whereby you can help to make her lot easier, and a man who is loyal to his wife and cherishes her, goes a long way at preserving a loving relationship throughout their married life."

In her chats with the young couple she told them how important it was always to talk quietly in front of their children and never to let on that they might be at odds with each other. That was likely, God forbid, to have a bad influence on them and give rise to rebelliousness and disrespect.

It goes without saying that I myself was given the same talking-to. But ambitious to show off how much I already knew about marital relationships, I told her of a book I'd read about it called *Kiryat sefer* by one Mordechai-Aharon Günzburg.[11] It contained letters written to a recently married friend advising him how to relate to his wife.[12] I read those letters to Grandmother, who was deeply impressed and advised me also to read them to my young wife, which I did.

Each of us had some story to tell the others of how Grandmother had planted the seeds of domestic peace between husbands and wives. And those efforts proved fruitful in the long run. In our family, for instance, husbands and wives lived in perfect accord with one another, and no one ever spoke derisively about one or another member of our family.

Grandfather gradually calmed down and became his old self once more. He began drinking tea, but with every sip he lamented in a weepy voice, "Beyle-Rashe is in her grave and I'm having my cup of tea as usual."

None of those paying condolence visits earlier had dared to approach Grandfather. But now, seeing that he was more composed, they talked to him, trying to impress upon him how greatly he was sinning against God in his wrath. A man must never take his own life. "The Lord has given, and the Lord has taken away," they said. King David, they reminded Grandfather, wept when a child of his had taken ill, but when the child died, he washed himself and ordered his musicians to strike up a tune.[13] Those words had a calming effect on Grandfather and, instead of weeping, he began telling stories in praise of Grandmother, of how she had always related to him, what a heart of gold she had had, and what a loving wife she had been.

On the sixth day, feeling more relaxed after a good night's sleep, Grandfather poured himself a cup of tea and helped himself to some of the refreshments like all of us. News of Grandfather's recovery and self-control traveled fast and people now felt less restrained during their visits of condolence, were able to chat with him, and tell him things about Beyle-Rashe of which he had been altogether ignorant. People started coming to the house from eleven o'clock in the morning, and throughout the day hundreds of men and women came and went to express their sorrow and console Grandfather.

One of them told him of the long-standing row he'd been having with his wife and that they had even come to blows. He had come to Beyle-Rashe to pour out his heart to her. "With her wisdom," he related, "she succeeded in softening my heart and made me see my wife's conduct in a new and more conciliatory light. She described to me how sweet and pleasurable a peaceful marital relationship could be in contrast to the heartache and torment involved when a marriage is bad. Her words had such a calming effect on me that I felt like rushing home that very minute to patch up the quarrel with my wife, though barely a minute earlier I'd been determined to divorce her. Some time after I left and when Aharon-Leyzer was away from home, she asked my wife to come see her. She talked to her in the same wise and persuasive manner and advised her how to relate to me from then on. As a result, our married life took a decisive turn for the better and we realized that we had been at cross-purposes with each other over the most trivial things, that sometimes she was right and sometimes I was right. Nine years have passed since then and we have not had a serious squabble since. We came to thank her. May God grant her a peaceful life in the world to come. For with her wisdom and kindness she saved our marriage from breaking up."

Many more stories like the above were told during those visits. People also said that as a result of her constant mediation, no divorces took place in Kamenets during her lifetime.[14] She kept a watchful eye wherever she could, doing everything within her power to preserve the peace between fighting couples. Nowadays, when divorces keep cropping up like mushrooms after a rain,[15] when relationships are deteriorating, with each side tugging and tearing at the damaged fabric until it falls apart altogether, I must admit that Grandmother's endeavors seem rather naive. Nevertheless, she had a great talent and capacity to smooth out, to mend and restore broken relationships. Another example of this kind was when older children came to her to complain about their stepmother's treatment of them. She promptly asked the stepmother to come to her for a chat, and with wise and touching words succeeded in changing the stepmother's conduct toward those orphans. Soon afterward, the children themselves came to thank Grandmother for her kindly intervention.

Grandmother's house had been a hive of activities of that kind. Every hour of the day one came and another left, but only when Aharon-Leyzer was away on his round of the landowners' estates. When Grandfather was at home, she asked people not to call, for she didn't want to disturb him while he was resting from his business affairs.

Now people started talking about Grandmother's secret acts of charity, which she performed without her husband's knowledge. She didn't want it to be known that she came to the aid of formerly prosperous families that had become so impoverished that they even lacked money to buy the daily bread for their children. She sent them wagonloads of vegetables from the supplies the landowners sent her for her own household, such as potatoes, cabbages, beets, carrots, onions, fruit, and so on. When she told Grandfather that she had run out of all those provisions, he immediately had a new consignment delivered from the estate. No sooner did it arrive than she once again distributed it among the needy. She also sent whatever she had in her pantry to the poorhouse, even meat. During the winter, Grandfather used to slaughter a huge ox, many sheep, and calves. Meat cost him hardly anything and Grandmother immediately made the calculations: so much for the family, this much for the impoverished householders, this much for the poorhouse, and so on. Grandfather, who was absorbed in his own affairs, never took the trouble to find out why his family's food consumption was so great. Grandmother also used to fatten many geese and later rendered the fat, which she then distributed among her own family as well as among the poor.

During the summer, she prepared quantities of preserves, jams, and juices from various kinds of fruit, using up at least sixty *funt* of sugar for them! If someone in the township fell ill, they came to her for those health-giving mixtures. Some needed it against constipation, others, to strengthen the heart. Those were Grandmother's preoccupations, and her chief concern was the welfare of the township's poor and the needy. She had little money to spare, however, for charitable causes, because she needed most of it to meet the expenses of her large household. Her husband was not too generous with it and kept her rather short of ready cash.

If she asked him occasionally for twenty-five rubles and he said, "I haven't got it," although he could have given it to her, she never said another word, showed no resentment, but put up a smiling front. That's why she was always short of money. So she went and borrowed some from her brother-in-law Mordechai-Leyb. However, instead of cash, her husband would send her a barrel of vodka worth one hundred rubles.[16] When, a couple of days later, she told him that she'd sold all the vodka, he would order more barrels to be sent to their tavern straight from the distillery on one of the estates. From the sale of the vodka she managed to pay back the loan she'd taken from her brother-in-law.

She never contradicted her husband either in word or in deed. If he said "yes" it was "yes," and if he said "no" it was "no." That was why he always listened to what she had to say. And if, occasionally, he fell out with her, he would appease her by saying: "To tell you the truth, my darling wife, when I don't follow your advice, I make a real mess of things."

She would then play down his admission with a good-humored smile, saying, "Never mind, you've got plenty of good sense yourself and certainly don't need a simple woman like me to teach you what to do. But one is no more than human, and everyone is likely to make mistakes now and again. No one is an angel, so forget it. . . ."

That's what Grandmother was like, and no wonder Grandfather almost lost his reason at her death.[17]

At the end of the shivah our eyes were swollen from weeping and our cheeks hollow from lack of food.

This is how a Jewish woman lived and behaved in those days, her lofty virtues barely noticeable in a woman of today. Women of such virtuous conduct used to be rare even in those days. Today there isn't even one.

I have mentioned on another occasion what a significant role my beloved grandmother had played within our family. The reader will understand it better if I add that after her death our large family fell apart. The bonds of unity weakened, relationships cooled off, and nothing remained of the once famous "Tsar's Regiment." If this "Regiment" had a commander—a quiet and invisible one without whom it could not function—it was Grandmother, who safeguarded her soldiers with her life. Grandfather was merely the brave and blustering captain.

CHAPTER 29

HASIDISM AND
MITNAGGEDISM

Hasidism and Mitnaggedism—What was the secret of Hasidism that cast such a spell over the entire Jewish world?—Mitnaggedism as a method—*Shulhan arukh*—The disadvantages of being a mitnagged—Hasidism—The Ba'al Shem Tov—The accessibility of Hasidism to all social classes—Moshe-Hayyim Luzzatto's *Mesillat yesharim*—The democratic conduct of the hasidim—The rebbe and hasidic rejoicing—The disadvantages of being a hasid—Conclusion

I ought to have concluded the first part of my memoirs with Grandmother's death. However, I feel obliged to explain the roles played by Hasidism and Mitnaggedism. The reader may have noticed how often I kept referring to the struggle between hasidim and mitnaggedim. Since I was personally involved in this conflict, which caused me a great deal of suffering, I cannot but pose the question: What was the charm exercised by Hasidism, which caused such an upheaval within the Jewish world, attracting to its ranks so many Jews in the larger and smaller towns? How was Hasidism capable of alienating the sons of sworn mitnaggedic rabbis and thus bringing about the ruin of their families? I shall try to clarify these questions to the best of my ability. Since not everyone is familiar with the essence of Hasidism, or even of Mitnaggedism, I will try to expand on and elucidate this subject.

The mitnaggedim observe to the letter the written and oral laws of the Torah as codified in the *Shulhan arukh*. These are practical commandments—what a person is prohibited or permitted to do.

But the *Shulhan arukh* does not say what a person should think, or even ask himself, as the Talmud states: *Rahamana liba ba'ei*,[1] meaning that God looks on the heart. But of that there is no mention whatsoever in the *Shulhan arukh*. That is why all the rabbis and the most outstanding among them, who lived after the *Shulhan arukh*, referred in their writings only to what a Jew must do and how he is to behave, making the already difficult laws more so, turning their observance into an insufferable hardship. Although the famous *Hovot ha-levavot*, written by Rabbi Bahya the Elder eight centuries ago,[2] which deals clearly and explicitly with how a person ought to purify his heart by means of virtuous conduct, is still popular today, the *Shulhan arukh*, written much later, has become the central code of behavior among the Jews. It has become the very life and soul of Jewishness, demanding the exercise of practical commandments; in other words, prescribing how religious obligations are actually to be performed and fulfilled. All precepts relating to the soul and the spirit of man such as pride, humility, love, hatred, envy, wrath, flattery, peace, or personal enmity—as understood in the Torah and the Prophets—were turned into mere trivialities and matters of secondary importance. Their value was recognized, but still they were passed over and easily ignored.

According to the *Shulhan arukh* and other rabbinic literature, a Jew must spend his life praying, learning, fasting, and tormenting himself, strictly avoiding all the pleasures of this world. He must behave like the Gaon of Vilna, the leader of the struggle against the hasidim,[3] who, when imposing upon himself a period of wandering,[4] did not chew his bread, but swallowed it whole so that he would not experience the taste of food.[5]

The devout mitnagged, therefore, kept praying and learning, fulfilling many precepts, tormenting himself, and weeping endlessly. In spite of all that, he lived in constant terror of the Angels of Destruction, who subject the dead to indescribable tortures in hell.

The pious mitnagged was always melancholy, dejected, and of solemn countenance. He was barred from enjoying this world, and terrified of the next. He never seemed to be able to do justice to all the precepts laid down in the *Shulhan arukh* and other rabbinical books. He always felt that he fell short in matters of faith, and was in constant fear of never being able to meet its requirements.

And what about those mitnaggedim who lacked the required piety by nature? They were certainly dejected on account of their weakness and lived in constant fear of the Day of Judgment, when they would be called to account and condemned to hell over the least infringement of the law committed on earth.

That is how every mitnagged carried within himself the sadness of his faith, and not a bit of joy was visible on his face. This was a sad people, suffering from exile and troubles, and for whom still more torments were waiting—after death—in a world to come full of tremendous hardship, compared to which the trials of this world were just a drop in the ocean.

According to the mitnaggedic faith, an *am ha-aretz,* meaning an ignorant person, unable to learn, was not considered a proper Jew. A Jew must learn and know all the laws, and in general he must learn, and learn, and learn. It goes without saying that an *am ha-aretz* had no standing whatsoever in anyone's eyes. He was looked down upon by all and, if he was poor as well (which should have been understood as the reason for his illiteracy), he was invariably thought of as someone of an even lower order. Such a Jew felt humiliated, seeing himself as nothing but a base-born creature, whereas everyone else was God's very own child.

It was always the craftsmen and the workers who occupied this low status. They came from poverty-stricken homes and were apprenticed to learn a trade from early boyhood. It was no wonder that they didn't learn, remained illiterate as well as poor![6] A mitnagged, therefore, regarded craftsmen and laborers with contempt and always related to them with overbearing arrogance.

This arrogance was the hallmark of a mitnagged. Prestige was nothing to be trifled with! So it was prestige they were after, and they pursued it in every possible way. Every mitnagged gauged his own lineage against that of a fellow-mitnagged according to two criteria: lineage of wealth and lineage of learning. Here is how it works: he who learns better, or he who has a thousand rubles, thinks himself more respectable than someone who has only one hundred rubles, and he who has ten thousand rubles sees himself as far superior to someone who has only a thousand rubles, and so on.

It is therefore easy to understand that the penniless and the illiterate felt degraded and humiliated by their treatment in the synagogues and study houses (in the end, the shame of ignorance was only the lot of the poor, for the wealthy boors were forgiven this fault by virtue of their money). Because everyone was embarrassed even to be seen talking to them, the poor and ignorant were always relegated to places near the door, and nobody took the least notice of them.

In addition, the mitnaggedim lacked the quality of unity and concord. Each was out for himself, not caring about the lot of his fellow man. Such a sense of exaggerated pride often gave rise to envy of another man's wealth, prestige, or lineage. They were always involved in some kind of quarrel or dispute about communal issues or personal matters, and that went for the study houses as well.

The study houses were the only places where Jews gathered. At one time they spent most of their waking hours there. Three times a day they would gather to pray and to learn, and also just to chat. The study house is really the only "club" the Jews have.[7] But the mitnaggedim decided that everyone must have his own permanent seat, which he must purchase with his own money, and when he comes to pray he must take this seat only, which is called a *shtot*.[8] Everyone in the study house has his own *shtot*, which is passed down from father to son. These seating arrangements played an important part in matters of prestige and lineage. A mitnagged will do everything in his power to make certain that his seat is in a more prestigious location than that of his neighbor, or, at any rate, no less than his.

I recall that in the towns during my childhood the price paid for a seat along the *mizrah* often equaled that of a house. The acquisition of such a seat caused a great deal of bad blood among the mitnaggedim, and whoever writes the history of those people one day will have enough material to describe an ugly and piddling war rather than events relating to faith and synagogues.

The poor people, as mentioned above, had to stand near the door and had nothing to sit on as though they were mere stones, not human beings. And it never occurred to a single mitnagged to ask himself, if only fleetingly, if it was right to divide people in the House of God into "beautiful" and "repulsive," richer and poorer classes.

Even the calling up of a person to recite the blessings for the Torah reading was a matter of prestige. These blessings were distributed to the householders, and here, too, there were ranks. Thus, for example, to be the "third" or the "sixth" called up to the Torah was considered more prestigious than the "seventh," the "last," or the *maftir*, whereas the "fourth" or "fifth" were deemed of lesser rank.[9] The *gabbai* who stands alongside the Torah scroll and gives out the honors has to evaluate the importance of this or that house-holder and creases his brow accordingly: is this portion in our sacred Torah, of which each and every word is a treasure, befitting to this householder? How strange! And for the most part, unsuitable . . . and there would be arguments, even blows, and the synagogue of the mitnaggedim becomes filled with envy and hatred.

Altogether, only eight men are called up to the Torah. But in every synagogue, among the hundreds of congregants, were tens of wealthy, honorable, important householders or so-called "nice" Jews who stood uncompromisingly upon their right to be called up. Therefore, among the mitnaggedim, the readings after the first six were not divided into portions but into verses.[10]

The poor members of the congregation were rarely called up to the Torah. That, naturally, caused a great deal of discontent and resentment among them and probably accounted for the fact that most of the poor and the artisans set up their own minyans, where they could enjoy being called up to the Torah and breathe a sigh of relief, now that they had freed themselves from the insults they formerly had to endure in the synagogues and study houses.[11]

Harmony, peace, and cheerfulness were not to be found in the study houses of the mitnaggedim, neither on weekdays nor on the Sabbath or holidays. After the service, every mitnagged went to his own home, had his meal with his family, and lay down for a midday nap. There was no mirth, no singing, no dancing; one either prayed or learned, or did something else: ate or slept. Anything other than praying, learning, eating, or sleeping was forbidden. That was at the root of a mitnagged's lack of humor and gloomy countenance. He lived in a kind of wasteland where delight and exultation and true enjoyment of life could not possibly exist.

These, in short, are the drawbacks of being a mitnagged: isolation, alienation, constant terror of the next world and avoidance of any pleasure in this world, hatred and contempt for the innocent ignorant, directed only at the poor—though someone's boorishness was easily overlooked if his pockets were well-lined—contempt and hatred for the poor in general, pride, envy, hatred, discord, and lineage; and, above all, lack of any vitality, of joy, gladness, and ecstasy—which were so dear to the hearts of the democratically inclined of our people.[12] It is obvious, therefore, that under such circumstances a different system, a revolutionary one, was bound to spring up. And that did not take long.

It began 170 years ago with the Ba'al Shem Tov,[13] the founder of this revolution. The Ba'al Shem Tov introduced two fundamental changes: On the one hand, he eased the burden of faith, which had become unbearable and which, even if one succeeded in suffering it, left one in a state of uncertainty regarding one's place in the world to come.[14] On the other hand, he strengthened Judaism in a way that prevented the influence of the Enlightenment (which had begun to invade all European countries) from destroying the Jews as a people. Already, then, the ingenious Ba'al Shem Tov comprehended the significance of the talmudic phrase which he revitalized and spread among his followers: "Three things have redeemed Jews as a people—not altering their attire, their language, or their names."[15]

The Ba'al Shem Tov also related similarly to the Bible and the Talmud. First of all, he broke down the black wall erected by the mitnaggedim between Judaism and joyfulness, between faith and life. He told his followers that God delights in His creatures' joy of life; that the enjoyment of food and drink was part of one's faith in God;[16] thus, for example, the priests in the Temple were commanded to eat the sacrificial offerings in a holy place—the Tent of Meeting.[17] A Jew ought to serve his God with joy in his heart, as it is written in the book of Deuteronomy, in the chapter of the *Tokheha,*[18] verse 47:[19] "Because you would not serve the Lord your God in joy and gladness"—because of this you will be cursed. We find in the book of Samuel, that Samuel says to Saul: "you will encounter a band of prophets coming down from the shrine preceded by lyres, timbrels, flutes and harps, and they will be speaking in ecstasy [prophesying]" [1 Sam. 10:5]. That, too, is clear proof that the prophets could not prophesy without musical accompaniment, and in Chronicles it is written that David, after having presented much gold and silver to the Temple, said in his prayers: "and now Your people, who are present here—I saw them joyously making freewill offerings" [1 Chron. 29:17]. In Psalms 43 it is said, "That I may come to the altar of God, God, my delight, my joy; that I may praise You with the lyre, O God, my God" [v. 4], "My lips shall be jubilant, as I sing a hymn to You, my whole being, which You have redeemed" [Ps. 71:23].[20] And in Psalms 68 it is written, "But the righteous shall rejoice; they shall exult in the presence of God; they shall be exceedingly joyful" [v. 4]. With reference to that it says in the Midrash: "Whenever thou art about to pray, let thy heart rejoice that thou art about to pray to a God who is without a peer. Here, indeed, is cause for true rejoicing, that we are privileged to serve the Lord, blessed be He, who is incomparable."[21] In Psalms 100 it says: "Worship the Lord in gladness; come into His presence with shouts of joy" [v. 2]. And on this, in tractate *Shabbat* [30b] the Talmud states: "The Divine Presence rests only upon one who finds joy in the performance of a precept."[22] In Psalms 104 it is said: "May my prayer be pleasing to Him; I will rejoice in the Lord" [v. 34]. In Psalms 149 it is said: "Let Israel rejoice in its maker, let the children of Zion exult in their king" [v. 2]. In the Song of Songs, it is said: "Draw me after you, let us run! The king has brought me into his chambers, let us delight and rejoice in your love" [1:4].

The famous rabbi Moshe-Hayyim Luzzatto,[23] who lived before the Ba'al Shem Tov,[24] wrote in his book *Mesillat yesharim,*[25] that a Jew ought to purify his heart in the presence of the Lord. Already in the introduction to the book he says "that the majority of men will conceive saintliness to consist in reciting numerous Psalms and long confessionals, in fasting and ablutions in ice and snow. Such practices fail to satisfy the intellect, and offer nothing to the understanding. We find it difficult properly to conceive true saintliness, since we cannot grasp that to which we give no thought" [pp. 6–7]. In chapter 18 of his book, in which he elucidates the virtues of saintliness, he maintains that "such people render the very savor of saintliness repellent to the average person, as well as to the more intelligent. They give the impression that saintliness depends upon foolish practices that are contrary to reason and common sense, like reciting numerous supplicatory prayers and long confessionals, or weeping and genuflecting, or afflicting oneself with strange torments that are liable to bring one to death's door" [pp. 288–89]. No! That is not Hasidism! Luzzatto then enumerates the virtues to which man must aspire, of which the "hasid" is the highest degree, even more valuable than the "zaddik."[26] Hasidism comes from the joy of the heart and is practiced with a joyful spirit, as the Sages have already said: "The Divine Presence rests [upon man] neither through gloom, [nor through sloth . . .]" [*Shabbat* 30b].[27]

The Ba'al Shem Tov broadened and deepened the concept of serving God with joy in one's heart, not allowing dejection and melancholy to get the upper hand. A hasid should constantly be in a cheerful frame of mind; only then will he serve God genuinely. In addition, a Jew ought to keep clear of all vices, especially pride, which is the mother of all vice. Jews should live in unity and peace and not consider themselves superior to others—only then will redemption come.[28]

However, since Jews still do not live in their own land, but are dispersed over many countries and towns, each community should choose a rebbe, who will wield absolute authority within his particular realm, and whose word must be considered holy and obeyed unconditionally. He must never be contradicted even to the smallest degree. As it is written in the Talmud, tractate *Rosh Hashanah* 25b: "Jerubaal in his generation is like Moses in his generation, Bedan in his generation is like Aaron in his generation; Jepthah in his generation is like Samuel in his generation, and to teach you that the most worthless, once he has been appointed a leader of the community is to be accounted like the mightiest of the mighty."[29] The mind of every Jew who finds himself in such a community must be subordinated to that of his leader, all his secrets revealed to him, all his suffering and troubles confessed to him, and his heart and soul opened up to him. That is the only way to maintain unity and peace among the Jews. For peace is the essence, the very basis upon which the world stands.[30]

It is easy to understand that such words were specifically aimed at the somber and rancorous atmosphere surrounding the mitnaggedim in those days. They fell like refreshing rain upon parched soil, and Jews began to flock to the ranks of the hasidic movement in an unending stream. It was the same faith, the same religion, the same *Shulhan arukh,* and yet—easier, an easier way of life, a lighter burden of faith, mingled with joy, rapture, and ecstasy. And, above all, there was complete equality, without reference to one's origins or lineage.

Now there was no need to torment oneself to death and still feel inadequate in the performance of one's duties. On the contrary, one might now enjoy the best of food, drink the choicest of wines, so long as this was within one's reach. Eating and drinking were from now on considered no less acceptable to God than constant praying and learning, so long as one did so in the name of God and with a cheerful heart, with happiness and pleasure. Joy and happiness were to be the catchwords from now on, and one need not feel a lesser Jew for not knowing how to learn. One could serve God just as well by thinking of Him with affection—even with a sigh.

Among the mitnaggedim, the learners themselves did not even feel adequate in their religious observance. They believed in what

Rabbi Zera said in tractate *Shabbat* [112b]: "If the earlier [scholars] were sons of angels, we are sons of men, and if the earlier [scholars] were sons of men, we are like asses, and not [even] like asses of Rabbi Hanina ben Dosa and Rabbi Phinehas ben Jair, but like other asses. . . ."[31]

According to the Ba'al Shem Tov, however, all Jews were of equal birth. One did not have to be a genius or possess special talents. If they were or did, all the better; if not, it didn't matter. Every Jew could be pious, whether he was learned or illiterate; it was enough for him to have a kind heart. The mitnaggedim behaved according to the verse "an ignorant person cannot be pious."[32] That is wrong. An *am ha-aretz* with a kind heart could be a better and more pious Jew than the greatest scholar.

As I said, Jews were attracted to Hasidism. To the simple Jew Hasidism brought genuine happiness. He became worthy. Even more—hitherto, he was not even considered a human being, not in the study house, not in his own eyes, or in the eyes of others. But now, in the hasidic *shtibl,* as they called their study house, the unlearned man was on a par with the greatest scholar, the poorest with the wealthiest man in his community. Even the scholars were pleased with Hasidism, for they were now able to extricate themselves from the gloom of the mitnaggedim. They became livelier, more active, and independent in their intellectual pursuits, qualities they could never before have allowed themselves. A new field of mysticism and Kabbala opened up to them, which had the intoxicating effect of good wine. They were entranced by the free and easy atmosphere of Hasidism, and were thus drawn into it.

The mitnagged was always full of worries. With the approach of a holiday he knew he had to have a complete set of new garments tailored for himself, for in the study house, proper attire was strictly adhered to. If he did not have a nice outfit, he would be humiliated by his neighbor who showed off better quality clothes than his own. What one wore among the hasidim was of no consequence at all. Nice clothes played no role whatsoever in their *shtiblekh.* One couldn't care less what kind of *kapote* one's fellow hasid wore. There, one man's clothes were as good as another's.

In the hasidic *shtibl* there was no monopoly on seats, there were no *shtet,* and everyone sat down wherever a seat was vacant. Actually, hasidim don't stand still in a particular spot during their prayers. They keep moving about and swaying; their temperament doesn't allow them to stand still. Motion is necessary. And indeed, the hasidim walk about during the prayers. Someone might first stand beside the eastern wall, then by the door, then in the southern or northern section—in short, one is constantly on the move.[33]

Nor do the hasidim observe the rule of communal prayer. Some recite *barukh she'amar,* others *yishtabakh,* or *shmoneh esreh.*[34] Another smokes a pipe, for smoking is also considered a noble deed.[35] Over there, several hasidim stand in a corner while one pours out vodka into a glass to be passed around for a communal *lehayyim*—they have finished their prayers before the rest. Kotsker hasidim can even drink a *lehayyim* before their prayers. Meanwhile, someone starts chanting a tune, which is picked up by several youngsters—and it becomes quite joyful.

Among the hasidim, the sense of pride did not exist, as if there were no such thing in the world. All were equal, poor and rich, illiterate and learned, young and old. Most of them addressed each other familiarly, avoiding the formal "You." To use this formal form of speech was deemed antihasidic behavior.[36]

Only one who possessed a pleasant voice and prayed straight from the heart with genuine fervor was truly honored among the hasidim. They also appreciated the one who was always merry, loved the bitter drop, and started dancing all on his own, drawing other hasidim after him; so long as things got merry. He might be young, poor, or simply unlearned. It didn't matter, so long as he was capable of drawing the wealthiest, the greatest scholar, the oldest among them, into the circle, and all that in midweek. And if one elderly, wealthy man didn't feel like joining in—which rarely happened—he was thrust into the circle by a slap on his back or dragged in by his beard. He was forced to take a shot of schnapps, and then he'd already be tipsy, dancing and dancing for all he's worth.

Among the hasidim, every day was a holiday and a reason for making merry. If someone had a *yahrzeit,* the hasidim in the *shtibl* demanded a sip of schnapps,[37] and if he couldn't afford the vodka, it was donated by one of the wealthier hasidim. But if a wealthy man had a *yahrzeit* he had to provide plenty of drinks, and after the service, the bottles were passed around and things got lively. Indeed, every day was something like a holiday for them. Here— the *yahrzeit* of the rebbe and an opportunity to hold a feast, to sing and dance, or there—the arrival of a special guest, in whose honor the feasting, singing, and dancing were repeated, or just for the sake of having a good time.

On the Sabbath preceding the *selihot* prayers, at dusk, when every mitnagged was filled with gloomy foreboding in anticipation of the Day of Judgment and when they wept through the doleful *la-menatzeah*[38] prayer, the hasidic *shtibl,* on the other hand, resounded with genuine joy. During that same evening, the hasidim sang the Sabbath hymns until late into the night, much later than on an ordinary Sabbath. A *krupnik* soup with meat, cooked in the *shtibl* or at a neighbor's, was brought in together with numerous bottles of schnapps and beer, and they chanted a variety of melodies until the middle of the night. Then all the hasidim gathered together, recited the *selihot* quickly and in a happy mood, concluding them within half an hour. Then, they set the table—if the *krupnik* was ready, everyone partook, and if it wasn't ready, they went on singing and dancing with true religious fervor. Such riotous revelry usually went on until the small hours of the morning.

That same night, the journey to the rebbe was arranged, the number of coaches required, and so on, and the poor man "attached" himself to the rich man with whom he wished to travel. It is interesting to note that it was the poor man who did the choosing, and if, for example, the poor man chose Hayyim, Hayyim could not refuse him. On the contrary, the wealthy man would give the poor fellow a friendly slap on his back, which would promptly be returned by the poor man, and both would break into laughter. A well-to-do hasid might have two poor fellow travelers, and an especially wealthy one, three or even four. My father already had his fellow travelers—Avraham, Hirsh, and Motke—who had a monopoly on him and accompanied him to the rebbe every Rosh Hashanah.[39]

Over a third of all the hasidim traveled to the rebbe for Rosh Hashanah. Those who stayed at home came to see the others off. Then, many of those who remained behind handed the passengers petitions with requests to the rebbe to appeal to God to help them overcome the troubles of their everyday lives. How hasidim lived throughout the year I have already described in sufficient detail in earlier chapters of my memoirs.[40]

As I mentioned above, Hasidism suited every class of people, from poor to rich, from ignorant to learned, from old to young. The simple wealthy hasid lived an enviable life compared to that of the wealthiest mitnagged. And that applied not only to the Jews.

A wealthy and pious Christian was also unaware of the pleasures experienced by a wealthy hasid. The home of the latter was always full of song, ecstasy, and great rejoicing.

But I couldn't be a hasid. My heart was not in it. First of all, I was repelled by the adherence to a rebbe, something completely alien to the character of a mitnagged. A rebbe, on his own, may, perhaps, be tolerated. But the hurly-burly around him, his extraordinary status, and the fact that his office passes from father to son, like royalty, puts me off altogether. I absolutely and most definitely do not believe that there is anyone who has not been elected, but has acquired his position by virtue of his lineage, to whom one can pour out one's heart, reveal all one's shortcomings, and who is capable of advising a distraught person of how to rid himself of the bad traits in his character and mend his ways, and so on, and so on, and that there is anyone willing to follow such advice.

Another thing that distanced me from Hasidism when I was still a young boy was witnessing the miserable conditions in which the wives of poverty-stricken hasidim had to live. Their husbands led a happy, joyful life, eating and drinking their fill, dancing and singing in the company of their fellow hasidim while their wives and children suffered cold and hunger at home.[41]

There were some hasidic laborers who earned ten gulden or two rubles[42] a week at most. In the winter they would wash sheep hides by the river,[43] and their wives and children would suffer from hunger and cold. But after work the men would go off to the *shtibl*, to rejoice, revel, and sing. The starving wife and children, who stayed behind in the cold rooms, worried them, it would seem, very little. All that spoiled my enthusiasm for Hasidism. Perhaps from the psychological point of view the poor man is right: what would be gained if he too were to sit at home with his doleful wife and his children? Could he warm them? Could he make them happy? But this influenced me greatly. I felt closer to the dour-faced mitnaggedim, who were never happy, who never danced or sang, but who nevertheless stayed with their wives and children and who carried on their backs the difficult burden of earning a living.

As I have already noted,[44] I had, of course, other theoretical objections to Hasidism, but here it is important to remember the practical side, which it would seem was the main reason I could not accept the hasidic faith. The hasid had to be able to totally disregard the practical side of life, and devote himself entirely to singing and to a carefree existence. I could never do that, and therefore I would never have made much of a hasid.

There is one more failing of Hasidism which I must bring up, which at the time made a very bad impression on me: great scholars would never spring from their midst. The good intellect of a gifted hasidic boy was bound to be wasted. He was discouraged from learning, allowed to let the days slip by in idleness, and that was a great pity. On the other hand, the children of the mitnaggedim devoted most of their time to sharpening their wits; they worked hard at it and knew a great deal. One could be proud of them. A boy like that worked hard, and I, too, was keen on working hard and acquiring knowledge, and that was why I rejected Hasidism outright as a way of life.

YEKHEZKEL KOTIK:
LIST OF PUBLICATIONS

As a community activist Kotik initiated and founded many societies, for which he wrote, edited, and published various pamphlets, in Hebrew and in Yiddish. For the most part, prior to the writing of his memoirs, his publications were detailed bylaws for welfare societies; a minority of these publications were moral-didactic in nature. Some of these brochures are extremely rare; others may have been lost without being recorded in any bibliographical listing. A list of the publications I was able to locate follows. The titles have been abbreviated. For the full titles, see Assaf, *What I Have Seen,* Appendix B, 389–92.

1. *Hatza'at hukei agudat Ahi ezer.* . . . (Proposed bylaws for the Achiezer society). Warsaw: Halter and Eisenshtadt, 1896, 46pp. (H & Y).[1]

2. *Aseret ha-dibrot li-venei tziyyon* (The ten commandments to the sons of Zion). Warsaw: Halter, 1899, 129pp. (H & Y).[2]

3. *Hatza'at hukei Ezrat Yetomim* (Proposed bylaws for Ezrat Yetomim [orphans' fund]. Warsaw: Halter, 1900, 24pp. (H).

4. *Proyektirte takones fir der khevre Ezras Yesoymim* (Proposed bylaws for the Ezrat Yetomim society). Warsaw: Halter, 1901, 32pp. (Y).

5. *Hatza'at hukei agudat Ezrat Holim* (Proposed bylaws for the Ezrat Holim [sick fund] society). Warsaw: Halter, 1902, 24pp. (H).[3]

6. Portions of an unpublished pamphlet in Kotik's handwriting are found in the YIVO library. Its title page reads, *Sefer torat adam . . . by Yekhezkel ben Moshe Kotik, Warsaw* [5]666 [1906]. Kotik evidently began writing this pamphlet in 1906 but never completed it. From its seven remaining pages, the

pamphlet's message is clear. Like its predecessor, *Aseret ha-dibrot* [no. 2 above], it proposed religious reforms. These reforms are none other than a proposal for a social existence based on the moral principles that should, according to Kotik, characterize modern Jewish existence.[4]

7. *Arbeyter-kalendar, a zamelbukh far arbeyter-interesen* (Workers' almanac, an anthology for workers). Warsaw: Edelstein, 1907, intermittent pagination (approximately 100 pp.).[5]

8. *Der yudisher deputat* (The Jewish deputy). Warsaw: Starovolski, 1909, 28pp.[6]

9. *Di lokatoren (shkheynim) mit di virtslayt, behandelt di frage fun di lokatoren un zeyre betsihungen tsu di balebatim* (The tenants with the landlords, treating the question of the tenants and their relationship to the landlords). Warsaw: Morgenstern, 1909, 24 pp.[7]

10. *Der proyektirter ustav far dem "Varshaver lokatoren fereyn"* (The proposed bylaws of the Warsaw tenants' association). Warsaw: Morgenstern, [1909], 13pp. (+ 10 pp.—the catalogue of Morgenstern books).[8]

11. *Proyektirte takones far der khevre Moyshev Zkeynim (hilf far alte leyt)* (Proposed bylaws for the Moshav Zekenim society [assistance for the elderly]. Warsaw, 1910, 16pp.[9]

12. *Instruktsyes far der khevre "Moyshev Zkeynim"* (Guidelines for the Moshav Zekenim society). Warsaw: Shriftgiser, 1913, 16pp.

13. *Mayne zikhroynes*. Part one, Warsaw: Gitlin, 1913, 415pp.; Part two, Warsaw: Gitlin, 1914, 327pp.

14. *Mayne zikhroynes*. 2d ed. Part one, Berlin: Klal-Verlag, 1922, 352pp. (with the addition of Sholem Aleichem's letter); Part two, Berlin: Klal-Verlag, 1922, 270pp.

15. Kotik published several articles in *Ha-melitz*.[10] Because of the lack of indexes to this newspaper I was unable to find more than one short article, which Kotik sent from Warsaw. The untitled article denigrated the practice of those Warsaw Jews who went to bars and other venues where antisemitic shows were shown, wondering how the same Jews who squabbled over "honors" in the synagogue voluntarily visited places where they were unwanted. The article appeared in *Ha-melitz*, 7 September 1891, no. 192: 1–2.

APPENDIX B

SELECTED BIBLIOGRAPHY
ON YEKHEZKEL KOTIK
AND HIS MEMOIRS

1. Ba'al Makshoves [Yisrael Elyashev, pseud.]. "Literarishe gesh-prekhn" (Literary talks). *Der fraynd,* 20 December 1912, no. 277.
2. Aharon Einhorn. "Amol" (Once). *Haynt,* 1 January 1913, no. 292: 4.
3. Noyekh Prylucki. "Yekhezkel Kotiks 'Zikhroynes' (notitsn)" (Notes on Yekhezkel Kotik's *Memoirs*). Parts 1–6. *Der moment,* 21 February 1913, no. 34: 5; 25 February, no. 37: 3; 4 March, no. 43: 3; 7 March, no. 46: 4–5; 11 March, no. 49: 3; 18 March, no. 55: 3.
4. Lipa Kestin. "A vikhtiker yidisher yubileum (25 yor ekzistents fun 'Akhiezer')" (A notable Jewish jubilee [25 years to the founding of Achiezer]). *Haynt,* 22 July 1913, no. 157: 5.
5. A. Yud. [Avraham Yuditski]. "Sirtutim sifrutiyyim" (Literary sketches). Parts 1–3. *Ha-zeman,* 28 August 1913, no. 182: 3; 2 September, no. 186: 4; 10 September, no. 193: 2–3.
6. Moshe Katz. "Bibliografye" (Bibliography). *Di tsukunft* 18, no. 9 (September 1913): 936–37.
7. Simon M. Dubnow. [Review of Kotik's *Memoirs*]. *Evreiskaia starina* 6 (1913): 413–14 (R).
8. Hirsh-David Nomberg. "Notitsn—Yekhezkel Kotik" (Notes—Yekhezkel Kotik). *Haynt,* 21 April 1914, no. 82: 3.

9. Zalman Reisen. *Lexicon of Yiddish Literature and Press.* Warsaw: Tsentral, 1914, 535–36 (Y). (See also no. 14, following.)

10. A. Litvin [Shmuel Hurwitz, pseud.]. "Yekhezkel Kotik un zayn kaviarnie" (Yekhezkel Kotik and his café). *Yudishe neshomes,* vol. 4: *Poyln,* 1–11. New York, 1917.

11. "Yekhezkel Kotik za"l" (The late Yekhezkel Kotik). *Der moment,* 15 August 1921, no. 185: 2 (unsigned obituary).

12. Avraham Goldberg. "Yekhezkel Kotik (A por verter nokh zayn toyt)—Tsu der kharakteristik fun a merkvirdikn lebn" (Yekhezkel Kotik: A few words after his death—A portrait of an extraordinary life). *Haynt,* 26 August 1921, no. 196: 9.

13. Avraham Kotik. *Dos lebn fun a idishn inteligent* (The life of a Jewish intellectual). New York: Toybenshlag, 1925.

14. Zalman Reisen. *Lexicon of Yiddish Literature, Press and Philology.* Vilna: Kletskin farlag, 1929, 3:424–26 (Y).

15. Avraham Reisen. *Epizodn fun mayn lebn* (Episodes from my life). Vilna: Kletskin farlag, 1929, 1:212–16.

16. Hirsh Greenbaum. "Undzer Kotik-ekspeditsye keyn Kamenets de-Lita" (Our Kotik expedition to Lithuanian Kamenetz). *Literarishe bleter* 31 (430), 29 July 1932: 492–93.

17. Shlomo Shrebrek. *Zikhronot ha-motzi la'or Shlomo Shrebrek* (The memoirs of the publisher Shlomo Shrebrek). Tel Aviv: Shrebrek, 1955, 144, 158–59.

18. Y. Gutkovitsh. *Oyf ale teg fun a gants yor* (On all the days of an entire year). Warsaw: Yidish bukh, 1966, 110.

19. *Encyclopaedia Judaica,* s.v. "Kotik, Yekhezkel."

20. Jack Kugelmass. "Yekhezkl Kotik: The Archetypal Jewish Middleman." In "Native Aliens: The Jews of Poland as a Middleman Minority," Ph.D. diss., New School of Social Research, New York, 1980, 125–64.

21. Yekhezkel Lifshitz. "Kotik, Yekhezkel." In *Lexicon of the New Yiddish Literature: Biographical Dictionary of Modern Yiddish Literature.* New York: Congress for Jewish Culture, 1981, 8:44 (Y).

22. Zevi Prylucki. "Mayne zikhroynes" (My memoirs), part 6. *Folks-shtime,* 19 March 1983, no. 11.

23. David Assaf. "'Nisu'ei behalah' be-mizrah eyropah: Perek mezikhronotav shel Yẹhezkel Kotik" (Panic weddings in Eastern Europe: A chapter from Yekhezkel's Kotik's memoirs). *Et ha-da'at* 2 (1998): 63–74.

24. Akiva Zimmerman. "Ma'asiyot ve-sipurim al toldot mishpakha ahat be-Polin" (Tales and stories regarding the history of a family in Poland). *Ha-tzofe,* 18 December 1998, 10.

25. David Assaf. "Mesaper ha-zikhronot ha-mufla" (The wonderful memoirist). *Etmol* 142 (January 1999): 14–16.

26. Yochanan Reshet [Yoram Bronovsky, pseud.]. "Shavua shel sfarim" (A week of books). *Ha-aretz,* 8 January 1999, section B, 15.

27. Yosef Friedlender. "A gan-eydn fun zikhroynes" (A memoir paradise). *Forverts,* 19 March 1999, 15, 23.

28. Ido Basok. "Ha-ayarah shelo hadla lamut" (The town that did not stop dying). *Ha-aretz: Sfarim,* no. 327, 2 June 1999, 11.

29. Shmuel Werses. [Review essay on *Mah she-ra'iti*]. *Gal-ed* 17 (2000): 141–46 (Hebrew section).

30. Shalom Luria. "Shivhei he-avar u-te'amav" (In praise of the past and its flavors). *Chulyot* 6 (summer 2000): 419–20.

31. "Zemanim kashim la-yehudim: Perek mi-zikhronotav shel Yehezkel Kotik" (Hard times for the Jews). In *The Broken Chain: Polish Jewry through the Ages,* ed. Israel Bartal and Israel Gutman, 447–52. Jerusalem: Merkaz Zalman Shazar, 2001.

Yekhezkel Kotik's Genealogy

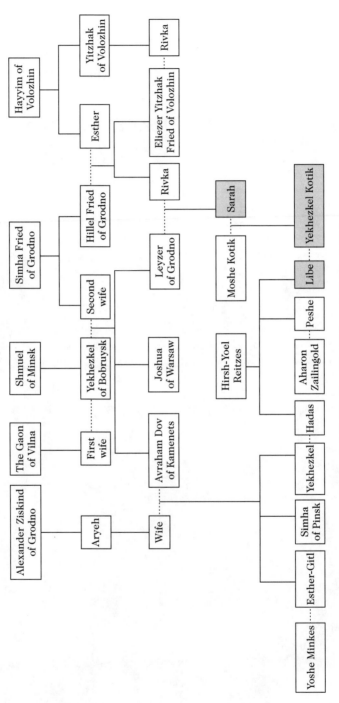

Yekhezkel Kotik's Family: Wife and Mother's Side

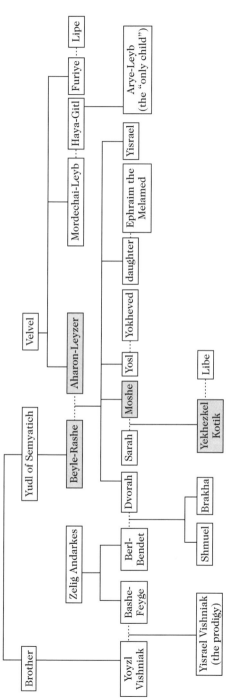

Yekhezkel Kotik's Family: Father's Side

Notes

Letter

1. On Sholem Aleichem's stay in Lausanne in January 1913, see Introduction.

2. I.e., Sholem Aleichem's first letter to Kotik, dated 6 January 1913. See Introduction.

3. Shmuel Niger (1883–1955)—pen name of Shmuel Charney, researcher and critic, one of the leading scholars in the field of Yiddish literature, a native of Belorussia who resided in New York from 1919. One of Sholem Aleichem's closest friends, Niger published dozens of articles about his work. See *LNYL* 6:190–210; Kressel, *Cyclopedia,* 2:450–51. At the beginning of 1913, Niger was staying in Berne, Switzerland, and Sholem Aleichem wrote to him on 8 January on this matter (see Introduction). In Niger's letters from these years I have found neither a reply nor any other comment regarding Kotik.

4. Avraham Reisen (1876–1953)—Yiddish poet and writer, born in Keidanov (Belorussia), Reisen lived in Warsaw and, from 1911, in the United States. See *LNYL,* 8:458–78; Kressel, *Cyclopedia,* 2:860–61.

5. In his previous letter to Kotik Sholem Aleichem had related how, in his great desire to read the book, he cut the pages in Niger's copy that was sent to him by mistake. See Introduction.

6. *Rendlekh* (sing. *rendl*)—a term for gold coins, ducats, or florins. Sholem Aleichem alludes here to the figure of the ascetic described in chapter 25, who compares the commandments to coins and calls upon youths to gather them.

7. I.e., Kotik's eldest son, Avraham-Hirsh. See Introduction, note 127, and below, in the continuation of the letter.

8. Zastavye—a suburb adjacent to Kamenets. See chapter 1, note 36.

9. *Ispravnik*—district governor with both civilian and police authority. See *RHT,* 32.

10. *Assessor*—a local government official. This post developed from the top administrative rank established by Peter the Great in 1722 and was preserved essentially in the Russian-annexed regions of Poland. The *assessor* was subordinate to the *ispravnik* and served as his representative to the local authority. See *RHT,* 2, 187 (*zasedateli*).

11. In the original *pritsim* (sing. *porets*)—a Yiddish term for a noble Polish estate owner (Polish: *pan*). Apparently, this expression was applied to them because of their ruthlessness and wild cruelty.

12. On the apikores Twersky, see chapter 15.

13. *Kerbl* is slang for ruble. This is a play on the folk proverb: "The *kerbl* is no bastard." That is, a person should not be ashamed of the money in his possession. See *Jüdische Sprichwörter,* 246, no. 3400. The apikores Twersky was known for distributing his money to his friends and to the poor.

14. Two "Yisraels"—two youths of the same name and age in Kotik's family. See chapter 8.

15. Three kidnappers employed by the Jewish communal board (Kahal), who forcibly drafted youths for the army. See chapter 9.

16. *Upravliaishche*—administrator; senior civil servant. See *RHT,* 171–72 (*upravlenie*). Berl-Bendet, Kotik's brother-in-law, was a village Jew (*yishuvnik*), and a noble's agent. See chapters 12–13.

17. See chapter 14.

18. See chapter 28.

19. Yiddish literature was considered "popular," while Hebrew literature was considered the "national" literature.

20. Joseph Izbitski (1876–1928)—Bund activist and Yiddish writer who was known by the pseudonym Beynish Mikhailovitch. See *LNYL,* 5:608–12.

21. "Kotik's coffee house was the gathering place for the Warsaw writers, and all the labor activists came there. One could run into Beynish Mikhailovitch and the Bund leader Alter Ehrlich, also H. D. Nomberg and Avraham Reisen were permanent guests there" (Shrebrek, *Zikhronot,* 158); see also Introduction.

22. Nalewki Street—a narrow street in the "Jewish" section of Warsaw, known for the density of its shops and people and for the many buildings with courtyards that branched off from it. A symbol for the spirit of commerce among Polish Jewry in general and Warsaw Jewry in particular.

23. Mordechai Spektor (1858–1925)—Yiddish writer and journalist. Born in Uman (Ukraine), he became known as a writer of novels and as an editor of literary collections, such as *Der Hoyzfraynd* (The friend of the house). See *LNYL,* 6:518–27.

24. Mikhail Artzibashev (1878–1927)—well-known Russian writer, famous for the novel *Sanin,* which caused literary debates because of its pessimism as well as for its advocacy of decadent egoism and hedonism. On Sholem Aleichem's negative attitude toward Artzibashev, see Bartal, "Gentile Society," 235–36, and note 114.

25. Someone full of rage and anger, who threatens but does not carry out his threats; see *Jüdische Sprichwörter,* 126, no. 1813. "Der yudisher gazlan" was also a pseudonym Sholem Aleichem used occasionally.

CHAPTER 1

1. *Slup* (Polish *słup*)—Yiddish for column. This tower, which was painted white and could be seen at a distance, was probably built in the late thirteenth century as part of the system of Polish fortifications against the Tartar threat. The tower was thirty-seven meters high, and measured thirty-five meters in circumference.

See *Słownik,* 3:764; *Kamenetz Memorial Book,* 22–23. In Jewish folklore Kamenets was thus identified with the "slup." See Prylucki, *Zamlbikher,* 61, no. 825.

2. *Funt*—pound. Measuring weight used in Russia (one-fortieth of a *pud;* see note 21 below), equivalent to 409 grams See *RHT,* 19.

3. Alexander II (1818–81) ascended to the throne in 1855 after the death of his father, Tsar Nicholas I. Early in his reign comprehensive political, economic, and social reforms were instituted, the most important of which were the liberation of the peasants and the abolition of their perpetual servitude in 1861. The restrictions against the Jews also were lightened and many of the brutal and degrading statutes that had characterized the days of Nicholas were nullified or ameliorated, especially the military draft statute, which was changed in 1856 (to equalize the Jewish draft with that of the general population). See Dubnow, *History of the Jews,* 321–30; Shochat, "Yahas ha-rusim."

4. Białowieska Forest (Polish: Puszcza Białowieska). One of the largest forested areas in Europe (1,140 square kilometers), which served as permanent hunting grounds for Polish kings and Russian tsars. The town of Białowieża, in the middle of the forest, 35 kilometers north of Kamenets, was the site of one of the tsar's summer residences. On this forest, see Schama, *Landscape,* 37–74.

5. I.e., Russian miles, which equal seven versts. Each verst is 1.0668 kilometers. See note 22 below.

6. *Skazka* (Russian *revizski skazki*)—the reported results of the population census within a local jurisdiction (generally only the number of males) presented to the higher authorities, used for purposes of tax collection and the military draft. See *RHT,* 126. According to the 1847 census, the number of Jews in Kamenets was 1,451: 645 men and 806 women (*EJD,* 2:425). This number is certainly not exact. As Kotik notes, one must add to it an unknown number of unregistered Jews who evaded registration to avoid military service and taxes.

7. The year 1874 saw a wide-ranging reform in the draft system—forced military service was abolished, and the Jewish communities were freed from the responsibility for drafting a quota of recruits. It was the personal responsibility of all twenty-year-old male subjects of the state to appear before a draft board that functioned according to fixed criteria, with the power to exempt sons from poor families or only sons. See Slutsky, "Military Service Act"; Klier, *Jewish Question,* 332–49. The negative reaction of Orthodox Jews, who viewed this reform as an even more pernicious decree than that of the cantonists in the days of Nicholas I, is reflected in the memoir literature. See, for example, Kaufmann, *Zikhronot,* 43–47; Friedman, *Zikhronot,* 112–14.

8. "What did it mean to be 'hidden'? This was the invention of a wise and clever people. The sages of Israel saw that the authorities collect tariffs and property taxes from the public funds of every community according to its population, and impose upon them the physical obligation to provide a number of soldiers according to the census of its individuals. Therefore, it is surely a simple matter: let us reduce the number of our individuals and we will avoid many problems. But how to reduce the numbers? . . . We'll quietly downplay the known births and not record them in the roster. The 'hidden' will grow up and reach the age of Torah and the wedding canopy, and in turn give birth to sons and daughters and these too will not appear in the population roster" (Chemerinsky, *Motele,* 131).

9. Wysokie (Wysokie Litewskie)—about 27 kilometers southwest of Kamenets. In the 1847 census, it had 1,475 registered Jews: 780 men and 695 women. See *Pinkas ha-kehillot: Poland,* 5:249–50; *EJD,* 2:425.

10. "Herring" is a cognomen for lower-class individuals of little importance, since only they could be dragged into a store in such a fashion. See Sadan, *Yerid,* 81–86.

11. *Szlachcic*—a nobleman of the *szlachta* class. As opposed to the magnates, who owned large estates, they were neither wealthy nor property owners. See Maimon, *Autobiography,* 11; Lipschitz, *Me-dor le-dor,* 23.

12. Kotik's descriptions of Jewish domestic occupations provide a more balanced picture than the tendentious and dichotomous one many maskilim sketched. According to the maskilic view, the women supported the men, who spent most of their time sitting on the benches of the study houses. Gottlober, for example, states, "For the Jewish income in those days was brought in by the women, women of valor, while the men sat hidden in their houses or in the study house, learning and praying . . . and even the men who left Torah study after many years . . . could only help their wives in the stores by retrieving the merchandise for them" (*Memoirs,* 1:86; see also Levin, *Social and Economic Values,* 151–53).

13. On the relations between Jews and lords, see the summation in *Beit Yisrael be-Polin,* 1:95–98. For a more extensive treatment, see Rosman, *Lords' Jews.*

14. "The happy ones among the craftsmen were those whose diligence or success enabled them to become close to the lords who, in turn, tolerated the craftsmen's presence, for as long as it benefited the lord. Such craftsmen were appropriately called 'the lords' craftsmen' and they were considered superior to their brethren" (Lipschitz, *Me-dor le-dor,* 53–54).

15. "A house like this was not only (in general) a dwelling for the owner's family, but also (one will not believe it, but this is how it was) for a few neighbors. Many families dwelled in one house. With the rent at five, ten or even fifteen silver rubles a year, a family found refuge in this kind of house" (ibid., 45–46). This overcrowding had its consequences: unsanitary conditions, noise, jealousy, and constant bickering.

16. Brisk (Brest; Brześć Litewski)—capital of the Brisk district (Grodno province), to which Kamenets belonged, located 35 kilometers south of Kamenets. It was also the seat for the regional authorities, with the *ispravnik* at their head.

17. Russian *gubernator*—the ruler of a province (*guberniia*). See *RHT,* 28, and note 31 below.

18. Yiddish *yishuvnikes*—a term for Jews living in villages or isolated estates who were generally cut off from Jewish communal life. Jews in such remote areas were affiliated with a neighboring Jewish community, to whom they paid taxes and, in exchange, from whose services they benefited. They brought their legal disputes to the communal rabbinical courts and prayed with the congregation on the holidays. See Lipschitz, *Me-dor le-dor,* 93–95.

19. Stereotypical names used by Polish nobles to refer to Jews. See Shpirn, "Names," 180; Friedman, *Zikhronot,* 258.

20. In the Yiddish original, Kotik used the terms *morg,* a Lithuanian mea-

surement equal to two acres (*RHT,* 63), and "four *shok,*" a Lithuanian measurement equal to sixty units.

21. *Pud*—old Russian weight equal to forty *funts* (see note 2 above) or 16.38 kilograms (see *RHT,* 109–10).

22. A square verst equals 1.138 square kilometers (see ibid., 175).

23. Kotik uses the word *kelipah,* an expression derived from Jewish mysticism, meaning a demon or an evil spirit that rules a person.

24. The Trinkovskis (Khaytshe [Haya] and Yonye [Yonah]) were one of the most respected families in the town. They ran the tavern and inn frequented by the nobility.

25. *Arenda*—the leasing of the privilege to collect taxes or income, usually granted by a noble to an agent. The lessee was called *arendar* or *arendator* and this word usually specified a Jew. Varied types of *arenda* arrangements formed one of the main livelihoods of Polish Jewry for generations. In these agreements, the lord or owner of an asset granted the lessee an estate, property, or parts thereof, or the right to farm taxes for an agreed-upon amount. During the timeframe for the agreement, the lessee had the right to profit from said assets to his best advantage. See Rosman, *Lords' Jews,* 106–42. The Kotiks' lease, which Kotik will discuss in detail below, was a "general" one within whose framework the lord leased all his property—the town, the surrounding holdings, agricultural lands, and the serfs living within its area. In actuality, the lessee substituted for the lord, supervising and controlling nearly all aspects of life in the property leased to him. He was also permitted, as Kotik's ancestors had been, to sublease privileges to secondary lessees.

26. *Komissar* in the original—a noble-appointed official who managed the estate and its holdings. The official responsible for all the noble's estates and holdings was the chief commissioner (*hoypt-komissar*).

27. *Shlimazel*—unlucky, slovenly. The word probably stems from the German *schlimm* (bad, awful). See *Jüdische Sprichwörter,* 281–82; Sadan, "Shlumiel."

28. This apparently refers to the 1794 Polish uprising against the Russian conquerors (additional rebellions took place in 1830–31 and 1863) led by Tadeusz Kościuszko. Following its suppression Poland was partitioned for the third time. I have not been able to find details regarding Osserevski, and it is possible that the name has been corrupted. Kamenets lost its status as a royal possession in the mid-eighteenth century, when it was placed under the authority of a Lithuanian noble named Vilkhorski. See *Kamenetz Memorial Book,* 26–27.

29. *Pruska*—the site of Osserevski's mansion. There was another estate with the same name in the Kamenets region. See chapter 22, following note 9; and *Słownik,* 9:83.

30. *Nomiestnik* in the original. Until 1874 *namestnik* was the title given the military governor of Poland, whose role paralleled that of the general-governor. See *RHT,* 66–67.

31. General-governor (*general-gubernator*)—the provincial ruler. This important official often governed several provinces. See *RHT,* 19. For example, the general-governor in Vilna was responsible for the northwestern provinces of Vilna, Grodno, Minsk, Kovno, and Vitebsk.

32. This was not an unusual phenomenon. On the practice of betting on women in card games, see Rivkind, *Gambling,* 55–68.

33. *Voyt* in the original (Polish *wójt*), or *klyutsch-voyt* (*kliuch* means estate in Polish). See *RHT,* 38 (*kliuchnik*), 178 (*voit*). On *klyutsch-voyt,* see note 110 below.

34. Yiddish *shtetl-gelt,* the town money, meaning the income the lord received from leasing agreements with Jews. See Rivkind, *Jewish Money,* 269.

35. The Lesna, a tributary of the Bug.

36. Zastavye (*Zastawie;* beyond the lake in Polish)—also called *Zamosty.* A suburb of Kamenets separated from the town by the Lesna River. See *Pinkas hakehillot: Poland,* 5:250.

37. See note 25 above.

38. Kalish (Kalisz) province, located in western Poland on the Prussian border, was part of the Duchy of Warsaw from 1807–15, and subsequently part of the Kingdom of Poland under Russian administration.

39. Tsar Alexander II abolished serfdom in 1861. See note 3 above.

40. Kotik probably confused two different issues: Jews indeed used circumventions to purchase land, such as through Christian middlemen, but that was before the abolishment of serfdom, when land ownership was restricted to the nobility. The use of Christian names in order to purchase land resumed after the announcement of "temporary rules" in May 1882 that stressed that Jews should be prevented from land purchases in their names outside of the towns. See Dinur, "Ignatiev," 19–21.

41. *Revisor* in the original—an inspector dispatched by the central government whose role was to check on bureaucratic procedures, taxation, and population registration, in order to prevent corruption. The local clerks' consternation at the visit of the big-city inspector who could expose corruption is satirized in N. Gogol's famous play *Revisere,* first produced in 1836 by special permission of Tsar Nicholas I.

42. *Dyesyatnikes*—local gendarmes subject to the *assessor*'s authority whose role was to preserve law and order. See *RHT,* 11 (*desiatskii*).

43. Sokolka (Sokółka)—a district town in the Grodno province, about 38 kilometers northeast of Bialystok.

44. *Eyn Ya'akov*—a compilation of talmudic legends with commentary by Yaakov ben Haviv (fifteenth century). Its simplicity of style and content made it a popular book, and it was published in many editions. In many communities special societies were devoted to its study. It also became a widespread custom to study this book in synagogues, either alone or in groups.

45. Catherine, probably Catherine II, Empress of Russia from 1762 until her death in 1796; Peter, probably Tsar Peter III, Catherine's husband, who reigned for only a few months in 1762; Paul, the son of Catherine and Peter, tsar from 1796 until his assassination in 1801.

46. Napoleon's Russian campaign started with his invasion of Russia in June 1812 and lasted for six months until his withdrawal. This war has been described in many literary works (such as L. Tolstoy's *War and Peace*) and played a major role in shaping the modern Russian national identity.

47. *Prushim*—in the nineteenth century this term denoted Lithuanian Jews who left their wives and families, devoting themselves to Torah study according to the doctrines of the Gaon of Vilna and his disciple Hayyim of Volozhin. See Etkes,

Lita; and Stampfer, *Lithuanian Yeshiva.* On the *prushim* who filled the yeshivot of Lithuania and Belorussia, see Wengeroff, *Memoiren,* 1:143–53; and Shochat, "Cantonists."

48. Eating days—Yiddish *esen teg.* A popular Eastern European arrangement that enabled out-of-town yeshiva students to be hosted in the homes of local inhabitants. Local Jews invited the students to eat in their homes, and each was assigned a specific day with a particular family. It was considered a privilege to host a young Torah scholar, and families competed for the right to host the most promising students, while the students covertly competed to be hosted by the wealthiest families. See, for example, Kasovich, *Our Years,* 23–24, 35–38; and Salzmann, *Min he-avar,* 115.

49. *Kest*—Yiddish *esen kest.* A popular Eastern European arrangement in which the Torah study of gifted young men was financed after their marriage by the bride's father, who was interested in having his daughter marry a talented Torah scholar. See Etkes, *Lita,* 63–84. These young men were also called *lomdim,* a term which originally meant a ripe scholar, but was also applied to someone engaged in the study of Torah in his community's study house whose livelihood was supplied, fully or partially, by the public, his wife's parents, or individual patrons. See Katz, "Marriage," 26; and Reiner, *"Kloiz."*

50. *Treyfe bikhlekh*—forbidden books, a term for Enlightenment books, novels, and all tracts other than religious literature. Anyone reading such books was considered a heretic.

51. On Białowieska Forest, see note 4 above.

52. Groshen (*grosz, gadol;* lit. "big")—a small copper coin worth half a Russian kopeck, which is one two-hundredth of a silver ruble. In the nineteenth century this term connoted a worthless coin (the Yiddish expression *nit vert keyn groshen* means 'it isn't even worth a penny'). See *RHT,* 28.

53. Praga—a suburb on the east bank of the Vistula River opposite Warsaw. Until 1764 Jews were not allowed to reside on a permanent basis in the capitol, Warsaw, and therefore most Jews who had business in Warsaw were forced to settle in Praga, a commercial center which enjoyed the status of a town. Praga was annexed to Warsaw in 1791.

54. On this type of tavern, which also functioned as an inn for lords and merchants, see Lipschitz, *Me-dor le-dor,* 31.

55. Bialystok (Białystok), located about 100 kilometers northwest of Kamenets, was a large commercial town that underwent rapid development during the latter half of the nineteenth century. The number of resident Jews, who were an absolute majority in the general population, increased from 761 in 1765 to 45,905 in 1897. See Leshtchinsky, *Yidishe folk,* 71.

56. Tiktin (Tykocin) was an old established Jewish community in Podlasie, on the border between Poland and Lithuania, about 26 kilometers west of Bialystok.

57. Yitzhak Zabludovski (1781–1865) was a famous wealthy Jew who made his fortune in the lumber trade and received the honorary and hereditary Russian title of "Respected Citizen" in his lifetime. See Hershberg, *Bialystok,* vol. 1, s.v. "Zabludovski."

58. Grodno, one of the oldest and important Lithuanian Jewish communities,

was the capitol of Grodno province, about 142 kilometers north of Kamenets. See *EJD*, vol. 9.

59. Kobrin (Kobryń)—about 40 kilometers southeast of Kamenets. See *Kobrin*; and *Pinkas ha-kehillot: Poland*, 5:305–10.

60. Ivan Paskevich served as Russian high commissioner in Poland after the suppression of the 1831 Polish uprising. He lived in Warsaw and maintained a good relationship with the Jewish community's elders. See Shatzky, *Warsaw*, vol. 2, s.v. "Paskevich."

61. On Shepsl (Shabbetai) and his band, see Stutschewsky, *Klezmorim*, 117–19.

62. In Yiddish, *badkhn* (from the Hebrew *badhan*) means master of the wedding ceremony. The *badkhn* improvised rhymes, sometimes funny and even vulgar, at other times sad and remorseful, which he tailored to the specific circumstances. We find many critical descriptions of these professionals. See, for example, Günzburg, *Aviezer*, 69–72; and Gottlober, *Memoirs*, 1:101–6. See also Rivkind, "Badchan"; Yaari, "Badchanim"; and Krasney, *Badkhan*.

63. Twenty groshen equals ten kopecks.

64. The Polish uprising against the Russian authorities began in January 1863. The Poles succeeded in establishing a national government in Warsaw; however, a year and a half later the rebellion was brutally suppressed along with the total abolition of any remnants of Polish sovereignty. Some of the rebellion's events and their effect on the Jews are described in chapters 5, 13, and 21–22.

65. Talmud Torah—poor Jewish children received their basic education within the framework of this institution, financed by the Jewish communities in the town and the surrounding villages. Children of wealthy families studied either in their own homes with private tutors or with a small group of children in a heder in the melamed's house (on heder and melamed, see below).

66. On *prushim*, see note 47 above. The meaning of this nickname may be related to the Polish word for socks: *pończochy*. As an itinerant, he may have gone barefoot or in socks. In chapters 15 and 25 he is called "Patshoshnik."

67. The Maggid of Kelme—Moshe-Yitzhak ben Noah Darshan of Kelme—was a disciple of Yisrael Salanter, the founder of the *Musar* movement, and one of the famous preachers of his day (on preachers, see note 130 below). He traveled among the Jewish communities of Lithuania and usually virulently attacked Haskalah and Jewish nationalism. See Deinard, *Zikhronot*, 1:100–102, 109; Friedman, *Zikhronot*, 8; Etkes, *Israel Salanter*, 183–89; and *Pinkas Slonim*, 1:66–67.

68. A government-sponsored lottery whose tickets were printed in Saxony and also distributed in Russia. See Rivkind, *Gambling*, 105–21.

69. According to BT *Ketubbot* 50a: "If a man desires to spend liberally he should not spend more than a fifth [since by spending more] he might himself come to be in need [of the help] of people."

70. According to Job 28:5–6: "Earth, out of which food grows . . . Its rocks are a source of sapphires; It contains gold dust too."

71. In the original: Shmuel. This was, however, probably a mistake on Kotik's part for the prophet Elijah.

72. Compare Lipschitz, *Me-dor le-dor*, 59.

73. *Krupnik* was one of the most popular foods in Lithuania. On the many kinds and methods of preparation, see Chemerinsky, *Motele*, 182.

74. Hikes in fish prices caused intermittent scandals in Eastern European Jewish communities and sometimes even led to boycotts on buying fish for the Sabbath until prices were lowered. See Agnon, *Ir u-melo'ah*, 589–91, 612, 615 (The case described there was based on a responsum found in *Hesed le-Avraham* [Lemberg, 1898], *Orah hayyim*, no. 26).

75. Compare Lipschitz, *Me-dor le-dor*, 13.

76. On the different types of candles, see ibid., 47–48.

77. For another description of the Sabbath, see ibid., 90–92.

78. *Shulhan arukh* (lit. "set table") is the code of Jewish law compiled in Safed by Joseph Karo (1488–1575), which governs all aspects of Jewish life and is still considered the authoritative source for the codification of Jewish law.

79. According to Jewish law, it is obligatory to eat three meals on the Sabbath. The third meal (in Hebrew *se'udah shlishit*) was usually eaten at home before the conclusion of the Sabbath. Hasidism transformed this meal into a special spiritual and social occasion, removing it from the family circle to the hasidic *shtibl*. However, in Kamenets, with its nonhasidic majority, most families ate the third meal at home.

80. Psalm 119, the longest chapter of the Bible (176 verses), begins with this verse. It was the custom to read this psalm in synagogue at sundown on Saturday.

81. *Pshetlekh* in the original (from the Hebrew *pshat*, lit. "simple"). Paradoxically, these "simple" interpretations mean casuistic readings of talmudic issues. Usually, this word carries negative connotations since these "simple" interpretations are far removed from the text's original meaning. *Harifut* (sharpness) or *pilpul* (casuistry) characterize scholarly ability to raise difficult questions and supply answers regarding talmudic issues based upon a large spectrum of sources, and to interpret these problems in a surprising, new light. This methodology attracted scholars to its intellectual sophistication and creativity, but also drew fire from critics because of its distance from the text's literal meaning and the dangers of meaningless hairsplitting.

82. See notes 47–49 above. Compare the atmosphere of Torah study in Kamenets as described by Kotik to S. Y. Abramovitsh's (Mendele Mokher Seforim) description of the town of Kapulie, in his story "Of Bygone Days," 284–85.

83. The period when Tsar Nicholas I's forced conscription decree was in effect (1827–56) is remembered as one of the most traumatic eras in Russian Jewish history and has been dealt with extensively both in memoir literature and scholarly research. Kotik himself returns to this subject in chapter 9.

84. Lit. "catcher." Special deputies hired by the community elders (Kahal) to kidnap young boys, especially unregistered ones, for forced army conscription. See Shochat, "Kahal," 181–83; Stanislawski, *Nicholas and the Jews*, 29–31; and chapter 9, note 6 below.

85. Hebrew *parnas ha-hodesh* (lit. "Elder of the Month"). The Eastern European Jewish communities were administered by a body of elders (Kahal) headed by one "head elder" in monthly rotation. After 1844, when the Russian government abolished the Kahal, this title continued to identify the communal leader even

though he was now not replaced on a monthly basis. See Shochat, "Kahal," 144–53; and chapter 2, near note 2.

86. *Sborshchik*—a Russian term for the tax collector who was also in charge of the conscription of army recruits from the community. Usually nominated by the district governors, the holders of this office wielded a great deal of power. After the abolishment of the Kahal the *sborshchiks* continued to hold important positions within the Jewish communal leadership, serving as de facto heads of the communities. See Shochat, "Kahal," 161–65; *RHT,* 119; and chapter 2, following note 18.

87. Relying on this passage, Shochat emphasizes the connection between the exemptions received by Torah scholars from army service through the intervention of the community elders and the atmosphere of Torah study prevalent in the northwestern provinces of the Pale of Settlement. See Shochat, "Cantonists."

88. *Maharsha*—Hebrew acronym for "our teacher Shmuel Eliezer" (1555–1631), one of the great talmudic commentators in Poland. Among his most important works are *Hidushei halakhot* and *Hidushei agadot,* commentaries on difficult halakhic issues and unexplained midrashic sections in the Talmud. These works, found in most printed editions of the Talmud, were studied systematically in Eastern Europe along with *Rashi* and *Tosaphot,* as an integral part of Talmud study. *Maharsha-keplekh*—lit. "heads able to decode *Maharsha's* commentaries," common praise for a brilliant Torah scholar. In his memoirs Moshe Lilienblum relates that when he was ten years old, "I understood *Maharsha* by myself, and sometimes I tired my teacher with my questions." (Lilienblum, *Autobiography,* 1:84); see also Friedman, *Zikhronot,* 60.

89. This paragraph, which has no connection to the preceding or following paragraphs, is an example of the lack of editing found throughout Kotik's memoirs.

90. Informer—Hebrew *moser,* a term for a Jew who supplied information to the authorities regarding illegal activities. Most informers were motivated by greed, either for the payment received from the authorities or for money extorted from the Jewish communities to buy their silence. According to Jewish law an informer has the legal status of *rodef* (persecutor) and it is therefore permissible to kill him before he brings disaster upon the entire community. Such cases are documented in Russia for the regime of Tsar Nicholas I. See Ginsburg, *Ktavim,* 152–78; and Assaf, *Regal Way,* 105–15.

91. "Unfortunately, and to the misfortune of the whole nation, within every town one can find a professional informer, a smooth-tongued fellow who chose informing as his livelihood and from it earned his bread . . . and everybody pays him respect and relates to him with great deference because he is an informer" (Sholem Aleichem, *Hebrew Writings,* 113).

92. This motif—the informer who breaks other people's hearts with his mournful prayers—predates Kotik. See, for example, the story about the killing of an informer in Shklov in Peretz Smolenskin's novella "An Ass's Burial." Of this informer, drowned in the river by the order of the community elders of Shklov, it was recounted that "when he prayed, his prayers came from a pure and innocent heart, and during the High Holidays he prayed with tears and trembling like one of the innocents" (*Ha-shahar* 5 [1874], 393–94).

93. St. Petersburg was the Russian capital and the seat of the tsar until 1918.

94. *Katorga*—a sentence of hard labor and exile, usually to Siberia.

95. Selets (Sielec)—a town near Pruzhany, about 114 kilometers west of Pinsk. See Salzmann, *Min he-avar;* and *Pinkas ha-kehillot: Poland,* 5:273–74.

96. Danzig (Gdańsk)—an international port city in northern Poland on the Baltic seacoast. Danzig was a timber-trading center; lumber was floated down the Vistula, which bisects Poland from south to north.

97. On study in the heder and its accompanying folklore, see Shtern, *"Khey-der,"* 37–130; Lifschitz, "Ha-heder," 307–80; Katz, *Tradition and Crisis,* 159–64; Scharfstein, *Heder;* and Stampfer, "Heder Study," 271–89.

98. *Lekah tov* (lit. "good lesson")—an anthology of selected easy passages from the Talmud along with commentaries from *Rashi, Tosaphot,* and *Maharsha.* See Nissenbaum, *Alei heldi,* 10.

99. This humiliating punishment is described in a variety of sources. See Sadan, *Ir va-em,* 79; Braver and Braver, *Zikhronot,* 234; *Belz,* 210; and Bergner, *Long Winter-Nights,* 62–63. See also Lifschitz, "Ha-heder," 327; Scharfstein, *Heder,* 127, 130–31; *EJD,* 9:463; and Kaufmann, *Zikhronot,* 20.

100. On the weekly examinations of heder students, see Lifschitz, "Ha-Heder," 321–22.

101. Such cases indeed happened. Yehudah-Leib Levin (Yehalel) tells us that his oldest brother died when he was six as a result of his melamed's beatings (Levin, *Zikhronot,* 37). The cruelties of the melamdim and the indifference with which these beatings were accepted by the community as part of everyday life are frequently mentioned in the memoir literature. See Maimon, *Autobiography,* 31–34; Gottlober, *Memoirs,* 1:66–67; Berman, *Al neharot,* 123–24; and Kaufmann, *Zikhronot,* 19–21. See also Lipschitz, *Me-dor le-dor,* 63; and Levitats, *Jewish Community in Russia,* 2:121.

102. *Tena'im* in the original (lit. "conditions"). Official contract in which the parents of the engaged couple specified the time and place of the wedding and their mutual financial commitments, generally the conditions and duration of the *kest,* the monetary worth of the dowry, and the specific property with which the couple was to be provided. The signing ceremony—today called the engagement ceremony—took place months, sometimes years, before the wedding. See Gottlober, *Memoirs,* 1:88–89; and Lilienblum, *Autobiography,* 1:88–90.

103. Shmaryahu Levin tells the exact same story about his sixteen-year-old uncle: "During the *heder* hours the news was suddenly brought to him that his wife had borne him his first child. But the messenger of the happy tidings found the new father, his nether garments down, lying across the bench, receiving the ministrations of his Rebbi. He was asked to dress himself at once and hurry home to his wife. But Ziskind, the Rebbi, met the situation coolly. He gravely requested the messenger to wait: 'Time enough,' he said. 'I'm not through yet' "(Levin, *Childhood in Exile,* 60–61).

104. Kotik refers to a well-known phenomenon: in most East European hed-ers—there was no instruction in writing. Writing was taught by scribes (Yiddish *shraybers*) who came to the homes of boys and girls after school hours and taught Yiddish or Russian writing skills. Sometimes the scribes established small classes in their own homes, where they also taught calligraphy and letter writing. See

Rakowski, *Lo nichna'ati,* 14; Scharfstein, *Heder,* 115–17; and chapter 20, note 27.

105. The weekly Torah portion was part of the heder curriculum. However, due to lack of time the portion was not studied in its entirety; rather, the pupils studied only the first few paragraphs of each portion.

106. The Hebrew Bible is called *Esrim ve-arba'ah* in Yiddish (lit. "Twenty-Four"), as it contains twenty-four books.

107. Bible study was indeed uncommon in traditional Eastern European Jewish society, especially in hasidic society, in which a fragmentary teaching of the Pentateuch generally sufficed. There were, however, heders in which the study of Prophets formed an important part of the curriculum (see, for example, Kasovich, *Our Years,* 8). On the overt and covert reasons why Bible study was considered heretical, see Parush, "Ha-ba'arut," 65–106. Compare chapter 26, following note 13.

108. A school year had two terms (Hebrew and Yiddish *zman,* lit. "time"), a winter term and a summer term, each of which lasted between four and six months, depending on how the Jewish holidays fell. See Lifschitz, "Ha-heder," 323–24.

109. Such a banquet, called *se'udat humash* (lit. "Pentateuch feast"), took place at the heder or in the family circle. See ibid., 357–59. On this custom's ancient roots in Ashkenazic society, see Marcus, *Rituals of Childhood.*

110. On these types of gendarmes (*dyesyatnikes*), see note 42 above. In the original text Kotik uses *klyutsch-voyt* to describe the bailiff (see note 33 above). As Deinard has written, "In the small towns there were no policemen and no police department and no government officials with the exception of one Christian who held the office of '*klyutsch-voyt*,' and his job was to imprison every evildoer, thief or murderer. He had no jail and he would lock up the sinner by placing his feet in a wide wooden pillory . . . and this sinner would sit in this officer's house until escorted to the district capital" (*Zikhronot,* 1:24).

111. Kotik uses the word "doctor" to refer to a medical doctor and the word *royfe* to refer to a healer without formal medical training. In Kotik's childhood Russian Jews were not allowed to study medicine—a right granted only in the 1860s—and this explains why most of the doctors came from the Polish gentry. See Lipschitz, *Me-dor le-dor,* 64–65.

112. This refers to *gehakte bankes,* that is, a method of medicinal cupping that involves making small incisions in the skin before applying the heated cup and allowing the suction to draw out blood. On cupping in the public bathhouse, see ibid., 52, 60.

113. Compare Mendele, *Collected Works,* 266.

114. On the custom of collecting money during Hanukkah from the villages in order to finance melamdim and other religious functionaries, see the sources in Rivkind, *Jewish Money,* 102–7.

115. On the bathhouse and its regulations, see Lipschitz, *Me-dor le-dor,* 49–53. On the associated folklore, see Mendele, *Collected Works,* 97–99.

116. Synagogue courtyard—Yiddish *shulhoyf.* As Lipshitz has described it, "Alongside of the synagogue stood the study house, and next to that more study houses called *kloyzn,* and in most of the towns the public bathhouse, within which was the ritual bath, and the *hekdesh* were situated there as well. This area was called the 'synagogue courtyard' " (*Me-dor le-dor,* 87). See also *Beit Yisrael be-Polin,* 1:65.

117. The statute of 1804, which established the legal status of Jews in tsarist Russia, legislated that all rabbis must subsist on only their salaries and forbade them to collect fees for performing any religious ceremonies (Ettinger, *Essays,* 256). In order to circumvent this law many communities had two budgets—one for the public record submitted to the authorities for confirmation and the other, a hidden one, where money was reserved for institutions or activities (such as bribery) not recognized by the authorities. For example, according to Tchernowitz, "In the budget presented to the government, the bathhouse always took first priority, apparently for the purposes of repairs and improvements. But, in fact, this money was used for the hiring of rabbis and for the purposes of bribing the government officials, so that grievous misfortunes might be avoided" (*Autobiography,* 67). See also Shochat, "Kahal," 195; and Rivkind, *Jewish Money,* 40.

118. *Draier*—lit. "three." A three-groshen copper coin worth one and a half kopecks. Jews in many towns and villages in the Pale of Settlement continued to keep their accounts based on the old Polish currency—gulden (*zloty*) and groshen—and consequently, they sometimes mixed these two different currencies together. See Chemerinsky, *Motele,* 59–60.

119. The poorhouse—*hekdesh* in the Yiddish original. A community-financed shelter, usually found on the outskirts of the town next to the bathhouse and considered a dirty and terrifying place. As Deinard has described it, it was "a house which was a disgrace among our people. In every small or big town, there was a house by that name that was used to accommodate itinerants and as a hospital. Upon arriving in town a poor wanderer knew that he should go to the *hekdesh* and when he fell ill he would find himself there. . . . The *hekdesh* was generally at the edge of the town or outside of its borders. Nobody cared for its upkeep and no one knew what went on inside" (*Zikhronot,* 1:64). See also Lipschitz, *Me-dor le-dor,* 49–51; and Levin, *Social and Economic Values,* 134.

120. Although not specified in Kotik's memoirs, the name of the Kamenets rabbi was Avraham Dov Halevi (d. 1866; on his death, see chapter 27). His wife was the granddaughter of Alexander Ziskind of Grodno. Some of his literary works were collected by his grandson and entitled *Zekher Avraham* (Nissenbaum, *Nahalat avot*); see also *Karnei or* (his son's introduction); and *Melitzei esh,* 15 Tishri, no.116.

121. Refers to Alexander Ziskind of Grodno (d. 1794). His book, *Yesod ve-shoresh ha-avodah* (lit. "The foundation and root of worship"), first published in Novidvor in 1782, is an ethical kabbalistic guide for proper daily behavior, prayer, and the appropriate way of observing the commandments. See Klausner, "He-hasid," 427–32; and Piekarz, *Beginning of Hasidism,* 51–53. The rabbi of Kamenets was not his son-in-law but his grandson-in-law.

122. Refers to Yekhezkel Halevi of Bobruysk (d. 1812), son of Shmuel Halevi of Minsk. His first wife was the Gaon of Vilna's daughter (her name is unknown). His second wife was the daughter of Simha Fried of Grodno. See *Karnei or* (introduction); and *Melitzei esh,* 29 Shevat, no. 297.

123. Elijah, the Gaon of Vilna (1720–97), known by the Hebrew acronym *Ha-Gra* (Ha-Gaon Rabbi Eliyahu), was one of the greatest spiritual personalities in Eastern European traditional Jewish society. His dedication to Torah study and his widespread Torah erudition made him a legend in his own lifetime. The Gaon also became known as one of the most bitter antagonists of Hasidism and the founder of

the adversarial movement (Mitnaggedism), with which most Lithuanian Jewry was affiliated. See Ben-Sasson, "The Gaon"; Nadler, *Mithnagdim;* Etkes, *The Gaon;* and *The Gaon of Vilna.*

124. Refers to Shmuel Halevi of Minsk, Yekhezkel of Bobruysk's father. He was the rabbi of the Minsk region and a fourth-generation descendent of the *Maharsha.* See *Karnei or* (introduction).

125. Pious and devoted Jews used to take upon themselves a life of wandering and deprivation (Hebrew *galut*) in order to expiate their own sins and the sins of the nation of Israel, which caused the exile of God.

126. A well-known Polish family of lords that possessed many holdings throughout Lithuanian Poland. Here Kotik is probably referring to the Lithuanian governor, Prince Karol Stanislaw Radziwiłł (1734–90). His brutal and impulsive character was portrayed in Maimon, *Autobiography*, 62–67.

127. Refers to Simha Fried of Grodno (d. 1813), Mordechai of Bobruysk's son. See *Melitzei esh,* 8 Elul, no. 192; and chapter 4, following note 7. For his epitaph, see *Ir giborim,* 68. Kotik's tale of the loans that he gave to Radziwiłł and the attempt to imprison him are not known from other sources and it is probable that Kotik's rendition reflects confusion with other texts, including the story of the *dzierżawce* (chief lessor), two powerful Jewish brothers from Slutsk who worked in the service of the duke Hieronim Radziwiłł, and were arrested in 1745 because of their large debts. See Halpern, *Eastern European Jewry,* 277–78; and Teller, "Słuck."

128. Only three of Yekhezkel's sons are known by name: Leyzer of Grodno (see chapter 4, note 2); Avraham Dov of Kamenets; and Yehoshua Segal of Warsaw (d. 1855; see Kotik, *Memoirs*, 2, chapter 4; *Melitzei esh,* 2 Shevat, no. 26).

129. This translates into the paltry salary of 150 rubles a year. For comparative data on the annual incomes of various professionals in the fields of commerce and services, see Levin, *Social and Economic Values,* 285–86 n. 39.

130. In Hebrew *maggid* (pl. *maggidim*), a term for preachers and admonishers who usually spoke in synagogues on moral and religious issues, calling for repentance and performance of good deeds. Large communities hired permanent preachers who were retained especially for the purpose of preaching in the main synagogue every Sabbath. Smaller communities usually hired itinerant preachers who drew their salaries after the Sabbath. See Piekarz, *Beginning of Hasidism,* 96–172. With the spread of Hasidism this profession declined; however, in the Lithuanian towns it continued throughout the nineteenth century, and itinerant preachers played an important role in spreading modern Jewish nationalism and Zionism. See Luz, *Parallels Meet,* 149–53.

131. Hebrew *meshorerim* (singers). On cantors and choirboys, see Lipschitz, *Me-dor le-dor,* 80–82.

132. The preacher's obligation to obtain the rabbi's permission to preach was based on an old regulation practiced in the Lithuanian communities. See *Pinkas medinat Lita,* 33, no. 130; 144, no. 596.

133. Yisrael Shkuder (1804–40)—little is known about him. His full name was Yisrael-Yaakov and his surname most probably stems from the town Skuodas (Kretinga district, Lithuania), where he served as a cantor. See Zaludkowski, *Liturgye,* 26–27; and Harris, *Hebrew Liturgical Music,* 410.

134. Baruch Karliner (d. 1871)—despite his inability to read music he was

considered one of the outstanding hasidic cantors of his day. He served as a cantor in his native town of Karlin and also in Kovno, Brisk, and Kamenets Podolsk. See Chemerinsky, *Motele,* 127–31; *EJD,* 2:106–7; Zaludkowski, *Liturgye,* 215–16; and Harris, *Hebrew Liturgical Music,* 418.

135. This custom of leave-taking was also reported by M. A. Günzburg, who told of his own leave-taking in 1810 of his native Lithuanian town of Salant. See idem, *Aviezer,* 67.

136. *Droshe geshank*—a gift bestowed for delivering a sermon. A term for the presents the young couple received from the wedding guests, ostensibly a fee for the sermon delivered by the groom. As Gottlober describes it, "In the meantime the groom delivers his sermon and everyone listens. Then the *badkhn* stands up and interrupts the groom in the middle of his speech and begins his own ridiculous rendition . . . after this jesting the *badkhn* announces: '*Droshe geshank*'! and all the guests, from the couples' parents through close and distant relatives and friends, present their gifts, some in gold, some in silver, and others in utensils, and the *badkhn* announces each giver's name" (*Memoirs,* 1:104).

137. The burial society—or *hevrah kadishah* (lit. "sacred society")—was a volunteer society which saw to all the needs of the deceased: ritual purification of the body, shrouds, the funeral ceremony, and the burial. Such a society was an integral part of every Jewish community, and the most respected members of the community were among its members as well, including the rabbi. It was the most prestigious and wealthy society in the community. See Katz, *Tradition and Crisis,* 133–40; and Mann, "Symbols," 153–62.

138. Mead (miód)—a sweet alcoholic drink made from fermented honey mixed with water. See Toussaint-Samet, *Food,* 34–37.

139. The burial society's annual feast usually took place on the 7th of Adar (there were communities where it was held on the 15th of Kislev) at the end of a fast day declared by society members. The custom of the triennial Hanukkah feast to which Kotik refers is not known from other sources. These feasts, including the enormous amount of food and drink consumed, were described in many literary works, including "An Ass's Burial" by Peretz Smolenskin, and "The Brave Pandrei" by Zalman Schneor. See Lipschitz, *Me-dor le-dor,* 63–64; and Deinard, *Zikhronot,* 1:66–67.

140. For explanations of the custom of placing the deceased on the floor, see Shperling, *Minhagim,* no. 1015; and Chayes, "Customs," 300–301. See also chapter 28, where the death of Kotik's grandmother is described.

141. The Angel Dumah—lit. "angel of silence," the angel who was in charge of *Sheol* (hell): "The dead cannot praise the Lord, nor any who go down into silence" (Ps. 115:17). On the heder pupils, whose heads were filled with superstitious imaginings, Günzberg states, "The children barraged me with stories about striking the corpse in the grave, the angel of death who is full of eyes, the angel Dumah who can awaken dead bodies from their sleep with his angry whip, angels of terror, devils, demons, evil spirits and Lillith, sorcerers and magicians, and more of such nonsense" (*Aviezer,* 13).

142. This motif—the deceased who has forgotten his name—is already found in medieval midrashic sources. See Zlotnik, "Nameless Ones," 217–25.

143. Refers to coins in circulation under Tsar Nicholas I. Kotik adds that those

were coins called *draiers* (three groshen) and *firers* (four groshen); see note 118 above.

144. The custom of giving charity at a funeral is ancient and its sources date back to the talmudic period. See Chayes, "Customs," 316; and Glick, *A Light Unto the Mourner*, 127–33.

CHAPTER 2

1. The Jewish community usually elected its leadership once a year. The triennial election and the official approval of those elected were mandated in the statute of 1804. See Shochat, "Kahal," 146–47; and Ettinger, *Essays*, 255–56, no. 50.

2. It was in the authorities' interest that all Jewish affairs be managed by reliable and trustworthy permanent representatives. For additional examples, see Shochat, "Kahal," 146–49.

3. In Russia, this term referred specifically to the government tax levied on alcohol. This tax was enacted in early 1850 by Tsar Nicholas I, and its collection was leased to the excise-man (*akciznikes*). See Lipschitz, *Zikhron Ya'akov*, 2:54–55; Mahler, *History*, 5:18–22; Shochat, "Günzburg," 317; and chapters 4 (following note 19) and 7 below.

4. In the absence of vineyards in Eastern Europe, alcoholic beverages—vodka, brandy, and beer—were usually made from barley or rye. The waste products of alcohol production were used as cow feed, and it was therefore common to raise cows in proximity to distilleries.

5. *Korobkeh* in the original (lit. "box"), a term for the indirect tax that Jewish communities in Russia levied on commercial transactions or food products, usually meat. Tax collection was leased from the Kahal and the income used to cover communal expenses, payment of government taxation, and charitable needs. See Halpern, *Eastern European Jewry*, 333–39.

6. *Kahal-shtub* in the original. A hall, usually in the synagogue complex, in which the meetings of the community elders were convened. See Lipschitz, *Me-dor le-dor*, 79.

7. From the sixteenth century, it was the custom among the pious to fast on the eve of the new moon, as this was considered a time conducive to the absolution of sins. This fast, called the "Minor Day of Atonement," usually ended after the afternoon prayers.

8. *Hatzot*, or *tikkun hatzot*, usually refers to an ancient custom involving rising at midnight in order to pray and mourn the destruction of Jerusalem and the Temple. It is possible, however, that in using the term *hatzot* Kotik meant the midday service of the "Minor Day of Atonement" (see previous note).

9. Semyatich (Siemiatycze)—about 60 kilometers west of Kamenets.

10. *Militaire-podriatchic* in the original (on this term, see *RHT*, 89). Jewish contractors and army suppliers, such as Yudl, were entrepreneurs who played important roles in the Russian economy, especially during the Napoleonic Wars (see, for example, Wengeroff, *Memoiren*, 1:9–10). During their stay in St. Petersburg to develop their connections with army and government officials, some also were able to intercede for the benefit of Jewish communities in the Pale of Settlement; see, for example, *EJD*, 9:74–75.

11. Beyle-Rashe is the Yiddish form of the name Bella [beautiful]-Rachel.

12. This refers to the official abolishment of the Kahal in 1844. For a detailed treatment, see Shochat, "Kahal."

13. Someone paid to fill out official forms, documents, or letters to be submitted to the authorities on behalf of individuals.

14. See BT *Pesahim* 49b: "An *am ha-aretz*, it is permitted to stab him [even] on the Day of Atonement which falls on the Sabbath."

15. See Stanislawski, *Nicholas and the Jews,* 161.

16. Deputies—a body established after the abolishment of the Kahal, comprised of the important householders of the community, who advised the *sborshchik* and assisted him in fulfilling his duties. See Shochat, "Kahal," 165–74.

17. On the district of Slonim (Grodno province), see Introduction, "Kamenets and Its Environs." The town of Slonim (Słonim) was situated about 150 kilometers northeast of Kamenets.

18. On the election of the *sborshchik* and the deputies, see Shochat, "Kahal," 174–75.

19. On the recruitment arrangements between Kamenets and Wysokie, see chapter 1, following note 9; on recruitment into the tsarist army, see chapter 9.

20. It was customary to invite the poor to a special feast during the wedding celebrations and to reserve special tables for them. The poor flocked especially to the weddings of the wealthy, where they could be assured of a hearty feast. See Trunk, *Poyln,* 1:97–103; and Kalish, *Etmoli,* 65.

21. On the musicians of Kobrin, see chapter 1, following note 59.

22. It is customary to arrange ceremonial feasts in honor of the newly married couple every evening of the week after the wedding ceremony. The seven benedictions of the marriage ceremony are again recited during the Grace after Meals.

CHAPTER 3

1. Kotik's dating is incorrect. This decree was in fact issued in 1835. Although Dubnow pointed out this error in his review of the book (*Evreiskaia starina* 6 [1913]: 413–14), it was not corrected in the second edition of Kotik's memoirs. On "panic" marriages, see Halpern, *Eastern European Jewry,* 289–309. Kotik's sympathetic-humorous account should be compared to other satiric-critical descriptions, such as Mendele's "Of Bygone Days," 285, 313–14, or Isaac Meir Dik's *"Ha-behalah asher haytah be-ir ha-heres,"* describing similar events in the town of Nesvizh (Vilna province). See Ginsburg, "Panic."

2. According to Eastern European Jewish custom only married men wore prayer shawls (tallit). Thus the just-married boy here had to wear a prayer shawl, but was exempt from putting on phylacteries (tefillin), as he was not yet thirteen, bar-mitzvah age, when the putting on of phylacteries became obligatory.

3. On Eastern European women's headdresses, see Frankel, "Costume," 50–57. The custom of a woman covering her hair for reasons of modesty dates back to talmudic times (see BT *Berakhot* 24a); however, according to Jewish law only married women are obligated to cover their hair. A bride's hair was usually cut the day after the wedding, although some had their hair cut before the wedding, prior to their immersion in the ritual bath. Since a girl's hair was left to grow from birth until

her marriage, this haircut became a traumatic event, described in many memoirs, novels, and stories. See, for example, Gottlober, *Memoirs,* 1:101; and Singer, *Yoshe Kalb,* 24–25.

4. Seclusion (*yihud*)—leaving the bride and groom alone in a closed room. The custom was to seclude the newlyweds immediately after the wedding, generally so that they could break their wedding day fast. Its main purpose was, however, to impart legal force to the marriage.

5. For reasons of modesty, Kotik used the letter "p," an abbreviation for *pishn* (urinate) in the original.

6. The weekly Torah reading is divided into seven portions. It was considered an honor to be called up for the sixth portion.

7. Playing with nuts on Passover is an ancient custom, whose origins are noted in BT *Pesahim* 109a: "It was related of Rabbi Akiba that he used to distribute parched ears [of corn] and nuts to children on the eve of Passover, so that they might not fall asleep but ask [the four questions]." See also Elzet, "Me-minhagei yisrael," 351.

8. The asking of the "four questions" is one of the most famous and beloved parts of the traditional Passover Seder. They are usually recited by the youngest child present.

9. In the Diaspora, an extra day—a "second festival day of the Diaspora"—is added to each of the biblical festival days (Passover, Shavuot, and Sukkot).

10. According to Jewish law, from age twelve a girl, with certain restrictions, is no longer considered a child and can be engaged to marry (Maimonides, *Code: Book of Women,* "Laws Concerning Marriage," 2:1–3). See chapter 5, following note 22.

11. Elsewhere the panic was of shorter duration—weeks or months. See Halpern, *Eastern European Jewry,* 306. Halpern estimated that during the panic of 1835 some twenty to thirty thousand people were married in the Pale of Settlement.

12. This daughter, Dvorah, married Berl-Bendet. See chapters 12 (following note 2) and 13 (beginning and end).

CHAPTER 4

1. About the rabbi of Kamenets, Avraham Dov Halevi, see chapter 1, following note 120.

2. Refers to Rabbi Eliezer Halevi of Grodno (d. 1853), son of Rabbi Yekhezkel of Bobruysk. In 1833, after the death of his father-in-law, Rabbi Hillel Fried, he served as a rabbinical judge (*dayan*) in Grodno. See *Melitzei esh,* 5 Adar, no. 62; and *Ir giborim,* 87–88.

3. Refers to Rabbi Hillel Fried of Grodno (d. 1833). From 1813, after the death of his father, Rabbi Simha, he served as *dayan* in Grodno (because of a controversy regarding the rabbinate, there were no rabbis in Grodno from 1818, only rabbinical judges. See *Ir giborim,* 55). His second marriage was to Esther, the daughter of Rabbi Hayyim of Volozhin. See also *Ir giborim,* 77–78; *Melitzei esh,* 2 Adar, no. 26; and Eliach, *Avi ha-yeshivot,* s.v. "Hillel Fried."

4. Rabbi Hayyim of Volozhin (1749–1821) was the Gaon of Vilna's most famous disciple, founder of the famous yeshiva in Volozhin, and one of the leading

Jewish scholars in Lithuania. See Stampfer, *Lithuanian Yeshiva*, 25–54; and Eliach, *Avi ha-yeshivot*, s.v. "Hayyim of Volozhin." After his death, his son Yitzhak assumed the post of head of the yeshiva.

5. Refers to Rabbi Eliezer-Yitzhak Fried of Volozhin (1809–53), son of Rabbi Hillel of Grodno. He married his niece Rivkah, Rabbi Yitzhak of Volozhin's daughter, inheriting his uncle's post as head of the rabbinical court and of the Volozhin yeshiva. See *Melitzei esh*, 19 Elul, no. 249; Stampfer, *Lithuanian Yeshiva*, 60, 66–72; and Eliach, *Avi ha-yeshivot*, s.v. "Eliezer-Yitzhak Fried."

6. Rabbi Yitzhak of Volozhin (1790–1849) was the son and student of Rabbi Hayyim of Volozhin, and replaced him as the head of the yeshiva. See Stampfer, *Lithuanian Yeshiva*, 55–66; and Eliach, *Avi ha-yeshivot*, s.v. "Yitzhak of Volozhin."

7. On Rabbi Yekhezkel of Bobruysk, Rabbi Shmuel of Minsk, and Rabbi Simha, son of Mordechai Fried (father of Rabbi Hillel and father-in-law of Rabbi Yekhezkel), see chapter 1, notes 120, 122, and 124.

8. On Rabbi Moshe Polier of Kobrin (d. 1858), see Kleinman, *Or yesharim*, 50–167; idem, *Mazkeret*, 189–98; Levin, *Zikhronot*, 32, 36–39; and Rabinowitsch, *Lithuanian Hasidism*, 169–83.

9. Shivah (lit. "seven"), the Hebrew term for the seven-day period of mourning for the death of an immediate family member. Orthodox Jews used to sit shivah as well for relatives who disgraced their family through deeds such as conversion to Christianity or, in radical mitnaggedic families, by joining a hasidic sect. See, for example, the case of two brothers from Brisk who fled to the rebbe of Neshkiz (Volhynia) and whose father sat shivah for them (*EJD*, 2:174–75).

10. Zelig was a local tavern keeper. His son, Berl-Bendet, married Aharon-Leyzer's eldest daughter (see chapter 12). The word *Andarkes*—probably Zelig's nickname—means women's woolen clothes. See *Dictionary of the Yiddish Language*, s.v. "andarek."

11. This case had a happy ending; others, however, ended badly. About a boy drawn to Moshe of Kobrin and his mitnaggedic father's declaration never to allow his son in his sight again, see *Pinkas Slonim*, 3:105.

12. Ze'ev (lit. "wolf") is the Hebrew name for Velvel.

13. Kotik was born in 1847, which means that his father Moshe was born in 1832 or 1833.

14. Arele of Kamenets (1810–66) was an important figure among the Kobriner and Slonimer hasidim (see also below, chapter 15, near note 20). Scant information on him is provided by his grandson, Moshe Hayyim Kleinman of Brisk, in his *Or yesharim*. It is worth noting Kleinman's adaptation from Kotik's memoir. See ibid., 62–63.

15. On Yekhezkel, the rabbi's son, see chapter 20.

16. On the importance of ritual bathing in Hasidism, see Wertheim, *Law and Custom*, 102–5, 215–16. On the importance of singing in Hasidism, see Geshuri, *Music and Dance*.

17. The name *Daitsch* (lit. "German"), refers to someone influenced by modern trends, at that time identified closely with modern German culture and lifestyle. It was also an expression used by traditional Jews for maskilim.

18. As mentioned above (chapter 1, note 25), this refers to a "general lease," which in this case meant a monopoly on the production and sale of vodka.

19. The excise tax, legalized in 1850, granted only to first guild merchants the right to lease taverns for a period of four years. In exchange they were required to pay the treasury a small tax on the vodka they sold. This new arrangement upset the former economic system, which had been based on small tavern keepers distributed over large areas, but also allowed for the rise of a new, though small, wealthy class. Thousands of Jewish families in the Pale of Settlement were involved in vodka leasing and associated spheres. The lessor (usually known as the *aktziznik* or the *otkupchik*), also exercised a certain amount of influence in the promotion of enlightenment and russification. Thus, he earned the hatred of members of the traditional Jewish society. Many descriptions of this type are found in the contemporary literature (see, for example, Gordon, *Collected Works,* 95; and Mendele, *Collected Works,* 234–36). See also Friedman, *Zikhronot,* 22; Tsherikover, *Yehudim,* 181–84; Slutsky, *Russian-Jewish Press,* 2:18–19; and Levin, *Social and Economic Values,* 88–89, 96, 105, 240–42. After the Crimean War, the excise was placed in the hands of a single lessor, Baron Joseph (Yozel) Günzburg, who retained this position until 1865. See chapter 7, note 1.

20. *Smotritel* in the original. See *RHT,* 130. On the excise inspectors appointed by the lessors, see Lipschitz, *Zikhron Ya'akov,* 2:54–55; and Dinur, *Mapu's Letters,* 36. For the memoirs of a Russian excise inspector who visited a brewery run by Jew in Lubavitch, see Mondshine, "Ha-tzadik mi-Lubavich."

21. The population registries (*skazka*) were intended to improve tax collection and to update the quota of army recruits each community was required to supply. Jews who were not legally registered and had no documents or papers were considered "hidden." See chapter 1, notes 6–8.

22. Kivke (Yiddish nickname for Akiva), Khatskl (Yekhezkel), Moshke (Moshe), and Berke (Ber), were Aharon-Leyzer's personal strongmen. See chapter 7.

23. Jews in different towns developed various cunning ruses to escape paying the excise tax. See, for example, Chemerinsky, *Motele,* 78.

24. The leftovers (*shirayim*) from the rebbe's own plate were much sought after by the hasidim, who tried to grab pieces of the food the rebbe had tasted. Those who succeeded in grabbing a crumb thought this a great honor. See Wertheim, *Law and Custom,* 252–54.

25. *Sochowisz* in the original. Kotik was probably referring to Neshkhiz (Niesuchojeże), at that time home to the zaddik Yitzhak (1790?-1868). See *Pinkas ha-kehillot: Poland,* 5:139; and chapter 22, note 7. On the various hasidic sects in Kamenets, see chapters 5 (Kotsk), 14 (Slonim and Karlin), 15, 20, and 24.

26. *Yahrzeit*—the annual memorial day for a close relative, on which special customs are observed, such as lighting a candle, reciting the kaddish prayer, studying portions from the Mishnah, and visiting the graveside. Hasidim are known for their fondness for commemorating the memorial days of zaddikim. On such days hasidim refrain from reciting *tahanun* (a daily prayer not recited on holidays) and hold a special feast. See Wertheim, *Law and Custom,* 252–54.

27. According to BT *Megillah* 13b, Moses was born and died on the seventh of Adar.

28. On the Ninth of Av, the congregants usually sat on the synagogue floor barefoot as a sign of mourning. This mischievous custom of pouring water on the floor is not known to me from any other sources.

29. *Berelekh* in the original. Children used to throw burrs at the congregants while the latter were reciting *kinot* (elegiac poems). This custom is well documented in the memoir literature; see, for example, Salzmann, *Min he-avar,* 73; and Levin, *Childhood in Exile,* 83.

30. The playful atmosphere on the Ninth of Av, so contradictory to the traditional mournful spirit of this day, indeed raised many eyebrows. As Yehudah-Leib Maimon remembers, "When I was six or seven years old, I also participated in this 'game,' but when I was nine years old I wondered about this strange custom and was ashamed of myself: how could it be possible that on such a day of mourning for the nation . . . children would play in front of our eyes with thorns and burrs, and none of the mournful congregants, among them important rabbis . . . would protest?" (*Lema'an tziyyon,* 1:103–4).

31. The Fifteenth of Av is an ancient joyous holiday. See M. *Ta'anit* 4:8: "There were no happier days for Israel than the fifteenth of Av and the Day of Atonement." This day, as well as the fifteenth of Shevat, marked the last days of the term in the heder and the yeshiva before the summer and winter recess, respectively. See Hannover, *Abyss of Despair,* 112.

32. *Selihot* (lit. "forgiveness")—special penitential hymns, recited mainly (according to the Ashkenazic custom) during the week before Rosh Hashanah and during the Ten Days of Penitence between the New Year and Yom Kippur. The recitation of *selihot* begins on the Saturday night preceding Rosh Hashanah.

33. Lit. "Rejoicing of the 'drawing of water.'" A festivity held during the intermediate days of Sukkot, in commemoration of an ancient water ceremony celebrated in the Jerusalem Temple.

CHAPTER 5

1. Kotsk (Kock)—a Polish town about 50 kilometers northeast of Lublin, where the zaddik Menahem-Mendel Morgenstern (1787–1859) resided. The Kotsker rebbe was one of the most fascinating personalities of nineteenth-century Polish Hasidism. His many followers abandoned their families and lived near their charismatic rebbe for long periods of time. The lifestyle of Kotsker hasidim provoked a great deal of criticism, even within hasidic circles. The radical demands they made on themselves caused their numbers to dwindle and gave rise to many splinter groups, especially against the background of the rebbe's seclusion (around 1840) and his severing of all contact with the outside world.

2. According to Jewish law, a daughter does not inherit equally with sons. Sarah-Beyle probably received a promissory note of inheritance at her wedding, called *shtar hatzi zachar* (lit. "half-male promissory note"). In this note, common practice among Ashkenazi Jewry at least since the fourteenth century, the father promised his daughter that after his death she would inherit her share along with her brothers, at the rate of half of their portion. See Yuval, *Scholars in Their Time,* 29–32.

3. *Shovavim tat* in the original, a Hebrew acronym for the first eight portions of the book of Exodus, enumerated in the text. Both pious individuals and sinners who wished to repent would fast every Monday and Thursday during the weeks when these portions were read (usually January-February).

4. *Omer*—a biblical commandment (Lev. 23:15–16) to count forty-nine days from the second night of Passover until Shavuot (the Feast of Weeks). According to Jewish law women are exempt from this duty, thus we have here an example of an especially pious woman who goes beyond the letter of the law.

5. Both books were intended primarily for a female readership. *Taytsh-khumash:* an edition of the Pentateuch where the Hebrew text is followed by a translation (Yiddish: *taytsh*) into Yiddish. *Tse'enah u-re'enah* (lit. "go out and see")—a popular didactic book in Yiddish written by Yaakov Ashkenazi of Janov, which presents midrashic commentaries on the weekly Torah reading in simple story form. Because of its prose style and nature, this book became widely popular, among women especially. It was first published in the late sixteenth century, and up until the present has appeared in more than two hundred editions. Women's reading of this book during the Sabbath became a widespread custom in Eastern Europe. See Shmeruk, *Yiddish*, 115–17.

6. See chapter 1, note 88.

7. *Pshetlekh* and *shpitslekh* in the original. On *pshetlekh*, see chapter 1, note 81. *Shpitslekh* are also clever explanations of talmudic issues.

8. Siedlce is a Polish town about 95 kilometers east of Warsaw.

9. This question seems unclear and must be missing some details. Kotik probably wanted to demonstrate Yisrael's mathematical abilities *ad absurdum*, presenting him as someone who could answer even meaningless mathematical questions.

10. On the 1863 uprising see chapter 1, note 64, and chapters 13 and 21–22 below. Even though Jews in general tried not to openly identify with one side or another, there were in fact many Jews like Yisrael who were swept up in the wave of Polish patriotism. On the manifestations of Jewish-Polish brotherhood in those years, see Dubnow, *Jews in Russia*, 2:177–83; Gelber, *Polnische Aufstand;* Shatzky, "Yidn," 423–68; and Duker, "Polish Insurrection," 144–53. For a comprehensive article, which makes use of Kotik's memoirs, see Fajnhauz, "Ludność żydowska." On the uprising as reflected in Jewish and Polish literature, see Altbauer, "Revolt," 27–36 (on Kotik: 33–34); and Opalski and Bartal, *Brotherhood.*

11. Louis Napoleon III (1808–73), the nephew of Napoleon I Bonaparte, was elected president of the Republic of France in 1848 and crowned emperor in 1852. He fought against Russia in the Crimean War and strengthened France's standing as a world power.

12. Pesah Kaplan (1870–1943) was a Hebrew and Yiddish writer and journalist. See *LNYL*, 8:98–100.

13. Kotik mentioned that in his youth he knew about two hundred hasidic melodies, most of which he did not like, except for Yisrael's tunes that always moved him (Kotik, *Memoirs*, 2, chap. 2).

14. On 3 May 1791, after the first partition of Poland (1772), the Polish parliament approved a constitution, which is considered the first modern constitution ratified in Europe. This constitution was nullified by Parliament after the second partition (1793).

15. Czemeryn was a small village next to Kamenets. See *Słownik*, 1:792.

16. Most probably refers to Prince Ireneusz Kleofas Ogiński (1808–63), son of a famous aristocratic family from the Vilna region; see *Słownik Biograficzny,*

610–11. On his positive attitude toward the Jews in Retovo (Kovno province), a town which belonged to him, see *Ha-karmel* (1862), no. 11, 162. Kotik's naming of Oginski as the rebel leader in Lithuania is apparently incorrect. This is not mentioned in Polish sources. See Altbauer, "Revolt," 34 n. 7. On his escape to Pinsk, see chapter 21, following note 19.

17. At the outbreak of the uprising, Prince Nicholas Michael Muravyov (1791–1866), known as the "hangman," was appointed governor-general of the Vilna, Grodno, Kovno, Vitebsk, Minsk, and Moghilev provinces. He established his headquarters in Vilna and cruelly suppressed the uprising through brutal terror and forced russification. See *Cambridge History of Poland*, 380–86, and chapters 13 (following note 4) and 21 (following note 16) below.

18. The drinking of this strange concoction—a tried and true remedy for hangovers—is a documented custom among Ruzhiner hasidim, mentioned by the zaddik, Avraham-Yaakov of Sadgora, Yisrael of Ruzhin's son: "I remember that in Ruzhin it was the custom to drink mead with olive oil at the holy table on the last day of Hanukkah . . . and I remember that in my childhood with my holy father of blessed memory, this custom was a duty . . . only later when there was wine there was no more need for this drink" (*Emet le-Ya'akov*, 89).

19. A son to recite the mourner's prayer (*kaddish yatom*) after his death.

20. According to BT *Kidushin* 41a, "one may not give his daughter in betrothal when a minor, [but must wait] until she grows up and says 'I want so-and-so,'" but the reality was that parents of the social and economic elite did betroth their children at a very young age (see *Tosaphot*, ad loc., "*Assur*": "And we are now used to betrothing our daughters, even minors, because the exile is becoming more difficult from day to day"). However, in order to avoid infringing on Jewish law, the actual betrothal ceremony was celebrated only after the onset of puberty (twelve-and-a-half for girls, thirteen for boys). In Polish Jewish society very early marriages were common and attested to from the late eighteenth century: "There in Poland marriages of children are very common" (*Noda bi-yehudah*, part two, *Even ha-ezer*, par. 54). See Katz, "Marriage," 21–54; and Goldberg, "Marriage," 3–39. During the nineteenth century, early marriage was a main motif in maskilic criticism of traditional Jewish society. See Stampfer, "Early Marriage," 76–77; and chapter 20, note 1 below.

21. This refers to Miedzyrzec Podlaski in Poland, 88 kilometers north of Lublin, and not to the famous town in Volhin.

22. This account's reliability is questionable, as the Kotsker rebbe was in seclusion during that period and refused to receive any of his hasidim.

23. The term *kest* usually refers to the groom, who receives full board and lodgings at his wife's parents' home (see chapter 1, note 49). In this instance, however, since the groom's father was wealthier, the couple received their *kest* there.

24. Yisrael composed special melodies in honor of the zaddik Avraham of Slonim's visit to Kamenets (Kotik, *Memoirs*, 2, chapter 2). He also composed a Cossack march for the wedding of the zaddik Asher of Stolin (the second)'s daughter, which was sung every year on Simhat Torah in the hasidic *shtibl* in Kamenets (ibid., chapter 18; *EJD*, 2:104).

25. An approbation (*haskamah*) was a letter of approval important rabbis

granted to an author in which they praised him and his book, declared his copyright, and called upon the public to purchase the book. Despite a continuous decline in the importance of approbations, a book printed without one was considered suspicious. See Halpern, *Eastern European Jewry,* 78–107.

26. Refers to Rabbi Yehoshua Yitzhak Shapira (1801–72), known as Eizel Harif. He served as a rabbi in Slonim from 1852 and was known for his scholarship and sharp tongue. He was miserly in the granting of approbations, and many witticisms have been linked to him in this context. See Levin, *Harif,* 139–47.

27. Rabbi Menahem Mendel of Kotsk died in 1859, so Kotik is evidently referring to his eldest son and successor, Rabbi David of Kotsk (1809–73). In any case, it is difficult to believe that the zaddik traveled to Yisrael's deathbed, because Kotsk was a considerable distance from Warsaw.

CHAPTER 6

1. For a similar use of this expression, see Chayes, "Customs," 285.

2. Selling of shares in the world to come is a well-known motif in Jewish folklore. For examples, see Sadan, *Egozim,* 50–52. See also documents and signed testimonies from the nineteenth century in *Pinkas Slonim,* 4:403–4; and Beit-Halevi, *Vaks,* 104–5.

CHAPTER 7

1. Baron Yozel (Joseph) Günzburg (1812–78)—progenitor of three generations of bankers and intercessors on behalf of Jews living in the Pale of Settlement. During the 1840s he made a fortune as the excise lessee of the liquor monopoly for all of Russia. In 1857 he moved to Paris, from whence he continued to manage his business in Russia. In 1859 he established a bank in St. Petersburg which was one of the major credit suppliers in Russia and which financed large development projects such as railroads, mines, and the like. He was one of the founders of the society for the promotion of Enlightenment among the Jews of Russia (1863) and lent financial support to its activities. His son Naphtali Herz (Horace) was awarded a title of nobility in 1871, and he himself received one in 1874. See Ginsburg, *Historishe verk,* 2:117–59; Shochat, "Günzburg."

2. The collection of the excise tax passed into the hands of Yozel Günzburg in 1857, after the Crimean War. See Lipschitz, *Zikhron Ya'akov,* 2:55.

3. For example, Mattityahu, the writer Avraham Mapu's brother (see Dinur, *Mapu's Letters,* s.v. "Baron Joseph Günzburg"), or Pauline Wengeroff's father-in-law (Wengeroff, *Memoiren,* 2:81–82). See also chapter 4, note 19.

4. A contemporary estimate according to which nearly eight thousand Jews were employed in the excise business seems inflated. See Tsherikover, *Yehudim,* 181–84. In his memoirs, Avraham Yaakov Paperna notes that Baron Günzburg's clerks made an annual profit of between four hundred and five hundred rubles— proportionately more than other Jews' incomes. See Ginsburg, *Historishe verk,* 2:122–23; Levin, *Social and Economic Values,* 285–86 n. 39.

5. *Ben yakhid* in the original (lit. "only son"), but in the present context only child. The expression also implies a special relationship and treatment.

CHAPTER 8

1. *Dardakei-melamed* in the original (lit. "teacher of small children"). This was the common name for the entry level of the heder system, which concentrated on teaching the Hebrew alphabet. On Yaakov-Ber, see chapter 1, following note 97.

2. *Belfer* in the original (lit. "helper"). His basic responsibility was to escort the children to and from the heder. This was considered a low-status position, and those who held this post were stereotyped as stupid and mean-spirited. See Gottlober, *Memoirs,* 1:66–70.

3. Refers to the Hebrew alphabet, where the difference between the possible pronunciations of the second letter, *beys* (pronounced *bo* and *vo*), and the sixth letter, *vav* (pronounced *voo*) with the long vowel *komets,* may not be distinguished by the young ear. This technique, rote recitation of the letter and the vowel, was typical of all heders and caused didactic difficulties. See Lifschitz, "Ha-heder," 352–54; and Bialik, "Alphabet."

4. Compare to a similar dialogue between the young Solomon Maimon and his father, as found in Maimon, *Autobiography,* 65–66.

5. Refers to the biblical commentary composed by Rabbi Shlomo Yitzhaki (acronym: *Rashi;* 1040–1105), which was the most popular and widely studied basic commentary in the heder.

6. Every Thursday the melamed reviewed the material studied throughout the week, in preparation for the exam he would give on Saturday in the boys' homes. See chapter 1, note 100.

7. For a more comprehensive treatment of Yisrael Vishniak, see chapter 16.

8. *Ha-mafkid* (lit. "he who entrusts")—the third chapter of BT *Bava Metziah.*

9. *Hai* (lit. "life")—an acronym spelled from the letters *het* and *yod,* which in Hebrew numerology equals eighteen.

10. Many ethical and kabbalistic books contain descriptions of the various sections of Hell. Some of these books, such as Elijah de Vidas's *Reshit hokhmah,* or Zvi-Hirsch Koidanover's *Kav ha-yashar,* were translated into Yiddish and enjoyed a wide distribution, and the melamed apparently gleaned his tales from them. Such stories were widespread among Lithuanian Jewry: "We would tell each other tales without end: about Paradise below and Paradise above, about Hell, the Dark Mountains, and the Sambatyon . . . about marine creatures, demons and spirits and transmigration of souls, things that made one's hair stand on end and set your very soul atremble" (*Lithuanian Jewry,* 1:612).

11. The series of torments the deceased suffers in his grave, mainly from the blows administered by the angels of destruction. Ethical and kabbalistic books devoted many pages to this topic, and special tracts such as *Hibut ha-kever* and *Masekhet gehenom* treat these matters in detail. These tracts are also found in the *Zohar,* in *Reshit hokhmah* (*Sha'ar ha-yir'ah,* chapters 12–13), and elsewhere. See Zlotnik, "Nameless Ones," 217–25. On *hibut ha-kever* suffered by the righteous, see Shperling, *Minhagim,* 438.

12. See the end of chapter 1.

13. According to M. *Eduyot* 2:10: "The judgment of the wicked in hell [endures] twelve months."

14. See *Reshit hokhmah,* 1:246–47.

15. A Hebrew phrase paralleling the seven liberal arts, the traditional medieval curriculum of secular learning. Metaphorically, it refers to one who is well versed in universal knowledge. The myth regarding the enormous secular knowledge of the Gaon, begun during his lifetime, was inflated after his death by Orthodox and maskilic authors, with each group using it to its own advantage. See Etkes, *The Gaon,* 44–83.

16. On the possible source for this story, see *Aliyot Eliyahu,* 234.

17. This story is probably based on the Gaon's purported knowledge of the "musical arts." See *Pe'at ha-shulhan,* 5a.

18. In Lithuanian mitnaggedic society, the stories praising the Gaon—both oral and written—served the same purpose as the hagiographic literature surrounding the Ba'al Shem Tov and the other hasidic zaddikim did for Hasidism. See Lilienblum, *Autobiography,* 1:90–92, 99, where he recounts his fondness for stories about the Gaon. One example of such a hagiographic work is *Aliyot Eliyahu.* On the place of magic and sorcery in traditional Eastern European Jewish society, see Etkes, "Magic," 69–104.

19. *Shul-rufer* in the original, i.e., "synagogue crier." Refers to the beadle, whose duties—particularly in small towns—were connected to the upkeep of the synagogue; errands on behalf of the community's leaders, such as delivering messages and announcing the beginning of the Sabbath or the arrival of a maggid in town; as well as the waking of people for prayers and *selihot* by rapping on the windows of their houses with a hammer and crying *in shul arayn!* (Get into the synagogue!). See Chemerinsky, *Motele,* 38–40.

20. Imaginary creatures, half-human and half-fish.

21. Embedded in this tale is the kabbalistic-mystical concept of metempsychosis, in which sinners' souls may return to earth, even in animals' bodies. Metempsychosis as an animal purportedly effected repentance for serious sins. See Scholem, *Kabbalah,* 344–50; idem, *Symbolism,* 334–37; and Nigal, *Magic,* 67–133.

22. Once again, the background is the concept of metempsychosis. See *In Praise of the Ba'al Shem Tov,* 218–19; *Lithuanian Jewry,* 1:603.

23. Shereshov (Szereszów)—a town in Grodno province, about 34 kilometers northeast of Kamenets. See *Pinkas ha-kehillot: Poland,* 5:318–20.

24. In his story "The Fathers and the Sons," Mendele relates a similar tale about a Jewish woman who turns to a gypsy witch for help in bringing her husband back to her, and indeed that very night he returns home, riding on the end of a poker and holding a broom in his hand. See Mendele, *Collected Works,* 24.

25. Tallow—the harder fat of sheep, cattle, and pigs, whose ingestion is forbidden by biblical injunction (Lev. 3:17) but may be used to manufacture soap, candles, and the like.

26. See *Reshit hokhmah,* 1:247; Kasovich, *Our Years,* 41; and Lieberman, "Sin."

27. Refers to Doctor Lassovski and Yoshke the healer, mentioned in chapter 1, following note 110.

28. A term meaning possession of a living person's body by spirits of the dead or demonic forces. The dybbuk phenomenon—both in Jewish society (from its reflection in the kabbalistic concept of metempsychosis to the well-known play

by S. An-Sky) and in non-Jewish society—was widely known and accepted as a form of insanity. Most of the dybbuk stories from Eastern Europe originated in hasidic circles. See Scholem, *Kabbalah*, 349–50; Nigal, *Dybbuk*; and Bilu, "Dybbuk."

29. *Avarodek* in the original. Refers to Novogrodek (Nowogródek), about 120 kilometers southwest of Minsk. The dybbuk tale referred to here probably occurred in 1848, and is known from other sources, which present different versions. The main version is found in a Yiddish booklet *Ma'aseh nora'ah* (Warsaw 1911), which places the event in a village near Stolovitz (Stolbtsy), about sixty kilometers southeast of Novogrodek. See Sadan, "Anshei Mirmah," 224; Nigal, *Dybbuk*, 146–62. The story was first recorded in 1849 by Yisrael Solomon Zalman Katz, a ritual slaughterer in Shereshov. Interestingly, the latter was none other than the uncle of Arele of Kamenets, Moshe Kotik's teacher and rabbi. See Kleinman, *Or yesharim*, 62.

30. Special incantations were written for exorcism ceremonies, ordering the dybbuk to exit "according to the commands of the holy angels."

31. Refers to Rabbi Yaakov-Meir Padva (1797–1855), head of the rabbinical court in Brisk from 1840 until his death. See Feinstein, *Ir tehilah*, 221.

32. The participation of the rabbis of Kamenets and Brisk in the exorcism described here is doubtful, but seems to be one of the many tales connected to this dybbuk that "Lithuania was in turmoil over," according to Kotik. Lithuanian rabbis, as opposed to hasidic zaddikim, generally did not deal with dybbuk exorcism, and similar cases are almost unheard of (see, however, Nigal, *Dybbuk*, 186–96).

33. On a dybbuk's exit via the little toe of the left foot, see Nigal, *Dybbuk*, 188–89, 195, 243.

34. *Kaf ha-kelah* in the original (1 Sam. 25:29). The middle of the sling—as opposed to the bundle of life (*tzror ha-hayyim*)—is interpreted in the Talmud (compare BT *Shabbat* 152b) and the *Zohar* as the site where evil souls on their way to Hell were tortured, and as a place where the sinner's soul was thrown from one side of the world to the other.

35. Probably refers to the zaddik Mordechai (the second) of Lachovich, who, from 1832, led a hasidic community in Lyakhovichi, about sixty kilometers east of Slonim. See Rabinowitsch, *Lithuanian Hasidism*, 150–61.

Chapter 9

1. The recruitment decree for Jews, first enacted in 1827 by Tsar Nicholas I, remained in effect until abolished by Tsar Alexander II on 26 August 1856. Kotik was eight years old in 1855, at the height of the Crimean War, and he refers here to the decree issued in July 1853 expanding the recruitment quota for Jews to ten instead of seven Jews out of a thousand, and granting permission to kidnap anyone without a legal passport and turn him over to the army. See Shochat, "Günzburg," 307–18; and Stanislawski, *Nicholas and the Jews*, 30, 184. On the recruitment system, see *RHT*, 115. Kidnapping of Jewish children during the Crimean War (1853–56) is well documented in many memoirs. See, for example, Levin, *Zikhronot*, 30–35; Friedberg, "Zikhronot"; Paperna, "Ka-afikim ba-Negev," 440–50; and Zunser, *Works*, 2:673–84. On forced recruitment to the tsar's army in light of memoir literature, see Levin, *Kantonistn*, 119–212; and Ofek, "Cantonists," 153–78.

2. According to the law, recruitment of boys younger than twelve was not

permitted; however, eight-year-olds and up were kidnapped and passed off as adults. See Baron, *Russian Jew,* 30. See also the description of Jewish cantonists by the famous Russian thinker Alexander Herzen: "They brought the children and formed them into regular ranks: it was one of the most awful sights I have ever seen, those poor, poor children! Boys of twelve or thirteen might somehow have survived it, but little fellows of eight and ten. . . . Not even a brush full of black paint could put such horror on canvas" (*Memoirs,* 170).

3. Although the conversion of Jews was never formally articulated as a policy goal, that was in fact the aim of the recruitment system. There are no accurate statistical data regarding Jewish conversion rates; however, it appears that as opposed to Kotik's view, the number was relatively high. About half of the seventy thousand Jews who were forcibly recruited from 1827 to 1855 converted, among them about twenty-five thousand children under the age of eighteen. See Stanislawski, *Nicholas and the Jews,* 25; and idem, "Apostasy," 193–94. Despite the fact that during the thirty years the recruitment decree was in effect no more than seventy thousand Jews were recruited—a low number, given the size of the Jewish population in the Pale of Settlement (about three million)—this was an unforgettably traumatic period in the history of Russian Jewry. On the recruitment policy and its consequences, see Dubnow, *History of the Jews,* 153–61; Levin, *Kantonistn;* Ginsburg, *Historishe verk* 3:3–135; Levitats, *Jewish Community in Russia,* 1:68–78, 2:36–44; Mahler, *History,* 122–38; Baron, *Russian Jew,* 29–32; and Stanislawski, *Nicholas and the Jews,* 13–34.

4. "Cantonist" was a term coined for children who were kidnapped for pre-army service. These boys lived in army camps (cantons), which served as schools for the soldiers' children. They lived in extremely difficult physical conditions and under strict discipline, aimed chiefly at forcing them to convert.

5. See chapter 1, note 84.

6. Under the quota system, Jewish communities were forced to provide fixed numbers of recruits, with the *sborshchik* and the elders held personally responsible for fulfilling this obligation. When volunteers were not found, the elders preferred to forcibly recruit either "negative" or weak elements in the community (such as itinerants, the poor, orphans, the violent, Sabbath desecraters, etc.). This brutal and discriminatory policy, which peaked in 1854 (when some 7,500 Jews were recruited), provoked a great deal of social tension, resentment, and criticism of the elders.

7. The recruitment system legislated that the child recruit remain in the canton until reaching the proper age for official military service—eighteen years old. From the age of eighteen he was drafted for another twenty-five years; the years previously spent in the canton did not count as part of the required service.

8. Refers to the provinces east of the Jewish Pale, where Jewish settlement was forbidden. Herzen, for example, (see note 2 above) met Jewish cantonists in the environs of the town of Perm, in the foothills of the Urals.

9. Saratov—a town on the banks of the Volga River, outside of the Jewish Pale of Settlement. The Jewish community there was established in the second quarter of the nineteenth century by veterans of Nicholas's army.

10. Arye-Leyb is the "only child"; see chapter 7, note 5.

11. The cantonists' decree, that is, the discriminatory recruitment of the

Jews, was abolished in a special manifest issued by Tsar Alexander II on his coronation day, 26 August 1856. The terms of Jewish recruitment were now equivalent to those for the rest of the population.

12. Kotik is imprecise here. Permission to kidnap an individual without a passport instead of registered townsmen was granted earlier, in July 1853; however, the kidnappings reached their peak during the Crimean War period. In September 1854 Baron Günzburg wrote to Nicholas I: "Already in the last recruitment there were not enough youngsters in many communities to satisfy all the requirements of the recruitment laws; only the permission given to every Jew to kidnap a co-religionist from another town who had no passport and hand him over instead of a family member saved him from the responsibility for filling the deficit in the number of recruits" (Shochat, "Günzburg," 316). This decree was abolished by Alexander II in August 1856.

13. On violent resistance to recruitment, see Tsherikover, *Yehudim*, 109–16.

14. In 1874 the entire recruitment system underwent a comprehensive reform. See chapter 1, note 7.

15. The term "hangman" refers to the regime of the last Russian tsar, Nicholas II, who ruled from 1894 to 1917. Kotik is probably referring here to the brutally oppressive measures enacted by the government (under Prime Minister P. A. Stolypin) from 1906 to 1911 to stamp out potential revolutionaries by means of mass murder.

16. See above, following note 6.

CHAPTER 10

1. On the troublemakers of Zastavye who never accepted Kotik's family's leadership, see chapters 1–2.

2. About this *sborshchik,* who replaced Aharon-Leyzer, see chapter 2, following note 18, where Kotik presents another version regarding the circumstances surrounding his grandfather's reassumption of this post.

3. *Kittel*—a white linen robe worn on the High Holidays as well as by bridegrooms under the wedding canopy, also used for shrouds. On its source, see A. Druyanow's note to Elzet, "Me-minhagei yisrael," 357–58; and Prylucki, *Dos gevet,* s.v. *"kitl."*

4. This ritual was deliberately designed to resemble the traditional excommunication ceremony, whose origins lay in the geonic period (see *Teshuvot ha-geonim* [Lyck, 1864], no. 10).

5. See Baron, *Russian Jew,* 108–9.

6. The tax on the sale of cattle hides was traditionally part of the meat tax (*korobkeh*) subleased by the community. See chapter 2, note 5; and Shmeruk, "Hasidic Ritual Slaughter," 54.

7. For more about Twersky, see chapter 15, following note 19.

8. *Hamon* in the original, a Yiddish term for the simple people—those belonging to the lowest socioeconomic level, that is, the poor and usually unemployed.

9. Although formally subjects of the Russian regime, most Polish Jews could neither speak nor understand Russian (see Deinard, *Zikhronot,* 1:126–27). This state of affairs changed from the 1860s with the increasing russification of Polish Jews.

10. This lord is mentioned again in chapter 12. His estate was four versts from Kamenets. See chapter 22, following note 9.

11. This estate was located some kilometers northeast of Kamenets, near Zastavye. Kotik's aunt and her family lived there later. See Kotik, *Memoirs,* 2, chapter 1.

12. The Russian serfs were liberated in 1861; the Polish rebellion was suppressed during 1863 and 1864.

13. See chapter 22, following note 9.

CHAPTER 11

1. Leyzer was appointed rabbi in Grodno in 1833. On his family lineage see chapter 4, notes 2–7.

2. On this strict code of modesty adhered to by the ultrapious, see Kalish, *Etmoli,* 40.

3. On scholarly women of this sort in Lithuania, see Epstein, *Mekor Barukh,* 4:1948–77.

4. The two most important sections of the morning prayer service.

5. Refers to Aharon-Leyzer's request that the rabbi of Kamenets arrange the match or else be run out of town. See the beginning of chapter 4.

6. On this book, written by Alexander Ziskind of Grodno, who was Kotik's mother's great-grandfather, see chapter 1, note 121.

7. *Hovot ha-levavot* (lit. "duties of the hearts")—a philosophical-ethical book written by Bahya ibn Paquda (Spain, eleventh century) concerning how a person is to fulfill his obligations to God, here subsumed mainly in virtuous and well-mannered behavior. This book's popularity is attested to by its repeated printings, including in Yiddish translation.

8. *Menorat ha-ma'or* (lit. "candelabrum of light")—a fundamental Jewish ethical-homiletical tract, written by Isaac Aboab (Spain, fourteenth century), a compilation of homilies and legends arranged topically (Torah study, repentance, etc.). Also a popular book, it was printed in many editions, including in Yiddish translation (first edition: Amsterdam, 1722), and became an important source shaping the worldview of women and simple folk to whom the Hebrew original was inaccessible.

9. Kotik referred to this match earlier. See chapter 4, following note 17.

10. *Sefer hasidim* (lit. "book of the pious")—a compendium of ethical homilies and sayings edited mainly by Yehudah ben Shmuel he-Hasid of Regensburg (d. 1217) that encapsulates the religious and social ideals of the twelfth- to thirteenth-century circle of Ashkenazic pietists. It guided the reader toward rigorous observance of the commandments and the moral values of Judaism. This book, an important source shaping the values of Ashkenazic Jewry as a whole for centuries, was translated and printed in Yiddish several times from the eighteenth century.

11. This epigram refers to one who is inefficient, or slow. Although the source of this particular saying is obscure, many popular sayings combine inefficient wives and cats; see, for example, "when the housewife is a *shlimazel*—the cat is a woman of valor" (*Jüdische Sprichwörter,* 34, no. 469).

CHAPTER 12

1. Berl-Bendet is the Yiddish form for the Hebrew name Dov-Baruch; Bendet is a shortened form of the Latin Benedictus.

2. See chapter 3, note 12.

3. This estate was about three miles northeast of Kamenets, halfway between Kamenets and Shereshov. See chapter 22, following note 3.

4. On the negative image of village Jews as ignorant and simpleminded, see Lipschitz, *Me-dor le-dor*, 94–95.

5. Potatoes were a main ingredient in vodka production.

6. On beer production and the connection between the brewery and cows, see chapter 2, following note 4.

7. On the enlightened merchant who used technical journals in order to familiarize himself with economic trends and to succeed in his business, see Levin, *Social and Economic Values*, 145.

CHAPTER 13

1. On Shepsl and his band, see chapter 1, following note 59.

2. This phrase was used to threaten little children, as a means of cautioning them to behave properly or else the satanic Jew would come and kidnap them. See Cohen, *Shpola*, 19.

3. Refers to the rebellion of 1863. See chapter 5, note 10.

4. For more about Muravyov, see chapter 5, note 17, and chapter 21, following note 16.

CHAPTER 14

1. Village Jews, who did not have a chance to pray in a quorum during the year, used to travel—especially for the High Holidays—to the nearest town, in order to pray with the community and to hear the blowing of the shofar. This phenomenon is extensively documented in the memoir literature; see Lipschitz, *Me-dor le-dor*, 94; Levin, *Childhood in Exile*, 87–88; and Kotik, *Memoirs, 2*, chapter 8.

2. Piroshki—Fruit-, cheese-, potato-, or meat-filled pockets of dough. See Kosover, *Food and Beverages*, 115–16.

3. Because of the biblical prohibition against counting the Israelites (see Rashi on Exod. 30:12), it was the custom to count indirectly, such as "not one, not two," and so on.

4. On Kotik's father's travels to his rebbe on Rosh Hashanah, see chapter 24 and chapter 29, note 39.

5. The number of strokes should be forty less one, in commemoration of the ancient custom of thirty-nine punitive lashes administered by the Sanhedrin to sinners (M. *Makot* 3:10; *Kitzur shulhan arukh*, chap. 131, par. 11). See, for example, Maimon's discription: "Of this kind, for example, was the *Malkoth* (Beating) before Yom Kippur, in which every Jew lays himself on his face in the synagogue, while another with a narrow strip of leather gives him thirty-nine lashes" (*Autobiography,* 83). See also Paperna, "Ka-afikim ba-Negev," 443–44.

6. While being flogged, the penitent recited confessional prayers, including a prayer enumerating his sins, during which he beat his breast for each sin.

7. On this custom, see *Kitzur shulhan arukh,* chap. 131, par. 16.

8. See ibid., chap. 131, par. 15.

9. Being called up to read the Torah, as well as the opening and closing of the Torah ark on Yom Kippur, were considered great honors. It was customary to auction off these honors, with the pledges earmarked for synagogue maintenance.

10. Refers to the Habad movement, whose rebbes settled in the town of Lubavitch (White Russia) in 1813. During the period in question, the Lubavitcher rebbe was Menahem Mendel Schneersohn, known as *Tzemah Tzedek* (1789–1866).

11. Tzimmes—a mixture of stewed or fried vegetables and fruits (usually carrots, prunes, and pumpkin), a holiday or Sabbath specialty. See A. Druyanow's note to Elzet, "Me-minhagei yisrael," 344.

12. On card playing during Hanukkah, see ibid., 353; Rivkind, *Gambling,* 48–54; Salzmann, *Ayyarati,* 115–24; and Agnon, *Bridal Canopy,* 184.

13. *Nitl*—a term for Christmas eve. Found in medieval Hebrew sources, this word is probably derived from the Latin *dies natalis* (day of birth); however, folk etymology linked it to Hebrew *nitlah* (lit. "the hanged"), an allusion to the crucifixion. It was a widespread custom not to study Torah on Christmas eve. See Elzet, "Me-minhagei yisrael," 350; Rivkind, *Gambling,* 54.

14. *Okeh* (probably from Slavic: lit. "eye")—a type of card game. See Chemerinsky, *Motele,* 178–81; Rivkind, *Gambling,* index, s.v. "okeh"; Friedman, *Zikhronot,* 61–62; and Salzmann, *Ayyarati,* 119–21.

15. *Purim-shpil* (lit. "Purim play")—one of the most popular Purim amusements in Eastern European Jewish communities was the mounting of comic amateur productions on subjects taken from the Book of Esther. On this custom's source, see Shmeruk, *Plays.*

16. *Schmaltz*—rendered goose fat. As the most commonly available fat, lard, was prohibited by Jewish dietary law, Jews used to fatten geese instead and slaughter them around Hanukkah-time, preparing enough fat to last through the winter, until Passover. Fattening geese and chickens, especially for Passover, was common in Jewish Pale of Settlement shtetls. See Ginsburg, "Panic," 61; Elzet, "Me-minhagei yisrael," 342–43; and Salzmann, *Min he-avar,* 86–87.

17. Latkes—during Passover, these fried or baked potato pancakes were made with matzah meal instead of breadcrumbs.

18. Ell—a unit of length for cloth, about sixty-eight centimeters.

CHAPTER 15

1. Avraham of Slonim—the zaddik Avraham Weinberg (1804–83), a disciple of Moshe of Kobrin and founder of the Slonimer branch of Hasidism.

2. See chapter 1, note 66.

3. The third- to fourth-century talmudic sage Rabbah bar Bar Hanah was well known for his hyperbolic legends based on events he had witnessed during his travels. His astonishing miraculous stories received both literal and mystical interpretations. For the story of the goose, see BT *Bava Batra* 73b [=*Book of Legends,* 785, no. 258].

4. A general term attributing physical or psychological damage to an act of magic, a curse, or an "evil look." Various precautions were taken against the "evil eye," mostly incantations and amulets. The use of incantations against the evil eye was widespread in Lithuanian Jewish communities late into the nineteenth century. See, for example, Nissenbaum, *Alei heldi,* 75–76; and *Lithuanian Jewry,* 1:606.

5. BT *Sanhedrin* 101a reports the use of incantations recited over eggs as a magical practice (*sarey beitzim*). See also Rashi, ad loc.; and Mendele, "Of Bygone Days," 292.

6. The famed Volozhin yeshiva (Vilna province, about seventy kilometers northwest of Minsk) was founded in 1802 by Rabbi Hayyim, the head of the town's rabbinical court, and a close disciple of the Gaon of Vilna. This new model of yeshiva, independent of the local community, relied for its financial survival on fund-raising efforts throughout the Jewish Diaspora. Special emissaries, appointed by the yeshiva administration, traveled among Jewish communities, collecting money for the yeshiva and spreading its fame. For the history of this yeshiva, its rabbis and students, see Stampfer, *Lithuanian Yeshiva,* 25–217.

7. On Rabbi Hayyim of Volozhin's attitude toward Hasidism, see Etkes, *The Gaon,* 164–222.

8. Moshe of Kobrin died in 1858 (on him see chapter 4, note 8). Since in Yiddish a melamed is also called a *rebbe,* the young Kotik (then eleven years old!) naively and surprisingly jumped to the hasty conclusion that his father's hasidic rebbe was like his teachers.

9. *Kolel* refers specifically to the hasidim who lived in Eretz-Israel with the financial support of their fellow hasidim in the Diaspora. The actual name of the *kolel*—of which the Kobrin sect was only part—was Kolel Reisen [White Russia], headed first by Moshe of Kobrin and afterward by Avraham of Slonim. In using the wrong term Kotik probably meant to hint at the overall framework of the Kobrin hasidic sect; however, the number six thousand seems greatly exaggerated.

10. On Rabbi Avraham and Slonimer Hasidism, see Kleinman, *Or yesharim,* 167–230; Levin, *Zikhronot,* 47–49; Rabinowitsch, *Lithuanian Hasidism,* 188–94; and Suraski, *Yesod ha-ma'alah,* vol. 1. The maskil Avraham-Yaakov Paperna, who was related to Rabbi Avraham, also mentioned in his memoirs that in 1848 the latter was still "half-*melamed* and half-*preacher* and lived in poverty, but was already known as one of the more important Kobriner hasidim, so at the death of the Kobriner zaddik his hasidim cast their eye on him and made him their leader . . . the ascension of this *melamed* provoked jealousy even in the heart of the greatest hasidic rebbe of that time, Aharon of Karlin" (Paperna, "Zikhronot," 71; emphases in the original).

11. On Noah-Naphtali (d. 1889) see Rabinowitsch, *Lithuanian Hasidism,* 183–87. On the inheritance controversy between Noah and Avraham of Slonim, see also Levin, *Zikhronot,* 36, 48–50 (the author was Moshe of Kobrin's grandson, and Noah was his brother-in-law).

12. Refers to money collected in the Jewish communities for the inhabitants of Eretz-Israel. This money (also known as *Erets-Yisroel-gelt* or *khalukeh-gelt*) enjoyed a special status. It could not be diverted to any other charitable purpose, but had to be directly utilized for the needs of members living in Eretz-Israel.

13. Refers to the zaddik Yisrael of Ruzhin (1796–1850), who was well known for his regal lifestyle (see Assaf, *Regal Way*). For the saying attributed to him, see Zack, *Beit yisrael*, 14.

14. Probably refers to the zaddik Noah of Lachovich (1774–1832), who led Lachovicher Hasidism from 1810 and was Avraham of Slonim's teacher. See Rabinowitsch, *Lithuanian Hasidism,* 156–60.

15. On this Sabbath's events, see also Kotik, *Memoirs,* 2, chapter 2.

16. On Avraham of Slonim's charitable activities on behalf of Eretz-Israel, see Suraski, *Yesod ha-ma'alah,* 1:350–57. This one-sided hasidic description ignores the split between the disciples of Rabbi Avraham and Rabbi Noah-Naphtali. No other evidence has come to light on Avraham's imprisonment due to the informer, but Suraski (ibid., 352) mentions an ambiguous tradition about "the great deal of contempt" the zaddik aroused while on his first charity mission for Eretz-Israel.

17. One of the most important Mishnaic sages, who lived in the first half of the first century, founder of the school of thought known as *Beit Hillel* (school of Hillel). His dicta, as found in talmudic literature, portray him as a spiritual-halakhic leader whose views leaned toward a more moralistic and liberal interpretation of Jewish law.

18. Probably to be identified as Yehudah Arkader, leader of the mitnaggedim in Brisk, about whom it was related that he died brokenhearted after having sat shivah for his two sons, who had become followers of the Neshkhizer zaddik. See *EJD,* 2:174–75.

19. See BT *Shabbat* 31a. This saying is attributed to Hillel the Elder, whom Twersky, as mentioned above, greatly admired.

20. On Arele, see chapter 4, note 14. See also Kleinman, *Or yesharim,* 63.

21. According to the statute of 1804, which was reaffirmed in the statute of 1835, rabbis were forbidden to impose bans. Nevertheless, Jewish communal boards and other Jewish groups (such as hasidim) continued to impose bans and excommunication. See Shochat, "Kahal," 211–15.

CHAPTER 16

1. *Di Kliatshe,* a well-known Yiddish story by Shalom-Yaakov Abramovitsh (1835–1917), known as Mendele Mokher Seforim [The bookseller], first published in Vilna in 1873 (and later in two different versions). Mendele depicts the Jewish bookseller—from whom he took his pseudonym—in his introduction to the first edition of his collected works in Yiddish (Odessa, 1907). (For an English translation, see Neugroschel, *Great Works of Jewish Fantasy,* 545–663.) On Jewish booksellers, see Lipschitz, *Me-dor le-dor,* 60–62.

2. Slavuta (Sławuta)—a town in Volhynia, which became famous for its Hebrew printing press (founded in 1791) managed by descendants of the zaddik Pinhas Shapira of Koretz (Korzec). They were renowned for the magnificent editions of the Babylonian Talmud they produced. A controversy over printing rights for the Talmud between the printers of Slavuta and Vilna was one cause of the 1836 order closing all Hebrew presses in Russia (with the exception of Vilna). In 1847, after this decree was cancelled, the Slavuta printers moved to Zhitomir. In actuality,

the edition of the Talmud referred to here was printed in Zhitomir between 1858 and 1864.

3. Talmudic tractates were usually sold unbound, in order to lower their price and to enable yeshiva students to purchase only the particular tractate needed for their studies. For a description of binding talmudic tractates sent by mail, see Agnon's "My Grandfather's Talmud" (*Elu ve-elu,* 217–18).

4. On the many other associations that Kotik, the adult, later founded, see the introduction. It is noteworthy that children's associations dedicated to Torah study or for purchasing volumes of the Talmud were not unusual. See Lilienblum, *Autobiography,* 1:85; Lipschitz, *Me-dor le-dor,* 83; and Friedman, *Zikhronot,* 49.

5. Refers to Yehoshua-Heshl ben Meshulam-Zalman Ashkenazi (d. 1867), head of the rabbinical court in Grodno prior to his move to Lublin (1852). Not much is known about him. His only published work is *Midbar naveh,* a public homily he presented in 1862, published after his death by his son in 1881 in Vilna.

6. No responsa book compiled by Yehoshua-Heshl of Lublin is extant, though there is indeed a tradition that he wrote ten books, which were never printed. The manuscripts, kept by his son, were burned in a fire in Grodno. See Nissenbaum, *Lublin,* 127–28.

7. Yisrael Vishniak was a historical figure. A little may be learned about him from his only book *Sefer bekhi u-misped* (Vilna 1868, 28 pp.), which he published at the age of twenty-two. Based on an obituary he delivered in the new study house in Bielsk in the year 1867, the book was dedicated to the memory of his teacher Yehoshua-Heshl of Lublin (with whom he studied for only one year—1861) and to two other rabbis who died in the cholera epidemic a year earlier (1866). On the opening page he refers to this epidemic, which was responsible for the deaths of many people in his hometown, Kamenets, including the rabbi, Avraham-Dov (on the epidemic and the rabbi's death, see chapter 27). From his book and its appended approbations, we may draw a picture of a typical young Lithuanian Jew with extensive knowledge of rabbinical literature. In his introduction he also declares his intention of publishing a book of responsa he had compiled, in the near future.

8. Refers to Tzvi-Hirsh Orenstein of Lemberg (Lwów), who, in 1865, was appointed rabbi in Brisk. In 1874 the Russian authorities deported him back to Galicia, where he served as rabbi in Lemberg until his death in 1888. See Feinstein, *Ir tehilah,* 221–22; and Wunder, *Meorei Galicia,* 1:74–78. Kotik mixed up either the time or the place: Vishniak, who was two years Kotik's senior (see chapter 8), was born in 1846 (note 7 above), so if he was about twelve when he came to Brisk, this greatly preceded Rabbi Orenstein's arrival.

9. The rabbi of Karlin was probably Shmuel-Avigdor Tosfa'ah (d. 1866), who served as rabbi there from 1855. See Nadav, "Pinsk," 290–92.

10. Refers to Leyb, who was accused of informing on the zaddik of Slonim; see chapter 15.

11. In addition to the regular talmudic discussion printed on this particular page, it appears that Yisrael's examiners intended to call his attention to the following dictum: "Whoever is boastful, if he is a sage, his wisdom departs from him, if he is a prophet, his prophecy departs from him."

12. *Pnei Yehoshua*—refers, probably, to a book of responsa compiled by

Yehoshua-Heshl ben Yosef of Kraków (d. 1648), first printed in Amsterdam in 1705, and later, with some additions, in Lemberg in 1860.

13. As mentioned previously (note 7), Vishniak published only one book, and this was not a kabbalistic work.

14. Bielsk Podlaski is located fifty-four kilometers south of Bialystok.

15. Refers to Eliezer-Elimelech Vishniak of Bielsk, a Torah scholar who died in Warsaw in 1870 at the age of fifty-five. See Yevnin, *Nahalat olamim,* 56–57.

16. Accounts of the practice of laying four pairs of phylacteries exist (see Gartner, *Customs,* 166–69), but none about such an unusual custom of twelve. It seems to be a fabrication based on the confusion of two traditions: the pietistic practice of laying two pairs of phylacteries (one according to Rashi's opinion and the other according to Rabbenu Tam) in order to be certain of fulfilling the obligation, and kabbalistic customs related to the number twelve, such as the custom of baking twelve loaves of hallah for the Sabbath (see Wertheim, *Law and Custom,* 224–26).

17. In the introduction to *Bekhi u-misped* (note 7 above), Vishniak hints at his poverty-stricken state: "I won't deny that right now (while *Yisrael* is in beggary, may God improve his condition) it is difficult to cover the cost of postage" (my emphasis).

18. Refers to Yehudah-Leyb Eger of Lublin (1816–88), a descendant of a prominent rabbinic family, who became a hasid in his youth. He was a disciple of the zaddik Menahem-Mendel of Kotsk and later the zaddik Mordechai-Yosef of Izbica. In 1860 he began to lead a hasidic community and became the founder of a hasidic dynasty active in Lublin until the Holocaust.

CHAPTER 17

1. On these two melamdim, see chapter 1, following notes 100–101.

2. Neither of these books is relevant to the talmudic tractate *Hulin. Magen Avraham,* written by Avraham-Abale Gombiner (Poland, seventeenth century), is a commentary on the *Orah hayyim* section of the *Shulhan arukh. Shitah meku-betzet,* written by Bezalel Ashkenazi (Eretz-Israel, sixteenth century), is a broad anthology of commentaries on some talmudic tractates but does not include *Hulin.*

3. The exact meaning of this word is not clear; however, from the context it seems to refer to a tarpaulin-like cloth that can be used even in the rain (in Yiddish *regn* = rain). This is probably a misspelling, and Kotik evidently meant *regn-kamlet,* which is cloth made of goat's wool. See Prylucki, *Dos gevet,* 101; and Chemerinsky, *Motele,* 65.

4. On the tradition of handing down clothes from one generation to the next, see Lipschitz, *Me-dor le-dor,* 39–40.

5. May refer to sheepskin (German: *Schur*). The 1761 regulations of the Jewish council of Lithuania explicitly prohibited women from adorning themselves in *shoorkes* (*Pinkas medinat Lita,* 272, no. 1026).

6. On men and women's clothing in Eastern Europe and women's jewelry, see Prylucki, *Dos gevet;* Ginsburg, *Historishe verk,* 3:273ff.; *Beit Yisrael be-Polin,* 1:72; and Frankel, "Costume."

7. Refers to Rabbi Aryeh-Leyb ben Asher Gunzberg, known as *Sha'agat Aryeh* for his book of responsa. See following note.

8. This is far from the truth, since the Gaon—who, in fact, had no official role in the community—received a very high annual contribution from the Kahal of Vilna as well as accommodations. See Mondshine, "Parnasei Vilna," 185.

9. A book of responsa (Frankfurt on the Oder, 1755) written by Aryeh-Leyb Gunzberg (1695?-1785), a famous eighteenth-century rabbi and head of yeshiva. His assertive personality led to many controversies, one of which forced him to leave Minsk in 1742. He relocated to Volozhin; however, there, too, he became embroiled in conflicts with the elders. He returned to Minsk and again was embroiled in conflict with the local rabbi. In 1765, after years of wandering, he settled in Metz (France), where he lived out his days. See Maggid, *Günzburg,* 35–50; Eisenstadt, *Minsk,* 15–22; and *Minsk,* 92–93.

10. On his expulsion, see Gordon, *Collected Works,* 329; and Maggid, *Günzburg,* 35–37. Maggid, in citing two different versions regarding the reasons for his expulsion, noted: "We heard people tell different stories . . . for which we are not responsible." However, his accounts are of interest, since Kotik probably used one of these stories either directly or indirectly: "They took a simple wagon from the village tied to two oxen . . . and drove him shamefully and publicly out of the town . . . And they didn't pay attention that it was Friday afternoon, and consequently Rabbi Aryeh-Leyb would be forced to spend the Sabbath in the forest or in the field. However among the public . . . was a woman, her name was Blumke, who pitied the poor rabbi, and she made her living selling challahs for the Sabbath. This woman waded through the masses and approached the rabbi with her two big baskets, from which she gave him three loaves for the Sabbath. The rabbi was greatly moved by what this simple woman did and blessed her from the depths of his heart." Expulsion from a town, on Friday or in a refuse wagon, is known from other tales of expulsion, especially of hasidic zaddikim, and is a central motif in S. Y. Agnon's story "Ha-nidah" (*Elu ve-elu,* 9–56). See also idem, *A Guest for the Night* (New York, 1968), 202.

11. On the Sabbath, the blessing over bread is recited over two loaves, but the custom was to bake three which would suffice for two meals. Sometimes the extra loaf was given to the poor; compare *Kobrin,* 136.

12. This story preserves, as noted in note 10 above, an echo of the real Blumke Wilenkin, who supported the Sha'agat Aryeh financially and established a famous *kloyz* in Minsk, named Blumke's Kloyz. On her, see Maggid, *Günzburg,* 37; Eisenstadt, *Minsk,* 21–22; and *Minsk,* index, s.v. "Blumke Wilenkin."

13. Refers to Rabbi Joel Sirkes (1561–1640), known by the acronym BaH for his most famous book (*Bayit hadash*). Although Kotik refers to it as a work on the Talmud, it is, in fact, a comprehensive commentary on Jacob ben Asher's *Arba'ah turim.*

14. Joel Sirkes served as rabbi in Brisk from 1611 to 1618, and then moved to Kraków. The story of his expulsion is probably fabricated (see Feinstein, *Ir tehilah,* 24–25). Similar accusations, that the local rabbi was not constantly studying Torah, were made against other rabbis, such as Samuel ben Avigdor of Vilna (see Fuenn, *Kiryah ne'emanah,* 141). It is noteworthy that Rabbi Aryeh-Leyb (Sha'agat Aryeh) was a descendent of Sirkes and also served as a rabbi in Brisk (in 1713); consequently, the expulsion tale referred to previously may have confused the two.

CHAPTER 18

1. See the Yiddish folk expression "Every melamed is a bit of a *shlimazel*" (*Jüdische Sprichwörter,* 162, no. 2300). Being a melamed was considered the lowest rung on the professional ladder, and a position any individual without luck, skills, or intellectual acumen could almost always find.

2. See the beginning of chapter 16.

3. This chamber was mentioned previously. See chapter 9, following note 7. On a similar chamber in Kobrin, see *Kobrin,* 55.

4. Adolina—a street in Kamenets. On the study house there, see chapter 1, following note 43.

5. See chapter 16, note 2; as mentioned there, the Slavuta edition of the Talmud was printed in Zhitomir.

6. In early nineteenth-century Eastern European communities, the lack of complete sets of the Talmud in the study houses was common. Usually only wealthy householders possessed complete sets. See Assaf, *Mekorot,* 178–79.

7. A delay in the Torah reading (*ikuv keri'ah*) is an ancient Ashkenazic custom that allows anyone with a personal or communal grievance to postpone the weekly Torah reading until his claim is clarified. See Elzet, "Me-minhagei yisrael," 346; Grossman, "Stopping-the-Service."

8. This reference to Kopust (Kopys, White Russia) is evidently a mistake, as the first of three Hebrew presses was not established there until 1797. The Babylonian Talmud was printed in Kopust from 1816 to 1828.

9. Kotik's reference is not clear. He most probably means stories about Jesus included in the earliest printed editions of the Babylonian Talmud (sixteenth century), such as the Venice edition. See, for example, the stories about Jesus in BT *Sanhedrin* 43a, 107b and *Sotah* 47a, which were censored in later editions.

10. The term philosophy (Hebrew *hakirah*) refers to rationalistic works produced by medieval Jewish philosophers, whose focus was a systematic and critical discussion of faith. Outstanding among these works are Maimonides' (twelfth century) *Moreh nevukhim* (Guide of the perplexed), which offers a critical-rationalist approach to issues of faith and the existence of God, and the poet Yehudah Halevi's (eleventh to twelfth century) philosophical work, *The Kuzari,* set in the framework of a theological-apologetic debate between representatives of the three monotheistic religions.

11. *Behinot olam*—an ethical tract written by Yedaiah Bedersi, a fourteenth-century poet and philosopher, espousing rationalist thinking and lust for knowledge, which enjoyed widespread popularity among scholars over the generations and had many "excellent commentaries" written on it.

12. Homilies are a fundamental branch of Hebrew ethical literature that subsequently influenced the development of hasidic teachings and literature. *Hovot ha-levavot* (see chapter 11, note 7) is considered the seminal work of this genre.

13. Kotik refers to the three typical types of Torah scholars: the youngest, unmarried students (*bahurim*); young married students who live on *kest* (*lomdim*); and married scholars from other towns who have left their families and come to study in Kamenets (*prushim*).

14. Yosl (or Yosele; see chapter 16, following note 2) was the son of the well-

to-do scholar Simha-Leyzer. His father's rich library is mentioned in chapter 1, following note 70. On Shmuel Meirims, see Kotik, *Memoirs, 2*, chapter 3. After his marriage he moved to Brisk, where he made his living as a cloth merchant. He became a maskil and was considered a heretic.

15. A Yiddish expression (*feygl milkh*) denoting something of superior quality, so rare as to be unobtainable (such as bird's milk).

CHAPTER 19

1. Izbica Hasidism was a radical sect founded by Rabbi Mordechai-Yosef Leiner (1800–1854), one of the most important disciples of the zaddik Menahem-Mendel of Kotsk. Circa 1840 he split off from his rebbe and established his own court in Izbica (Poland), about fifty-two kilometers southeast of Lublin. On this branch of Hasidism, see Trunk, *Poyln*, 1:121–40; Mahler, *Hasidism*, 303–11; Weiss, *Studies*, 209–48; Faierstein, *Izbica*; and Elior, "Polish Hasidism," 402–32.

2. In the original: *zikhrono li-srakha*, instead of *zikhrono li-vrakha* ("may his memory be blessed").

3. The Vilna Gaon was seen as the leader of the mitnaggedic camp that opposed Hasidism. On the social and aesthetic function of rabbis' portraits, see Cohen, *Jewish Icons*, 114–53.

4. This two-volume work was edited by the grandsons of Mordechai-Yosef of Izbica. However, Kotik could only have seen the first, published in Vienna in 1860 (the second part was published in Lublin in 1922). The publication of *Mei ha-shiloah* provoked a controversy even within the hasidic camp; see Elior, "Polish Hasidism," 431–32.

5. Numbers 25 relates how the Israelites whored with Moabite women, and how Zimri son of Salu, a prince from one of the chief families of the tribe of Simeon, committed adultery with a Moabite woman named Cozbi daughter of Zur. Both were stabbed to death by Pinhas, son of Eleazar, the High Priest. Pinhas was rewarded for his actions and became a symbol of religious zealotry, whereas Zimri became synonymous with whoredom and adultery, from which the talmudic saying "Their deeds are the deeds of Zimri, but they expect a reward like Pinhas" derives (BT *Sotah* 22b).

6. Pinhas was the grandson of the first High Priest, Aaron, Moses' brother. In *Mei ha-shiloah*, 1:54a, we find: "It would be improper to call Zimri an adulterer . . . because God would never have allowed a portion of the Torah to be devoted to an adulterer, but there is a secret in all of this. . . . Zimri in fact guarded himself against all bad, lustful desires, but now he realized that she was his soulmate . . . and hence Pinhas was acquitted, because he was related to Moses . . . and from him [Pinhas] was hidden the deep foundation to which Zimri was privy, which was that she was his partner from the six days of creation." See Weiss, *Studies*, 229–30; Elior, "Polish Hasidism," 402–32.

7. Refers to Rabbi Gershon-Tanhum ben Eliyahu-Binyamin (1812–81). See Eisenstadt, *Minsk*, 54–55.

8. Refers to Baron Amschel-Mayer Rothschild (1773–1855) of Frankfurt am Main, who was close to Orthodox circles.

9. *Ha-maggid*, the first of the modern Hebrew weekly newspapers, published

between 1856 and 1903, circulated mainly in Poland and imperial Russia. Its first editors were Eliezer Zilberman and David Gordon. Because of *Ha-maggid*'s non-radical approach to religious issues, it enjoyed a wide readership among moderate Orthodox circles in Eastern Europe.

10. From its inception *Ha-maggid* promoted settlement of Eretz-Israel out of nationalistic sentiments and published news and reports regarding daily life in Eretz-Israel as well as the activities of land-purchasing societies. Kotik is probably referring to the Colonisationverein für Palästina (Society for the Settlement of Eretz-Israel), established in 1860 in Frankfurt an der Oder, and to its plans, which were heatedly discussed in the columns of *Ha-maggid*. This colonization scheme was abandoned when the society disbanded in 1864. See Eliav, *Love of Zion*, 128–33; and Salmon, *Religion and Zionism*, 44–96.

11. On Jewish woodcutters, see Chemerinsky, *Motele*, 52–53.

12. A town in east Prussia, close to the Russian border, where *Ha-maggid* was edited and printed.

13. According to Exod. 10:9. Kotik's words also echo J. L. Gordon's famous Hebrew poem, *Bi-ne'arenu u-vi-zkenenu nelekh,* written in 1881 in the wake of pogroms in Russia.

CHAPTER 20

1. "When a boy reached the age of twelve and was still not a groom, he was ashamed to face other boys his age who were already married . . . even his parents began to be concerned and this worry did not let them sleep nights" (Gottlober, *Memoirs,* 1:86). On the early age of marriage and its reflection in Hebrew and Yiddish literature, see Knaani, *Ha-batim she-hayu,* 11–114; and chapter 5, note 20.

2. On Yekhezkel, the rabbi's son, and his attraction to Hasidism, see chapter 4, following note 14.

3. On the denunciation, see chapter 15. In the second volume of his memoirs, Kotik tells us more about Yekhezkel: He would travel nine months of the year collecting funds for Kolel Slonim in Eretz-Israel, and reside at the Slonimer court for the other three months, where he became the rebbe's closest confidant. In the early 1880s he divorced his wife, Hadas, by order of the rebbe, emigrated to Eretz-Israel, and settled in Safed. See Kotik, *Memoirs,* 2, chapter 2; and Suraski, *Yesod ha-ma'alah,* 1:264–65, 346 (Suraski did not identify this figure correctly).

4. Aharon Zailingold was later known as a publisher of hasidic books (see, for example, Zailingold, *Me'orot ha-gedolim,* introduction, 8–10). Around 1875 Zailingold moved from Pinsk to Kiev, where he managed a guesthouse. Business flourished and he encouraged his brother-in-law Kotik to move to Kiev (See Kotik, *Memoirs,* 2, chapter 16). Like Kotik, Zailingold left Kiev after the pogroms of the 1880s and moved to Warsaw, where he managed a bookstore at 32 Nalewki Street; Kotik lived at 31 Nalewki Street.

5. Refers to the zaddik Aharon Perlov "the second" (1802–72), grandson of Aharon "the great" and head of Karliner Hasidism from 1826. See Rabinowitsch, *Lithuanian Hasidism,* 80–99; and Nadav, "Pinsk," 280–85.

6. According to the Midrash, God finished creating the world in six days,

and since then "has been busy making matches—the daughter of Such-and-such to So-and-so" (*Book of Legends,* 510, no. 56).

7. Prior to the engagement it was customary to test the prospective groom's knowledge of the Talmud: "And I was approached by the examiner in whose hands was the tractate *Bava Metziah,* and he showed me the first Mishnah, 'Two persons hold a garment' with the Gemara and *Tosaphot . . .* and I read it aloud before him, and he asks and I answer in the manner in which young Jewish grooms are tested" (Gottlober, *Memoirs,* 1:84, 88).

8. The tractate *Kiddushin* (lit. "the legal act of marriage") concentrates on marital issues, and was a popular source for testing young husbands-to-be.

9. Reitzes—son of Reitze (from German *Reiz,* meaning charm; grace). On a wealthy man from Ostróg named Zvi-Hirsh son of Meir Reitzes (d. 1797), see Bieber, *Ostraha,* 228–29, seemingly the father of Mordechai mentioned here (Bieber hints that this man acquired his wealth illicitly).

10. Ostróg (Ostraha)—one of the oldest and most respected Jewish communities in Volhin. Bieber tells of a "wealthy and respected member of our town, a great Torah scholar and charitable," by the name of Mordechai ben Gershon, who worked for the wealthy householder Meir Hakohen Sussmann, and "every year he traveled to Prussia to sell the rafts and the grains packed thereon." This description fits what is told above; however, this Mordechai died in 1845 and "left neither sons nor daughters . . . all his wealth and possessions were divided among his relatives" (ibid., 304, 311–13) .

11. Refers to Baron Amschel-Mayer Rothschild. See chapter 19, note 8.

12. An expression denoting great wealth.

13. Some famous zaddikim lived in Ostróg, among them Pinhas Shapira of Koretz and the preacher Yaakov-Yosef ben Yehudah (Yibi), but here Kotik refers to zaddikim who came from other towns in Volhin and were guests at Mordechai's home. In the first half of the nineteenth century the most important zaddikim in Volhin were connected to the dynasties of Friedman (Ruzhin-Sadgóra) and Twersky (Chernobyl), but no references to Mordechai of Ostróg were found in the pertinent sources.

14. It is difficult to pinpoint this event. It is known, however, that on 26 August 1813 the Vistula flooded its banks, heavily damaging Kraków's Jewish quarter (see *Pinkas ha-kehillot: Poland,* 3:15). On the role of Jews in river trade with Danzig, see Rosman, *Lords' Jews,* 89–104, and chapter 1, following note 96.

15. Dubno—a town in Volhin, west of Ostróg, thirty-eight kilometers southwest of Rovno.

16. On Baron Günzburg and the excise tax, see chapter 7.

17. In fact, three daughters: Hadas—Yekhezkel's wife; Peshe—Aharon Zailingold's wife; and Libe—Kotik's wife.

18. Ritual circumcisers (*mohalim*) used to record the babies' names and the dates of their circumcision in a special ledger; however, the number five thousand seems greatly exaggerated.

19. The borders of the Jewish Pale of Settlement within the Russian empire were set after the partitions of Poland, in the late eighteenth century; however, the final borders were set only in 1835, during Nicholas I's reign. Fifteen provinces (*gubernii*) were included in the framework of the Russian Pale, and another ten

provinces, of varying legal and administrative status, in Poland. As mentioned before, in 1857 Baron Günzburg leased collection of the excise tax, but in 1865 the government itself took over collection of this tax.

20. Fort (Polish *gród*)—the residence of the municipal governor and also generally the seat of the court. The fort in Brisk, mentioned here, was built during the 1830s as part of Russia's western defense lines. The military government of Brisk functioned within the fort as well as the quartermaster's stores that negotiated with various contractors. See *Pinkas ha-kehillot: Poland*, 5:229–30.

21. Refers to the Crimean War (1853–56), fought between Russia and Turkey and its allies (Britain and France). This war ended through the mutual weakening of all fighting parties and the exposure of Russian bureaucratic inefficiency. Sebastopol, a fortress port town on the banks of the Black Sea (south of Crimea), was a Russian navy base and the site of many bloody battles.

22. The spice box (Hebrew *hadas*) used in the *havdalah* ceremony marking the conclusion of the Sabbath.

23. Refers to the commentary on the Mishnah comprised by Rabbi Yisrael Lipschitz of Danzig (1782–1860). This popular commentary was originally printed in separate volumes. All six volumes were published together for the first time in Berlin in 1862, and Kotik is probably referring to this edition.

24. It was customary for the engaged couple to exchange "little presents" prior to the wedding; for example, "They had . . . to hand over to him the so-called little presents for me, namely, a cap of black velvet trimmed with gold lace, a Bible bound in green velvet with silver clasps, and so on" (Maimon, *Autobiography,* 51, 55). See also Gottlober, *Memoirs,* 1:88–89.

25. Kotik, like other Yiddish-speaking Jewish children, did not know how to write Hebrew (*lashon kodesh;* i.e., the traditional Hebrew, mixed with Aramaic, which is the language of the liturgy and most of rabbinic literature). Since the custom was that letters be written in Hebrew, there were special letter-writing guidebooks (known as *brievensteller* or *igronim*), which contained variations on set letters for different occasions (such as letters of commerce or letters from a groom to his bride-to-be). One could copy the sample letter and simply insert the appropriate names. On this genre, see Zwick, *Briefsteller.*

26. Kotik quotes this letter in slightly faulty Hebrew, followed by a Yiddish translation. The introduction to the letter is made up of strings of biblical metaphors, typical of the phrases found in the above-mentioned letter-writing guidebooks. This, however, is not traditional rabbinic Hebrew, but rather a maskilic modern Hebrew.

27. After the suppression of the 1863 Polish Revolt, russification in the northwestern provinces of the empire increased. Public use of Polish and Lithuanian was prohibited, and children up to the age of eighteen (including Jews) were forced to learn Russian. Though this decree was not completely enforced, during this period—the age of Alexander II's reforms, a period of relative tolerance toward Jews, as well as ideological changes within Jewish society itself toward education and professional progress—many Jews worried that girls who did not know how to write Russian might not be assured of an appropriate match (see Salzmann, *Min he-avar,* 82–83 and *Kobrin,* 123–27). Among traditional families it was more acceptable that females (and not males) study Russian and receive a modern education.

28. In fact, this letter, as was common among maskilim who wrote love letters at that time, was in Germanized Yiddish. For example, this teacher used the terms *Bräutigam* (bridegroom) and *Braut* (bride). Compare to a story by A. S. Friedberg (*"Ahavah bi-mesirat kulmos"*), where he humorously described the correspondence between two maskilim who penned letters in very elegant German in the names of a bride and groom. Each betrothed was convinced that the other was fluent in German, while the truth was that both the groom and bride-to-be were entirely ignorant of that language (Friedberg, *Sefer ha-zikhronot*, 2:30).

29. *Daitsch*—lit. "German," generally used to refer to someone influenced by the German Enlightenment, who modernized his dress and appearance. From the viewpoint of Orthodox society such a man was considered almost a heretic. On the German character of the Russian Jewish Enlightenment in its early years, see Slutsky, *Russian-Jewish Press*, 1:15–18.

30. The rabbi's son's name was Simha; see chapter 22.

31. Calling off a match caused the bride great humiliation, suggesting some apparent fault in her family's lineage, which endangered her chances of a future match. This strict attitude regarding the cancellation of a betrothal agreement is found in the regulations of Ashkenazic communities as early as the eleventh century. See Grossman, *Ashkenaz*, 406–8; Elzet, "Me-minhagei yisrael," 353–54. See also Agnon, *Bridal Canopy*, 177: "Let him write a divorce . . . and not return the Engagement Contract to the bride, the shame being too great for a daughter of Israel."

32. The promised dowry was generally deposited with a trustee, often a rabbi or relative, who was supposed to keep the money and hand it over to the couple after the conclusion of the period of *kest*. See chapter 26, where Kotik describes his trip to Kobrin in order to receive his dowry money.

33. Serfdom was abolished in 1861; see the following chapter.

34. Avraham-Dov of Kamenets had a brother living in Warsaw—Rabbi Yehoshua Halevi (d. 1885). See *Melitzei esh*, 2 Shevat, no. 26.

CHAPTER 21

1. For the background to the liberation of the peasants and the reforms of Tsar Alexander II, see Dubnow, *History of the Jews*, 5:321–30; Kluchevsky, *Divrey yemey Rusiyah*, 3:392–409; and Klier, *Jewish Question*, 13ff.

2. See chapter 1, notes 33, 110.

3. The proclamation was issued on 19 February 1861, which fell on a Sunday, according to the Julian calendar then in use in tsarist Russia. The date according to the Gregorian calendar—which is twelve days ahead of the Julian—would have been 3 March 1861.

4. On the collapse of the old economic order during the 1860s and its background (abolition of the duty taxes between Poland and Russia, the failure of the Crimean War, the emancipation of the serfs, the Polish rebellion, the accelerated development of the railroad, etc.), see Slutsky, *Russian-Jewish Press*, 1:19–21.

5. According to the reform, in principle the tsar was to free the peasant-serfs along with their land. The land was to be granted to the peasants in perpetuity, in order that they, through hard work, might keep up the payment of local and state

taxes. The lands were indeed divided, generally by agreement between the peasant and landlord, with the peasant committing himself to pay its worth either in cash or through labor. The peasants could not, of course, afford to pay immediately, and the government granted them special loans, repayable within forty-nine years (and not within forty, as Kotik writes), at 6 percent interest. Until payment was made to the landlord in its entirety, the peasants were still tied to the land and to the supervision and the authority of the lords. See Kluchevsky, *Divrey yemey Rusiyah,* 3:399–406.

6. *Volost* in the original, according to the Russian, that is, the rural governmental center. See *RHT,* 179–81.

7. The double-headed eagle was one of the symbols of the Russian government. The Poles who tore them down replaced them with their own symbol, a double-headed white eagle. S. Y. Agnon beautifully recounts a similar event, but from the point of view of the Jews of Galicia, who were forced to change the eagle atop their synagogue candelabra according to the changing regimes. See *Ir u-melo'ah,* 32–33.

8. *Polkovnik* in the original; see *RHT,* 91.

9. In the original: "in the chicken hothouse." In many homes a chicken coop was placed beneath the stove and floor of the house; see Lipschitz, *Me-dor le-dor,* 45.

10. See Baron, *Russian Jew,* 41; Glatstein, *Yash,* 70.

11. In Hebrew *viduy,* a deathbed penitential prayer. See M. *Sanhedrin* 6:2; *Shulhan arukh, Yoreh de'ah,* chap. 338.

12. In his novel *1863* (Tel Aviv 1929, 186–88), Joseph Opatoshu provides a harrowing description of the hanging by a Russian of a Jew suspected of aiding the Polish rebels.

13. Chernavchitsy (Czerniawczyce)—a town in Grodno province, about twenty kilometers southeast of Kamenets. See *Słownik,* 1:819–20; *Pinkas ha-kehillot: Poland,* 5:305.

14. A battalion consisted of about five hundred soldiers, made up of infantry, cavalry, and artillery. An infantry regiment—which was the basic unit within the nineteenth-century Russian army—consisted of four battalions (about two thousand soldiers). See *RHT,* 91.

15. Squadron—a cavalry unit consisting of about 150 horsemen. A Russian cavalry regiment was usually made up of six squadrons; see ibid.

16. See Zunser, *Works,* 2:687–88; Friedman, *Zikhronot,* 37–38. On Muravyov, see chapter 5, note 17.

17. He was, in fact, never a candidate. On the battles in the Czemeryn Forest and Oginski, see chapter 5, following notes 15–16.

18. In 1648–49 bloody riots erupted throughout most parts of Poland when the Ukrainians, under the leadership of Bogdan Chmielnicki, rebelled against their Polish lords. In the course of these uprisings, tens of thousands of Jews were either killed or maimed, and hundreds of Jewish communities were ruined. Until the Holocaust, the Chmielnicki massacres remained etched in the collective Jewish memory as the most traumatic and cruelest attempt to destroy the Jewish people. Horror stories of Jews slaughtered in synagogues, recounted by survivors, were recorded in contemporary testimonies such as the famous chronicle of Nathan

Hannover, *Abyss of Despair*. On the place of this event in historical memory, see Shmeruk, "Collective Memory," 173–83; Raba, *Between Remembrance and Denial*.

19. On Oginski's escape to Pinsk, see chapter 5, following note 16.

20. On Aharon-Leyzer's brother-in-law Lipe, see chapters 6–7.

21. Refers to the prodigy Yisrael Vishniak's father-in-law. See chapter 16, following note 13.

22. *Sotnia*—a unit of about one hundred soldiers. See *RHT*, 139.

23. As almost occurred on Sikhowski's manor. See chapter 13.

CHAPTER 22

1. Industry in Odessa expanded dramatically as a result of the Crimean War. On the migration of Jews from towns and villages in the Pale of Settlement to Odessa, see Zipperstein, *Odessa*, 70–75.

2. Volhin province was established in 1797, with Zhitomir as its capitol. Despite the low level and the small number of those employed in industry in Volhin, several branches of production were almost entirely in Jewish hands (leather, candles, tobacco, paper, paint). See *Pinkas ha-kehillot: Poland*, 5:6–7. From the 1840s, Jewish industry in Volhin declined until sparked again by the rapid success of the sugar industry in the Kiev province. See Mahler, *History*, 41, and note 22 below.

3. Refers to charity boxes (Yiddish *pushkes*) scattered throughout synagogues, study houses, and private homes, used to collect money for the indigent living in Eretz-Yisrael. See Stampfer, "Collection Box," 89–102. The identity of Meir Ba'al ha-Nes (the miracle worker) is uncertain.

4. Yosef Rozin, head of the rabbinical court in Telz, was described in similar terms. Although a mitnaggedic rabbi, nevertheless in Lithuania and White Russia the common people considered him a miracle worker and a sort of hasidic zaddik; see Friedman, *Zikhronot*, 63–65.

5. Kotik used the hasidic terminology *kvitlekh* and *tsetlekh* here, referring to the notes the hasidim passed to the zaddik, in which they wrote their name and their needs—health, livelihood, matches, and so on—for which they asked the zaddik's blessing and prayer. See Assaf, *Regal Way*, 316–18.

6. Many people were illiterate and needed the aid of the rabbi's son, who wrote (probably for a fee) these formulaic notes of request. See ibid., 428.

7. Refers to the zaddik Yitzhak of Neshkhiz, who became known—as was his father, Mordechai of Neshkhiz—as a miracle worker. See chapter 4, note 25.

8. On the underlying context for these paragraphs, see Slutsky, *Russian-Jewish Press*, 1:19–21.

9. On Osserevski's estate "Pruska," see chapter 1, following note 29. On Vilevinski's estate of the same name, see chapter 10, following note 10.

10. See Dubnow, *History of the Jews*, 327. Nevertheless, favorable reports were recorded in the Jewish press concerning Muravyov's meetings with Jews in various communities; see, for example, *Ha-karmel* 4 (1864): 33–34, 45.

11. On these measurements, see chapter 1, note 20.

12. See the end of chapter 12, where Kotik notes Berl-Bendet's subscription to German agricultural journals in order to improve and update the management and production techniques on the estate.

13. A shift toward modern education had already begun in the 1840s with attempts by the Russian government (in cooperation with maskilim) to promote secular education among the Jews. The plan was to establish special elementary schools for Jews along with rabbinical seminaries (in Vilna and Zhitomir), whose graduates would be awarded the equivalent of a Russian gymnasium diploma. These institutions met with the opposition of Orthodox Jews, who were worried by their secular tendencies and were therefore determined to protect the old heder system. In the 1860s, as part of the intensive russification, the doors of Russian gymnasia and universities were also opened to Jewish students. See Dubnow, *History of the Jews,* 321–30; Tsherikover, *Yehudim,* 185–87; Slutsky, *Russian-Jewish Press,* 1:21–29; and Levitats, *Jewish Community in Russia,* 2:45–55. On the intensive russification in the northwestern provinces inspired by Muravyov, see Klier, *Jewish Question,* 159–81.

14. *Sledovateli sudebnyi* in Russian. This position was created in 1860 in order to take the investigation of criminal cases out of police hands (*RHT,* 127). From 1864, with the implementation of reforms in the judicial system, Jews were permitted to become examining magistrates. See Genkin, "Practitioners of Law."

15. From 1861 Jews with higher education (physicians and lawyers, for example) were permitted to settle throughout Russia, even outside the Jewish Pale. Within a short time this permission was extended to the paramedical professions (pharmacists, medical assistants, and midwives) as well as to various craftsmen. See Slutsky, *Russian-Jewish Press,* 1:24.

16. For an analysis of the demographic and economic trends among Russian Jewry from the 1860s until the late nineteenth century, see Ettinger, *Essays,* 257–79.

17. The Jewish community of Moscow was established in the 1860s by veterans of Nicholas I's army, who had been granted permission to reside there permanently. With the extension of this authorization to include other professions, many Jewish merchants arrived in Moscow along with maskilim and craftsmen. The community grew rapidly; however, in Kotik's day its numbers never neared fifty thousand: in 1871 the estimated number of Jews living in Moscow was eight thousand, and in 1890 about thirty-five thousand. In 1891–92 most of the city's Jews were exiled and only some five thousand remained. It was not until the 1920s that their numbers began to rise. Among the famous Jews who contributed to Moscow's industrial development were the banker and railroad magnate Samuel Poliakoff and the tea baron Kalonymus Ze'ev Wissotzky. Kotik visited Moscow in the 1870s and lived there for a short period of time (Kotik, *Memoirs,* 2, chapter 23).

18. From the beginning of the seventeenth century, when the citizens of Kiev were granted the right to exclude Jews from the city (*Privilegium de non tolerandis Iudaeis*), until the time of Alexander II, only a small number of Jews lived within the city itself, whereas a large Jewish community, composed mostly of traders, lived outside the city's walls. From 1861 wealthy Jews and their employees, accredited Jews with higher education, merchants, and craftsmen were permitted to live in every quarter of the city; however, most of the Jews settled in two quarters: Podil and Demievka. On Jewish Kiev, see Hamm, *Kiev,* 117–34. Kotik moved to Kiev in 1876; see introduction.

19. Nikolayev was a seaport on the east bank of the Bug River, about seventy

kilometers from the Black Sea. On Pinsk river trade in the nineteenth century and its central role in the export of agricultural surplus (mainly grains) and forest produce of southwest Russia, see Nadav, "Pinsk," 227–35. This trade declined as the Russian railway system developed.

20. Kotik probably alludes here to the increasingly antisemitic atmosphere accompanying the Mendel Beilis blood libel case (Beilis was accused of the ritual murder of a twelve-year-old boy in Kiev). The investigation and trial lasted for two years (1911–13), and the ensuing controversy formed a central issue on the Russian-Jewish agenda.

21. See note 18 above. Here, too, Kotik gives an inaccurate count of the Jewish population. In 1863, according to official estimates, the number of Jews living in Kiev was 3,013; in 1897, 31,801; and only in 1910 did their number reach 50,792. See Leshtchinsky, *Yidishe folk,* 71; Hamm, *Kiev,* 120, 128. Since many Jews lived in Kiev without residence permits, one must assume that these numbers are also inexact. It would appear that prior to the pogroms of 1881 more than 18,000 Jews lived in Kiev. See Slutsky, "Geography," 17.

22. Among the sugar magnates in Kiev were Yisrael Brodsky (1823–88) and his sons (especially Lazar, who was known as "the sugar king of the south"). Their factories supplied over a quarter of the empire's sugar consumption and employed hundreds of workers. See Hamm, *Kiev,* 129–30; Ettinger, *Essays,* 276–77; and Friedman, *Zikhronot,* 206–14. Kotik depicts Kiev's wealthy Jews in the second volume of his memoirs; see Kotik, *Memoirs,* 2, chapter 17.

CHAPTER 23

1. It was customary for the wedding ceremony to be held at the bride's residence, but here, because the bride was an orphan, it took place in the groom's hometown.

2. *Pantofl*—lit. "slippers"—flat-bottomed shoes without laces, traditionally worn by hasidim; "stockings"—in hasidic dress, three-quarter-length pants were tied below the knee, atop knee-high white socks. See Prylucki, *Dos gevet,* 86–93; and Kaufmann, *Zikhronot,* 34.

3. On the musicians of Kobrin, see chapter 1, following note 59. On the musicians from Brisk, see *EJD,* 2:111–12.

4. See Gottlober, *Memoirs,* 1:101–3. For a wonderful description of an Eastern European wedding and its particular customs, see Saul Tchernichowsky's poem "Elka's Wedding."

5. The ancient custom was to refrain from holding weddings on Fridays (in order not to run the risk of desecrating the Sabbath), and it was permitted only for the poor (see Roth, "Shelo le-vayesh," 6). It was explicitly prohibited in the 1761 regulation issued by the Jewish council of Lithuania (*Pinkas medinat Lita,* 268, no. 992). Hasidic circles, however, preferred to marry on this day.

6. This extreme custom was in contradiction with talmudic law, which states that a man may not marry unless he has first seen the bride (BT *Kiddushin* 41a); hasidim preferred, however, that the groom not set eyes upon the bride until the *badekns.* See Kaufmann, *Zikhronot,* 35.

7. The source of this custom is evidently the seventeenth-century kabba-

listic work of Avraham Azulay, *Hesed le-Avraham* (Jerusalem, 1996), 166. See, for example, Maimon's description: "I had read in a Hebrew book of an approved plan for a husband to secure lordship over his better half for life. He was to tread on her foot at the marriage ceremony; and if both hit on the stratagem, the first to succeed would retain the upper hand. Accordingly, when my bride and I were placed side by side at the ceremony this trick occurred to me, and I said to myself, now you must not let the opportunity pass of securing for your whole lifetime lordship over your wife. . . . While I was in this irresolute state, I felt the slipper of my wife on my foot with such force that I should almost have screamed aloud if I had not been checked by shame" (*Autobiography,* 59). See also Gottlober, *Memoirs,* 1:104; and Elzet, "Me-minhagei yisrael," 360–61.

8. On this custom, see Shomer and Shomer, *Avinu Shomer,* 32.

9. Grooms customarily wore a *kittel* to their wedding—generally a gift from the bride—and many explanations have been tendered for this custom. See Shperling, *Minhagim,* 407, no. 907; Elzet, "Me-minhagei yisrael," 357; and Gottlober, *Memoirs,* 1:103.

10. A nickname for the bowl of chicken soup served to the bride and groom, who generally fasted on their wedding day. See Gottlober, *Memoirs,* 1:104.

11. This is a halakhic requirement called *yihud.* The bride and groom are placed in a side room for a short time, where they break their wedding day fast. See chapter 3, note 4.

<h2 style="text-align:center">Chapter 24</h2>

1. Refers to Aharon Zailingold. See chapter 20, note 4.

2. On Aharon of Karlin, see chapter 20, note 5.

3. In Yiddish this means "vinegar maker," probably his family's profession.

4. On this custom see chapter 14, near note 11.

5. Gen. 2:24. The hasid intimated that immediately after his marriage Kotik left his father and mother in the religious-spiritual sense as well.

6. The hasid wanted to insult Kotik by the humoristic use of the German translation of this passage, in which he purposely confused the word *und* (German for "and") with the word *Hund* (German for "dog"). In the German translation of Genesis written by Shlomo Dubna (Berlin, 1783) this passage was translated differently, and the citation here clearly reflects a contemporary popular joke condemning the maskilic *Be'ur* (see following note). Moreover, hasidim insultingly referred to maskilim as "dogs"; see Perl, *Bohen tzaddik,* 26.

7. The philosopher Moses Mendelssohn (1729–86), father of the German-Jewish Enlightenment movement, was so named on account of his birthplace, Dessau, though he resided in Berlin for most of his life. One of his greatest achievements was the *Be'ur* (lit. "commentary")—a German translation of the Bible with a new commentary. The volumes, edited by Mendelssohn and his disciples, began to be published from 1783 under the title *Netivot ha-shalom,* and the translation itself was printed in Hebrew characters alongside the biblical text. While the commentary usually conformed to traditional exegesis, it was not accepted by rabbis or leaders of Orthodoxy (though it was never banned), and it became a symbol of maskilic heresy. See Sandler, *Mendelssohn's Pentateuch,* 194–218.

8. On the preacher's house, which was the center for opposition to Hasidism in the township, see chapter 19.

9. Refers to both Kotik's sister and his aunt, who died during the 1866 cholera epidemic. See chapter 27, note 4.

10. Kotik here uses the same reasoning he attributed earlier to Leyb Meirs, who had denounced the Slonimer rebbe, and on whom the hasidim, out of revenge, wanted to force a hasidic lifestyle. See the end of chapter 15.

11. In the original, "I have already danced my dance."

12. Kotik was a great-grandson (on his mother's side) of Hillel Fried, who had married Hayyim of Volozhin's daughter. The famous Volozhin Yeshiva was not a communal institution but rather the property of the founder's family. Thus the heads of the yeshiva and its leaders were always family members. In 1865 the head of the Volozhin Yeshiva was Naphtali-Tzvi-Yehuda Berlin (*Ha-netziv*), the son-in-law of Yitzhak of Volozhin. His assistant was Hayyim-Hillel Fried, Hillel Fried's grandson. See Stampfer, *Lithuanian Yeshiva,* 72–88.

CHAPTER 25

1. The town of Volozhin was situated in Vilna province, while Kamenets was in Grodno province. According to an 1857 law, a passport, to be issued by the municipal council on the recommendation of the *sborshchik,* was required for interprovincial travel. See Shochat, "Kahal," 163, 183.

2. Scripture mandates: "When a man has taken a bride, he shall not go out with the army or be assigned to it for any purpose; he shall be exempt one year for the sake of his household, to give happiness to the woman he has married" (Deut. 24:5). The following declaration was made to those about to go into battle: "Is there anyone who has spoken for a woman in marriage, but who has not yet married her? Let him go back to his home, lest he die in battle and another marry her"(Deut. 20:7).

3. The Volozhin Yeshiva was mainly an institution of learning, but Kotik's plan reflects its public image as an Orthodox institution for rabbinical training. See Stampfer, *Lithuanian Yeshiva,* 99–102.

4. See Maimonides, *Code,* Book One: *Knowledge,* "Laws Concerning the Study of Torah," 3:12–13. (See *Maimonides Reader,* 68–69, for an English translation.)

5. See Maimonides, *Code,* Book Four: *The Book of Women,* "Marriage," 14:1.

6. The belief that the souls of the dead come to pray in the synagogue at night stems from the literature of the medieval German pietists (*Hasidey Ashkenaz*). See *Sefer hasidim,* no. 271; Elzet, "Me-minhagei yisrael," 374; and Chayes, "Customs," 328. On this widespread belief in Eastern Europe, see Friedman, *Zikhronot,* 32; and Lewinsky, "Night Prayers by the Dead," 149–57.

7. Written by Alexander Ziskind of Grodno, a forebear of Kotik's (on his mother's side). See chapter 1, note 121.

8. This book provides step-by-step spiritual guidance for the reader on how he is supposed to feel while praying, such as: "When he says 'Our Lord,' his heart should fill with tremendous joy . . . And when he prays with a very broken heart,

how good it would be if his eyes were to well up with tears as springs of water" (*Yesod ve-shoresh ha-avodah*, 40a).

9. A reference to the discussion in the Talmud: "Rabbi [Judah ha-Nasi] was asked, why were you called 'Our holy Teacher'? Said he to them, I have never looked at my membrum . . . [i.e.,] he did not insert his hand beneath his girdle" (BT *Shabbat* 118b); see also, "Whosoever puts his hand below his belly that hand shall be cut off" (BT *Niddah* 13b).

10. On the *patshoshnik*, see chapter 1, note 66.

11. According to BT *Megillah* 7b "It is the duty of a man to mellow himself [with wine] on Purim until he cannot tell the difference between 'cursed be Haman' and 'blessed be Mordecai,' " meaning one must drink wine on Purim until one cannot differentiate between good and bad. See Maimonides, *Code,* Book Three: *The Book of Seasons,* "Megillah and Hanukkah," 2:15.

12. *Bava Kama*—lit. "first gate"; *Bava Metziah*—"middle gate"; *Bava Batra*—"last gate." These three talmudic tractates, which deal with various issues regarding civil law, were a popular part of the curriculum among Torah scholars and yeshiva students.

CHAPTER 26

1. Refers to Yosef-Shlomo Sheinbaum, also known by the nickname Yoshe Minkes (Mina's son). He married Esther-Gitl, the daughter of Avraham-Dov, the rabbi of Kamenets and Kotik's uncle. For the few known details about him, see Ilana'eh, *Me'ever la-hushiyut,* 5; and *Kobrin,* 50.

2. *Torah u-gedulah* (lit. "Torah and greatness") in the original. See BT *Gittin* 59a for the ascription of these qualities to Judah ha-Nasi.

3. One of the sons, Eliezer-Yitzhak Sheinbaum (1855–1929), emigrated to Jerusalem in 1921, changed his name to Ilana'eh, and turned to philosophical writing. See Ilana'eh, *Me'ever la-hushiyut,* 5–22.

4. His full name was Eliezer Edelstein. See ibid., 5–6.

5. Meaning he was attracted to secular studies.

6. Refers to Zalman-Sender Kahana-Shapira (1851–1923), born in Nesvizh, twice related to Kotik: he married the daughter of Kotik's cousin Esther-Gitl, and he was the great-grandson of Hayyim of Volozhin. He lived in Kobrin until 1885. In that year he was appointed head of the rabbinical court in Malech, and opened a well-respected yeshiva there in 1898. In 1903 he moved to Krinki, and in 1921 he immigrated to Palestine along with his brother-in-law Sheinbaum (see note 3 above) and settled in Jerusalem. See *Pinkas Krinki,* 83–84; Tzinowitz, *Etz hayyim,* 449–54; and Shapira, *Hidushey ha-Garzas,* 13–29.

7. Krinki—about thirty-eight kilometers northeast of Bialystok.

8. On the miraculous deeds attributed to Zalman-Sender, see Shapira, *Hidushey ha-Garzas,* 18–19.

9. Referring, of course, to the exchange of responsa on halakhic matters. Among the rabbis with whom he corresponded were Yosef-Baer Soloveichik of Brisk and his son Hayyim, Naphtali-Tzvi-Yehuda Berlin (Ha-Netziv of Volozhin), and Yeruham-Yehudah Perlman (*Ha-gadol* [The Great] of Minsk). For the extant responsa, see Shapira, *Hidushey ha-Garzas,* 262ff.

10. Among these scholars was, for example, Yaakov-David Willowski (1845–1913; known as Ridbaz). See *Kobrin*, 233.

11. One can learn about the contrast between these two brothers-in-law from the life of Eliezer-Yitzhak Sheinbaum (note 3 above), who, in his youth, was influenced by both: For a long time he was under Leyzer's influence, who tried to send him to a gymnasium; later—with the support of his father Yoshe Minkes—he went to study Torah under Zalman-Sender's supervision. See Ilana'eh, *Me'ever la-hushiyut*, 5–7.

12. *Mirovoi posrednik* (lit. "peacemaker") in the original. This post, established with the liberation of the serfs in 1861, entailed the settling of disputes that arose between the freed serfs and the landowners. The position was abolished in 1874 (*RHT*, 97–98).

13. See chapter 1, note 107.

14. Kotik quotes the biblical verses here and below in the original Hebrew (with some minor mistakes) and interprets them literally in Yiddish. For the biblical citations in English, *Tanakh: A New Translation of the Holy Scriptures according to the Traditional Hebrew Text* (Philadelphia: Jewish Publication Society, 1985) has been used.

15. Refers to Isa. 1:14–15: "Your new moons and fixed seasons fill Me with loathing; they are become a burden to Me, I cannot endure them. And when you lift up your hands, I will turn my eyes away from you; though you pray at length, I will not listen."

16. It was the custom to donate a tenth of the dowry money to charity, in remembrance of the biblical tithe. See Rivkind, *Jewish Money*, 157–67, esp. 160.

17. The prayer recited in memory of the dead; also an expression meaning to lose hope.

18. A term for a maskilic rabbi appointed to the governmental post of "crown rabbi" in order to act as the official religious representative of the Jewish community to the Russian authorities. Although Russian attempts to initiate reforms in the rabbinate date back to the early nineteenth century, its formal legal realization dates only to the statutes of 1835. From the government's point of view, the rabbi's main duty—apart from religious instruction and supervision of religious ceremonies—was to manage the communal registry, noting all births, marriages, divorces, and deaths. According to the law only rabbis with secular education, able to read and write Russian, and who swore allegiance to the tsar, would be eligible for this position. Very few rabbis met these rigid criteria, and it was often necessary to hire individuals to serve alongside the regular rabbi. The importance of the "crown rabbis" increased after 1847 with the establishment of rabbinical seminars in Vilna and Zhitomir, whose graduates were supposed to supply the new model of maskilic rabbis; however, these rabbis generally did not enjoy the trust of the Orthodox, who viewed them as ignorant, heretics, and government agents. On this post and its history, see Shochat, *Crown Rabbinate*.

19. On Yosl, see the end of chapter 18.

20. Eliezer Halberstam (1819–99) arrived in Bialystok in 1833 and was "one of the first of the ten greatest Hebrew modern writers and poets in our land" (Nahum Sokolow in his introduction to Halberstam's *Aley higayon ve-kinor* [Warsaw, 1895]).

On him, see Hershberg, *Bialystok,* 1:214–20. Kotik describes him again in his *Memoirs,* 2, chapter 3.

21. On Zabludovski, see chapter 1, note 57.

22. An example of such a divorce is found as early as 1829, the case of Avraham-Dov Gottlober, who was forced by a hasidic rabbi to divorce his wife after he was found in possession of maskilic books (Gottlober, *Memoirs,* 1:243–45). Kotik later described (*Memoirs,* 2, chapter 3) a huge wave of divorces that swept over Bialystok in the mid-1860s, making it famous as a city of heretics and a Haskalah center.

23. On the cholera epidemic see the following chapter. The exact number of victims is unknown, but estimates of three million were posited for the 1848 cholera epidemic. See Baron, *Russian Jew,* 65–66.

CHAPTER 27

1. On the outbreak of cholera in Brisk in 1866, see *EJD,* 2:168–69. Unlike the plague, cholera reached Europe only in the nineteenth century. The death rate was astounding and reached into the millions. Many local outbreaks of this deadly contagious intestinal disease were reported in Russia throughout the nineteenth century, especially the widespread outbreak of 1848. Another wave swept over the country from 1865 to 1875. These epidemics sometimes wiped out entire towns, creating thousands of refugees, and wreaking havoc with demography.

2. These months (September–November 1866) indeed saw increased reports on the epidemic in the Hebrew press, though it probably broke out several months earlier. An article on how to safeguard one's health against cholera had already appeared eight months earlier (*Ha-karmel* 5:290–91; 6:137). On the enormity of this epidemic and the protective measures (including some strange and unusual remedies) taken by various communities, see the reports printed in *Ha-karmel* 6 (1866–67) from towns like Grodno (147), Vilna and Bialystok (154–55), Shavl (156), Utian (162), Vilkomir (171, 177–78, 194–95), Ponivez (203), and Konstantin-Yashan (178). See also Katsnelson, *Ha-milhamah ha-sifrutit,* 176.

3. According to Jewish law, the body of the deceased must be purified before burial, and the ritual washing was performed by members of the burial society (see chapter 28, note 3). See also Chayes, "Customs," 301–2; Benayahu, *Ma'amadot.*

4. See chapter 24, note 9. In chapter 1, following note 132, Kotik mentions his young sister Faygele's death during an epidemic, but it seems that he was referring there to an outbreak of measles which occurred when he, too, was a child.

5. During epidemics, it was customary to marry off the poor, cripples, orphans, and unfortunate, because such deeds, considered the ultimate expression of charity, were thought to be powerful enough to stop the outbreak. The wedding ceremonies, paid for by the community, were sometimes conducted in the graveyard with the entire community in attendance. See Lipietz, *Sefer mat'amim,* 73; Michelsohn, *Ohel Elimelekh,* no. 153; Mendele, *Collected Works,* 97–98; Kasovich, *Our Years,* 56–57; Zuckerovitch, "Zambrow," 13–14; and Lewinsky, "Hatunot magefah," 60–63. For example, "The righteous women gathered from the marketplace a dirty virgin maid who stalks in doorways . . . whose countenance could make one vomit, and they found for her a mate of short stature, blind, with a huge nose . . .

and joyfully they led them both to the graveyard to be married" (Friedberg, *Sefer ha-zikhronot*, 2:75). See also Lilienblum, *Collected Works*, 413 (refers to the plague in Vilkomir in 1869). "Plague weddings" were performed in Poland up until 1925, at least; see Caspi, "Shedlitz," 101–2.

6. *Ketoret* (lit. "incense")—a prayer recited during the morning service, based on a talmudic passage (BT *Kritot* 6a-b) regarding the aromatic spices that made up the incense in the Temple. The belief in the power of this prayer to stave off the plague was derived from the Bible (Num. 17:11–15). See Emden, *Siddur beit Yaakov*, 36a; Shperling, *Minhagim*, 574; Lewinsky, "Hatunot magefah," 62. In an epistle written by Israel Ba'al Shem Tov (printed at the end of *Ben porat Yosef* [Korets, 1881]), he noted that when he heard of the approaching epidemic he recited the *ketoret* prayer along with his disciples.

7. Kotik was probably referring to a severe cholera epidemic that erupted in Lublin in 1892. See, for example, Stern, *Kitvei agadah*, 50.

8. *Lulav* (lit. "palm branch")—used for ceremonial purposes during Sukkot. Magical powers to counteract evil were attributed to waving the palm frond (BT *Sukkah* 37b-38a). Even after the festival of Sukkot the *lulav* retained its status as a sacred artifact, and it was customary to save it for use in the fulfillment of other commandments, such as for stoking the oven to bake matzah for Passover. Lilienblum also reported the use of *lulav* rings in Vilkomir during the plague of 1866. See his report in *Ha-karmel* 6 (1866): 178; idem, *Collected Works*, 413.

9. I found no other evidence for such a practice. There were places where it was customary to perform charity weddings in the four corners of the town in order to halt the advance of the evil from any direction. See *Ha-karmel* 6 (1866): 147 (Grodno), 154 (Bialystok), 178 (Vilkomir).

10. *Tu niema miejsca* (Polish) in the original.

11. *Tu jest dosyć miejsca* (Polish) in the original.

12. The death of the rabbi of Kamenets in the epidemic of 1866 is mentioned in the eulogy delivered by the "prodigy" Yisrael Vishniak of Bielsk. See chapter 16, note 7.

13. This was a group of volunteers who scrubbed the bodies of the sick with saline solution, vodka, and alcohol, in order to ease their spasms and raise their blood pressure. On the "society of scrubbers," see, for example, Zuckerovitch, "Zambrow," 13–14.

14. Turna—a town in the Brisk district (about twenty-two kilometers north of Brisk), property of the noble Radziwiłł family. See *Słownik*, 12:646.

15. Kotik's father was forced to settle on this estate, and Kotik and his wife followed him there. Kotik describes his life there in detail in *Memoirs*, 2, chapter 2.

16. According to PT *Shekalim* 48c.

17. Avraham-Hirsh Kotik, born in 1867.

18. See chapter 26, note 18.

19. It is difficult to identify this person, perhaps he was Aryeh-Leib Feinstein (1821–1903), author of the book *Ir tehilah*, who was suspected of being a heretic by the ultra-Orthodox of Brisk. See Sokolow, *Sefer zikaron*, 166–68; and *EJD*, 2:173–74.

20. Kotik did not study in either of the two rabbinical seminars (in Vilna and Zhitomir), whose graduates were trained for the post of "crown rabbi." In order to

be awarded this position he must, according to the law, have been able to pass a gymnasium-level Russian fluency exam.

21. Kotik refers here to Russian language textbooks written especially for Jews, such as Shmuel Yaakov Fuenn, *Talmud leshon Rusiyah* (Vilna, 1847) or Avraham Yaakov Paperna, *Moreh sefat Rusiyah* (Warsaw, 1869). See Lilienblum, *Autobiography,* 1:128.

CHAPTER 28

1. On Yoshke the "doctor" and the healers in the township, see chapter 1, following note 111.

2. See, for example, the description of his weeping in chapter 14.

3. For reasons of modesty the purification of a woman was performed only by female members of the local burial society.

4. The ceremony of requesting forgiveness from the deceased described here is a folk custom, which has no basis in Jewish law. See Chayes, "Customs," 301.

5. See *Shulhan arukh, Yoreh de'ah,* chapter 343, paragraph 1.

6. His uncle's death and funeral were described in the previous chapter.

7. This custom, which came about for reasons of modesty, derives from a saying attributed to Rabbi Joshua ben Levi: "Three things were told me by the Angel of Death . . . do not stand in front of women when they are returning from the presence of a dead person, because I go leaping in front of them with my sword in my hand, and I have permission to harm" (BT *Berakhot* 51a). See *Kitzur shulhan arukh,* chapter 198, paragraph 10. On various customs related to funerals, see Chayes, "Customs"; Benayahu, *Ma'amadot.*

8. During the shivah, mourners sit either on the floor, on a mattress, or on a low stool. Sitting on benches or chairs is not permitted. See *Kitzur shulhan arukh,* chapter 211, paragraph 1; Glick, *A Light unto the Mourner,* 77–79.

9. See the description of the blessing ceremony in the Kotik household on Yom Kippur eve, chapter 14, following note 7.

10. Based on *Pirkei avot* (Ethics of the Fathers), 2:4. The original meaning refers to the will of God (i.e., fulfilling the commandments), but Kotik's grandmother interpreted this passage as emphasizing man's relationship to his fellow man.

11. Mistakenly printed *Kiryat sofer* in the original. This book, which is actually a *brievensteller* (see chapter 20, note 25), was printed in Vilna in 1835 and thereafter in a number of editions. See Klausner, *Ha-sifrut ha-ivrit ha-hadashah,* 3:148; Zwick, *Briefsteller,* 117–29. M. A. Günzburg (1795–1846) was one of the most important maskilic figures in Vilna. See Klausner, *Ha-sifrut ha-ivrit ha-hadashah,* 3:129–85; Bartal, "Günzburg."

12. In his book Günzburg presents a series of letters "from father to son, from lover to his beloved friend, on difficulties and obstacles on the path to betrothal." Nathan shares with his friend Shmuel, who has recently married, his experiences and thoughts regarding married life and love. See *Kiryat sefer,* 74–77.

13. See 2 Sam. 12:16–24. The order "to strike up a tune" is not mentioned in either the biblical source or in the Midrash.

14. This idyllic description is hard to accept. A different picture emerges

from available statistics regarding marriage and divorce in other Pale of Settlement Jewish communities. For example, in Berdichev (Volhin province), there were a reported 1,004 divorces from 1861 to 1868, as opposed to 3,078 marriages; that is, a three-to-one ratio of marriages to divorces (Tzederbaum, *Berditchov*, 88).

15. This, too, seems hyperbolic and not grounded in reality. According to the census of 1897, within the Jewish population in the Pale there were 12,589 divorced women and 3,975 divorced men. Although these numbers do not include those who remarried, the numbers are still small considering the overall Jewish population in the Pale (over five million). See Stampfer, "Remarriage," 99.

16. As mentioned earlier, Aharon-Leyzer and his wife ran a tavern in Kamenets. See chapter 4.

17. However, it turned out that his grandfather's bitter mourning period did not last long. Three months after his wife's death, his announcement that he had remarried took the entire family by surprise. See Kotik, *Memoirs, 2*, chapter 1.

CHAPTER 29

1. BT *Sanhedrin* 106b: "The Holy One, blessed be He, requires the heart as it is written 'But the Lord looketh on the heart [1 Sam. 16:7]' " (see also *Hovot ha-levavot*, 10; *Sefer hasidim*, 21, no. 15). This saying became a kind of hasidic slogan encapsulating its basic spiritual message—the centrality of devotion during prayer, study, and in all aspects of daily life.

2. On this book and its author (Bahya ibn Paquda), see chapter 11, note 7.

3. On Elijah, the Gaon of Vilna, see chapter 1, note 123. For the background to his struggle against Hasidism from 1772 to 1797, see Etkes, *The Gaon*, 84–108; and Mondshine, "Parnasei Vilna."

4. On the meaning of wandering (*galut* in Hebrew), see chapter 1, note 125. On the Gaon' s wanderings, see *Aliyot Eliyahu*, 84. See also *Pe'at ha-shulhan*, 5b. He then settled in Vilna (circa 1748), where he remained until his death.

5. This story is based on the Gaon's sons' testimony, found in their foreword to their father's commentary on the *Shulhan arukh* (*Orah hayyim*): "When he was thirteen and a day, he committed himself to a life of piety and abstinence . . . from then until his death he never looked beyond his four walls and didn't want to enjoy this world. He ate only a small piece of dry bread . . . morning and evening, and didn't taste it in his palate, but swallowed it whole" (*Aliyot Eliyahu*, 179).

6. As opposed to the myth of the "poor Torah scholar," in traditional Ashkenazic society the chances of a poor man's son becoming an outstanding scholar were quite small. See Katz, "Marriage," 32–33.

7. The term "study house" (Hebrew *beit midrash*) applied to any building dedicated to the study of Torah and prayer. On the mutual influence of the religious and the social functions of synagogues and study houses, see Katz, *Tradition and Crisis*, 147–55; and Lipschitz, *Me-dor le-dor*, 82–87.

8. *Shtot* (lit. "city," "town")—a synagogue pew purchased for exclusive use by its owner. On *shtotgelt* (the money with which the seat was bought), see Rivkind, *Jewish Money*, 268. On the history of "inheritance" of synagogue seats, see Krauss, *Batei ha-tefilah*, 254–55. On the reflection of social stratification within the synagogue, see Katz, *Tradition and Crisis*, 133, 210–11. Social stratification was more

defined in synagogues than in the more "democratic" study houses. See Lipschitz, *Me-dor le-dor,* 84.

9. The first two honors of being called up to the Torah reading are reserved for a Priest (*kohen*) and a Levite (*levi*), respectively; thus the third, reserved for those of nonlevitical lineage (*yisrael*), is considered the most prestigious and is given to a respected Torah scholar, communal leader, well-to-do householder, or the like (but see Friedman, *Zikhronot,* 73). Generally, the number of portions read on the Sabbath is no less than seven plus *maftir,* but more may be added, in which case the final portion is called "last" (*aharon*). The *maftir* is the person who is called up to recite the blessings before and after the reading of the *haftarah,* a chapter taken from the Prophets. At regular Sabbath morning services, the *maftir* also recites the blessings on the Torah and reads at least the last three verses of the weekly portion. It is noteworthy that in the synagogue Kotik established in Warsaw this custom of "hefty" honors was done away with; see introduction, following note 37.

10. As mentioned above, it is possible to call up a greater number of persons to read from the Torah by "shrinking" the customary division; however, the minimum length for each portion is three verses.

11. Scholars classify this "opposition" phenomenon, mainly the establishment of artisan societies' prayer groups, as a reflection of the crisis that swept over traditional Eastern European Jewish society during the eighteenth century. See Dinur, "Hasidism," 130–32; and Katz, *Tradition and Crisis,* 133–34.

12. Kotik uses the term "democracy" here, not in its modern sense, but to denote those commoners who opposed the tyrannical rule of the communal leaders who despised the poor and ignored their religious rights.

13. In the original *ba'al shem* (lit. "master of the [Holy] name")—an honorific usually conferred on miracle workers and healers who utilized holy names, amulets, and folk healing. This name was bestowed on Rabbi Israel ben Eliezer (d. 1760), the founder of Hasidism, also known as the Besht—an acronym for Ba'al Shem Tov (the addition of the word *tov* [good] has no special connotation, and there were others with the same honorific). On *ba'aley shem* and the Besht, see Etkes, "Magic"; and Rosman, *Founder of Hasidism,* 11–26.

14. This view, that Hasidism aimed to ease the "burden" of the practical commandments, also espoused by some historians, Simon Dubnow in particular, is obviously not true, for in fact the religious and halakhic demands of Hasidism were far from being "easy." Indeed, in many aspects hasidim were more demanding than their opponents. In addition, hasidic and prehasidic writings contain no trace of complaints regarding the heavy burden of fulfilling religious obligations, from which the Jewish lower classes seemingly wished to be freed.

15. This saying, found not in the Talmud but in the Midrash, is quite different: "Thanks to four reasons the Israelites were redeemed from Egypt: they did not change their names, they did not change their language, they did not go talebearing, and none of them was found to have been immoral." For references and different versions, see Sever, *Mikhlol ha-ma'amarim,* 1:348, s.v. "bizekhut arba'ah devarim."

16. The concept of "worship in corporeality" was central to hasidic thought and was generally understood as an expansion of the normative framework of worship by exposing the positive religious potential in daily activities, such as eating, drinking, sleeping, sexual relations, earning a livelihood, and so on. See, for

example, Schatz, *Hasidism as Mysticism,* s.v. "avodah be-gashmiyut," especially 28–30; Piekarz, *Beginning of Hasidism,* s.v. "gashmiyut"; and Tishby, *Studies,* 3:967–70. On the concept of "worship in joy," see Shochat, "Joy in Hasidism," where he showed that although this was one of the famous trademarks of Hasidism, it did not originate with this movement.

17. Hebrew *ohel moed.* For this matter, see Exod. 29: 31–32, among others.

18. Lit. "exhortations." Refers to Deuteronomy 27–28, which enumerates curses and punishments to be brought upon the Israelites if they fail to obey the divine commandments.

19. Kotik mistakenly wrote verse 44; the correct reference is Deut. 28:47. The majority of the biblical quotations that follow were taken by Kotik from Luzzatto's *Mesillat yesharim,* chapter 19, 342–47. On this book, see notes following.

20. Kotik combined these two verses into one.

21. *Mesillat yesharim,* 344–45.

22. The reference mistakenly reads fol. 66 in the original.

23. Moshe Hayyim Luzzatto (b. Padua, 1707—d. Acre, 1744)—kabbalist, poet and author. Leader of a kabbalistic circle by virtue of his outstanding knowledge in all fields of Judaism, his charismatic personality, and his personal messianic outlook, his activities created an acrimonious controversy regarding his personality and his kabbalistic teachings. Suspected of Sabbatian leanings, he was forced to conceal some of his writings, and eventually to leave his home. He wandered throughout various western European cities and emigrated to Eretz-Israel in 1743. His writings greatly influenced Hasidism. See Tishby, *Studies,* 3:961–94.

24. Luzzatto did not live before, but was contemporary with the Ba'al Shem Tov.

25. *Mesillat yesharim*—a didactic ethical book, a guide to the moral behavior leading to spiritual perfection. This well-known book, written clearly and eloquently, without complex kabbalistic discourse, was first printed during Luzzatto's lifetime (Amsterdam, 1740) and enjoyed widespread popularity among many circles, including hasidic and mitnaggedic ones.

26. *Mesillat yesharim,* chapter 13. Luzzatto used the term *hasid* to refer to "saintliness" (the word stems from *gomel hasadim;* i.e., performs acts of kindness), and the term *zaddik* to refer to almsgiving. Kotik attributes these terms to Hasidism.

27. See note 22 above.

28. On the messianic attitudes of the Ba'al Shem Tov and his disciples, see Dan, *Messianism,* 118–63.

29. This quotation begins: "The Scripture places three of the most questionable characters [Jerubaal, Bedan, Jepthah] on the same level with three of the most estimable characters [Moses, Aaron, Samuel]." Bedan was one of the biblical Judges (1 Sam. 12:11).

30. According to *Pirkei avot* (Ethics of the Fathers) 1:18: "On three things does the world stand: on justice, on truth, and on peace." Kotik refers in this passage to the hasidic leader, the zaddik.

31. This is the most popular saying used to describe "the decline of the generations," providing an excuse for the stagnation and inability to make significant changes in the normative religious system, which idolizes its past.

32. According to *Pirkei avot* 2:5: "An uncultured person is not sin-fearing, neither is an ignorant person pious." The simple meaning of this saying is that one who has no Torah knowledge cannot be pious; the mitnaggedim used it to ridicule hasidim, who, in their eyes, were all ignoramuses.

33. On the hasidic way of prayer with shaking and dancing, see Wertheim, *Law and Custom*, 157–62.

34. Passages from the daily morning prayers. The congregation usually prays in unison.

35. On the importance of pipe smoking in Hasidism, see Wertheim, *Law and Custom*, 340–41; and Jacobs, "Tobacco."

36. Like many languages, Yiddish requires the respectful use of the second person plural—*ir*—when addressing a person of seniority in age, rank, or position, including ones' parents. Hasidim, however, used to address anyone using the direct second person singular form, *du*. This was considered vulgar and impolite, especially when a young hasid addressed an elder in this manner. See Levin, *Zikhronot*, 49.

37. On *yahrzeit*, see chapter 4, note 26; Wertheim, *Law and Custom*, 252–54, 335–40.

38. Psalm 67, which is recited on Saturday night before the evening prayers, according to the Ashkenazi rite.

39. "It is like a law for the rich person, not to travel by himself to Liady . . . and according to his wealth he should take with him poor people who desire to fill their thirst of Hasidism" (Rabinowitsch, "Schneerson," 170). During the nineteenth century, group travel to the zaddik's court became one of the most important hasidic experiences; see Assaf, *Regal Way*, 310–15. On Moshe Kotik's travels to the rebbe around Rosh Hashanah, see chap. 14 near note 4 and the beginning of chapter 24.

40. See especially chapters 14–15.

41. Accusations against hasidim, that they had caused the destruction of family units, were heard from the inception of the hasidic-mitnaggedic controversy; see, for example, Katz, *Tradition and Crisis*, 211–12.

42. Ten gulden equals 150 kopecks or two-and-a-half rubles.

43. Kotik refers here to tanners, whose profession entailed soaking animal skins in water. For this reason and because working with hides gave off foul smells, tanners' workshops were generally located near rivers or lakes, outside the town, and the tanner became a symbol of a contemptible and despised craft.

44. See chapters 24–25.

Appendix A

1. This publication is evidently related to the "Lithuanian" minyan founded by Kotik in Warsaw, which he called Achiezer. It contains the "bylaws of the synagogue known as the Achiezer Synagogue for its aim of using its revenues to assist and support members of the congregation harmed by circumstances" (p. 10). Kotik later used these detailed bylaws as a basis for other societies he founded.

2. Although bilingual, Yiddish far outweighs Hebrew in this publication. The publisher Shlomo Shrebrek wrote that Kotik originally approached him with a Yiddish pamphlet titled *Aseres ha-dibros li-vnos* [sic] *tsiyyon.* Only after ascertaining

that Shrebrek knew Hebrew, did he give him the Hebrew version. See Shrebrek, *Zikhronot*, 159. Shrebrek appears to have been mistaken; there is no evidence for the existence of separate editions of this brochure. Although because of its title this publication is often assumed to be a Zionist pamphlet, the role of Zionism in it is marginal (see Assaf, *What I Have Seen*, 389–90 n. 10).

3. It appears that Kotik also published these bylaws in Yiddish (see the advertisement in *Der proyektirter* [no. 10], 15), as he did for many of the other societies he promoted. I was unable, however, to locate a copy of these bylaws in Yiddish.

4. YIVO Archives, Rabbinic and Historical Manuscripts Collection, RG 128, fol. 244. Kotik suggests twenty-four pluralistic principles, which he calls "the guiding principles and foundations of religious life." Each Jew is obliged to observe these principles, alongside the pentateuchal Ten Commandments. A report on Kotik's funeral ("Yekhezkel Kotik"; Goldberg, "Kotik") noted that in a eulogy delivered at the graveside it was mentioned that while ill Kotik was engaged in working on his composition called *Sefer ha-midot*. This work was to contain quotations of talmudic and rabbinic dicta on the proper behavior to which a Jew should adhere. Evidently, the reference here is to *Sefer torat adam* [no. 6], on which Kotik was apparently working during the final year of his life.

5. This publication, a workers' almanac edited by Kotik's son Avraham, contains information along socialist lines. It includes a detailed calendar for 1907–8; an article by Avraham Kotik; programs of the Bund, Poalei Zion, and Jewish workers' parties in Germany, Belgium, and Russia; stories; a bibliography; and advertisements.

6. This publication is of especial interest. It is divided into two parts. In part one Kotik relates to criticism of one of his commandments (integration into non-Jewish society) found in his *Aseret ha-dibrot* (note 2 above) and defends his views on antisemitism. Part two treats the question of the involvement of Jews in the elections to the Russian parliament (Duma). Kotik took issue with the dominant right wing National Democrats' hostility toward Jews, their strong opposition to Jewish representation in the Duma. For background, see *EJD, Warsaw* 1:87–89. On page 28 Kotik declared his intention of publishing another booklet on the same topic; however, it appears that he never did so.

7. In this pamphlet Kotik presented a plan to relieve the severe housing shortage affecting Warsaw Jews. He suggested ways in which renters could become owners of their apartments. See also Rivkind, *Jewish Money*, 67–68.

8. This pamphlet is not found in JNUL. It was the late Professor Chone Shmeruk who was kind enough to make it available to me.

9. This publication is not held by JNUL. A copy is found in YIVO, New York.

10. See the necrology "Yekhezkel Kotik."

Works Cited

Where an English title page was available for a Hebrew or Yiddish source, this was cited, with the original language noted in the key. Where no such title page was available, references have been provided in transliteration with a translation of the title in the key (with the exception of many older rabbinic works whose titles are not easily translated).

(H=Hebrew; Y=Yiddish; E=English; R=Russian)

Agnon, *Bridal Canopy*
    Shmuel Yosef Agnon. *The Bridal Canopy.* Translated by Israel Meir Lask. New York: Schocken, 1967.

Agnon, *Elu ve-elu*
    ———. *Elu ve-elu* (This and that). Jerusalem: Schocken, 1969.

Agnon, *Ir u-melo'ah*
    ———. *Ir u-melo'ah* (A city in its fullness). Jerusalem: Schocken, 1973.

Aksenfeld, "The Headband"
    Yisroel Aksenfeld. "The Headband." In *The Shtetl.* Translated and edited by Joachim Neugroschel, 49–172. New York: Richard Marek, 1979.

Aliyot Eliyahu
    Joshua-Heshel Levin. *Aliyot Eliyahu* (Elijah's ascensions). Vilna, 1856. Reprint, Jerusalem: n.p., 1989.

Altbauer, "Revolt"
    Moshe Altbauer. "The Revolt of 1863 in Jewish Literature and Folklore." *He'avar* 11 (1964): 27–36 (H).

Ascheim, "East European Jew"
    Steven E. Ascheim. "The East European Jew and German Jewish Identity." *Studies in Contemporary Jewry* 1 (1984): 3–25.

Assaf, *Regal Way*
David Assaf. *The Regal Way: The Life and Times of Rabbi Israel of Ruzhin.* Stanford, CA: Stanford University Press, 2002.

Assaf, *What I Have Seen*
————, trans. and ed. *What I Have Seen: The Memoirs of Yekhezkel Kotik.* Tel Aviv: Tel Aviv University, 1998 (H).

Assaf, *Mekorot*
Simha Assaf. *Mekorot le-toldot ha-hinukh be-yisrael* (Sources on the history of Jewish education). Vol. 4. Jerusalem: Mossad Harav Kook, 1943.

Ba'al Makhshoves, "Literarishe geshprekhn"
Ba'al Makhsoves [Yisrael Elyashev, pseud.]. "Literarishe geshprekhn" (Literary talks). *Der fraynd,* 20 December 1912, no. 277.

Ba'al-Makhshoves, "Memuarn-literatur"
————. "Memuarn-literatur" (Memoir literature). *Shriftn,* 3: 58–70. Vilna, [1913].

Ba'al-Makhshoves, *Skirot u-reshamim*
————. *Skirot u-reshamim* (Reviews and impressions). Vol. 1. Warsaw: Sifrut, 1912.

Baron, *Russian Jew*
Salo W. Baron. *The Russian Jew under Tsars and Soviets.* New York: Macmillan, 1976.

Barros, *Autobiography: Narrative of Transformation*
Barros, Carolyn A. *Autobiography: Narrative of Transformation.* Ann Arbor: University of Michigan Press, 1998.

Bartal, "Gentile Society"
Israel Bartal. "Non-Jews and Gentile Society in East-European Hebrew and Yiddish Literature, 1856–1914." Ph.D. diss., Hebrew University, Jerusalem, 1980 (H).

Bartal, "Günzburg"
————."Mordechai Aaron Günzburg: A Lithuanian Maskil Faces Modernity." In *From East and West: Jews in a Changing Europe, 1750–1870,* ed. Frances Malino and David Sorkin, 126–47. Oxford: Blackwell, 1990.

Bartal, "Non-Jews"
————. "Non-Jews and Gentile Society in East European Hebrew and Yiddish Literature, 1856–1914." *Polin* 4 (1989): 53–69.

Beit-Halevi, *Vaks*
Israel David Beit-Halevi. *Toldot Rabbi Hayyim Elazar Vaks, ha-Rav me-Kalish* (The life of the Kalisher rabbi Hayyim Elazar Vaks). Tel Aviv: privately printed, 1950.

Beit Yisrael be-Polin
> *Beit Yisrael be-Polin* (The Jews in Poland). Edited by Israel Halpern. 2 vols. Jerusalem: Youth Department of the Zionist Organization, 1948–54.

Belz
> *Belz: Sefer zikaron* (Belz memorial book). Edited by Yosef Rubin. Tel Aviv, 1974.

Benayahu, *Ma'amadot*
> Meir Benayahu. *Studies in Memory of . . . Yitzhak Nissim.* Vol. 6: *Ma'amadot u-moshavot.* Jerusalem: Yad Harav Nissim, 1985 (H).

Ben-Sasson, "The Gaon"
> Haim Hillel Ben-Sasson. "The Personality of Elijah Gaon of Vilna and His Historical Influence." *Zion* 31 (1966): 39–86, 197–216 (H).

Bergner, *Long Winter-Nights*
> Hinde Bergner. *In the Long Winter-Nights . . . Memoirs of a Jewish Family in a Galician Township (1870–1900).* Montreal, 1946 (Y).

Berkowitz, *Ha-rishonim*
> Yitzhak Dov Berkowitz. *Ha-rishonim ki-vnei adam* (Portraits of our forefathers). In *Collected Writings of Y. D. Berkowitz.* Vol. 2. Tel Aviv: Dvir, 1964 (H).

Berman, *Al neharot*
> Israel Berman. *Al neharot Ukrayna* (By the rivers of the Ukraine). Tel Aviv: Twersky, 1946.

Bialik, "Alphabet"
> Hayyim Nahman Bialik. "The Alphabet and What Lies between the Lines." In *Random Harvest: The Novellas of Bialik,* trans. David Patterson and Ezra Spicehandler, 32–35. Boulder, Colo.: Westview, 1999.

Bieber, *Ostraha*
> Menahem Mendl Bieber. *Mazkeret li-gedolei Ostraha* (Memorial volume to the great men of Ostróg). Berdichev, 1907.

Bilu, "Dybbuk"
> Yoram Bilu. "Dybbuk Possession and Mechanisms of Internalization and Externalization: A Case Study." In *Projection, Identification, Projective Identification,* ed. Joseph Sandler, 163–78. Madison, Conn.: International University Press, 1987.

Birstein, *A Face in the Clouds*
> Yossel Birstein. *A Face in the Clouds.* Tel Aviv: Hakibbutz Hameuchad, 1991 (H).

Book of Legends
> *The Book of Legends (Sefer Ha-Aggadah).* Edited by Hayyim Nahman Bialik

and Yehoshua Hana Ravnitzky. Translated by William G. Braude. New York: Schocken, 1992.

Braver and Braver, *Zikhronot*
Michael Braver and Avraham Yaakov Braver. *Zikhronot av u-vno* (Memoirs of a father and son). Jerusalem: Mossad Harav Kook, 1966.

Buckley, *Turning Key*
Jerome Hamilton Buckley. *The Turning Key: Autobiography and the Subjective Impulse since 1800.* Cambridge, Mass.: Harvard University Press, 1984.

Cambridge History of Poland
The Cambridge History of Poland, 1697–1935. Edited by W. F. Reddaway et al. Cambridge: Cambridge University Press, 1941.

Caspi, "Shedlitz"
Yitzhak Caspi. "Shalosh hatunot mitzva be-Shedlitz" (Three weddings in Siedlce). *Reshumot,* n.s., 2 (1946): 101–2.

Chayes, "Customs"
Hayyim Chayes. "Beliefs and Customs in Connection with Death." *Filologishe shriftn* 2 (1928): 281–328 (Y).

Chemerinsky, *Motele*
Hayyim Chemerinsky. *My Town Motele.* Edited by David Assaf. Jerusalem: Magnes, 2002.

Cohen, *Shpola*
David Cohen. *Shpola: Masekhet hayyei yehudim ba-ayyarah* (Shpola: The life of the Jews in the town). Haifa: Irgun Yotzei Shpola be-Yisrael, 1965.

Cohen, *Jewish Icons*
Richard I. Cohen. *Jewish Icons: Art and Society in Modern Europe.* Berkeley and Los Angeles: University of California Press, 1998.

Dan, *Messianism*
Joseph Dan. *The Modern Jewish Messianism.* Tel Aviv: Ministry of Defence, 1999 (H).

Dawidowicz, *Golden Tradition*
Lucy S. Dawidowicz, ed. *The Golden Tradition: Jewish Life and Thought in Eastern Europe.* Boston: Beacon, 1967.

Deinard, *Zikhronot*
Ephraim Deinard, *Zikhronot bat ami: Memoirs of Jewish Life in Russia.* 2 vols. St. Louis: Moinester, 1920 (H).

Der Nister, *The Family Mashber*
Der Nister. *The Family Mashber.* Translated by Leonard Wolf. New York: Summit, 1987.

Dictionary of the Yiddish Language
   Great Dictionary of the Yiddish Language. Edited by Yudel Mark. Vol. 3. New York: Yiddish Dictionary Committee, 1971 (Y).

Dinur, "Hasidism"
   Benzion Dinur. "The Origins of Hasidism and its Social and Messianic Foundations." In *Essential Papers on Hasidism: Origins to Present,* ed. Gershon D. Hundert, 86–208. New York: New York University Press, 1991.

Dinur, "Ignatiev"
   ———. "The 'Projects' of Count Ignatiev to Solve the Jewish Question." *He'avar* 10 (1963): 5–60 (H).

Dinur, *Milhamah u-mahapekha*
   ———. *Bi-yemei milhamah u-mahapekha* (In days of war and revolution). Jerusalem: Bialik Institute, 1960.

Dinur, *Mapu's Letters*
   ———, ed. *The Letters of Abraham Mapu.* Jerusalem: Bialik Institute, 1970 (II).

Dubnow, *Evreiskaia starina*
   Simon M. Dubnow. [Review of Kotik's *Memoirs*]. *Evreiskaia starina* 6 (1913): 413–14 (R).

Dubnow, *History of the Jews*
   ———. *History of the Jews.* Translated by Moshe Spiegel. Vol. 5. New York and London: Thomas Yoseloff, 1973.

Dubnow, *Jews in Russia*
   ———. *History of the Jews in Russia and Poland.* 3 vols. Translated by I. Friedlaender. Philadelphia: Jewish Publication Society, 1916–20.

Dubnow, "Nahpesa ve-nahkora"
   ———. "Nahpesa ve-nahkora" (Let us search and examine). *Pardes* 1 (1892): 221–42. First published in Russian in *Voskhod* 11 (1891).

Duker, "Polish Insurrection"
   Abraham G. Duker. "Jewish Participants in the Polish Insurrection of 1863." In *Studies and Essays in Honor of Abraham A. Neuman,* 144–53. Leiden: Brill, 1962.

Eakin, *Fictions in Autobiography*
   John Paul Eakin. *Fictions in Autobiography: Studies in the Art of Self-Invention.* Princeton, N. J.: Princeton University Press, 1985.

Einhorn, "Amol"
   Aharon Einhorn. "Amol" (Once). *Haynt,* 1 January 1913, no. 292: 4.

Eisenstadt, *Minsk*
   Benzion Eisenstadt. *Rabanei Minsk ve-hakhamehah* (The rabbis and scholars of Minsk). Vilna, 1899.

EJD
> *Encyclopaedia of the Jewish Diaspora: A Memorial Library of Countries and Communities, Poland Series.*
>
> Vol. 1: *Warsaw,* vol. 1, edited by Itzhak Gruenbaum. Jerusalem: Encyclopaedia of the Jewish Diaspora Co., 1953 (H).
>
> Vol. 2: *Brest-Litovsk,* edited by Eliezer Steinman. Jerusalem, 1954 (H).
>
> Vol. 9: *Grodno,* edited by Dov Rabin. Jerusalem, 1973 (H & Y).

Eliach, *Avi ha-yeshivot*
> Dov Eliach. *Avi ha-yeshivot* (Father of the yeshivot). 2 vols. Jerusalem: Machon Moreshet ha-Yeshivot, 1991.

Eliav, *Love of Zion*
> Mordechai Eliav. *Love of Zion and Men of Hod: German Jewry and the Settlement of Eretz Israel in the 19th Century.* Tel Aviv: Hakibbutz Hameuchad, 1970 (H).

Elior, "Polish Hasidism"
> Rachel Elior. "The Innovation of Polish Hasidism." *Tarbiz* 62 (1993): 381–432 (H).

Elzet, "Me-minhagei yisrael"
> Yehudah Elzet. "Me-minhagei yisrael" (Jewish customs). *Reshumot* 1 (Odessa, 1918): 335–77.

Emden, *Siddur beit Yaakov*
> Yaakov Emden. *Siddur beit Yaakov.* Lemberg, 1904.

Emet le-Yaakov
> Avraham-Yaakov Friedman of Sadgora. *Emet le-Yaakov.* Edited by Alexander S. Bistritzky. Jerusalem: Ha-merkaz le-hotza'at sifrei hasidut mi-beit Ruzhin, 1993.

Epstein, *Mekor Barukh*
> Baruch Epstein. *Mekor Barukh.* 4 vols. Vilna, 1928.

Etkes, *The Gaon*
> Immanuel Etkes. *The Gaon of Vilna: The Man and His Image.* Jerusalem: Zalman Shazar Center for Jewish History, 1998 (H).

Etkes, *Israel Salanter*
> ———. *Rabbi Israel Salanter and the Mussar Movement.* Philadelphia: Jewish Publication Society, 1993.

Etkes, *Lita*
> ———. *Lita bi-Yerushalayim: The Scholarly Elite in Lithuania and the Prushim of Jerusalem as Reflected in the Writings of Shmuel of Kelme.* Jerusalem: Yad Izhak Ben-Zvi, 1991 (H).

Etkes, "Magic"
———. "The Role of Magic and *Ba'alei-Shem* in Ashkenazic Society in the Late 17th and Early 18th Centuries." *Zion* 60 (1995): 69–104 (H).

Ettinger, *Essays*
Shmuel Ettinger. *On the History of the Jews in Poland and Russia: Collected Essays.* Jerusalem: Zalman Shazar Center for Jewish History, 1994 (H). *Evreiskaya entsiklopediia.* 16 vols. St. Petersburg, 1908–13.

Faierstein, *Izbica*
Morris M. Faierstein. *All Is in the Hands of Heaven: The Teachings of Rabbi Mordecai Joseph Leiner of Izbica.* Hoboken, N.J.: Ktav, 1989.

Fajnhauz, "Ludność żydowska"
Dawid Fajnhauz. "Ludność żydowska na Litwie i Bialorusi a powstanie styczniowe." Parts 1 and 2. *Biuletyn Żydowskiego Institutu Historycznego* 37 (1961): 3–34, 108; 38 (1961): 39–68, 150.

Feingold, "Autobiography as Literature"
Ben-Ami Feingold. "Autobiography as Literature: An Examination of M. L. Lilienblum's *Youthful Sins.*" *Mehqarei Yerushalayim be-sifrut ivrit* 4 (1984): 86–111 (H).

Feinstein, *Ir tehilah*
Aryeh Leib Feinstein. *Ir tehilah* (City of glory). Warsaw, 1885.

Jacob Fichmann, "Nusah Polin"
Jacob Fichmann. "Nusah Polin" (Polish style). In *Ruhot menagnot: Sofrei Polin.* Jerusalem: Bialik Institute, 1953.

Finkelstein, *Haynt*
Chaim Finkelstein. *Haynt: A Jewish Daily, 1908–1939.* Tel Aviv: I. L. Peretz, 1978 (Y).

Frankel, "Costume"
Giza Frankel. "Notes on the Costume of the Jewish Woman in Eastern Europe." *Journal of Jewish Art* 7 (1980): 50–57.

Frankel, "Russian-Jewish Crisis"
Jonathan Frankel. "The Emergence of the New Politics: The Russian-Jewish Crisis, 1881–1882." In *Prophecy and Politics: Socialism, Nationalism, and the Russian Jews, 1862–1917,* 49–132. Cambridge: Cambridge University Press, 1981.

Freid, *Yamim ve-shanim*
Meir Yaakov Freid. *Yamim ve-shanim: Zikhronot ve-tziyurim mi-tekufah shel hamishim shanah* (Days and years: Memoirs and vignettes from a fifty-year period). Vol. 2. Tel Aviv: Dvir, 1939.

Friedberg, *Sefer ha-zikhronot*
Avraham Shalom Friedberg, *Sefer ha-zikhronot* (Book of memoirs). 2 vols. Warsaw, 1899.

Friedberg, "Zikhronot"
————. "Zikhronot mi-yemei ne'urai: Ha-hatufim" (Memoirs of my youth: The Cantonists). In *Sefer ha-shanah,* ed. Nahum Sokolow, 3:82–101. Warsaw, 1902.

Friedman, *Zikhronot*
Eliezer Elijah Friedman. *Sefer ha-zikhronot (1858–1926)* (Book of memoirs [1858–1926]). Tel Aviv, 1926.

Fuenn, *Kiryah ne'emanah*
Shmuel Yaakov Fuenn. *Kiryah ne'emanah* (A faithful city). Vilna, 1915.

Fuks and Fuks, "Yiddish Publishing"
Leo Fuks and Renate Fuks. "Yiddish Publishing Activities in the Weimar Republic, 1920–1933." *Leo Baeck Institute Year Book* 33 (1988): 417–34.

The Gaon of Vilna
The Gaon of Vilna: The Man and His Legacy. Edited by Rachel Schnold. Tel Aviv: Beth Hatefutsoth, 1998.

Gartner, *Customs*
Yaakov Gartner. *The Evolvement of Customs in the World of Halacha.* Jerusalem: Hemed, 1995 (H).

Gelber, *Polnische Aufstand*
Nathan Michael Gelber. *Die Juden und der Polnische Aufstand 1863.* Vienna: R. Löwit, 1923.

Genkin, "Practitioners of Law"
B. Genkin. "Jews as Practitioners of Law in Czarist Russia." *He'avar* 3 (1955): 111–15 (H).

Geshuri, *Music and Dance*
Meir Shimeon Geshuri. *Music and Dance in Hassidism.* Vol. 1. Tel Aviv: Netzach, 1955 (H).

Ginsburg, *Historishe verk*
Saul M. Ginsburg. *Historishe verk* (Historical works). 3 vols. New York: Ginsburg Testimonial Committee, 1937.

Ginsburg, *Ktavim*
————. *Ktavim Historiyim* (Historical works). Tel Aviv: Dvir, 1944.

Ginsburg, "Panic"
————. "On the Panic of 1835." *He'avar* 2 (1918): 34–44. Reprint, *Chulyot: Journal of Yiddish Research* 1 (1993): 56–69 (H).

Ginsburg and Marek, *Yiddish Folksongs*
Saul M. Ginsburg and Pesach Marek. *Yiddish Folksongs in Russia.* St. Petersburg, 1901. Reprint, Ramat Gan: Bar-Ilan University Press, 1991 (Y).

Glatstein, "Di letste fun a dor"
Yaakov Glatstein. "Di letste fun a dor" (Last of a generation). *Yidisher kemfer,* no. 1027, 9 October 1953, 14–15.

Glatstein, *Yash*
————. *Kshe-Yash nasa* (When Yash traveled). Translated by Dan Miron. Tel Aviv: Hakibbutz Hameuchad, 1994.

Glick, *A Light unto the Mourner*
Shmuel Glick. *A Light unto the Mourner: The Development of Major Customs of Mourning in the Jewish Tradition.* Jerusalem, 1991 (H).

Goldberg, "Kotik"
Avraham Goldberg. "Yekhezkel Kotik (A por verter nokh zayn toyt)—Tsu der kharakteristik fun a merkvirdikn lebn" (Yekhezkel Kotik: A few words after his death—A portrait of an extraordinary life). *Haynt,* 26 August 1921, no. 196: 9.

Goldberg, "Marriage"
Jacob Goldberg. "Jewish Marriage in Eighteenth-Century Poland." *Polin* 10 (1997): 3–39.

Gordon, *Collected Works*
Yehudah Leib Gordon. *Collected Works: Prose.* Tel Aviv: Dvir, 1960 (H).

Gottlober, *Memoirs*
Abraham Bear Gottlober. *Memoirs and Travels.* 2 vols. Jerusalem: Bialik Institute, 1976 (H).

Govrin, "Geografia sifrutit"
Nurit Govrin. "Geografia sifrutit: Darkhei itzuvan shel arim al mapat ha-sifrut ha-ivrit" (Literary geography: Shaping images of places in Hebrew literature). In *Ketivat ha-aretz,* 15–25. Jerusalem: Carmel, 1998.

Graetz, "Autobiography"
Michael Graetz. "Autobiography: On the Self-Understanding of the Maskilim." In *German Jewish History in Modern Times,* ed. Michael A. Meyer, 1: 324–32. New York: Columbia University Press, 1996.

Grafstein, *Panorama*
Melech Grafstein. *Sholom Aleichem Panorama.* New York: Jewish Observer, 1948.

Green, "Hasidic Homilies"
Arthur Green. "On Translating Hasidic Homilies." *Prooftexts* 3 (1983): 63–72.

Greenbaum, "Undzer Kotik-ekspeditsye"
Hirsh Greenbaum. "Undzer Kotik-ekspeditsye keyn Kamenets de-Lita" (Our

Kotik expedition to Lithuanian Kamenetz). *Literarishe bleter* 31 (430), 29 July 1932: 492–93.

Grossman, *Ashkenaz*
Avraham Grossman. *The Early Sages of Ashkenaz.* Jerusalem: Magnes Press, 1981 (H).

Grossman, "Stopping-the-Service"
———. "The Origins and Essence of the Custom of Stopping-the-Service." *Milet* 1 (1983): 199–219 (H).

Günzburg, *Aviezer*
Mordechai Aaron Günzburg. *Aviezer.* Vilna, 1863.

Günzburg, *Kiryat sefer*
———. *Kiryat sefer.* Vilna, 1835. Reprint, Vilna, 1848.

Gurshteyn, "Der yunger Mendele"
Aaron Gurshteyn. "Der yunger Mendele in kontekst fun di sekhtsiker yorn" (Young Mendele in the context of the sixties). In *Di yidishe literatur in nayntsetn yorhundert,* ed. Chone Shmeruk and Chava Turniansky, 485–510. Jerusalem: Magnes Press, 1993.

Halpern, *Eastern European Jewry*
Israel Halpern. *Eastern European Jewry: Historical Studies.* Jerusalem: Magnes Press, 1968 (H).

Hamm, *Kiev*
Michael F. Hamm. *Kiev: A Portrait, 1800–1917.* Princeton, N.J.: Princeton University Press, 1993.

Hannover, *Abyss of Despair*
Natan Neta ben Moshe Hannover. *Abyss of Despair (Yven metzulah).* Translated by Abraham J. Mesch. New Brunswick, N.J.: Transaction Books, 1983.

Harris, *Hebrew Liturgical Music*
Hyman H. Harris. *Hebrew Liturgical Music.* New York: Bitzaron, 1950 (H).

Harshav, "Chagall"
Benjamin Harshav, "Marc Chagall: Tsiyur, teatron, olam: Arba'ah prakim im perek ptihah." *Alpayim* 8 (1994): 9–97 (portions of which appeared in English in Guggenheim Museum, *Marc Chagall and the Jewish Theater* [New York, 1992], 15–63).

Hershberg, *Bialystok*
Abraham Samuel Hershberg. *Pinkas Bialystok (The Chronicle of Bialystok).* 2 vols. New York: Bialystok Jewish Historical Association, 1949–50 (Y).

Herzen, *Memoirs*
Alexander Herzen. *My Past and Thoughts: The Memoirs of Alexander Herzen.* Translated by Constance Garnett. Berkeley: University of California Press, 1982.

Hovot ha-levavot
Bahya ibn Paquda. *Hovot ha-levavot.* Jerusalem, 1928. (English: *Duties of the Heart,* trans. Yaakov Feldman. Northvale, N.J.: J. Aronson, 1996).

Ilana'eh, *Me'ever la-hushiyut*
Eliezer Yitzchak Ilana'eh. *Me-ever la-hushiyut* (Beyond senses). Jerusalem: Darom, 1930.

In Praise of the Ba'al Shem Tov
In Praise of the Baal Shem Tov (Shivhei ha-Besht). Translated and edited by Dan Ben-Amos and Jerome R. Mintz. Bloomington and London: Indiana University Press, 1970.

Ir giborim
Shimon Eliezer Fridenstein. *Ir giborim . . . Korot ir Horodna* (Town of heroes . . . The history of Grodno). Vilna, 1880.

Jacobs, "Tobacco"
Louis Jacobs. "Tobacco and the Hasidim." *Polin* 11 (1998): 25–30.

Jüdische Sprichwörter
Jüdische Sprichwörter und Redensarten (Yiddish proverbs and sayings). Compiled by Ignaz Bernstein. Warsaw, 1908.

Kalish, *Etmoli*
Ita Kalish. *Etmoli* (My yesterday). Tel Aviv: Hakibbutz Hameuchad, 1970.

Kamenetz Memorial Book
Kamenetz Litovsk, Zastavye and Colonies Memorial Book. Edited by Shmuel Eisenshtadt and Mordecai Gelbert. Tel Aviv: Townsmen Organization in Israel and the United States, 1967 (E, H, & Y).

Karnei or
Alexander Ziskind of Grodno. *Karnei or.* Vilna, 1883.

Kasovich, *Our Years*
Israel Isser Kasovich. *The Days of Our Years: Personal and General Reminiscence (1859–1929).* Translated by Maximilian Hurwitz. New York: Jordan Publishing, 1929.

Katsnelson, *Ha-milhamah ha-sifrutit*
Gideon Katsnelson. *Ha-milhamah ha-sifrutit beyn ha-haredim ve-ha-maskilim* (The literary war between the ultra-Orthodox and the maskilim). Tel Aviv: Dvir, 1954.

Katz, "Marriage"
Jacob Katz. "Marriage and Sexual Life among Jews at the Close of the Middle Ages." *Zion* 10 (1945): 21–54 (H).

Katz, *Tradition and Crisis*
————. *Tradition and Crisis: Jewish Society at the End of the Middle Ages.* Translated by Bernard Dov Cooperman. New York: Schocken, 1993.

Katz, "Bibliografye"
  Moshe Katz. "Bibliografye" (Bibliography). *Di tsukunft* 18, no. 9 (September 1913): 936–37.

Kaufmann, *Zikhronot*
  Shmuel Kaufmann. *Zikhronot (Toldot yemey hayyai)* (Memoirs [My life history]). Tel Aviv: privately printed, 1955.

Kestin, "Yidisher yubileum"
  Lipa Kestin. "A vikhtiker yidisher yubileum (25 yor ekzistents fun 'Akhiezer')" (A notable Jewish jubilee [25 years to the founding of Achiezer]). *Haynt,* 22 July 1913, no. 157: 5.

"Kinderhochzeit"
  "Kinderhochzeit." *Menorah* 6/7 (June 1927) (=*Die Juden in Polen*): 384–88.

Kirshenblatt-Gimblett, Introduction
  Barbara Kirshenblatt-Gimblett. Introduction to *Life Is with People: The Culture of the Shtetl,* by Mark Zborowski and Elizabeth Herzog. New York: Schocken, 1995.

Kitzur shulhan arukh
  Solomon Ganzfried. *Code of Jewish Law: A Compilation of Jewish Laws and Customs by Rabbi Solomon Ganzfried.* Translated by Hyman E. Goldin. Revised ed. 4 vols. New York: Hebrew Publishing Co., 1961 (H & E).

Klausner, *Ha-sifrut ha-ivrit ha-hadashah*
  Joseph Klausner. *Historiyah shel ha-sifrut ha-ivrit ha-hadashah* (The history of a new Hebrew literature). 6 vols. Jerusalem: Magnes Press, 1930–50.

Klausner, "He-hasid"
  ———. "R. Aleksander Ziskind mi-Horodna: He-hasid beyn ha-mitnaggedim" (Alexander Ziskind of Grodno: The hasid among the mitnaggedim). In *Sefer Assaf,* ed. M. D. Cassuto, Joseph Klausner, and Joshua Gutman, 427–32. Jerusalem: Mossad Harav Kook, 1953 (H).

Kleinman, *Mazkeret*
  Moshe Hayyim Kleinman. *Mazkeret shem ha-gedolim.* Piotrkow, 1908. Reprint, Bnei Brak, 1967.

Kleinman, *Or yesharim*
  ———. *Or yesharim.* Piotrkow, 1924.

Klier, *Jewish Question*
  John Doyle Klier. *Imperial Russia's Jewish Question, 1855–1881.* Cambridge: Cambridge University Press, 1995.

Klier, "What Exactly Was a Shtetl"
  ———. "What Exactly Was a Shtetl?" In *The Shtetl: Image and Reality,* ed. Gennady Estraikh and Mikhail Krutikov, 23–35. Oxford: Legenda, 2000.

Klier and Lambroza, *Pogroms*
John D. Klier and Shlomo Lambroza, eds. *Pogroms: Anti-Jewish Violence in Modern Russian History,* 39–134. Cambridge: Cambridge University Press, 1992.

Kluchevsky, *Divrey yemey Rusiyah*
Vasili O. Kluchevsky. *Divrey yemey Rusiyah* (A history of Russia). Vol. 3. Tel Aviv: Hakibbutz Hameuchad, 1978.

Knaani, *Ha-batim she-hayu*
David Knaani. *Ha-batim she-hayu: Studies in History of the Jewish Family.* Tel Aviv: Sifriat Poalim, 1986 (H).

Kobrin
Sefer Kobrin: Megilat hayyim ve-hurban (Book of Kobrin: A scroll of life and destruction). Edited by Bezalel Schwartz and Yisrael H. Biletzky. Tel Aviv: [Defus he-hadash], 1951.

"Kolonye fun 'Moment' "
"Di lustrayze tsu der kolonye fun 'Moment' " (A pleasure trip to *Der moment*'s neighborhood). *Der moment,* 14 July 1911, no. 151: 4–5.

Kosover, *Food and Beverages*
Mordecai Kosover. *Food and Beverages: A Study in History of Culture and Linguistics.* New York: YIVO, 1958 (Y).

Kotik, *Lebn*
Avraham Kotik. *Dos lebn fun a idishn inteligent* (The life of a Jewish intellectual). New York: Toybenshlag, 1925.

Kotik, *Aseret ha-dibrot*
Yekhezkel Kotik. *Aseret ha-dibrot li-venei tziyyon* (The ten commandments to the sons of Zion). Warsaw, 1899 (H & Y).

Kotik, *Das Haus meiner Grosseltern*
———. *Das Haus meiner Grosseltern.* Translated by Leo Hirsch. Berlin: Schocken, 1936.

Kotik, *Memoirs, 2*
———. *Mayne zikhroynes* (My memoirs). Vol. 2. Warsaw: Gitlin, 1914.

Kotik, *Der proyektirter*
———. *Der proyektirter ustav far dem "Varshaver lokatoren fereyn"* (The proposed bylaws of the Warsaw tenants' association). Warsaw, 1909.

Krasney, *Badkhan*
Ariela Krasney. *The Badkhan.* Ramat Gan: Bar-Ilan University, 1998 (H).

Krauss, *Batei ha-tefilah*
Samuel Krauss. *Korot batey ha-tefilah be-yisrael* (A history of synagogues). New York: Ogen, 1955.

Kressel, *Cyclopedia*
    G. Kressel. *Cyclopedia of Modern Hebrew Literature.* Vols. 1–2. Merchavia: Sifriat Poalim, 1965–67 (H).

Kugelmass, "Native Aliens"
    Jack Kugelmass. "Native Aliens: The Jews of Poland as a Middleman Minority." Ph.D. diss., New School of Social Research, New York, 1980.

Kugelmass and Boyarin, *From a Ruined Garden*
    Jack Kugelmass and Jonathan Boyarin, eds. *From a Ruined Garden: The Memorial Books of Polish Jewry.* New York: Schocken, 1983.

Lejeune, *On Autobiography*
    Philippe Lejeune. *On Autobiography.* Edited by Paul John Eakin. Translated by Katherine Leary. Minneapolis: University of Minnesota Press, 1989.

Leshtchinsky, *Yidishe folk*
    Jacob Leshtchinsky. *Dos yidishe folk in tsifern* (The Jewish people in numbers). Berlin: Klal-Verlag, 1922.

Levin, *Kantonistn*
    Avraham Levin. *Kantonistn* (Cantonists). Warsaw, 1934.

Levin, *Social and Economic Values*
    Mordechai Levin. *Social and Economic Values: The Idea of Professional Modernization in the Ideology of the Haskalah Movement.* Jerusalem: Bialik Institute, 1975 (H).

Levin, *Childhood in Exile*
    Shmarya Levin. *Childhood in Exile.* Translated by Maurice Samuel. London: Routledge, 1929.

Levin, *Harif*
    Yehudah Leib Levin. *Rabbi Eizel Harif.* 2d ed. Jerusalem: Mossad Harim Levin, 1973.

Levin, *Zikhronot*
    Yehudah Leib Levin [Yehalel]. *Zikhronot ve-hegyonot* (Memoirs and thoughts). Jerusalem: Bialik Institute, 1968.

Levitats, *Jewish Community in Russia*
    Isaac Levitats. Vol. 1: *The Jewish Community in Russia, 1772–1844.* New York: Columbia University Press, 1943.
    Vol. 2: *The Jewish Community in Russia, 1844–1917.* Jerusalem: Posner and Sons, 1981.

Lewinsky, "Hatunot magefah"
    Yom Tov Lewinsky. Hatunot magefah be-minhagey Ashkenaz" (Plague weddings in Ashkenazi custom). *Mahanayim* 83 (1963): 60–63.

Lewinsky, "Night Prayers by the Dead"
———. "Night Prayers by the Dead." *Mehqarey ha-merkaz le-heker ha-folklor* 3 (1972): 149–57 (H).

Lieberman, "Sin"
Saul Lieberman. "Sin and Its Punishment: A Study in Jewish and Christian Visions of Hell." In *Louis Ginzberg Jubilee Volume,* Hebrew section, 249–70. New York: American Academy for Jewish Research, 1945 (H).

Lifschitz. "Ha-heder"
Eliezer Meir Lifschitz. "Ha-heder" (The heder). *Ketavim* 1: 307–80. Jerusalem: Mossad Harav Kook, 1947.

Lilienblum, *Autobiography*
Moshe Leib Lilienblum. *An Autobiography.* 3 vols. Jerusalem: Bialik Institute, 1970 (H).

Lilienblum, *Collected Works*
———. *Kol kitvey Moshe Leib Lilienblum.* Vol. 2. Kraków, 1912.

Lipietz, *Sefer mat'amim*
Yitzhak Lipietz, comp. *Sefer mat'amim.* Warsaw, 1890.

Lipschitz, *Zikhron Ya'akov*
Yaakov Halevi Lipschitz. *Zikhron Ya'akov* (Jacob's memoirs). 3 vols. Kovno, 1924–30. Reprint, 1968.

Lipschitz, *Me-dor le-dor*
Zvi H. Lipschitz. *Me-dor le-dor* (From generation to generation). Warsaw, 1901.

Lis, *Briv*
Abraham Lis, ed. *Briv fun Sholem Aleykhem, 1879–1916* (Sholem Aleichem's letters, 1879–1916). Tel Aviv: Beth Sholem Aleichem, 1995.

Lithuanian Jewry
Lithuanian Jewry. 3 vols. Tel Aviv: Am Hasefer, 1959–67 (H).

Litvin, "Kotik"
A. Litvin [Shmuel Hurwitz, pseud.]. "Yekhezkel Kotik un zayn kaviarnie" (Yekhezkel Kotik and his café). *Yudishe neshomes,* vol. 4: *Poyln,* 1–11. New York, 1917.

LNYL
Lexicon of the New Yiddish Literature: Biographical Dictionary of Modern Yiddish Literature. 8 vols. New York: Congress for Jewish Culture, 1956–81 (Y).

Luz, *Parallels Meet*
    Ehud Luz. *Parallels Meet: Religion and Nationalism in the Early Zionist Movement (1882–1904)*. Translated by Lenn J. Schramm. Philadelphia: Jewish Publication Society, 1988.

Maggid, *Günzburg*
    David Maggid. *Toldot mishpahat Günzburg* (A history of the Günzburg family). St. Petersburg, 1899.

Mahler, *Hasidism*
    Raphael Mahler. *Hasidism and the Jewish Enlightenment.* Philadelphia: Jewish Publication Society, 1985.

Mahler, *History*
    ———. *History of the Jewish People in Modern Times.* Vol. 5. Merchavia: Sifriat Poalim, 1970 (H).

Mahler, *Toldot ha-yehudim be-Polin*
    ———. *Toldot ha-yehudim be-Polin (ad ha-meah ha-19): Kalkalah, hevrah, ha-matzav ha-mishpati* (History of the Jews of Poland [to the nineteenth century]: Economy, society, legal status). Merchavia: Sifriat Poalim, 1946.

Maimon, *Autobiography*
    The Autobiography of Solomon Maimon. Translated by J. Clark Murray. Oxford: East and West Library, 1954.

Maimon, *Lema'an tziyyon*
    Yehudah Leyb Maimon. *Lema'an tziyyon lo eheshe.* 2 vols. Jerusalem: Mossad Harav Kook, 1954.

Maimonides, *Code*
    The Code of Maimonides (Mishneh Torah). 13 vols. Yale Judaica Series. New Haven, Conn.: Yale University Press, 1949–79.

Maimonides Reader
    Isadore Twersky, ed. *A Maimonides Reader.* New York: Behrman, 1972.

Mann, "Symbols"
    Vivian Mann. "Symbols of the Legacy: Community Life." In *The Precious Legacy: Judaic Treasures from the Czechoslovak State Collections,* ed. David Altschuler, 111–62. New York: Summit, 1983.

Marcus, *Rituals of Childhood*
    Ivan G. Marcus. *Rituals of Childhood: Jewish Acculturation in Medieval Europe.* New Haven, Conn.: Yale University Press, 1996.

Marcus, *Auto/biographical Discourses*
    Laura Marcus, *Auto/biographical Discourses: Theory, Criticism, Practice.* Manchester: Manchester University Press, 1994.

"Materyaln"
"Materyaln far a leksikon fun der yidisher sovetisher literatur" (Material for a lexicon of Soviet-Yiddish literature). *Sovetish heymland* (1983), no. 9: 169.

Meisel, "Geshikhtlekher shtof"
Nachman Meisel. "Geshikhtlekher shtof in der yidisher literatur (biz der velt-milkhome)" (Historical material in Yiddish literature [until the world war]). *Fun noenten avar* 1 (1937): 71–76.

Melitzei esh
Avraham Stern. *Melitzei esh*. 3 vols. Voranov, 1932–38. Reprint, Brooklyn: Grossman, 1962.

Mendele, *Collected Works*
Kol kitvey Mendele Mokher Sfarim. Tel Aviv: Dvir, 1966.

Mendele, "Of Bygone Days"
Mendele Mokher Seforim. "Of Bygone Days" (Shloyme reb khayims). Translated by Raymond P. Scheindlin. In *A Shtetl and Other Yiddish Novellas,* ed. Ruth R. Wisse, 249–358. Detroit: Wayne State University Press, 1986.

Mendes-Flohr, "*Ostjuden*"
Paul Mendes-Flohr. "*Fin-de-siècle* Orientalism, the *Ostjuden,* and the Aesthetics of Jewish Self-Affirmation." *Studies in Contemporary Jewry* 1 (1984): 96–139.

Mesillat Yesharim
Moses Hayyim Luzzatto. *Mesillat Yesharim: The Path of the Upright*. Edited and translated by Mordecai M. Kaplan. Philadelphia: Jewish Publication Society, 1936.

Michelsohn, *Ohel Elimelekh*
Avraham Hayyim Michelsohn, comp. *Ohel Elimelekh*. Przemsyl, 1915.

Minsk
Minsk: Jewish Mother-City: Memorial Anthology. Edited by Shlomo Even-Shoshan. Vol. 1. Tel Aviv: Hakibbutz Hameuchad, 1975 (H).

Mintz, "Shape of Haskalah Autobiography"
Alan Mintz. "Guenzburg, Lilienblum, and the Shape of Haskalah Autobiography." *AJS Review* 4 (1979): 71–110.

Mintz, *Tabenkin*
Mattityahu Mintz. *Haver ve-yariv: Yitzhak Tabenkin be-mifleget Poalei Tziyyon, 1905–1912* (Friend and rival: Yitzhak Tabenkin and the Poalei Zion party). Tel Aviv: Yad Tabenkin, 1986.

Miron, *Loners*
Dan Miron. *When Loners Come Together: A Portrait of Hebrew Literature at the Turn of the Twentieth Century.* Tel Aviv: Am Oved, 1987 (H).

Mondshine, "Ha-tzadik mi-Lubavich"
Yehoshua Mondshine. "Ha-tzadik mi-Lubavich" (The Lubavitcher rebbe). *Kerem Chabad* 2 (1987): 80–87.

Mondshine, "Parnasei Vilna"
———, "Parnasei Vilna ve-ha-Gra, u-milhamtam ba-hasidut" (The elders of Vilna and the Gaon Rabbi Elijah and their struggle against Hasidism). *Kerem Chabad* 4 (1992): 182–221.

Moseley, "Jewish Autobiography"
Marcus Moseley. "Jewish Autobiography in Eastern Europe: The Pre-History of a Literary Genre." Ph.D. diss., Trinity College, Oxford University, 1990.

Nadav, "Pinsk"
Mordekhai Nadav. "History of the Jews of Pinsk: 1506–1880." In *Pinsk: Historical Volume,* 1: 15–334. Tel Aviv-Haifa: Association of the Jews of Pinsk in Israel, 1973 (H).

Nadler, *Mithnagdim*
Allan Nadler. *The Faith of the Mithnagdim: Rabbinic Responses to Hasidic Rapture.* Baltimore: Johns Hopkins University Press, 1997.

Nalbantian, *Aesthetic Autobiography*
Suzanne Nalbantian. *Aesthetic Autobiography.* London: Macmillan, 1994

Neugroschel, *Great Works of Jewish Fantasy*
Joachim Neugroschel. *Great Works of Jewish Fantasy and Occult.* Woodstock, N.Y.: Overlook Press, 1976.

Nigal, *Dybbuk*
Gedalyah Nigal. *"Dybbuk" Tales in Jewish Literature.* Jerusalem: Rubin Mass, 1983 (H).

Nigal, *Magic*
———. *Magic, Mysticism and Hasidism: The Supernatural in Jewish Thought.* Northvale, N.J.: J. Aronson, 1994.

Niger, "Fun Sholem Aleykhems korespondents"
Shmuel Niger. "Fun Sholem Aleykhems korespondents" (From Sholem Aleichem's correspondence). *Gedank un lebn* 4, no. 4 (January 1947): 223–38.

Niger, "Di noente fargangenheyt"
———. "Di noente fargangenheyt" (The recent past). *Literarishe bleter* 101, 9 April 1926, 224–26.

Niger, *Shalom Aleikhem*
———. *Shalom Aleikhem: Iyyunim be-yetzirotav* (Sholem Aleichem: Studies in his works). Tel Aviv: Hakibbutz Hameuchad, 1975.

Nissenbaum, *Nahalat avot*
Mordecai Aryeh Nissenbaum. *Nahalat avot.* Jerusalem, 1926.

Nissenbaum, *Lublin*
Shlomo Baruch Nissenbaum. *Le-korot ha-yehudim be-Lublin* (A history of the Jews of Lublin). Lublin, 1900.

Nissenbaum, *Alei heldi*
Yitzhak Nissenbaum. *Alei heldi, 1869–1929* (My life, 1869–1929). Jerusalem: Rubin Mass, 1969.

Noda bi-yehudah
Yehezkel Landa. *Responsa noda bi-yehudah.* Part two. Prague, 1811. Reprint, Jerusalem, 1961 (H).

Nomberg, "Kotik"
Hirsh-David Nomberg. "Notitsn—Yekhezkel Kotik" (Notes—Yekhezkel Kotik). *Haynt,* 21 April 1914, no. 82: 3.

Nun, "Nussbaum"
Nun [H. D. Nomberg]. "Dr. Nussbaum un Kotiks a khevre" (Dr. Nussbaum and Kotik's society). *Der fraynd,* 29 November 1910, no. 270: 2.

Ofek, "Cantonists"
Adina Ofek. "The Cantonists: Remnants of Collective Memory Reflected in Literature." *Dappim: Research in Literature* 11 (1998): 153–78 (H).

Ofek, *Leksikon le-sifrut yeladim*
Uriel Ofek. *Leksikon Ofek le-sifrut yeladim* (Ofek lexicon of children's literature). Tel Aviv: Zemora Bitan, 1985.

Opalski and Bartal, *Brotherhood*
Magdalena Opalski and Israel Bartal. *Poles and Jews: A Failed Brotherhood.* Hanover, N.H.: University Press of New England, 1992.

Oysgeveylte briv
Oysgeveylte briv (Selected letters). Vol. 15 of Sholem Aleichem's *Oysgeveylte verk.* Moscow: Emes, 1941.

Paperna, "Ka-afikim ba-Negev"
Avraham Yaakov Paperna. "Ka-afikim ba-Negev." *Sefer ha-yovel likhvod Nahum Sokolow,* 440–50. Warsaw, 1904.

Paperna, "Zikhronot"
———. "Zikhronot" (Memoirs). In *Sefer ha-shanah,* edited by Nahum Sokolow, 1:60–75. Warsaw, 1900.

Parush, "Ha-ba'arut"
Iris Parush. "Mabat aher al 'hayyei ha-ivrit ha-metah': Ha-ba'arut ha-mekhuvenet ba-lashon ha-ivrit ba-hevrah ha-yehudit ha-mizrah eropit ba-me'ah ha-19" (A different look at the life of "dead Hebrew": Deliberate ignorance of Hebrew in nineteenth-century Eastern European society). *Alpayim* 13 (1996): 65–106.

Pascal, *Design and Truth in Autobiography*
Roy Pascal. *Design and Truth in Autobiography*. Cambridge, Mass.: Harvard University Press, 1960.

Pe'at ha-shulhan
Yisrael of Shklov. *Pe'at ha-shulhan*. Safed, 1836. Reprint, Jerusalem, 1959.

Perl, *Bohen tzaddik*
Joseph Perl. *Bohen tzaddik* (The test of the righteous). Prague, 1838.

Piekarz, *Beginning of Hasidism*
Mendel Piekarz. *The Beginning of Hasidism: Ideological Trends in Derush and Musar Literature*. Jerusalem: Bialik Institute, 1978 (H).

Piekarz, "Testimony Literature"
————. "On Testimony Literature as a Historical Source for Persecution during the 'Final Solution.'" *Kivvunim* 20 (1983): 129–57 (H).

Pinkas ha-kehillot: Lithuania
Pinkas ha-kehillot: Encyclopedia of Jewish Communities from Their Foundation till after the Holocaust: Lithuania. Edited by Dov Levin. Jerusalem: Yad Vashem, 1996 (H).

Pinkas ha-kehillot: Poland
Pinkas ha-kehillot: Encyclopaedia of Jewish Communities—Poland.
Vol. 3: *Western Galicia and Silesia,* ed. Abraham Wein and Aharon Weiss. Jerusalem: Yad Vashem, 1984 (H).
Vol. 4: *Warsaw and Its Region,* ed. Abraham Wein. Jerusalem: Yad Vashem, 1989 (H).
Vol. 5: *Volhynia and Polesie,* ed. Shmuel Spector. Jerusalem: Yad Vashem, 1990 (H).

Pinkas Krinki
Pinkas Krinki (Krinki memorial book). Edited by Dov Rabin. Tel Aviv: Irgun Yotzei Krinki, 1970.

Pinkas medinat Lita
Pinkas medinat Lita (Minute book of the Lithuanian council). Edited by Simon Dubnow. Berlin: Ayanot, 1925.

Pinkas Slonim
Pinkas Slonim (Slonim memorial book). Edited by Kalman Lichtenstein. 4 vols. Tel Aviv: Irgun Yotzei Slonim, 1962–79 (H & Y).

Prylucki, *Dos gevet*
Noyekh Prylucki. *Dos gevet: Dialogn vegn shprakh un kultur* (The wager: Dialogues on language and culture). Warsaw, 1923.

Prylucki, "Kotiks 'Zikhroynes' "
———. "Yekhezkel Kotiks 'Zikhroynes' (notitsn)" (Notes on Yekhezkel Kotik's *Memoirs*). Parts 1–6. *Der moment,* 21 February 1913, no. 34: 5; 25 February, no. 37: 3; 4 March, no. 43: 3; 7 March, no. 46: 4–5; 11 March, no. 49: 3; 18 March, no. 55: 3.

Prylucki, *Zamlbikher*
———. *Noyekh Prilutskis zamlbikher far yidishn folklor, filologye un kulturgeshikhte* (Noah Prylucki's anthology on Yiddish folklore, philology, and cultural history). Vol. 1. Warsaw, 1912.

Prylucki, "Mayne zikhroynes"
Zevi Hirsh Prylucki. "Mayne zikhroynes" (My memoirs). Part 6. *Folks-shtime,* 19 March 1983, no. 11.

R-n, "Akhiezer"
Y. R-n. "Di farzamlung fun 'Akhiezer' " (The meeting of the Achiezer society). *Haynt,* 4 May 1914, no. 93: 5.

Raba, *Between Remembrance and Denial*
Joel Raba. *Between Remembrance and Denial: The Fate of the Jews in the Wars of the Polish Commonwealth during the Mid-Seventeenth Century as Shown in Contemporary Writings and Historical Research.* New York: Boulder, 1995.

Rabinowicz, "Fifty Years Ago"
S. Rabinowicz. "Fifty Years Ago." In *Historishe shriftn,* ed. F. Kursky, A. Menes, A. Rosin, and E. Tscherikower, 3: 314–47. Vilna, 1939 (Y).

Rabinowitsch, "Schneerson"
Alexander Ziskind Rabinowitsch. "Toldot Mishpahat Schneerson" (A history of the Schneerson family). *He-asif* 5 (1889): 163–80.

Rabinowitsch, *Lithuanian Hasidism*
Wolf Zeev Rabinowitsch. *Lithuanian Hasidism from its Beginning to the Present Day.* London: Vallentine, Mitchell, 1970.

Rakowski, *Lo nichna'ati*
Puah Rakowski. *Lo nichna'ati* (I did not falter). Tel Aviv: Twersky, 1952.

Reiner, "*Kloiz*"
Elchanan Reiner. "Wealth, Social Position and the Study of Torah: The Status of the *Kloiz* in Eastern European Jewish Society in the Early Modern Period." *Zion* 58 (1993): 287–328 (H).

Reisen, *Epizodn*
Avraham Reisen. *Epizodn fun mayn lebn* (Episodes from my life). 2 vols. Vilna: Kletskin farlag, 1929.

Reisen, *Lexicon*
Zalman Reisen. *Lexicon of Yiddish Literature, Press and Philology*. 4 vols. Vilna: Kletskin farlag, 1928–29 (Y).

Reshit hokhmah
Elijah De Vidas: *Reshit hokhmah ha-shalem*. 3 vols. Edited by Hayyim Yosef Waldman. Jerusalem: Or Hamusar, 1984.

RHT
Russian Historical Terms: Dictionary of Russian Historical Terms from the Eleventh Century to 1917. Compiled by Sergei G. Pushkarev. New Haven and London: Yale University Press, 1970.

Rivkind, "Badchan"
Isaac Rivkind. "From a Notebook of a Badchan and a Cantor." In *Mincha le-Yehudah . . . Presented to Rabbi Yehudah L. Zlotnik*, 235–57. Jerusalem: Mossad Harav Kook, 1950 (H).

Rivkind, *Gambling*
———. *The Fight against Gambling among Jews*. New York: YIVO, 1946 (Y).

Rivkind, *Jewish Money*
———. *Jewish Money in Folkways, Cultural History and Folklore: A Lexicological Study*. New York: American Academy for Jewish Research, 1959 (Y).

Robertson, "From Ghetto to Modern Culture"
Ritchie Robertson. "From the Ghetto to Modern Culture: The Autobiographies of Solomon Maimon and Jakob Fromer." *Polin* 7 (1992): 12–30.

Roskies, *Against the Apocalypse*
David Roskies. *Against the Apocalypse: Responses to Catastrophe in Modern Jewish Culture*. Cambridge, Mass.: Harvard University Press, 1984.

Roskies, *Jewish Search for a Usable Past*
———. *The Jewish Search for a Usable Past*. Bloomington: Indiana University Press, 1999.

Roskies, "Peretses zikhroynes"
———. "A shlisl tsu Peretses zikhroynes" (A key to Peretz's memoirs). *Di goldene keyt* 99 (1979): 132–59.

Roskies, "Sholem Aleichem's *From the Fair*"
———. "Unfinished Business: Sholem Aleichem's *From the Fair*." *Prooftexts* 6 (1988): 65–78.

Roskies, "Shtetl"
———. "The Shtetl in Jewish Collective Memory." In *The Jewish Search for a Usable Past*, 41–66. Bloomington: Indiana University Press, 1999.

Roskies and Roskies, *Shtetl Book*
Diane K. Roskies and David G. Roskies, eds. *The Shtetl Book*. 2d ed. New York: Ktav, 1979.

Rosman, *Founder of Hasidism*
Moshe J. Rosman. *Founder of Hasidism: A Quest for the Historical Ba'al Shem Tov.* Berkeley and Los Angeles: University of California Press, 1996.

Rosman, *Lords' Jews*
————. *The Lords' Jews: Magnate-Jewish Relations in the Lithuanian-Polish Commonwealth during the Eighteenth Century.* Cambridge, Mass.: Harvard Ukrainian Research Institute and the Center for Jewish Studies, 1990.

Roth, "Shelo le-vayesh"
Ernst Roth. "Shelo le-vayesh" (Not to shame). *Yedah-Am* 10 (1965): 6.

Sadan, "Anshei mirmah"
Dov Sadan. "Anshei mirmah" (Treacherous men). *Orlogin* 8 (1953): 222–26.

Sadan, *Egozim*
————. *Ke'arat egozim* (A bowl of nuts). Tel Aviv: Newman, 1953.

Sadan, *Ir va-em*
————. *Ir va-em be-eney banehah* (A city in its sons' eyes). Tel Aviv: Am Oved, 1981.

Sadan, "Shlumiel"
————. "La-sugyah: Shlumiel" (On the question of "Shlumiel"). *Orlogin* 1 (1950): 198–203.

Sadan, *Yerid*
————. *Yerid ha-sha'ashu'im* (The amusement fair). Tel Aviv: Massada, 1964.

Salmon, *Religion and Zionism*
Yosef Salmon. *Religion and Zionism: First Encounters.* Jerusalem: Hassifria Haziyonit, 1990 (H).

Salzmann, *Ayyarati*
Shlomo Salzmann. *Ayyarati: Zikhronot ve-reshumot* (My town: Memoirs and impressions). Tel Aviv, 1947.

Salzmann, *Min he-avar*
————. *Min he-avar: Zikhronot ve-reshumot* (From the past: Memoirs and impressions). Tel Aviv: privately printed, 1943.

Sandler, *Mendelssohn's Pentateuch*
Perez Sandler. *Mendelssohn's Edition of the Pentateuch.* Jerusalem: Rubin Mass, 1984 (H).

Sarid, "Kamenetz"
Levi Sarid. "A Short History of Kamenetz-Litovsk." In *Kamenetz Memorial Book,* ed. Shmuel Eisenshtadt and Mordecai Gelbert, English section, 26–28. Tel Aviv: Townsmen Organizations in Israel and the U.S., 1967.

Schama, *Landscape*
Simon Schama. *Landscape and Memory.* New York: Knopf, 1995.

Scharfstein, *Heder*
Zevi Scharfstein. *The Heder in the Life of the Jewish People.* New York: Shilo, 1943 (H).

Schatz, *Hasidism as Mysticism*
Rivka Schatz Uffenheimer. *Hasidism as Mysticism: Quietistic Elements in Eighteenth-Century Hasidic Thought.* Translated by Jonathan Chipman. Jerusalem: Princeton University Press and Magnes Press, 1993.

Scholem, *Kabbalah*
Gershom Scholem. *Kabbalah.* Jerusalem: Keter, 1974.

Scholem, *Symbolism*
————. *Elements in the Kabbala and Its Symbolism.* Jerusalem: Bialik Institute, 1976 (H).

Schreuder and Weber, *Der Schocken Verlag*
Saskia Schreuder and Claude Weber, eds. *Der Schocken Verlag/Berlin, Jüdische Selbstbehauptung in Deutschland, 1931–1938.* Berlin: Akademie-Verlag, 1994.

Schwarz, *Memoirs of My People*
Leo W. Schwarz. *Memoirs of My People.* New York: Rinehart, 1945.

Sefer hasidim
Sefer hasidim. 2d ed. Compiled by Jehuda Wistinetzki. Frankfurt am Main: Wahrmann, 1924.

Sever, *Mikhlol ha-ma'amarim*
M. Sever. *Mikhlol ha-ma'amarim ve-ha-pitgamim* (Compendium of proverbs and sayings). 3 vols. Jerusalem: Mossad Harav Kook, 1961–62.

Shalev, *Be-ikar al ahavah*
Meir Shalev. *Be-ikar al ahavah* (Mostly about love). Tel Aviv: Am Oved, 1995.

Shapira, *Hidushey ha-Garzas*
David Shapira, ed. *Hidushey ha-Garzas al seder Kodashim* (Novellae of Solomon Zalman Sender Kahana-Shapira). Jerusalem: Machon Yerushalyim, 1983.

Shatzky, *Warsaw*
Jacob Shatzky. *The History of the Jews in Warsaw.* 3 vols. New York: YIVO, 1947–53 (Y).

Shatzky, "Yidisher memuarn literatur"
————. "Yidisher memuarn literatur" (Yiddish memoir literature). *Di tsukunft* 30, no. 8 (August 1925): 483–88.

Shatzky, "Yidn"
————. "Yidn in dem poylishn oyfshtand fun 1863" (Jews in the 1863 Polish uprising). *Historishe shriftn* 1 (1929): 423–68.

Shinan, "Aggadic Literature"
    Avigdor Shinan. "The Aggadic Literature: Written Tradition and Transmission." *Mehqarey Yerushalayim be-folklor yehudi* 1 (1981): 44–60 (H).

Shmeruk, "Collective Memory"
    Chone Shmeruk. "Yiddish Literature and Collective Memory: The Case of the Chmielnicki Massacres." *Polin* 5 (1990): 173–83.

Shmeruk, "Hasidic Ritual Slaughter"
    ———. "The Social Significance of Hasidic Ritual Slaughter." *Zion* 20 (1955): 47–72 (H).

Shmeruk, "Menakhem-Mendl-serye"
    ———. "Vegn Sholem Aleykhems letster Menakhem-Mendl-serye" (About Shalom Aleichem's last Menakhem-Mendl series). *Di goldene keyt* 56 (1966): 22–55.

Shmeruk, *Plays*
    ———. *Yiddish Biblical Plays, 1697–1750.* Jerusalem: Israel Academy of Sciences and Humanities, 1979 (H & Y).

Shmeruk, "Schund Literature"
    ———. "On the History of 'Schund' Literature in Yiddish." *Tarbiz* 52 (1983): 325–54 (H).

Shmeruk, *Yiddish*
    ———. *Yiddish Literature: Aspects of Its History.* Tel Aviv: Porter Institute, Tel Aviv University, 1978 (H).

Shmeruk, *Jewish Publications*
    ———, ed. *Jewish Publications in the Soviet Union, 1917–1960.* Jerusalem: Historical Society of Israel, 1961 (H & Y).

Shochat, "Cantonists"
    Azriel Shochat. "The Cantonists and the 'Yeshivot' of Russian Jewry during the Reign of Nicholas I." *Jewish History* 1, no. 1 (1986): 33–38 (H).

Shochat, *Crown Rabbinate*
    ———. *The "Crown Rabbinate" in Russia.* Haifa: University of Haifa, 1975 (H).

Shochat, "Günzburg"
    ———. "Le-gezerot ha-giyusim shel Nikolai ha-rishon (Reshit shtadlanuto shel ha-Baron Günzburg)" (Nicholas I's conscription decrees [the initiation of Baron Günzburg's intercession]). In *Sefer Shalom Sivan,* ed. A. Even-Shoshan et al., 307–18. Jerusalem: Kiryat Sefer, 1979.

Shochat, "Joy in Hasidism"
    ———. "On Joy in Hasidism." *Zion* 16 (1951): 30–43 (H).

Shochat, "Kahal"
    ———. "Leadership of the Jewish Communities in Russia after the Abolition of the 'Kahal.'" *Zion* 42 (1977): 143–233 (H).

Shochat, "Yahas ha-rusim"
    ———. "Yahas ha-rusim el ha-yehudim bi-yemei Aleksander ha-sheni" (The Russian attitude toward the Jews in the days of Alexander II). In *Sefer Peninah Sivan,* ed. Shraga Abramson and Ben-Zion Luria, 179–88. Jerusalem: Kiryat Sefer, 1989.

Sholem Aleichem Book
    The Sholem Aleichem Book. Edited by Yitzhak Dov Berkowitz. 2d ed. New York: YKUF, 1958 (Y).

Sholem Aleichem, *From the Fair*
    ———. *From the Fair: The Autobiography of Sholom Aleichem.* Translated by Curt Leviant. New York: Penguin, 1986.

Sholem Aleichem, *Hebrew Writings*
    ———. *Hebrew Writings.* Edited by Chone Shmeruk. Jerusalem: Bialik Institute, 1976 (H).

Sholem Aleichem, *Menakhem-Mendl*
    Sholem Aleichem. *Menakhem-Mendl (Nyu York—Varshe—Vin—Yehupets).* Tel Aviv: Beth Sholem Aleichem, 1977 (Y).

Sholem Aleichem, *Menahem-Mendel be-Varshah*
    ———. *Menahem-Mendel be-Varshah* (Menahem Mendl in Warsaw). Translated by Arieh Aharoni. Tel Aviv: Aleph, 1977.

Sholem Aleichem, "Oyfn himl a yarid"
    ———. "Oyfn himl a yarid: A tragedye fun premyes" (Nonsense: A tragedy of premiums). *Haynt,* 14 July 1913, no. 151.

Shomer and Shomer, *Avinu Shomer*
    Rosa Shomer-Batshelis and Miryam Shomer-Zunser. *Avinu Shomer* (Our father, Nahum Meir Shaykevitsh). Jerusalem: Ahiassaf, 1953.

Shperling, *Minhagim*
    Abraham Yitzhak Shperling. *Te'amei ha-minhagim u-mekorei ha-dinim* (Explanations for customs and sources for laws). Jerusalem: Eshkol, 1957.

Shpirn, "Names"
    Tsvi Shpirn. "Proper Names and Their Importance in Yiddish." *Filologishe shriftn* 2 (1928): 175–86 (Y).

Shrebrek, *Zikhronot*
    Shlomo Shrebrek. *Zikhronot ha-motzi la'or Shlomo Shrebrek* (The memoirs of the publisher Shlomo Shrebrek). Tel Aviv: Shrebrek, 1955.

Shtern, *"Kheyder"*
Yekhiel Shtern. *"Kheyder and Beys-Medresh."* *YIVO Bleter* 31–32 (1948): 37–130 (Y).

Singer, *Yoshe Kalb*
Israel Joshua Singer. *Yoshe Kalb*. Translated by Maurice Samuel. New York: Schocken, 1988.

Słownik
Słownik geograficzny Królestwa Polskiego. 12 vols. Warsaw, 1880–92.

Słownik Biograficzny
Polski Słownik Biograficzny. Vol. 23. Kraków, 1978.

Slutsky, "Geography"
Yehuda Slutsky. "The Geography of the 1881 Pogrom." *He'avar* 9 (1962): 16–25 (H).

Slutsky, "Military Service Act"
———. "The Russian Military Service Act (1874) and the Jews." *He'avar* 21 (1975): 3–19 (H).

Slutsky, *Russian-Jewish Press*
———. Vol. 1: *The Russian-Jewish Press in the Nineteenth Century*. Jerusalem: Bialik Institute, 1970 (H).

Vol. 2: *The Russian-Jewish Press in the Twentieth Century*. Jerusalem: Tel Aviv University, 1978 (H).

Sokolow, *Sefer zikaron*
Nahum Sokolow, ed. *Sefer zikaron le-sofrei yisrael ha-hayim itanu ka-yom* (A memoir book of contemporary Jewish writers). Warsaw, 1889.

Stampfer, "Collection Box"
Shaul Stampfer. "The 'Collection Box': The Social Role of Eretz Israel Charity Funds." *Cathedra* 21 (1982): 89–102 (H).

Stampfer, "Early Marriage"
———. "The Social Implications of Very Early Marriage in Eastern Europe in the Nineteenth Century." In *Studies on Polish Jewry: Paul Glikson Memorial Volume*, ed. Ezra Mendelsohn and Chone Shmeruk, 65–77. Jerusalem: Hebrew University, 1987 (H).

Stampfer, "Heder Study"
———. "Heder Study, Knowledge of Torah, and the Maintenance of Social Stratification in Traditional East European Jewish Society." *Studies in Jewish Education* 3 (1988): 271–89.

Stampfer, *Lithuanian Yeshiva*
———. *The Lithuanian Yeshiva*. Jerusalem: Zalman Shazar Center for Jewish History, 1995 (H).

Stampfer, "Remarriage"
———. "Remarriage among Jews and Christians in Nineteenth-Century Eastern Europe." *Jewish History* 3/2 (1988): 85–114.

Stanislawski, "Apostasy"
Michael Stanislawski. "Jewish Apostasy in Russia: A Tentative Typology." In *Jewish Apostasy in the Modern World,* ed. Todd M. Endelman, 189–205. New York: Holmes & Meier, 1987.

Stanislawski, *Nicholas and the Jews*
———. *Tsar Nicholas I and the Jews: The Transformation of Jewish Society in Russia, 1825–1855.* Philadelphia: Jewish Publication Society, 1983.

Stern, *Kitvei agadah*
Avraham Stern. *Kevutzat kitvei agadah* (Collection of aggadic works). Montreal: Nartern Printing Vesteyshaneri, 1947.

Stutschewsky, *Klezmorim*
Joachim Stutschewsky. *Klezmorim: History, Folklore, Compositions.* Jerusalem: Bialik Institute, 1959 (H).

Suraski, *Yesod ha-ma'alah*
Aaron Suraski. *Yesod ha-ma'alah.* 2 vols. Bnei Brak: Zivtanim, 1991 (H).

Tchernowitz, *Autobiography*
Chaim Tchernowitz [Rav Tzair]. *Autobiography.* New York: Bitzaron, 1954 (H).

Teller, "Słuck"
Adam Teller. "The Słuck Tradition Concerning the Early Days of the Besht." In *Studies in Hasidism* [Jerusalem Studies in Jewish Thought 15], ed. David Assaf, Joseph Dan, and Immanuel Etkes, 15–38. Jerusalem, 1999 (H).

Tian-Shanskaia, *Village Life*
Olga Semyonova Tian-Shanskaia. *Village Life in Late Tsarist Russia.* Edited and translated by David L. Ransel. Bloomington: Indiana University Press, 1993.

Tishby, *Studies*
Isaiah Tishby. *Studies in Kabbala and Its Branches.* 3 vols. Jerusalem: Magnes Press, 1982–93 (H).

Toussaint-Samet, *Food*
Maguelonne Toussaint-Samet. *A History of Food.* Translated by Anthea Bell. Oxford: Blackwell, 1994.

Tracing An-sky
Tracing An-sky: Jewish Collections from the State Ethnographic Museum in St. Petersburg. 2d ed. Edited by Mariella Beukers and Renee Waale. Zwolle: Waanders, 1992.

Trunk, *Poyln*
Jehiel Isaiah Trunk. *Poyln: Zikhroynes un bilder* (Poland: Memoirs and pictures). 7 vols. New York: Unzer Tsait, 1946–53.

Tsherikover, *Yehudim*
> Elijah Tsherikover. *Yehudim be-itot mahapekhah* (Jews in revolutionary times). Tel Aviv: Am Oved, 1957.

Tzederbaum, *Berditchov*
> Alexander Tzederbaum [Erez]. *Di geheymnise fun Berditchov* (Secrets from Berdichev). Warsaw, 1870.

Tzinowitz, *Etz hayyim*
> Moshe Tzinowitz. *Etz hayyim: Toldot yeshivat Volozhin* (Tree of life: A history of the Volozhin yeshiva). Tel Aviv: Mor, 1972.

"Vider in Milosna"
> "Vider in Milosna" (Miłosna again). *Der moment,* 18 August 1911, no. 181: 2.

Warsaw
> *History of the Jews of Warsaw: From Their Beginnings to the Present.* Edited by Gideon Greif. Jerusalem: Keter, 1991 (H).

Weinreich, "Unpublished Letters"
> Max Weinreich. "Thirty Unpublished Letters of Sholem Aleichem." *Filologishe shriftn* 3 (1929): 153–72 (Y).

Weiss, *Studies*
> Joseph Weiss. *Studies in Eastern European Jewish Mysticism.* Edited by David Goldstein. Oxford: Oxford University Press, 1985.

Wengeroff, *Memoiren*
> Pauline Wengeroff. *Memoiren einer Grossmutter: Bilder aus der Kulturgeschichte der Juden Russland im 19. Jahrhundert.* 2 vols. Berlin: Verlag von M. Poppelauer, 1922.

Werses, "Agnon"
> Shmuel Werses. "Tahalikhei ha-higud shel sipurei am bi-yitzirat Agnon" (Folk narrative processes in the work of Agnon). In *S. Y. Agnon Literally: Studies of His Writings,* 3–22. Jerusalem: Bialik Institute, 2000. (H)

Werses, "Haskalah Autobiography"
> ———. "Autobiography during the Haskalah Period." In *Trends and Forms in Haskalah Literature,* 249–60. Jerusalem: Magnes Press, 1990 (H).

Wertheim, *Law and Custom*
> Aaron Wertheim. *Law and Custom in Hasidism.* Translated by Shmuel Himelstein. Hoboken, N.J.: Ktav, 1992.

Wunder, *Meorei Galicia*
> Meir Wunder. *Meorei Galicia: Encyclopedia of Galician Rabbis and Scholars.* 5 vols. Jerusalem: Institute for Commemoration of Galician Jewry, 1978–97 (H).

Yaari, "Badchanim"
> Abraham Yaari. "Badchanim Literature." *Kiryat Sefer* 35 (1959–60): 109–26 (H).

Yakhinson, *Sotsyal-ekonomisher shteyger*
    Y. Yakhinson. *Sotsyal-ekonomisher shteyger ba yidn in Rusland in XIX yor-hundert* (The socioeconomic condition of the Jews in nineteenth-century Russia). Kharkov: Tsentraler Verlag, 1929.

Yassif, *Hebrew Folktale*
    Eli Yassif. *The Hebrew Folktale: History, Genre, Meaning.* Translated by Jacqueline S. Teitelbaum. Bloomington: Indiana University Press, 1999.

"Yekhezkel Kotik"
    "Yekhezkel Kotik za"l" (The late Yekhezkel Kotik). *Der moment,* 15 August 1921, no. 185: 2.

Yerushalmi, *Zakhor*
    Yosef Hayim Yerushalmi. *Zakhor: Jewish History and Jewish Memory.* Seattle: University of Washington Press, 1982.

Yesod ve-shoresh ha-avodah
    Alexander Ziskind of Grodno. *Yesod ve-shoresh ha-avodah* (The foundation and root of worship). Novidvor, 1782. Reprint, Warsaw, 1814.

Yevnin, *Nahalat olamim*
    Shmuel Yevnin. *Nahalat olamim* (Eternal inheritance). Warsaw, 1882.

A. Yud., "Sirtutim sifrutiyyim"
    A. Yud. [Avraham Yuditski]. "Sirtutim sifrutiyyim" (Literary sketches). Parts 1–3. *Ha-zeman,* 28 August 1918, no. 182: 3; 2 September, no. 186: 4; 10 September, no. 193: 2–3.

Yuval, *Scholars in Their Time*
    Israel Jacob Yuval. *Scholars in Their Time: The Religious Leadership of German Jewry in the Late Middle Ages.* Jerusalem: Magnes Press, 1988 (H).

Zack, *Beit yisrael*
    Reuben Zack, comp. *Beit yisrael.* Piotrkow, 1913.

Zailingold, *Me'orot ha-gedolim*
    Aaron Zailingold, comp. *Me'orot ha-gedolim.* Edited with an introduction by Gedalyah Nigal. Jerusalem: Carmel, 1997.

Zakhor nizkor
    Zakhor nizkor: Zikaron netzah le-kehilah kedoshah Kamenetz Litovsk-Zastavye asher nehrevah ba-shoah (We will remember: An eternal memorial to Kamenetz-Litovsk-Zastavye). Beit ha-Sefer ha-Mamlakhti al shem H. N. Bialik. Tel Aviv, 1964.

Zakovitch, "From Oral to Written Tale in the Bible"
    Yair Zakovitch. "From Oral to Written Tale in the Bible." *Mehqarey Yerushalayim be-folklor yehudi* 1 (1981): 9–43 (H).

Zalkin, "Hasidism in Nineteenth-Century Lithuania"
Mordechai Zalkin. "Between Dvinsk and Vilna: The Spread of Hasidism in Nineteenth-Century Lithuania." In *Be-maagalei hasidim: Kovets mehqarim le-zikhro shel Professor Mordecai Wilensky,* ed. Immanuel Etkes et al., 21–50. Jerusalem: Bialik Institute, 1999 (H).

Zaludkowski, *Liturgye*
Elijah Zaludkowski. *Kultur-treger fun der yidisher liturgye* (Cultural agents of Yiddish liturgy). Detroit: privately printed, 1930.

Zborowski and Herzog, *Life Is with People*
Mark Zborowski and Elizabeth Herzog. *Life Is with People: The Culture of the Shtetl.* New York: Schocken, 1952.

Zeidman, "Yeshiva Kneset Beit Itzchak"
Hillel Zeidman. "Yeshiva Kneset Beit Itzchak of Kamenitz." In *Jewish Institutions of Higher Learning in Europe and Their Development and Destruction,* ed. Samuel K. Mirsky, 307–24. New York: Ogen, 1956 (H).

Zeitlin, "Fun fraytog biz fraytog"
Aaron Zeitlin, "Fun fraytog biz fraytog" (From Friday to Friday). *Der tog— Morgen zhurnal,* 19 February 1971, 6.

Zerubavel, *Recovered Roots*
Yael Zerubavel. *Recovered Roots: Collective Memory and the Making of Israeli National Tradition.* Chicago: University of Chicago Press, 1994.

Zipperstein, *Odessa*
Steven J. Zipperstein. *The Jews of Odessa: A Cultural History, 1794–1881.* Stanford, Calif.: Stanford University Press, 1985.

Zlotnik, "Nameless Ones"
Yehudah Leib Zlotnik. "The Nameless Ones." *Edoth* 2 (1946–47): 217–25 (H).

Zolf, *Oyf fremder erd*
Falk Zolf. *Oyf fremder erd* (On foreign soil). Winnepeg: Israelite Press, 1945.

Zuckerovitch, "Zambrow"
Meir Zuckerovitch. "Kalat ha-ir be-Zambrow" (The bride of Zambrow). *Yedah-Am* 1 (1948): 13–14.

Zunser, *Works*
The Works of Elyokum Zunser. 2 vols. Edited by Mordkhe Schaechter. New York: YIVO, 1964 (Y).

Zwick, *Briefsteller*
Judith Halevi Zwick. *The Hebrew Briefsteller (Sixteenth–Twentieth Century).* Tel Aviv: Papyrus, 1990 (H).

GLOSSARY

am ha-aretz— Ignoramus. A derisive term for an unlearned person.

apikores—Freethinker.

assessor—A local government official, subordinate to the *ispravnik*.

badekns—A ceremony in which the groom covers the face of the bride with her veil before proceeding to the wedding canopy.

badkhn—Lit. "entertainer." Professional jester and entertainer who sings and recites rhymes at a wedding celebration.

bet midrash—Study house

cantonist—Children kidnapped for pre-army service in the Russian army.

chametz—Leaven or leavened food banned during Passover.

dayan—A rabbinical judge.

dessiatine—Russian land measurement (1,092 hectare; about 10 dunam).

din Torah—A hearing before a rabbinical court, mainly in civil disputes.

funt—Pound. Measuring weight used in Russia, equivalent to 409.5 grams.

gabbai (pl. gabbaim)—A trustee in charge of the management of the synagogue affairs or of a social-religious association.

gartl—Lit. "belt" or "girdle." A cloth belt used to keep the *kapote* tightly closed. Among Hasidim and the more pious, wrapping the *gartl* around the body was an important part of preparation for prayer, since it symbolized separating the heart (which turned to God) from the genitals.

Gemara—An alternate term for the Talmud (usually the Babylonian Talmud), which refers not only to the deliberations of the talmudic sages but also to a series of medieval commentaries printed in the margins (such as *Rashi* and *Tosaphot*).

goy (pl. goyim)—A non-Jew.

groshen—A small copper coin worth half a Russian kopeck, which is one two-hundredth of a silver ruble.

gulden—A coin worth fifteen Russian kopecks.

hakhnasat kallah—Lit. "bringing in the bride," i.e., under the wedding canopy), a rabbinic commandment to provide a dowry for brides and to rejoice at their weddings, popularly applied to providing dowries for poor brides.

Hanukkah—Eight-day celebration commemorating the victory of Judah Maccabee over the Syrian king Antiochus Epiphanes and the subsequent rededication of the Temple.

Hanukkah gelt—Hanukkah money, the gift traditionally given on this holiday.

hasid (pl. hasidim)—A follower of a hasidic *rebbe* (zaddik), affiliated with the hasidic movement established by Rabbi Israel Ba'al Shem Tov (eighteenth century).

Haskalah—Enlightenment. A sociocultural trend in Jewish society that had its inception in late-eighteenth-century Berlin, aimed at spreading modern European culture and emancipation among Jews. Its leaders proposed radical reforms in many aspects of traditional Jewish society.

havdalah—Ceremony marking the end of the Sabbath.

heder (kheyder)—Lit. "room." A private elementary school in traditional Eastern European Jewish society.

hekdesh—Poorhouse. A community-financed shelter.

hibut ha-kever—Torments administered to the deceased in his grave, mainly by angels of destruction.

hol ha-moed—The intermediate days of the Passover and Sukkot festivals, which have the status of a half-holiday.

Humash—Lit. "the five books." The Five Books of Moses or the Pentateuch.

huppah—A canopy under which bride and groom stand during a Jewish wedding ceremony.

ispravnik—District governor with both civilian and police authority.

Kabbalah—Jewish mystical tradition.

kaddish—An Aramaic prayer praising God, recited several times during the daily service. Primarily used to refer to the mourners' prayer. Sometimes used to refer to a son (who is obligated to recite this prayer after a parent's death).

Kahal—Jewish communal board.

kapote—A long black coat traditionally worn by observant Jewish men in Eastern Europe.

kapparot—Ceremony of atonement performed early in the morning on the eve of Yom Kippur whose purpose is to symbolically transfer a person's sins to a chicken. The fowl is swung over the penitent's head three times. The chicken is then slaughtered and used for the pre-fast meal.

kest—A popular Eastern European Jewish arrangement that provided food, lodging, and tuition to gifted young married men, thereby enabling them to continue their Torah study, usually financed by the bride's family.

khapers—Special deputies hired by the community elders to kidnap young boys, especially unregistered ones, for forced conscription to the army.

kiddush—Prayer of sanctification recited on the Sabbath and holiday; also used to refer to the light meal that follows.

kittel—White linen robe worn on the High Holidays, by bridegrooms under the wedding canopy, and also used for shrouds.

klezmer (pl. klezmorim)—A member of a band of folk musicians hired to play at weddings or other family or community celebrations. In the plural often used to refer to the band as a whole.

kloyz—Study house.

Kol Nidre—Lit. "all vows." A prayer recited by the entire community on the eve of Yom Kippur canceling all vows and oaths taken the previous year that could not be fulfilled, one of the high points of the High Holiday ritual.

kopeck (kopeika)—A small brass coin. From 1774 each silver ruble contained one hundred kopecks.

kugel—A pudding made of noodles, either sweet or savory.

Lag ba-omer—The thirty-third day of the fifty-day period between Passover and Shavuot; a semi-holiday.

lehayyim—Cheers. A traditional toast over wine.

Lekah tov—An anthology of selected easy passages from the Talmud with commentaries.

lomed (pl. lomdim)—A term which originally meant a mature scholar, also applied to a person engaged in Torah study in his local study house whose livelihood was supplied, fully or partially, by the public, his wife's parents, or individual patrons.

Ma'ariv—The evening prayer.

maggid (pl. maggidim)—Preacher.

Maharsha—An acronym for Rabbi Shmuel Eliezer (sixteenth century, Poland). His work, of the same name, printed in most editions of the Talmud, is a commentary on difficult halakhic issues.

maskil (pl. maskilim)—An adherent of the Haskalah movement that often criticized traditional Jewish society (especially Hasidism).

melamed (pl. melamdim)—A teacher in the traditional elementary school (*heder*).

Melaveh malkah—Lit. "escorting the queen." A festive meal eaten after the conclusion of the Sabbath during which the participants figuratively bid farewell to the Sabbath queen in song and dance.

Midrash (pl. midrashim)—An anthology of homiletic Bible exegesis as well as a compendium of rabbinic stories, parables, and teachings, written and compiled in the talmudic period.

minyan—Prayer quorum, the minimum required being ten adult men.

Mishnah—Earliest codification of Jewish oral law, edited during the first quarter of the second century, which contains six orders. It served as the basis for the discussions found in the Gemara.

mitnagged (pl. mitnaggedim)—Lit. "opponent." An ardent opponent of Hasidism (generally a Lithuanian) who followed traditional rabbinical authority.

mitzveh—A good deed.

mizrah—Lit. "east." The wall in the synagogue facing Jerusalem (usually the eastern wall), next to the Torah Ark, where the most respected members of the community sat.

mohel (pl. mohalim)—A ritual circumciser.

Musaf—Lit. "additional." An additional service recited following the morning service on the Sabbath and holidays.

Neilah—Lit. "to close." The closing prayer service on Yom Kippur.

Ninth of Av—Fast day commemorating the destruction of the First and Second Temples.

parnas—An elected lay leader.

parnas khodesh—Lit. "elder of the month." The Eastern European Jewish communities were administered by a body of elders (see *Kahal*) whose head served in monthly rotation. After 1844, when the Russian government abolished the Kahal, this title continued to be used for the head of the town's elders, even though he was no longer replaced on a monthly basis.

Pirkei avot—Ethics of the Fathers. A Mishnaic tractate, a collection of rabbinic parables and dicta.

piyyutim—Hebrew term for special liturgical hymns (often in complicated Hebrew or Aramaic) included in the daily and festival prayer books.

porush (pl. prushim)—Lit. "chaste." A Lithuanian Jew who leaves his wife and family in his hometown and devotes himself to Torah study elsewhere.

pud—Old Russian weight, equal to forty *funts* or to 16.38 kilograms.

Rabiner—Crown rabbi. A rabbi appointed by the Russian authorities to be the Jewish community's official representative.

Rashi—An acronym for Rabbi Shlomo Yitzhaki (eleventh century, France), and shorthand for his extremely popular commentaries on the Bible and the Talmud.

rebbe—A hasidic leader (zaddik), admired by his followers as a perfect model of religious behavior.

rebbetzin—A rabbi's wife.

Rosh Hashanah—The Jewish New Year festival.

ruble—Russian currency. One silver ruble contains one hundred kopecks.

sborshchik—Russian term for tax collector, who was also in charge of the conscription of army recruits from the community. These officeholders wielded a great deal of power.

selihot—Special penitential prayers recited during the week before Rosh Hashanah and during the Ten Days of Penitence from Rosh Hashanah to Yom Kippur.

Shavuot—Pentecost; Festival of Weeks; second of the three annual pilgrim festivals, commemorating the receiving of the Torah at Mt. Sinai.

shivah—The Jewish mourning period lasting seven days.

shlimazel—An unlucky or slovenly individual.

shmurah matzah—Matzah baked from wheat kept from contact with water from the time it was harvested.

shtetl (pl. shtetls; Yiddish *shtetlekh*)—Lit. "small town." A popular term, especially in the nineteenth century, used to describe small East European towns where most of the inhabitants were Jews, and where the atmosphere and character of the town were typically "Jewish."

shtibl (pl. shtiblekh)—A small house or room where hasidim prayed.

shtrayml—an expensive round hat made from sable or fox tails. Its origins are obscure. Over time it became a beloved symbol proudly worn by pious Jews. Usually given as a wedding present, the groom cherishes it throughout his lifetime.

Shulhan arukh—The code of Jewish law compiled in Safed by Joseph Karo (1488–1575); the most authoritative of the Jewish legal codes.

Simhat Torah—A festival marking the completion of the annual cycle of the Torah reading, celebrated immediately after the conclusion of the Sukkot festival.

Sukkot—Festival of Tabernacles; last of the three pilgrim festivals, celebrated in the Jewish month of Tishri, after the Days of Awe.

szlachta—The lower Polish nobility, who did not own large estates or possess great wealth.

Talmud Torah—The traditional community-financed Jewish elementary school, which provided education to the poor.

top (pl. tep)—A liquid measurement, about four and a half liters.

Tosaphot—Critical and explanatory glosses on the Babylonian Talmud written by a school of scholars in France and Germany in the twelfth and thirteenth centuries, found in the printed editions of the Talmud.

tsholnt—A stew of beans, potatoes, and cubes of beef, eaten at the midday Sabbath meal, which was slow-cooked in the oven overnight in a sealed pot. Families usually brought their individual pots to the local bakery before the beginning of the Sabbath.

tzitzit—A four-cornered vestlike garment with ritual fringes worn by males either under or on top of clothing.

verst (versta)—Russian distance measurement, equal to 1.0668 kilometers.

yahrzeit—Anniverary of death of a parent, a near relative, or a religious leader.

yeshiva (pl. yeshivot)—Traditional academy for advanced talmudic studies.

yishuvnik—A village Jew.

Yom Kippur—The Day of Atonement.

zaddik (pl. zaddikim)—Lit. "a righteous man." The spiritual leader of a hasidic sect. (See *rebbe.*)

INDEXES OF NAMES,
PLACES, AND SUBJECTS

NAMES

In these indexes an "f" after a number indicates a separate reference on the next page, and an "ff" indicates separate references on the next two pages. *Passim* is used for a cluster of references in close but not consecutive sequence. Kotik's family members (with the exception of Yekhezkel, who is not indexed) are indexed under "Kotik, family of Yekhezkel." Short parenthetical explanations were usually provided only for persons mentioned in the memoirs.

PLACES

SUBJECTS

Books in the Raphael Patai Series
in Jewish Folklore and Anthropology

For an updated listing of books in this series, please visit our Web site at http://wsupress.wayne.edu.